Handbook of Research on Digital Innovation and Networking in Post-COVID-19 Organizations

Ana Pego
Nova University of Lisbon, Portugal

A volume in the Advances in Business Strategy
and Competitive Advantage (ABSCA) Book Series

Published in the United States of America by
IGI Global
Business Science Reference (an imprint of IGI Global)
701 E. Chocolate Avenue
Hershey PA, USA 17033
Tel: 717-533-8845
Fax: 717-533-8661
E-mail: cust@igi-global.com
Web site: http://www.igi-global.com

Library of Congress Cataloging-in-Publication Data

Names: Pego, Ana, 1969- editor.
Title: Handbook of research on digital innovation and networking in
  post-Covid-19 organizations / Ana Pego, editor.
Description: Hershey, PA : Business Science Reference, 2022. | Includes
  bibliographical references and index. | Summary: "This book of research
  chapters highlight the broad potential and adaptation that organizations
  faced during the Covid-19 crisis of the past few years"-- Provided by
  publisher.
Identifiers: LCCN 2022023430 (print) | LCCN 2022023431 (ebook) | ISBN
  9781668467626 (hardcover) | ISBN 9781668467633 (ebook)
Subjects: LCSH: Technological innovations. | Business networks--Management.
  | COVID-19 Pandemic, 2020--Influence.
Classification: LCC HD45 .H29376 2022 (print) | LCC HD45 (ebook) | DDC
  658.4063--dc23/eng/20220627
LC record available at https://lccn.loc.gov/2022023430
LC ebook record available at https://lccn.loc.gov/2022023431

This book is published in the IGI Global book series Advances in Business Strategy and Competitive Advantage (ABSCA) (ISSN: 2327-3429; eISSN: 2327-3437)

British Cataloguing in Publication Data
A Cataloguing in Publication record for this book is available from the British Library.

For electronic access to this publication, please contact: eresources@igi-global.com.

Advances in Business Strategy and Competitive Advantage (ABSCA) Book Series

Patricia Ordóñez de Pablos
Universidad de Oviedo, Spain

ISSN:2327-3429
EISSN:2327-3437

Mission

Business entities are constantly seeking new ways through which to gain advantage over their competitors and strengthen their position within the business environment. With competition at an all-time high due to technological advancements allowing for competition on a global scale, firms continue to seek new ways through which to improve and strengthen their business processes, procedures, and profitability.

The **Advances in Business Strategy and Competitive Advantage (ABSCA) Book Series** is a timely series responding to the high demand for state-of-the-art research on how business strategies are created, implemented and re-designed to meet the demands of globalized competitive markets. With a focus on local and global challenges, business opportunities and the needs of society, the **ABSCA** encourages scientific discourse on doing business and managing information technologies for the creation of sustainable competitive advantage.

Coverage

- Value Creation
- Outsourcing
- Competitive Strategy
- Value Chain
- Joint Ventures
- Economies of Scale
- Cost Leadership Strategy
- Foreign Investment Decision Process
- Business Models
- Adaptive Enterprise

IGI Global is currently accepting manuscripts for publication within this series. To submit a proposal for a volume in this series, please contact our Acquisition Editors at Acquisitions@igi-global.com or visit: http://www.igi-global.com/publish/.

Titles in this Series

For a list of additional titles in this series, please visit: www.igi-global.com/book-series/advances-business-strategy-competitive-advantage/73672

Antecedents and Outcomes of Employee-Based Brand Equity
Muhammad Waseem Bari (Government College University, Faisalabad, Pakistan) Muhammad Abrar (Government College University, Faisalabad, Pakistan) and Emilia Alaverdov (Tbilisi State University, Georgia)
Business Science Reference • © 2022 • 297pp • H/C (ISBN: 9781668436219) • US $250.00

Cases on Emerging Market Responses to the COVID-19 Pandemic
Raj K. Kovid (Sharda University, India) and Vikas Kumar (Central University of Haryana, India)
Business Science Reference • © 2022 • 332pp • H/C (ISBN: 9781668435045) • US $240.00

Impact of Digital Transformation on the Development of New Business Models and Consumer Experience
Maria Antónia Rodrigues (Polytechnic of Porto, Portugal & CEOS.PP, Portugal & SIIS Porto, Portugal) and João F. Proença (Faculty of Economics, University of Porto, Portugal & Advance/CSG, University of Lisbon, Portugal & ISEG, University of Lisbon, Portugal)
Business Science Reference • © 2022 • 347pp • H/C (ISBN: 9781799891796) • US $240.00

Cases on Survival and Sustainability Strategies of Social Entrepreneurs
Charles Oham (University of Greenwich, UK)
Business Science Reference • © 2022 • 312pp • H/C (ISBN: 9781799877240) • US $215.00

Career Re-Invention in the Post-Pandemic Era
Shalin Hai-Jew (Kansas State University, USA)
Business Science Reference • © 2022 • 332pp • H/C (ISBN: 9781799886266) • US $230.00

Handbook of Research on Cross-Disciplinary Uses of Gamification in Organizations
Oscar Bernardes (ISCAP, ISEP, Polytechnic Institute of Porto, Portugal & University of Aveiro, Portugal) Vanessa Amorim (ISCAP, Polytechnic Institute of Porto, Portugal) and António Carrizo Moreira (University of Aveiro, Portugal)
Business Science Reference • © 2022 • 657pp • H/C (ISBN: 9781799892236) • US $325.00

Critical Analysis and Architecture for Strategic Business Planning
James McKee (Independent Researcher, Australia)
Business Science Reference • © 2022 • 289pp • H/C (ISBN: 9781799880738) • US $240.00

701 East Chocolate Avenue, Hershey, PA 17033, USA
Tel: 717-533-8845 x100 • Fax: 717-533-8661
E-Mail: cust@igi-global.com • www.igi-global.com

List of Contributors

Table of Contents

Detailed Table of Contents

Social enterprises have business models that aim to solve social, health, and environmental issues in communities. Drawing on theoretical perspectives in political science, neo-classical economists, and third sector management, the research seeks to understand organisation-level explanation of the types of networking and collaborative strategies small social enterprises employed pre-COVID-19 and post-COVID-19 lockdown. This rapid response research combines interviews with 22 third sector chief executive officers and analysis of policy measures announced during the COVID-19 lockdown. The findings suggest identifiable benefits of networking and collaboration between organisations and across sectors during the COVID-19 lockdown. The study represents an original contribution to knowledge and understanding of organisations networking and collaboration strategies employed to drive the transformation of health and social care services in communities.

Chapter 2

Offering experiences—memorable exchanges and interactions with a brand—has become a top priority for companies of any sector and dimension over the last decades, especially in the light of the advent of digital technologies. However, to date both academic and practitioner attention is mostly limited to B2C contexts, thus calling for a deeper investigation of the opportunities that experiences offer also to B2B firms. After a brief review of the literature on customer experience and the role of digitalization—especially after COVID-19—this chapter focuses on digitally enabled experiences to improve B2B customer relationships. The chapter is based on a three case vignettes analysis that emphasizes how B2B firms can make use of digital tools to craft more effective and impactful customer experiences. Three digitally enabled B2B experiential strategies are identified—downstream empowerment, farsighted customization, and relational flexibility—that ultimately support B2B companies in improving their customer relationships in the long run.

    Andrey I. Pilipenko, Russian Presidential Academy of National Economy and Public
       Administration, Russia
    Zoya A. Pilipenko, Bank of Russia, Russia
    Olga I. Pilipenko, The Russian Presidential Academy of National Economy and Public
       Administration, Russia

The self-sufficient companies are dialectically complex formations capable of self-movement through downward and upward causation mechanisms. They become drivers for constructing the future reality. As backbone elements of the economic system, resilient companies change both the internal structure and the external one. Under the influence of the pandemic, the technological revolution 4.0, the downward causation mechanism induces organizational changes within the companies while the upward causation one does the same with their external networking interactions. Thus, they build new structural relationships as the future economic system basis, distinguished by the dialectical interaction of the economy and society with the dominance of social preferences of individuals. Such a transformation occurs as self-sufficient companies build up intangible assets; build corporate ecosystems based on technological platforms; introduce diversity, equity, and inclusion principles into intra-company structures; and include ecological, social, and governance issues in their development strategies.

    Caglar Dogru, Ufuk University, Turkey

The world is facing one of its hardest pandemics ever with COVID-19. It has been a very tough challenge since the pandemic urged radical changes and transformations in every aspect of life and especially in the work life. During the pandemic, teleworking has gained a vital role for sustaining the production of goods and services. Although teleworking has both positive and negative outcomes, it has been a life jacket for not only organizations but also for employees all around the world during the COVID-19 pandemic. In this chapter, the role of teleworking in the human resources during the pandemic, between May 2020 and January 2022, is evaluated monthly on the basis of analyzing the descriptive statistics of people teleworking or working at home for pay in the United States, by their specific characteristics grouped as age, gender, full-time/part time job status and occupations.

    Yusuf Bayraktutan, Department of Economics, Kocaeli University, Turkey
    Ali Rıza Solmaz, Department of Economics, Kocaeli University, Turkey

The first COVID-19 case in Turkey was seen on March 11, 2020. Various measures have been taken and restrictions have been introduced to reduce the rate of spread since then. International and intercity transport of goods and passengers were limited and/or stopped and curfews/restrictions were applied. The activities of the service sector were regulated/stopped, and their activities were allowed on the condition that certain criteria were met. Working style and hours in public and private sector were designed. The restrictions on economic and social life were gradually lifted. In addition to the loss of people and workforce caused by the pandemic, the reflections of the measures put in effect in terms of economic concerns on national economy have been clearly observed. In this chapter, the economic effects of the pandemic process in Turkey; the short-term results in selected/main indicators, like inflation, unemployment, GDP, trade, etc.; and economic recovery due to policy measures will be evaluated.

Aslisah Senak, Eskişehir Osmangazi University, Turkey
Nuray Girginer, Eskisehir Osmangazi University, Turkey

This chapter aims to demonstrate the value co-created by local ventilator production amid pandemic and how fast a technological product can be co-manufactured by interaction and resource integration among actors. The aim is to discuss the manufacturing process of ventilators as an emerging healthcare strategy amid pandemic with a service dominant logic lense and how well this case fits Gummeson and Mele's value co-creation model in a many-to-many network setting. Formation of a self-governed network of resource-integrating and service-exchanging actors by domestic production of intensive care ventilators dempnstrate the importance of network-based perspective for post-COVID-19 era.

Andrea Girardi, University of Modena and Reggio Emilia, Italy

Performance measurement systems such as KPIs are necessary managerial tools to set targets and monitor performances. During the outbreak of COVID-19, some companies experienced threats to traditional and consolidated business lines. The retail sector saw no decline in turnover. The aim of the chapter is to uncover and analyse the challenges imposed by COVID-19 to the retail sector as well as possible solutions implemented in order to overcome such difficulties. The chapter reports the case study of the largest retailer in Italy during the COVID-19 pandemic. Although seeing sales increase, the managers had many difficulties on the side of procurement and distribution of goods. The performance monitoring system was suddenly insufficient to manage the emergency. The solutions concerned the adjustment of the algorithms with dynamic components addition to KPIs and the conversion of some efficiency targets into effective ones. The chapter suggests insights on how performance measurement systems can be designed and developed in advance to allow more dynamism during emergencies.

Marcelo Amaral Dionisio, Pontifical Catholic University of Rio de Janeiro (PUC-Rio),
Brazil

The COVID-19 pandemic promoted a sudden impact on businesses across the globe, leaving strong concerns about how it will affect SMEs that contribute with 40% of GDP in emerging economies, where they already operate in challenging circumstances due to institutional voids and scarce resources, in a continuous struggle to survive. In this scenario, Brazilian SMEs accelerated their digital transformation (DT) to maintain their economic activity, moving from physical stores to the virtual environment using websites, social networks, and messaging applications, in a context where effective digital inclusion becomes essential, with the effective appropriation of digital technologies. The purpose of this work is to examine in 20 Brazilian SMEs, challenges, strategies, and activities they had faced to deal with this digital transformation. This chapter is expected to fill a gap in literature as studies into SME development through social media are still in the early stages and to be a practical contribution by demonstrating true challenges and results faced in this process.

Chapter 9

Andrey I. Pilipenko, The Russian Presidential Academy of National Economy and Public Administration, Russia
Zoya I. Pilipenko, Bank of Russia, Russia
Olga I. Pilipenko, The Russian Presidential Academy of National Economy and Public Administration, Russia

The COVID-19 global pandemic had a shock effect on all spheres of human activities: technology, society, and economy. They are distinguished by the fact that they are structural integrities capable of self-movement. All systemic changes in the economy before COVID-19 are interpreted in terms of statics and, post pandemic, in dynamics. Self-sufficient companies are the main drivers of modern system formation processes. They form the entire structure of interactions in static economic systems, mediating the mechanism of their self-organization. Their functions of "creative destruction" of organizational interactions mediate the mechanism of self-movement of systems both in statics and in dynamics. A model of the structure formation in the economy by resilient companies is presented as horizontal structure interactions of dialectical pairs and hierarchical structural levels according to the upward and downward causation principles. The mechanism of system self-movement is regulated by the dialectical laws.

Chapter 10

Sara Elouadi, Hassan II University, Morocco
Nariman Elouadi, Univesidad de Almeria España, Spain

This research focuses on the practice of teleworking during the COVID-19 pandemic. The objective is to analyze its effects on employees and companies, in particular the creation of the feeling of blurring between private life and professional life. The chapter begins with a theoretical analysis of telework by borrowing the framework of the theory of social regulation and the theory of conventions. Both make it possible to understand and situate the formation and control of the rules established by telework. Then the authors present their questionnaire survey and its main results.

Chapter 11

Regina G. Diaz, EGADE Business School, Mexico
Raul F. Montalvo, EGADE Business School, Mexico

With the pandemic, digital transformation (DT) was accelerated, and consumers adopted new consumption patterns. Therefore, suppliers had to adapt their business models quickly. This study aims to understand the strategies of large suppliers on Mexican corner stores (CS) during the pandemic and show the perception of CS about these DT strategies. Many digital platform initiatives that were developed by both the government and large suppliers are introduced in this chapter. Additionally, interviews with large suppliers' executives were consulted to clarify their activities that were developed in favor of CS. By conducting 20 interviews with CS, the authors found their perception of large suppliers' DT actions. Findings reveal that the lack of training, investment, and incentives are key factors for the entire virtuous cycle to be fulfilled.

Olukemi Adedokun Fagbolu, National Open University of Nigeria, Nigeria
Kikelomo Aminat Abdulkadir, Kwara State University, Malete, Nigeria

This chapter explores the effects of the COVID-19 pandemic on tourism business. This exploratory research adopts a structured questionnaire and purposive sampling method to gather primary data from the respondents at the study organization. Data collected are presented on tables and further analyzed using descriptive statistics through PSPP analytical free software tool comprising means (M) and simple percentages. The outcomes of the study reveal that the COVID-19 pandemic has a negative significance on the tourism industry.

Alicia Blanco, Rey Juan Carlos University, Spain
Gabriel Cachón-Rodríguez, Rey Juan Carlos University, Spain
Ana Cruz-Suárez, Rey Juan Carlos University, Spain
Cristina Del-Castillo-Feito, Rey Juan Carlos University, Spain

COVID-19 has generated a context full of questions about the effects of mental health in the economic or social sphere. Significant changes in consumer behavior have been investigated. As consumers reduced their purchases in physical establishments and increased online purchases, retailers took measures to minimize health risks, but also to retain consumers. The objective of this research is to identify the intellectual structure of the research field on anxiety and consumption, including the main lines of research in the area, the sources of knowledge, and the connection points that are helping to spread this knowledge. To do this, this research uses a bibliometric methodology based on co-citations. This research concludes that academics must incorporate anxiety in their models and that companies must take this variable into account in the design of their business strategies. We have to legitimize anxiety as one more variable influences on consumer behavior.

Chapter 14

Carlos Silva, NOS Inovação, Portugal
Joana Coutinho Sousa, NOS Inovação, Portugal
Nuno Cid Ponte, NOS Inovação, Portugal
Nuno Martins, NOS Inovação, Portugal
Nuno Miguel Felizardo, NOS Inovação, Portugal
João Miguel Ferreira, NOS Inovação, Portugal

This chapter presents insights about how NOS Inovação has reshaped their teams to get a more horizontal and holistic overview about their services (from development to operations) and how this change has positively impacted the development of new services targeting internet personalisation. Furthermore, this chapter also describes the NOS vision about Industry 5.0, where digital transition is a key enabler and presents a critical role in the future.

The technology known as augmented reality (AR) adds virtual elements to a real physical environment observed through a screen of a mobile device. This innovative and relatively new technology can be used and adapted to other applications that in turn generate new consumption habits. The main objective of these applications is to surprise the consumer and get their full attention and interest. In other words, an AR-based consumer environment will, first of all, arouse the customer's desire to purchase and, subsequently, will motivate him to own a product that he has already viewed through an application, generally through a mobile device with access to internet, new and innovative as AR is. This new approach to consumption allows innovative and efficient marketing strategies because it depends on the way a product or service is displayed beyond the traditional forms such as a window display in a store, a commercial on television, a catalog with images 2D or the box that contains the product.

The COVID-19 pandemic outbreak is considered one of the most serious crises. It affected the education industry causing huge complications and high levels of uncertainty. The pandemic crisis led governments worldwide to rapidly proceed into mandatory emergency measures to restrict physical interactions between people and prevent the virus from spreading extensively. One of the measures was the immediate closure of universities. This unpleasant action hit hard and interrupted education at every rank. To maintain its educational continuity, the Cyprus Government responded immediately to the emerging educational needs, driving higher education institutions to terminate all conventional courses and turn to online education. This chapter aims to evaluate the readiness of the academic staff in high education institutions in Cyprus for shifting the instructional mode from face-to-face to emergency remote teaching (ERT). Methodologically, the research adopted the quantitative approach, collecting data from academics (n=146) in the higher education institutions in Cyprus.

Chapter 17

The COVID-19 pandemic brought many challenges to people, organizations, and governments, and businesses were impacted by social isolation measures and falling consumption. To cope with this situation, it was not only necessary to send the workforce out of offices into remote working or telecommuting, but it was also imperative to innovate to retain customers. In this context, this exploratory study was elaborated to better understand teleworking, workers' behavior, and the usefulness of agile management methods to innovate and help companies stay competitive in the Brazilian scenario. The chapter discusses the results of three surveys conducted during the most critical period of the pandemic, which showed that working from home, despite its great economic and social advantages, needs the companies' attention to employees' potential health problems, and that companies that adopted agile management earlier were able to adapt and innovate faster to overcome the challenges imposed by the pandemic.

Chapter 18

This chapter investigates the impact of the COVID-19 pandemic on the Japanese service sector and the resulting innovations to manage and respond to the difficult situation. Specifically, this study illustrates how e-commerce is emerging as a leading channel for retailers, examines the ethical awareness of both businesses and consumers, and studies the new business models resulting from this trend. Based on several case studies, this study examines the service sector's response to a series of disasters, the cultural background of consumers, and age-long corporate cultures. Additionally, the future direction of innovation in Japan's service sector is discussed and forecasted.

Chapter 19

The impact of the COVID-19 pandemic has not been uniform across industries. In some, we have witnessed a remarkable degree of innovation which has seen the establishment of a vast array of business models. By contrast, in others innovation has been rather slack. These conflicting trends raise the questions of whether the COVID-19 pandemic has accelerated the demise of certain industries or hastened the emergence of others. By coupling the crisis management literature with organizational learning theory and by relying on 23 in-depth interviews, the chapter provides a taxonomy of the various types of innovation responses to the existing crisis and disruption. The taxonomy is instrumental to gain a better understanding of how companies across countries and industry sectors respond to disruption by innovating and the valuable lessons that can be drawn from this experience.

Chapter 20

The COVID-19 pandemic in Bangladesh tells us that economic activities and alternative livelihoods have been disturbed. There are challenges in the areas of equitable distribution of resources and providing economic support to the disadvantaged groups (cash and kind support, food supports, social safety net). This research explores the short term livelihood coping strategies to respond to and recover from COVID-19 with a special focus on socio-demography, socio-economy, food security, and health aspect.

As the crisis develops, future rounds of representative monitoring data on the same respondents will help us understand the evolving impacts and potential recovery.

Chapter 21

The tourism sector is a wide-ranging industry that provides myriad job opportunities worldwide, especially for countries whose economies depends on tourism, like Greece, Spain, and Lebanon. However, the COVID-19 pandemic has tremendously affected this sector. To better understand the post-COVID-19 situation on tourism, the research is mainly based on different sources (articles, papers, reports, and statistics based on the UNWTO, WTO, WHO, etc.) collected through secondary and primary data interpretation. The methodology has been adapted accordingly to collect data from expert interviews and semi-structured surveys following Saunders et al. As a result, this study aims to gather information about the post-COVID-19 impact on the tourism sector through exploring sustainable tourism as one of the solutions for the speedy recovery of the industry in terms of recovery. The main findings presented in this research have shown that domestic tourism will be more sustainable until international tourism gets back on its feet.

Chapter 22

Currently, the use of information and communication technologies (ICT) in the various sectors of the economy faces the challenge of improving specialization and competitiveness; it also promotes the ability to deal with decision-making processes in education and the possibility of "trying out" new ways of being with others in school. The aim of the chapter is to investigate how teachers deal with the new forms of teaching methodology based on online teaching during the era of COVID-19 in secondary schools in the Algarve region, based on the following research question: What are teachers' perceptions regarding the impact of the use of digital technologies and platforms on students? To test the research question, an electronic questionnaire was sent to teachers in randomly selected schools in the Algarve region between July 1 and July 15, 2020. The results show that, according to teachers' perceptions, some students were willing to use new digital methods to allow more networking, and on the other hand, other students had difficulties in learning and applying knowledge.

Chapter 23

The agricultural sector was one of the most important sectors in the economy during COVID-19. The potential of agriculture and the needs of consumers were the main factors in changing the way agriculture supplied the market. Circular products in agriculture were important due to the fact that consumer needs changed during COVID-19. This chapter shows which products have been more important to consumers and how the market has changed to improve the strategy in this sector. Therefore, the perspective of producers to supply the market is the main point of this chapter, as it shows that there is an adjustment in the type of products and services, and therefore, this research will help to understand the circular economy in the agricultural sector during COVID-19.

Chapter 24
Doni Maryono, Muhammadiyah University of Sidoarjo, Indonesia
Rita Ambarwati, Muhammadiyah University of Sidoarjo, Indonesia

The pandemic has an impact on almost all sectors of people's lives, both in the economic, political, and socio-cultural sectors. The government has implemented large-scale social restrictions (PSBB) as an effort to stop the spread of the COVID-19 virus. With the PSBB, it causes disruption to the hospital supply chain management. As a step to anticipate the hospital's impact on the PSBB, the hospital needs to evaluate the performance of supply chain management. The purpose of this chapter is to describe the performance evaluation of hospital supply chain management using a balanced scorecard approach. A new finding from this study is to measure the performance of hospitals experiencing various disruptions in their supply chain management caused by the COVID-19 pandemic with a balanced scorecard. The author concludes that measurements with the balanced scorecard approach can provide information about the performance of hospital supply chain management broadly in areas experiencing disruption due to the COVID-19 pandemic.

Chapter 25
Vítor João Pereira Domingues Martinho, Agricultural School (ESAV) and CERNAS-IPV
Research Centre, Polytechnic Institute of Viseu (IPV), Viseu, Portugal

Considering the specific scenario of the Portuguese framework, it seems interesting to perform a research focused in this context. In fact, the Portuguese economic crisis after 2010/2011 created serious socioeconomic difficulties to the country, but in the recent years, the situation performed significant improvements. This new shock brought to the Portuguese society, again, new challenges and the need of new supports for the policies design by the public institutions and government. In this way, the objective of this research is to assess the Portuguese economic dynamics and, from here, discuss potential impacts from the COVID-19 frameworks, considering data disaggregated at regional and municipal level. For that, it considered the developments from the new economic geography, namely those related with the agglomeration processes and circular and cumulative phenomena. As main conclusions, with the social confinement, a greater economic impact around the Lisbon municipalities than in the north is expected.

Preface

As the evidence shows, the impact of COVID-19 in society has been known since 2019. This book provides an overview of the impact of the pandemic on society in terms of digital adaptation across all sectors of the economy. The authors present the ability of organizations to cope with digital challenges, but also the management strategy to improve the ability to deal with technologies. In fact, most sectors have adopted a new work methodology in relation to their needs. The topics presented in the book are useful for a better understanding of the challenges of COVID-19 time. Nevertheless, new facts and new approaches can be used for a new organizational strategy, in parallel with marketing, management, teaching and sector performance. The target audience is students, researchers, organizations, and citizens. In summary, the digital challenges in organizations, schools, and manufacturing provide a comprehensive opportunity to use digital tools for better performance, although some authors unanimously agreed that more time is needed to be sure of this challenge.

CHAPTER 1: EFFICACY OF NETWORKING AND COLLABORATION – EVIDENCE FROM SOCIAL ENTERPRISES

Chi Maher

Social enterprises have business models that aim to solve social, health and environmental issues in communities. Drawing on theoretical perspectives in political science, neo-classical economists and third sector management, the research seeks to understand organization -level explanation of the types of networking and collaborative strategies small social enterprises employed pre-Covid-19 and post-Covid-19 lockdown. This rapid response research combines interviews with 22 third sector Chief Executive Officers and analysis of policy measures announced during Covid-19 lockdown. The findings suggest identifiable benefits of networking and collaboration between organisations and across sectors during Covid-19 lockdown. The study represents an original contribution to knowledge and understanding of organisations networking and collaboration strategies employed to drive the transformation of health and social care services in communities

CHAPTER 2: STRATEGIES TO IMPROVE B2B CUSTOMER RELATIONSHIPS THROUGH DIGITALLY ENABLED EXPERIENCES

Laura Ingrid Maria Colm

Offering experiences – memorable exchanges and interactions with a brand – has become a top priority for companies of any sector and dimension over the last decades, especially in the light of the advent of digital technologies. However, to date both academics' and practitioners' attention is mostly limited to B2C contexts, thus calling for a deeper investigation of the opportunities that experiences offer also to B2B firms. After a brief review of the literature on customer experience and the role of digitalization – especially after Covid-19 – this chapter focuses on digitally enabled experiences to improve B2B customer relationships. The chapter is based on a three case vignettes analysis, which emphasizes how B2B firms can make use of digital tools to craft more effective and impactful customer experiences. Three digitally enabled B2B experiential strategies are identified – downstream empowerment, farsighted customization, and relational flexibility – that ultimately support B2B companies in improving their customer relationships in the long run.

CHAPTER 3: PATTERNS OF SELF-SUFFICIENT COMPANIES' NETWORK INTERACTIONS REORGANIZATION DUE TO COVID-19 – DIALECTICS OF ORGANIZATIONAL STRUCTURES OPTIMIZATION

Andrey I. Pilipenko, Zoya A. Pilipenko, Olga I. Pilipenko

The self-sufficient companies are dialectically complex formations capable of self-movement through downward and upward causation mechanisms. They become drivers for constructing the future reality. As backbone elements of the economic system, resilient companies change both the internal structure and the external one. Under the influence of the pandemic, the technological revolution 4.0, the downward causation mechanism induces organizational changes within the companies while the upward causation one does the same with their external networking interactions. Thus, they build new structural relationships as the future economic system basis, distinguished by the dialectical interaction of the economy and society with the dominance of social preferences of individuals. Such a transformation occurs as self-sufficient companies build up intangible assets, build corporate ecosystems based on technological platforms, introduce diversity, equity, and inclusion principles into intra-company structures, and include ecological, social and governance issues in their development strategies.

CHAPTER 4: TELEWORKING AS AN EMERGING STRATEGY DURING COVID-19 – EVIDENCE FROM THE UNITED STATES

Caglar Dogru

The World is facing one of its hardest pandemics ever in the history with Covid-19. It has been a very tough challenge since the pandemic urged radical changes and transformations in every aspect of life and especially in the work life. During the pandemic, teleworking has gained a vital role for sustaining the production of goods and services. Although teleworking has both positive and negative outcomes, it has been a life jacket for not only organizations but also for employees all around the world during the Covid-19 pandemic. In this chapter, the role of teleworking in the human resources during the pandemic, between May 2020 and January 2022, is evaluated monthly; on the basis of analyzing the descriptive statistics of people teleworked or worked at home for pay in the United States, by their specific characteristics grouped as age, gender, full-time/part time job status and occupations.

CHAPTER 5: COVID-19 POLICY MEASURES AND REFLECTIONS ON TURKISH ECONOMY AND FOREIGN TRADE

Yusuf Bayraktutan, Ali RızaSolmaz

The first Covid-19 case in Turkiye was seen on March 11, 2020. Various measures have been taken and restrictions have been introduced to reduce the rate of spread since then. International and intercity transport of goods and passengers were limited, and/or stopped, curfews/restrictions were applied. The activities of service sector were regulated/stopped, and their activities were allowed on the condition that certain criteria were met. Working style and hours in public and private sector were designed. The restrictions on economic and social life were gradually lifted. In addition to the loss of people and workforce caused by the pandemic, the reflections of the measures put in effect in terms of economic concerns on national economy have been clearly observed. In this chapter, the economic effects of the pandemic process in Turkiye, the short-term results in selected/main indicators, like inflation, unemployment, GDP, trade, etc., and economic recovery due to policy measures will be evaluated.

CHAPTER 6: VENTILATOR PRODUCTION IN TURKEY AMID PANDEMIC THROUGH SERVICE DOMINANT LOGIC LENSES

AslisahSenak, NurayGirginer

This chapter aims to demonstrate the value co-created by local ventilator production amid pandemic and how fast a technological product can be co-manufactured by interaction and resource integration among actors. The aim is to discuss the manufacturing process of ventilators as an emerging healthcare strategy amid pandemic with a service dominant logic lense and how well this case fits Gummeson and Mele's value co-creation model in a many to many network setting. Formation of a self governed network of resource-integrating and service-exchanging actors by domestic production of intensive care ventilators dempnstrate the importance of network-based perspective for post Covid-19 era.

CHAPTER 7: PERFORMANCE MEASUREMENT SYSTEMS THREATENED BY PANDEMIC OPPORTUNITIES IN RETAIL – HOW MANAGERS STRUGGLED TO BALANCE GROWING SALES WITH UNEXPECTEDLY INADEQUATE SUPPLY CHAIN KPIS

Andrea Girardi

Performance measurement systems such as KPIs are necessary managerial tools to set targets and monitor performances. During the outbreak of the Covid-19, some companies experienced threats to traditional and consolidated business lines. The retail sector saw no decline in turnover. The aim of the chapter is to uncover and analyse the challenges imposed by the Covid-19 to the retail sector as well as possible solutions implemented in order to overcome such difficulties. The chapter reports the case study of the largest retailer in Italy during the covid-19 pandemic. Although seeing sales increase, the managers had many difficulties on the side of procurement and distribution of goods. The performance monitoring system was suddenly insufficient to manage the emergency. The solutions concerned the adjustment of the algorithms with dynamic components addition to KPIs and the conversion of some efficiency targets into effective ones. The chapter suggests insights on how performance measurement systems can be designed and developed in advance to allow more dynamism during emergencies.

CHAPTER 8: ANALYZING DIGITAL TRANSFORMATION IN BRAZILIAN SMES

Marcelo Amaral Dionisio

The COVID-19 pandemic promoted a sudden impact on businesses across the globe, leaving strong concerns about how it will affect SMEs that contribute with 40% of GDP in emerging economies, where they already operate in challenging circumstances due to institutional voids and scarce resources, in a continuously struggle to survive. In this scenario, Brazilian SMEs accelerated their digital transformation (DT) to maintain their economic activity, moving from physical stores to the virtual environment using websites, social networks, and messaging applications, in a context where effective digital inclusion becomes essential, with the effective appropriation of digital technologies. The purpose of this work is to examine in 20 Brazilian SMEs, challenges, strategies, and activities they had faced to deal with this digital transformation. This chapter per the authors expect to fill a gap in literature as studies into SMEs development through social media are still in early stages, along with a practical contribution by demonstrating true challenges and results faced in this process.

CHAPTER 9: DIALECTICS OF SELF-MOVEMENT OF RESILIENT COMPANIES IN THE ECONOMY AND SOCIETY POST COVID-19 – PATTERNS OF ORGANIZATIONAL TRANSFORMATIONS OF NETWORKING INTERACTIONS

Andrey I. Pilipenko, Zoya I. Pilipenko, Olga I. Pilipenko

The COVID-19 pandemic promoted a sudden impact on businesses across the globe, leaving strong concerns about how it will affect SMEs that contribute with 40% of GDP in emerging economies, where they already operate in challenging circumstances due to institutional voids and scarce resources, in a continuously struggle to survive. In this scenario, Brazilian SMEs accelerated their digital transformation (DT) to maintain their economic activity, moving from physical stores to the virtual environment using websites, social networks, and messaging applications, in a context where effective digital inclusion becomes essential, with the effective appropriation of digital technologies. The purpose of this work is to examine in 20 Brazilian SMEs, challenges, strategies, and activities they had faced to deal with this digital transformation. These chapters per the authors expect to fill a gap in literature as studies into SMEs development through social media are still in early stages, along with a practical contribution by demonstrating true challenges and results faced in this process.

CHAPTER 10: TELEWORKING DURING THE PANDEMIC OF COVID-19 – EMPIRICAL STUDY OF ITS EFFECTS

Sara Elouadi, Nariman Elouadi

The research focuses on the practice of teleworking during the Covid-19 pandemic. Our objective is to analyze its effects on employees and companies, in particular the creation of the feeling of blurring between private life and professional life. The chapter begins with a theoretical analysis of telework by borrowing the framework of the theory of social regulation and the theory of conventions. Both make it possible to understand and situate the formation and control of the rules established by telework. Then we present our questionnaire survey and its main results.

CHAPTER 11: INNOVATIVE DIGITAL TRANSFORMATION STRATEGIES OF LARGE SUPPLIERS FOR MEXICAN CORNER STORES DURING A PANDEMIC – CHALLENGES AND OPPORTUNITIES

Regina G. Diaz, Raul F. Montalvo

With the pandemic, digital transformation (DT) was accelerated, and consumers adopted new consumption patterns. Therefore, suppliers had to adapt their business models quickly. This study aims to understand the strategies of large suppliers on Mexican corner stores (CS) during the pandemic and show the perception of CS about these DT strategies. Many digital platform initiatives that were developed by both the government and large suppliers are introduced in this chapter. Additionally, interviews with large suppliers' executives were consulted to clarify their activities that were developed in favor of CS. By conducting 20 interviews with CS, the authors found their perception of large suppliers' DT actions. Findings reveal that the lack of training, investment, and incentives are key factors for the entire virtuous cycle to be fulfilled.

CHAPTER 12: SIGNIFICANCE OF THE COVID-19 PANDEMIC ON TOURISM BUSINESS IN NIGERIA – PERSPECTIVES FROM AIRPORTS, HOTELS, AND RECREATIONAL CENTRES

Olukemi Deborah Fagbolu, Kikelomo A. Abdulkadir

This chapter explores the effects of covid-19 pandemic on tourism business. This exploratory research adopts a structured questionnaire and purposive sampling method to gather primary data from the respondents at the study organization. Data collected are presented on tables and further analyzed using descriptive statistics through PSPP analytical free software tool comprising means (M) and simple percentages. The outcomes of the study reveal that covid-19 pandemic has a negative significance on the tourism industry.

CHAPTER 13: COVID-19 WELCOMES A NEW VARIABLE THAT INFLUENCES CONSUMER BEHAVIOR –ANXIETY

Alicia Blanco, Gabriel Cachón-Rodríguez, Ana Cruz-Suárez, Cristina Del-Castillo-Feito

Covid-19 has generated a context full of questions about the effects of mental health in the economic or social sphere. Significant changes in consumer behavior have been investigated as consumers reduced their purchases in physical establishments and increased online purchases, retailers took measures to minimize health risks, but also to retain consumers, or we live in moments in which panic selling occurred. The objective of this research is to identify the intellectual structure of the research field on anxiety and consumption, including the main lines of research in the area, the sources of knowledge, and the connection points that are helping to spread this knowledge. To do this, this research uses a bibliometric methodology based on co-citations. This research concludes that academics must incorporate anxiety in their models and that companies must take this variable into account in the design of their business strategies. Definitely, we have to legitimize anxiety as one more variable that influences the consumer behavior.

CHAPTER 14: FAST-PACED TECHNOLOGY EVOLUTION FACED BY OPERATORS WITH THE NEEDS EMERGING FROM WORK MODEL CHANGES AND GENERAL INFORMATION ACCESS FOR CUSTOMERS

Carlos Silva, Joana Coutinho Sousa, Nuno Cid Ponte, Nuno Martins, Nuno Miguel Felizardo, João Miguel Ferreira

The remote working demands, a more and more agile mindset to build multidisciplinary teams to get a holistic approach about telecom services, products and network, sustained in transversal service quality KPIs ensuring that the industry was able to respond faster to the customer's needs in the digital world. This chapter presents insights about how NOS Inovação has reshaped their teams to get a more horizontal and holistic overview about their services (from Development to Operations) and how this change has positively impacted the development of new services targeting Internet personalisation. Furthermore, this chapter also describes NOS' vision about Industry 5.0, where digital transition is a key enabler and presents a critical role in the future.

CHAPTER 15: AUGMENTED REALITY AS AN EFFICIENT MARKETING STRATEGY IN A NEW CONSUMPTION MODEL DURING THE COVID-19 PANDEMIC

Gerardo Reyes Ruiz

The technology known as Augmented Reality (AR) adds virtual elements to a real physical environment observed through a screen of a mobile device. This innovative and relatively new technology can be used and adapted to other applications that in turn generate new consumption habits. The main objective of these applications is to surprise the consumer and get their full attention and interest. In other words, an AR-based consumer environment will, first of all, arouse the customer's desire to purchase and, subsequently, will motivate him to own a product that he has already viewed through an application, generally through a mobile device with access to internet, new and innovative as AR is. This new approach to consumption allows innovative and efficient marketing strategies because it depends on the way a product or service is displayed beyond the traditional forms such as a window display in a store, a commercial on television, a catalog with images. 2D or the box that contains the product.

CHAPTER 16: THE READINESS OF HIGHER EDUCATION ACADEMIC STAFF IN CYPRUS FOR SHIFTING THE INSTRUCTIONAL DELIVERY MODE FROM FACE-TO-FACE TO EMERGENCY REMOTE TEACHING

George Yiapanas, Maria Constantinou, Elena Marcoulli

The Covid-19 pandemic outbreak is considered one of the most serious crises, which affected the education industry causing huge complications and high levels of uncertainty. The pandemic crisis led governments worldwide to rapidly proceed into mandatory emergency measures, to restrict physical interactions between people, and prevent the virus from spreading extensively. One of the measures was the immediate closure of universities. This unpleasant action hit hard and interrupted education at every rank. To maintain its educational continuity, the Cyprus Government responded immediately to the emerging educational needs, driving higher education institutions to terminate all conventional courses and turn to online education. This book chapter aims to evaluate the readiness of the academic staff in high education institutions in Cyprus for shifting the instructional mode from face-to-face to emergency remote teaching [ERT]. Methodologically, the research adopted the quantitative approach, collecting data from academics [n=146] in the higher education institutions in Cyprus.

CHAPTER 17: THE COVID-19 PANDEMIC AND HOW BRAZILIAN ORGANIZATIONS FACED ITS CHALLENGES – FROM REMOTE EMPLOYEE BEHAVIOR TO INNOVATION USING AGILE MANAGEMENT

Bruno Luiz Bucci Bandeira, Caio Eduardo Doná Araújo, Jonas William Barros Godoy, João Pinheiro de Barros Neto

The COVID-19 pandemic brought many challenges to people, organizations, and governments, and businesses were impacted by social isolation measures and falling consumption. To cope with this situation, it was not only necessary to send the workforce out of offices into remote working or telecommuting, but it was also imperative to innovate to retain customers. In this context, this exploratory study was elaborated to better understand teleworking, workers' behavior, and the usefulness of agile management methods to innovate and help companies stay competitive in the Brazilian scenario. The article discusses the results of three surveys conducted during the most critical period of the pandemic, which showed that working from home, despite its great economic and social advantages, needs the companies' attention to employees' potential health problems, and that companies that adopted agile management earlier were able to adapt and innovate faster to overcome the challenges imposed by the pandemic.

CHAPTER 18: INNOVATIONS IN THE SERVICE INDUSTRY DURING THE COVID-19 PANDEMIC – THE CASE OF JAPAN

Mitsunori Hirogaki

This chapter investigates the impact of the COVID-19 pandemic on the Japanese service sector and the resulting innovations to manage and respond to the difficult situation. Specifically, this study illustrates how e-commerce is emerging as a leading channel for retailers, examines the ethical awareness of both businesses and consumers, and studies the new business models resulting from this trend. Based on several case studies, this study examines the service sector's response to a series of disasters, the cultural background of consumers, and age-long corporate cultures. Additionally, the future direction of innovation in Japan's service sector is discussed and forecasted.

CHAPTER 19: TURNING A CRISIS INTO AN OPPORTUNITY – INNOVATIONS DURING THE PANDEMIC

Francesca Bonetti, Alessandra Vecchi

The impact of the C19 pandemic has not been uniform across industries. In some, we have witnessed a remarkable degree of innovation which has seen the establishment of a vast array of business models. By contrast, in others innovation has been rather slack. These conflicting trends raise the questions of whether the C19 pandemic has accelerated the demise of certain industries or hastened the emergence of others? By coupling the crisis management literature with organizational learning theory and by relying on 23 in-depth interviews, the paper provides a taxonomy of the various types of innovation responses to the existing crisis and disruption. The taxonomy is instrumental to gain a better understanding of how companies across countries and industry sectors respond to disruption by innovating, and the valuable lessons that can be drawn from this experience.

CHAPTER 20: SUSTAINABILITY ISSUES AND LIVELIHOOD COPING STRATEGIES IN THE COVID-19 PANDEMIC

Shafiqul Islam

COVID-19 pandemic in Bangladesh tells us that economic activities and alternative livelihoods have been disturbed. There are challenges in areas of equitable distribution of resources and providing economic support to the disadvantageous groups (cash and kind support, food supports, social safety net). These researches explores the short term livelihood coping strategies to response and recover COVID-19, with a special focus on socio-demography, socio-economy, food security and health aspect. As the crisis develops, future rounds of representative monitoring data on the same respondents will help understand the evolving impacts and potential recovery.

CHAPTER 21: ESTIMATING THE IMPACT OF COVID-19 ON THE FUTURE OF THE TOURISM SECTOR – IMPLICATIONS ON TOURISM AND SUSTAINABILITY POST PANDEMIC

Viana Imad Hassan, Georges Bellos

The tourism sector is a wide-ranging industry that provides a myriad of job opportunities worldwide; and especially for countries whose economy depends on tourism, like Greece, Spain and Lebanon. However, the COVID-19 pandemic has tremendously affected this sector, To better understand the post COVID-19 situation on tourism the research is mainly based on different sources (articles, papers, reports, and statistics based on the UNWTO, WTO WHO, etc.) collected through secondary and primary data interpretation the methodology has been adapted accordingly to collect data from expert interviews and semi structured surveys following Saunders et al. (2019). As a result, this study aims to gather information about the Post COVID impact on the tourism sector, through exploring sustainable tourism as one of the solutions for the speedy recovery of the industry in terms of recovery the main findings presented in this research have shown that domestic tourism will be more sustainable till this current time until international tourism will get back on its feet.

CHAPTER 22: PERSPECTIVE FOR A DIGITAL TEACHING METHOD – A CASE STUDY ABOUT SECONDARY SCHOOLS DURING THE COVID-19 ERA IN THE ALGARVE REGION

Ana Pego

Currently, the use of information and communication technologies (ICT) in the various sectors of the economy faces the challenge of improving specialization and competitiveness; also promotes the ability to deal with decision-making processes in education and the possibility of "trying out" new ways of being with others in school. The aim of the article is to investigate how teachers deal with the new forms of teaching methodology based on online teaching during the era COVID-19 in secondary schools in the Algarve region, based on the following research question: what are teachers' perceptions regarding the impact of the use of digital technologies and platforms on students? To test the research question, an electronic questionnaire was sent to teachers in randomly selected schools in the Algarve region between July 1 and July 15, 2020. The results show that, according to teachers' perceptions, some students were willing to use new digital methods to allow more networking, and on the other hand, other students had difficulties in learning and applying knowledge.

CHAPTER 23: THE CIRCULAR AGRICULTURE PRODUCTS DURING COVID-19 – A PORTUGUESE ANALYSIS

Ana Pego

The agricultural sector was one of the most important sectors in the economy during COVID -19. The potential of agriculture and the needs of consumers were the main factors in changing the way agriculture supplied the market. Circular products in agriculture were important due to the fact that consumer needs changed during COVID -19. This article shows which products have been more important to consumers and how the market has changed to improve the strategy in this sector. Therefore, the perspective of producers to supply the market is the main point of this article, as it knows that there is an adjustment in the type of products and services and therefore, this research will help to understand the circular economy in the agricultural sector during COVID-19.

CHAPTER 24: EVALUATION OF SUPPLY CHAIN PERFORMANCE USING THE BALANCED SCORECARD APPROACH DURING THE COVID-19 PANDEMIC – A CASE STUDY OF JS GENERAL HOSPITAL

Doni Maryono, Rita Ambarwati

The pandemic has an impact on almost all sectors of people's lives, both in the economic, political, and socio-cultural sectors. The government has implemented large-scale social restrictions (PSBB) as an effort to stop the spread of the COVID-19 virus. With the PSBB, it causes disruption to the hospital supply chain management. As a step to anticipate the hospital's impact on the PSBB, the hospital needs to evaluate the performance of supply chain management, is the supply chain management performance going well or not? The purpose of this chapter is to describe the performance evaluation of hospital supply chain management using a balanced scorecard approach. A new finding from this study is to measure the performance of hospitals experiencing various disruptions in their supply chain management caused by the COVID-19 pandemic with a balanced scorecard. The author concludes that measurements with the balanced scorecard approach can provide information about the performance of hospital supply chain management broadly in areas experiencing disruption due to the COVID-19 pandemic.

CHAPTER 25: DYNAMICS OF ECONOMIC SECTORS AND HUMAN MOBILITY BEFORE AND DURING COVID-19 – THE PORTUGUESE CONTEXT

Vítor João Pereira Domingues Martinho

Considering the specific scenario of the Portuguese framework, it seems interesting to perform a research focused in this context. In fact, the Portuguese economic crisis after 2010/2011 created serious socioeconomic difficulties to the country, but in the recent years the situation performed significant improvements. This new shock brought to the Portuguese society, again, new challenges and the need of new supports for the policies design by the public institutions and government. In this way, the objective of this research is to assess the Portuguese economic dynamics and, from here, discuss potential impacts from the Covid-19 frameworks, considering data disaggregated at regional and municipal level. For that, it was considered the developments from the New Economic Geography, namely those related with the agglomeration processes and circular and cumulative phenomena. As main conclusions, of highlighting that, considering the Portuguese economic structure, it is expected, with the social confinement, a greater economic impact around the Lisbon municipalities than in the North.

Ana Pego
Nova University of Lisbon, Portugal

Introduction

Digital applications in COVID-19 and their impact on social and economic values are presented in this book. The importance of a new challenge in terms of the use of technologies and digital tools is presented in all chapters of the book, giving the reader the opportunity to understand how consumers, organizations and other sectors. The author also provides an important contribution about the strategies that organizations have implemented and the ability to deal with digital planning. In addition, digital influence is seen as a positive aspect in society. The book is a good tool for teachers, policy makers and citizens as it provides an overview of how society has changed towards a comfortable COVID -19 discussions.

The book is divided into 25 chapters that present a new way of dealing with COVID-19. The main structure of each chapter is a new way of dealing with society and its performance based on research during and after COVID-19. The authors describe study cases and their implications, such as: Chapter 1 provides an overview about the Efficacy of Networking and Collaboration: Evidence from Social Enterprises; Chapter 2 describes the Strategies to Improve B2B Customer Relationships Through Digitally Enabled Experiences; Chapter 3 point out the patterns of Self-Sufficient Companies' Network Interactions Reorganization due to COVID-19: Dialectics of Organizational Structures Optimization; Chapter 4 indicates the teleworking as an Emerging Strategy During Covid-19: Evidence from the United States; Chapter 5 presents the Covid-19 Policy Measures and Reflections on Turkish Economy and Foreign Trade; Chapter 6 discusses the ventilator Production in Turkey Amid Pandemic Through Service Dominant Logic Lenses; Chapter 7 describes the performance Measurement Systems Threatened by Pandemic Opportunities in Retail: how Managers Struggled to Balance Growing Sales with Unexpectedly Inadequate Supply Chain KPIs; Chapter 8 analyses the digital transformation in Brazilian SMEs; Chapter 9 indicates the dialectics of Self-Movement of Resilient Companies in the Economy and Society Post COVID-19: Patterns of Organizational Transformations of Networking Interactions; Chapter 10, describes the teleworking during the Pandemic of Covid-19: Empirical Study of its Effects; Chapter 11 addresses the innovative Digital Transformation Strategies of Large Suppliers for Mexican Corner Stores during a Pandemic: Challenges and Opportunities; Chapter 12 provides the significance of covid-19 pandemic on tourism business in Nigeria: Perspectives from airport, hotel and recreational centre; Chapter 13 expresses the Covid welcomes a new variable that influences consumer behavior. The anxiety; Chapter 14 describes the Fast paced Technology Evolution faced by Operators with the needs emerging from Work Model Changes and General Information Access for Customers; Chapter 15 indicates the augmented reality as an efficient marketing strategy in a new consumption model during the covid-19 pandemic; Chapter 16 expresses the readiness of higher education academic staff in Cyprus for shifting the instructional delivery mode from face-to-face to emergency remote teaching; Chapter 17 indicates how Brazilian Organizations faced its Challenges: from Remote Employee Behavior to Innovation using Agile Management; Chapter 18 describes the Innovations in the service industry during the COVID-19 pandemic: the case of Japan; Chapter 19 identifies the crisis into an Opportunity – Innovations during the Pandemic; Chapter 20 shows the sustainability issues and Livelihood Coping Strategies in COVID-19 Pandemic: COVID-19 and Livelihood Coping Strategies; Chapter 21 estimates the impact of the Covid 19 on the future of the tourism sector: Implications on Tourism and Sustainability Post pandemic; chapter 22 gives a perspective for a Digital Teaching Method. A Case Study about Secondary Schools during COVID 19 Era in the Algarve Region; Chapter 23 presents the circular Agriculture products during COVID 19. A Portuguese Analysis; Chapter 24 describes the evaluation of Supply Chain Performance Using the Balanced Scorecard Approach during the Covid-19 Pandemic: A Case Study of Js General Hospital; Chapter 25 presents the dynamics of economic sectors and human mobility, before and during the Covid-19: The Portuguese specific context.

The findings from all these chapters are incorporated into a comprehensive study COVID -19 of digital influence in all areas of the economy and also the social impact of its use.

CONCLUSION

The authors conclude that digital innovation and networking are essential in post- COVID -19 organisations. The authors suggest that given that the COVID 19 was responsible for rethinking the planning process, but also implementing new methods, the sector should innovate. This means that the areas presented in the 25F chapters cover a wide range of new techniques related to resilience capability after the COVID 19 recession. In summary, according to the authors, COVID -19 will open a new path to improve citizens' well-being and ability to change economic and social patterns toward sustainability in the future. Digital innovation and networking of organisations became an important aspect of sustainability.

Chapter 1
Efficacy of Networking and Collaborations:
Evidence From Social Enterprises

Chi Maher
York St. John University, London, UK

ABSTRACT

Social enterprises have business models that aim to solve social, health, and environmental issues in communities. Drawing on theoretical perspectives in political science, neo-classical economists, and third sector management, the research seeks to understand organisation-level explanation of the types of networking and collaborative strategies small social enterprises employed pre-COVID-19 and post-COVID-19 lockdown. This rapid response research combines interviews with 22 third sector chief executive officers and analysis of policy measures announced during the COVID-19 lockdown. The findings suggest identifiable benefits of networking and collaboration between organisations and across sectors during the COVID-19 lockdown. The study represents an original contribution to knowledge and understanding of organisations networking and collaboration strategies employed to drive the transformation of health and social care services in communities.

INTRODUCTION

The coronavirus (COVID-19) is an etiological agent and human-to-human transmission of the (SARS-COV-2) virus has affected several countries around the world. It has been labelled as a pandemic by the World Health Organization (WHO) (WHO: Situation Report-97). Combatting the COVID-19 pandemic involves public health, social services, private sector and third sector organisations, all collaborating to provide services to the community. The UK went into lockdown on March 23rd, 2020, with rules coming into place stating the following:

i) shopping for necessities; ii) a day for exercise; iii) medical need or providing care and iv) travelling to or from work (if you cannot work from home) (Ogden, 2020).

DOI: 10.4018/978-1-6684-6762-6.ch001

These rules mainly affected the way in which public services were delivered. The Government introduced the Coronavirus Job Retention Scheme and provided the £750 million Coronavirus Business Interruption Loan to organisations to help keep them afloat. However, there was a lack of clarity about how the £750 million would be allocated, small third sector social enterprise organisations were unclear about their eligibility and how they should apply (NVCO, 2020). Nearly two weeks after the Government announced £750 million of funding for the third sector, the Secretary of State was still unable to provide sufficient detail or clarity about the eligibility criteria for allocating that loan. An announcement of funding was of limited benefit when small social enterprises were facing imminent closure and were unclear whether they were eligible or how to apply (NVCO, 2022).

The need for several sector organisations to continue to deliver services throughout the Covid-19 lockdown meant that they were limited in the extent to which they could make use of the Government's Coronavirus Job Retention Scheme.

These organisations were concerned that the parameters for any loan provided by the government favoured those working in the private sector, which meant that they would receive limited support (Hyndman, 2020). Furthermore, the difficulty was that the Government Coronavirus Job Retention scheme, or 'laying staff off', meant that organisations can stand down staff at exactly the time when they want staff to stay on and deliver the increase in demand for services.

This study provides an original contribution to literature by explaining networking activities undertaken by social enterprises, pre-Covid-19 lockdown, first lockdown and collaborative actions taken at local, national, and international levels during the lockdown to assist the most vulnerable in our societies. Future research could empirically examine small social enterprises networking and collaboration activities and intended outcomes through longitudinal studies cross-sector and cross borders.

The UK Third Sector Social Enterprises

The UK's third sector social enterprises are highly diverse in terms of structure and service delivery. The sector is comprised of organisations of vastly different sizes, operating under different funding models, and providing a tremendous range of services. Many social enterprises perform vital work supporting the vulnerable in society. Yet, several small social enterprises were fighting for survival within weeks of the first Covid-19 lockdown as traditional methods of generating income dried up overnight with social distancing making delivering services difficult and more costly. Financial interest sustainability is a major concern for several Third sector small social enterprises with limited reserves and limited income generating mechanisms in place. As a result, they depend predominately on government contracted services (NVCO, 2020).

Academic Notion of the Third Sector

Academics within the sector have increased in the last three decades as the understanding of the benefits and the contributions of the sector to the economy increases (Vickers, 2010). For instance, neo-classical economists view the existence of the sector in terms of the market and the state failures (Weisbord, 1997). Neo-classical economists suggest that the state has failed to fulfil the demand for public services, and therefore, the sector organisations emerge to fill the gaps (Maher, 2018a).

Another explanation of the existence of the sector is the privatisation of public services rooted in the market-based philosophies of the Conservative government (1979 – 1997) (Hopkin and Shaw,201 6).

The Conservative government made explicit recommendations that the sector organisations take a greater role in delivering public services, leading to a significant increase in government funding to the sector for many years. The Labour Government (1997 to 2010) continued this momentum as part of their programme of welfare reforms. The Labour government encouraged partnerships and collaborations between the sector and government to frame policy and deliver services. In 1998, Labour government policies such as Compact (Macmillan, 2011; Maher, 2018c) influenced by the Deakin Report (1996 (citied in Lewis, 1999) suggested that the state and the sector organisations should develop a closer relationship guided by 'Compact'. The Compact document sets out a framework agreement that outlines a shared vision and values with a commitment by both the government and the sector organisations to work together to build a positive relationship between the government and the third sector in the development and delivery of public services (Maher, 2019). A combination of this approach and pluralist provision of services led to a reduction in state responsibility, with an increased expectation of service provision from the private sector and the third sector organisations.

There is also evidence that the third sector can be flexible and effective because it values profitability in a different way from the private sector (Lewis, 1999; Maher, 2016). The third sector, for example, places people and community benefits above financial benefits. Some authors (Kendall, 2004; Macmillan, 2011) view the sector social enterprise organisations as effective because they target the unmet needs of local people which the public or private sector often do not provide if these individuals' needs do not meet their service provision inclusion criteria. The sector organisations provide services where there are gaps in statutory services provision. The sector identifies innovative ways of service delivery.

Taking into consideration, these differing academic perspectives, on the existence of the third sector, it is also possible that the growth and continuing development of the third sector social enterprises, is that their role includes creating employment for people and generating social capital (Maher, 2018b, 2019a). The sector also plays a key role in tackling inequalities in access to health and social care; promoting social and economic inclusion of disadvantaged individuals and local communities (Hudson, 2009; MacMillan, 2011). It is important for this chapter briefly discusses third sector's distinctiveness from the private and public sectors. This will enable us to understand the importance and the reasoning fastening the sector organisation's networking and collaboration activities with other sectors during the Covid-19 pandemic lockdown.

Differentiation Between the Third, Public and Private Sectors

The uniqueness of the sector from the public and private sectors was first conceptualised by Polanyi (1968) in his work entitled: 'Primitive, Archaic and Modern Economies'. According to Polanyi (1968), there are three integrations of economic circulation: a) market exchange, ii) redistribution, iii) reciprocity.

1. Market exchange in 'primitive economies' entailed recognising a product as something that has exchange value and involves the separation of buyer and seller. Hence, market exchange used a universal equivalent: money. In modern economies the private sector undertakes the role of market exchange, as the private sector's mode of economic integration is that of the market.
2. Redistribution in 'primitive economies' involved a third party (in the centre) between the giver and the recipient. In modern economies the state (welfare system) assumes this role. The mode of circulation involves contributions to the centre through taxation and payments out of it, through social security benefits and pensions.

3. Reciprocity in 'primitive economies' entailed people producing goods and services for which they were best suited, and they shared them with those around and others reciprocated. The objective is to produce and share, not for personal gain or profit, but fear of social contempt. The third sector shares some of these features, as it works on the principle of non-profit provision of services for the community (Polanyi, 1968). Birkhoelzer (1998) developed Polanyi's (1968) ideas by suggesting that the third sector is a form of collective self-organisation by citizens who start to produce self-help on local, regional, national, and international levels (Maher, 2016).

Other authors (Ciucescu, 2009, Maher, 2019a) also suggest that the sector is distinct from the private and public sectors because third sector organisations are flexible and responsive to individualised care (tailored care to meet individual needs rather than providing a standardised service for all clients) and changes in community needs which contrasts with the public sector (Local Government) service and provision of care which is centred around the 'median citizen' (Ciucescu, 2009).

Third sector organisations encourage citizen participation in the delivery of community services that is otherwise minimised or denied in the public sector (Local Government) provision. However, many third sector organisations close each year due to lack of funding. Others have survived because they adapted to varying their service provision in response to economic, political changes and austerity programmes (NVCO, 2020).

LITERTURE REVIEW

The Government recognises third sector social enterprises for their ability to engage with grassroots communities and to develop needs-led services that are not provided by public sector services (Ciucescu, 2009; Maher, 2009c).Yet, these organisations constantly network with other organisations and sectors as they understand the many benefits that networking between organisations can offer, such as: knowledge exchange, expanding services outreach; value creation, improve leadership skills, enhanced organisational capabilities and collaboration activities (Jones, 2013; Shumate, Fu and Cooper, 2018; Lalzai and Rana, 2020).

Bingham and O'Leary (2008) define 'collaboration' as a set of evolving relationships between stakeholders, who share certain mutual goals. Thus, collaboration involves exchange of resources between service providers to implement policy or joint planning and delivery of services. Therefore, collaboration signifies a closer relationship to the point of "co-labour" which emphasises new structures, shared resources, creating, enhancing, and building on social and organisational capital in pursuit of shared purposes (Bingham and O'Leary, 2008).

Theoretical Rationale for Collaboration

The theoretical rationale for collaborations can be identified from various experiences and attitudes of diverse factors within these interactions; macro forces and micro factors (Mattessich and Monsey, 1992). The macro perspective assumes that organisations' collaborations are formed due to decreased trust in the state's ability to solve social problems, as well as access to limited state funding, and one organisation's inability to single-handedly tackle the growing complex societal issues (Mattessich and Monsey, 1992). On the other hand, the micro perspective presents two compelling explanations of strategic intents, which are rooted in either a utilitarian rationale or an altruistic argument (Mattessich and Monsey, 1992). The utilitarian rationale can be associated with the notion that collaborations are formed due to a lack of critical competencies.

Several authors (Thomson and Perry, 2006; Batley and Rose, 2011) argue that there are several benefits organisations can achieve from collaborations including; resource and expertise acquisitions, value creation, market positioning and access to new markets. On the other hand, the altruistic rationale suggests that collaborations are formed due to the need for tackling environmental, health and social problems that exceed the scope of a single organization. Thus, a utilitarian perspective of collaboration, emphasises competitive results, whilst the altruistic approach emphasises efforts to address health, environmental and social issues successfully.

Previous studies revealed that collaboration which exists between non-profits and Government (Boris and Steuerle, 2006) provides improved access to resources (Shaw and de Bruin 2013), facilitates knowledge and information exchange (Chalmers and Balan-Vnuk, 2013). These studies confirm that collaboration 'exists', but there is a scarcity of research explaining how the COVID-19 pandemic lockdown is influencing networking and collaboration activities, strategies and outcomes for small third sector social enterprises. Thus, this study's aim is to enhance our understanding of the types of collaborative strategies and networking activities small social enterprises employed during Covid-19 lockdown to support and engage with emerging and existing services users.

The research objectives are to:

1. Understand networking activities small third sector social enterprises were undertaking pre-Covid-19 first lockdown.
2. Ascertain changes to networking and collaborative strategies employed by small third sector social enterprises during Covid-19 first lockdown.
3. Identify small third sector social enterprises collaboration activities post-covid-19 first lockdown.

The next section discusses the research design, data collection and data analysis approach, employed to understand small third sector social enterprises networking activities and collaboration strategies during Covid-19 first lockdown.

METHOLOGY

This section explains the research strategy, data collection methods, data analysis, as well as time horizons, relating to the empirical work of the study. The section concludes with a discussion of the issues of methodological rigour, as well as the ethical considerations from the empirical work. Following a detailed review of the literature and consideration of the aim and objectives of the study, a purposeful sample of key informants were recruited from the authors network and from "WhatsApp" calls for participants in the UK. The author employed a qualitative research strategy to obtain data from 22 key informants (Chief Executive Officers) working in small third sector social enterprises to gain their views, experiences, networking activities and collaboration strategies in a pre-Covid-19 lockdown environment, during and post Covid-19 pandemic lockdown.

Interviews ranged from 48 to 62 minutes, at the end of the interview the author asked participants if they were satisfied with the interview. The author also gave participants the opportunity to add any additional information that they considered relevant for the study. Utilising on-line semi-structured interviews allowed the author to ask questions designed to address each of the study research questions in section 2.1.

Methods

The author reviewed Government policy published during the covid-19 lockdown and secondary data of small social enterprises involvement in delivering health, social care, and support services in the UK. Yin (2009) suggests that, except for studies of preliterate societies, documentary information is likely to be relevant to every research topic. The most important use of documents for the study was to form a general overview of the context of the research and to support and validate evidence from information gathered from semi- structured interviews with key informants.

In addition, information was gathered from online sources (the websites of various third sector, public social media accounts, online mass-media publication, etc.). Databases such as, google and google Schola search were applied to cover "government support" and "state funding", networking and collaboration activities linked to the COVID-19 lockdown (search string: Corvid 19 pandemic OR Coronavirus) focusing on published articles between December 30, 2019, and March 31, 2021. A total of 102 articles were analysed. On-line semi-structured interviews were conducted between January 2021 and March 2021.

The study employed a rapid response research method intended to produce evidence in a timely manner rather than to explain the pandemic and its effects after the event. Rapid response research lends itself to fastmoving developments and has, for instance, been employed to support rapid policy responses to riots (Doern, 2016) or earthquakes (Williams and Shepherd, 2016). The immediacy of the pandemic demanded rapid response research, sharing actionable findings in real time. Rapid Response Research provides a unique opportunity to provide real-time information, useful data, and up to date information for policy makers. In the longer term, data captured during rapid response research can become an essential element of scientific research that will explain economic recovery, changes in organisation's processes and will improve our understanding of this phase of the pandemic.

The method is employed to help answer the three pressing research questions that are linked to the research aim. The research questions are:

1.   (RQ1) What type(s) of networking activities did small third sector social enterprises undertake pre-Covid-19 first lockdown?
2.   (RQ2) How did small third sector social enterprises develop collaborations strategies during Covid-19 first lockdown?
3.   (RQ3) Why are small third sector social enterprises continuing networking and collaborations activities post-covid-19 first lockdown?

The semi-structured interview approach allows for flexibility with a preference for posing questions so that the interview is like a conversation whilst maintaining focus on issues contained in the research questions. The author began each interview with a general conversation about the purpose of the study and how the study will benefit organisations and the sector. In following this remit, the author created a space for the participants to share their experiences as openly as possible.

The study allows participants to contribute to research at the interface of third sector social enterprise pre-Covid-19 and post-the Covid-19 pandemic networking activities and collaboration strategies to provide a unique view just as the situation unfolds rather than after the event, by asking the study participants questions such as:

1. "How is your organisation affected by the COVID-19 outbreak?"
2. Did your organisation form new networking and collaboration activities to respond to challenges posed by Covid-19 lockdown?
3. "Are there any State policies that influenced your decisions to develop pre and post networking and collaborations strategies during this period? ".

Through their responses the aim is to gain a deeper understanding of networking and collaborative activities of small third sector social enterprises pre and post Covid -19 pandemic first lockdown.

Ethical Considerations

Prior to commencing the interviews, the author contacted each participant in writing and in advance about the purpose of the research, and the duration & time of the interview. The author obtained a signed informed consent form from each participant stating their willingness to participate in the research. Each participant was informed that they had the option to withdraw at any time from the research but none of the participants chose to do so. To maintain anonymity, the author did not name the participants and their organisations to ensure that readers of the chapter could not identify the views of specific individuals (Maher, 2013). Ensuring that participants did not restrict their disclosure was an important consideration for the research and involved the assurance of confidentiality (Bryman, 2016). To minimise inaccuracies in the interview data, interviews were digitally recorded (with participant permission) and transcribed verbatim. After transcribing each interview, the author read and manually checked the transcripts for accuracy and subsequently sent them to participants and invited them to check them as an accurate representation of what they said at the interview before starting data analysis.

We can consider the information verification process that the author employed during data collection as contributing to the methodological rigour of the research. Participants tended to give personal examples during the interview of what they did to pursue networking and collaborative activities. When they did not give examples, the author asked them to think of a recent action or events to justify their statements. The author made every effort to test the reliability of evidence from participants by seeking corroborative information from other sources such as documented evidence of organisational policy, organisation website and Government published literature on the Covid-19 pandemic. Collected evidence from the participants constituted most data for analysis and interpretation on the findings.

The study's validity issue relies on analytical generalisation rather than statistical generalisation. For this study, the author will be generalising gathered data from the semi-structured interviews with the study participants and literature which was discussed in section 2. Yin (2009) affirms that a study cannot rely on a single data collection method and advocates the need to use multiple sources of evidence. When one uses multiple methods, the researcher can place more confidence in the relationships that he or she uncovers in the research findings. Using multiple sources of evidence (semi-structured interviews, documentary evidence and UK Government Covid-19 pandemic published information) increases the validity of the findings as the strengths of one approach compensated for the limitations of the other evidence source (Yin, 2009).

Data Analysis

To satisfy the research aim and objectives, the author followed Huberman and Miles' (1994) process of data analysis. After transcribing each interview, the author read and manually checked the data to check the accuracy of the transcribed interviews. The author employed computer-assisted qualitative data analysis software NVivo 10 to facilitate the data coding and clustering of themes. Data was directly imported from a word processing package into NVivo 10, simultaneously creating cases with each interview transcript. It provided a disciplined structure to search and analyses of data. All the responses were coded to a particular interview question. New codes were interrogated through the search facilities. It added to the validity of the results by ensuring that the author found all instances of word usage (Maher, 2018b). It also helped provide a transparent data analysis process and a quick way of demonstrating who said what and when which in turn, provided a reliable general picture of the data (Miles and Huberman, 1994).

We can consider the information verification process that the author employed during data collection and analysis as contributing to the methodological rigour of the research. Participants tended to give examples during the interview of what they did to pursue networking and collaborative activities. When they did not give examples, the author asked them to think of an action or events to justify their statements. The author made every effort to test the reliability of evidence from participants by seeking corroborative information from other sources such as documented evidence of organisation website, policy, and procedures. Collected evidence from the participants constituted the major portion of data for analysis and interpretation in the study.

Some methodology limitations should be acknowledged. The most important limitation of the research **was** that only the Chief Executive of organisations participated. Another limitation was that organisational setting was not observed due to logistic limitations resulting from the Covid-19 pandemic lockdown restrictions.

Furthermore, the use of rapid response research could be interpreted as a limitation; however, the immediacy of the COVID-19 lockdown demanded this strategy in order to share actionable findings through recommendations in real time (Vindrola-Padros, et al.; 2020). The next section will explain and discuss the results and findings.

FINDINGS

This section explains the result of the fieldwork undertaken to understand networking activities and collaboration strategies, employed by small third sector social enterprises during the first Covid-19 lockdown, in order to overcome challenges exacerbated by the pandemic. The study represents an original contribution to knowledge and understanding of small third sector social enterprise networking and collaboration strategies pre and post Covid-19 first lockdown. The results will be discussed under the heading of each research question.

Research Question 1: What type(s) of networking activities did small third sector social enterprises undertaking pre-Covid-19 first lockdown?

The UK went into Lockdown on March 23rd, 2020, with rules coming into place stating the following: shopping for necessities; once a day for exercise; medical need or providing care and travelling to or from work (if you cannot work from home) (Ogden, 2020). These rules **mainly** affected the way in which social enterprises were able to continue networking and delivering essential services.

The study participants reported:

"We networked with organisations in same buildings to share ideas and sometimes we work on projects together ... it helps to share the load" (Participant: 2).

Our networks were far reaching geographically and across sectors. We always endeavour to attend most networking meetings they help us to build relationships with others in the sector but most importantly funders and local authority officers. This helped us to know who to speak with ... talk to and collaborate with when the Government announced the lockdown" (Participant: 4)

To support service recipients third sector social enterprises have formed formal and informal networks that developed directly into formal collaboration with other organisations to response to issues brought about by Covid-19 lockdown. The COVID-19 pandemic triggered the sharpest and deepest economic contraction in the 21st century (WHO: Situation Report-97).

Since the beginning of the first lockdown, there were more people requiring health and social care support. The demand for third sector services escalated. The first lockdown manifested uncertainty and threat to these organisations which resulted in increased networking with other organisations in the same difficult situation. This led to organisations hastily developing new networking activities.

The urgency of the situation combined with an organisation's survival need enabled greater sharing of information, open dialogue and working jointly to deliver services to the community. One of the most positive consequences of the pandemic lockdown has been organisations were able to disregard competitive practices exacerbated by UK commissioning rules (Maher, 2019b). This brings enormous networking opportunities to harness and maximise their strengths allowing them to work effectively together.

Research Question 2: Are there changes to the type(s) of networking and collaborative strategies employed by small third sector social enterprises during Covid-19 first lockdown?

Collaboration is about working together to achieve an agreed outcome in a mutually beneficial way. It requires a group of independent organisations working together to achieve a common purpose (Bingham and O'Leary, 2008). Furthermore, collaboration requires knowledge, internal assessments, assuming responsibilities and value creation. Evidence of how small social enterprises developed collaborations strategies during the Covid-19 lockdown are discussed below.

Several participants reported:

The collaboration with various organisations on a joined-up approach to service delivery has helped, and we see the greater good and synergies of working together during this crisis (Participant: 8).

To provide much needed support for the community we are collaborating and engaging with the National Health Service and Local Authority to share data and to identify and address gaps in service provision (Participant: 11).

We have threats to our existence, which we must fight for by working with others. I must say that the dedication and commitment demonstrated by all our collaborative partners is very inspiring ... we are collaborating with local, national and international based organisations (Participant: 15).

There is increasing evidence that collaborations across sectors, within sectors and across borders were established to deliver front line and community services during this period. These organisations were working together to improve health outcomes, social care, and wellbeing for all communities. The evidence suggests that building collaborations helped these organisations to survive the turmoil of the pandemic and restrictions put in place by the Government during the lockdown. It also supports the altruistic approach affirmation that organisations form collaborations to address social issues successfully. Collaborative activities form a significant part of an organisation's survival tactics, much of which was moving to intentional gathering resources required to provide support for services' recipients. Organisations were having to consider ways of delivering services using on-line services and working collaboratively with public and private sector organisations. Furthermore, these organisations were able to share their experiences and ideas to address health inequalities and drive transformation of health and social care services, this will stand them in good stead post lockdown.

Research Question 3: Why are small third sector social enterprises maintaining collaboration activities post covid-19 lockdown?

During the first Covid-19 lockdown third sector organisations were facing a dramatic fall in income and were facing increasing demands of their services due to the pandemic. Therefore, collaboration with other organisations was a strategy to support their survival. The evidence suggests that most organisations are continuing to maintain and develop such collaboration in preparation for future crisis and lockdown. There was concern over financial security when there were increasing demands on the organisation's services, which meant that these organisations maintained and continued to develop collaborative alliances locally, nationally, and globally post-Covid-19 first lockdown.

Although, the Government introduced the Coronavirus Job Retention Scheme and provided £750 million Coronavirus Business Interruption Loan to organisations to help them survive. To be eligible for the Coronavirus Business Interruption Loan Scheme, an organisation must generate at least 50% of its income from trading.

This excluded "a large proportion" of small third sector social enterprises. Some may have been eligible for the loan scheme but many of these small organisations were not able to take on debt finance as they did not generate the level of surplus income with which to repay loans and service interest incurred (NVCO,2020).

Participants reported:

Although we have received a small amount of funding from the government.... It's doesn't cover increasing staff hours to deliver the high demand for our services right now ... demand for our services is still increasing and people with long-term Covid are banging on our doors (Participant: 19).

We are a relatively small organisation we have less funding coming in now than we did a year ago, we don't know if we will be able to pull together the funding required to see us through this financial year if our collaborative partners pull out (Participant: 22).

We are in a critical situation. More than half of our staff have been put on Coronavirus Job Retention scheme. The level of uncertainty is painful. Organisations we are collaborating with are our lifeline (Participant: 16):

Throughout the lockdown, social enterprise organisations have been forced to collaborate with others. Hence, they have completely broken-down barriers within and between sectors to successfully form collaborative partnerships. However, these organisations are in desperate need for their organisations to survive beyond the lockdown period. Therefore, there is an urgent call for the Government to increase the support available to small social enterprises by setting up a comprehensive stabilisation fund, and to ensure that support is made available to these organisations as they are facing a dramatic fall in income. They are also experiencing financial hardship. Astonishingly, there were some CEOs petrified of losing their organisation's funding and as a result will not comment on Government funding policy during Covid-19 first lockdown. For instance, a participant stated:

Government policies relates to our funders … so I'm not prepared to say anything about our funding … or how government policies are affecting our funding right now … what I say here could affect our future funding … I am not prepared to comment (Participant: 1).

The onus should not be on individual enterprises to be fearful of making their needs known to the Government. There was a lack of clarity at sector-level about how the Government is determining which organisation should and can apply for the Coronavirus Business Interruption Loan. This lack of transparency meant that several organisations were missing out on much-needed funding. In future, funding criteria should be published to coincide with the announcement of public funding to minimise distress and uncertainty within the sector organisations.

DISCUSSIONS AND CONCLUSIONS

Covid-19 restrictions affected the functioning of many organisations, particularly small third sector social enterprises that have become largely dependent on state funding (Maher, 2018c). These organisations had to formulate collaborative arrangements from their networks and work consistently in collaboration with private and public sector organisations during the Covid-19 pandemic lockdown.

Their actions clearly support the altruistic collaboration notion which suggests that collaborations are formed due to the need for tackling health and social problems that exceed the scope of a single organisation; rather than a utilitarian perspective of collaboration, which emphasises on competitive reasons. Most organisations continued to implement creative methods, such as the use of technology as a more efficient networking and collaboration tool to deliver services rather than face-to-face support which were mostly restricted during the lockdown.

The UK Government was exposed to being unable to provide adequate financial support to the sector organisations and frontline staff. These insufficiencies were caused by years of austerity programmes introduced by the Conservative Party in 2015 (Maher, 2019a). This led to the fragmentation and displacement of a wide range of systems in the UK. These difficulties were further exacerbated by the lack of state planning capacity for pandemics such as Covid-19.

Going forward, the state should not view organisations networking and collaboration as a means of cost-cutting and reduction in public sector funding. Collaboration should be recognised as a means of improving efficiency and effectiveness. The state should support third sector organisations that collaborated with other third sector organisation, private and public sector organisation locally and globally to monitor their effectiveness, prepare to respond to changes in demand for services and future pandemics.

Networking and collaboration require organisations to share and learn across sectors and across all types of local and international organisations. It requires the intentional application of resources (staff time, funding, organisational infrastructure, etc.) by third sector organisations, funders, and the state.

There are, however, barriers to small social enterprises engaging in collaboration activities. These include:

1.   Lack of financial resources for collaboration and a lack of recognition by funders of the need to fund such activities.
2.   Inadequate resourcing due to funders only funding project-based work, inflexible funding parameters.
3.   Complexity of funding applications when multiple organisations are applying for the same funding.
4.   Funders competitive tendering approach, emphasising organisations competition rather than collaboration; this approach limits organisation openness to collaborate with other organisations in the sector.
5.   Limited expertise and staffing capacity to manage complex collaboration strategies.

During **the** Covid-19 pandemic lockdown, networking and collaboration were viewed as a means of addressing challenges, both from the organisation's perspectives (Banting, 2000; Brock & Banting) funders perspectives. The research supports the view that collaboration is a potentially powerful strategy to build small third sector social enterprises capacity locally, nationally, and globally for their long-term survival.

CONCLUSION

The world of networking and collaboration are complex, challenging, and contingent on many organisational and contextual factors such as, size and funding streams. It requires exploration and organisation's willingness to have open minded determination and ability to change processes that will affect the organisation's policy and funding application practices. Additionally, the use of research to make decisions about every stakeholder working with and the types of funding the organisation requires. Appropriate funding for infrastructure to support the collaborative process is needed. Funders could consider funding small social enterprise organisations infrastructure to initiate the collaboration and to support ongoing infrastructure and investment of resources.

This study makes a significant contribution to the current scholarly third sector literature. The existing literature has not explored the networking and collaborative activities of small social enterprises locally or globally pre or post Covid-19 pandemic lockdown. The research fills this void by examining organisation-level explanation of the types of networking and collaborative strategies they employed during Covid-19 lockdown to support and engage with services recipients.

The study findings echo argument of neo-classical economists' views that the existence of third sector organisations is due to the state failing to fulfil the demand for public services. This has been clearly demonstrated by the role small third sector enterprises played during Covid-19 lockdown. They provided urgent and much needed health, social and community services that the state was unable to provide such as, home delivery services and 24 hours counselling services. Although, there is distinctiveness between the third sector, the private and public sectors, there is **much** evidence to demonstrate how third sector organisations supplemented public sector services and worked collaboratively with the private sector during and after Covid-19 lockdown.

Networking and collaborative actions taken at international level in several countries with World Health Organisation (WHO) have been reinforced at national and local levels. For instance, UK small social enterprises were developing collaboration with the National Health Service, Local Authorities, Social Enterprise UK, and the World Association of Non-Governmental Organisations to support and assist the most vulnerable in our societies. As these collaborations are continuing post Covid-19 lockdown, this could have implications for building social capital in the third sector.

IMPILCATIONS FOR POLICY AND PRACTICE

The Coronavirus Job Retention Scheme and Business Interruption Loan Schemes promptly addressed an urgent need across the business sector. The Government was consistently referring to them as a solution for third sector organisations in financial hardship. There is a clear need to ensure such schemes are suited to the needs of the small third sector social enterprises before the information are published by the Government. The Government needs to recognise that some organisations may take some time to recover following the ending of the crisis and may need on-going support post-Covid-19 lock down for organisations to establish sustainable collaboration and networking strategies.

The Government should establish **a** further funding support scheme to help the sector organisations to stay afloat throughout post Covid-19 crisis. This should be available particularly to small social enterprises facing huge financial pressures.

Funders should allocate a portion of future funding envelopes to collaboration and networking activities – starting with a minimum target of 5% of the overall funding and increase funding year by year in accordance with inflation rate. This funding should address a specific framework that ensures measurable outcomes of organisation's networking and collaborative activities.

State funding bodies should facilitate integrated networking and collaborative arrangements between all sectors to co-produce solutions for tackling health and social care problems during a pandemic to inform public policy.

Similarly, third sector organisations should identify and assess possible networking and collaborative activities that will improve service delivery and create more efficient service delivery before a crisis or pandemic such as Covid-19. The sector organisations should be proactive not reactive.

There may be a need for the sector organisations to analyse CEO's networking and collaboration skills, this may make it possible organisations to identify CEO's developmental needs. Such actions could require re-visiting CEO's roles and responsibilities to accommodate the organisation's needs to develop collaborative capabilities.

The sector organisations should build evidence based **on** sustainable collaboration strategies and scalable networking support systems to prevent the next crisis or pandemic impacting on the health and social care needs of communities.

RECOMMENDATIONS FOR FUTURE RESEARCH

This study is an initial attempt to systematically examine small third sector social enterprises, during the COVID-19 fist lockdown, networking activities and collaborative strategies to strategies employed to drive the transformation of health and social care services in communities. The study provides a timely and detailed account of events from small third sector Social Enterprise CEOs.

Further research is required to empirically explore the cause-and-effect of networking and collaboration activities and intended outcomes through longitudinal studies cross-sector and cross borders. Future studies will also allow analysis, not only qualitatively, but also quantitatively; especially focusing on the dimensions and the effects of the actions of these organisations in other countries across the globe.

REFERENCES

Batley, R., & Rose, P. (2011). Analysing collaboration between non-governmental service providers and governments. *Public Administration and Development*, *31*(4), 230–239. doi:10.1002/pad.613

Boris, E. T., & Steuerle, C. E. (Eds.). (2006). *Nonprofits & government: Collaboration & conflict*. The Urban Institute.

Bryman, A. (2016). *Social research methods*. Oxford university press.

Chalmers, D. M., & Balan-Vnuk, E. (2013). Innovating not-for-profit social ventures: Exploring the micro foundations of internal and external absorptive capacity routines. *International Small Business Journal*, *31*(7), 785–810. doi:10.1177/0266242612465630

Ciucescu, N. (2009). The role and importance of Non-Profit Organizations. *Studies and Scientific Research. Economics Edition*, (14).

Doern, R. (2016). Entrepreneurship and crisis management: The experiences of small businesses during the London 2011 riots. *International Small Business Journal*, *34*(3), 276–302. doi:10.1177/0266242614553863

Hopkin, J., & Alexander Shaw, K. (2016). Organized combat or structural advantage? The politics of inequality and the winner-take-all economy in the United Kingdom. *Politics & Society*, *44*(3), 345–371. doi:10.1177/0032329216655316

Hyndman, N. (2020). UK charities and the pandemic: Navigating the perfect storm. *Journal of Accounting & Organizational Change*.

Jones, H. (2013). Collaboration and Mutual Support in the Third Sector. In *Community Research for Community Development* (pp. 197–218). Palgrave Macmillan. doi:10.1057/9781137034748_11

Kendall, J. (2004). The Mainstreaming of the Third sector into UK Public Policy in the late 1990s: Whys and Wherefores. In *Strategy Mix for Nonprofits Organisations* (pp. 41–70). Springer. doi:10.1007/978-1-4419-6858-6_3

Lalzai, K., & Rana, M. B. (2020). *Understanding MNC-NGO collaboration in emerging markets: Investigating how MNC-NGO collaboration evolves, creates and co*. Academic Press.

Lewis, J. (1999). Reviewing the relationship between the voluntary sector and the state in Britain in the 1990s. *Volantes: International Journal of Voluntary and Nonprofits Organizations*, *10*(3), 255–270. doi:10.1023/A:1021257001466

Macmillan, R. (2011). 'Supporting 'the voluntary sector in an age of austerity: The UK coalition government's consultation on improving support for frontline civil society organisations in England. *Voluntary Sector Review*, *2*(1), 115–124. doi:10.1332/204080511X560666

Maher, C. (2009). Managing career development in the not-for-profit sector. *Business Leadership Review, 6*(4).

Maher, C. (2013). *A qualitative case study approach to understanding third sector managers' career orientations*. Work Based Learning e-Journal International.

Maher, C. (2016). Career anchors of social enterprise managers in the UK-an empirical analysis. *Journal for International Business and Entrepreneurship Development*, *9*(4), 398–416. doi:10.1504/JIBED.2016.080019

Maher, C. (Ed.). (2018a). *Handbook of Research on Value Creation for Small and Micro Social Enterprises*. IGI Global.

Maher, C. (2018b). *Understanding Managerial Career Anchors and Career Path Preferences: A Case Study of Third Sector Social Enterprise Managers*. Scholars' Press.

Maher, C. (2018c). *Influence of Public Policy on Small Social Enterprises*. Academic Press.

Maher, C. (2019a). Public Policy and the Sustainability of Third Sector Social enterprises. *International Journal of Sustainable Entrepreneurship and Corporate Social Responsibility*, *4*(1), 42–56. doi:10.4018/IJSECSR.2019010103

Maher, C. (2019b). *Handbook of Research on Value Creation for Small and Micro Social Enterprises*. IGI Global. doi:10.4018/978-1-5225-6298-6

Maher, C. (2019c). Social Value and Public Services Procurement. In Handbook of Research on Value Creation for Small and Micro Social Enterprises (pp. 293-310). IGI Global. doi:10.4018/978-1-5225-6298-6.ch015

Maher, S. M. (2019). The Development of National Health Service Social Enterprises in England. In *Handbook of Research on Value Creation for Small and Micro Social Enterprises* (pp. 95–108). IGI Global. doi:10.4018/978-1-5225-6298-6.ch005

Mattessich, P. W., & Monsey, B. R. (1992). Collaboration: what makes it work. A review of research literature on factors influencing successful collaboration. Amherst H. Wilder Foundation.

Miles, M. B., & Huberman, A. M. (1994). *Qualitative data analysis: An expanded sourcebook*. Sage.

NVCO. (2020). *The UK Voluntary Sector Almanac*. NVCO Publications London.

O'Leary, R., & Bingham, L. B. (Eds.). (2009). *The collaborative public manager: New ideas for the twenty-first century*. Georgetown University Press.

Ogden, R. S. (2020). The passage of time during the UK Covid-19 lockdown. *PLoS One*, *15*(7), e0235871.

Polanyi, K. (1968). Our Obsolete Market Mentality. In *Primitive, Archaic, and Modern Economies: Essays of Karl Polanyi*. Academic Press. (Original work published 1947)

Shaw, E., & de Bruin, A. (2013). Reconsidering capitalism: The promise of social innovation and social entrepreneurship. *International Small Business Journal*, *31*(7), 737–746. doi:10.1177/0266242613497494

Shumate, M., Fu, J. S., & Cooper, K. R. (2018). Does cross-sector collaboration lead to higher non-profit capacity. *Journal of Business Ethics*, *150*(2), 385–399. doi:10.100710551-018-3856-8

Thomson, A. M., & Perry, J. L. (2006). Collaboration processes: Inside the black box. *Public Administration Review*, *66*(s1), 20–32. doi:10.1111/j.1540-6210.2006.00663.x

Vickers, I. (2010). *Social enterprise and the environment: A review of the literature*. ESRC Third Sector Research Centre, Working paper No 22. http://www.tsrc.ac.uk/Linkclick.aspx?fileticket=ecjpzwhq e4%3D&tabid=654

Vindrola-Padros, C., Chisnall, G., Cooper, S., Dowrick, A., Djellouli, N., Symmons, S. M., Martin, S., Singleton, G., Vanderslott, S., Vera, N., & Johnson, G. A. (2020). Carrying out rapid qualitative research during a pandemic: Emerging lessons from COVID-19. *Qualitative Health Research*, *30*(14), 2192–2204. doi:10.1177/1049732320951526 PMID:32865149

Weisbord, B. A. (1997). The future of the nonprofits sector: Its entwining with private enterprise and government. *Journal of Policy Analysis and Management: The Journal of the Association for Public Policy Analysis and Management*, *16*(4), 541–555. doi:10.1002/(SICI)1520-6688(199723)16:4<541::AID-PAM2>3.0.CO;2-G

Williams, T. A., & Shepherd, D. A. (2016). Building resilience or providing sustenance: Different paths of emergent ventures in the aftermath of the Haiti earthquake. *Academy of Management Journal*, *59*(6), 2069–2102. doi:10.5465/amj.2015.0682

World Health Organization Coronavirus Disease. (2019). *COVID-19 Situation Report-97*. Available from: https://www.who.int/docs/default-source/coronaviruse/situation-reports/20200426-sitrep-97-covid-19.pdf

Yin, R. K. (2009). How to do better case studies. The SAGE handbook of applied social research methods, 2, 254-282.

APPENDIX: ABBREVIATIONS

Each abbreviation has been defined in the text within which it first occurs.

CEO: Chief Executive Officer
NHS: National Health Service
NVCO: National Voluntary and Community Organisations
UK: United Kingdom
PCT: Primary Care Trusts
SE: Social enterprises
TSOs: Third sector organisations
U.K.: United Kingdom
U.S.A.: United states of America
WHO: World Health Organisation

Chapter 2
Strategies to Improve B2B Customer Relationships Through Digitally Enabled Experiences

Laura Ingrid Maria Colm

SDA Bocconi School of Management, Italy

ABSTRACT

Offering experiences—memorable exchanges and interactions with a brand—has become a top priority for companies of any sector and dimension over the last decades, especially in the light of the advent of digital technologies. However, to date both academic and practitioner attention is mostly limited to B2C contexts, thus calling for a deeper investigation of the opportunities that experiences offer also to B2B firms. After a brief review of the literature on customer experience and the role of digitalization—especially after COVID-19—this chapter focuses on digitally enabled experiences to improve B2B customer relationships. The chapter is based on a three case vignettes analysis that emphasizes how B2B firms can make use of digital tools to craft more effective and impactful customer experiences. Three digitally enabled B2B experiential strategies are identified—downstream empowerment, farsighted customization, and relational flexibility—that ultimately support B2B companies in improving their customer relationships in the long run.

INTRODUCTION

Experiences have become increasingly important over the last decades for companies of any sector and dimension. Offering the own customers meaningful and memorable exchanges and interactions with a brand (e.g., company, salespeople, offer itself, communications, etc.) is an important driver of business success and competitive advantage (Lemon & Verhoef, 2016). This has become especially true with the advent of digital technologies, as the empowerment of customers through digitalization has driven

DOI: 10.4018/978-1-6684-6762-6.ch002

organizations to focus more attentively on customer relationships, customer satisfaction, service quality and overall customer buying preferences and behavior (Batra, 2017).

Even though the concept has increasingly received attention both by academics and practitioners, it has been mostly limited to B2C contexts and relationships (Zolkiewski et al., 2017; Pandey & Mookerjee, 2018). However, especially with the uncertainty raised by and surrounding Covid-19, as well as its impact on global industries, B2B companies are starting to see the benefits of investing in customer experience and the advantage it can give them over the competition. Indeed, during the pandemic also B2B buyers got used to interact with their customers through digital tools, trying to replicate the strengths of in-person exchanges also via online or remote interactions with the supplier company. The concurrent progressions in terms of digital experiences in the B2C market have raised the bar even more, as B2B customers now expect the same kind of seamless, omnichannel "shopping" experiences they are confronted with as consumers, also in their business relationships.

After a brief review of the literature on customer experience both in B2C and B2B settings, and the role of digitalization in shaping them to create better customer relationships, this chapter focuses on strategies to improve customer relationships in B2B settings through digitally enabled experiences. In particular, the chapter is based on a three case vignette analysis, that highlight how B2B firms can employ digital tools to create meaningful experiences that can positively impact the relationships with their customers. The three cases – *Paulstra*, *TeamViewer Frontline*, and *Doosan Machine Tools* – do not necessarily present examples of strategies that were undertaken *because* of Covid-19, but they were offered and/or turned out as an effective response to market needs during that period, and indeed, they do not represent short-term buffers to handle the emergency, but forward-looking strategies for improving customer relationships in the post-pandemic future.

This chapter emphasizes how digitally enabled experiences can innovate and positively impact a company's relationships with its customers not only in B2C but also in B2B settings. From an academic standpoint the chapter responds to recent calls to further investigate customer experiences, and especially digital ones, in business and industrial contexts. The chapter also speaks to managers operating in several B2B industries, offering insights about how to improve buyer relationships and overall value chain relations by creating effective, long-lasting strategies that offer better experiences with the aid of digital tools.

CUSTOMER EXPERIENCE: A CONCEPT BORN IN B2C CONTEXTS

Customer experience is defined as a journey consisting of multiple interactions between a company and its customers across a series of touchpoints over time (Lemon & Verhoef, 2016). These touchpoints include all the moments and instances of customer-firm contact along the customer journey. They can elicit multidimensional responses – cognitive, emotional, behavioral, social, and sensorial ones – and can have a social, physical, or digital format, or a combination thereof (De Keyser et al., 2020).

The notion of *experience* grounds its roots in a variety of scientific disciplines, such as philosophy, anthropology, and sociology. The concept of *customer experience* goes back to the 1980s, when literature on consumer behavior in business and management studies was rapidly growing. Those were the early years in which the customer started to be envisioned and understood not only as a rational decision maker, who is solely interested in a product's functional benefits, but also as an emotional human being with feelings and individual preferences. Therefore, customer experiences include the role of emotions in consumption behavior and have been labelled as a subjective state of consciousness with "a variety of symbolic meanings, hedonic responses, and aesthetic criteria" (Holbrook & Hirschman, 1982, p. 132).

A decade later, in the 1990s, the customer experiences became more salient in the marketing field thanks to Pine and Gilmore, who coined the term *experience economy* (Pine & Gilmore, 1999). With this concept they recognized and referred to a new category of economic offering, which requires companies to craft and deliver memorable events for their customers, in order to stay relevant for them.

In the same period, Schmitt (1999), a pioneer in experiential marketing, developed a conceptual framework distinguishing among five types of experiences that companies can (and should) create for their customer base: sense, feel, think, act, and relate (a mix of all or some of the previous four experiences). This early framework emphasizes the importance of experiences not only for the customers – who have the opportunity to enjoy better interactions with their favorite brands – but also for organizations – who have the opportunity to generate greater value for their customers, thus getting value back in return (e.g., through loyalty, higher spending on the firm's products, and positive word of mouth).

Indeed, from then onwards, the marketing and management literatures acknowledge several contributions emphasizing the role of customer experiences as value generators for both customers and companies (see for instance Addis & Holbrook, 2001; Carù & Cova, 2003; LaSalle & Britton, 2003). For the latter they can ultimately be a source of long-term competitive advantage, especially if the experiences are personalized and co-created (Bolton et al., 2014; Jain et al., 2017). Thus, companies should take an active role in "orchestrating" the delivery of extraordinary experiences (Arnould & Price, 1993), especially as the value that marketers can provide entirely depends on the experiential evaluation of customers and co-creation with them (Vargo & Lusch, 2004). This requires paying attention in the conception and design of every small detail of the experience in each touchpoint involved.

Another framework (Cupman, 2016) has therefore tried to encapsulate the "recipe" of developing effective customer experiences by condensing them into six "ingredients" (or pillars): commitment (manifesting enthusiasm in satisfying customers through experiences), fulfillment (consistence of the experience with customer needs), seamlessness (experiences should be pleasurable and make life easier to the customer), responsiveness (timely response, delivery, and resolution of the experience), proactivity (anticipating customer needs and going beyond them in the experience delivery), and evolution (seeking constant changes and improvements of the offered experiences).

This tendency has eventually resulted in the creation of the "7Es" framework (Batat, 2019) a response to the traditional 4Ps marketing framework (and its various evolutions over time), putting the customers and their experiences at the very heart of companies' offerings through the "experiential marketing mix" – which relies on experience, exchange, extension, emphasis, empathy, emotional touchpoints, emic/etic process. In contrast to conventional marketing approaches, for which the ultimate goal is to maximize the customer's utility from a functional standpoint through quality and price (outcome-focus), from an experiential marketing perspective the goal is to maximize the lived experience (process-focus), incorporating also additional criteria, such as symbolic, emotional, relational, and aesthetic ones.

Overall, these major frameworks were all (more or less explicitly) designed for B2C situations and typically have the end customer (that is, the consumer) in mind – which can be explained against the backdrop of experiences' and experiential marketing theory's origins. Indeed, none of these models takes a clear B2B perspective, as they did not originate in or for B2B companies' needs. Nonetheless, with appropriate contextual adaptations, they can speak as well to B2B firms and help improving industrial supplier-customer relations – which increasingly feature similarities with B2C relationships, especially in the light of digitalization and Covid-19's acceleration in the adoption of digital tools also in B2B contexts.

THE RELATIONAL OPPORTUNITIES OFFERED BY B2B CUSTOMER EXPERIENCES

The lack of attention that has characterized the concept of customer experiences in B2B settings, both by researchers and practitioners, can have a twofold explanation. First, experiences and experiential marketing literature ground their roots in consumer research, where the concept got established primarily. Second, the B2B buying process has been traditionally viewed as highly rational, while customer experience has rather been envisioned as an emotional concept (see for instance Kemp et al., 2018). Indeed, the B2B purchasing process is often lengthy, planned (and not impulse-triggered), characterized by a high degree of complexity, and frequently involves multiple actors as decision makers, with a strong focus on elements such as technical features, performance, and value for money. In addition to this, the impact of experiences on a company's offer quality is difficult to measure and hard to quantify, as it relies on both intangible outcomes and long-term payoffs, which makes the concept elusive.

However, this gap is now starting to be addressed, as managers are acknowledging the relevance that customer experience management can have in improving relationships with their customers (Zolkiewski et al., 2017). Indeed, one recent attempt that goes in this direction is the exploratory study by Pandey and Mookerjee (2018), indicating that the experiential value for B2B decision-making comes from cost, functional, emotional, and symbolic values. Cost value refers to an experience able to minimize transaction costs (monetary and non-monetary ones) in an industrial purchase; functional value derives from experiences supporting an industrial offer's performance; emotional value builds on sensory and socio-relational cues; and symbolic value arises from positive associations between brand and company that are triggered during an experience. Altogether, these values build the concept of experiential value in B2B, which can be pursued especially through co-creation and customer involvement.

Indeed, literature highlights at least two relational benefits for business companies investing in experiential initiatives for their customers. First, they can help increasing repurchase (Russo et al., 2017), customer satisfaction (Madaleno et al., 2007), supplier brand equity (Biedenbach & Marell, 2010), overall business performance (Ulaga, 2018), profitability (Kuppelwieser & Klaus, 2020; McColl-Kennedy et al., 2019), as well as competitive advantage (Kushwaha et al., 2021). As shown by McKinsey (Maechler et al., 2016), B2B companies that were able to transform their customer experience processes earned benefits similar to those of B2C companies, including a 10 to 15% revenue growth and a 10 to 20% reduction in operational costs. This is particularly important for B2B companies, who typically rely on lasting relationships, where repeated purchases, satisfaction, and trust play a key role for the organization's long-term survival. Second, by offering satisfactory, high-quality experiences, B2B firms can improve the offer's value for both their customers, as well as their customers' customers (Pine 2015; Dahlquist & Griffith, 2014). This aspect is becoming increasingly important as shorter connections to the final demand are determining more frequently a business strategy's success, especially in the light of radical changes in the end markets, that have been triggered or accelerated by Covid-19.

Achieving these benefits is of paramount importance for B2B companies, especially in the light of their difficulties in performing well on the six customer experience pillars (see Cupman, 2016). Indeed, a study by B2B International (Hauge & Hauge, 2018) shows that none of the B2B companies surveyed claims to perform better than 48% on any of those dimensions. The worst scores go to proactivity (25%) and seamlessness (27%), indicating a substantial lack of industrial firms to adequately identify with customers and their needs. However, possessing these very skills would be important, considering that the conception of the traditional B2B buying process is evolving, including more frequently also experience-based information (Aarikka-Stenroos & Makkonen, 2014). Investing in experiences can therefore be a fundamental step towards improved industrial customer relationships.

This is all the more so, as products' features and pricing are becoming increasingly less effective as differentiators, due to higher commoditization and a globally more intense competition. Consequently, B2B managers are turning to customer experiences as the backbone of long-lasting, successful customer relationships, even though their limited familiarity with experiences implementation makes their deployment often a challenging task, thus requiring further knowledge on the topic.

THE ROLE OF DIGITAL EXPERIENCES TO IMPROVE CUSTOMER RELATIONSHIPS ESPECIALLY AFTER COVID-19

Over the last decade customer experience has become a dominant phenomenon in relational marketing and customer relationship management (CRM) – two concepts which got widely established in organizations in the 1990s, both in the B2C and the B2B domain. These notions have been criticized for being still too strongly sales- and product-oriented, and not adequately encompassing and addressing the intangible and symbolic needs and expectations of customers (in addition to rational ones). Thus, experiences can play a central role in responding to these shortcomings, by construing a customer-centric approach, as they encompass both the customer's rational and emotional perception of a firm, on the basis of multiple interactions through the whole customer journey (Verhoef et al., 2009).

Digitalization and digital marketing have dramatically increased the number of touchpoints along the customer journey that companies have at their disposal to effectively interact with their markets of reference in a multi- and, ideally, omnichannel manner. As digital technologies are becoming more widespread, managers are especially interested in understanding their influence and impact on the creation of customer-centric experiences (Batat, 2019). Indeed, a continuous access to the web through more stable and faster internet connections, as well as the diffusion of smartphones, the rise of big data and the subsequent level of personalization of the offer that can be obtained through them, the ascension of artificial intelligence, virtual reality, bots and robots, all represent powerful enablers of customer relationships through digital levers. Such technologies make goods and services more convenient and available to customers, allow more direct and efficient customer-company interactions, and also increase companies' opportunities to deliver more tailor-made experiences to their current and prospective customers (Smilanski, 2017). These opportunities go much beyond transactional digital marketing, centered on just the purchase of products online, for instance through e-commerce. In fact, this is just the top of the iceberg, as the content and information, services, and activities that can be made available through the digital sphere to both B2C and B2B customers need to be considered as well. These represent precious sources to craft customer experiences and can also act as amplifiers for physical experiences. Thus, digital experiences and experiences enabled through digital tools are becoming more and more central in today's marketing strategies – with a significant increase after the pandemic shock.

Covid-19 has given a strong boost to companies in the adoption of digital channels to reach and interact with their customers, as such means were the only available ones to maintain and sustain customer relationships and customer contact. Especially during the more severe phases of the pandemic, in which most countries worldwide were trying to contain the spread of the virus as much as possible through lockdowns, digital tools were the only opportunity firms had not only to keep their operations running. So, digital channels represented the sole solution to ensure *business continuity* during the pandemic shock.

This term refers to the "capability of an organization to continue the delivery of products and services within acceptable time frames at predefined capacity during a disruption" (International Organization for Standardization, 2019). However, Covid-19 did not only hamper companies from an organizational, productive, and logistical standpoint: it also (and especially) had dramatic consequences on *relational continuity*, that is, on maintaining regular contact and interactions with customers (Colm & Ordanini, 2021) – an aspect being particularly crucial for B2B firms, who rely on constant, cooperative, long-term relationships with their customers.

This situation has boosted the relevance and role of digital experiences in at least two ways. First, individuals got used in their everyday life to a more intense usage of virtual and online tools, which thus became more pervasive for both routinary (e.g., online grocery shopping in B2C or business meetings in B2B) and extraordinary activities (e.g., interactions with virtual shopping assistants for investment purchases in B2C or online deal signatures in B2B), in the private and in the professional sphere. Both consumers and industrial clients thus got used to spend time in digital environments – which can be defined as settings or "places" produced through computer technology – including websites, mobile applications, social media, audio and video content, and other web-based resources – that allow social interaction (Andrade Braga, 2009). As a consequence, they expect to digitally interact with firms through high(er)-quality experiences compared to the past, precisely because of their pervasiveness. So, companies should try to fully leverage digital technology's potential in order to meet the expectations of their increasingly demanding customers. In other words, the pandemic and the subsequent spread of digitalization have raised the bar in terms of intensity and quality of customer exchanges, leading to significant consequences at the relational level.

Second, while the complete online shift that businesses and their customers faced (almost overnight) during the pandemic is not likely to stay, a full comeback to physical exchanges is not likely to be restored either (McKinsey, 2020). This means, that individuals will still use and expect to employ digital tools in their private lives and at work, for efficiency and convenience reasons, but also as they can allow to better enjoy a company's offer and improve the interaction with the firm itself. Digital and digitally enabled experiences therefore shift to the center of attention of organizations, as companies are competing for an increasing share of their competitive advantage online, in digital environments, or in physical environments that are augmented with the aid of digital technologies. To fully seize the opportunities offered by digital innovation from an experiential standpoint, companies need to understand how to design forward-looking, well-crafted digital strategies, that are able to improve both offline and online relationships. This is particularly important from a long-term perspective, as the introduction of such digital innovations will impact permanently firms' business models, requiring and implying also radical changes to their DNA (Leeflang et al., 2014).

THE ROLE OF DIGITALLY ENABLED EXPERIENCES TO IMPROVE B2B CUSTOMER RELATIONSHIPS: A MULTIPLE CASE VIGNETTES ANALYSIS

The following section focuses on how B2B firms can make use of digital tools to craft and offer more effective and impactful customer experiences in B2B contexts. More specifically, with the aid of three successful examples, it aims at shedding light on how digitally enabled experiences can have the power to enhance the overall relationship between a company and its customers. This chapter is based on a three case vignette analysis, that highlight strategies through which B2B firms can effectively employ digital technologies to offer successful customer experiences that have positive reverberations at the relational level.

Through a multiple case vignettes approach (Holland & Naudé, 2004), examples of B2B firms from different industries – industrial components, software, and machine tools – are selected to highlight how digitally enabled experiential strategies can prove effective to improve a B2B firm's relationships with its industrial customers. For each case a detailed account is provided of how the companies employ digitally enabled experiences together with their underlying strategy, emphasizing the positive outcomes on the overall relationship against the backdrop of Covid-19. More specifically:

- The first case deals with *Paulstra*, a French company part of the Hutchinson group, which manufactures industrial components to solve vibro-acoustic problems in several industries. Paulstra introduced a mobile phone app called PaulstraSoft Mobile, that allows its customers and prospects to choose the right product by placing a mobile phone with the app on the machine tool. At the end of the process, the app suggests the best Paulstra solution for the specific customer-situation.
- The second case is about the software (productivity solution platform) *TeamViewer Frontline*, allowing to improve the workflow and remote interactions (e.g., for testing, repair, etc.) with industrial customers through augmented reality (AR).
- The third case features the Korean company *Doosan Machine Tools* who created virtual tours of their factories with virtual reality (VR), making them available for customers and prospects who are not able to visit their facilities physically and/or prefer to gain a deeper understanding of the company's offer in a digital fashion.

It is worth mentioning that the three cases – *Paulstra*, *TeamViewer Frontline*, and *Doosan Machine Tools* – do not necessarily present examples of strategies that were deployed *because* of Covid-19, but they were offered and/or turned out as an effective response to market needs during that period. In fact, they do not represent short-term buffers to handle the emergency, but forward-looking strategies for improving customer relationships in the post-pandemic future with the aid of digital tools.

Paulstra's Mobile App: How to Empower Business Customers and Improve their Experiences through Early Digital Interactions

In addition to rapidly changing market conditions, over the last decades industrial companies are constantly facing a situation in which the complexity of products and technologies is increasing, and their functionalities are continuously expanding (Dussauge et al., 1992; Christopher, 1998), and on top of this, recent exogenous shocks such as Covid-19 generated additional difficulties. In the light of such uncertain future market conditions, industrial companies need to put particular effort in being innovative and staying up to date, while nurturing long-term relationships with their customers. Indeed, offering products that are at the edge of technology while being easy – and even enjoyable – to employ for the customer, becomes the ultimate challenge to stay relevant in the market.

It is against this backdrop that the French company Paulstra launched the PaulstraSoft software some years ago. Paulstra is part of the Hutchinson group and is a leading player in Europe in the industrial components industry, more specifically in the vibro-acoustic field. The company produces articles and technical solutions for vibration and acoustic insulation through five types of products: elastomer mounts, metal mounts, flexible bushes, flexible coupling, and dynamic sealing. These are catered to the most diverse sectors, including automotive, rail, aerospace, and marine.

The PaulstraSoft software is meant to be an antivibration support selection tool and aims at offering an additional service to customers: helping them in determining the right vibratory solution in growingly complex business scenarios. For instance, it allows to make several calculations (e.g., the needed shock damping or the required vibration attenuation for a specific machine tool) and to visualize product sheets (for a better understanding of their technical features). The software can be downloaded and used free of charge and offers customers the chance to do computations and assessments to identify the components they need even before entering directly in contact with Paulstra, thus streamlining requests for technical consultations before possibly placing an order.

An evolution of the desktop version of the software, that proved particularly useful during the pandemic, consists in the smartphone application called PaulstraSoft Mobile. The app, which can be used independently on the desktop software, represents an extension of the original service, and is completely designed from the customer's standpoint, to offer an improved experience. Indeed, the company explains that PaulstraSoft's mobile version has been introduced since the use of smartphones is constantly increasing and a more agile and accessible software, suitable for all internet users, was needed. The app – which is free of charge as the desktop version – is handy and intuitive to use, with additional advantages. For instance, just by placing the smartphone with the PaulstraSoft mobile app on a machine tool while it is working, vibrations are registered through the smartphone's accelerometer. At the end of the process, the interface suggests the most suitable Paulstra solution (e.g., metal mount, flexible bush) on the basis of the customer's machine characteristics.

From an experiential standpoint, this supplier-led digital tool offers at least three benefits to the customer in addition to the possibility to measure directly the vibrations transmitted by the own devices – which is something that the desktop version cannot offer. First of all, it gives the customer time autonomy, as the application can be used anywhere and anytime, independently on Paulstra. Moreover, the application does not require a Wifi or 4G connection to use its features: once it has been downloaded, it works without internet connection. Finally, it also allows the customer to use it as a simulation tool between different Paustra vibration control solutions and to make first a benchmarking and comparison in an independent manner. So, the app enables the customer to do early digital interactions with the (potential) supplier without needing to ask immediately and directly for support. This experience gives customers higher degrees of freedom and encourages them to interact with Paulstra when it best fits their own journeys. This has been particularly helpful during the pandemic, where suppliers and customers could not meet in person – i.e., the supplier could not visit the customer to test and verify directly which solutions are most suitable for the customer's machines and workspace. However, the introduction of the app is a useful strategy far beyond Covid-19, as it improves the customers' experience – empowering them to do the first analyses of the decision process autonomously and independently on supplier suggestions – while increasing cost and time efficiency also for the supplier – who does not necessarily need to travel for basic evaluations, but "jumps in" when the customer can make clearer requests and has a higher readiness to adopt Paulstra's solutions.

Table 1. Paulstra's mobile app – PaulstraSoft: main information

Company and Digitally Enabled Experiential Strategy Information	
Industry	Industrial components (vibro-acoustic field) catered to the automotive, rail, aerospace, marine, offshore, defense, and general industry sectors
Location	Paris, France
Core offer	Articles and technical solutions for vibration and acoustic insulation through five types of products: elastomer mounts, metal mounts, flexible bushes, flexible coupling, and dynamic sealing.
Brand Positioning/Mission	"Paulstra is the specialist in noise and vibration reduction. With more than 80 years of experience, we are able to offer ranges of anti-vibration and acoustic products."
Revenues	About EUR 203 million (2020)
Number of Employees	650 (2021)
Digitally Enabled Experiential Strategy (PaulstraSoft Mobile)	Allow industrial customers and prospects to choose the right anti-vibration solution by themselves, by placing the mobile phone with the PaulstraSoft Mobile app on the machine tool. At the end of the process, the app suggests the best Paulstra-solution for the specific customer-situation.

TeamViewer Frontline: How to Customize Business Customers' Customers Experiences through Augmented Reality

In many cases, B2B suppliers manage relationships not only with their customers but also with their customers' customers (Dahlquist & Griffith, 2014) or influence them indirectly, for instance by creating product preferences (Webster, 2000) through the characteristics of the products they sell to their direct customers. This is particularly relevant in today's fast evolving business context, where the final market's needs change quickly, thus requiring the whole value chain to provide timely responses.

An outstanding case that helps shedding light on how the employment of digital technologies can help suppliers improve their customers' and especially their customers' customers experiences, is provided by TeamViewer's Frontline software. TeamViewer is a German company founded in 2005, who operates in the software development sector and is a leading company in cloud-based technologies, that enable online remote support and collaboration. The product range of the company includes Frontline, a productivity software platform, that enables the frontline workforce (typically operating in the factory) to operate with industrial augmented reality (AR) solutions that improve work quality. Indeed, processes are digitalized and streamlined for frontline employees in deskless workspaces through AR-empowered solutions (that include wearables, such as smartglasses, and mobile devices). These allow the companies employing them to increase work productivity, procedures' efficiency, and output quality not only in terms of internal operations, but along the entire value chain. For instance, such solutions create high potential for cost savings, due to reduced error rates in logistics, production, and assembly processes, while reducing complaints and improving the quality delivered to the own customers. So, through Frontline, TeamViewer puts its customers a position to create better working experiences for its employees (while improving the delivered performance), but also to create more valuable experiences (and higher quality offers) for their own customers.

For instance, Frontline includes a "See What I See" feature that allows technical assistance specialists to provide live support to their customers. They can initiate remotely an AR-session by wearing smartglasses on site, through which they can share with the technicians what they are looking at in real-time.

Table 2. TeamViewer frontline: main information

Company and Digitally Enabled Experiential Strategy Information	
Industry	Software development
Location	Göppingen, Germany
Core offer	Productivity solution platform
Brand Positioning/Mission	"TeamViewer focuses on cloud-based technologies to enable online remote support and collaboration globally."
Revenues	About EUR 514 million (2020)
Number of Employees	615 (2020)
Digitally Enabled Experiential Strategy (TeamViewer Frontline)	TeamViewer's Frontline software enables the frontline workforce to operate with industrial augmented reality solutions that enable remote support to and customized collaboration with their customers.

The technical assistance specialists can provide on-screen annotations and other information directly into the customer's viewer, they can also zoom in, share their screen, record the session, and even turn on electronic torches remotely, if needed. This way, the customer's technicians can receive indications about how to proceed and fix the problem in a timely manner. This example highlights how TeamViewer allows its customers to improve their customers' experience in receiving prompt assistance through the Frontline software.

In January 2022 the fourth release of Frontline was launched, which integrates additional new technologies that TeamViewer acquired in 2021. These features have further improved the service offered by Frontline, in particular, in terms of customizability of the software by the customer. This way, the customer can further personalize the software to offer in turn a highly customized service to their own customers, thus improving their experience. So, while Frontline's adoption grew during the pandemic, this strategic move suggests that the software's potential goes far beyond Covid-19. Indeed, the software contributes significantly to the improvement of the supplier-customer relationship, as it allows customers to be more responsive to their own customers' requests, while saving time and money (e.g., on travel). This kind of service seems especially important considering the growing predictive maintenance phenomenon, that has the power and potential to significantly enhance the customers' experience at all levels.

Doosan Machine Tools: How to Offer Business Customers Flexibility in Their Experiences through Virtual Tours

While physical interactions between supplier and customer are always relevant in B2B as they facilitate reciprocal understanding and alignment, it is even more important when the relationship is young (and the customer is still a prospect who does not know the provider), or when a new project needs to be started (and trust needs to be developed while the customer needs to be re reassured about the provider's competences) (Cousins & Menguc, 2006).

During the pandemic, however, in-presence encounters faced an abrupt interruption, since reciprocal visits were not possible at all during lockdown-periods, or only limitedly and with many constraints thereafter, as business was slowly but steadily "coming back to normal". This condition has caused a series of major difficulties to B2B companies, and especially to firms offering complex products and solutions, that are difficult to explain and represent typically expensive investments. These two characteristics make it very challenging for managers to sell such products remotely, without any physical trigger that can help build trust and prove the supplier's superior quality compared to the market average. In addition to this, the deal signature is another "moment of truth" that business customers typically prefer to happen in person, also for symbolic reasons.

An industry in which the above-described situation perfectly applies is the industrial machine tools sector, to which Doosan Machine Tools belongs. Doosan is a South Korean multinational company, founded in 1896 and specialized in manufacturing and selling metalworking machinery for diverse sectors, such as automotive, aerospace, IT, and energy. Its market is for about 50% Asian, but the share of sales from Europe and other Western regions is steadily growing.

With the outbreak of Covid-19, Doosan had to renounce all of a sudden to the opportunity of inviting prospects and customers to visit their headquarters and factory. These touchpoints are very important for the customer acquisition process, especially for a firm that is striving to expand internationally entering new markets in which its brand is less known and established. This is all the more so, as Doosan's facilities and factories represent an excellent business card, as they convey well the firm's innovativeness and high-quality standards.

As a response to the problem, Doosan resorted to shooting high-end corporate and factory videos, labelling them as virtual tours, as they offered online visitors the chance to get in touch with the company and better understand their characteristics and offer. First, a short, introductory virtual tour (lasting less than a minute) was made available on the company's website under the section "about us", as well as on Doosan's YouTube channel. The video was meant to provide a remote tour of the company's factory, displaying some representative products that the Doosan manufactures, as well as to show the main productive sites, the sales subsidiaries, and the established global service network for assistance. Then, the two main, South Korean factories could be further explored through virtual tours: the Seongju factory – presented externally through an aerial video and internally through drone-shot footages, integrated with text; and the Namsan factory – which was presented through an interactive map, allowing to click on several areas of interest (e.g., the system shop, the spindle grinding room) and choose the videos to watch. Eventually, a longer (lasting about ten minutes) virtual factory tour with virtual reality (VR) was also shot: VR gives the opportunity to interact with the video, by clicking on four directional arrows (up, down, left, and right) to better frame specific areas of interest in the company's facilities or in the displayed activities, according to the user's preferences.

Thanks to the virtual tours, Doosan aimed at allowing customers and prospects to live a first, visual, experience with the company even in absence of a regular on-site visit. Indeed, through a video many more information can be conveyed about a firm's values and philosophy, working procedures and product aspect, than through a traditional PDF-presentation. Another main advantage of the video is that it gives customers the flexibility to establish a first, autonomous, contact with a (potential) supplier, without having necessarily to ask for information beforehand. At the same time, as a repository is built through those videos, since they are saved on the company's YouTube channel, they can also be retrieved later in the relationship, if needed. So, the virtual tours allowed to "enter" the company in a moment in which it was not possible to do this otherwise but proved effective also after the Covid-19's travel restrictions. Indeed, these videos give customers the flexibility to decide if and when in their customer journey they prefer to plan a virtual or a physical visit. Additional flexibility is provided through the VR-integration, that ensures participation on the users' side by giving them the freedom to decide on what to focus.

Table 3. Doosan machine tools: main information

Company and Digitally Enabled Experiential Strategy Information	
Industry	Industrial metalworking machinery for the automotive, aerospace, IT, and energy sectors
Location	Changwon, South Korea
Core offer	Machine tools manufacturing and selling
Brand Positioning/Mission	"We build your tomorrow today: based on a customer-oriented approach it has pursued for the last 40 years, Doosan Machine Tools continues to strive to provide products with the highest quality in order to maximize customer satisfaction."
Revenues	About EUR 1.02 billion (2020)
Number of Employees	About 37,500 (2020)
Digitally Enabled Experiential Strategy (Doosan Machine Tool's Virtual Tours)	Doosan Machine Tools offers virtual tours of their factories – integrated also with virtual reality – to prospects and customers who are not able to come for an in-person visit or prefer to gain a deeper understanding of the company and its offer in a digital fashion.

MAIN EVIDENCE FROM THE EXAMINED CASE VIGNETTES: DOWNSTREAM EMPOWERMENT, FARSIGHTED CUSTOMIZATION, AND RELATIONAL FLEXIBILITY AS DIGITALLY ENABLED B2B EXPERIENTIAL STRATEGIES

The three case vignettes presented in this chapter focused on how B2B companies in different industries (industrial components, software, and machine tools) can effectively use digital technologies to craft meaningful experiences for their industrial customers, thus improving the overall supplier-customer relationship. Each vignette highlights the relevance of creating significant customer experiences not only in B2C, but also in B2B contexts, as these can impact the supplier-customer relationship in a positive way. More specifically, the digital dimension plays a major role to achieve this goal, as digitally enabled customer experiences have the power to improve the perception of the supplier's offer, increase customer satisfaction, and thus enhance the relational dimension between industrial buyer and seller. In fact, evidence points to the identification of three different *digitally enabled B2B experiential strategies* that B2B firms can employ to this end.

Paulstra's case offers an example of how digitally enabled service experiences can be used as a powerful instrument to create *downstream empowerment*, that is, enabling customers to do some initial steps by themselves before having to turn to the supplier with more specific requests. Indeed, through the PaulstraSoft mobile app, prospective and actual customers get a free tool that allows them to perform some tests and preliminary verifications in a self-service fashion. This way, customers are empowered, as they are given the opportunity to "break free" from the supplier – at least until they are not sure that the supplier's product range is suitable to satisfy their needs. While it might seem that the provider is giving up degrees of control with such a strategy, the likelihood to increase customers' satisfaction thanks to a seamless experience (Cupman, 2016) and to improve the relational bond with the supplier is actually higher, as the customer's role has been elevated by the provider itself. So, power shifts downstream in the value chain, but the deriving benefits are for the upstream players (B2B suppliers) as well, thanks to the employment of a digital self-service technology, that made this virtuous circle possible. This strategy proved effective as it did not only provide a solution to a short-term pandemic problem – the opportunity to establish what kind of products the customer needs without having to meet physically –

but responded to the broader need to make industrial relationships simultaneously more efficient and pleasant for all parties involved.

In the case of TeamViewer's Frontline software platform, the strategic purpose of the digitally enabled experience provided through the software – and especially through its latest release – is a different one. Frontline owes much of its success to its *farsighted customization*, that is, to the fact that it enables customers to improve and personalize the experience lived by their own customers through the employment of this tool. For instance, through the AR embedded in the Frontline application, TeamViewer's customers can better support their own customers remotely, by providing tele-guided and computer-aided assistance. This assistance provided through a cutting-edge technological experience that was well-conceived upfront by the original supplier provides three benefits. First, it permits to fix problems in a more efficient and effective way, potentially improving overall business performance (Ulaga, 2018) and competitive advantage (Kushwaha et al., 2021). Second, it also provides a pleasurable experience to those in need of the assistance (Dahlquist & Griffith, 2014), thanks to a user-friendly interface. Third, the provided experience is highly customizable, which enables Frontline's customers to contribute actively to the value generated downstream. This kind of strategy has certainly paid off during Covid-19, when remote interactions (and especially guidance and support to keep operations running) were the only available alternative to in-person meetings. However, its success is likely to last as the pandemic has shown that there was room for streamlining operations, without renouncing to high-level experiences in the supplier-customer relationship. On the contrary: digitally enabled experiences make augmented interactions possible, that are even more effective than the traditional, physical ones.

Eventually, the motivation underlying the employment of digital experiences in Doosan Machinery Tool's case, can be attributed to the need to infuse *relational flexibility* into the relationships with its customers. The virtual tours have allowed the company to continue looking for new leads also during the pandemic, when receiving prospects' visits was not possible because of sanitary restrictions. However, this kind of digital experience also gives the opportunity to get in touch with a potential supplier without needing to invest significant amounts of time and money when the customer is still unsure. So, this additional flexibility offered by the digital visit is an advantage that will remain beyond the pandemic. From the provider's standpoint, it allows to have a strong control over the image, capabilities, and values it wants to convey – to some extent even more than in a physical visit. From the customers' standpoint, it allows to be engaged through a simple and intuitive yet innovative experience, which involves the use of VR – possibly making more decision makers participate than it would have been possible in a physical visit. So, the chance of "tangibilizing" the offer (Thomsen et al., 2020) through digital technologies has provided long-term benefits for both parties involved.

Figure 1 provides a visual summary of the three digitally enabled B2B experiential strategies that act as catalysts for better supplier-customer relationships.

Summing up, the three examined case vignettes allow to shed light on different strategic functions of digitally enabled experiences in B2B contexts. B2B managers should consider which kind of digital tools can best fit the experiences they want to deliver to their industrial clients according to the specific situation they are confronted with and depending on the goals they want to achieve – i.e., making their customers more autonomous, helping them in getting established in the eyes of their own demand, or giving them several flexible options for getting accustomed with the supplier's offer.

It is worth highlighting, that digital tools contributed to both sustaining and improving customer relationships temporarily, during a crisis, but are not limited to that. Indeed, the companies featured in the three case vignettes all adopted forward-looking strategies, that could help them offer better experiences also in a long-term view. This is made possible as all three strategies rely intensely on co-creation (Vargo & Lusch, 2004) and thus concretely involve customers, by delegating some tasks to them (Paulstra), strengthening their core capabilities (TeamViewer Frontline), and making them choose the way they want to be engaged (Doosan Machine Tools). in addition to this, in all three cases the B2B company's key to successful digitally-enabled experiences relied in the consideration of the customers' underlying needs – the need to be more independent and (pro)active decision makers (Paulstra), the need to improve downstream relationships (TeamViewer Frontline), the need for flexibility (Doosan Machine Tools). As a consequence, putting the customer at the very center of the company's strategies, also from an experiential (and not only a rational-functional) standpoint, with the help of digital technologies, seems to be an optimal way to boost B2B relationships.

Figure 1. The three digitally enabled B2B experiential strategies

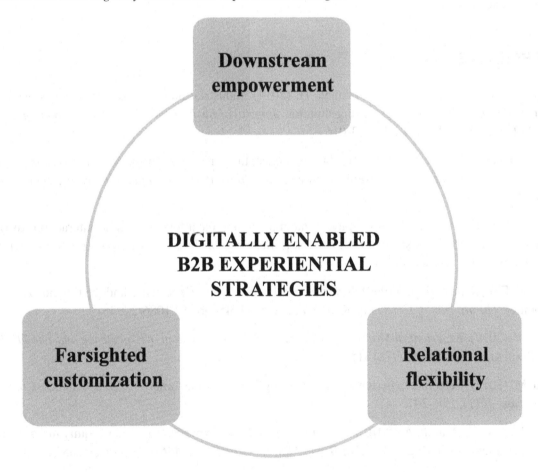

CONCLUSION

This chapter emphasizes how digitally enabled experiences can improve, innovate, and positively impact a company's relationships with its customers not only in B2C but also in B2B settings. Indeed, there is the need to maintain a balance between two tensions: preserving long-lasting customer relationships and replicating strategies that proved successful, while innovating the customers' experience. Digital technologies can significantly contribute to addressing this tension successfully, as depicted in the three case vignettes: through downstream empowerment (elevating the role of the own customers), farsighted customization (allowing customers to better respond to their own customers' needs), and relational flexibility (allowing customers to co-determine the interaction modes with the supplier). However, there are two important preconditions for digitally enabled experiential strategies to work. First, B2B managers must believe that they have the true potential to improve the overall buyer-seller relationship holistically, and not envision them just as a "nice to have" to modernize interactions. Second, the specific digital technology chosen should be coherent with the company's positioning, success factors, and values, in order to amplify them in the eye of the customer. This provides an important step to reach a better understanding of customer experiences, and especially digital ones, in business and industrial contexts (see Zolkiewski et al., 2017), that managers can rely on for fostering their B2B market relationships in the post-pandemic future.

REFERENCES

Aarikka-Stenroos, L., & Sakari Makkonen, H. (2014). Industrial buyers' use of references, word-of-mouth and reputation in complex buying situation. *Journal of Business and Industrial Marketing*, *29*(4), 344–352. doi:10.1108/JBIM-08-2013-0164

Addis, M., & Holbrook, M. B. (2001). On the conceptual link between mass customisation and experiential consumption: An explosion of subjectivity. *Journal of Consumer Behaviour*, *1*(1), 50–66. doi:10.1002/cb.53

Andrade Braga, A. (2009). Netnography: A naturalistic approach towards online interaction. In B. J. Jansen, A. Spink, & I. Taksa (Eds.), *Handbook of Research on Web Log Analysis* (pp. 488–505). IGI Global. doi:10.4018/978-1-59904-974-8.ch024

Arnould, E. J., & Price, L. L. (1993). River Magic: Extraordinary Experience and the Extended Service Encounter. *The Journal of Consumer Research*, *20*(1), 24–45. doi:10.1086/209331

Batat, W. (2019). *Experiential Marketing: Consumer Behavior, Customer Experience and The 7Es* (1st ed.). Routledge. doi:10.4324/9781315232201

Batra, M. (2017). Customer experience – an emerging frontier in customer service excellence. *Competition Forum*, *15*(1), 198–207.

Biedenbach, G., & Marell, A. (2010). The impact of customer experience on brand equity in a business-to- business services setting. *Journal of Brand Management*, *17*(6), 446–458. doi:10.1057/bm.2009.37

Bolton, R. N., Gustafsson, A., McColl-Kennedy, J., Sirianni, N. J., & Tse, D. K. (2014). Small details that make big differences: A radical approach to consumption experience as a firm's differentiating strategy. *Journal of Service Management*, *25*(2), 253–274. doi:10.1108/JOSM-01-2014-0034

Carù, A., & Cova, B. (2003). Revisiting consumption experience: A more humble but complete view of the concept. *Marketing Theory*, *3*(2), 259–278. doi:10.1177/14705931030032004

Christopher, M. (1998). *Logistics and Supply Chain Management – Strategies for Reducing Cost and Improving Service* (2nd ed.). Pitman Publishing.

Colm, L., & Ordanini, A. (2021). Facing supply chain disruptions: Strategies to ensure relational continuity. In R. Wilding (Ed.), *The impact of Covid-19 on supply chain management* (pp. 55–72). Proud Pen. doi:10.51432/978-1-8381524-2-0-4

Cousins, P. D., & Menguc, B. (2006). The Implications of Socialization and Integration in Supply Chain Management. *Journal of Operations Management, 24*(5), 604–620. doi:10.1016/j.jom.2005.09.001

Cupman, J. (2016). The Six Pillars of B2B Customer Experience Excellence. *MarketingProfs*. Available at: https://www.marketingprofs.com/articles/2016/29806/the-six-pillars-of-b2b-customer-experience-excellence

Dahlquist, S. H., & Griffith, D. A. (2014). Multidyadic industrial channels: Understanding component supplier profits and original equipment manufacturer behavior. *Journal of Marketing, 78*(4), 59–79. doi:10.1509/jm.13.0174

De Keyser, A., Verleye, K., Lemon, K. N., Keiningham, T. L., & Klaus, P. (2020). Moving the customer experience field forward: Introducing the touchpoints, context, qualities (TCQ) nomenclature. *Journal of Service Research, 23*(4), 433–455. doi:10.1177/1094670520928390

Dussauge, P., Hart, S., & Ramanantsoa, B. (1992). *Strategic Technology Management – Integrating Product Technology into Global Business Strategies for the 1990s*. Wiley.

Hauge, N., & Hauge, P. (2018). *B2B Customer Experience: A Practical Guide to Delivering Exceptional CX*. KoganPage.

Holbrook, M. B., & Hirschmann, E. C. (1982). The experiential aspects of consumption: Consumer fantasies, feelings and fun. *The Journal of Consumer Research, 9*(2), 132–140. https://www.jstor.org/stable/2489122. doi:10.1086/208906

Holland, C. P., & Naudé, P. (2004). The metamorphosis of marketing into an information-handling problem. *Journal of Business and Industrial Marketing, 19*(3), 167–177. doi:10.1108/08858620410531306

International Organization for Standardization. (2019). *Security and resilience – Business continuity management systems – Requirements* (ISO 22301:2019). https://www.iso.org/obp/ui#iso:std:iso:22301:ed-2:v1:en

Jain, R., Aagja, J., & Bagdare, S. (2017). Customer experience–a review and research agenda. *Journal of Service Theory and Practice, 27*(3), 642–662. doi:10.1108/JSTP-03-2015-0064

Kemp, E., Borders, A., Anaza, N., & Johnston, W. (2018). The heart in organizational buying: Marketers' understanding of emotions and decision-making of buyers. *Journal of Business and Industrial Marketing, 33*(1), 19–28. doi:10.1108/JBIM-06-2017-0129

Kuppelwieser, V. G., & Klaus, P. (2020). Measuring customer experience quality: The EXQ scale revisited. *Journal of Business Research, 126*(C), 624–633. doi:10.1016/j.jbusres.2020.01.042

Kushwaha, A. K., Kar, A. K., & Dwivedi, Y. K. (2021). Applications of big data in emerging management disciplines: A literature review using text mining. *International Journal of Information Management Data Insights*, *1*(2), 100017. doi:10.1016/j.jjimei.2021.100017

LaSalle, D., & Britton, T. A. (2003). *Priceless: Turning ordinary products into extraordinary experiences*. Harvard Business School Press.

Leeflang, P. S. H., Verhoef, P. C., Dahlström, P., & Freundt, T. (2014). Challenges and solutions for marketing in a digital era. *European Management Journal*, *32*(1), 1–12. doi:10.1016/j.emj.2013.12.001

Lemon, K. N., & Verhoef, P. C. (2016). Understanding customer experience throughout the customer journey. *Journal of Marketing*, *80*(6), 69–96. doi:10.1509/jm.15.0420

Madaleno, R., Wilson, H., & Palmer, R. (2007). Determinants of Customer Satisfaction in a Multi-Channel B2B Environment. *Total Quality Management & Business Excellence*, *18*(8), 915–925. doi:10.1080/14783360701350938

Maechler, N., Sahni, S., & van Ooostrun, M. (2016). *Improving the business-to-business customer experience*. https://www.mckinsey.com/business-functions/marketing-and-sales/our-insights/improving-the-business-to-business-customer-experience

McColl-Kennedy, J., Mohamed Zaki, M., Lemon, K. N., Urmetzer, F., & Neely, A. (2019). Gaining customer experience insights that matter. *Journal of Service Research*, *22*(1), 8–26. doi:10.1177/1094670518812182

McKinsey & Company. (2020). *The path to the next normal*. https://www.mckinsey.com/~/media/McKinsey/Featured%20Insights/Navigating%20the%20coronavirus%20crisis%20collected%20works/Path-to-the-next-normal-collection.pdf

Pandey, S. K., & Mookerjee, A. (2018). Assessing the role of emotions in B2B decision making: An exploratory study. *Journal of Indian Business Research*, *10*(2), 170–192. doi:10.1108/JIBR-10-2017-0171

Pine, B. (2015). How B2B companies create economic value by designing experiences and transformations for their customers. *Strategy and Leadership*, *43*(3), 2–6. doi:10.1108/SL-03-2015-0018

Pine, B. J. II, & Gilmore, J. H. (1999). *The experience economy*. Harvard Business School Press.

Russo, I., Confente, I., Gligor David, M., & Cobelli, N. (2017). The combined effect of product returns experience and switching costs on B2B customer re-purchase intent. *Journal of Business and Industrial Marketing*, *32*(5), 664–676. doi:10.1108/JBIM-06-2016-0129

Schmitt, B. (1999). Experiential marketing. *Journal of Marketing Management*, *15*(1-3), 53–67. doi:10.1362/026725799784870496

Smilanski, S. (2017). *Experiential Marketing* (2nd ed.). KoganPage.

Thomsen, T. U., Holmqvist, J., von Wallpach, S., Hemetsberger, A., & Belk, R. W. (2020). Conceptualizing unconventional luxury. *Journal of Business Research*, *116*, 441–445. doi:10.1016/j.jbusres.2020.01.058

Ulaga, W. (2018). The journey towards customer centricity and service growth in B2B: A commentary and research directions. *AMS Review*, *8*(1/2), 80–83. doi:10.100713162-018-0119-x

Vargo, S. L., & Lusch, R. F. (2004). Evolving to a New Dominant Logic for Marketing. *Journal of Marketing*, *68*(1), 1–17. doi:10.1509/jmkg.68.1.1.24036

Verhoef, P. C., Lemon, K. N., Parasuraman, A., Roggeveen, A., Tsiros, M., & Schlesinger, L. A. (2009). Customer experience creation: Determinants, dynamics and management strategies. *Journal of Retailing*, *85*(1), 31–41. doi:10.1016/j.jretai.2008.11.001

Webster, F. E. (2000). Understanding the relationships among brands, consumers, and resellers. *Journal of the Academy of Marketing Science*, *28*(1), 17–23. doi:10.1177/0092070300281002

Zolkiewski, J., Story, V., Burton, J., Chan, P., Gomes, A., Hunter-Jones, P., O'Malley, L., Peters, L. D., Raddats, C., & Robinson, W. (2017). Strategic B2B customer experience management: The importance of outcome-based measures. *Journal of Services Marketing*, *31*(2), 172–184. doi:10.1108/JSM-10-2016-0350

KEY TERMS AND DEFINITIONS

B2B Relationship: The relationship between a firm and its industrial customers.

Case Vignette: Short, written summary of a case study.

Customer Experience: The interaction between firm and customer over the duration of their relationship through a series of physical and digital touchpoints.

Digital Environment: A setting or place produced through computer technology – including websites, mobile applications, social media, audio and video content, and other web-based resources.

Digitally Enabled Experience: A customer experience made possible, improved, and/or augmented thanks to the aid of digital technologies.

Relational Continuity: A specific form of business continuity that refers to a company's capability and effort of maintaining regular contact and interactions with customers in all conditions, also when an exogenous shock (such as the COVID-19 pandemic) occurs.

Relational Marketing: Marketing efforts dedicated to maintaining, sustaining, and improving over time the relationships between a firm and its customers.

Chapter 3
Patterns of Self–Sufficient Companies' Network Interaction Reorganization Due to COVID–19:
Dialectics of Organizational Structures Optimization

Andrey I. Pilipenko
https://orcid.org/0000-0001-9446-345X
Russian Presidential Academy of National Economy and Public Administration, Russia

Olga I. Pilipenko
The Russian Presidential Academy of National Economy and Public Administration, Russia

Zoya A. Pilipenko
https://orcid.org/0000-0001-5734-5673
Bank of Russia, Russia

ABSTRACT

The self-sufficient companies are dialectically complex formations capable of self-movement through downward and upward causation mechanisms. They become drivers for constructing the future reality. As backbone elements of the economic system, resilient companies change both the internal structure and the external one. Under the influence of the pandemic, the technological revolution 4.0, the downward causation mechanism induces organizational changes within the companies while the upward causation one does the same with their external networking interactions. Thus, they build new structural relationships as the future economic system basis, distinguished by the dialectical interaction of the economy and society with the dominance of social preferences of individuals. Such a transformation occurs as self-sufficient companies build up intangible assets; build corporate ecosystems based on technological platforms; introduce diversity, equity, and inclusion principles into intra-company structures; and include ecological, social, and governance issues in their development strategies.

DOI: 10.4018/978-1-6684-6762-6.ch003

BACKGROUND

The COVID-19 pandemic has radically changed the prevailing ideas about the possibility of extraordinary changes in the economy, society, and companies, which were expressed in the calls of the World Economic Forum for Great Reset. At the same time, many obstacles arose on the way to the New Normal after COVID-19, which are due to the absolute uncertainty of the future reality (Okamoto, 2020). In this regard, there is an urgent need to rethink fundamental changes in the past and present in order to understand the patterns of formation of post-COVID-19 reality. In the chapter of this book titled "Dialectics of self-movement of resilient companies in the economy and society post COVID-19: patterns of organizational transformations of networking interactions" the authors present their vision of the main driver of the processes of system formation of the future reality and justify theoretically their choice of self-sufficient companies in this capacity. They have demonstrated their ability to change their internal structure and participate in the organization of the system's structure at the macro level. This is explained by the fact that, having become self-sufficient, these companies have acquired the ability to quickly adapt to the changed conditions of their functioning by "destroying" non-working interactions and by "creating" new structural ties. Of great importance is the fact that as a result of "creative destruction", according to J. Schumpeter (1949), the object, subjective and process components of the processes of system formation change. The object component of the organizational relations of self-sufficient companies is associated with an increase in the variety of new assets in the exchange, the subject component concerns the participants of the exchange, and the process component is represented by the interaction of downward and upward causation mechanisms at the disposal of companies.

With the help of the downward causation mechanism resilient companies structure their internal organization as to object and subject components. In fact, self-sufficient companies do the same in connection with the objective and subjective components of the processes of structure formation through the upward causation mechanism. Based on the developments of such representatives of institutional theory as O.E. Williamson (1985), R.H. Coase (1988), G.M. Hodgson (1988b), the authors identified a dialectical pair of causation mechanisms in the hands of self-sufficient companies that are able to transform both the internal organizational structure of their business and external networking interactions with their help. At the same time, the difference in the operation of these mechanisms at the dispose of these companies lies in the fact that in a static economic system these changes complicate its structure, reproducing the constant relationships, both at its horizontal level and in the formation of a vertical structural hierarchy. In other words, downward and upward causation mechanisms strengthen the integrity of a static economic system, but up to its certain limit state. The dialectical leap of the system from statics to dynamics is also mediated by self-sufficient companies. It only begins with the destruction of the structure of a static economy, when the levels-causes and levels-effects, built in the form of upward vertical structures, change the vector of their movement to the opposite - towards downward causation relationships. As a result, the structure of system integrity is destroyed and it loses the mechanism of its own self-organization. This is how the conditions are formed for the dialectical leap of a static economic system into the complete uncertainty of a future dynamic reality. And the main role in breaking the evolutionary continuity is played by the structure-forming elements of the system, which are self-sufficient companies. The most important moment of such creative transformation by companies of internal and external networking interactions is their role as the demiurge of structuring post-COVID-19 reality both in terms of the object and subjective components, and in the context of the process component of these organizational transformations. It is they who, from a theoretical point of view, are called upon to construct new organizational ties that are adequate to the dynamic post-COVID-19 reality.

The authors build methodological approaches to interpreting the special role of self-sufficient companies in the processes of structuring post-pandemic reality involving the theoretical developments of representatives of general systems theory (Hacken, 1977), of synergetics (Bertalanffy, 1968), tectology (Bogdanov, 1934), the catastrophe theory (Arnold, 1975, 1979; Guckenheimer, 1973; Zeeman, 1977; Thom, 1969; 1974), of the modern theory of complexity economics (Arthur, 1999; Arthur, et al., 1997; Anderson, et al., 1988; Hausmann, et al., 1996), etc. Besides much was inspired by the geniuses of the past and present who anticipated the distant future: G.W.F. Hegel (1892), K. Marx and F. Engels (1955-1974), J. M. Keynes (1936), Joseph A. Schumpeter (1949), D. North (1990, 1997, 2005), and many other brilliant researchers.

For the in-depth understanding of this phenomenon, the authors use dialectical logic in interpreting the organizational potential of self-sufficient companies and the mechanisms for its implementation at the stage of the jump of existing economic systems from statics to their dynamics post COVID-19 (Pilipenko, at al., 2021). In other words, all network interactions with the participation of such companies can be interpreted from the point of view of the interaction of integration (cooperation, association, inclusion) and disintegration (differentiation, separation, diversity), regulated by dialectical laws. The optimization mechanism of these universal organizational processes is described by the authors using the dynamic set model (Smit, et al., 2020; Davies, et al., 2019; Ghose, 2020; Dixon-Fyle, 2020).

For the authors' generalizations, specific developments of such consulting companies as McKinsey & Co, McKinsey Global Institute, PwC, KPMG, BCG Henderson Institute, The Economist Group were used, which made it possible to differentiate the national practices of self-sufficient companies in a sample of individual countries of the world.

The authors analyze specific trends that have become real during the pandemic and which, to a greater or lesser extent, should be considered in the context of constructing a future reality as a form of organizing a dynamic economy. At the same time, based on systemic theories, it should be recognized that the progress of a dynamic economy in comparison with its past static state will be determined by the possibilities of its "expansion" as a condition for its self-development. With regard to the modern economy, it is about the restoration of its dialectical interaction with society within the framework of the socio-economic systemic integrity. A special role belongs to self-sufficient companies, since it is they who will mediate this expansion of the capabilities of the new system, integrating into it dialectically both the economy and society. This is what will largely determine the much greater opportunities for progress in the new, more complex, dynamic economy. At the same time, the growth in the variety of organizational solutions that will be used by self-sufficient companies in the context of self-development of system integrity will be largely determined by new products, services, processes and businesses, new breakthrough technological tools such as cloud technologies, big data, the internet of things (IoT), artificial intelligence (AI). On this basis, self-sufficient companies have stepped up their networking interactions by building corporate ecosystems, technological platforms, etc. The logical consequence of the digital transformation of their business processes was the problem of a shortage of workers with the necessary qualifications, which are qualitatively different from the needs of a static economy (Boston Consulting Group, 2019). At the same time, the problem of socialization of talented employees in intra-company teams has become more acute, which has demanded the latest corporate strategies for optimizing diversity, equity, and inclusion principles. And expanding the sphere of interests of self-sufficient companies by including environmental, social and governance (ESG) issues in them makes it possible to understand the mechanism for restoring the dialectic of interaction between the economy and society in the sense of constructing a new dynamic reality of the future.

Thus, the interdependence of the phenomenon of the technological revolution 4.0 with the labor force necessary to implement its results leads to the problem of replacing the principles of capital-centrism with human-centrism in the organization of structural ties both within companies and in the system as a whole. For an in-depth understanding of this phenomenon, the authors use dialectical logic in interpreting the organizational potential of self-sufficient companies and the mechanisms for its implementation at the stage of the jump of existing economic systems from statics to their dynamics in the post-COVID-19 future. At the same time, the authors interpret all network interactions with the participation of companies in terms of the interaction of integration (cooperation, association, inclusion) and disintegration (differentiation, separation, diversity), and equity, the optimization of which is regulated by dialectical laws.

The material of the chapter is structured as follows. First, the theoretical problems associated with self-sufficient companies and their mediation of the downward and upward causation mechanisms are considered. Then, a change in the technological base of self-sufficient companies is revealed due to their digital transformation. The authors were interested in the growth trends of their intangible assets and the introduction of corporate ecosystems based on technological platforms. The conclusions obtained through the study of specific practices of self-sufficient companies allowed the authors to determine the technology for expanding their networking interactions in the context of forming the structure of a future dynamic reality. Further, the authors investigated the subjective component of the processes of system formation with the participation of self-sufficient companies. In this context, a new trend is visible in their strategic interests, related to the optimization of the principles of socialization of talented employees in intra-company teams. Their high level of education and a certain social position necessitate cardinal changes in the internal organization of their work. It is about the priority of the principles of diversity, equity and inclusion in the processes of socialization of employees with the qualities of intellectually autonomous individuals. In the results and discussion section, the authors discussed the mediation by self-sufficient companies of the upward causation mechanism through the prism of expanding their interests by incorporating ESG issues into their CEOs strategies. As a result, the authors offer a model representation of the functioning of a self-sufficient company at the stage of self-organization and during its expansion through the formation of corporate ecosystems and technological platforms. As a result, the authors formulate some conclusions on the chapter.

INTRODUCTION

An adequate understanding of the patterns of optimizing the organizational structures of self-sufficient companies will minimize uncertainty and accelerate the progress of dynamic socio-economic systems post pandemic. The specificity of constructing a post-COVID-19 reality is due to the fact that we are talking about the formation of a new systemic integrity with dynamic characteristics, including the economy and society in their dialectical interaction and with human-centric (socially oriented) principles of organization. Moreover, the drivers of these fundamental changes are self-sufficient companies, whose CEOs were the first to include in their agenda the atypical issues of diversity, equity, and inclusion in terms of organizing the internal structure and ecological, social and governance issues in the context of changing the external environment of their functioning. In addition, self-sufficient companies are quickly implementing the possibilities of the technological revolution 4.0, which, from a theoretical point of view, means the formation of a new technological foundation for the socio-economic system of the post-COVID-19 future. In addition, self-sufficient companies become capable of quickly implementing the possibilities of the technological revolution 4.0, which theoretically means the formation of the new technological foundation for the socio-economic system of the post-pandemic future.

On the way to the digital transformation of their business processes, self-sufficient companies faced the fundamental problem of a lack of personnel with the necessary qualifications, able to replicate in practice the latest breakthrough technological solutions when structuring networking interactions that correspond to the dynamic reality of the future. The huge demand for talented, creative employees today and its high growth rates in the short term have forced CEOs of rapidly adapting companies to rethink the object, subject and process aspects of their business reorganization. In this list, a person came out on top in the context of his education, adequate socialization, ability to seamlessly integrate into intra-company teams, motivational aspects of professional activity, taking into account the performance indicators of the entire team. As a result, human-centric diversity, equity, and inclusion principles of organizing internal interactions of talented employees have become a priority for top managers of self-sufficient companies. Moreover, all of the above applies to processes within self-sufficient companies, which are regulated by the downward causation mechanism. From a theoretical point of view, it mediates the self-organization of these companies in the conditions of the urgent requirements of a dynamic economy to its dialectically complex backbone elements. In fact, the internal restructuring of their organizational structure is a reorganization of elements as a starting button for changing the quality of the economic system itself. This statement corresponds to the philosophical interpretations of the elements of the system, according to which the organizational structure, the most conservative characteristic of the system as the integrity can change only if its structure-forming elements change qualitatively. Actually, this process is happening today before our eyes.

The pandemic and all the phenomena generated by it are forcing self-sufficient companies to change qualitatively in order to fulfill their fundamental mission of "creative destruction" according to Joseph A. Schumpeter (1949). It is about the final destruction of the organizational structure of the static economy by them and of the creation of the structure with the dynamic characteristics for the new socio-economic systemic integrity. In this case, the downward causation mechanism implements an internal restructuring of the organizational structure of self-sufficient companies in order to launch the upward causation mechanism in relation to external networking interactions. It is they who regulate the organization of a new horizontal level of structure by them, followed by a vertical structural hierarchy, corresponding to the dynamic system as an organic integrity of society and the economy in the future. It turns out that it is self-sufficient companies that form networking interactions, which will include broader social preferences for their employees as consumers, savers, investors, spokesmen for their civic positions, voters, fighters for the equity, and the brighter future for their children. Thus, the behavioral aspects of the actions of the companies themselves implement the dialectic of interaction between the economic and social value priorities of individuals, which, under certain circumstances, put the principles of a fair community in the first place. Under these conditions, the theoretical significance of understanding the patterns of restructuring the network interactions of self-sufficient companies that mediate the dialectical leap of the socio-economic system from statics to dynamics increases many times.

Self-Sufficient Companies in Downward and Upward Causation Processes: Network Interactions' Reorganization

The phenomenon of self-sufficient companies was formed long before the coronavirus pandemic. However, in the context of the coronavirus infection, it is these companies that have proven their viability as sustainable forms of business organization. Moreover, it was they who turned out to be capable of "creative destruction", i.e. to the destruction of the structural ties of a static economy under the influence of the coronavirus pandemic and to the creation of new networking interactions as a result of the dialectical leap of the economy from statics to dynamics (Pilipenko O.I., et al., 2021). Based on the provisions of systemic theories, the authors identified self-sufficient companies as backbone elements of the economic system that can act as drivers for the formation of a post-COVID reality with dynamic characteristics.

McKinsey Global Institute study lets the authors to identify self-sustaining companies from a sample of 5,000 large corporations across different areas of economic activity and 37 OECD countries, taking into account the dynamics of indicators of their economic activity over the past 25 years (Manyika, June 2021). In 2018 all together they had $40 trillion in revenue and represented $17 trillion in gross value added. Those companies underpin 85 percent of technology investment and 85 percent of labor productivity growth since 1995, which greatly exceeds their GDP contribution. Thus for the past 60 years the size of the business sector varies only modestly within each of the major economies, but its share has remained steady. Such a stable position of companies in various segments of national economies allows the authors to associate it with the qualities of self-sufficiency and with the upward and downward causation mechanisms at their disposal.

McKinsey Global Institute experts concretize the specifics of the business of these companies clustering eight distinct company archetypes that differ in their patterns of impact on the nation economy and households. It is about *Discoverers, Technologists, Experts, Deliverers, Makers, Builders, Fuelers,* and *Financiers*. This clustering is of great interest in terms of companies' factor inputs (labor and both tangible and intangible capital), their creation of economic value (cost structure and R&D spending), and their relative impacts on the economy via the eight pathways (Figure 1).

Discoverers have high R&D, intellectual property (IP), and capital income. Self-sufficient companies of this archetype are common in pharmaceutical and biotechnological sectors as well as in some household goods production that relied on R&D and intellectual property to differentiate their products. *Technologists* have high R&D and have enabled productivity growth in the economy. Self-sufficient companies of this archetype range across hardware, software, digital retailers, and media. They have also contributed to consumer surplus through steep price reductions (as well as quality improvements) over time. *Experts* include for-profit hospitals, health services, business services companies, including private universities. Self-sufficient companies of this archetype particularly rely on high-skill workers and devote the highest share of their value added to employee compensation. *Deliverers* have high employment levels and large supplier costs typical of retail and distribution. Self-sufficient companies of this archetype include some manufacturers, such as footwear and luxury, apparel firms with high marketing costs. They account for 16 percent of revenue, and employ 29 percent of the workers in a sample of companies of all archetypes. *Makers* include other manufacturers and represent the largest 2 McKinsey Global Institute archetype, with about 25 percent of the revenue of all self-sufficient companies and with 27 percent of employment. Self-sufficient companies of this archetype are close to or above average in their impacts across all the pathways, because the make their contribution through each pathway high and larger than most in absolute terms. *Builders* include utility, telecommunications, and transportation companies that

Figure 1. General characteristics of self-sufficient companies according to eight distinct company archetypes
Source: Manyika, James, Michael Birshan, Sven Smit, Jonathan Woetzel, Kevin Russell, Lindsay Purcell, Sree Ramaswamy. (June 2021). Companies in the 21st century. A new look at how corporations impact the economy and households. Discussion paper. McKinsey Global Institute. Retrieved from:
Note: The eight archetypes are based on a clustering of companies by their production characteristics and pattern of contributions through pathways. The data set consists of about 5,000 parent companies headquartered in OECD economies with more than $1 billion in revenue.

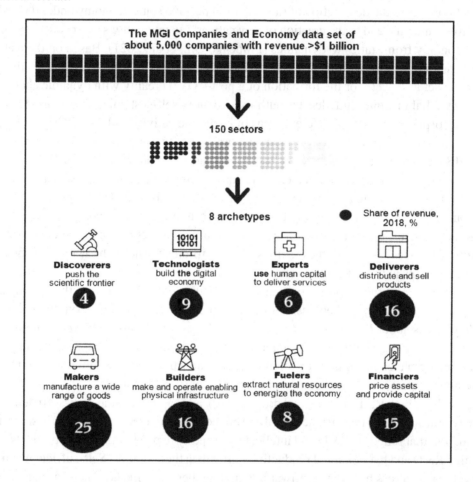

construct, use, and operate physical infrastructure, as well as manufacturers of materials and chemicals. Self-sufficient companies as *Builders* have double the physical assets of the average and, along with *Fuelers*, the highest scope of emissions.

Actually, these archetypes represent the specifics of self-sufficient companies in all sectors of the economy, united by their common quality to serve as drivers of system formation processes in a pandemic and structuring reality with dynamic qualities in the future. In addition, according to the conclusion of the McKinsey Global Institute experts, over the past quarter-century (and longer) these companies continue to be the dominant contributor to the economy and its growth in all the above business areas. *Technologists, Financiers,* and *Discoverers* had the highest growth in the capital income and labor income pathways as they widened their gross value added (GVA) share of revenue and decreased their supplier payments (Manyika, at al., June 2021).

It is with these self-sufficient companies in different archetypes that the structuring of the post-COVID-19 reality will be associated through the upward and downward causation mechanisms at their disposal. It is the latter that mediate organizational changes both within self-sufficient companies and in the external environment of their functioning.

So, self-sufficient companies as backbone elements of the economic system are able to form networking interactions at its micro and macro levels as structures of the future dynamic post-COVID-19 reality. In other words, the dialectic of destruction and creation of new structures by self-sufficient companies is implemented due to the mechanisms of downward and upward causation. Roger W. Sperry, Nobel laureate, psychologist and biologist, was the first to formulate the concept of "downward causation" (Sperry, 1964; 1969). In his opinion, any higher levels of organization in systems are formed due to causal processes occurring at lower levels. Such dependences surprisingly repeat themselves during the self-organization of economic systems in the process of forming an ascending hierarchy of structural levels generated by the basic horizontal level, represented by dialectical pairs of exchange partners (Pilipenko, O.I., et al., 2021).

Being backbone elements of the economic system, self-sufficient companies are capable of self-movement through downward and upward causation mechanisms (Argyris, et al., 1996; Levitt, et al., 1988). These processes are complex and include subject, object and process components. It is necessary to consider the subjective component of the processes of organizational complication of self-sufficient companies, the institutional support (maintenance) of which should be interpreted in the context of those structures that determine the integrity of organizations in business (Hodgson, at al., 2004). The fact is that such companies provide a certain social environment for the generation and manifestation of the habits of team members. As a result, the subjective component of the processes of self-organization of companies is involved in the formation of their internal structural relationships that ensure their integrity through self-organization. In this process, a self-sufficient company forms, reproduces and constructs new organizational routines and the individual habits of employees corresponding to them (Blitz, 1992; Kontopoulos, 1993; Hodgson, 1988, 1988b; Weissman, 2000). Understanding the mechanisms of self-enforcing companies and the economic system as a whole (Aldrich, 1999) allowed the authors to highlight the dialectics of the downward and upward causation mechanisms in relation to the subjective component of self-organization processes in its constancy and change. Moreover, this specificity of organizational changes in companies is of fundamental importance in generating the dialectic of interaction between the economy and society in the post-COVID-19 reality. It is in this context that it becomes possible to understand the phenomenon of the expansion of the economic system and the acquisition of dynamic characteristics by it.

In the context of constructing an uncertain reality as the COVID-19 pandemic ends, it is self-sufficient companies that begin to structure the individual habits of their employees, as well as collective "meta-habits" as routines at the level of the entire organization to transcend them into the external environment. Mutually influencing each other in the course of intra-company interaction, individuals structure the internal environment of the company, thereby mediating the downward causation mechanism. G.M. Hodgson (2003) identified the fundamental role of habits in the reproduction of forward and backward connections in the rule-like behavior of individuals. In other words, it is about the formation of internal structural interactions at the stage of self-organization of self-sufficient companies. This is how a relatively long-lived system of rules for the behavior of company employees arises, capable of forming habits and reproducing them in the behavior of individuals through the downward causation mechanism inside the company and through the upward causation mechanism outside the companies.

In this interpretation, institutions (as norms of behavior, mechanisms of encouragement and punishment) are both objective "external" structures and subjective, "out of a person's head", products of human behaviour (Hodgson, 2003). In this sense, "downward causation" is realized when structuring interactions, when the company affects the team, and "upward" causation is mediated by companies and their employees, which transcend (objectify outside the firm) organizational structures and rule-driven behavior of companies in the economy, and of individuals in society (Hodgson, 2002). Thus, the dialectics of the interaction of these two processes of causation is realized by the subjective component in the process of self-movement of self-sufficient companies. It is about the self-organization of a self-sufficient company through downward causation and their self-development with the help of upward causation and with the participation of their subjective component.

American theorist T.B. Veblen described this more specifically in relation to the psychological mechanisms involved in these processes. In his opinion, today's situation shapes tomorrow's institutions through a process of coercion and selection, influencing the habitual human vision of things (Veblen, (1899), P. 190). The individual is limited in his actions. In this regard, he acquires habits that are compatible with restrictions both at the level of firms and the entire society. In the modern societal crisis, the subjective component is also represented by company CEOs, whose importance is growing due to their ability to increase the stability of the organization during a long period of uncertainty and even turn the crisis into an opportunity, or a catalyst for positive changes (Mendy, et al., 2020).

In accordance with the methodological developments of the representatives of the institutional theory, institutions, due to their fundamental status in the socio-economic system (Hodgson, 1998, 1988b), ensure the reproduction of basic forms of economic behavior, determine the content of habits of thinking and acting (Hodgson, 1988). This corresponds to the fact that if there are certain system's properties and development trends, then the individual components of the systems function in accordance with them. At the same time, the reverse "ascending" causality is realized, which, according to G.M. Hodgson means that institutions in their existence depend on individuals, and individuals can change them (Hodgson, 2003). As a result, the individual is limited in his actions and acquires habits that are compatible with restrictions both at the level of firms and the entire society.

These provisions are of exceptional importance for understanding the role of self-sufficient companies in the formation of structural links in the external environment of companies, in their interactions with all stakeholders in connection with market transactions and social interactions. This means that self-sufficient companies are able not only to destroy, but also to create networking interactions both within themselves and at the system level. In our case, it is about structuring interactions for a dynamic economy post the pandemic. The new dynamic system will be distinguished not only by new structural ties, dialectically complex self-sufficient companies, but also by the resulting expansion due to the restoration of the dialectic of interaction between society and the economy. And this organic interaction is realized by the subjective component of the mechanisms of upward and downward causation at the disposal of self-sufficient companies.

Intangible Assets of Self-Sufficient Companies and Technology of Their Networking Interactions Expansion: Formation of the Structure for the Future Dynamic Reality

From a theoretical point of view, self-sufficient companies are organizational entities capable of self-movement. These include large companies that determine the dynamics in their segments of the economy and have a significant impact on the economy as a whole and its growth. In the pandemic and various regimes of economic lockdown, these companies have proved to be stable and quite successful, capable of radically transforming intra-company structural ties. This demonstrates the ability of these companies to self-move: to self-organize through the mechanism of downward causation and to self-develop through upward causation mechanism. Moreover, all the changes that occur in self-sufficient companies predetermine the transformation of the structural ties of the economic system in a dialectical leap from statics to dynamics. In other words, the vector of change in self-sufficient companies determines the direction of structuring the economic system. This means that transformations within self-sufficient companies and in their external environment form the general contours of a dynamic economy post COVID-19.

As noted above, the dynamic state of the future economic system will be largely associated with the formation of a new technological foundation. It should be emphasized that technological progress is embedded into the mechanism of self-development of the economic system, i.e. technological revolution 4.0 and new disruptive technologies are endogenous factors in the formation of the future reality that self-sufficient companies construct. The well-known economic historian Joel Mokyr (2005) adhered to the same point of view. He identified technological progress with the determinant of the mechanism of self-movement of economic systems, inherent in them genetically. It turns out that structure formation in the economy occurs as a self-regulating process, the main participants of which are self-sufficient companies that perform the function of backbone elements of the economic system. Taking into account all the above, they can be defined as drivers for constructing a post-COVID-19 reality, mediating the mechanism of its self-development.

That is why, in the pandemic, self-sufficient companies were the first to quickly respond to the changed external environment of their operation. For these purposes, the CEOs of these companies have focused on new products and services, new processes and new business, the implementation of which becomes possible as a result of the technological revolution 4.0. This is confirmed by surveys of CEOs of the largest companies about new-business building, according to McKinsey Global Survey. Thus, by 2026 self-sufficient companies are planning coming of half of their revenues from products, services, or businesses that haven't yet been created (Leap by McKinsey, December 2021). These data indicate that new-business building is considered by self-sufficient companies as a means of supporting sustainable, inclusive growth in the indefinite future (Fig. 2).

Figure 2 shows, that more than 80 percent of respondents see new-business building as a way to adapt to potential disruptions and changing demand, while 62 percent consider it to generate one or more new revenue streams. Accelerating this trend will mean that in five years, half of the revenues of self-sustaining companies will most likely come from new products, services and business models. In other words, during the pandemic companies are forced to diversify their sources of income, taking advantage of the opportunities of the technological revolution 4.0 to strengthen their position.

So, objectively, in the interconnections of self-sufficient companies, new objects of exchange and network interactions mediating them appear, due to the challenges of digital business transformation. Theoretically, it is about the formation of a new object component of the processes of self-development of self-sufficient companies, associated with the increase of intangibles (Krishnan, et al., June 2018; Roth, 2019; Corrado, et al. 2018). This trend emerged long before the coronavirus pandemic. And later it turned out that national companies that mastered the deployment of intangibles strengthened their position in the market and are already displaying above-average growth rates. The COVID-19 pandemic has strengthened the role of intangible assets in accelerating the development and spread of the knowledge economy at the national level. A significant investments of the self-sufficient companies in

Figure 2. CEOs of self-sufficient companies are looking to bring in half of their companies' revenues from new products, services, or business by 2026

Notes: [1]Respondents were asked, "To achieve your organization's enterprise-wide revenue ambitions for 5 year from now, what share of that revenue do you expect will come from its current products and/or services (including upgrades and new versions)?"; n = 1,178.

[2] Questions were asked only of respondents who said new-business building is at least a top 10 strategic priority for their companies; n = 1,069.

[3] n = 1,178.

Source: Leap by McKinsey. (December 2021). 2021 Global Report: The State of New-Business Building. McKinsey&Co

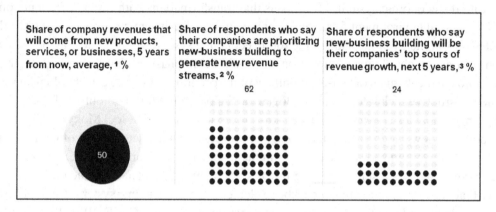

various categories of intangible assets have given them an edge over their competitors and strengthened their resilience (Fig. 3).

Top growers are investing 2.6 times more in intangibles than low growers (Figure 3). The gap between them increases to between five and seven times in sectors such as financial services where competitive advantage is anchored in knowledge. This multiple is stable in all categories of intangibles. McKinsey Global Institute experts conventionally identified the following four major types of intangible assets:

- *Innovation capital as a result of* investments in the company's IP, including R&D. It is about new product development in industries from manufacturing to biotechnology; design, such as new product interfaces — digital (payment gateways in apps) or physical (larger iPhone screens); and entertainment and artistic originals as to book publishing and movie production. In the case of electronics' company it could be the design of a new device; and as to a mining company it is about geological intelligence for exploration.

- *Digital and analytics capital* includes building software such as the installation and maintenance of customer relationship management software; developing databases as to building a data lake and a data management platform; digital platforms such as a front-end e-commerce interface; and analytics models and algorithms. The latter could include a personalization process enabling real time and tailored social media campaigns.

- *Human and relational capital* spans two subcategories. The first one, organizational and managerial capital includes building individual or organizational skills through training, advancing the working skills of particular specialty and developing capabilities. The latter is about a talent strategy connected with building employees' critical digital and cognitive capabilities, their social and emotional skills, and their adaptability and resilience. The second subcategory is associated with ecosystems and networks including activities connected with developing and improving

Figure 3. Self-sufficient companies as top growers invest 2.6 times more in intangibles than low growers across sectors
Notes: 1. Median by sector. Survey included other sectors not shown here.
Figures may not sum to 100% because of rounding.
Source: Hazan, Eric, Sven Smit, Jonathan Woetzel, and Shanghai Biljana Cvetanovski, Mekala Krishnan, Brian Gregg, Jesko Perrey, and Klemens Hjartar, (June 2021). Getting tangible about intangibles: The future of growth and productivity? Discussion Paper. McKinsey Global Institute. Retrieved from: www.mckinsey.com/mgi

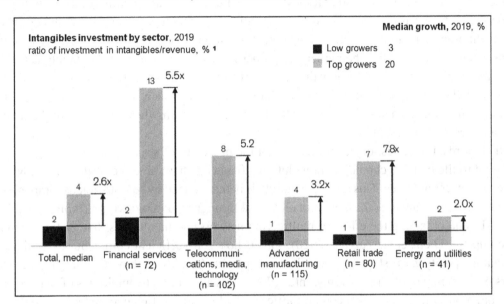

privileged relationships. It is about partnerships with key suppliers and networks including an ecosystem of data partners and etc.

- *Brand capital* deals with investments in marketing and sales. It is about building and improving brand equity, including a TV campaign for brand awareness improvement; convening consumer panels to gain customer insights and better understand the customers' voice; as well as targeting promotions aimed at preventing customer churn or offering excellent customer service to retain clients.

Higher investment in intangible assets makes top growers more likely to create new forms of competitive strength. In many ways, it is investing in intangibles what strengthens the resilience of self-sustaining companies, accelerating their technological progress and digital transformation of their business processes.

Thus, in the context of the pandemic, a new object component of the processes of structure formation begins to rapidly form with the self-sufficient companies as main participants. It is they who have increased capital investments in intangible assets that objectify new products and services, new processes and new business-building. These new objects of exchange allow self-sufficient companies to actively form more branched structural ties about market transactions with them. And these processes are accelerated by the latest technological tools capable of providing diverse, hitherto unknown configurations of technologically interconnected partners. Thus the technological revolution 4.0 has brought a new technological base for corporate structural ties, mediated by new objects of exchange and a new technology for combining them. It is about corporate ecosystems on technology platforms. They are often complex to build and replicate but they enable self-sufficient companies-partners to create enduring competitive strength, to outperform their peers and to develop resilience. Intangible assets are interdependent, and self-sufficient companies achieve greater synergies by investing in all of them.

So, new and innovative products, services and processes have emerged as a result of technological revolution 4.0. Being for the most part represented by intangible assets, they differ in that the greatest economic return from them is provided if they mediate multivariate interactions of as many participants in the market exchange as possible. The new quality of their technological service involving such breakthrough technologies as cloud computing, big data, the Internet of things (IoT) and artificial intelligence (AI) makes it possible to realize their emergent properties and launch the networking interactions multiplication mechanism. In fact, this is how the process of forming dialectical ties in business and in market exchange with the participation of self-sufficient companies takes place. Thus, these companies mediate the upward causation mechanism already for the purpose of ensuring the conditions for the functioning of a dynamic economic system.

In other words, the newest object component of the processes of structuring intercompany relations was brought to life by the technological revolution 4.0 and can have an effect if they are provided with new interaction technologies. This new opportunity is being realized by self-sufficient companies whose digital transformation involves the merger of all 4 breakthrough technologies (cloud computing, big data, IoT and AI), and obtaining the effect of multiplying networking interactions that go far beyond limits of one company (Dietz, et al., August, 2020). This is how self-sufficient companies expand already in their dynamic quality at the stage of their self-development. As a result, they start shaping the structural contours of the future dynamic economy. Intangible assets and digital technologies of multiplication of network interconnections of market counterparties will allow self-sufficient companies to quickly build new networking relationships in place of those destroyed in a static economy. In turn, a critical mass of such self-sufficient companies will predetermine the possibilities for expanding the entire economic system.

Actually, this model confirms the logic of the complication of macro-systems, according to W. Brian Arthur (1999), which is quite applicable to the design of a future dynamic reality. The model for such a qualitative transformation of intangibles in the form of new products, services, processes and new business using the latest breakthrough technologies is modern corporate ecosystems, which Ludwig von Bertalanffy (1968) endowed with the ability to self-organize and self-develop. According to Thomas M. Siebel (2019), by 2025, of the total global business revenue of $190 trillion, about 30% of corporate income will be generated by ecosystems.

An ecosystem can be thought of as a customer-centric business model that combines two or more groups of products, services, and information to meet the ultimate needs of customers (Chung, et al., September 2020). The main idea underlying it is to collect on one technological platform services that could satisfy a variety of human needs, for example, from shopping for goods to entertainment. The main providers, as a rule, are self-sufficient companies as large players that concentrate ideas, talents and other resources on their existing ecosystems and add platform infrastructure to them. A complete technology platform integrates disruptive cloud computing, big data, IoT, and AI technologies through a model-driven architecture (Karalee, et al., 2020). Models are automatically implemented on one or more clouds, taking into account the platform-specific implementation.

Since all services are interconnected, the cost of attracting customers (CAC - customer acquisition cost) to each next service of the ecosystem is reduced and the company's profit received from one user for the entire time of interaction with him (LTV - lifetime value) is growing. In other words, corporate ecosystems mediate the implementation of the digital transformation of the external environment of interaction between companies and customers, which allows participants to spend less on marketing and earn more per client, but not by raising prices, but by providing them with a wider range of services. In this case, win-win relations (mutually beneficial cooperation) of partners are implemented in the ecosystem, which interconnects all its services on a unified technological platform. In the future, the speed and deepening of technological progress depend on the quality of the digital transformation of self-sufficient companies, which, in turn, is predetermined by their ability to provide conditions for the unlimited expansion of the intellectual abilities of their own talented employees.

Realization of Employees' Intellectual Abilities as a Condition for Successful Digital Transformation of Self-Sufficient Companies: Diversity, Equity, and Inclusion (DEI) Principles of Organizing Intra-Company Teams

The groups of intangibles mentioned above are not equivalent in their impact on the speed and vector of structuring networking interactions by self-sufficient companies. This is due to the fact that of the three components of the mechanism of their self-movement – object, subject and process – it is the subject that has a special role in the digital transformation of the business environment. This is due to the fact that all currently known intangible assets and 4 latest tools (cloud technologies, big data, IoT, AI) for their integration on a corporate technological platform can deepen and expand only with the participation of creative individuals and subject to adequate organization of their professional activities within firms. Only in this case, the intellectual abilities of a person will make the possibilities of implementing the technological revolution 4.0 truly limitless. This is what Klaus Schwab (Schwab, 2016; Schwab, et al., 2020), when he wrote that the modern technological revolution is changing not only "what" and "how" we do, but also "who" we are. That is why human and relational capital, as one of the four groups of modern intangibles, plays a key role in modern technological progress, in the digital transformation of self-sufficient companies and in the formation of a dynamic economy as a whole. In other words, human capital and optimal forms of organizing the professional activities of talented employees are able to implement a full-fledged digital transformation of self-sufficient companies, expand its multiplier effect through corporate ecosystems capable of self-organization and self-development. W.B. Arthur (2009) saw this as a process of system complexity that begins with the fact that new technology in the form of technological complexes generates unceasing waves of perturbation, causing new perturbations both in technology and in all areas of human activity. Thus, if a self-sufficient company mediates the mechanism of self-propulsion of the economic system, transforming the possibilities of technological revolution 4.0 into new organizational solutions, then its own progress is determined by how successfully CEOs can unite talented employees with diverse abilities into a single in-house team.

Despite the apparent simplicity of this problem, it belongs to the fundamental ones, since today it requires a theoretical rethinking of the human phenomenon (Pierre Teilhard de Chardin, 1959) and the implementation of the findings in the practice of self-sufficient companies. According to the authors, a person should be considered as a complex systemic integrity, capable of both self-organization (primarily, by receiving education and appropriate socialization), and self-development (when implementing individual abilities in professional activities and civic positions in society). If in the process of education the society "creates" its future member from a person, then becoming highly educated (or not having received an adequate education), the individual develops himself, adapting the society to his individual value preferences. Human capital, the bearer of which is an intellectually autonomous person, is capable of infinitely multiplying technological breakthroughs and ensuring socio-economic progress, but under certain conditions. His desire to create for the benefit of the company or society is due to complete co-incidence or in large part of his personalized values with social norms of justice (equity).

The quality of modern education leaves much to be desired. Even before the COVID-19 pandemic, international think tanks noted the crisis state of education (World Bank, 2018). And this has turned into a serious problem for self-sufficient companies due to the lack of talented personnel in the context of the coronavirus. No less serious becomes the problem of adequate socialization of people, which turned into a societal crisis accelerated by COVID-19. It expressed itself in the anti-social (opportunistic) behavior of growing number of citizens who opposed economic lockdown and social distancing in the course of the struggle of nation states against the pandemic. As a result, citizens began to refuse to trust their governments. Self-sufficient companies were the first to face the problems of low educational level and inadequate socialization of employees adapting to new operating conditions.

Low-quality education has caused a growing shortage of specialists who meet the requirements of the technological revolution 4.0. So, back in 2019 according to the Mckinsey&Company' experts (McConnell, 2019), the resulting job displacement could be massive affecting as many as 800 million people globally by 2030 and requiring up to 375 million of them to switch occupational categories and learn new skills. As a whole the companies lack the talent they will need in the future: 44 percent of respondents say their organizations will face skill gaps within the next five years, and another 43 per-cent report existing skill gaps (Agrawal, et al., 2020). As a result 87 percent of the companies surveyed confirmed that they either are experiencing gaps now or expect them within a few years (Figure 4). For CEOs today it becomes obvious that achieving strong performance in the new reality will require more than a rapid crisis response to the shortage of adequate personnel.

The task of attracting talented employees with the qualities of an intellectually autonomous person-ality is of particular importance when choosing a form of digital transformation of business processes and models for organizing the professional activities of employees in a pandemic (Figure 5). However, the problem of the shortage of highly qualified personnel has a second side associated with the social-ization of talented workers. The fact is that intellectually autonomous individuals are more difficult to socialize. It is about their inclusion in a well-coordinated intra-company team that optimally combines the dialectically opposite principles of organizing one's professional activities – diversity and inclusion. The principle of inclusion mediates the socialization of employees at the micro level of the company, and diversity expands its capabilities due to the diversity of different specialists (Figure 6). The optimal combination of diversity and inclusion is what reinforces the organizational structure and implements the mechanism of downward causation (Taplett, et al., 2019).

As a result, the socialization of employees at the level of firms is determined by the coordination of the principles of disintegration (diversity) and integration (inclusion) as to the organization of their professional activities. In publications on this issue, such a strategy of companies to form teams of employees was called "Inclusion & Diversity" (I&D) (Dixon-Fyle, et al., 2020). Although these phe-nomena are dialectically interdependent, the priority still belongs to diversity (separation, specialization, differentiation). This is due to the fact that inclusion (association, integration, socialization) becomes possible only if there is the variety of diverse (specialized, differentiated) phenomena, subjects, objects, processes, and etc. (Taplett, et al., 2019). The more diverse, for example, the subjects in terms of their abilities, specialization, professionalism the more effective their inclusion (integration, socialization) into intra-company teams can be, and vice versa.

Figure 4. Respondents' expectations for skill shortages due to market and technology trends that are changing the talent needs of organizations
Source: Küpper, Daniel, Tom Reichert, Tom Reichert, Vaishali Rastogi, and Ryoji Kimura (2020). How CEOs (chief executive officer) Can Win the Fight and Transform to Win the Future. Boston Consulting Group. June 8
Note: [1] Figures may not sum to 100%, because of rounding; n=1,216

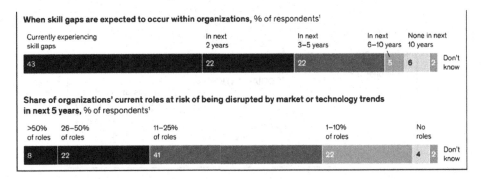

The problem of socialization of talented workers within companies was maturing even before the pandemic. Since the mid-2010s, it has been actively discussed both at the macro level (WEF, 2015, 2016, 2017, 2018; Breen, 2016), as well as at the company level (Hunt, et al., 2015; Hunt, et al., 2018; The business case for inclusive growth, 2018). Today it has become obvious that the importance of adequate socialization of talented employees at the firm level is increasing many times over (Garcia-Alonso, et al., 2020), since it is a necessary condition for the social consolidation of society. It is in this

Figure 5. The companies' need of building employees' skills in critical thinking, leadership and management, and advanced data analysis
Source: Agrawal, Sapana, Aaron De Smet, Pawel Poplawski, and Angelika Reich (2020). Beyond hiring: How companies are re-skilling to address talent gaps. Organization Practice and McKinsey Accelerate. January. McKinsey & Company
Note: [1]Out of 35 skills included in the Survey. Question was asked only of respondents who say their organizations have a re-skilling program currently under way or have already re-skilled >1 group, or class of employees; n= 394

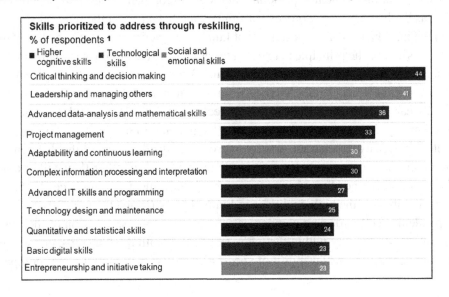

Figure 6. Socialization of employees in self-sufficient companies: dialectical interaction of the principles of diversity and inclusion in the processes of downward causation
Note: *Frances Brooks Taplett, Matt Krentz, Justin Dean, and Gabrielle Novacek. (2019). Diversity is just the first step. Inclusion comes next. 4/19. Boston Consulting Group.*

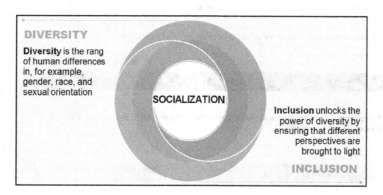

dialectic that the interaction of upward and downward causation processes is realized in the formation of a dynamic economy.

In the context of the COVID-19 pandemic, self-sufficient companies were forced to optimize the implementation of human intellectual capabilities and the potential of new breakthrough technologies. At the same time, the motivational aspects of the professional activity of talented employees come to the fore. Numerous studies have shown a close relationship between the stated needs of employees and the factors of their involvement, well-being and performance in the company. Table 1 represents the main motivational preferences of employees and those results, grouped by key elements of their experience, which can be obtained if they are satisfied. Based on the data obtained, it can be judged that the socialization (inclusion) of highly qualified personnel within the company is predetermined by such personalized values as trust, inclusiveness, openness, involvement (empathy, complicity, belonging), etc. (Smit, et al., 2020; Davies, et al., 2019; Ghose, 2020; Dixon-Fyle, et al., 2020). These parameters predetermine the success of the implementation of the "Inclusion & Diversity" strategy by companies in the context of the optimal socialization of talented personnel at the intra-company level. Boston Consulting Group experts see this as the beginning of a process of fundamental changes in the internal structure of companies through the introduction of the principles of human centricity (Boston Consulting Group, 2019).

Forms of expression of the principles of socialization of creative employees manifest themselves in different ways. So, according to the Boston Consulting Group, more than 50% of potential employees would decline a job if the company not have same environmental or diversity views, especially important over the last year (Fig.7) (BCG Executive Perspectives, July 2021). And the problem of adequate socialization of employees is aggravated as their intellectual autonomousness grows. Thus, as a whole, ten elements of employee experience account for approximately 60 percent of the differences in results. It follows that if companies cannot achieve an immediate positive result, then they will be able to provide it at the expense of non-financial means, increasing the involvement of employees by 55%, satisfying their need for recognition of the high quality of individual work (Emmett, et al., 2020).

So, in the pandemic, self-sufficient companies can optimize the socialization of their employees by ensuring their safety and security within the team, stabilizing team relationships, enhancing corporate culture and demonstrating the achievability of specific goals. As a result, CEOs of companies put the

Table 1. Employees' engagement, well-being, and effectiveness, driven by a set of employee experience factors

Top employee needs and experience factors by core themes of employee experience				Improvement	
Theme	Need (rank)	Employee experience factors	Work effectiveness	Engagement	Well-being
Stable, secure work experience	Job security (1)	Organizational stability	+16.9%	+52.9%	+53.3%
	Financial stability (2)				
	Physical and mental health (6)	Compensation and benefits	+21.2%	+45.6%	+44.5%
	Being rewarded (8)				
Trusting relationships	Working with people I can trust (5)	Trust in leadership	+23.7%	+47.6%	+45.4%
		Relationship with company	+20.9%	+49.9%	+51.3%
	Being recognized for my work (10)	Nonfinancial recognition	+20.4%	+55.1%	+49.3%
Social cohesion and inclusion	Being treated fairly (4)	Fairness	+22.3%	+48.0%	+52.3%
		Involvement	+14.8%	+32.4%	+51.1%
	Having supportive coworkers (9)	Respect	+15.7%	+51.8%	+49.8%
		Equality	+16.2%	+50.8%	+50.9%
Individual purpose and contribution	Achieving work goals (7)	Alignment with organizational purpose and values	+20.3%	+49.0%	+49.3%
	Balance of work and private life (3)				
	Fulfilling my personal purpose at work (12)				

Source: Emmett, Jonathan, Gunnar Schrah, Matt Schrimper, and Alexandra Wood. (2020). COVID-19 and the employee experience: How leaders can seize the moment. Organization Practice. June. McKinsey & Company

most difficult problems before the team of their best employees and understand that if they cannot solve them, then no one can. In these circumstances, top managers of self-sufficient companies interpret the strategy of "Inclusion & Diversity" (essentially socialization) as the art of the possible (COVID-19: Briefing materials, 2020).

As a result, theoretical conclusions and practical results are reduced to the same. The problem of talented employees (with the qualities of an intellectually autonomous personality) is put forward in the first place, since it is they who, adequately socializing through optimal inclusion in the company's team, mediate technologies for minimizing the uncertainty of the future reality and are able to model the variety of mechanisms for strengthening business positions in the post-COVID-19 reality. In this connection companies must re-recruit current talent and attract new talent by investing in improved

Figure 7. Importance of workplace factors ranked according to a Future Forum[4] study
Source: BCG Executive Perspectives. (July 2021). Investing to Win Talent. Boston Consulting Group
Note: 1. Percentage of respondents who agree with the statement "I would exclude companies that do not match my beliefs in environmental responsibility/diversity and inclusion". 2. Respondents who agree that "The issue of environmental responsibility/ diversity and inclusion became more important to me over the last year". 3. For environment, 55% ages 21-30 would exclude companies that do not match beliefs versus 47% for ages 60+. Number of respondents = 208,807. 4. Future Forum consortium was launched by Slack and is also led by BCG, Herman Miller, and MLT

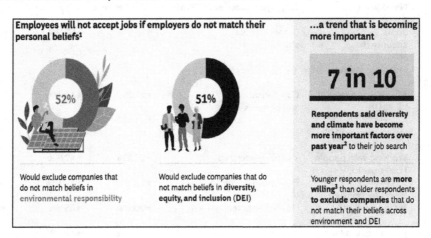

employee value proposition. Moreover, they are forced to solve the problem of adequate socialization (inclusion) of talented employees (who are differentiated) in intra-company teams, taking into account those individual preferences that separate them. In this context, it is of interest to expand the strategy of I&D by adding another very personalized value – equity. Then the socialization strategy harmonizes the three principles of organization – diversity, equity, and inclusion (DEI) (Figure 7).

Their CEOs have to invest in building a DEI capability that supports talents' diverse identities throughout their careers (Figure 8).

It is symptomatic that the adjustment of the internal self-organization of companies is carried out, first of all, in connection with the conditions for attracting and socializing talents. It is with them that companies attribute both their accelerated digital transformation and their future success in an uncertain reality. This proves, in general, the validity of the above theoretical conclusions of the authors about the dialectic of the interaction between education and socialization of the individual and their role in the construction of a future dynamic reality. Under these conditions, CEOs of self-sufficient companies are forced to rebuild the internal structure, taking into account the principles of inclusion of intellectually autonomous individuals who differ not only in professional abilities, but also in individual preferences. Serious changes in the organizational structures of self-sufficient companies are coming due to the fact that the socialization of talented individuals, as an optimization of the principles of inclusion and diversity, is predetermined by their personalized assessments of the implementation of the principle of equity. With the advent of equity in the inclusion and diversity strategy, self-sufficient companies are forced to start organizing in-house teams with a focus on human-centrism (Fig. 8) (Novacek, et al., May 2021).

Figure 8. Investing in DEI principles to support employees' diverse inclusion in the intra-firm team organization
Source: *BCG Executive Perspectives. (July 2021). Investing to Win Talent. Boston Consulting Group*

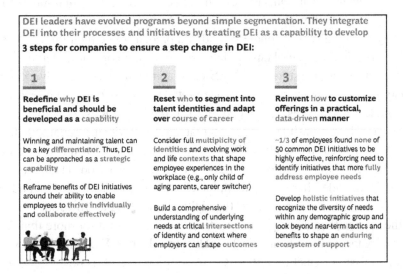

RESULTS AND DISCUSSION

The processes of socialization that accompany the integration of workers into the composition of intra-company teams are the result of the organization of their internal structure due to downward causation mechanism. Its specificity is expressed in the fact that self-sufficient companies capable of self-organization change their own structure, adapting to new technologies and models for the exchange of new assets, increasingly intangible. In this context, these companies are adapting to the changing external environment as a result of the pandemic, while adapting to it and changing it according to their requirements. In the latter case, they mediate the upward causation mechanism, forming new networking interactions for an economic system with dynamic properties.

In other words, self-sustaining companies that can mediate upward and downward causation mechanisms act as drivers of the future post-COVID-19 reality. However, in this capacity, they only mediate the processes of system formation, being themselves complex structures for organizing the professional activities of workers, capable of both self-organization and self-development. The main protagonists of all these processes are the subjects that are capable of self-organization due to education and socialization, and of self-development - thanks to the abilities of an intellectually autonomous person who, socializing into the company and society, changes their structural ties, taking into account their preferences. Thus, the subjective factor of system formation processes is able to ensure the expansion of self-sufficient companies through their ESG strategy and restore the dialectic of interaction between the economy and society, expanding the economic system and giving it dynamic properties.

Self-sufficient companies include large and the largest companies that have successfully survived all the economic lockdowns and social distancing caused by the COVID-19 pandemic. And, second, they are distinguished by the integration of ESG-principles of "responsible investment" into their development strategies. The authors expressed this hypothesis, following the dialectical logic, according to which a static system has backbone elements in the face of private business with the definite characteristics. As for the dynamic economy, it is distinguished by the "expansion" provided by self-sufficient companies, mediating the dialectical relationship between society and the economy, as well as all human-created systems and the natural environment. Only those (self-sufficient) companies that adhere to ESG-principles in their business will be able to implement this dialectics. At the same time, these characteristics will turn them into major players in the socio-economic field and predetermine their quality of self-sufficiency.

However, today there is no comprehensive database of such companies. Deloitte estimates that the total portfolio of "responsible investors" (self-sufficient companies) has already exceeded $50 billion. According to existing data, such investors are concentrated mainly in traditional sectors, and IT companies are still far from ESG-principles. At the end of 2021, the MSCI KLD 400 Social index (introduced in 1990 and unites socially responsible firms), calculated on American companies, showed an increase of 30%, and the MSCI World ESG Leaders - 25%. By comparison, the Dow Jones Sustainability World Index, which includes 323 companies, rose only 20% over the same period. The largest companies in the MSCI KLD 400 Social include Microsoft and Alphabet, which saw growth of 43% and 60% respectively over the past year. These same companies have the highest weight in the Dow Jones Sustainability World Index, although the IT, healthcare and pharmaceutical sectors account for more than 50%.

According to Morgan Stanley, during 2022-2027 the oil giant ExxonMobil plans to spend more than $15 billion on emission reduction initiatives. In addition, Exxon is developing hydrogen projects in Canada, Texas and the Netherlands. As a global energy company, ExxonMobil operates across the whole value chain and is uniquely positioned to deploy low-carbon technologies at scale.

However, these are just a few examples of companies that, according to the authors, meet the characteristics of self-sufficient companies. So far, there is no comprehensive database that would allow proving the connection of self-sufficient companies with their ESG investment principles, as well as assessing the degree of influence of ESG principles in companies' strategies on solving, for example, climate problems or creating an adequate social environment in national communities. Reasonable answers to these questions will be given only in the future, subject to the introduction of common standards and metrics. National regulators and professional associations around the world have already begun to develop them, but are at the very beginning of the journey. Meanwhile, only the emergence of such tools will make it possible to adequately assess and confirm the characteristics of self-sufficient companies in the context of their use of the ESG-principles of "responsible investment" and playing the role of drivers in the "expansion" of the dynamic post-COVID-19 reality.

For now, there is only a feeling that many markets already understand that it is necessary to increase the positive impact of investments on the planet and society, and some numbers speak for it. Thus, 19% of institutional and 10% of private investors choose instruments whose issuers take into account ESG factors in their activities. At the same time, 2/3 of investors from both categories declare their interest in "responsible investing" and agree to sacrifice profitability if new value targets are achieved. So only in the future it will be possible to deepen the theoretical understanding of the criteria for identifying self-sufficient companies and reinforce these conclusions with practical examples.

In fact, the root cause of all these cardinal changes in self-sufficient companies and socio-economic systems in a pandemic is the increasing importance of an individual with the qualities of an intellectually autonomous personality. Without them, it is impossible to realize the possibilities of the technological revolution 4.0, and they tend to personify their values as a condition for their full socialization into society. That is why the fact of the appearance of the equity parameter in the implementation of the principles of diversity and inclusion in the organization of structural ties at the firm level is so significant (Novacek, et al., May 2021). The point is that, despite the objectivity of the interaction of the principles of diversity and inclusion, they are implemented with the participation of the subjective component of the processes of system formation of the future reality. It is the personalized idea of equity that makes it possible to socialize or not to socialize individuals, especially if they are prone to diversity due to their intellectual autonomousness.

John Bordley Rawls (Rawls, 1971) called social equity "the first virtue of social institutions", which is embodied in the institutionalization of the rules of the game in the processes of system formation. According to philosophers and sociologists, equity is the highest social good, because if you create conditions for a fair structure of society, then the solidarity of citizens will come by itself, as its objective consequence. It is in this context that equity should be associated not just with a person, but should be interpreted as a social phenomenon that performs the function of the foundation of any society. This problem is very complicated, and today such tectological shifts (Bogdanov, 1934) can be observed in society, only thanks to the acceleration that the coronavirus pandemic has given them. Under these conditions, the interest of large self-sufficient companies in improving environmental, social and governance (ESG) aspects of their functioning has become objectified. The Economist Group experts have identified 9 areas of manifestation of ESG issues that have a well-defined economic return. It is about innovation acceleration factors, operational efficiency, sales and marketing, customer loyalty, risk management, employees' relations, suppliers' relationships, media and stakeholders' involvement (Economist Impact, 2022).

Socially responsible investing based on ESG principles became the mainstream in the 2010s, when global institutional investors faced increasing risks associated with ESG problems with their assets. In addition, opportunities for new green investment opened up. In addition, there has been growing public awareness of key ESG-principle investing issues such as climate changes, the diversity of human rights, and the need for greater corporate accountability and transparency in the new era. Now Milton Friedman's "shareholder primacy" is gradually making way for "stakeholder capitalism". This concept has been coined by the World Economic Forum with an explanation that the companies are shifting to the goal of seeking long-term value creation by taking into account the needs of all their stakeholders, and society at large.

In order to act as responsible owners and, ultimately, to benefit from strong investment returns, investors need to understand if companies are effectively managing the environmental and social impacts of their operations. In the very near future, sustainability principles and an ESG approach will be as important to doing business as financial reporting, as consumers, shareholders, and regulators "insist" on this. Many companies have already taken the first steps to develop a circular economy, support responsible consumption, and if earlier it was more of a business desire, now it is becoming one of the competitive advantages and an important factor for attracting investment. In this context, the ESG approach should be carried out as systematically as business digitalization or strategy development of diversity, equity and inclusion.

Considering that almost everyone is faced with a shortage of quality personnel, a drop in the number of responses to a vacancy and changing employee expectations, businesses will be forced to seriously work on their employee value proposition (EVP) in terms of strengthening non-material motivation and opportunities for staff development. And here the most important role will be played by ESG issues. Today it is important to have a mission, take on social, environmental or other obligations, including for the attitude of employees, and to ask what you are doing to make the world around us a better place (Business in the era of stakeholders, 28.02.2022).

In theoretical terms, it is about fundamental changes in the structuring of the economic system at the stage of its dynamics. Today, before our eyes, it is expanding due to the "firmware" of the dialectical interaction of the economic system and society. And the essence of this process is expressed in a change in the priority of the motives of the professional activity of talented workers, i.e. in replacing economic utilities with social ones. And these preferences of individuals move beyond the companies into the economy and society in the process of upward causation.

At the same time, we should not forget that human capital in the person of a person with special qualities of intellectual autonomousness is not just a factor, but a person with his own views, values, desires and developed norms of individual behavior. Understanding by such a person of his significance aggravates the situation in society, since a talented worker will strengthen the society with his behavior only if he shares its values and is convinced that they are fair and he is satisfied with a society with such norms of behavior. That is why human-centrism, as a principle of organizing systems created by man, involves a fundamental change in priorities: first, society demonstrates the fair principles of collective coexistence in society, and only then talented individuals choose for themselves the sphere in which they will serve such a society, the conditions of work for an employer in a particular organization and the priority of creative activity in the form that suits him. And the expansion of the strategy of self-sufficient companies through ESG issues indicates that the conditions for the socialization of intellectually autonomous individuals are changing dramatically in order to change the static economic system and society.

EMPIRICAL EVIDENCE

From mathematical models of self-movement of systems suitable for describing self-sufficient companies, the authors chose a model of small oscillations of a mechanical system near its steady state, provided that there are no dissipation processes

$$m\ddot{x}(t) + kx(t) = 0. \tag{1}$$

Here m – is the mass, for example, of an oscillating material point;
k – a positive coefficient characterizing the elasticity (or stiffness) of an oscillatory system;
x – Cartesian coordinate, for example, of an oscillating material point;

symbol $\ddot{x}$ means the second time derivative of the coordinate x, or $\ddot{x} \equiv \dfrac{d^2 x}{dt^2}$.

Dividing both parts of the model (**1**) by the mass m we obtain the simplest autonomous model of an oscillatory system, the (self-motion) movement of which is described by a linear differential equation of the form

$$\ddot{x} + \acute{E}_0^2 x = 0. \tag{2}$$

Here $\acute{E}_0^2 = \dfrac{k}{m}$ – square of natural cyclic frequency of a linear oscillator $\acute{E}_0$.

In physics, such a system (**2**) is usually called a *linear harmonic oscillator.*

To analyze the self-organization process of self-sufficient companies oscillating near a steady state, we transform model (**2**) to the form

$$\ddot{q} + \acute{E}_0^2 q = 0 \,, \tag{3}$$

where q – generalized coordinate, since the oscillatory processes occurring in a self-sufficient company cannot be described in Cartesian coordinates.

The authors proceed from the fact that a self-sufficient company is a backbone element of the economic system and is characterized by a rather complex internal organization. Since it is self-sufficient, at the stage of its self-organization there are mechanisms in it to maintain its stability due to oscillatory changes in its internal structural bonds. The authors propose to consider the totality of such self-sufficient companies with the presence of internal ties that act as elements of the economic system as a quasi-elastic environment. In this case, in the first approximation, it is expedient to introduce the assumption that there are no dissipative processes in a quasi-elastic medium.

In this context the meaning of positive coefficients m and k changes.

Thus, m is advisable to understand it as a generalized measure of inertia (the phenomenon of inertia) in the self-movement (at the stage of self-organization) of a self-sufficient company. Its adaptive capabilities (properties) as a quasi-elastic medium are characterized by the generalized coefficient k, which can also be understood as quasi-rigidity. Paying tribute to the terminology adopted in the theory of oscillations, we will call $\acute{E}_0^2 = \dfrac{k}{m}$ generalized *internal static rigidity* of the system with respect to its oscillatory properties. Thus, the natural cyclic frequency $\acute{E}_0 = \sqrt{\dfrac{k}{m}}$ of free oscillations of a self-sufficient company, considered as a generalized oscillator (3), is directly proportional to the square root of k and inversely proportional to the square root of m. Attention should be paid to the meaning of the relationship $\dfrac{k}{m}$ – is the generalized quasi-rigidity per unit of the generalized inertia of the system. It is easy to verify that $q_1(t) = \cos \acute{E}_0 t$ and $q_2(t) = \sin \acute{E}_0 t$ are particular solutions of the linear differential equation (3). Therefore, the general solution can be represented as

$$q(t) = c_1 \cos \acute{E}_0 t + c_2 \sin \acute{E}_0 t \,, \tag{4}$$

where c_1 and c_2 arbitrary positive constants.

The general solution (4) can be written in a more compact form

$$q(t) = A \cos (\acute{E}_0 t - \varphi) \,, \tag{5}$$

where the constants A (amplitude) and φ (initial phase) are related to arbitrary constants c_1 and c_2 by the relations

$$A = \sqrt{c_1^2 + c_2^2} \,, \ tg\varphi = \frac{c_2}{c_1} \tag{6}$$

The evolution of differential equations of the form (**3**) or a system of equations of the form (**6**), introduced into consideration below, can be qualitatively represented *in the phase space of these mathematical objects*. This is an abstract space in which the quantities describing the state of the system serve as coordinates. In our case, these are the generalized coordinate **q** and the generalized speed $\dot{q}$. The movement of a point $(q, \dot{q})$ along a curve in phase space (along the trajectory of a phase point) describes the movement of the entire system. The speed of the phase point along this trajectory is determined by the point itself. We use the introduced concept of phase space to represent in it the set of movements of a self-sufficient company, considered as a generalized harmonic oscillator (**3**).

To construct generalized phase trajectories, consider a system of two (equations) equalities

$$\begin{cases} q(t) = A\cos(\acute{\mathbf{E}}_0 t - \varphi) \\ \dot{q}(t) = -A\acute{\mathbf{E}}_0 \sin(\acute{\mathbf{E}}_0 t - \varphi) \end{cases} \tag{6}$$

We introduce dimensionless time $\dfrac{t}{T_0}$, guided by the fact that $\acute{\mathbf{E}}_0 = \dfrac{2\pi}{T_0}$, where T_0 – generalized period of fluctuations within a self-sufficient company. All calculations and construction of phase trajectories of self-sufficient companies are performed in MS Excel based on the system (**6**).

Fig. 9 shows typical phase portraits of self-organization and expansion of self-sufficient companies.

The phase point moves along the phase trajectory in the direction indicated by the arrow. The choice of direction is determined by the fact that the positive generalized velocity ($\dot{q} > 0$) that corresponds to an increase in the generalized coordinate **q** over time (in our case, dimensionless time), and negative ($\dot{q} < 0$) – to the reduction of the generalized coordinate **q**.

Note that in our case the integral curves coincide with the phase trajectories.

Summarizing the result obtained, we emphasize that it is about generalized natural oscillations and specific characteristics of a self-sufficient company as a linear oscillator. In this case, the entire phase plane is filled with nested ellipses (with the exception of the singular point $(q = \dot{q} = 0)$.

The developed theory makes it possible to unambiguously interpret the curve **1** as a process of self-organization of a self-sufficient company in its static state while mediating the downward causation processes. The curve **2** describes the expansion of a self-sufficient company through the formation of new structural links within the corporate ecosystem on a new technological platform.

In the new conditions, a self-sufficient company expands its strategy by including ESG issues in it. Thus, self-sufficient companies acquire dynamic characteristics due to their mediation of upward causation processes. All this together forms new networking interactions for the post-COVID-19 dynamic reality in the economy and society.

So the objective factors for expanding the activities of companies have changed over the years of entrepreneurship development, but as for the essence they have not undergone significant adjustments. It is about profit maximization in any form: by increasing the rate of return, expanding market share, increasing the market value of shares, etc. Without this desire, there would be no commercial firms. As for the digital companies and big pharmaceuticals in the conditions of speculative demand growth for their products they behave in full accordance with the objective laws of business development. However, at present, a new trend has become more and more clear. It is very promising as it increasingly calls for the need to follow Environmental, Social and Corporate Governance (ESG) investment principles. What

Figure 9. The phase plane of a self-sufficient company as a harmonic oscillator - a family of nested ellipses
Source: the authors' development

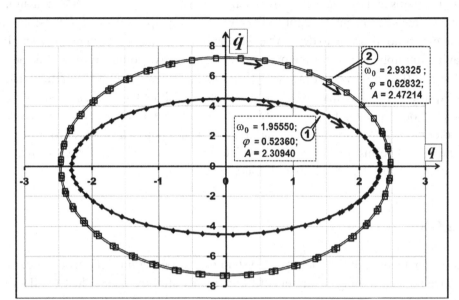

is the reason for this? Before the COVID-19 pandemic the static economy (yes, and society) became more complicated due to the deepening of internal structural ties.

Under the influence of the laws of self-organization, all players, including private business, have maximized utility by following the principles: "structure your business, maximize profits based on the repetition of forward and backward connections." The authors explained this by the specifics of the dialectical pairs functioning. Amidst uncertainty, the COVID-19 pandemic has forced companies to move away from old causal practices and start building new structures based on direct connections. In other words, what was good for a static economy – expand, repeating – has lost its relevance in the case of dynamic change. In the new conditions, only those companies that are able to destroy stereotypes and create something new can become successful (Schumpeter, 1949). Thus, digitalization and breakthrough technologies have changed priorities: physical and financial capital is gradually being replaced by intellectual capital. The carriers of the latter are intellectually autonomous individuals with socialization oriented towards the high ethical principles of behavior in society.

Therefore, according to the authors, all the "foam raised by the coronavirus pandemic" in the sense of the euphoria of digital companies and big pharmaceuticals, caught in a jet of high market conjuncture, will undoubtedly end. And if these large and largest companies neglect the laws of structuring a new dynamic reality, they will not be able to become self-sufficient and will lose the chance to become drivers of system formation processes. Ultimately, it will depend on their CEOs whether they will be successful in passing between the Scylla of quick profit from the problems of their citizens and the Charybdis of constructing a society with high social standards of living together.

The authors understand that only the future will prove the correctness of their conclusions. But, based on dialectical logic, the post-COVID-19 reality will be distinguished by dynamic characteristics, which the authors called "expansion". It is about restoring the dialectic of interaction between society and the economy, subject to the dominance of the first, about the return of harmony in the interaction between human-created systems and the Nature, from which mankind emerged many millennia ago.

In fact, these new phenomena brought to life the ESG-principles of the "responsible investment". Therefore, today it is not possible to determine whether the current digital companies and big pharmaceuticals, having multiplied their income on the crest of a positive conjuncture, will be able to acquire the status of self-sufficient. It takes time, analytical data and their in-depth theoretical understanding. The authors express an opinion that has yet to be proven. It is about the struggle of self-sufficient companies in the field of combining the incompatible: greed and integrity (like choosing between evil and good). Only the interaction of the interests and desires of the society and self-sufficient companies in the field of the ethical norms of behavior will predetermine a bright future for business giants capable to self-sufficiency, and for the prosperity of society.

CONCLUSION

A theoretical understanding of the patterns of system formation within self-sufficient companies is of great importance for determining the drivers of future reality after the end of the COVID-19 pandemic. A society organized on the principles of human-centrism is able to multiply it in building structural links in the economy and technology. At the same time, the role of an intermediate link in the organization of human-centric organizations in society, economy and technology is performed by self-sufficient companies. This is due to the fact that they represent those dialectically complex elements that were generated by socio-economic systems before pandemic. And it is they who are able to structure the new post-COVID-19 reality, since they are represented by companies that have acquired their own self-movement mechanism. Inside the company, it is represented by the mechanism of downward causation, which sets in motion the processes of self-organization of dialectically complex companies (internal structures), and outside, by the mechanism of upward causation, which implements their self-development. Moreover, transforming from within, private companies become capable of creatively destroying the external environment, integrating into society, the economy and technology to implement the mechanism of their own self-movement.

In the new dynamic reality, self-sufficient companies are strengthening their positions, since investing in intangibles is a way to expand them by generating a huge number of networking interactions. Companies that have invested across all categories of intangibles are further ahead in their digitization journey, less likely to be disrupted because they are highly innovative, and highly likely to be able to attract and retain top talent. All of this can create value and, importantly, value that can be defended even amid a deep market and economic disruption. And besides, investments in different types of intangibles interact with a high correlation, creating synergies. Thus, self-sufficient companies become dynamic, gaining enlargement and new opportunities for self-development by expanding ecosystems, forming technological platforms and expanding their strategies by introducing ESG issues into them.

Meanwhile, the process of expansion of self-sufficient companies occurs through the object, subject and process components of system formation both at the micro and macro levels of the economy and society. In this context, priority is given to the subject component, which mediates technological progress and the dynamic characteristics of the economy and society. The fundamental nature of this problem is predetermined by its complexity and the dialectical interconnectedness of the two mechanisms of human self-organization: its education as the basis of diversity (diversity) and socialization (the basis for inclusiveness, involvement, integration). Without each other, these phenomena will not provide the equity parameter as a quality of the social environment, and their combination is a fundamental problem that has not been solved in any country in the world. The national community that will be the first in this race for a creative person capable of autonomously solving the most complex problems, and striving to serve the fatherland with all his talent, will become the indisputable leader of future progress.

The subjective aspect of organizational changes within the firm, including the institutionalization of individual and collective behavior, comes to the fore in understanding the strategic actions of companies in the uncertain environment of post-COVID-19 reality. Self-sufficient companies survive economic crises more easily if they quickly change the organizational structure of their in-house teams. Moreover, they, as a rule, demonstrate the best results not only during the post-crisis recovery, but also after the end of the crisis in the long term. It is in this context that the main drivers of organizational change processes in the economy and society are self-sufficient companies that understand the importance of the principles of diversity, equity and inclusion, ensure their structural stability and adjust the individual habits and behavior of their employees through causation mechanisms.

In the newest conditions, those companies will be successful that, by experience in the crisis situation of the coronavirus pandemic, have come to the need to organize their teams on the principles of human-centrism with the involvement of highly qualified personnel to form a new quality of professional alliances in the form of super-teams from a variety of specialized groups of people and groups of specialized computers. Today it is difficult even to predict the prospects for such fundamental transformations, but the priority of a person capable of self-development, whose intellectual asset will be very expensive, and from a theoretical point of view, invaluable, is indisputable (Malone, 2018).

REFERENCES

Agrawal, S., De Smet, A., Poplawski, P., & Reich, A. (2020). *Beyond hiring: How companies are re-skilling to address talent gaps. In Organization Practice and McKinsey Accelerate.* McKinsey & Company.

Aldrich, H. E. (1999). *Organizations Evolving* (Vol. L). Sage.

Anderson, K., Arrow, J., & Pines, D. (Eds.). (1988). *The Economy as an Evolving Complex System.* Addison-Wesley.

Argyris, C., & Schön, D. A. (1996). *Organizational Learning II: Theory, Method, and Practice.* Addison-Wesley.

Arnold, V. I. (1979). Catastrophe theory. *Nature,* (10), 54–63.

Arnold, V. I. (1975). Critical points of smooth functions, *Proc. of International Congress of Mathematicians,* 19-40.

Arthur, W. B., Durlauf, S. N., & Lane, D. A. (Eds.). (1997). *The Economy as an Evolving Complex System II.* Addison-Wesley.

Arthur, W. B. (1999). Complexity and the economy. *Science, 284,* 107-109.

Arthur, W. B. (2009). *The Nature of Technology: What it Is and How it Evolves.* Free Press.

BCG Executive Perspectives. (2021). *Investing to Win Talent*. Boston Consulting Group.

von Bertalanffy, L. (1968). General System Theory: Foundations, Development, Applications. University of Alberta.

Blitz, D. (1992). *Emergent Evolution: Qualitative Novelty and the Level of Reality*. Kluwer. doi:10.1007/978-94-015-8042-7

Bogdanov, A. A. (1934). Tectology or General Organizational Science. Academic Press.

Boston Consulting Group. (2019). *Mission Talent: Mass Uniqueness. A global challenge for one billion workers*. BCG.

Breen, K. (2016). *Why does inclusive growth matter?* The World Economic Forum.

Business in the Era of Stakeholders. (2022). *Harvard Business Review Russia*. Retrieved from: https://hbr-russia.ru/ management/strategiya/biznes-v-eru-steykkholderov/

Chardin. (1959). *The Phenomenon of Human Being*. Harper & Brothers.

Chung, Dietz, Rab, & Townsend. (2020). *Ecosystem 2.0: Climbing to the next level*. McKinsey & Co.

Coase, R.H. (1988). The nature of the firm: origin, meaning, influence. *Journal of Law, Economics and Organization, 4*.

Corrado, Haskel, Jona-Lasinio, & Iommi. (2018). Intangible investment in the EU and US before and since the Great Recession and its contribution to productivity growth. *Journal of Infrastructure, Policy and Development, 2*(1).

COVID-19. Briefing Materials. (2020). Global health and crisis response. McKinsey & Company.

Davies, Diemand-Yauman, & van Dam. (2019, Feb.). Competitive advantage with a human dimension: From lifelong learning to lifelong employability. *McKinsey Quarterly*.

Dietz, Khan, & Rab. (2020). *How do companies create value from digital ecosystems?* McKinsey & Company.

Dixon-Fyle, Hunt, & Prince. (2020). *Diversity wins: How inclusion matters*. McKinsey & Company.

Impact, E. (2022). *The ESG conundrum: How investors and companies can find common purpose in ESG*. The Economist Group.

Emmett, J., Schrah, G., Schrimper, M., & Wood, A. (2020). *COVID-19 and the employee experience: How leaders can seize the moment. Organization Practice*. McKinsey & Company.

Garcia-Alonso, J., Krentz, M., Lovich, D., & Mingardon, S. (2020). Diversity, equity, and inclusion still matter in a pandemic. Boston Consulting Group.

Ghose, B. (2020). *Why 2020 will see the birth of the 'trust economy'*. World Economic Forum.

Guckenheimer, J. (1973). Bifurcation and catastrophe. In M. Peixoto (Ed.), *Dynamical Systems*. Academic Press.

Haken, H. (1977). *Synergetics. An Introduction.* Springer-Verlag.

Hausmann, R., & Gavin, M. (1996). *Securing stability and growth in a shock prone region: the policy challenge for Latin America.* Inter-American Development Bank. Working Paper. No. 315. Office of the Chief Economist.

Hegel, G. W. F. (1892). The science of logics. In The Logic of Hegel (2nd ed.). Oxford University Press.

Hodgson, G.M. (1988). Competence and control in the theory of the firm. *Journal of Economic Behavior and Organization, 35*(2), 179-201.

Hodgson, G. M. (1988b). *Economics and Institutions. A Manifesto for a Modern Institutional Economics.* Polity Press. doi:10.9783/9781512816952

Hodgson, G.M. (1998). The approach of institutional economics. *Journal of Economic Literature, 36*(1), 166-192.

Hodgson, G. M. (2002). Reconstitutive downward causation: social structure and the development of individual agency. In Intersubjectivity in Economics: Agents and Structures. Routledge.

Hodgson, G. M. (2003). The hidden persuaders: Institutions and individuals in economic theory. *Cambridge Journal of Economics, 27*(2), 159–175. doi:10.1093/cje/27.2.159

Hodgson, G. M., & Knudsen, T. (2004). The firm as an interactor: Firms as vehicles for habits and routines. *Journal of Evolutionary Economics, 14*(3), 281–307. doi:10.100700191-004-0192-1

Hunt, Layton, & Prince. (2015). *Diversity matters.* McKinsey & Company.

Hunt, Prince, Dixon-Fyle, & Yee. (2018). *Delivering Through Diversity.* McKinsey & Company.

Karalee, A., Gourévitch, M. S., Sterman, M., Quarta, L., & Close, A. S. (2020). Digital acceleration is just a dream without a new approach to tech. Boston Consulting Group.

Keynes, J. M. (1936). *The General Theory of Employment? Interest and Money. The Selected Works.* Harcourt, Brace and Company.

Kontopoulos, K. M. (1993). *The Logic of Social Structure.* Cambridge University Press. doi:10.1017/CBO9780511570971

Krishnan, Mischke, & Remes. (2018). Is the Solow paradox back? *McKinsey Quarterly.*

Leap by McKinsey. (2021). *Global Report: The state of new-business building.* McKinsey & Co.

Levitt, B., & March, J. G. (1988). Organizational learning. *Annual Review of Sociology, 14*(1), 319–340. doi:10.1146/annurev.so.14.080188.001535

Malone, T. W. (2018). *Superminds. The Surprising Power of People and Computers Thinking Together.* Little, Brown Spark.

Manyika, J., Birshan, M., Smit, S., Woetzel, J., Russell, K., Purcell, L., & Ramaswamy, S. (2021). *Companies in the 21st century. A new look at how corporations impact the economy and households.* Discussion paper. McKinsey Global Institute. Retrieved from: www.mckinsey.com/mgi

McConnell, M., & Schaninger, B. (2019, Jan.). *Are we long—or short—on talent? McKinsey Quarterly.*

Mendy, A., Stewart, M. L., & VanAkin, K. (2020). *A leader's guide: Communicating with teams, stakeholders, and communities during COVID-19. April. In Organization Practice.* McKinsey & Company.

Mokyr, J. (2005). The intellectual origins of modern economic growth. *Journal of Economic History, 65*(2), 285 – 351.

North, D. (1997). *The process of economic change.* Research Paper. 128. World Institute for Development Economics Research.

North, D. (2005). *Understanding the Process of Economic Change.* Princeton University Press.

North, D. C. (1990). *Institutions, Institutional Change and Economic Performance.* Cambridge University Press. doi:10.1017/CBO9780511808678

Novacek, Lee, & Krentz. (2021). *It's time to reimagine diversity, equity, and inclusion.* Boston Consulting Group.

Okamoto, G. (2020). Knightmare Uncertainty. *IMF Finance & Development, 57*(3).

Pilipenko, A. I., Pilipenko, Z. A., & Pilipenko, O. I. (2022). Dialectics of self-movement of resilient companies in the economy and society post COVID-19: patterns of organizational transformations of networking interactions. In Challenges and Emerging Strategies for Global Networking Post COVID-19. IGI Global.

Pilipenko, A. I., Pilipenko, Z. A., & Pilipenko, O. I. (2021). Rebuilding a stronger business in the uncertain post-COVID-19 future: Factor of intellectually autonomous and adequately socialized employees. In Adapting and Mitigating Environmental, Social, and Governance Risk in Business. IGI Global.

Pilipenko, O. I., Pilipenko, Z. A., & Pilipenko, A. I. (2021). Theory of Shocks, COVID-19, and Normative Fundamentals for Policy Responses. IGI Global.

Rawls, J. B. (1971). *A Theory of Justice.* Harvard University Press. doi:10.4159/9780674042605

Roth, F. (2019). Intangible capital and labor productivity growth: A review of the literature. *Hamburg Discussion Papers in International Economics*, 4.

Schumpeter, J. A. (1949). *The Theory of Economic Development: An Inquiry into Profits, Capital, Credit, Interest, and the Business Cycle.* Harvard University Press.

Schwab, K. (2016). *The Fourth Industrial Revolution.* Geneva: World Economic Forum.

Schwab, K., & Malleret, T. (2020). *COVID-19: The Great Reset.* World Economic Forum.

Siebel, T. M. (2019). *Digital Transformation: Survive and Thrive in an Era of Mass Extinction.* Rosetta Books.

Smit, S., Hirt, M., Dash, P., Lucas, A., Latkovic, T., Wilson, M., Greenberg, E., Buehler, K., & Hjartar, K. (2020). *Crushing coronavirus uncertainty: The big 'unlock' for our economies. To safeguard lives and livelihoods, we must restore confidence. In Strategy & Corporate Finance Practice.* McKinsey & Company.

Sperry, R. W. (1964). *Problems Outstanding in the Evolution of Brain Function*. American Museum of Natural History.

Sperry, R. W. (1969). A modified concept of consciousness. *Psychological Review, 76*(6), 532–536. doi:10.1037/h0028156 PMID:5366411

Taplett, F. B., Krentz, M., Dean, J., & Novacek, G. (2019). Diversity is just the first step. Inclusion comes next. Boston Consulting Group.

The business case for inclusive growth. (2018). In *Deloitte Global Inclusive Growth Survey*. Deloitte Touche Tohmatsu Limited.

The Economist Intelligence Unit. (2020). *COVID-19 and the crisis for higher education*. Report. London: The Economist Intelligence Unit Limited.

Thom, R. (1969). Topological models in biology. *Topology, 8,* 313-36.

Thom, R. (1974). Catastrophe theory: its present state and future perspectives. Dynamical Systems-Warwick. Lecture Notes in Mathematics. Math., 468, 366–372.

Veblen, T. B. (1899). *The Theory of the Leisure Class: An Economic Study in the Evolution of Institutions*. Macmillan.

WEF. (2018). *The Inclusive Growth and Development Report*. World Economic Forum.

Weissman, D. (2000). *A Social Ontology*. Yale University Press.

Williamson, O. E. (1985). *The Economic Institutions of Capitalism: Firms, Markets, Relational Contracting*. Academic Press.

World Bank. (2018). *World Development Report 2018: Learning to Realize Education's Promise*. World Bank.

Zeeman, E. C. (1977). *Catastrophe Theory: Selected Papers*. Addison-Wesley.

Chapter 4
Teleworking as an Emerging Strategy During COVID-19:
Evidence From the United States

Caglar Dogru
https://orcid.org/0000-0002-4215-8979
Ufuk University, Turkey

ABSTRACT

The world is facing one of its hardest pandemics ever with COVID-19. It has been a very tough challenge since the pandemic urged radical changes and transformations in every aspect of life and especially in the work life. During the pandemic, teleworking has gained a vital role for sustaining the production of goods and services. Although teleworking has both positive and negative outcomes, it has been a life jacket for not only organizations but also for employees all around the world during the COVID-19 pandemic. In this chapter, the role of teleworking in the human resources during the pandemic, between May 2020 and January 2022, is evaluated monthly on the basis of analyzing the descriptive statistics of people teleworking or working at home for pay in the United States, by their specific characteristics grouped as age, gender, full-time/part time job status and occupations.

INTRODUCTION

For the first time, a pandemic has had such impacts on every aspect of the life in our modern society. The Covid-19 pandemic has had negative effects to a very wide spectrum from for example businesses (Donthu and Gustafsson), and especially small businesses (Humphries, Neilson and Ulyssea, 2020), international trade (Hayakawa and Mukunoki, 2021), local (Yang, Ning, Jiang, & He, 2021) and global logistics (Hohenstein, 2022), agriculture (Štreimikienė, Baležentis, Volkov, Ribašauskienė, Morkūnas, & Žičkienė, 2021), gross domestic products of countries (Korneta and Rostek, 2021), and to workplace (Carnevale and Hatak, 2020) and outdoor socialization (Xie, Luo, Furuya and Sun, 2020), and employee psychology (Lin, Shao, Li Guo and Zhan, 2021).

DOI: 10.4018/978-1-6684-6762-6.ch004

Much has been written about the covid-19 pandemic and its effects on daily and business life as well as transformation of doing business into a new form. Besides other very important effects, one of the vital effects has been witnessed on the work life. When the covid-19 pandemic began, the business world all around the globe, tried to take cautions in order to protect people from getting infected with covid-19. Organizations have obeyed the rules and procedures set by the governments but at the same time they have had the responsibility to sustain production and distribution. At this point since workplaces closed for a while and most of the companies applied called fewer employees to offices than they did before the pandemic, new forms of work have been implemented. Among them remote work has been very popular since the beginning of the covid-19 pandemic due to its flexibility and benefits (Tursunbayeva, Di Lauro and Antonelli, 2022). The dominant way of remote working all around the world has been applied by teleworking (Bérastégui, 2021). During the covid-19 pandemic, teleworking has gained a vital role and been an emerging strategy to cope with the negative effects of this pandemic all around the world.

The primary goal of this chapter is to analyze the descriptive statistics of the teleworking employees and to reveal the position of teleworking compared to the total work force during the covid-19 pandemic. In order to reach this study aim, the United States was chosen as the sample research. The reason for selecting the United States to observe the effects of the pandemic on teleworking is that, United States was the only country when the research began, which measured teleworking or working at home for pay on various demographic criteria specifically due to the covid-19 pandemic. Throughout this chapter, firstly teleworking concept will be defined and discussed in the background section, and immediately afterwards, the scope of the research, the measures of teleworking in the United States and the analysis of teleworking in this country will be done. Consequently, future research directions covering teleworking during and post covid-19 will be given right before the conclusions.

BACKGROUND

Teleworking as an Alternative Form of Work

Teleworking is accepted as an alternative and a new form of work since the end of the twentieth century (Baruch, 2001). Teleworking can be defined as an alternative form of work which needs technological infrastructure in terms of information technologies and equipment enhancing employees to work from anywhere they are which opens a door to the virtual offices (Davenport and Pearlson, 1998). From the early contributions to our time, teleworking has been given important role in the literature by the researchers. So far scholars have linked teleworking to for example human resources functions (Pulido-Martos, Cortés-Denia and Lopez-Zafra, 2021), employee productivity (Hoornweg, Peters and Van der Heijden, 2016), employee health (Lunde et al., 2022), workplace flexibility and organizational performance (Sánchez, Pérez, de Luis Carnicer and Jiménez, 2007), role overload (Duxbury and Halinski, 2014), and even traffic and air pollution (Giovanis, 2018).

As the literature suggests, teleworking has both advantages and disadvantages in general. Among the disadvantages, there exist generally employees' having health problems for example sitting down longer hours, looking at the monitor or other electronic devices for longer time (Rodríguez-Nogueira et al., 2021). Besides, employees may suffer from some psychological problems due to their loneliness due to teleworking (Mann and Holdsworth, 2003). Also there is some trust problem with the employees and their organizations based on electronic surveillance (Doğru, 2021). Apart from these, work flexibility

(Sánchez, et al., 2007) and productivity (Kazekami, 2020) due to use of technology, can be counted among the advantages of teleworking.

TELEWORKING DURING THE COVID-19 PANDEMIC

As the pandemic began, governments and organizations around the world took many actions covering the employment issues in their own countries. To prevent people from getting infected with covid-19, remote work alternatives have been put into practice. During the pandemic, there have been a vast number of reports and researches (e.g. Dörr, Licht and Murmann, 2021) signaling small and medium enterprises' closing due to bankruptcies or their dismissing some of their employees (e.g. Turnea, Neştian, Tiţă, Vodă and Guţă, 2020). So in this context, teleworking has been used as an emerging strategy to cope with the challenges of the covid-19 pandemic.

With the help of teleworking, first of all, many lives have been saved since the pandemic began. Additionally, organizations have had the opportunity to sustain productivity of employees using information technologies. Moreover, employees have had the occasion of working at home for pay, except for the ones who lost their job due to the pandemic. But it is well understood that, we are now about to come over this pandemic in the near future with the vital role of teleworking and information technologies. In the next section, it is intended to reveal the demographic statistics of employees who has teleworked or worked at home for pay just because of the covid-19 pandemic.

MAIN FOCUS OF THE CHAPTER

The Scope of the Research

In this research, in accordance with the objectives of the study, it was intended to investigate the effects of the covid-19 pandemic on the way of working. The scope of the research is limited to analyzing these effects on teleworking and working at home for pay during the pandemic. By this approach, it is planned to reveal the real effects of the pandemic on the new forms of work, from the perspective of one of the most preferred type of work during covid-19 that is teleworking. In this context, the research consists of measuring teleworking in the United States beginning from May 2020, the first month in which the statistics were available, to January 2022, the last month in which this chapter was updated.

Measuring Teleworking in the United States

In this research secondary data monthly obtained by the United States Bureau of Labor Statistics between May 2020 and January 2021 were used. These data were retrieved from the statistical results of the U.S. Bureau of Labor Statistics based on the Current Population Survey (CPS). With the help of these surveys, we had the chance to investigate from multiple points of view based on demographics of the employees in the United States. The selected characteristics are stated in the next section.

Table 1. Descriptive statistics about employees who teleworked at home during COVID-19 (May 2020)

Characteristic	Total Employed (numbers in thousands)	Teleworking due to Covid-19*		Percentage	
		Total	Percentage	Total Employed	Teleworking due to Covid-19*
Total, 16 years and over	137.461	48.703	35,4	100,0	100,0
Age					
16 to 24 years	14.352	2.715	18,9	10,4	5,6
25 to 54 years	90.147	34.983	38,8	65,6	71,8
55 years and over	32.963	11.005	33,4	24,0	22,6
Gender					
Men, 16 years and over	74.004	22.774	30,8	53,8	46,8
Women, 16 years and over	63.457	25.929	40,9	46,2	53,2
Full-time / Part-time					
Full-time workers	116.620	44.334	38,0	84,8	91,0
Part-time workers	20.841	4.369	21,0	15,2	9,0
Occupation					
Management, professional, and related occupations	62.330	35.786	57,4	45,3	73,5
Service occupations	19.087	1.507	7,9	13,9	3,1
Sales and office occupations	26.931	9.487	35,2	19,6	19,5
Natural resources, construction, and maintenance occupations	12.362	937	7,6	9,0	1,9
Production, transportation, and material moving occupations	16.751	987	5,9	12,2	2,0

Source: U.S. Bureau of Labor Statistics, (2022). Labor Force Statistics from the Current Population Survey, https://www.bls.gov/cps/effects-of-the-coronavirus-covid-19-pandemic.htm#table1

*: Only who teleworked or worked at home for pay at some point in the past 4 weeks specifically due to Covid-19.

Note: Data are not seasonally adjusted.

Analysis of the Teleworking Statistics in the United States

The teleworking statistics obtained from the United States Bureau of Labor Statistics, are selected and classified into groups as; 'age', 'gender', 'fulltime and part time job status', and 'occupation' that includes management, professional and related occupations, service occupations, sales and office occupations, natural resources, construction, and maintenance occupations, production, transportation, and material moving occupations. These descriptive statistics are demonstrated in the following tables below beginning with May 2020 in Table 1.

May 2020 is the beginning of the selected period for observing the teleworking statistics. As it is seen in Table 1, in May 2020, 35,4% of the employees teleworked specifically due to Covid-19. If we evaluate the age composition among teleworkers in this month, we see that the majority belongs to the age group between 25 and 54 years with 71,8% which is higher than the age group of 55 years and over with 22,6%. In May 2020, in total workforce, women (40,9%) teleworked more than men (30,8%) due to the pandemic. Among the teleworkers, again women (53,2%) are slightly higher than men (46,8%).

Table 2. Descriptive Statistics about employees who teleworked at home during COVID-19 (June 2020)

Characteristic	Total Employed (numbers in thousands)	Teleworking due to Covid-19*		Percentage	
		Total	Percentage	Total Employed	Teleworking due to Covid-19*
Total, 16 years and over	142.811	44.644	31,3	100,0	100,0
Age					
16 to 24 years	16.553	2.490	15,0	11,6	5,6
25 to 54 years	92.407	32.147	34,8	64,7	72,0
55 years and over	33.851	10.008	29,6	23,7	22,4
Gender					
Men, 16 years and over	76.425	20.772	27,2	53,5	46,5
Women, 16 years and over	66.386	23.872	36,0	46,5	53,5
Full-time / Part-time					
Full-time workers	120.169	40.252	33,5	84,1	90,2
Part-time workers	22.642	4.393	19,4	15,9	9,8
Occupation					
Management, professional, and related occupations	63.336	33.001	52,1	44,3	73,9
Service occupations	21.164	1.421	6,7	14,8	3,2
Sales and office occupations	28.458	8.731	30,7	19,9	19,6
Natural resources, construction, and maintenance occupations	12.779	717	5,6	8,9	1,6
Production, transportation, and material moving occupations	17.074	775	4,5	12,0	1,7

Source: U.S. Bureau of Labor Statistics, (2022). Labor Force Statistics from the Current Population Survey, https://www.bls.gov/cps/effects-of-the-coronavirus-covid-19-pandemic.htm#table1

*: Only who teleworked or worked at home for pay at some point in the past 4 weeks specifically due to Covid-19.

Note: Data are not seasonally adjusted.

This may be stemmed from the social roles in the families, for example childcare at home. Also, full-time workers at a percentage of 38 and part-time workers at a percentage of 21 of the total workforce have teleworked or worked at home in May. Among these teleworkers, 91% is full-time workers. This points out that, due to the pandemic, teleworking has gained importance mostly because of the full-time workers. This may be due to the fact that, part-time workers had already used some alternative forms of work even before the pandemic. Also, among the occupation groups, the highest number of teleworkers belongs to the management, professional and related occupations (%73,5). This may be explained by the fact that, management and professional occupations are mostly suitable for remote work and teleworking. The statistics of the following month is shown in Table 2.

In June, the ratio of teleworking employees to the total employees in the United States started to fall from 35,4% to 31,3%. Among the employees teleworked or worked at home, the majority belongs to the age group between 25 and 54 years with 72%, which is very close to the number in May 2020. The percentages in age, gender, full or part-time work and occupations are very close to the previous month's numbers. But at this point we should underline that, they started to decrease due to the re-openings of

Table 3. Descriptive statistics about employees who teleworked at home during COVID-19 (July 2020)

Characteristic	Total Employed (numbers in thousands)	Teleworking due to Covid-19*		Percentage	
		Total	Percentage	Total Employed	Teleworking due to Covid-19*
Total, 16 years and over	144.492	38.194	26,4	100,0	100,0
Age					
16 to 24 years	17.507	2.169	12,4	12,1	5,7
25 to 54 years	92.504	27.347	29,6	64,0	71,6
55 years and over	34.481	8.677	25,2	23,9	22,7
Gender					
Men, 16 years and over	77.375	18.511	23,9	53,5	48,5
Women, 16 years and over	67.117	19.683	29,3	46,5	51,5
Full-time / Part-time					
Full-time workers	121.198	34.565	28,5	83,9	90,5
Part-time workers	23.294	3.629	15,6	16,1	9,5
Occupation					
Management, professional, and related occupations	62.494	27.932	44,7	43,3	73,1
Service occupations	21.929	1.188	5,4	15,2	3,1
Sales and office occupations	29.472	7.742	26,3	20,4	20,3
Natural resources, construction, and maintenance occupations	13.183	609	4,6	9,1	1,6
Production, transportation, and material moving occupations	17.414	723	4,2	12,1	1,9

Source: U.S. Bureau of Labor Statistics, (2022). Labor Force Statistics from the Current Population Survey, https://www.bls.gov/cps/effects-of-the-coronavirus-covid-19-pandemic.htm#table1

*: Only who teleworked or worked at home for pay at some point in the past 4 weeks specifically due to Covid-19.

Note: Data are not seasonally adjusted.

business in June. To see if this movement is a premise of a trend, we should have a look at the numbers of July 2020, which is present in Table 3.

The percentage of teleworking due to Covid-19 again fell in July 2020 from June's 31,3% to 26,4%. This is due to the summer's effects, such as rising temperatures, open air, etc., on the decrease of the Covid-19 cases. The other demographic statistics are similar to the previous months, only slight differences occur. But here we understand that in July, the number of male teleworkers (48,5%) is closing the gap with females (51.5%) when compared with May and June this year. We may have a look at the statistics of the following summer month of August in Table 4.

In August, teleworking due to the Covid-19 falls to 24,3% of total employees in the United States. According to the data, we reveal a decreasing trend in the number of employees who teleworked because of the pandemic in the last four months. As it is seen in Table 4, the share of management, professional and related occupations rose to 75,1%. This may be due to the working conditions in natural resources, construction, and maintenance occupations and also in production, transportation, and material moving

Table 4. Descriptive statistics about employees who teleworked at home during COVID-19 (August 2020)

Characteristic	Total Employed (numbers in thousands)	Teleworking due to Covid-19*		Percentage	
		Total	Percentage	Total Employed	Teleworking due to Covid-19*
Total, 16 years and over	147.224	35.800	24,3	100,0	100,0
Age					
16 to 24 years	17.577	1.954	11,1	11,9	5,5
25 to 54 years	94.500	25.922	27,4	64,2	72,4
55 years and over	35.147	7.925	22,5	23,9	22,1
Gender					
Men, 16 years and over	78.711	17.226	21,9	53,5	48,1
Women, 16 years and over	68.513	18.573	27,1	46,5	51,9
Full-time / Part-time					
Full-time workers	123.619	32.816	26,5	84,0	91,7
Part-time workers	23.605	2.984	12,6	16,0	8,3
Occupation					
Management, professional, and related occupations	63.095	26.876	42,6	42,9	75,1
Service occupations	22.673	943	4,2	15,4	2,6
Sales and office occupations	30.434	7.044	23,1	20,7	19,7
Natural resources, construction, and maintenance occupations	13.559	385	2,8	9,2	1,1
Production, transportation, and material moving occupations	17.464	551	3,2	11,9	1,5

Source: U.S. Bureau of Labor Statistics, (2022). Labor Force Statistics from the Current Population Survey, https://www.bls.gov/cps/effects-of-the-coronavirus-covid-19-pandemic.htm#table1

*: Only who teleworked or worked at home for pay at some point in the past 4 weeks specifically due to Covid-19.

Note: Data are not seasonally adjusted.

occupations. This is because the latter two occupations are mostly active in summer months and naturally teleworking is not as suitable as in management, professional and related occupations.

The decreasing trend in the percentage of teleworking due to the Covid-19 pandemic lasted also in September to 22.7%. Similar to the previous months, in September, the highest number of teleworking employees was in the group of '25 to 54 years' with 72,8%. The eye-catching point in in Table 5 is the increasing percentage difference of male and female teleworkers. In September, the percentage of male teleworkers fell from 48,1% to 46,9% whereas the percentage of female teleworkers rose from 51,9% to 53,1%. The statistics about upcoming month are presented in Table 6.

The lowest rate of teleworking so far (21,2%) occurred in October 2020 as seen in Table 6. This may be due to the fact that more workplaces practiced in-person attendance in the offices. Keeping other teleworking statistics classification, there is an important point in occupations. As it is noticed in Table 6, the percentage of employees working at services fell from 3% to 2,7%, whereas sales and office occupations rose to 18,9% from 18,2%. This can be explained as more employees teleworked in sales and office occupations, whereas less employees teleworked in services occupations. This may be realized as

Table 5. Descriptive statistics about employees who teleworked at home during COVID-19 (September 2020)

Characteristic	Total Employed (numbers in thousands)	Teleworking due to Covid-19*		Percentage	
		Total	Percentage	Total Employed	Teleworking due to Covid-19*
Total, 16 years and over	147.796	33.501	22,7	100,0	100,0
Age					
16 to 24 years	17.342	1.801	10,4	11,7	5,4
25 to 54 years	95.026	24.394	25,7	64,3	72,8
55 years and over	35.428	7.307	20,6	24,0	21,8
Gender					
Men, 16 years and over	78.817	15.720	19,9	53,3	46,9
Women, 16 years and over	68.979	17.781	25,8	46,7	53,1
Full-time / Part-time					
Full-time workers	122.998	30.531	24,8	83,2	91,1
Part-time workers	24.798	2.970	12,0	16,8	8,9
Occupation					
Management, professional, and related occupations	62.759	25.418	40,5	42,5	75,9
Service occupations	23.428	1.010	4,3	15,9	3,0
Sales and office occupations	29.696	6.096	20,5	20,1	18,2
Natural resources, construction, and maintenance occupations	13.683	423	3,1	9,3	1,3
Production, transportation, and material moving occupations	18.231	555	3,0	12,3	1,7

Source: U.S. Bureau of Labor Statistics, (2022). Labor Force Statistics from the Current Population Survey, https://www.bls.gov/cps/effects-of-the-coronavirus-covid-19-pandemic.htm#table1

*: Only who teleworked or worked at home for pay at some point in the past 4 weeks specifically due to Covid-19.

Note: Data are not seasonally adjusted.

a signal of rising Covid-19 cases, which in turn affected managerial and professional employees since they were the most appropriate group to telework in their forms of work.

After witnessing the lowest rate of teleworking in the covid-19 pandemic so far in October, a slight increase to 21,8% in November seems like a new start in the increasing trend. This may be based on the seasonal effects on the covid-19 pandemic and the increasing numbers of cases in the United States. There is also a slight increase in the full-time workers who teleworked or worked at home for pay. The same is applicable for the management, professional and related occupations as well as natural resources, construction, and maintenance occupations. In contrast there is a slight decrease in the sales and office occupations. The statistics related to December 2020 is given in Table 8.

As it was noted for the November statistics, the rise in the number of employees who teleworked in December, starts to form an increasing trend since it was recorded as 23,7%. Besides, in December, among teleworkers, the share of the men increased to 47,1% from 46,9%. Additionally, the full-time

Table 6. Descriptive statistics about employees who teleworked at home during COVID-19 (October 2020)

Characteristic	Total Employed (numbers in thousands)	Teleworking due to Covid-19*		Percentage	
		Total	Percentage	Total Employed	Teleworking due to Covid-19*
Total, 16 years and over	150.433	31.954	21,2	100,0	100,0
Age					
16 to 24 years	18.219	1.674	9,2	12,1	5,2
25 to 54 years	96.365	23.133	24,0	64,1	72,4
55 years and over	35.850	7.147	19,9	23,8	22,4
Gender					
Men, 16 years and over	79.794	14.978	18,8	53,0	46,9
Women, 16 years and over	70.639	16.975	24,0	47,0	53,1
Full-time / Part-time					
Full-time workers	124.165	28.761	23,2	82,5	90,0
Part-time workers	26.269	3.193	12,2	17,5	10,0
Occupation					
Management, professional, and related occupations	63.277	24.132	38,1	42,1	75,5
Service occupations	24.137	869	3,6	16,0	2,7
Sales and office occupations	30.501	6.044	19,8	20,3	18,9
Natural resources, construction, and maintenance occupations	13.956	361	2,6	9,3	1,1
Production, transportation, and material moving occupations	18.562	547	2,9	12,3	1,7

Source: U.S. Bureau of Labor Statistics, (2022). Labor Force Statistics from the Current Population Survey, https://www.bls.gov/cps/effects-of-the-coronavirus-covid-19-pandemic.htm#table1

*: Only who teleworked or worked at home for pay at some point in the past 4 weeks specifically due to Covid-19.

Note: Data are not seasonally adjusted.

workers who teleworked or worked at home for pay in December increased to 90,9%. This shows us, teleworking was used extensively in this period to come over the problems of the covid-19 pandemic.

To understand the benefits of teleworking or working from home throughout the covid-19 pandemic, it was understood so far that, the percentage of teleworking, the percentage of men teleworkers, full-time teleworkers and management, professional and related occupations can be accepted to be pioneer characteristics. This is due to the nature of remote work, and their having flexible characteristics in general. Because when there was impossible to work in person, males, full-time workers and management, professional and related occupations switched more to teleworking based on the results so far. So in January, it was witnessed that the numbers of men, 16 years and over, full-time workers and management, professional and related occupations increased. To see if this is the same case in February, we can see the Table 10.

In the second month of the new year, the percentage of teleworking due to Covid-19 fell from 23,2% to 22,7%. And as it is seen in Table 10, full-time workers teleworked or worked at home more than they did in January. In February, the decrease among teleworkers in management, professional and related

Table 7. Descriptive statistics about employees who teleworked at home during COVID-19 (November 2020)

Characteristic	Total Employed (numbers in thousands)	Teleworking due to Covid-19*		Percentage	
		Total	Percentage	Total Employed	Teleworking due to Covid-19*
Total, 16 years and over	150.203	32.737	21,8	100,0	100,0
Age					
16 to 24 years	18.062	1.765	9,8	12,0	5,4
25 to 54 years	96.394	23.745	24,6	64,2	72,5
55 years and over	35.748	7.226	20,2	23,8	22,1
Gender					
Men, 16 years and over	79.291	15.339	19,3	52,8	46,9
Women, 16 years and over	70.913	17.398	24,5	47,2	53,1
Full-time / Part-time					
Full-time workers	124.325	29.588	23,8	82,8	90,4
Part-time workers	25.879	3.149	12,2	17,2	9,6
Occupation					
Management, professional, and related occupations	63.387	24.855	39,2	42,2	75,9
Service occupations	23.822	915	3,8	15,9	2,8
Sales and office occupations	30.632	5.984	19,5	20,4	18,3
Natural resources, construction, and maintenance occupations	13.677	428	3,1	9,1	1,3
Production, transportation, and material moving occupations	18.685	555	3,0	12,4	1,7

Source: U.S. Bureau of Labor Statistics, (2022). Labor Force Statistics from the Current Population Survey, https://www.bls.gov/cps/effects-of-the-coronavirus-covid-19-pandemic.htm#table1

*: Only who teleworked or worked at home for pay at some point in the past 4 weeks specifically due to Covid-19.

Note: Data are not seasonally adjusted.

occupations from 76,1 to 75,5% was compensated with the increase in sales and office occupations from 18,5 to 19,1%. Although these numbers seem to be slight differences, they can be viewed as early signals of re-openings in the United States in the spring season.

In March 2021, teleworking due to the Covid-19 pandemic fell to a level of 21,0%. This is seen as a decreasing trend in teleworking and working at home, which means in turn, working in-person in the offices was gaining its importance again. All of the groups of the characteristics are similar to the previous month except for a special group of occupations. In March, the teleworkers in natural resources, construction, and maintenance occupations group decreased to 0,9%. This is important but also acceptable since the nature of this occupation group needs actual existence of the employees in the workplace.

Since the beginning of the Covid-19 pandemic, for the first time the percentage of teleworking because of covid -19 fell below 20% to a level of 18,3%. In April 2021 roughly a year after the pandemic begins, it seems that work life began to normalize. As seen in Table 12, the teleworkers or workers from home

Table 8. Descriptive statistics about employees who teleworked at home during COVID-19 (December 2020)

Characteristic	Total Employed (numbers in thousands)	Teleworking due to Covid-19*		Percentage	
		Total	Percentage	Total Employed	Teleworking due to Covid-19*
Total, 16 years and over	149.613	35.501	23,7	100,0	100,0
Age					
16 to 24 years	17.795	1.838	10,3	11,9	5,2
25 to 54 years	96.427	25.754	26,7	64,5	72,5
55 years and over	35.391	7.908	22,3	23,7	22,3
Gender					
Men, 16 years and over	78.955	16.728	21,2	52,8	47,1
Women, 16 years and over	70.658	18.773	26,6	47,2	52,9
Full-time / Part-time					
Full-time workers	124.415	32.272	25,9	83,2	90,9
Part-time workers	25.197	3.228	12,8	16,8	9,1
Occupation					
Management, professional, and related occupations	64.007	26.812	41,9	42,8	75,5
Service occupations	22.490	1.043	4,6	15,0	2,9
Sales and office occupations	30.712	6.603	21,5	20,5	18,6
Natural resources, construction, and maintenance occupations	13.191	450	3,4	8,8	1,3
Production, transportation, and material moving occupations	19.212	592	3,1	12,8	1,7

Source: U.S. Bureau of Labor Statistics, (2022). Labor Force Statistics from the Current Population Survey, https://www.bls.gov/cps/effects-of-the-coronavirus-covid-19-pandemic.htm#table1

*: Only who teleworked or worked at home for pay at some point in the past 4 weeks specifically due to Covid-19.

Note: Data are not seasonally adjusted.

still pioneered by the management, professional and related occupations. Additionally, still workers aged between 25-54 dominated the teleworkers with a percentage of 72,5%.

A year after the first data available in May 2020 about working from home, in May 2021 it seems that work life accelerated to be back into normal days. This is because the share of the teleworking or working from home due to the pandemic is 16,6% in May 2021. The majority of the teleworkers was full-time workers constituting 91,6% of teleworking. The gap between male and female workers from home in this month was smaller than the previous month, April. This means more female employees entered into the workforce and started working in the workplace rather than working at home.

At this point we should also underline that there was a decrease in the percentage of teleworking due to the pandemic stemmed from both increasing number of employees entered into labor force and less employee worked as teleworkers in this period so far. For example the number of the total employees increased from 151.778.000 (May 2021) to 152.283.000 (June 2021) and at the same time, number of the teleworkers decreased from 25.168.000 (May 2021) to 22.004.000 (June 2021). So we can note

Table 9. Descriptive statistics about employees who teleworked at home during COVID-19 (January 2021)

Characteristic	Total Employed (*numbers in thousands*)	Teleworking due to Covid-19*		Percentage	
		Total	Percentage	Total Employed	Teleworking due to Covid-19*
Total, 16 years and over	148.383	34.484	23,2	100,0	100,0
Age					
16 to 24 years	17.462	1.710	9,8	11,8	5,0
25 to 54 years	95.871	25.194	26,3	64,6	73,1
55 years and over	35.050	7.580	21,6	23,6	22,0
Gender					
Men, 16 years and over	78.535	16.341	20,8	52,9	47,4
Women, 16 years and over	69.848	18.143	26,0	47,1	52,6
Full-time / Part-time					
Full-time workers	123.717	31.516	25,5	83,4	91,4
Part-time workers	24.666	2.968	12,0	16,6	8,6
Occupation					
Management, professional, and related occupations	63.886	26.247	41,1	43,1	76,1
Service occupations	22.366	975	4,4	15,1	2,8
Sales and office occupations	30.295	6.376	21,0	20,4	18,5
Natural resources, construction, and maintenance occupations	13.235	386	2,9	8,9	1,1
Production, transportation, and material moving occupations	18.601	499	2,7	12,5	1,4

Source: U.S. Bureau of Labor Statistics, (2022). Labor Force Statistics from the Current Population Survey, https://www.bls.gov/cps/effects-of-the-coronavirus-covid-19-pandemic.htm#table1

*: Only who teleworked or worked at home for pay at some point in the past 4 weeks specifically due to Covid-19.

Note: Data are not seasonally adjusted.

that, there was also a decrease in teleworking or working from home among the new employees in the workforce in this period. In this month there was again an increase in the number of the men, full-time and management, professional and related occupations classes of teleworking.

In July, there was still a decrease in the ratio of teleworking employees to the total employees in the United States to a level of 13,2%. Additionally, the male and female teleworkers were very close to each other, 49,8% and 50,2% respectively. In this month, part-time teleworkers tended to be present at the workplaces, since their share in teleworking continued to decrease. Lastly, although the number of employees teleworked or worked from home in management, professional and related occupations decreased to 15.790.000 in July, its share among teleworking employees increased to 77.9%. This stemmed from other occupations' decreasing more in terms of employee numbers.

There was a slight increase in the number of employees teleworked because of covid-19 from 20.271.000 to 20.562.000 in August 2021. But this increase stemmed from 25 and more years old employees since their number increased in August and on the contrary the number of employees who were between 16

Table 10. Descriptive statistics about employees who teleworked at home during COVID-19 (February 2021)

Characteristic	Total Employed (numbers in thousands)	Teleworking due to Covid-19*		Percentage	
		Total	Percentage	Total Employed	Teleworking due to Covid-19*
Total, 16 years and over	149.522	33.893	22,7	100,0	100,0
Age					
16 to 24 years	17.808	1.521	8,5	11,9	4,5
25 to 54 years	96.364	24.536	25,5	64,4	72,4
55 years and over	35.350	7.835	22,2	23,6	23,1
Gender					
Men, 16 years and over	78.855	16.139	20,5	52,7	47,6
Women, 16 years and over	70.667	17.753	25,1	47,3	52,4
Full-time / Part-time					
Full-time workers	123.981	30.783	24,8	82,9	90,8
Part-time workers	25.541	3.109	12,2	17,1	9,2
Occupation					
Management, professional, and related occupations	64.471	25.581	39,7	43,1	75,5
Service occupations	22.574	937	4,1	15,1	2,8
Sales and office occupations	30.450	6.468	21,2	20,4	19,1
Natural resources, construction, and maintenance occupations	13.209	408	3,1	8,8	1,2
Production, transportation, and material moving occupations	18.818	499	2,7	12,6	1,5

Source: U.S. Bureau of Labor Statistics, (2022). Labor Force Statistics from the Current Population Survey, https://www.bls.gov/cps/effects-of-the-coronavirus-covid-19-pandemic.htm#table1

*: Only who teleworked or worked at home for pay at some point in the past 4 weeks specifically due to Covid-19.

Note: Data are not seasonally adjusted.

and 24 years old decreased in this month. The reflections of the first month of autumn on teleworking due to the pandemic can be seen in Table 17.

Similar to August, there was witnessed a slight decrease in the number of employees teleworked due to the pandemic in September. The number of the workers between 16 and 24 years old decreased from 907.000 in August to 777.000 in September. On the contrary, the workers between 25 and 54 years old increased from 15.147.000 in August to 15.270.000 in September. There was also a slight decrease in the number of full-time teleworkers whereas a slight increase in the number of part-time teleworkers in September.

In October 2021, the decreasing trend in both numbers and the percentage of the workers teleworked or worked at home for pay seemed to continue since, the numbers fell to 18.052.000 which means the 11,6% of the total employees in the United States. From the perspective of age, the number of employees teleworked in September between 25 and 54 ages decreased which is opposite to the situation for the

Table 11. Descriptive statistics about employees who teleworked at home during COVID-19 (March 2021)

Characteristic	Total Employed (numbers in thousands)	Teleworking due to Covid-19*		Percentage	
		Total	Percentage	Total Employed	Teleworking due to Covid-19*
Total, 16 years and over	150.493	31.553	21,0	100,0	100,0
Age					
16 to 24 years	17.900	1.517	8,5	11,9	4,8
25 to 54 years	96.911	22.964	23,7	64,4	72,8
55 years and over	35.682	7.072	19,8	23,7	22,4
Gender					
Men, 16 years and over	79.188	15.124	19,1	52,6	47,9
Women, 16 years and over	71.305	16.428	23,0	47,4	52,1
Full-time / Part-time					
Full-time workers	124.840	28.646	22,9	83,0	90,8
Part-time workers	25.653	2.906	11,3	17,0	9,2
Occupation					
Management, professional, and related occupations	64.503	23.778	36,9	42,9	75,4
Service occupations	23.194	934	4,0	15,4	3,0
Sales and office occupations	30.520	6.027	19,7	20,3	19,1
Natural resources, construction, and maintenance occupations	13.402	293	2,2	8,9	0,9
Production, transportation, and material moving occupations	18.875	520	2,8	12,5	1,6

Source: U.S. Bureau of Labor Statistics, (2022). Labor Force Statistics from the Current Population Survey, https://www.bls.gov/cps/effects-of-the-coronavirus-covid-19-pandemic.htm#table1

*: Only who teleworked or worked at home for pay at some point in the past 4 weeks specifically due to Covid-19.

Note: Data are not seasonally adjusted.

employees between 16 and 24 ages and also 55 and over age. Other characteristics of employees were similar to the previous month in October.

According to Table 19, it is understood that previously mentioned decreasing trend in the numbers of employees who teleworked or worked at home for pay continued in November 19. There were some slight differences in age, gender and occupation characteristics. The percentage of men increased to 49,5% and also the number of full-time teleworkers increased to 92,1%. Here, teleworking can be viewed as a transition for new forms of remote work, since it is witnessed that, not only women but also men and not only part-time but also full-time employees chose to telework or work from home even after one and half year after the pandemic began.

In December 2021, the number and the percentage of teleworking employees decreased to a record low during the covid-19 pandemic. Among the 155.732.000 employees only 17.358.000 teleworked or worked from home because of covid-19. This number is nearly one third of the first month we gather data of teleworking in May 2020. This is a strong signal for returning back to ordinary work life before

Table 12. Descriptive statistics about employees who teleworked at home during COVID-19 (April 2021)

Characteristic	Total Employed (numbers in thousands)	Teleworking due to Covid-19*		Percentage	
		Total	Percentage	Total Employed	Teleworking due to Covid-19*
Total, 16 years and over	151.160	27.643	18,3	100,0	100,0
Age					
16 to 24 years	18.126	1.344	7,4	12,0	4,9
25 to 54 years	97.234	20.048	20,6	64,3	72,5
55 years and over	35.800	6.251	17,5	23,7	22,6
Gender					
Men, 16 years and over	79.965	13.325	16,7	52,9	48,2
Women, 16 years and over	71.195	14.319	20,1	47,1	51,8
Full-time / Part-time					
Full-time workers	125.635	25.166	20,0	83,1	91,0
Part-time workers	25.524	2.478	9,7	16,9	9,0
Occupation					
Management, professional, and related occupations	64.264	21.309	33,2	42,5	77,1
Service occupations	24.203	609	2,5	16,0	2,2
Sales and office occupations	29.993	5.019	16,7	19,8	18,2
Natural resources, construction, and maintenance occupations	13.969	339	2,4	9,2	1,2
Production, transportation, and material moving occupations	18.731	368	2,0	12,4	1,3

Source: U.S. Bureau of Labor Statistics, (2022). Labor Force Statistics from the Current Population Survey, https://www.bls.gov/cps/effects-of-the-coronavirus-covid-19-pandemic.htm#table1

*: Only who teleworked or worked at home for pay at some point in the past 4 weeks specifically due to Covid-19.

Note: Data are not seasonally adjusted.

the pandemic. The majority of these teleworkers in December 2021 belonged to the occupation group of management, professional and related occupations.

The last month of our research interval, January 2022 provided the most updated data about teleworking due to the covid-19 pandemic. In January 2022, there was a severe increase in the both the number and the percentage of the teleworking employees from 17.358.000 in December to 23.938.000 in January. This might be due to the new variant named 'omicron' which was introduced as a more contagious variant (WHO, 2022). Although there was such an increase in January 2022, it was still low when compared to one year ago in January 2021 in which there were 34.484.000 employees who teleworked or worked from home.

Table 13. Descriptive statistics about employees who teleworked at home during COVID-19 (May 2021)

Characteristic	Total Employed (numbers in thousands)	Teleworking due to Covid-19*		Percentage	
		Total	Percentage	Total Employed	Teleworking due to Covid-19*
Total, 16 years and over	151.778	25.168	16,6	100,0	100,0
Age					
16 to 24 years	18.410	1.250	6,8	12,1	5,0
25 to 54 years	97.419	18.487	19,0	64,2	73,5
55 years and over	35.949	5.431	15,1	23,7	21,6
Gender					
Men, 16 years and over	80.430	12.189	15,2	53,0	48,4
Women, 16 years and over	71.348	12.979	18,2	47,0	51,6
Full-time / Part-time					
Full-time workers	126.579	23.051	18,2	83,4	91,6
Part-time workers	25.199	2.117	8,4	16,6	8,4
Occupation					
Management, professional, and related occupations	64.268	19.288	30,0	42,3	76,6
Service occupations	24.023	546	2,3	15,8	2,2
Sales and office occupations	30.363	4.655	15,3	20,0	18,5
Natural resources, construction, and maintenance occupations	14.100	291	2,1	9,3	1,2
Production, transportation, and material moving occupations	19.025	388	2,0	12,5	1,5

Source: U.S. Bureau of Labor Statistics, (2022). Labor Force Statistics from the Current Population Survey, https://www.bls.gov/cps/effects-of-the-coronavirus-covid-19-pandemic.htm#table1

*: Only who teleworked or worked at home for pay at some point in the past 4 weeks specifically due to Covid-19.

Note: Data are not seasonally adjusted.

FUTURE RESEARCH DIRECTIONS

The covid-19 pandemic has transformed many aspects of life permanently. It is still questionable if new forms of work, especially teleworking will last after the pandemic. So since this research showed that teleworking was used as an emerging strategy to cope with the difficulties of the pandemic, other benefits of teleworking should be investigated in the future especially the ones undermined so far. Among these benefits researchers should concentrate on the sustainability for both organizations and society. Although there have been researches on these topics lately, there is still a need for the environmental consequences of teleworking.

Besides these, the new solutions to existing problems of teleworking should be examined in the near future. Researches should generate new recommendations by their studies on the employee perceptions of teleworking. This can be achieved by investigating new ways for decreasing teleworking's negative effects on employee mental and physical health. This can generate fruitful consequences for lowering their degree of resistance to teleworking.

Table 14. Descriptive statistics about employees who teleworked at home during COVID-19 (June 2021)

Characteristic	Total Employed (numbers in thousands)	Teleworking due to Covid-19*		Percentage	
		Total	Percentage	Total Employed	Teleworking due to Covid-19*
Total, 16 years and over	152.283	22.004	14,4	100,0	100,0
Age					
16 to 24 years	19.701	1.041	5,3	12,9	4,7
25 to 54 years	97.028	16.331	16,8	63,7	74,2
55 years and over	35.554	4.632	13,0	23,3	21,1
Gender					
Men, 16 years and over	80.994	10.789	13,3	53,2	49,0
Women, 16 years and over	71.289	11.214	15,7	46,8	51,0
Full-time / Part-time					
Full-time workers	127.156	20.288	16,0	83,5	92,2
Part-time workers	25.127	1.716	6,8	16,5	7,8
Occupation					
Management, professional, and related occupations	64.316	17.306	26,9	42,2	78,7
Service occupations	24.631	453	1,8	16,2	2,1
Sales and office occupations	29.839	3.747	12,6	19,6	17,0
Natural resources, construction, and maintenance occupations	14.234	255	1,8	9,3	1,2
Production, transportation, and material moving occupations	19.263	241	1,3	12,6	1,1

Source: U.S. Bureau of Labor Statistics, (2022). Labor Force Statistics from the Current Population Survey, https://www.bls.gov/cps/effects-of-the-coronavirus-covid-19-pandemic.htm#table1

*: Only who teleworked or worked at home for pay at some point in the past 4 weeks specifically due to Covid-19.

Note: Data are not seasonally adjusted.

CONCLUSION

Since the covid-19 appeared in 2019 and the World Health Organization declared a pandemic, much has been written about it including teleworking. This chapter intended to contribute to the literature of teleworking by analyzing the monthly teleworking characteristics of employees from the first month when the data was available until the last month in which this chapter lastly updated. A comprehensive and detailed statistics from the U.S. Bureau of Labor Statistics was used in this research.

According to the results, in May 2020 the number of employees teleworking or working at home for pay was 35,4% of total employees in the United States. This result fell to a degree of 11,1%, the lowest percentage during the pandemic, in December 2021. But right after this month, it again increased to 15,4% in January 2022. It was witnessed in the research that, except for the data in January 2022, when time passed during the pandemic, teleworking and working from home was decreased in terms of employee numbers and teleworking percentage to total employee numbers. This may be due to the fact that, as the whole world experienced covid-19, work life has begun to turn back to old days. But it is now

Table 15. Descriptive statistics about employees who teleworked at home during COVID-19 (July 2021)

Characteristic	Total Employed *(numbers in thousands)*	Teleworking due to Covid-19*		Percentage	
		Total	Percentage	Total Employed	Teleworking due to Covid-19*
Total, 16 years and over	153.596	20.271	13,2	100,0	100,0
Age					
16 to 24 years	20.268	1.013	5,0	13,2	5,0
25 to 54 years	97.586	15.071	15,4	63,5	74,3
55 years and over	35.741	4.187	11,7	23,3	20,7
Gender					
Men, 16 years and over	81.918	10.088	12,3	53,3	49,8
Women, 16 years and over	71.678	10.183	14,2	46,7	50,2
Full-time / Part-time					
Full-time workers	128.863	18.764	14,6	83,9	92,6
Part-time workers	24.732	1.507	6,1	16,1	7,4
Occupation					
Management, professional, and related occupations	64.179	15.790	24,6	41,8	77,9
Service occupations	25.695	562	2,2	16,7	2,8
Sales and office occupations	29.527	3.346	11,3	19,2	16,5
Natural resources, construction, and maintenance occupations	14.549	282	1,9	9,5	1,4
Production, transportation, and material moving occupations	19.646	290	1,5	12,8	1,4

Source: U.S. Bureau of Labor Statistics, (2022). Labor Force Statistics from the Current Population Survey, https://www.bls.gov/cps/effects-of-the-coronavirus-covid-19-pandemic.htm#table1

*: Only who teleworked or worked at home for pay at some point in the past 4 weeks specifically due to Covid-19.

Note: Data are not seasonally adjusted.

unquestionable that teleworking was used as an emerging strategy by organizations all around the world. Now it is time to think post covid-19. Will teleworking be used in an effective way in the near future?

It is possible to carry teleworking to a higher level in the work life after the covid-19 pandemic. In order to do so, firstly negative effects of teleworking must be minimized. The majority of these negative effects are associated with the employees themselves. They can be negatively affected either mentally or physically when they are teleworking. So teleworking conditions should be improved. Employees should feel themselves more comfortable while teleworking. Moreover, by using information technologies while teleworking, employees should be directed to effective productivity without ineffective use of electronic surveillance. Last but not least, employees should be directed to social programs or open-air sports after the hours they spend while teleworking. Because we do not know whether another pandemic is at the door or not.

Table 16. Descriptive statistics about employees who teleworked at home during COVID-19 (August 2021)

Characteristic	Total Employed (numbers in thousands)	Teleworking due to Covid-19*		Percentage	
		Total	Percentage	Total Employed	Teleworking due to Covid-19*
Total, 16 years and over	153.232	20.562	13,4	100,0	100,0
Age					
16 to 24 years	19.165	907	4,7	12,5	4,4
25 to 54 years	97.881	15.145	15,5	63,9	73,7
55 years and over	36.186	4.509	12,5	23,6	21,9
Gender					
Men, 16 years and over	81.670	10.114	12,4	53,3	49,2
Women, 16 years and over	71.562	10.447	14,6	46,7	50,8
Full-time / Part-time					
Full-time workers	128.664	18.978	14,7	84,0	92,3
Part-time workers	24.568	1.584	6,4	16,0	7,7
Occupation					
Management, professional, and related occupations	64.122	15.740	24,5	41,8	76,6
Service occupations	24.940	539	2,2	16,3	2,6
Sales and office occupations	29.671	3.582	12,1	19,4	17,4
Natural resources, construction, and maintenance occupations	14.588	317	2,2	9,5	1,5
Production, transportation, and material moving occupations	19.911	383	1,9	13,0	1,9

Source: U.S. Bureau of Labor Statistics, (2022). Labor Force Statistics from the Current Population Survey, https://www.bls.gov/cps/effects-of-the-coronavirus-covid-19-pandemic.htm#table1

*: Only who teleworked or worked at home for pay at some point in the past 4 weeks specifically due to Covid-19.

Note: Data are not seasonally adjusted.

Table 17. Descriptive statistics about employees who teleworked at home during COVID-19 (September 2021)

Characteristic	Total Employed (numbers in thousands)	Teleworking due to Covid-19*		Percentage	
		Total	Percentage	Total Employed	Teleworking due to Covid-19*
Total, 16 years and over	154.026	20.348	13,2	100,0	100,0
Age					
16 to 24 years	18.545	777	4,2	12,0	3,8
25 to 54 years	98.702	15.270	15,5	64,1	75,0
55 years and over	36.778	4.301	11,7	23,9	21,1
Gender					
Men, 16 years and over	81.731	10.080	12,3	53,1	49,5
Women, 16 years and over	72.295	10.268	14,2	46,9	50,5
Full-time / Part-time					
Full-time workers	128.484	18.607	14,5	83,4	91,4
Part-time workers	25.542	1.741	6,8	16,6	8,6
Occupation					
Management, professional, and related occupations	65.163	15.480	23,8	42,3	76,1
Service occupations	25.674	612	2,4	16,7	3,0
Sales and office occupations	29.593	3.582	12,1	19,2	17,6
Natural resources, construction, and maintenance occupations	14.295	330	2,3	9,3	1,6
Production, transportation, and material moving occupations	19.301	345	1,8	12,5	1,7

Source: U.S. Bureau of Labor Statistics, (2022). Labor Force Statistics from the Current Population Survey, https://www.bls.gov/cps/effects-of-the-coronavirus-covid-19-pandemic.htm#table1

*: Only who teleworked or worked at home for pay at some point in the past 4 weeks specifically due to Covid-19.

Note: Data are not seasonally adjusted.

Table 18. Descriptive statistics about employees who teleworked at home during COVID-19 (October 2021)

Characteristic	Total Employed (numbers in thousands)	Teleworking due to Covid-19*		Percentage	
		Total	Percentage	Total Employed	Teleworking due to Covid-19*
Total, 16 years and over	154.966	18.052	11,6	100,0	100,0
Age					
16 to 24 years	18.937	808	4,3	12,2	4,5
25 to 54 years	99.355	13.387	13,5	64,1	74,2
55 years and over	36.674	3.857	10,5	23,7	21,4
Gender					
Men, 16 years and over	82.163	8.812	10,7	53,0	48,8
Women, 16 years and over	72.803	9.240	12,7	47,0	51,2
Full-time / Part-time					
Full-time workers	128.848	16.596	12,9	83,1	91,9
Part-time workers	26.119	1.456	5,6	16,9	8,1
Occupation					
Management, professional, and related occupations	65.335	13.840	21,2	42,2	76,7
Service occupations	25.458	476	1,9	16,4	2,6
Sales and office occupations	29.914	3.233	10,8	19,3	17,9
Natural resources, construction, and maintenance occupations	14.258	228	1,6	9,2	1,3
Production, transportation, and material moving occupations	20.001	275	1,4	12,9	1,5

Source: U.S. Bureau of Labor Statistics, (2022). Labor Force Statistics from the Current Population Survey, https://www.bls.gov/cps/effects-of-the-coronavirus-covid-19-pandemic.htm#table1

*: Only who teleworked or worked at home for pay at some point in the past 4 weeks specifically due to Covid-19.

Note: Data are not seasonally adjusted.

Table 19. Descriptive statistics about employees who teleworked at home during COVID-19 (November 2021)

Characteristic	Total Employed (numbers in thousands)	Teleworking due to Covid-19*		Percentage	
		Total	Percentage	Total Employed	Teleworking due to Covid-19*
Total, 16 years and over	155.797	17.533	11,3	100,0	100,0
Age					
16 to 24 years	18.949	712	3,8	12,2	4,1
25 to 54 years	100.032	13.204	13,2	64,2	75,3
55 years and over	36.815	3.617	9,8	23,6	20,6
Gender					
Men, 16 years and over	82.474	8.671	10,5	52,9	49,5
Women, 16 years and over	73.323	8.862	12,1	47,1	50,5
Full-time / Part-time					
Full-time workers	129.322	16.154	12,5	83,0	92,1
Part-time workers	26.475	1.379	5,2	17,0	7,9
Occupation					
Management, professional, and related occupations	66.060	13.485	20,4	42,4	76,9
Service occupations	25.252	370	1,5	16,2	2,1
Sales and office occupations	30.883	3.187	10,3	19,8	18,2
Natural resources, construction, and maintenance occupations	13.890	186	1,3	8,9	1,1
Production, transportation, and material moving occupations	19.712	305	1,5	12,7	1,7

Source: U.S. Bureau of Labor Statistics, (2022). Labor Force Statistics from the Current Population Survey, https://www.bls.gov/cps/effects-of-the-coronavirus-covid-19-pandemic.htm#table1

*: Only who teleworked or worked at home for pay at some point in the past 4 weeks specifically due to Covid-19.

Note: Data are not seasonally adjusted.

Table 20. Descriptive statistics about employees who teleworked at home during COVID-19 (December 2021)

Characteristic	Total Employed (numbers in thousands)	Teleworking due to Covid-19*		Percentage	
		Total	Percentage	Total Employed	Teleworking due to Covid-19*
Total, 16 years and over	155.732	17.358	11,1	100,0	100,0
Age					
16 to 24 years	18.825	620	3,3	12,1	3,6
25 to 54 years	100.016	12.988	13,0	64,2	74,8
55 years and over	36.891	3.750	10,2	23,7	21,6
Gender					
Men, 16 years and over	82.024	8.599	10,5	52,7	49,5
Women, 16 years and over	73.708	8.759	11,9	47,3	50,5
Full-time / Part-time					
Full-time workers	129.824	16.041	12,4	83,4	92,4
Part-time workers	25.908	1.317	5,1	16,6	7,6
Occupation					
Management, professional, and related occupations	66.366	13.521	20,4	42,6	77,9
Service occupations	24.821	328	1,3	15,9	1,9
Sales and office occupations	30.949	3.065	9,9	19,9	17,7
Natural resources, construction, and maintenance occupations	13.774	171	1,2	8,8	1,0
Production, transportation, and material moving occupations	19.821	273	1,4	12,7	1,6

Source: U.S. Bureau of Labor Statistics, (2022). Labor Force Statistics from the Current Population Survey, https://www.bls.gov/cps/effects-of-the-coronavirus-covid-19-pandemic.htm#table1

*: Only who teleworked or worked at home for pay at some point in the past 4 weeks specifically due to Covid-19.

Note: Data are not seasonally adjusted.

Table 21. Descriptive statistics about employees who teleworked at home during COVID-19 (January 2022)

Characteristic	Total Employed (numbers in thousands)	Teleworking due to Covid-19*		Percentage	
		Total	Percentage	Total Employed	Teleworking due to Covid-19*
Total, 16 years and over	155.618	23.938	15,4	100,0	100,0
Age					
16 to 24 years	18.478	1.025	5,5	11,9	4,3
25 to 54 years	100.214	17.659	17,6	64,4	73,8
55 years and over	36.927	5.254	14,2	23,7	21,9
Gender					
Men, 16 years and over	82.376	11.744	14,3	52,9	49,1
Women, 16 years and over	73.242	12.194	16,6	47,1	50,9
Full-time / Part-time					
Full-time workers	129.747	22.191	17,1	83,4	92,7
Part-time workers	25.871	1.747	6,8	16,6	7,3
Occupation					
Management, professional, and related occupations	66.740	17.969	26,9	42,9	75,1
Service occupations	24.232	729	3,0	15,6	3,0
Sales and office occupations	31.164	4.521	14,5	20,0	18,9
Natural resources, construction, and maintenance occupations	13.858	298	2,2	8,9	1,2
Production, transportation, and material moving occupations	19.624	421	2,1	12,6	1,8

Source: U.S. Bureau of Labor Statistics, (2022). Labor Force Statistics from the Current Population Survey, https://www.bls.gov/cps/effects-of-the-coronavirus-covid-19-pandemic.htm#table1

*: Only who teleworked or worked at home for pay at some point in the past 4 weeks specifically due to Covid-19.

Note: Data are not seasonally adjusted.

REFERENCES

Baruch, Y. (2001). The status of research on teleworking and an agenda for future research. *International Journal of Management Reviews, 3*(2), 113–129. doi:10.1111/1468-2370.00058

Bérastégui, P. (2021). *Teleworking in the aftermath of the Covid-19 pandemic: enabling conditions for a successful transition.* ETUI Research Paper-Policy Brief.

Carnevale, J. B., & Hatak, I. (2020). Employee adjustment and well-being in the era of COVID-19: Implications for human resource management. *Journal of Business Research, 116*, 183–187. doi:10.1016/j.jbusres.2020.05.037 PMID:32501303

Davenport, T. H., & Pearlson, K. (1998). Two cheers for the virtual office. *MIT Sloan Management Review, 39*(4), 51–65.

Doğru, Ç. (2021). The Effects of Electronic Surveillance on Job Tension, Task Performance and Organizational Trust. *Business Systems Research: International Journal of the Society for Advancing Innovation and Research in Economy, 12*(2), 125–143. doi:10.2478/bsrj-2021-0023

Donthu, N., & Gustafsson, A. (2020). Effects of COVID-19 on business and research. *Journal of Business Research, 117*, 284–289. doi:10.1016/j.jbusres.2020.06.008 PMID:32536736

Dörr, J. O., Licht, G., & Murmann, S. (2022). Small firms and the COVID-19 insolvency gap. *Small Business Economics, 58*(2), 887–917. doi:10.100711187-021-00514-4

Duxbury, L., & Halinski, M. (2014). When more is less: An examination of the relationship between hours in telework and role overload. *Work (Reading, Mass.), 48*(1), 91–103. doi:10.3233/WOR-141858 PMID:24763352

Giovanis, E. (2018). The relationship between teleworking, traffic and air pollution. *Atmospheric Pollution Research, 9*(1), 1–14. doi:10.1016/j.apr.2017.06.004

Hayakawa, K., & Mukunoki, H. (2021). The impact of COVID-19 on international trade: Evidence from the first shock. *Journal of the Japanese and International Economies, 60*, 101135. doi:10.1016/j.jjie.2021.101135

Hohenstein, N. O. (2022). Supply chain risk management in the COVID-19 pandemic: Strategies and empirical lessons for improving global logistics service providers' performance. *International Journal of Logistics Management*. Advance online publication. doi:10.1108/IJLM-02-2021-0109

Hoornweg, N., Peters, P., & Van der Heijden, B. (2016). Finding the optimal mix between telework and office hours to enhance employee productivity: A study into the relationship between telework intensity and individual productivity, with mediation of intrinsic motivation and moderation of office hours. In New Ways of Working Practices. Emerald Group Publishing Limited. doi:10.1108/S1877-636120160000016002

Humphries, J. E., Neilson, C., & Ulyssea, G. (2020). *The evolving impacts of COVID-19 on small businesses since the CARES Act.* Cowles Foundation Discussion Papers, EliScholar, Yale University. Retrieved from https://elischolar.library.yale.edu/cgi/viewcontent.cgi?article=1016&context=cowles-discussion-paper-series

Kazekami, S. (2020). Mechanisms to improve labor productivity by performing telework. *Telecommunications Policy, 44*(2), 101868. doi:10.1016/j.telpol.2019.101868

Korneta, P., & Rostek, K. (2021). The Impact of the SARS-CoV-19 Pandemic on the Global Gross Domestic Product. *International Journal of Environmental Research and Public Health, 18*(10), 5246. doi:10.3390/ijerph18105246 PMID:34069182

Lin, W., Shao, Y., Li, G., Guo, Y., & Zhan, X. (2021). The psychological implications of COVID-19 on employee job insecurity and its consequences: The mitigating role of organization adaptive practices. *The Journal of Applied Psychology, 106*(3), 317–329. doi:10.1037/apl0000896 PMID:33871269

Lunde, L. K., Fløvik, L., Christensen, J. O., Johannessen, H. A., Finne, L. B., Jørgensen, I. L., ... Vleeshouwers, J. (2022). The relationship between telework from home and employee health: A systematic review. *BMC Public Health, 22*(1), 1–14. PMID:34983455

Mann, S., & Holdsworth, L. (2003). The psychological impact of teleworking: Stress, emotions and health. *New Technology, Work and Employment, 18*(3), 196–211. doi:10.1111/1468-005X.00121

Pulido-Martos, M., Cortés-Denia, D., & Lopez-Zafra, E. (2021). Teleworking in Times of COVID-19: Effects on the Acquisition of Personal Resources. *Frontiers in Psychology, 12*, 2485. doi:10.3389/fpsyg.2021.685275 PMID:34248789

Rodríguez-Nogueira, Ó., Leirós-Rodríguez, R., Benítez-Andrades, J. A., Álvarez-Álvarez, M. J., Marqués-Sánchez, P., & Pinto-Carral, A. (2021). Musculoskeletal pain and teleworking in times of the COVID-19: Analysis of the impact on the workers at two Spanish universities. *International Journal of Environmental Research and Public Health, 18*(1), 31. doi:10.3390/ijerph18010031 PMID:33374537

Sánchez, A. M., Pérez, M. P., de Luis Carnicer, P., & Jiménez, M. J. V. (2007). Teleworking and workplace flexibility: A study of impact on firm performance. *Personnel Review, 36*(1), 42–64. doi:10.1108/00483480710716713

Štreimikienė, D., Baležentis, T., Volkov, A., Ribašauskienė, E., Morkūnas, M., & Žičkienė, A. (2021). Negative effects of covid-19 pandemic on agriculture: Systematic literature review in the frameworks of vulnerability, resilience and risks involved. *Economic Research-Ekonomska Istraživanja*, 1-17.

Turnea, E. S., Neştian, Ş. A., Tiţă, S. M., Vodă, A. I., & Guţă, A. L. (2020). Dismissals and Temporary Leaves in Romanian Companies in the Context of Low Demand and Cash Flow Problems during the COVID-19 Economic Lockdown. *Sustainability, 12*(21), 8850. doi:10.3390u12218850

Tursunbayeva, A., Di Lauro, S., & Antonelli, G. (2022). Remote work at the time of COVID-19 pandemic and beyond: A scoping review. *HR Analytics and Digital HR Practices*, 127-169.

United States Bureau of Labor Statistics. (2022). *Labor Force Statistics From the Current Population Survey*. Retrieved from https://www.bls.gov/cps/effects-of-the-coronavirus-covid-19-pandemic.htm#table1

World Health Organization. (2022). *Statement on Omicron sublineage BA.2*. Retrieved from https://www.who.int/news/item/22-02-2022-statement-on-omicron-sublineage-ba.2

Xie, J., Luo, S., Furuya, K., & Sun, D. (2020). Urban parks as green buffers during the COVID-19 pandemic. *Sustainability, 12*(17), 6751. doi:10.3390u12176751

Yang, S., Ning, L., Jiang, T., & He, Y. (2021). Dynamic impacts of COVID-19 pandemic on the regional express logistics: Evidence from China. *Transport Policy, 111*, 111–124. doi:10.1016/j.tranpol.2021.07.012

ADDITIONAL READING

Belostecinic, G., Mogoş, R. I., Popescu, M. L., Burlacu, S., Rădulescu, C. V., Bodislav, D. A., Bran, F., & Oancea-Negescu, M. D. (2022). Teleworking—An Economic and Social Impact during COVID-19 Pandemic: A Data Mining Analysis. *International Journal of Environmental Research and Public Health, 19*(1), 298. doi:10.3390/ijerph19010298 PMID:35010555

Belzunegui-Eraso, A., & Erro-Garcés, A. (2020). Teleworking in the Context of the Covid-19 Crisis. *Sustainability*, *12*(9), 3662. doi:10.3390u12093662

Chiru, C. (2017). Teleworkıng: Evolution and Trends in Usa, Eu And Romanıa. *Economics. Management & Financial Markets*, *12*(2), 222–229.

Contreras, F., Baykal, E., & Abid, G. (2020). E-leadership and teleworking in times of COVID-19 and beyond: What we know and where do we go. *Frontiers in Psychology*, *11*, 3484. doi:10.3389/fpsyg.2020.590271 PMID:33362656

Kontoangelos, K., Economou, M., & Papageorgiou, C. (2020). Mental health effects of COVID-19 pandemia: A review of clinical and psychological traits. *Psychiatry Investigation*, *17*(6), 491–505. doi:10.30773/pi.2020.0161 PMID:32570296

Morgan, R. E. (2004). Teleworking: An assessment of the benefits and challenges. *European Business Review*, *16*(4), 344–357. doi:10.1108/09555340410699613

Nilles, J. M. (1996). What does telework really do to us? *World Transport Policy and Practice, 2*(1-1), 15-23.

Pérez, M. P., Sánchez, A. M., de Luis Carnicer, M. P., & Jiménez, M. J. V. (2004). The environmental impacts of teleworking: A model of urban analysis and a case study. *Management of Environmental Quality*, *15*(6), 656–671. doi:10.1108/14777830410560728

Pulido-Martos, M., Cortés-Denia, D., & Lopez-Zafra, E. (2021). Teleworking in Times of COVID-19: Effects on the Acquisition of Personal Resources. *Frontiers in Psychology*, *12*, 2485. doi:10.3389/fpsyg.2021.685275 PMID:34248789

Que, J., Le Shi, J. D., Liu, J., Zhang, L., Wu, S., Gong, Y., ... Lu, L. (2020). Psychological impact of the COVID-19 pandemic on healthcare workers: A cross-sectional study in China. *General Psychiatry*, *33*(3), 1–12. doi:10.1136/gpsych-2020-100259 PMID:32596640

KEY TERMS AND DEFINITIONS

Employee: An individual working for pay in an organization.

Full-Time Work: An employee's working a number of maximum weekly work hours set by the government.

Pandemic: A disease's spreading to a whole country or around the world.

Part-Time Work: A form of work in which an employee works fewer hours than a full-time work.

Strategy: A broad and long-term plan for achieving organizational goals and objectives.

Teleworking: Working from home or another places other than an office using information technologies and needed equipment.

Chapter 5
COVID–19 Policy Measures and Reflections on the Turkish Economy and Foreign Trade

Yusuf Bayraktutan

Department of Economics, Kocaeli University, Turkey

Ali Rıza Solmaz

Department of Economics, Kocaeli University, Turkey

ABSTRACT

The first COVID-19 case in Turkey was seen on March 11, 2020. Various measures have been taken and restrictions have been introduced to reduce the rate of spread since then. International and intercity transport of goods and passengers were limited and/or stopped and curfews/restrictions were applied. The activities of the service sector were regulated/stopped, and their activities were allowed on the condition that certain criteria were met. Working style and hours in public and private sector were designed. The restrictions on economic and social life were gradually lifted. In addition to the loss of people and workforce caused by the pandemic, the reflections of the measures put in effect in terms of economic concerns on national economy have been clearly observed. In this chapter, the economic effects of the pandemic process in Turkey; the short-term results in selected/main indicators, like inflation, unemployment, GDP, trade, etc.; and economic recovery due to policy measures will be evaluated.

INTRODUCTION

The virus appeared in Wuhan, China in December 2019 and named as Covid-19 by the World Health Organization, has become the biggest pandemic of the last century with over 418 million cases and over 5.8 million deaths as of February 2022.

The first case in Turkiye was seen on March 11, 2020, and as of February 2022, the cumulative number of cases exceeded 13.2 million and the number of deaths exceeded 91 thousand in almost two years. Various measures have been taken and restrictions have been introduced to reduce the rate of

DOI: 10.4018/978-1-6684-6762-6.ch005

spread since the first detection. International transport of goods and passengers has been limited, and mutually stopped completely between many countries. While going online in education, curfews/restrictions were applied, and inter-city travels were subject to permission. The activities of venues such as cinemas, concert halls, weddings halls, cafes, coffee shops, massage parlours and gymnasiums have been regulated/stopped, and their activities are allowed on the condition that certain criteria are met. Remote working has been started in applicable areas, and working hours in public institutions have been reduced. Normalization measures were announced in March and June 2021, and restrictions on economic and social life were gradually lifted.

In addition to the loss of people and workforce caused by the pandemic, the reflections of the measures put in effect in terms of economic concerns, on society and individuals, as well as national economies have been clearly observed. Different reflections/effects of Covid-19 are handled by different disciplines and/or interdisciplinary studies. In this study, the economic effects of the pandemic process in Turkiye, the short-term results in selected/main indicators, and economic recovery due to policy measures will be evaluated[1]. Providing in detail information on policy measures of Turkish government this study aims to evaluate general tendency of main economic indicators during the period of pandemic. There are not much study with similar context in the related literature yet which makes this one valuable. As of the fist detection of Covid-19 in the country, Turkish government has taken immediate actions including effective measures and regulations on employment, production, foreign trade, etc., in terms of monetary, fiscal, social, and foreign trade policy instruments. Consequently, as the figures presented in this study and provided from trustworthy institutional sources, which collect and release data with the same methodology as the EUROSTAT and OECD, shows Turkiye has realized the highest growth rates among OECD member states during pandemic, being double digit annually in 2021, while keeping unemployment rate at relatively same level, and increased exports especially to the EU members making use of logistic advantages, and constraints in the supply chains. However, as seen almost every country in the world, inflation rate in Turkiye turned back its long term high levels, mostly because of expansionary monetary policy. As an emerging economy, Turkish case can be insightful to see reflections of policy measures against demand and supply shocks caused by pandemic on main economic variables.

This chapter consists of four sections. Following the theoretical background with a brief information on supply and demand shocks, the course of pandemic in Turkiye is presented. Under the third main subtitle, policy measures are explained in detail. Then, data on selected economic variables are presented with different figures and evaluated. Finally, this study is completed by conclusions and recommendations with the hope of contributing policy makers, and future research, as well.

THEORETICAL BACKGROUND

Like every unexpected event, Covid-19 led to uncertainties whose economic reflections can be evaluated in terms of demand and supply shocks. The course and possible duration of pandemic form its effects on demand and supply. Main factor with respect to supply side effects, the closure of workplaces, or limitations on, and differentiation in working hours and forms due to pandemic and quarantine. To the extent that digital technologies make telecommuting possible contraction of output can be reduced or prevented (Baldwin, and Mauro, 2020: 13). However, for those sectors, which telecommuting is not applicable, output reduction is inevitable.

Due to infection risk, among the most affected areas during pandemic, transportation, tourism, and education come first. Closure of schools and kindergartens brings the necessity of parental concerns over children. Not only the patients, but also the parents with children need to stay at home, and hence, the unavoidable decrease in labor supply will result in supply shocks (Wren-Lewis, 2020: 110). Those who have to take care of their infected relatives will also reduce labor supply. The reduction of employment might be because of voluntary concern on infected family members, as well as government mandated measures requiring individuals in ring to be in quarantine for a certain time period (Baldwin, and Mauro, 2020: 13).

Inactivation of critical components of a supply chain by pandemic more than a reasonable extend lead to the halt of production, and layoffs (Carlsson-Szlezak, et.al., 2020). On the other hand, the existence of sectors which increase output and turnover, such as suppliers of medical materials needed especially during pandemic, technology fields corresponding the demand for telecommuting, online education/ meeting, etc., cargo and e-commerce related businesses have to be addressed.

An important point regarding supply shocks is that they may result in demand shocks. The cases where negative supply shocks lead to great reductions in demand are called Keynesian supply shocks (Guerrieri, et.al., 2020: 2). Negative multiplier effect of supply shocks, and decreases in disposable incomes may trigger demand shocks.

Demand shock during pandemic is nourished by practical and psychological sources. Practically, when access to goods and services is restrained by lockdowns and closures, demand decreases; consumers, and goods and services league less together. Psychologically, consumers and firms tend to adapt a "wait and see" attitude when they come up against a high "Knight uncertainty" under covid-19 conditions (Baldwin, and Mauro, 2020: 16).

Pandemic greatly restrict especially the so-called "social consumption" which includes activities/ organizations requiring closeness of individuals (Wren-Lewis, 2020: 110), like cafes, restaurants, gyms, theatres, hotels, etc. As a matter of fact, restrictions on, or regulations of these types of activities are observed frequently during pandemic. Even if not forbiddance, suspension or cancellation of such consumption activities because of virus and infection risk/concern lead to negative demand shock. Cancelled social consumption may not be compensated with catch-up effect, after the infection risk disappeared. Because, consumption behaviors changes within this period.

With respect to demand during pandemic, stockpiling is another case to be addressed (Bofinger, et.al., 2020: 169). While some goods, like food, cleaning products, etc. are bought in beyond normal needs, expenditure on some durable goods might be reduced. Since individuals adapting precautionary approach prefer saving, consumption diversity will go down, and demand for certain items will be postponed.

Supply and demand shocks as a result of pandemic affect different sectors in different ways, while imposing implications on main indicators of the economy, such as employment, general price level, growth, government budget, balance of payments, etc. most of which included in this study.

PANDEMIC IN TURKIYE

According to the official data, the first Covid-19 case in Turkiye was seen on March 11, 2020. In mid-April, the number of new cases reached 4800. Curfews have been put into effect in order to prevent the increase in the number of cases. A curfew was imposed on those over the age of 65 on March 21 and under the age of 20 on April 3. A two-day curfew was imposed on 10-17 April and a four-day curfew

Figure 1. Number of patients/cases per day in Turkiye
Source: Ministry of Health (2021)

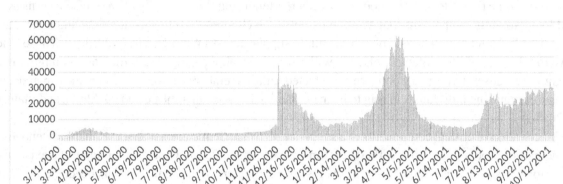

on 23 April in 31 provinces. In Figure-1, the reason for the severe increase in the number of cases as of November is that the number of cases was started to be given as of this date, while the number of patients was announced before 25 November.

Figure-2 shows the number of deaths per day. After March 17, 2017, when the first death due to Covid-19 occurred, the number of cases and deaths, which increased in the first month, decreased in the second month and followed a horizontal course for the next few months with the contribution of administrative measures. At the end of 2020 and in April 2021, new peaks were formed and the daily death toll approached 400. The highest number of deaths per day was 396 on April 30, 2021. The number of deaths, which increased to around 300 again in September 2021, decreased to 200 as of October 2021.

Figure 2. Daily number of deaths by COVID-19
Source: Ministry of Health (2021)

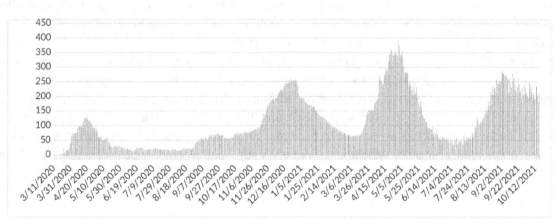

In Figure-3, the number of people vaccinated is given cumulatively. By February 12, 2021, 3 million people had been vaccinated. Vaccination, which slowed down in some periods due to disruptions in the supply process of the vaccine, accelerated again in June 2021. As of October 2021, the number

Figure 3. Daily vaccinated people
Source: Ministry of Health (2021)

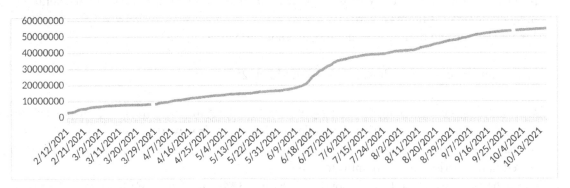

of people who received the first dose of vaccine is 55 million, and the number of people who received the second dose is approximately 48 million.

With the increasing vaccination rate, curfew and travel restrictions have been lifted as of July 1, 2021. The businesses, whose activities had been suspended, have started to operate since this date.

ECONOMIC MEASURES AND SUPPORTS IN TURKİYE IN PANDEMIC CONDITIONS

In order to minimize the negative economic effects of the pandemic, to prevent production activities, to avoid layoffs and to ensure normalization as soon as possible, a number of measures and supports have been announced based on reducing borrowing costs and protecting workers and employers. The various measures announced on different dates are outlined below.

Measures and Supports for Employment

Various measures and supports, which started with the detection of the first case in Turkiye and developed over time, were announced for both direct employees, workplaces and employers, with a proactive approach against the possible economic repercussions of employment losses and related income losses. The measures taken for employment are as follows (TOBB, 2021; KOSANO, 2021):

Initial Measures

On March 23, 2020, the following supports were announced:

1. No rent for 2 months from incubation companies and commercial enterprises in technoparks,
2. Failure to accrue rent by public administrations for workplaces whose activities are forcibly suspended,

3. The Short Working Allowance application, which allows the unemployed personnel to receive up to 60% of their gross salary from the Unemployment Fund; simplifying and accelerating the bureaucratic process in this regard,
4. Making flexible and remote working models more effective.

The following were added to these supports on March 25, 2020:

1. In the tourism sector, among the employees whose employment contracts are suspended, those who received insurance in April are included in the "short-time working allowance",
2. Increasing the compensatory working period granted for the compensation of the overtime not worked in this period from 2 months to 4 months,
3. In case the workplace rental fee cannot be paid between March 1, 2020 and June 30, 2020, this does not constitute a reason for termination of the lease agreement and eviction. All rent, revenue and retaliatory payments to be paid to the central government in the tourism sector for the specified period are postponed for 6 months,
4. Reducing the 600-day insurance premium requirement to 450 days and the last 120-day premium payment condition to 60 days, in order to facilitate the benefit of the short-time working allowance.

The Second Stage Employment Regulations

Dismissal of existing employees was prohibited for 3 months on April 17, 2020; with the renewals at the end of the period, this ban was extended until March 17, 2021. To this regulation, the following was added on 20 April 2020:

1. Paying 39.24 TL per day for 3 months to employees whose employment contract was terminated after 15 March 2020, but who could not benefit from unemployment insurance,
2. Extension of the authorization and collective bargaining procedures carried out under the trade unions and collective bargaining law for 3 months,
3. Without waiting for the completion of the eligibility determination for short-time working allowance applications, short-time working payment is made in line with the employers' declaration,
4. Recruitment of 32 thousand new personnel by the Ministry of Health.

The aforementioned regulations contributed to the reduction of economic disruptions caused by employment and income loss.

Tax Regulations and Subsidies

Various arrangements were made in March and April within the scope of reducing the tax burden of companies and employers during the pandemic period (TOBB, 2021; KOSANO, 2021).

The First Stage Regulations

With the President's decision dated 21.03.2020 and numbered 2004, all execution and bankruptcy proceedings were suspended until 30.04.2020, with the exception of execution proceedings regarding alimony receivable. On March 23, 2020, the following measures were announced:

1. For the retail, shopping mall, iron-steel, automotive, logistics-transportation, cinema, theatre, accommodation, food-beverage, textile-apparel and event-organization sectors, the withholding, VAT, SGK payments in April, May and June were postponed,
2. Accommodation tax not applied until November,
3. Reducing the VAT rate to 1% in air transport until 30.06.2020.

On March 24, 2020, the 6-month Withholding and VAT deferrals for March, April, May were extended to cover all sole proprietorships and some additional sectors (furniture, mining, construction, industrial kitchen, car rental, printing, health care); On March 25, 2020, the Accommodation tax has been postponed to January 1, 2021.

The Second Stage Tax Regulations

The merging of the SSI and Concise statements on April 6, 2020 was postponed to July 1, 2020; On April 20, 2020, the following regulations were made within the scope of compelling reasons related to the pandemic:

1. Postponing the usage permits and the fees to be collected from them for 3 months in the forests and recreation areas belonging to the state, without seeking the application condition,
2. Postponement of the amounts to be paid and the compensation for 3 months pursuant to the contract regarding the National treasury immovable assets,
3. iii. Postponing the fees to be collected from the rentals made in national parks for 3 months without seeking the application condition.

On 20 April 2020, the deadline for the submission of the Corporate Tax returns for the 2019 fiscal year and the payment periods of the taxes accrued on these returns until 1 June 2020; It has been announced that the annual announcement and advertisement taxes and environmental cleaning taxes of the businesses whose activities are stopped or that do not operate, should not be collected for the periods of inactivity.

Foreign Trade Regulations

During the pandemic period, various measures have been taken to ensure the domestic supply security of products that will provide food, cleaning and virus protection, and the materials used in their production. In addition, while incentives and facilities are provided to exporter companies, it is aimed to increase domestic added value and to protect domestic production against imported products.

Export Measures

The decisions announced to support exports are as follows (Ministry of Trade, 2021):

1. Export of mask fabric is subject to permission.
2. Approval of Trade Counsellors / Attachés has been removed for support applications of exporters.
3. Preliminary permit application has been started in the export of masks, overalls, liquid-proof aprons, glasses, gloves and fresh lemons.
4. The Covid-19 outbreak was accepted as a force majeure within the scope of the Outward Processing Regime; It has been made possible to give an additional period of up to 6 months for the outward processing permit documents/permits, provided that they are applied within 1 month from the end of the document/permit period at the latest.
5. The Covid-19 outbreak has been accepted as force majeure within the scope of undocumented export credit and tax, duty, fee exemption document.
6. The Covid-19 outbreak has been recognized as force majeure within the scope of the Inward Processing Regime
7. Between 8.03.2020-02.05.2020, the export of Disinfectant, Cologne, Hydrogen Peroxide and Ethyl Alcohol products has been temporarily registered.
8. Between 07.04.2020-31.08.2020, fresh lemon exports are subject to preliminary permission.
9. Stock financing support was started for the exporter.
10. Due to the disruptions observed in exports to certain countries, the repayment of the 7.6 billion dollar loan extended by exporters from Eximbank was postponed, while the terms were extended, maturity flexibility for export credit insurance and no additional fees were charged for maturity extensions. The magnitude of these flows is especially important when considering their demographic composition.

Import Measures

The measures taken within the scope of imports are as follows (Ministry of Trade, 2021):

1. The additional customs tax applied as 20% on disposable medical masks has been removed.
2. The additional 13% customs duty on respirators has been abolished.
3. The customs tax applied as 10% on the import of bulk ethyl alcohol, which is used as a raw material in the production of cologne and disinfectant, has been zeroed for the industrialists producing cologne and disinfectant.
4. The import of medical diagnostic kits is subject to the permission of the Turkish Medicines and Medical Devices Agency.
5. In order to ensure food supply security and price stability, the customs duty, which is currently 31.5% on molasses imports, has been reduced to 0% for the industrialists producing baker's yeast, provided that they submit the final use. A tariff quota with 0% customs duty has been opened for 100 thousand tons of paddy to be used until 31 May 2020. The surveillance value of $1,000/ton on crude sunflower oil imports has been reduced to $800/tonne until 1 July before the oil sunflower harvest. Until 1 June 2020, 30% customs duty on crude sunflower oil will be applied as 18%, and 13% customs duty on oil sunflower seeds will be applied as 9%.

6.   In order to maintain the continuity of employment and contribution of domestic companies to the economy, to protect them against import pressure and to increase domestic added value, additional customs duties have been applied to more than 5000 products from the beginning of 2020 and especially from April until 30.09.2020.

REFLECTIONS ON MAIN ECONOMIC INDICATORS AND FOREIGN TRADE OF TURKIYE

After the economic measures during the pandemic period are revealed, it will be useful to consider the developments in the country's economy separately at the general and sectoral level. In terms of basic variables, it is possible to see the general trend, deterioration and recovery with the data. It will be illuminating to monitor the changes in turnover, sales and number of companies on a sectoral basis.

Inflation

In Turkiye, inflation, which was reduced to single digits after many years, stuck in double digits with the 2018 exchange rate attack; The pandemic process was entered with the repeated 5% target in the context of efforts to bring inflation back to single digits and inflation targeting. When Figure-4 is analyzed, the inflation rate in Turkiye, which was 12.8% in February 2020, decreased to 11.86% in March, when the first case was announced, and to 10.94% in April While closures/restrictions due to the pandemic were expected to support the downward movement in prices by suppressing demand, and the general trend was shaped in this direction in the world, prices in Turkiye became sticky and increased in the following months. Expansionary approach in monetary and fiscal policies due to growth and employment concerns, especially the pulling of loan rates below inflation, increased the exchange rate along with the total expenditure tendency. Increasing demand and the cost of imported inputs, as well as deterioration in pricing behavior, created inflation pressure. In June, the inflation rate increased to 12.62 percent. The inflation rate, which remained flat during the summer months, started to rise as of November. Although the change in economic management and tightening in monetary policy led to a decline in the exchange rate, the delayed effects of food and energy costs and the increase in the exchange rate brought inflation to 15% on the anniversary of the pandemic. Inflation rate reached 19.58% as we entered the last quarter of 2021, thanks to the normalization steps as well as the exchange rate effect and the base effect of the previous period.

Employment

Although the unemployment rate followed a horizontal course during the pandemic period, a significant increase is observed in the idle labor force rate (broad unemployment rate). The idle labor force rate of 21.5% in January 2020 increased to 29.1% in April 2021.

When the data in Table-3 and Table-4 are evaluated together, the reason for the difference between unemployment rate and idle labor rate can be seen. The decrease in the labor force participation rate and employment rate in Table 3, and the increase in the rate of those who are able to work and are not looking for a job in Table 4, were the sources of the increase in the idle labor force rate. Relatively high continuing rates per 2020 have shown a decreasing trend over time. When the labor force participation

Figure 4. Inflation rate in Turkiye
Source: TURKSTAT (2021)

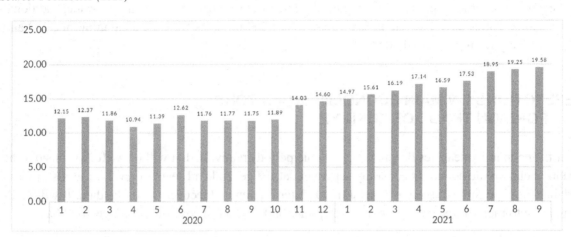

rate according to gender and age is evaluated, a decrease of 3.1 and 6.2 points is observed in the labor force participation rate of men and women aged 15-24, respectively.

Along with the normalization measures circular announced in June 2021, positive developments are observed in employment data. The unemployment rate, idle labor rate and youth unemployment rate decreased by 2.1, 4.2 and 1.4 points, respectively, compared to January 2021. The labor force participation rate, which was 46.7% at the start of the pandemic in March 2020, greatly recovered in 2021 and increased by 4.5 points.

The most severe effects of the pandemic on employment were felt especially in April, May and June 2020. The highest figures were recorded in April-May and June in terms of unemployment rate, broadly defined unemployment rate, youth unemployment rate, and increase rates of the population who are able to work but are not included in the labor force.

Industrial Production

When the monthly change data of the industrial production index in Figure-5 is evaluated, as in the employment data, the most severe negative effects are observed in the short term. In March, April and June, the change in the industrial production index was-1.6%, -31.4% and -19.4%, respectively. Industrial production started to recover as of June and with monthly increases of around 10% that continued until the end of the year, the industrial production index diverged from the general trend in the world and completed 2020 with an increase of 1.6% compared to the previous year. In March, April, May and June 2020, the industrial production index was realized as 16.8%, 66.3%, 41.1% and 24.1%, respectively, with the base effect of the previous year.

The Budget Balance

While public expenditures increased with the support provided on the one hand, and public revenues decreased with the postponed taxes on the other hand, the deterioration in the budget balance, which started

Table 1. Unemployment and labor force participation in Turkiye

		Unemployment Rate (%)	Idle Labor Ratio	Youth Unemployment Rate (%)	Employment Rate (%)	Labor force participation rate (%)				
						15+ Male	15+ Female	15-24 Male	15-24 Female	Total
2019	1	13.5	19.7	24.7	45.5	71.0	34.5	55.3	32.6	52.6
	2	13.9	19.2	24.4	45.7	72.0	34.7	55.7	33.3	53.1
	3	13.9	19.7	25.3	46.2	72.9	34.9	56.8	33.6	53.7
	4	13.7	19.0	25.1	45.6	71.4	34.7	56.9	33.7	52.8
	5	13.7	18.5	24.2	46.0	72.3	34.6	55.9	33.6	53.3
	6	13.7	19.1	25.2	45.7	72.1	34.3	56.1	32.7	53.0
	7	14.0	19.3	25.3	45.6	72.1	34.4	55.6	32.6	53.0
	8	14.1	19.3	26.6	45.3	71.8	34.1	56.2	32.0	52.7
	9	14.1	18.9	25.8	45.3	71.6	34.3	54.8	31.7	52.7
	10	13.4	18.7	25.0	45.4	71.3	34.0	54.2	31.6	52.4
	11	13.3	18.5	25.5	45.7	71.5	34.3	55.0	31.4	52.7
	12	13.3	18.6	24.4	45.6	71.7	33.9	53.7	31.1	52.6
2020	1	13.1	21.5	24.6	44.6	70.1	33.0	52.8	32.2	51.3
	2	12.7	20.8	23.6	44.4	70.0	32.2	51.9	29.2	50.9
	3	13.1	23.3	23.4	42.4	68.0	30.0	50.7	26.3	48.8
	4	13.4	27.7	24.7	40.4	64.8	29.0	49.8	26.0	46.7
	5	13.3	29.1	25.2	41.2	65.9	29.5	49.7	26.3	47.5
	6	13.4	25.8	25.4	42.4	67.5	30.8	51.2	26.8	48.9
	7	14.5	26.3	25.6	42.1	67.9	31.0	50.7	27.2	49.3
	8	13.0	25.2	24.7	42.8	68.0	30.8	49.8	27.5	49.2
	9	12.7	24.2	25.2	43.1	68.3	30.7	50.5	28.0	49.3
	10	12.9	25.5	24.6	43.1	68.3	30.9	50.8	27.4	49.4
	11	12.9	26.4	25.0	43.2	68.7	30.9	50.5	27.8	49.6
	12	12.7	28.4	25.6	42.9	67.5	31.1	50.9	28.3	49.1
2021	1	12.6	29.4	24.9	43.7	69.0	31.4	51.6	28.7	50.0
	2	13.2	28.0	25.2	43.7	69.1	31.9	51.9	27.9	50.3
	3	13.1	25.7	24.5	44.5	70.8	32.0	52.7	29.7	51.2
	4	13.5	27.2	24.3	44.2	70.3	32.4	53.3	30.3	51.1
	5	12.8	26.9	23.2	44.1	70.0	31.5	53.8	28.6	50.5
	6	10.7	22.5	22.8	44.9	69.2	31.8	53.5	29.7	50.3
	7	12.1	23.7	22.8	45.1	69.9	33.0	53.3	29.5	51.3
	8	12.1	22.0	22.7	45.0	70.4	32.3	54.2	29.7	51.2

Source: TURKSTAT (2021)

with the problems inherited from previous years, continued under the pandemic conditions. Except for August and October, the central government budget had a monthly deficit and ended 2020 with a deficit

Figure 5. Industrial production index
Source: TURKSTAT (2021)

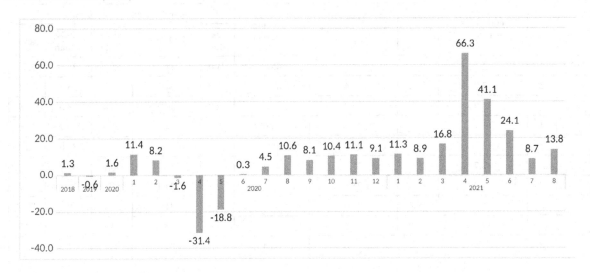

of 172 billion TL. The budget deficit, which was 7.4 billion TL in February 2020, was 43.7 billion TL in March, when the Covid-19 case was first detected in Turkiye, and 43.2 billion TL in April. One of the important reasons for the deepening of budget deficits at the beginning of the pandemic period is the loss of tax revenues as a result of the contraction in economic activities. Total tax revenues for March, April and May 2020 decreased by 5.6% compared to the same period of the previous year; on the other hand, transfer expenditures increased by 22.4% in the same period (TURKSTAT, 2021).

Figure 6. The budget balance in Turkiye
Source: TURKSTAT (2021)

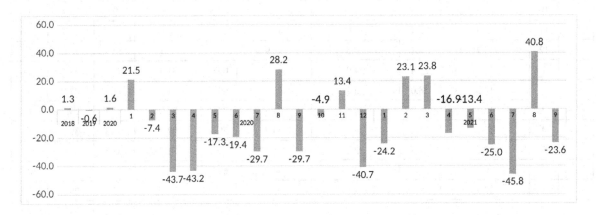

Current Account Balance

Current account deficit is one of the structural problems of the Turkish economy, such as unemployment and inflation. With the 2018 exchange rate attack and the weak growth performance in this process, a

Figure 7. Current account
Source: TURKSTAT (2021)

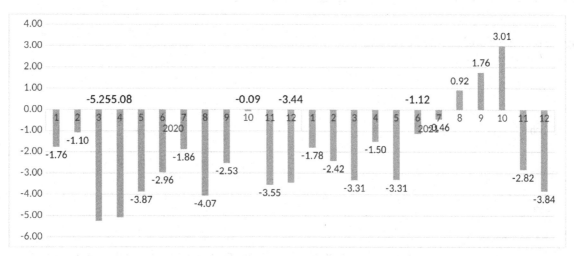

surplus of 5 billion 303 million dollars was formed in the current account in 2019. Despite the continuation of the exchange rate increase in 2020, the current account balance gave a deficit in all months; At the end of the year, the current account deficit was 35 billion 538 million dollars. In addition to dollarization and gold imports, the main sources of the increasing deficit in the current account are the decrease in foreign direct investments and portfolio inflows, as the deficit in the goods trade account increased by 126% compared to the previous year. Despite the deficit of 2.8 and 3.8 billion dollars in November and December, the cumulative current account deficit in 2021 was 58% less than the previous year.

Figure-8 shows the development of exports and imports in Turkiye. The effect of the epidemic, which was felt in the form of contraction in world trade, was also reflected in Turkiye's imports and exports from the first months. World trade volume contracted by 16.11% in April 2020 and by 17.5% in May (CPB, 2021). Similarly, foreign trade data, which had the lowest values in April and May in Turkiye, recovered in the second half of the year with the recovery provided by the supports. In 2021, the trend of exports and imports is upwards. As of August 2021, exports and imports increased by 37% and 25%, respectively, compared to the previous year. Foreign trade deficit decreased from 33 billion dollars to 28.9 billion dollars.

The share of the European Union, which is one of the most important markets for Turkiye, in Turkiye's total exports is over 40%. Turkiye's exports to the EU amounted to 72.3 billion dollars in 2019. However, in 2020, when the impact of the pandemic was felt, this number decreased to 66 billion dollars. In 2021, when the pandemic effect was largely overcome and economic activities increased relatively, exports to the EU exceeded the pre-pandemic period and reached 87.7 billion dollars.

In Figure-9, there are 5 countries to which Turkiye exports the most among EU members. As the pandemic spread in Europe and spread to Turkiye, as a result of the restrictions on foreign trade, Turkiye's exports shrank in all countries at the beginning of 2020. The period when the contraction is felt most severely is seen as April 2020. Between January 2020 and April 2020, exports to France contracted by 63%, to Italy by 55%, to Spain by 50%, to Germany by 39% and to the Netherlands by 38%. However, towards the end of the second quarter of 2020, it is seen that there is a significant recovery. As of December 2021, exports to all countries increased compared to before the pandemic.

Figure 8. Export and import in Turkiye
Source: TURKSTAT (2021)

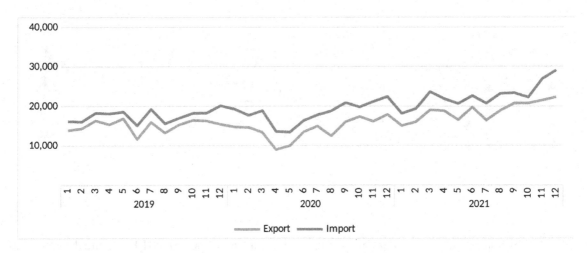

Figure 9. Top 5 importer EU members
Source: TURKSTAT (2021)

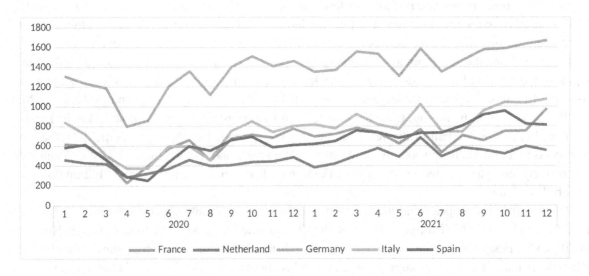

Currently, Turkiye and the EU are important foreign trade partners. Furthermore, the increase in container and freight costs during the pandemic, may make Turkiye more attractive to the EU. The China Containerized Freight Index (CCFI) increased from 854 in the second quarter of 2020 to 2164 in the second quarter of 2021 (UNCTAD, 2021: 59). This situation may enable Turkiye and similar peripheral countries to have higher potential in their trade relations with the EU. Especially, the increasing Euro/TL parity puts Turkiye in a more competitive position.

Figure 10. Companies engaged in e-commerce activities in Turkiye
Source: E-Commerce Info Platform (2022)

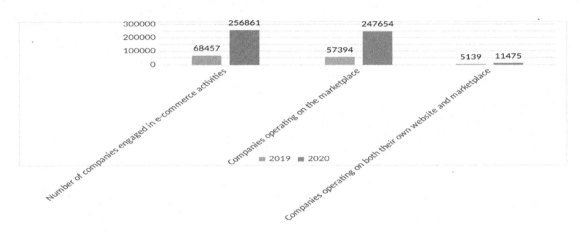

E-Commerce

The curfews and closure of businesses due to covid-19 pandemic, forced companies to find new ways to reach out their customers and buyers to change their purchasing and consumption habits. Digitalization has gained an obvious momentum in finance and trade. Figure-10 shows the change in the number of companies in Turkiye engaged in e-commerce during the pandemic. The number of companies engaged in e-commerce activities in 2020 has increased significantly compared to that of 2019. In 2020 only, the number of companies engaged in e-commerce activities increased by %375 with respect to previous year. The vast majority of e-commerce companies carry out their activities on certain marketplace websites. The companies operating on both their own websites and marketplace raised by %223 percent. Yet, only 4.5% of the companies operating in the marketplace has also served through their own websites.

Figure-11 shows the share of e-commerce in general trade on a monthly basis. While the share of e-commerce in total trade was 9.8% on average in 2019, it increased to 15.7% in 2020 and 17.6% in 2021. E-commerce, which had an increasing trend even before the pandemic, boomed especially in the months when the pandemic related restrictions were intense. At the beginning of the second quarter of 2020, the ratio of e-commerce to general trade increased to 16%. In 2020, the highest share was observed in May as 18%. Also, a slight decrease is observed in the periods when the measures are stretched and normalization steps are taken. Beyond the restrictions, the fear of individuals being infected with the virus is also a deterrent to shopping from stores.

When the 2020 growth rates of the sectors operating in e-commerce are evaluated, the highest growth is seen in food sector with 283%. This is followed by metallurgy and chemicals (189%), home appliances (129%), home, gardening furniture and decoration (105%). Due to the low share of metallurgy and chemicals in e-commerce, the increase in latter sectors, which already have a high share, had a significant impact on the volume (E-Commerce Info Platform, 2022).

It is possible to draw the following conclusion from all the information given about e-commerce: While the pandemic process indirectly and directly lead consumers to e-commerce, it also lead consum-

Figure 11. Ratio of e-commerce to general trade
Source: E-Commerce Info Platform (2022)

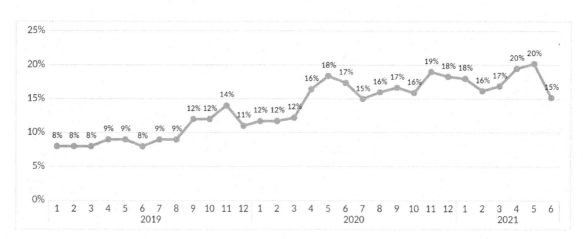

ers to spend more time at home, focusing on more daily needs and goods that change the environment they live in.

Gross Domestic Product and Growth

In Table 5, quarterly growth rates by sectors and expenditure groups are presented. As a first reaction to the pandemic conditions, Turkiye's exports decreased by -1.8% in the first quarter of 2020. The deepening of the contraction in the second quarter of 2020 spread across expenditure components. While a contraction was observed in all expenditure items, the contraction in exports of goods and services deepened; household consumption also decreased by -9.6%. As in other data, expenditure items other than exports (-22.1%) also recovered as of the 3rd quarter of 2020; especially fixed capital formation increased by 21.9%. When the 4th quarter is analysed, it is seen that the contraction in the exports of goods and services has come to an end and an increase of 0.05%, although at a low level.

In the 2nd quarter of 2020, the sectors with the highest contraction were services (-26.7%), manufacturing industry (-17.7%) and other service activities (-17.5%). Agriculture, forestry and fisheries sector (5.4%), information and communication sector (11.6%), finance and insurance activities (32.7%) and real estate activities (1.6%) were the sectors that showed growth. It is seen that the economy, which contracted in the 2nd quarter, when the effect of the pandemic increased, recovered with a growth rate of 6.3% in the 3rd quarter with the contribution of economic measures. While growth was observed in all sectors except services (-1.8%) and professional, administrative and support service activities (-6.5%), the growth in the manufacturing industry (8.6%) and industry (7.3%) also draws attention. In the 4th quarter, where the recovery continues, there is no sector that contracted except the construction sector (-12.5%). It is observed that the recovery took a relatively long time due to the continuation of the restrictions in the services sector, which was the sector that contracted the most in the 2nd quarter due to the pandemic. The services sector grew by 0.1% in the 3rd quarter and 4.6% in the 4th quarter.

In the pandemic conditions, despite the challenging conditions in the country and abroad, with the contribution of the policy stance and economic measures that prioritize growth and employment, Turkiye

Table 2. GDP growth rates by sectors and expenditure groups

	2020				2021	
	Q1	Q2	Q3	Q4	Q1	Q2
Gross Domestic Product	**4.4**	**-10.4**	**6.3**	**6.2**	**7.2**	**21.7**
Agriculture, forestry and fishing	3.1	5.4	6.7	5.5	8.7	2.3
Industry	7.5	-15.9	8.1	12.1	11.7	40.5
Manufacturing	8.2	-17.7	9.4	12.4	12.4	43.4
Construction	-5.1	-5.4	3.2	-15.0	3.3	3.1
Services (*)	1.2	-26.7	-1.8	2.9	6.0	45.8
Information and Communication	10.6	11.6	17.2	17.0	17.6	25.3
Financial and Insurance Activities	5.9	32.7	46.8	7.9	3.1	-22.7
Real Estate Activities	2.7	1.6	3.1	3.8	2.4	3.7
Professional, Scientific and Technical Activities	1.2	-17.5	-6.5	0.9	5.1	32.4
Administrative and Support Service Activities	5.0	-2.1	2.4	6.2	3.9	8.5
Other Service Activities	14.2	-17.7	6.3	10.6	15.4	32.3
Sectoral total	3.7	-11.3	5.1	5.1	7.1	23.5
Taxes-Subsidies	10.1	-2.1	17.2	15.1	8.7	7.9
Resident households final consumption expenditure	4.9	-9.2	8.4	7.8	7.0	22.9
Non-profit institutions serving households final consumption expenditure	18.2	-1.5	16.0	16.5	15.9	23.3
Government Final Consumption Expenditure	2.9	-0.3	2.0	3.7	0.7	4.2
Gross Fixed Capital Formation	-0.6	-5.9	22.6	11.7	12.4	20.3
Exports of Goods and Services	-1.1	-36.4	-21.4	0.5	3.0	59.9
Imports of Goods and Services (-)	21.6	-8.0	16.4	3.0	-1.8	19.2

Source: TURKSTAT (2021)

contracted by 10.3% in the 2nd quarter, had a growth rate of 6.3% and 5.9% in the 3rd and 4th quarters, respectively. With an annual growth rate of 1.8%, it has been one of the rare countries that completed 2020 with positive growth. The growth rates of the 1st and 2nd quarters of 2021 show the recovery in the economy. In particular, the services, manufacturing industry and industrial sectors grew by 45.8%, 45.3% and 40.5%, respectively, in the second quarter of 2021, due to the base effect of the contraction in the 2nd quarter of 2020.

CONCLUSION AND RECOMMENDATIONS

In this study, the economic reflections of the pandemic in Turkiye, the measures taken and the recovery process that started with the normalization steps were evaluated. In order to minimize the negative economic effects of the pandemic, policy measures of different kind, such as employment, tax exemption/postponement, reducing financing costs and facilitating their conditions, protecting the employed, regulating foreign trade and encouraging them in some sectors were taken. In addition, financial aid packages for households and employers were announced and implemented gradually. Increasing vaccination rates and the decrease in the number of cases in certain periods supported the gradual normalization of economic and social life and the success of the measures.

The economic recovery process has started as of the 3rd quarter of 2020. However, in parallel with the gradual reduction of restrictions in the normalization process, the increased vitality in the sectors, especially as of the middle of 2021, is seen in the changes in turnover.

In 2021, it has been observed that the production capacity in the economy has increased significantly compared to the beginning of the pandemic period. Especially when employment data is evaluated, positive developments in labor force participation, unemployment and idle labor force are striking. It can be considered that the increase in the labor force participation rate is partially related to the transition to face-to-face education and the decrease in the number of cases. As a matter of fact, Wren-Lewis (2010) pointed out that in case of a pandemic, in parallel with the number of patients, the obligation to care for the sick in the family and the closure of schools may cause a supply shock due to the inability of at least one of the parents to work.

World foreign trade volume, which contracted due to disruptions in supply chains, shrinkage and restrictions in production activities during the pandemic period, started to increase in 2021. In the Turkish economy, exports and imports have increased similarly. Despite periodic fluctuations, an increasing trend is observed in exports and imports in 2021 compared to the previous year.

Due to the decrease in tax revenues and the increase in transfer expenditures within the framework of the fiscal policy approach during the pandemic period, the trend of deterioration in the central government budget from the pre-pandemic period has deepened. Even though it is in a better situation compared to world examples and especially many EU member countries, the ratio of budget deficit to GDP has exceeded the Maastricht criteron (3%), which it has met for years. As of 2021, a trend towards balance in the budget has been realized; Compared to the previous year, the budget deficit decreased by 56%, and its ratio to GDP turned to be a level meeting the related Maastricht criterion, being 2,9%.

As of the 3rd quarter of 2020, Turkish economy has entered a relatively recovery trend. Although the 2nd quarter growth rate in 2021 was 21.7%, the rate of change compared to the previous quarter was 0.9%. Social awareness about vaccination and compliance with health measures supported the permanence of the recovery. In other words, it is of utmost importance to prevent the factors that will increase the spread of the pandemic. The subject requires awareness and sensitivity in the individual and social context as well as the political field in terms of its human and economic consequences. Finally, speed of digitalization has clearly increased during pandemic, e-trade and new payment forms are among the leading consequences of this tendency.

Main constraint of this study is the time period which covers two years yet, and is not long enough to obtain sufficient data to conduct econometrical analysis in order to reach empirical evidence on the outcomes of economic policy measures. Pandemic has affected different regions/cities, income groups, and genders at different levels. Rising concerns on equity, gender inequality, and regional disparity, etc. due to pandemic might be the subject of new researches. Meanwhile, the need for contactless payment, manless production of goods and services, etc. accelerated the tendency toward digitalization. Implications of this tendency on employment, production, trade (especially e-commerce), etc. are other issues to study. Management of supply chains and logistic costs during pandemic type crisis might also be discussed.

As of pandemic being effective, general economic policy framework has been revised worldwide in response to health related priorities and measures. Overall outcomes, and inflationary results of expansionary fiscal and monetary policies, the need for regulations in terms of foreign trade policy and their welfare implications through international trade, competitiveness, and efficiency; efforts to be self-sufficient at national level and its possibility to turn toward protectionism, provide new challenges for policy makers and economists during pandemic, and after. Turkish experience indicates that proper policy measures support employment and growth, but expansionary monetary policy leads to higher inflation. It has been observed that the rate of inflation has reached historically high levels due to economic measures during pandemic, even in the US, and the EU. Rising prices of basic necessities, especially food, and energy, and problems in supply chains, e.g. chips, and increases in logistic costs have negatively affected Turkiye, as well as every country globally. However, using geopolitical advantage, Turkiye has increased exports, especially to the EU, and undertaken a position of alternative supplier, instead of China and East Asia, for the EU member counties.

REFERENCES

Baldwin, R., & di Mauro, W. (2020). *Economics in the Time of COVID-19*. CEPR Press.

Bayraktutan, Y., & Solmaz, A. R. (2021). Türkiye'de Kovid-19 Salgını: İktisadi Önlemler ve Kısa Dönem Sonuçları Üzerine Bir Değerlendirme. In A. Çelik (Ed.), *Kovid-19 Sürecinde Türkiye'de Sosyal Politika* (pp. 17–46). Orion.

Bofinger, P., Dullien, S., Felbermayr, G., Fuest, C., Hüther, M., Südekum, J., & di Mauro, B. W. (2020). Economic Implications of the COVID-10 Crisis for Germany and Economic Policy Measures. In *Mitigating the COVID Economic Crisis: Act Fast and Do Whatever It Takes* (pp. 167–177). Centre for Economic Policy Research.

Carlsson-Szlezak, P., Reeves, M., & Swartz, P. (2020). *What Coronavirus Could Mean for the Global Economy*. https://hbr.org/2020/03/what-coronavirus-could-mean-for-the-global-economy/

E-Commerce Info Platform. (2022). *E-Commerce Statistics*. https://www.eticaret.gov.tr/istatistikler/

Guerrieri, V., Lorenzoni, G., Straub, L., & Werning, I. (2020). *Macroeconomic Implications of Covid-19: Can Negative Supply Shocks Cause Demand Shortages?* NBER Working Paper No: 26918.

KOSANO. (2021). *Koronavirüs (Covid-19)'a Yönelik Alınan Tüm Tedbirler*. https://kosano.org.tr/koronavirus-covid-19a-yonelik-alinan-tedbirler/

Ministry of Commerce. (2021). *Covid-19 Trade Precautions*. https://covid19.ticaret.gov.tr/

Ministry of Family and Social Services. (2021). https://www.ailevecalisma.gov.tr/tr-tr/haberler/bakan-selcuk-sosyal-koruma-kalkani-kapsaminda-yaptigimiz-yardimlarin-tutari-45-5-milyar-liraya-yaklasti/

Ministry of Health. (2021). *COVID-19 Bilgilendirme Platformu*. https://covid19.saglik.gov.tr/

TCMB. (2021). *Koronavirüsün Ekonomik ve Finansal Etkilerine Karşı Alınan Tedbirler*. https://www.tcmb.gov.tr/wps/wcm/connect/TR/TCMB+TR/Main+Menu/ Duyurular/Koronavirus/

TOBB. (2021). *İş Dünyası Korona İçin Ekonomik Tedbirler*. https://tobb.org.tr/Sayfalar/20200323-covid-destegi.php/

TURKSTAT. (2021). https://data.tuik.gov.tr/

UNCTAD. (2021). *Review of Maritime Transport 2021*. New York: United Nations Publications.

Wren-Lewis, S. (2020). The Economic Effects of a Pandemic. In *Mitigating the COVID Economic Crisis: Act Fast and Do Whatever It Takes* (pp. 109–112). Centre for Economic Policy Research.

ENDNOTE

[1] The authors have already contributed to Turkish literature on this issue with sectoral details (see Bayraktutan, and Solmaz, 2021).

Chapter 6
Ventilator Production in Turkey Amid Pandemic Through Service–Dominant Logic Lenses

Aslisah Senak
ⓘ https://orcid.org/0000-0003-2717-6850
Eskişehir Osmangazi University, Turkey

Nuray Girginer
Eskisehir Osmangazi University, Turkey

ABSTRACT

This chapter aims to demonstrate the value co-created by local ventilator production amid pandemic and how fast a technological product can be co-manufactured by interaction and resource integration among actors. The aim is to discuss the manufacturing process of ventilators as an emerging healthcare strategy amid pandemic with a service dominant logic lense and how well this case fits Gummeson and Mele's value co-creation model in a many-to-many network setting. Formation of a self-governed network of resource-integrating and service-exchanging actors by domestic production of intensive care ventilators dempnstrate the importance of network-based perspective for post-COVID-19 era.

INTRODUCTION

With coronavirus disease spreading the globe, the demand for healthcate equipments such as masks and ventilators sky rocketed. Patients with Covid-19 pneumonia not responding to non-invasive respiratory support need to be intubated and thus mechanical ventilators became the most needed equiment at intensive care units.

As mechanical ventilators appeared to be the most critical product for patients who need intensive care because of Covid-19 infection, countries that manufacture this product took measures of export restrictions to be able to answer the need of their own population. One of the main challenges faced for many emerging countries was to supply health care equipment to fight with pandemics. For countries

DOI: 10.4018/978-1-6684-6762-6.ch006

who already have ongoing production, the challenge was to meet the growing demand without importing critical components or the product itself. Before pandemics there was no mass production of ventilators locally in Turkey. Therefore Turkish Ministry of Industry and Technology and Ministry of Health started an initiation to manufacture local ventilators as an emerging strategy to be able to provide sustainable healthcare services to Turkish citizens during Covid 19 pandemics. Some similar co-operations to manufacture ventilators took place in other countries because of supply chain interruptions.

Ventilator manufacturing initiations in different countries due to restrictions on mobility of healthcare products show importance of networks and of the emerging strategies shaped by actors invloved such as the government, the private sector and other institutions and their networks during pandemics. These emerging strategies are cases of value co-creating within networks.

'Many studies about value co-creation are theoretically grounded in the marketing literature. Value co-creation is one of the main axioms of so called 'service dominant logic (S-D logic)' perspective which is a relatively new paradigm in the literature. S-D logic suggests that service is the fundamental basis of exchange and value is co-created by multiple actors always including the beneficiary through actor generated institutions and institutional arrangements. This perspective is based on the concepts of service ecosystems and institutions formed by actors within complex network structures. Accordingly the case study is evaluated with a marketing and service dominant lense within this chapter.

The study is derived from the PhD thesis of one of the authors and aims to explore constitution of an ecosystem through production of a specific product –ventilators- within a specific context – Covbid-19 Pandemic-. It demonstrates how fast a technological product can be co-manufactured with interaction and resource integration among actors within a network.

Data is collected by document analysis to respond the following research questions; 'Which are the actors invloved in local ventilator manufacturing ecosystem during pandemics and which are the outputs of this ecosystem'?

The chapter first outlines the urgent need of intensive care type ventilators and interruptions of healthcare equipment caused by trade restrictions amid Covid-19 pandemic. The challenges concerning supply chain of mechanical are explained to put forth the need for the manufacturing the ventilators locally. Further on the ecosystem formed to manufacture ventilators locally is presented. The main actors and their networks that constituted the ecosystem are defined. Subsequently, value co-creation through this ecosystem is linked with service dominant logic which emphasizes importance of institutons and institutional arrangements within networks. It is argued that the outcome of this ecosystem is not only the product itself but also the value co-created among actors in complex network relations. In the last part, the value co-creation process through ventilator manufacturing is adapted to Gummesson and Mele's value co-creation model. The chapter concludes by discussing the importance of networks in value co-creation in post Covid-19 era.

CHALLENGES AND EMERGING STRATEGIES CONCERNING MECHANICAL VENTILATORS AMID COVID-19 PANDEMIC

Throughout history, humanity has faced the threat of many epidemics and pandemics. While infectious diseases affecting a certain population in a certain region are described as epidemics, the emergence of a new virus that can easily spread, cause serious diseases and affect the global population is defined as a pandemic. It is known that globalization and related factors such as rapid population growth, industrialization and urbanization, migration, global trade, mobility, increased travel opportunities play a role in the spread of epidemics all over the world and are considered to increase the risk of pandemics. Although the duration and severity of pandemics may vary, their effects manifest themselves globally (Dündar, 2020).

Pandemics cause absenteeism in industry, service sector, education and training institutions, shrinkage of demand in certain sectors, closure of enterprises due to quarantine measures, decrease in production, increase in unemployment, decrease in incomes, and cause great losses in national economies and global markets. (İşsever et al., 2020)

There are two most important reasons why Covid-19 poses a great threat to the whole world. Firstly, the disease is destructive not only for a certain group of people -such as the elderly population with chronic diseases-, but also for healthy adults. The other feature that distinguishes Covid 19 pandemic from others is its exponential increasing rate of spread (Gates, 2020).

The global spread of the virus has caused economic and social negativities on a global scale. Due to the high spread rate, countries have had to take measures in order to reduce transmission and prevent collapse in the healthcare system. These measures are not limited to but include travel restrictions, remote work and education, banning social events where large numbers of people come together, and distributing financial support to households and businesses affected by the pandemic. These measures have brought along many economic and social changes that effected industry, foreign trade, tourism revenues, education, labor market and consumer behavior (Soylu, 2020).

In addition to its social and economic effects, with the spread of the Covid 19 pandemic all over the world in a short time, the supply of sufficient personal protective equipment and ventilators needed for patients who need to be intubated has become of great importance. Due to the sudden increase in demand, countries brought trade restrictions to meet their own needs that have led to difficulties in reaching sufficient amounts of medical supplies in countries not manufacturing ventilators (Ranney, 2020).

While the SARS-CoV-2 virus causes mild or moderate ventilatory tract infections in some infected people, it can cause severe acute ventilatory infections and pneumonia cases for some (Kutlu, 2020). In patients suffering from acute ventilatory distress due to infection, ventilatory devices called ventilators are used which artificially enable the person to breathe. Especially in intensive care units, these ventilators constitute an important part of the treatment (Ministry of Health Covid-19 Information Page, 2020).

Even countries where ventilators were manufactured by healthcare equipment companies have had difficulties in meeting suddenly increasing need for protective equipment and vital intensive care type ventilators, and the pandemic has revealed the importance of the health and medical device industry all over the world.

As a result of the spread of the Coronavirus disease all over the world in a short time, the demand for personal protective equipment and ventilators has increased all over the world with the first quarter of 2020, so manufacturing countries have imposed restrictions on the trade of these critical medical materials in order to meet their own needs (Ranney, 2020).

Among the products that have a global supply problem, the most technically complex is the ventilatory devices called mechanical ventilators. Severe cases cannot breathe naturally, artificial respiration of patients can only be achieved with medical ventilators. One of the most important factors that makes it difficult to cope with the Covid-19 pandemic effectively was the lack of sufficient numbers of these ventilators all over the world, including developed countries. (Malik et al., 2020)

The reason why countries could not reach sufficient number of ventilators during the crisis is the limitations on trade of these products and the lack of stock in the manufacturer countries. (Brem et al., 2021)

Before the pandemic, countries with low production costs such as China and Malaysia played an important role in the production and supply of personal protective products such as surgical gloves, masks, and surgical gowns that do not require advanced technology. Production of medical devices that require advanced technology instead were supplied by developed countries such as the USA, Germany, Switzerland to a large extent (Greffi, 2020).

Shifting production to low-cost countries is limited concerning high tech medical equipment. Production is mainly carried out in developed countries since regulations require manufacturers to strictly control their supply chains for the quality and performance of vital and technology-intensive medical devices such as ventilators. Developing countries can produce with their own means not technology-intensive protective materials that slow down the spread of the infection, but what plays a key role in reducing the death rate is the supply of mechanical ventilators, which is a more technology-intensive device. World's leading companies in the production of mechanical ventilators are listed as follows; BD (US), Philips (Netherlands), Hamilton Medical (Switzerland), Fishel&Paykel (New Zealand), Draeger (Germany), Medtronic (Ireland), GE Healthcare (US), Smiths (UK), Resmed (US), Maquet (Germany) (Bamber, 2020).

By the end of April 2020, as a result of Covid-19 pandemic, more than 70 countries have banned or restricted export of medical devices and drugs while they paid effort to increase production and imports (Pauwelyn, 2020). This situation has forced countries to increase ongoing production or find ways to manufacture ventilators by cooperations and consortia.

While developed and underdeveloped countries traded medical devices and protective materials before the pandemic, with the onset of the Covid-19 pandemic they have tended to look for production solutions as the need increased unpredictably (Greffi, 2020).

In parallel with the increasing need, major players in the market have developed strategies to increase production volumes of intensive care ventilators. GE (GE Healthcare) has signed a $64.1 million agreement with United States Department of Health and Human Services (HHS) on June 1, 2020 to deliver 2,410 ventilators. HHS also signed a purchase contract for 4000 units with Vyaire Medical, for 1,056 units with Medtronic, for 4518 units with Hamilton Medical, and for 12,300 units with Philips. The German government also signed purchase contracts with Draeger and the British government with Smiths Group Plc. for 10,000 units in 2020 (Nguyen and DarSantos, 2020).

In addition to the large, medium or small scale ventilator manufacturers in medical device sector who tended to increase their production in line with the rapidly growing demand, giant automotive manufacturers such as Tesla, Ford, GM have also co-operated with medical device manufacturers or started manufacturing ventilators at their facilities by adopting their production lines to ventilators to meet the needs of the US government (Brem et al., 2021). Similarly, NASA (National Aeronautics and Space Administration) designed a portable ventilator suitable for emergency use with a short lifespan and therefore partially responding to the need, and manufactured FDA (US Food and Drug Administration) approved ventilators in small quantities.

GE Healthcare, the world's leading medical device manufacturer, partnered with Ford to produce 50,000 units of a non-high-end ventilator model and has signed a contract worth 336 million dollars with HHS (Nguyen and Santos, 2020). Production is planned to be completed within 100 days (Malik et al., 2020).

Virgin Orbit, an American aerospace company from outside of medical device industry, mechanicalized the ventilators using a pump that can be easily manufactured. British vacuum cleaner manufacturer Dyson used the motors outsourced from Singapore to meet the needs of the British Ministry of Health and started production with a new ventilator brand just in 10 days. Mercedes-Benz, Formula 1 team and London College University have also collaborated for the mass production of an open source ventilator design (Bamber, 2020).

Giant manufacturers such as Fitbit, Microsoft and Tesla have also attempted to make fast-produced ventilators at their closed production facilities aiming to reinforce their brand awareness. Tesla and Microsoft did not commercialize their ventilators and Dyson did not resume production after the UK government was no longer in need of ventilators (Nguyen and Darsantos, 2020).

In the UK, the government-financed National Health Service (NHS) called on medical device manufacturers to increase their current production capacity by solidarity and joint production. The campaign was titled 'VentilatorChallangeUK'. A consortium of supplier networks arouse in response to the call. Companies such as Smiths Medical, Accenture, Unilever, Microsoft, AMRC Cymru, Arrow, DHL, Airbus, Ford, Haas F1, HVM Catapult, Rolls-Royce, GKN Aerospace, Inspiration Healthcare, McLaren, Meggitt, Newton, Penlon, PTC, Racing Point, Mercedes-AMG F1, Renault Sport Racing, Siemens UK & Siemens Healthineers, STFC Harwell, STI, Thales contributed to the production of ventilators in required quantities within their own means. In an article titled 'Creating Medical Miracles' and published in UK, it is stated that staff of the companies at the consortium worked in extra shifts seven days a week. An official from one of the critical component manufacturers declared that all actors invloved showed the same dedication to increase the current production, and reaching the goal would not have been possible without combining their capacities and competencies (Portway, 2020).

Smaller-scale local manufacturers have also contributed with innovative solutions to healthcare providers to save lives. In Italy, one of the most heavily affected countries by the pandemic in Europe, an engineering company used 3D printers to produce valves that connect patients to ventilators to be able to meet the urgent need of a hospital in Brescia (Singh et al., 2020).

These cases demonstrate the importance of sharing resources and integrating competencies and thus, the importance of networks in production ecosystems.

MECHANICAL VENTILATOR MANUFACTURING INITIATIVE IN TURKEY AMID COVID-19 PANDEMIC

Medical device industry is a vital, a multi-actor and multidisciplinary sector due to its relationship with health. It is directly related to research in medical sciences, R&D activities in the pharmaceutical industry, applied sciences such as the machinery manufacturing industry, engineering solutions and to technological developments in many different fields. The success of R&D activities for medical devices is in direct relation with collaboration of many different actors such as researchers, engineers, financiers, the public, health workers, patients, conformity assessment bodies and so on. A multi-actor and multi-disciplinary environment brings important advantages and success, while threats such as foreign dependency are encountered in the lack of this environment (Kiper, 2018).

At the onset of Covid-19 pandemic, a start up in Turkey, namely Biosys Biomedical Engineering Industry and Trade Ltd. Sti (Biosys) held the patent of an intensive care type mechanical ventilator prototype (UNDP, 2021). The 8 years old start-up patented the product with financial support of The Scientific and Technological Research Council of Turkey (Tübitak) and Small and Medium Industry Development Organisation (KOSGEB) a cople of years before the outbreak of the pandemic. But the company did not have means for mass production.

Turkish Ministry of Industry and Technology took action with the support of the Ministry of Health to start an initiative for manufacturing ventilators at local manufacturers to respond to the increasing need. The ministry brought together the start-up with big scale manufacturers from different industries to make us of their production capacity, supply chain network, know-how and human resources. Engineers employed at Baykar (manufacturer in defense industry), Aselsan (manufacturer in defense and healthcare industry) and Arçelik (household appliances manufacturer) worked together to maket he prototpe design suitable for mass production. Second step was to submit the cost-benefit calculations and production project to the Ministry for approval. As a result of Ministry of Health's approval, the preparations were completed and production started at Arçelik facilities in April 2020 within only a couple of weeks time (Anadolu Ajans, 2020).

All intellectual and industrial rights of the product have been transferred to the Presidency of Turkish Health Institutes (TÜRSEB). Production and commercialization rights have been transferred to International Health Services Inc. (USHAŞ), which was established as a company active under the Ministry of Health (UNDP, 2021).

In Turkey Ministry of Health is held responsible for handling a pandemic. However, in case of a disaster, governed by a Presidential Government System, the main actors in charge are the Ministry of Industry and Technology, the Ministry of National Education, the Ministry of Transport and Infrastructure, Ministry of Interior, Ministry of Environment and Urbanization, Ministry of Treasury and Finance, Ministry of Foreign Affairs, Ministry of Family, Labor and Social Services, Ministry of Environment and Urbanization, Ministry of Trade, Ministry of Culture and Tourism, Local Government Units, Governorships, Experts, Science Boards, Civil Community Organizations that deal with with health, security, economy, education, technology, social structure aspects of the crisis. In this context, a Pandemic Influenza National Preparation Plan was prepared in 2019 in order to combat the pandemic, and a Scientific Committee was constituted by the General Directorate of Public Health.

According to this plan, coordination between ministries and other institutions is carried out with the National Pandemic Advisory Board (NPAB) affiliated to the Ministry operations center. Provincial Pandemic Boards and Public Health Boards are authorized to advice according to the diverse situations of the provinces to help the Ministry take decisions. Planned pandemic measures to be taken in Turkey can be listed as social awareness activities, stay at home practices and restriction of religious, social, cultural and sports activities, restriction of transportation and movement, practices regarding migrants and refugees under temporary protection status, restriction of circulation, partial curfew, mask supply and transition to remote education. Along with these practices and policies, some economic measures and regulations such as tax and credit deferral and exemptions, strengthening of health infrastructure, strengthening of social assistance and social solidarity also take place in the plan (Turan and Çelikyay, 2020).

In the Medical Devices and Medical Equipment Working Group Report prepared by the Ministry of Development for the years 2014-2018, the institutions, concepts and policies that make up the medical device ecosystem are shown in Figure.1.

With Figure 1 illustrates actors in Turkish Medical Devices and Supplies industry listed within in the 10th Development Plan Report. These actors are; Ministry of Health, Ministry of Industry and Technology, Social Security Agency (SGK), Public Procurement Agency (KİK), Public Hospital Unions, Hospitals affiliated to the Ministry of Health, Private Hospitals, University Hospitals, Market Surveillance and Control Authorities affiliated to Provincial Health Directorates, Medicines and Medical Devices Agency, General Directorate of Health Researches, Notified Bodies, Accredited Laboratories, manufacturers

Figure 1. Elements of medical device ecosystem in Turkey
Source: The 10th Development Plan (2014-2018) Turkish Medical Devices and Supplies Report

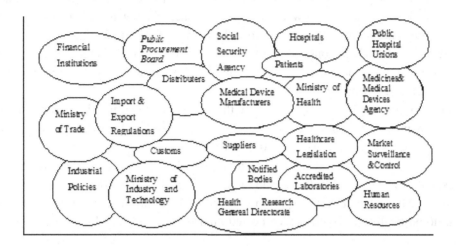

for medical devices, their suppliers, the sales channels of the manufacturers and the distributors and dealers that form the distribution network. The report also states that these institutions are expected to implement policies and practices that are compatible with each other (Ministry of Development, 2014).

As of March 2020, it has been determined that 15% of people infected with the coronavirus become patients and 20 percent of these patients will need intensive care. Accordingly with these estimations, 7500 intensive care ventilators were needed for every 1.000.000 people. Before the pandemic, 50 intensive care ventilators were available per every 100.000 people in Turkey (Hürriyet Newspaper, 20.04.2020).

On news it was announced that doctors had to choose patients to be connected to these devices as a result of the disease spreading much faster in Italy (Munyar, 2020 a) where there were 13 intensive care type ventilators for every 100.000 people. Examples of countries' attempts to manufacture ventilators and critical components in their own production ecosystems in order to avoid similar scenarios were mentioned in the previous section.

With the outbreak of the pandemic, there was no manufacturer of intensive care type ventilators in Turkey. Biosys Biomedical -the start-up founded in 2012 by a group of engineers and intensive care specialists- held a patent for a prototype itensive care type mechanical ventilator as a result of the R&D studies carried out with the support of Tubitak (Scientific and Technological Research Council of Turkey) and KOSGEB (Small and Medium Industry Development Organisation) " funds.

Deputy Minister of Industry and Technology held meetings with Biosys, Aselsan (the public owned largest defense electronics company), Baykar (manufacturer in defence industry), Arcelik (the biggest household appliances company in the country with an international supplier network) and discussed how to proceed with the mass production of the device.

It was decided that production lines of Arcelik were more suitable for mass production of the device in thousands of units (Munyar, 2020 a.) Thereupon, Minister of Health approved the project and guaranteed purchasing 10.000 units (Destici, 2020).

Arçelik made some of their LCD screen manufacturing lines available with required modifications for mass ventilator production. The workspace was isolated so that the team does not get infected and production does not get disrupted. Necessary adjustments on the design of the ventilator for mass production is carried out in joint efforts of Biosys, Baykar, Aselsan and Arcelik engineers. To start manufacturing phase, first orders to supply of some critical components were placed in the USA and China. However suppliers confirmed a minimum of 7-8 weeks of delivery time, which was too long to submit 2000 units of ventilators to the Ministry until the end of April 2020 and 3000 units in May 2020. To speed up the process, the Ministry officials announced that they would bring the components with Turkish Airlines in order to shorten the turnaround time. At the same time. Aselsan started working on production of some components locally (Munyar, 2020 b).

Other than arranging airway transportation with Turkish Airlines for the urgent supply of some components, the Ministry of Health has also contacted embassies to get in touch with manufacturers and speed up the process (Anadolu Ajans 28.04.2020).

With a campaign initiated by Baykar's CTO, more than 1000 ventilators were ordered by Aselsan, Baykar, Tusaş, Havelsan and the Central Union of Agricultural Credit Cooperatives of Turkey (Tarnet) and donated to the Ministry of Health. Approximate price of an intensive care ventilator was is 20.000 USD while a domestically produced device costed approximately 6.000 USD (Hürriyet Newspaper, 20.04.2020).

Apart from donating companies and those who offered to support production with their own means, SAHA Istanbul, a cluster of industrial companies in the Northern Marmara also announced to provide their engineering and production capabilities. Component suppliers opened despite curfew and staff worked on weekends and with both day and night shifts (ITO News, 06.04.2020).

In an interview dated April 28, 2020, Arcelik's CTO Oguzhan Ozturk, told the story of mass production as follows: 'Ministry of Industry and Technology, together with Biosys, Aselsan and Baykar contacted Arçelik to discuss how the prototype ventilators could be manufactured in high quantities. The first meeting with these corporations was held at Arçelik Garage, one of the best prototyping centers in the world. Then, the project plan was submitted to Health Minister who gave them an appointment to the core team at 02:00 on 25 March 2020 in Ankara due to his busy schedule.

After the approval of Health Ministry, Biosys, Baykar, ASELSAN and Arçelik shared their know-how to make the product safe and ready for mass production in two weeks. The device was in complience with national and international standards and manufactured in accordance with the TS EN ISO 80601-2-12. The product was certified as per CE 93/42/EEC by Biosys.

Engineers involved in the project worked 18-20 hours a day. Actors directly involved in production shared their resources based on their competencies. Baykar provided software support based on their aviation industry experience. Aselsan has worked on localizing components that are difficult to import. Ministry of Health called on ambassadors and Turkish Airlines (THY) for critical component supply. Arçelik and Aselsan manufactured the ventilators at their facilities. Delivery of the first batch by Arcelik was as early as April 20th with a ceremony attended by the Minister of Industry and Technology. In his interview, Öztürk stated that the production of ventilators would not have been possible without the R&D investments priorly made. Problems encountered during planning and manufacturing pheses were correctly handled by the parties involved. That is how a solution emerged in a very short time with contrubitions of strong engineering structure of three companies and the support of all their suppliers and stakeholders. It was also a case of solidarity within hard times faced due to pandemics (Anadolu Ajans, 28.04.2020).

At the course of June 2020, International Health Services Inc. (USHAŞ), which held the industrial and commercial rights of the ventilator ordered ASELSAN the second batch worth 31.315.000 USD (Anadolu Agency, 10.06.2020).

In Anadolu Agency's news dated April 20, 2021, Biosys founding partner was interviewed 1 year after the start of the Project. His statements were as follows:

A year ago, the software of the prototype ventilator was improved in Baykar, preparations were made for mass production in Arçelik, and production could start as early as in 2 weeks time. During the project, Baykar, ASELSAN and Arçelik engineers worked for 18-20 hours a day. First five thousand devices were manufactured in Arçelik. Then the production was transferred to ASELSAN. Approximately twenty thousand devices have been produced to date, and are actively used in 81 provinces of Turkey. Devices are also exported to more than 30 countries. (Anadolu Agency, 28.04.2021).

All actors involved in manufacturing the ventilator and their networks form an ecosystem that emerges as a healthcare strategy to cope with Covid-19 Pandemic. The output of this ecosystem is not only local ventilator device as an end product but also a set of values emerged with the processes of integrating resources of the interacting actors in the context of the pandemic. The value co-created is the know-how obtained for companies, experience for employees, improved health services for population, earned trust for ministries, the income for the country's economy and saved lives for the globe.

Creating value propositions is the foundation of the marketing discipline. Service Dominant Logic, a relatively new perspective in Marketing thought since early 2000, advocates that all parties are involved in creating the value and argues against the value delivered by the producer embedded to the product. This perspective sees the main subject of the exchange as the 'service' that emerges when one of the parties uses its competencies such as knowledge and skills for the benefit of the other party. The origins of this theory is based on the concepts of service ecosystems and institutions formed by actors within complex network structures. (Vargo and Lusch, 2017). It is observed that such institutional arrangments arouse within ventilator manufacturing ecosystem which enabled all parties to co-create value despite the fact that they had different corporote identities from different industries with different structuring and networks.

According to the dictionary of the Turkish Language Institution, ecosystem is defined as 'the ecological system that is formed by the mutual relations of living things in a certain area and the environment surrounding them' (Turkish Language Institution, 7 March 2022).

Many concepts and theories in economic and administrative sciences are explained using metaphors and concepts or theories from other scientific fields. In 1993, James Moore adapted the 'ecosystem', a concept in biology, to the business world, and defined the business ecosystem as 'the economic community formed by institutions and individuals, in other words, by the organisms of the business world'. According to Moore, this economic community produces services and products that have value for its customers, who are also members of the same ecosystem. The 'organisms' that make up the business ecosystem is consisted of customers and leading manufacturing companies, as well as suppliers, intermediaries, dealers, sales channels, suppliers of complementary products, competitor businesses and other stakeholders. Leading businesses play a key role in the evolution of the ecosystem. Although they fulfill the function of shaping investments in line with the common visions of the community members, their roles may change over time. (Letaifa et al., 2013: 22-29)

Figure 2. Actors in ventilator manufacturing ecosystem in Turkey amid pandemic
Source: Senak Duzarat and Girginer, 2021

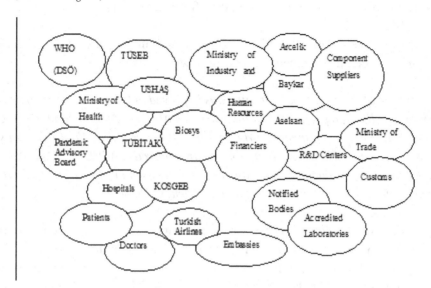

More argues that the concept of 'ecosystem' should be used instead of 'industry' and expands his first definition to include finance, standardization organizations, labor unions, professional chambers, public institutions and other relevant parties. Studies and contributions to business ecosystems continued after Moore. Power and Jerian (2001) stated that the ecosystem consists of interacting elements such as in the real world and also non-living things such as the internet surrounding this physical community. Iansiti and Levien (2004) suggest that participants in business networks in a business ecosystems share the same fate as they do in biological ecosystems and that an unhealthy ecosystem will affect all species it hosts (Moore, 1998; Power and Jerian, 2001; Iansiti and Levien, 2004; Peltoniemi and Vuori, 2004).

In the context of pandemic, ministries, institutions, companies and their stakeholders that co-operated for the production of ventilators created an ecosystem. That ecosystem also includes patients, hospitals, doctors, regulations concerning pandemic and related different corporations and institutions. The effective functioning of this ecosystem will affect the well being of it's components.

The figure 2 demonstrates network of the actors in the ventilator production in Turkey amid pandemic

Ministries, manufacturers, suppliers, hospitals, doctors, financial institutions, citizens are all the actors who will benefit from the outputs of this system in complex relationships.

The service ecosystem presents a dynamic perspective to social and organizational service structures, stating that innovation emerges within the repetitive interaction and resource integration relations between actors and institutional arrangements. Vargo and Lusch emphasize that the service ecosystem they conceptualize encompasses broader social systems beyond the interaction in the business world and markets (Vargo and Lusch 2011; Russo-Spena et al., 2016).

In this aspect, the Ventilator Manufacturing Ecosystem can be considered as a service ecosystem formed by networks of many different actors and regulations and institutions surrounding them. All public supervisory and regulatory bodies, manufacturers, national and multinational sales channels, intermediaries, dealers, hospitals, end consumers, suppliers, healthcare professionals and associations, standardization institutions, research and technology centers, test laboratories that concern the medical device industry, universities, start-ups, engineers, all other relevant stakeholders and the electronic data, policy, law and investment environment that frame them can be considered as acotrs of the service ecosystem that came into existence.

A succesfull outcome of the system was possible by the fact that all actors involved carried out production processes in coordination by interacting and integrating their tangible and untangible resources. Making use of both tangible and untangible resources of actors in a network is the essential theme of value co-creation. As our aim is to evaluate the ventilator production through so called 'service dominant logic' lenses and value co-creation concept in marketing, we will outline the main characteristics of this new paradigm and analyse value co-creation through ventilator manufacturing in a network setting in following sections of this chapter.

SERVICE DOMINANT LOGIC

Service Dominant Logic (S-D Logic) is one of the main pillars of this model.

The view that 'all actors, including the customers in the network of relations are actively involved in the production of the service' constitutes the basis of a new perspective called 'Service Dominant Logic (SD Logic)' in marketing theory (Vargo and Lusch, 2004).

The developments in the world economy in the last two hundred years have led to the transition from agricultural economies to industrial systems. Due to the fact that developed countries have become service-dominated economies, the service perspective has become widespread in the marketing literature. Marketing researchers, who have been dealing with exchange and profitability for a long time, argue that in the traditional product dominant marketing approach, businesses transfer value to the customer with the product. However, this approach does not take into account the consumption process after the product reaches the customer. Such an approach does not allow the customers of the business to know what they are doing with the product, and does not allow the marketers to interact with the customer during the consumption process. Over time, the marketing literature has shifted its focus from financial benefits to intangible benefits, such as the relationship and interaction between the producer and its customers. Activities that will facilitate relationship building and make it sustainable gained more importance. Interaction with customers in production processes and the view that they are consuming services during production have opened new horizons for businesses in innovation, relationship and learning (Grönroos, 2006).

Service Dominant Logic defines service as 'the process of doing something for others' and puts service on the basis of exchange. According to this understanding, products and services are tools of service. Unlike services, service is the use of knowledge and skills for the benefit of others (Vargo & Lusch, 2004). According to the so called S-D logic Vargo and Lusch presents, 'service' is the basis of Exchange. It is revealed by the integration of resources and the co-creation of value (Akaka & Vargo, 2013). The collaborative creation of value takes place not only between the manufacturers and its customers, but also within the network of actors comprising all stakeholders involved in the process. All economic actors access resources, adapt to the resources they reach, and integrate their resources to create value for themselves and others (Akaka et al., 2012).

The diversity (heterogeneity) of resources and specialization in different fields push institutions to combine their resources. In service dominant logic, 'suppliers' who provide inputs and 'consumers' who buy outputs are replaced by 'actors' who integrate their resources. Institutions are resource integrators that transform the knowledge and skills of their employees and other resources acquired from the market into services (Vargo and Lusch, 2008). Vargo and Lusch, who explain the evolution from the product-dominant point of view in the marketing discipline to the service-dominant point of view centered on relations, define the output of economic activity -whether it is based on goods or services- as service and value creation (Erdogan et al. 2011).

S-D logic is based on the resource-based theory that emphasizes the physical resources (operand) of the enterprises and the non-physical (operant) resources such as knowledge, skills, technology that are used to use these physical resources. Non-physical resources enable the use of physical resources and some other non-physical resources. These 'operant' resources determine the core competencies of businesses and are used to get results. Resources that directly deal with production outputs such as labor, capital, raw materials and materials are 'operand' resources (Vargo and Lusch, 2004).

Resources become valuable for an actor only when they are used and integrated. Therefore, service-dominant logic focuses on non-physical resources that enable the use of physical resources. The service-dominant logic, which points to the collaborative nature of value creation, is based on the propositions that value is always created among all actors including their networks and that all economic and social actors are resource integrators (Vargo and Lusch 2008).

The resource-based approach, which deals with the effects of organizational resources on the competitiveness and performance of businesses, began to take shape in the 1980s. While the common view was that the potential profitability was determined by industrial factors, researchers with the contributions of Wernerfelt (1984) reveal that the effects of internal resources and talents on the profitability of the enterprises come to the fore. In the 1990s, industrial organization theory, which is based on the assumption that businesses and their resources are homogeneous, and which bases its superiority on the external analysis of the business, has left its place to the resource-based theory, which argues that companies are heterogeneous because they have different resources (Güles and Ozilhan, 2010).

Resource-based theory argues that enterprises can provide sustainable competitive advantage when their resources are scarce, valuable, difficult and costly to imitate, and if their organizational processes and policies are suitable for the use of these resources. Although it is still considered as an approach for some researchers in the 2010s, most researchers argue that the resource-based approach has evolved into theory (Kozlenkova et al., 2014)

In the literature, it is observed that S-D logic focuses on the concepts of actor, context, innovation, institution, market, resources, service, systems, value co-creation and value propositions as a logic or theoretical lens, not as a testable theory. In S-D logic, from a system, service ecosystem perspective, service exchange and value creation mean simultaneous interaction at different levels and complex service systems. In the service ecosystem approach, for example, vehicle buying and selling is not just the legal ownership of the vehicle, but a complex set of activities under the influence of different institutions (legislative bodies, brand communities, etc.), technology (symbols and processes) and resources (knowledge and social roles). Thus, there are not only actors but also physical and non-physical elements in the co-creation of value (Pohlmann and Kaartemo 2017).

The service-dominant logic that emerged with the 2000s emphasizes multilateral relationship networks, not the bilateral relations between businesses (Business to Business - B2B) or between business and consumer (B2C) in relational marketing, and brings the consumer to the core in a functional way. It takes the service marketing that emerged in the 1980s and 90s one step further by redefining the supplier-customer roles, both are positioned as active parties in value creation. Instead of business, supplier, customer or consumer, the concepts of actor and the relationship between actors (Actor to actor – A2A) are used (Vargo and Lusch, 2016).

The logic, which Vargo and Lusch called service dominant logic, was developed by many researchers in the following process and 10 basic propositions were reduced to 4 basic axioms. These axioms are as follows; The basis of exchange is service. The customer is always the co-creator of value. All social and economic actors are resource integrators. Value is always uniquely and phenomenologically determined by the beneficiary.

In 2016, a more holistic, realistic and dynamic perspective on value creation was introduced, with inter-actor relations instead of business and customer. 'The co-creation of values is coordinated through the institutions and institutional arrangements created by the actors'. A new axiom has been added in the form of institutional structures (institutions) and institutional arrangements (institutional arrangments), which are more understandable rules, norms, meanings, symbols and practices that enable cooperation instead of dual structures, have become the pillars that form the basic foundations of common value creation (Vargo and Lusch, 2008).

VALUE CO-CREATION THROUGH VENTILATOR MANUFACTURING IN A MANY TO MANY NETWORK SETTING

In this section, value co-creation process through ventilator production will be evaluated within the framework of Gummeson and Mele's so called Value Co-Creation model (2010). In the following part of this section, first of all, we will briefly mention theoretical foundations of Gummesson and Mele's model and discuss how ventilator production fits within the framework of this model and S-D Logic.

Gummeson and Mele's (2010) Interaction and Resource Integration Model in a Many-to-Many Network Setting is primarily in line with S-D logic, and is in line with some aspects of relationship marketing and many-to-many marketing theories. Actors interact in a many-to-many structure and use each other's resources and competencies. This way they co-create value.

The model puts forward the role of interaction in value creation through resource integration in a relational framework. The most important premise of resource integration is the interaction of actors in the network structure. Actors communicate knowledge and other resources to each other through dialogue for organizational learning, resource creation, and innovation.

Services marketing based on long-term customer relationships is strengthened in Europe as a response to traditional marketing management and marketing mix approaches where marketing is viewed as a decision-making function concerning design, pricing, distribution and promotion of goods and services (Gronroos, 1989). Industrial marketing (Turnbull et al., 1996), in which the Purchasing Group (International Marketing and Purchasing Group - IMP) emphasizes the complex network structures that emerge as a result of interaction between businesses, and relational marketing, argues that value is created through relationships, including stakeholders and competitors, rather than the output of exchange. These new marketing approaches have realized a paradigm shift in marketing theory.

Gummeson and Mele relate their model to services marketing – which puts emphasis on services instead of product or service as a product-, industrial marketing -which deals not only with the relationship between the producer and the consumer, but also with industrial relations-, relational marketing -which is based on long term relationships instead of transactional relationships- as mid-range theories.

Mid-range act as a cornerstone or bridge in reaching broader theories based on empirical findings and observations in specific researches (Brodie et al. 2011).

Although there are overlapping aspects with above listed mid-range theories, the main foundations to the model is Hunt and Morgan's 'Resource Advantage Theory', 'Service Dominant Logic' and 'Many-to-many Marketing' theories put forward by Vargo and Lusch.

Another Grand theory, many-to-many marketing, prioritizes complex networks based on relationships and interaction (Lusch and Vargo, 2006). It introduces the concept of contextual value that covers all networks, instead of considering value as customer-oriented use value and supplier-oriented exchange value (Gummeson and Mele, 2010).

In the Resource Advantage theory associated with the model, Hunt and Morgan (1996) stated that suppliers have the opportunity to use relational resources that will increase their competitiveness by interacting with rival companies and other stakeholders. These resources can be classified as financial, physical, legal, human resources, corporate, data resources and relational resources.

As an extension of these medium and basic theories, Gummeson and Mele (2010) created the model in Figure 3, in which they show that actors interact in a many-to-many structure, using each other's resources and competencies jointly, and thus co-creating value. Figure 4 shows how the value created with the ventilator production process overlaps with the shared value creation model in Figure 3, which was created by associating these concepts and theories.

As seen in Figure 3, interaction between actors in Gummeson and Mele's (2010) model is realized through dialogue, knowledge transfer, sharing of other resources and learning. The social structures occured as a result of this interaction and are constantly reshaped by the actions of the actors.

Interaction

With the technological and digital revolution, the concepts of time and place are expanding nowadays; the roles of seller and buyer, producer and consumer are intertwined, buyers or consumers become partners in the decision-making processes of organizations and production (Sheth and Parvatiyar, 1995). Interaction is an important element of relationship marketing (Grönroos, 2004). By interacting, the parties can initiate a relationship and transfer resources (Johnston et al., 2006). This resource transfer may consist of physical elements as well as non-physical elements such as knowledge and know-how.

In Gummeson and Mele's (2010) model, interaction between actors is realized through dialogue, sharing of information and other resources, and learning.

Resource Integration

The transition from the conventional understanding of supply chain to the idea of value co-creation networks blurs the business boundaries. All actors can be considered as open systems dependent on the resources of others in order to exist.

This interdependence requires special exchange and interaction processes in which the actor combines his own resources with the resources of others for the health of the system. The systematic approach emphasizes the need to get rid of the shackles of the producer-customer duality to create value (Storbacka & Nenonen, 2011).

Resource integration can be defined as actors connecting their resources by interacting with actors (A2A) for the benefit of all parties. Integration occurs when resources differ in quality and quantity and

Figure 3. Value co-creation through A2A interaction and resource integration in a many to many network setting
Source: Gummeson and Mele (2010)

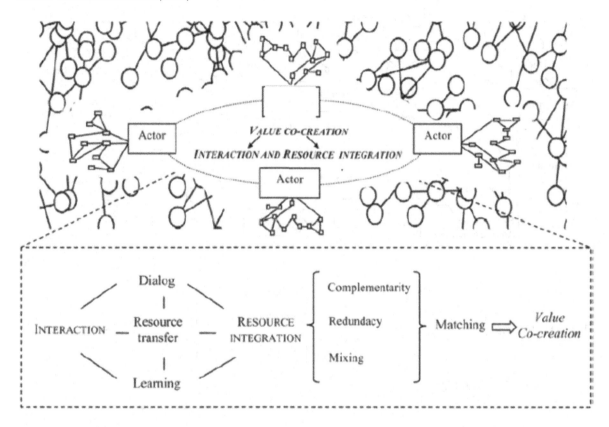

complementary resources are needed. In case the resources are similar, volumetric increase and abundance will be achieved with the combined resources. In all cases, interaction and co-creation between networks ensures better matching of resources, processes, and outputs, enabling service systems to function better. Resource integration; It can occur in three different ways, through complementary resources, where different resources make up for the deficiency of each other, similar resources in cooperation, or mixed resources that include comprehensive collaborations (Gummeson & Mele, 2010).

Value Co-Creation through Manufacturing Local Ventilators Amid Pandemic

As Covid-19 Pandemic and supply chain distruptions in healthcare equipment emerged, the ventilator was manufactured in Turkey by actors interacting and integrating their resources within an ecosystem of services and a complex network of actors, as depicted in Gummesson and Mele's model.

Figure 4 is the adoption of Gummesson and Mele's 'Value Co-Creation through A2A Interaction and Resource Integration in a Many to Many Network Setting' Model to value co-creation through manufacturing local ventilators in Turkey amid Pandemic.

As Figure 4 illustrates, Biosys, Arçelik, Aselsan, Baykar, Ministry of Health and Ministry of Industry and Technology are the main actors that took an active role in the production. Along with these main

Figure 4. Value co-creation through manufacturing local ventilators amid pandemic
Source: Adapted from Gummesson and Mele's Value Co-Creation through A2A Interaction and Resource Integration in a Many to Many Network Setting Model (2010)

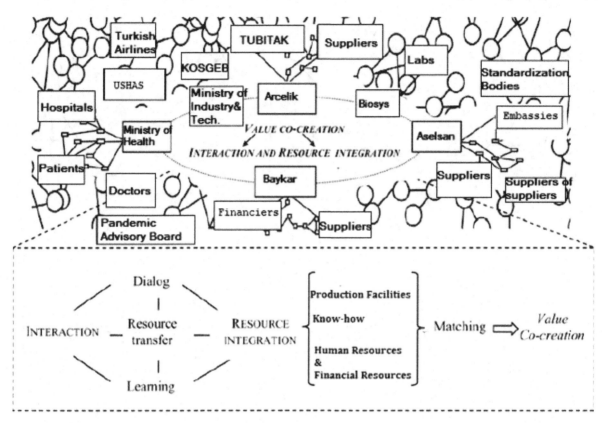

actors, suppliers, the World Health Organization (WHO), which provides data about the pandemic and promotes the relevant legal regulations, the Ministry of Commerce as an institution that regulates the import and export of products, the customs that implement these regulations, R&D centers, Tübitak, Turkish Airlines (THY) which is involved in the supply of critical components of the device, embassies, Baykar (250 units), ASELSAN (250 units), Roketsan (250 units), Havelsan (150 units), Arçelik (150 units), Amazon Turkey (100 units) as financing companies which supported donation campaign are all actors in the ecosystem (Hürriyet Newspaper, 2020). Also institutions such as accredited test laboratories, hospitals, patients and human resources are stakeholders who play a role and create value.

In service dominant logic, the importance of the contextuality and the dimensions of time and place in the creation and determination of value are emphasized together with network relations (Vargo & Akaka, 2009). The pandemic experienced in 2020 constitutes the contextual framework of the value created by the production of ventilators in Turkey.

The interactions between the structures and actors including resources and rules, that make sense of the exchange relations, are called structuring (Göğce and Özmen, 2020). Figure 4 shows those structurings created by the actors. As suggested by Gummesson and Mele (2010), this configuration takes place not only in bilateral relations but also between multiple actors and their connections. Similarly, the service-dominated logic defines a service system as 'networks that connect service-producing organizations' (Forsstorm, 2005). These service system networks, which are interconnected in the figure above, constitute the ventilator ecosystem.

The competencies of the actors are important in co-creating value. For co-creation, the parties must be both dependent and independent from each other. Institutions with heterogeneous resources cooperate by using each other's resources in a meaningful way (Forsstorm, 2005). In Figure 4, it can be seen that the actors in the structuring are both independent and dependent on each other. The healthcare industry is a sector that requires the coming together of multiple actors for innovation and value co-creation (Reypens et al. 2016).

According to Gummesson and Mele (2010), resource integration can be realized in three different ways; through complementary resources, where different resources make up for the deficiency of each other, similar resources in cooperation, or mixed resources that include comprehensive collaborations. In ventilator manufacturing ecosystem, production facilities suitable for mass production of medical devices and patent are complementary resources. Similar resources are engineering skills, know-how and experience. Financial resources and workforce used for production can be characterized as mixed resources.

It is observed that Arçelik, Baykar, Aselsan, Biosys and the Ministry of Health, which are the main actors in the production of ventilators, integrate both complementary and similar resources with their network structures consisting of their own suppliers and stakeholders. For example, Biosys obtained necessary certifications, Arçelik and Aselsan provided their production facilities, Baykar provided engineering and software support, and the Ministry of Health and Ministry of Industry initiated the project and urged Turkish Airlines and embassies for urgent procurement of some components (Anadolu Ajans, 2020).

Eventually, resources of actors are renewed and integrated. The key to value creation is resource integration. An actor's potential to create value stems not only from its core skills and unique resources, but also from its position in the network, its cohesion, its contribution to success and development. As seen in Figure 4, the value creation among actors in complex relationships in the ventilator manufacturing processes emerges when institutions, supplier companies and other stakeholders use their non- physical resources as well as physical resources such as their knowledge and sectoral expertise.

In Gummesson and Mele's model (2010), the resources of the parties are integrated in the process of value co-creation and something that one of the parties cannot achieve alone is provided. This applies to the ventilator production in Turkey during Covid-19 pandemic. Although Biosys was the company who received the patent, they were not capable of mass production. Production was realized thanks to integration of both tangible and untangible resources of actors and their networks involved. Whereas sharing know how or supplier data and costs among companies would be regarded as violance of confidential information, it is understood that all these processes were executed smoothly. Problems were solved immediately by high level management thanks to involvment of decision makers in all steps of the process. Advancement would have taken much longer in case of possible co-operations due to legal measures about confidentiality and competition. Pandemic and motivation of saving lives made all parties co-creating value consciously putting aside many aspects of business life such as profitability. Despite this fact, the end product was manufactured for less than half of what it would have costed in case of importing it.

Service exchange and resource integration among actors are key elements of service dominant logic. Within this perspective, resource-integrating and service-exchanging actors set off self governed networks through institutions and institutional arrangments. Covid 19 pandemic is thought to generate a natural service oriented mindset for actors involved in production of ventilators which accelerates interaction and resource integration processes. Co-creation is automatically coordinated through actor generated institutions and institutional arrangments as argued in service dominant logic. Observation of similar strategies emerging in different countries to meet the ventilator need fortifies this claim. Pandemics as triggering factor of service for service mind set helps forming new networks of value co-creation as well as forming of co-operations for a health care product.

Accordingly with above, multidimensional outputs of this ecosystem are improving healthcare services, fostering trust to the government, boosting morale to fight with pandemic, financial savings, international reputation and know how generating. The value emerging within the ecosystem is co-created by multiple actors and their networks.

CONCLUSION

The aim of this chapter was to demonstrate the importance of networks on value co-creation by defining the actors invloved in local ventilator manufacturing ecosystem during Covid-19 pandemic and the outputs of this ecosystem. Local production of ventilators in Turkey amid pandemic is analysed as a case study.

The outcome of the ventilator manufacturing ecosystem is not only the product itself but also the value co-created by these actors in context of pandemics. Value creation is the core subject of marketing discipline and value co-creation is one of the main axioms of so called 'service dominant logic' perspective which is a relatively new paradigm. Literature review for service dominant logic reveals that the value co-creation among actors in a many to many network setting instead of supplier -customer dyad gains recognition in marketing thought.

Upon the information obtained through newspapers, interviews broadcasted, websites and internal newsletters of the companies involved, it is observed that the pandemic created a service for service mindset for all parties involved in ventilator production. This mindset helped creation of institutional arrangements among actors involved and helped them to co-operate smoothly without concerns of confidentiality or profit.

Consequently, it is argued that ministries, manufacturers, employees, suppliers, hospitals, doctors, testing and certification institutions, financing institutions, all other stakeholders and citizens who will benefit from the outputs of local ventilator manufacturing initiative created a ventilator manufacturing ecosystem.

This ventilator ecosystem is constituted by the self governed network of resource-integrating and service-exchanging actors as described in Gummesson and Mele's value co-creation through Actor2Actor interaction in a many to many network model. The value emerged was co-created by multiple actors and their networks.

As a biological ecosystem determines the fate of the species living in it, the local ventilator ecosystem contributed to the sustainabilty of health services during Covid-19 Pandemic. With it's healthcare services aspects, it is also considered as a service ecosystem. On the other hand, as a biological ecosystem creates potential for new species, new types of medical devices were carried out in the local ventilator ecosystem.

Value derived in context of pandemics can be related to multidimensional outputs of the ecosystem such as improved healthcare services, fostered trust to the government, boosted morale to fight with pandemic, financial savings, international reputation and know how generated.

Based upon local ventilator production in Turkey as a case study, it is concluded that service ecosystems, value co-creation and network based stakeholder perspective will gain more importance for innovation and business strategies post Covid-19.

Furthermore, ventilator manufacturing initiations in different countries due to restrictions on mobility of healthcare products caused formation of new networks getting together around a shared aim – intensive care type ventilator production- and new ecosystems in many other countries. Thus, it is claimed that the outputs of this study can be evaluated in a larger extent than the local case in Turkey.

REFERENCES

Allee, V. (2009). Value-creating networks: Organizational issues and challenges. *The Learning Organization*, *16*(6), 427–442. doi:10.1108/09696470910993918

Anadolu, A. J. A. N. S. (2020). *AA Yerli Solunum Cihazının Üretim Aşamalarını Görüntüledi*. 30 Nisan 2021 tarihinde https://www.aa.com.tr/tr/bilim-teknoloji/aa-yerli-solunum-cihazinin-uretim-asamalarini-goruntuledi/1821021

Anadolu, A. J. A. N. S. (2020). *ASELSAN İle USHAŞ Arasında Sözleşme İmzalandı*. https://www.aa.com.tr/tr/ekonomi/aselsan-ile-ushas-arasinda-sozlesme-imzalandi/1871703

Bamber, P., Fernandez-Stark, K., & Taglioni, D. (2020). *Why Global Value Chains Remain Essential For COVID-19 Supplies*. VOX CEPR Policy Portal. https://voxeu.org/content/why-global-value-chains-remain-essential-covid-19-supplies

Brem, A., Viardot, E., & Nylund, P. A. (2021). Implications of the coronavirus (COVID-19) outbreak for innovation: Which technologies will improve our lives? *Technological Forecasting and Social Change*, *163*, 120451. doi:10.1016/j.techfore.2020.120451 PMID:33191956

Destici, A. (2020). Covid-19 Seferberliği Üretimde Dönüşümü Getirdi. *Koç Grubu Bizden Haberler Dergisi*, *482*, 11–13.

Dündar, N. (2020). Küresel salgınların makroekonomik etkileri üzerine bir araştırma. *Journal of Social and Humanities Sciences Research*, *7*(52), 837–852.

Düzarat Şenak, A. (2021). *Pandemi Sürecinde Yerli Solunum Cihazı Üretimi ve Ortaklaşa Değer Yaratımı*. Eskişehir Osmangazi Üniversitesi, Sosyal Bilimler Enstitüsü, İşletme ABD, Yayınlanmamış Doktora Tezi.

Düzarat Şenak, A., & Girginer, N. (2021). *Bir Hizmet Ekosistemi Örneği Olarak Yerli Solunum Cihazı Üretimi*. İktisadi ve İdari Bilimlerde Araştırma ve Değerlendirmeler-1. Gece Publishing.

Gates, B. (2020). Responding to Covid-19 - A once-in-a-century pandemic? *The New England Journal of Medicine*, *382*(18), 1677–1679. doi:10.1056/NEJMp2003762 PMID:32109012

Gögce, H., & Özmen, M. (2020). Hizmet Baskın Mantık ve Ortaklaşa Değer Yaratımı: Pazarlama Disiplini İçin Bütüncül Bir Değer Yaklaşımı. *Pazarlama Teorisi ve Uygulamaları Dergisi*, *5*(1), 1–18.

Gözen, M. (2019). Değer ve Değerleme Hakkında Kavramsal Ve Kuramsal Bir Çalışma. *Selçuk Üniversitesi Sosyal Bilimler Meslek Yüksekokulu Dergisi*, *22*(2), 374–382. doi:10.29249elcuksbmyd.481913

Grönroos, C. (2004). The Relationship Marketing Process: Communication, Interaction, Dialogue, Value. *Journal of Business and Industrial Marketing*.

Grönroos, C. (2006). Adopting a service logic for marketing. *Marketing Theory*, 6(3), 317–333. doi:10.1177/1470593106066794

Gules, H. K., & Özilhan, D. (2010). Kaynak Temelli Teori Bağlamında Üretim Ve Pazarlama Stratejilerinin İşletme Performansı Üzerine Etkisinin İncelenmesi. *Sosyal ve Ekonomik Araştırmalar Dergisi*, 13(19), 477–490.

Gummesson, E. (2006). Many-to-Many Marketing as Grand Theory: A Nordic School Contribution. Routledge.

Gummesson, E., & Mele, C. (2010). Marketing as Value Co-Creation Through Network Interaction and Resource Integration. *Journal of Business Market Management*, 4(4), 181–198. doi:10.100712087-010-0044-2

Haber, İ. T. O. (2020). *Yeni ekosistemin ilk bebeği doğdu*. https://www.itohaber.com/haber/sektorel/211582/yeni_ekosistemin_ilk_bebegi_dogdu.html

Hürriyet, G. (2020). *Yerli solunum cihazinin uretim aşamalari görüntülendi*. https://www.hurriyet.com.tr/teknoloji/yerli-solunum-cihazinin-uretim-asamalari-goruntulendi-41505171

İşsever, H., İşsever, T., & Öztan, G. (2020). COVID-19 Epidemiyolojisi. *Sağlık Bilimlerinde İleri Araştırmalar Dergisi*, 3, 1–13.

Kiper, M. (2018). *Dünyada Ve Türkiye'de Tıbbi Cihaz Sektörü Ve Strateji Önerisi*. TTGV – T/2013/002.

Kozlenkova, I. V., Samaha, S. A., & Palmatier, R. W. (2014). Resource-based theory in marketing. *Journal of the Academy of Marketing Science*, 42(1), 1–21. doi:10.100711747-013-0336-7

Kutlu, R. (2020). Yeni Koronavirüs Pandemisi ile İlgili Öğrendiklerimiz, Tanı ve Tedavisindeki Güncel Yaklaşımlar ve Türkiye'deki Durum. *Turkish Journal of Family Medicine and Primary Care*, 14(2), 329–344. doi:10.21763/tjfmpc.729917

Letaifa, S.B., Gratacap, A., & Isckia, T. (2013). Understanding Business Ecosystems: How Firms Succeed in the New World of Convergence. *De Boeck*, 22-29.

Malik, A., Masood, T., & Kousar, R. (2020). Reconfiguring and ramping-up ventilator production in the face of COVID-19: Can robots help? *Journal of Manufacturing Systems*, 15, 1–26. PMID:33082617

Munyar, V. (2020a). Yerli Ventilatörün Kolektif Öyküsü. *Dünya Gazetesi*.

Munyar, V. (2020b). O Solunum Cihazının Seri Üretimi İçin Milli Seferberlik Ruhu Oluştu. *Dünya Gazetesi*.

Nguyen, H., & Dar Santos, B. (2020). *Acute Impact of COVID-19 on the Global Ventilator Industry*. BlackOre Research Inc. http://www.blackore.com/sites/default/files/researchpdfs/blackore_hoovest_analytics__ventilator_industry_analysis_2020-11-22.pdf

Parvatiyar, A., & Sheth, J. N. (1995). The Evolution of Relationship Marketing. *International Business Review*, 4(4), 397–418. doi:10.1016/0969-5931(95)00018-6

Pauwelyn, J. (2020). Export Restrictions in Times of Pandemic: Options and Limits Under International Trade Agreements. *Journal of World Trade, 5*(5), 727–747. doi:10.54648/TRAD2020031

Peltoniemi, M., & Vuori, E.K. (2004). Business Ecosystem as the New Approach to Complex Adaptive Business Environments. *Frontier of e-Business Research*, 20-22.

Portway, K. (2021). Creating Medical Marvels: How Lasers Have Played Their Part in the pandemic, Including Making Medical Devices. Keely Portway Reports. *Europa ScienceLaser Systems Europe, 50*, 12.

Ranney, M. L., Griffeth, V., & Jha, A. K. (2020). Critical Supply Shortages— The Need for Ventilators and Personal Protective Equipment during the Covid-19 Pandemic. *The New England Journal of Medicine, 382*(18), 41–54. doi:10.1056/NEJMp2006141 PMID:32212516

Sağlik Bakanliği, T. C. (2020). *Covid-19 Bilgilendirme Sayfası*. https://covid19.saglik.gov.tr

Singh, S., Prakash, C., & Ramakrishna, S. (2020). Three-dimensional Printing in the Fight Against Novel Virus COVID-19: Technology Helping Society During an Infectious Disease Pandemic. *Technology in Society, 62*(06), 101–135. doi:10.1016/j.techsoc.2020.101305 PMID:32834232

Soylu, Ö. B. (2020). Türkiye Ekonomisinde Covid-19'un Sektörel Etkileri. *Avrasya Sosyal ve Ekonomi Araştırmaları Dergisi, 7*(5), 159–185.

Spena, T.R., Trequa, M., & Bifulco, F. (2016). Knowledge Practices For An Emerging Innovation Ecosystem. *International Journal of Innovation Technology Management, 13*.

Turan, A., & Çelikyay, H. H. (2020). Türkiye'de KOVİD-19 ile Mücadele: Politikalar ve Aktörler. *Uluslararası Yönetim Akademisi Dergisi, 3*, 1–25.

Türkiye Cumhuriyeti Cumhurbaşkanliği Strateji Ve Bütçe. (2020). *On Birinci Kalkınma Planı*. www.sbb.gov.tr

UNDP Istanbul International Center For Private Sector in Development. (2020). Lessons Learned and Strategies fro Local Manufacturing of PPE for Covid-19 Response Based on Literature Review. In *Experience and Case Study from Turkey*. USHAŞ.

Vargo, S. L., Akaka, M. A., & Vaughan, C. M. (2017). Conceptualizing value : A service-ecosystem view. *Journal of Creating Value, 3*(2), 1–8. doi:10.1177/2394964317732861

Vargo, S. L., Koskela-Huotari, K., & Vink, J. (2020). Service-Dominant Logic: Foundations and Applications. In E. Bridges & K. Fowler (Eds.), *The Routledge Handbook of Service Research Insights and Ideas* (pp. 3–23). Routledge. doi:10.4324/9781351245234-1

Vargo, S. L., & Lusch, R. F. (2004). Evolving toward a New Dominant Logic for Marketing. *Journal of Marketing, 68*(1), 1–17. doi:10.1509/jmkg.68.1.1.24036

Vargo, S. L., & Lusch, R. F. (2008). Service-Dominant Logic: Continuing The Evolution. *Journal of the Academy of Marketing Science, 36*(1), 1–10. doi:10.100711747-007-0069-6

Vargo, S. L., & Lusch, R. F. (2016). Institutions and axioms: An extension and update of service-dominant logic. *Journal of the Academy of Marketing Science, 44*(1), 5–23. doi:10.100711747-015-0456-3

Vargo, S. L., Maglio, P. P., & Akaka, M. A. (2008). On value and value co-creation: A service systems and service logic perspective. *European Management Journal, 26*(3), 145–152. doi:10.1016/j.emj.2008.04.003

Wernerfelt, B. (1984). A resource-based view of the firm. *Strategic Management Journal, 5*(2), 171–180. doi:10.1002mj.4250050207

Yanik & Ajans. (2020). *Yerli solunum cihazı 30'dan fazla ülkede insanlara nefes oluyor.* https://www.aa.com.tr/tr/saglik/yerli-solunum-cihazi-30dan-fazla-ulkede-insanlara-nefes-oluyor/2214339

Chapter 7
Performance Measurement Systems Threatened by Pandemic Opportunities in Retail:
How Managers Struggled to Balance Growing Sales With Unexpectedly Inadequate Supply Chain KPIs

Andrea Girardi
https://orcid.org/0000-0002-1589-7565
University of Modena and Reggio Emilia, Italy

ABSTRACT

Performance measurement systems such as KPIs are necessary managerial tools to set targets and monitor performances. During the outbreak of COVID-19, some companies experienced threats to traditional and consolidated business lines. The retail sector saw no decline in turnover. The aim of the chapter is to uncover and analyse the challenges imposed by COVID-19 to the retail sector as well as possible solutions implemented in order to overcome such difficulties. The chapter reports the case study of the largest retailer in Italy during the COVID-19 pandemic. Although seeing sales increase, the managers had many difficulties on the side of procurement and distribution of goods. The performance monitoring system was suddenly insufficient to manage the emergency. The solutions concerned the adjustment of the algorithms with dynamic components addition to KPIs and the conversion of some efficiency targets into effective ones. The chapter suggests insights on how performance measurement systems can be designed and developed in advance to allow more dynamism during emergencies.

DOI: 10.4018/978-1-6684-6762-6.ch007

INTRODUCTION

Performance measurement systems constitute a managerial tool belonging to the macro category of accounting practices (Merchant & der Stede, 2017). They are based on calculations and metrics meant to represent the reality of the results of processes and activities within the company. These systems are generally represented by ratios and percentages (KPIs) of goals achievement (Chan & Chan, 2004; Parmenter, 2020). The most crucial performance indicators can be numerous and divided into effectiveness and efficiency indicators (Almeida & Azevedo, 2016). Altogether they constitute the performance evaluation structure as a foundation for management and corporate strategy.

Managers use these tools for two reasons. On the one hand, they use them to represent the company's reality and take a picture of the business situation accurately and timely (Merchant & der Stede, 2017; Van gorp, 2005). On the other hand, they are essential tools for setting goals to be achieved, whether at the group, department (e.g., sales), office, or even individual level (Yuan et al., 2009).

During the outbreak of the Covid-19 pandemic, companies were overwhelmed by a profound disruption in their core businesses and activities. The performance measurement system, as structured in normal times, in most cases has proved to be entirely unsuitable for the sudden new challenges imposed by the pandemic.

Many recent contributions to the literature (Hohenstein, 2022; Parisi & Bekier, 2022; Rahman et al., 2021) have highlighted that performance measurement systems have encountered two significant categories of weakness in emergency times. The first was related to the timing of data calculation and reporting. The frequency with which data was calculated in normal times turned out to be insufficient during the emergency period. The second concerned the degree of dynamism of the measurements. During the emergency, measurements had to be removed quickly to focus attention on those processes or departments on which the pandemic had the most significant impact. Many companies in this field experienced a drop in turnover (Cowling et al., 2020; De Vito & Gómez, 2020; Hartmann & Lussier, 2020; J. Kim et al., 2021; R. Y. Kim, 2020), putting additional pressure on sales offices (Hartmann & Lussier, 2020) to develop strategies and, as a result, appropriate KPIs to compensate for the sudden extinction of certain established business lines.

The case study (Yin, 1983) reported in this chapter brings a more particular perspective by capturing a particular situation in which managers (heard during qualitative semi-structured interviews) of Italy's largest retail group faced the reverse problem. In this case, sales did not fall but instead increased significantly. At first glance, this seems a new opportunity brought by the pandemic (as it was the case for digital communications and entertainment companies (Barykin et al., 2021)), while actually, the company's managers experienced considerable difficulties in supplying goods (Ivanov, 2020; Ivanov & Das, 2020; Paul & Chowdhury, 2021). These difficulties in the specific context were due to a set of primary factors: the lockdown of some suppliers or suppliers of intermediate components, difficulties in delivering the goods to the shops, the sudden change in sales forecasts, the presence of a single supplier for a particular good (e.g., gift items), the unexpectedly high demand for products in the peripheral stores at the expense of the hypermarkets and the increased demand for non-food goods (because all other stores outside the supermarkets were closed). These factors undermined the system for measuring the performance mainly in two departments: the buyer department and the supplier logistics department. In these two business areas, the traditional performance measurement system quickly proved to be unsuitable to represent the new requirements.

The company's managers implemented the following solutions. Working groups consisting of the general managers were quickly established for the operational management of the emergency. In these teams, the most involved were buyers, personnel, and supplier logistics managers. These teams decided to replace the usual reporting regularly (Merchant & der Stede, 2017) with up-to-date spreadsheets that monitor product stock-outs in each shop in real-time. Typical efficiency KPIs were replaced with new effectiveness KPIs (Almeida & Azevedo, 2016; Parmenter, 2020) to monitor the actual arrival of goods at the point of sale. Completely reworked procurement budgets, bringing inbound freight costs to previously unimaginable levels (which reduced the sales margin in favour of getting the goods where they were needed). New KPIs have been created to monitor the possibility of purchasing a particular product from multiple suppliers as an exception to the company's traditional procurement policy. KPIs on hypermarket performances were reshaped to allow more room for unabsorbed fixed costs. General algorithms were adjusted to adapt to distribution needs and lead times changes.

Given the results obtained from the analysis of the interviews conducted, this chapter contributes to the management literature on performance measurement in times of emergency (Hohenstein, 2022; Parisi & Bekier, 2022; Rahman et al., 2021) by bringing to light the vital need for supply-side chain performance measurement systems (Ivanov, 2020; Ivanov & Das, 2020; Paul & Chowdhury, 2021). In particular, there is a need for managers and management scholars to reflect on the importance of designing dynamic performance monitoring systems in advance. Such dynamism should be expressed in terms of the ability to simultaneously monitor the efficiency and effectiveness of supply chains and the rapidity with which monitoring systems can be adjusted to adapt to unexpected jolts such as the one brought on by the covid-19 pandemic.

BACKGROUND

Performance Measurement Systems as Accounting Tools

Performance measurement systems represent a sub-category of accounting practices within organizations (Merchant & der Stede, 2017). Accounting practices are associated with data collection, calculations, metrics, and information dissemination necessary to represent organizational reality to external stakeholders (investors) and internal decision-makers (managers). Specifically, performance management systems are intended as accounting tools to monitor organizational activities and processes performances within companies and organizations (Parmenter, 2020). They are generally represented by ratios and percentages collected around general and company-specific Key Performance Indicators (KPIs). These KPIs constantly monitor companies' activity by collecting, calculating, and reporting their performances (Chan & Chan, 2004). The management of complex organizations requires numerous KPIs to capture macro and micro achievements toward efficiency and effectiveness (Almeida & Azevedo, 2016). The aggregate of all KPIs constitutes the performance evaluation structure that supports general management and corporate strategy.

Managers implement performance management systems to set goals and monitor their degree of achievement of them. In setting goals, these tools are translated into different dimensions to adapt at the group, department (for example, supply chain), office, and even individual level (Yuan et al., 2009). Most aspects of the corporate organization can be decomposed into small parts with single targets to achieve. On the other hand, performance measurement tools support managers to picture the business situation at a distance (Robinson, 1992), allowing timely information on potential issues to be solved and opportunities to be taken (Merchant & der Stede, 2017; Van gorp, 2005). The more accurate and timely this representation, the better the management reaction would be (Van gorp, 2005).

The Effect of the COVID-19 Pandemic on Performance Measurement Systems

The outbreak of the Covid-19 pandemic in march 2020 brought unexpected challenges to the performance measurement systems of many companies around the world (Aguinis & Burgi-Tian, 2021). Companies were overwhelmed by a significant change in their core businesses and activities, and the consequent pressures on performance measurements followed. Although appropriate for ordinary times, the structure of these performance measurement tools resulted suddenly unsuitable and insufficient in times of exception.

For this reason, recent literature focuses on the weaknesses of traditional performance measurement systems in representing organizational reality during pandemics (Hohenstein, 2022; Parisi & Bekier, 2022; Rahman et al., 2021). Firstly, the frequency with which data was collected and calculated typically resulted insufficiently and wholly detached from the new needs for urgency imposed by the emergency. Indeed, the situation of exception required more quickly and frequent measurements able to focus management attention on those processes or departments on which the pandemic had a more significant impact (Cowling et al., 2020; De Vito & Gómez, 2020; Hartmann & Lussier, 2020; J. Kim et al., 2021; R. Y. Kim, 2020). Generally, companies experienced increased pressure on the sales department (Hartmann & Lussier, 2020). These were expected to play a crucial role in quickly developing strategies, and proper KPIs in support, to reinvent possible business lines where traditional ones suddenly disappeared under the pandemic.

Some other companies experienced an opposite massive increase in demand for their products (or services) with a consequent positive impact on their sales performances. For example, this was the case of digital companies operating in the field of communication or entertainment (Barykin et al., 2021). Among companies that took advantage of the pandemic situation in Italy were undoubtedly listed in the retail sector (Burgos & Ivanov, 2021). In this case, retails experienced a substantial increase in the demand for their products as they represented one of the few categories allowed to operate during look down(s). However, although these companies were not experiencing a massive loss in their turnover, the pressure for change and adaptation on performance measurement systems was equally strong. This particular situation in which the pandemic, at first glance, seems to have brought new interesting opportunities to retail companies, while, in fact, undermined consolidated performance measurement systems similarly to other less fortunate type of companies as shown above.

It is interesting to analyze further this particular situation in which benefit on the sales side was balanced by increasing difficulties in setting KPIs and performance measurements, especially on the supply side (Ivanov, 2020; Ivanov & Das, 2020; Paul & Chowdhury, 2021). The following sections of the chapter show a case study conducted into the Italian largest retail business. The impacts of increasing sales brought into the company's strategy and the performance measurement system. Managers' answers to this new challenge reveal much on the role of performance measurement design and adjustment to support businesses in times of exception.

MAIN FOCUS OF THE CHAPTER

Case Study: Performance Measurement Systems in the Retail Sector during the COVID-19 Pandemic

The Context: The Retail Sector during COVID-19 Pandemic

The empirical part of this chapter was conducted during a case study (Yin, 1983) involving top managers of the Italian largest retailer. This particular situation challenged managers into a new problem. The decision of the government to prevent the spread of the Covid-19 virus concretized into the imposition of lockdown of all non-essential businesses activities. While many companies suffered a drop in sales, retailers increased their revenues. This was because citizens only had retailers as a source of goods of many kinds (except for medicines). Retailers suddenly became essential suppliers of all sorts of goods, from food to non-food products. Non-food products, in particular, represented an increasing line of business for retailers.

Methodology, Data Collection, and Analysis

The case study was conducted following Yin's (1983) framework. In particular, it implemented the use of semi-structured interviews with internal stakeholders. Semi-structured interviews as a research instrument (Drever, 2006; Schmidt, 2004) were chosen because they represent a "process in which the interviewer focuses her questions on some limited number of points. She may range quite widely around a point, but this would be done only as a means of getting the required information on that particular point" (Smith, 1972, p.119). The interviews were conducted in April 2020 during the peak of the Covid-19 pandemic emergency in Italy. A total of 4 top managers of the company were interviewed, and, on average, interviews lasted 40 minutes. The average length of the interviews was slightly shorter than usual as managers were interviewed using a zoom platform.

Furthermore, all interviews can be considered elite interviews (Aberbach & Rockman, 2002; Marshall & Rossman, 2016) as involved only directors. Elite interviews are fascinating as they allow a deep understanding of the organizational context narrated by subjects with much knowledge on policies and strategies. Indeed, "elites are also able to discuss an organization's policies, histories, and plans" (Marshall & Rossman, 2016, p.304).

All interviews were recorded using two electronic devices in parallel to reduce the risk of missing any word. During interviews, the researcher took detailed notes (O'Dwyer, 2004). After the interviews, the recordings were transcribed and coded. The coding was performed using the computer-assisted qualitative data analysis software (CAQDAS), Nvivo. The process of codes identification was mixed between previously known codes and new codes arising from interviews (Bazeley, 2014). Table 1 illustrates the subjects interviewed and their role in the organization.

The Case Study: The Largest Retailer in Italy

The case study involved the largest retailer in Italy. Italy was selected as it was the first country to be severely hit by the pandemic outbreak in spring 2020. The Italian government had to face a quickly spreading health. The institutional answer was to impose lockdown of non-essential business and private

Table 1. Subjects interviewed during the case study research

Number of interviewees	Role within the organization	Department	Length of the interview (min)
1	General Manager	Supply Logistics	36
2	General Manager	Sales	40
3	General Manager	HR	54
4	General Manager	Organization	31

activities. The effects of governmental response to the crisis reflected on the retail sector as explained in this chapter. However, although lockdown was imposed in Italy first, the most of western countries implemented a similar strategy immediately after. Other European countries as well as the USA stopped non-essential activities and introduced regulation to reduce social contact between people in order to prevent the spread of the virus. It could be expected that lockdown imposition affected the retail sector in other western countries.

The retail company analysed operates on all Italian territory (although mainly in the North) with one headquarter in Modena and 1350 shops. This supermarket chain manages a wide range of shop scales: small corner shops, medium city supermarkets, and large district megastores. The group has 22.000 employees, 1.000 of which operate at the heart quarter as administrative while the rest 21.000 work directly in the stores around the country. The logistic infrastructure serving all the 13500 shops is impressive and requires necessary managerial effort.

Case Study: Challenges to the Performance Measurement System during the Crisis

The interviews with directors revealed how managers, although understanding the great opportunity brought by the pandemic on the sales side (40 million euros increase in turnover compared to the same quarter of 2019), suddenly realized that their operations and costs would have been seriously challenged by the pandemic situation. Managers experienced issues on the human resources management side[1], digital infrastructure[2], and physical settings in stores[3]. However, this specific organization faced substantial challenges, primarily in its logistics. These activities included procuring goods and their supply to end stores from distribution centres. Figure 1 illustrates the supermarket's supply chain and highlights specific spots in which the crisis compromised operations.

In particular, issues brought about by the pandemic were divided into two main categories. Some problems were related to the procurement phase of the supply chain (KPI Procurement in Figure 1), while others concerned distribution to stores (KPI sales forecast and shipping in Figure 1).

Procurement challenges mainly were related to three main areas of concern. The first challenge that procurement managers faced during the pandemic was that many non-food products were suddenly unobtainable on the markets. However, customers' demand for these products was constantly rising. The cause for this was related to the fact that suppliers of non-essential goods were shot down cy Covid-10 restrictions and could not operate and supply those goods. Performance KPIs, such as transport costs, procurement margins, lead times, etc., suddenly assumed values never experienced before. Traditional targets and efficiency goals became unrealistic and unattainable.

From the very words of the company's supply logistics manager:

Figure 1. The representation of the supermarket supply chain and the KPIs affected by the pandemic
Source: Author's personal elaboration.

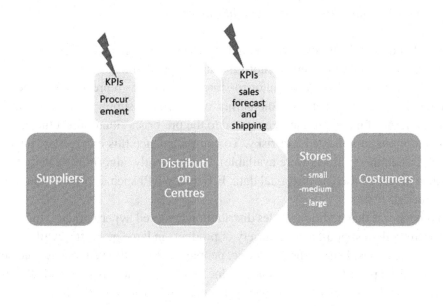

... Everybody wanted those [non-food] products because other shops were closed. However, we struggled to find those products on the market because [...] our suppliers were closed, and there was a lack of goods.... On KPIs? Well efficiency KPIs: lead time, the incidence of transport costs, shelf occupancy, etc., all of a sudden they went crazy! (Interviewee 1)

The second challenge concerned some specific food products. Products such as yeast, flour, lemons, and tomato sauce went quickly out of stock in all stores. This was due to the change in the cooking preferences of customers. Indeed, people locked in their houses used to spend some time cooling, and those ingredients are at the base of many Italian dishes. Furthermore, people tend to stock durable goods like flour and tomato sauce to cope with the difficult times ahead in crises. Then, the demand for those products quickly exceeded supply, and all stores experienced daily stock-outs of those goods, asking for timely replenishment. In this scenario, efficiency KPIs on the supply of these goods suffered. Extended lead times, increase in price due to scarcity, and empty shelves were some examples of the magnitude of the problem.

The third procurement challenge the company's supply department faced was traditional relationships of power between the supermarket and the suppliers. This phenomenon was more evident on private labels. Indeed, private labels are those products manufactured by one company for sale under the supermarket's brand. They are generally cheaper than traditional branded products because they are produced exploiting excess production capacity. In the situation in which excess production capacity is reduced to zero, the relative power of the supermarket on suppliers reduces. The supermarket's policy to reduce the number of suppliers per type of product was consequently anachronistic, as well as performance measurements associated.

In the past, we wanted to reduce the number of suppliers for our private label lines to reduce manage-ment costs, [...] generally we had a few suppliers for every type of product we label with our brand. Certainly, we could not think this was not enough! (interviewee 1)

On the other hand, on the distribution side, managers faced two main challenges when reorganizing material flows from distributor centers to shops during the pandemic.

The first challenge on the from-distributor-to-stores logistic was represented by the increased vari-ability of demand and consequent unpredictability of necessary supply. All stores, indeed, reported different sales patterns of many products compared to the pre-crisis situation. At the central level, sales forecasts became more complicated and risky. To counterbalance this emergency, buyers were prone to extra supply (when the products were available). Consequently, algorithms calculating stock needs are useless since they are based on historical data. Efficiency KPI such as product rotation on the shelf, was heavily affected.

The second issue was that traditional sales distribution favoured hypermarkets, whose infrastructures and facilities were built to support a wide variety of products in large quantities while allowing custom-ers fast access to the goods. During the pandemic, people were not allowed to leave the neighbourhood and addressed local shops instead of hypermarkets located far away to buy food and other products. This caused a massive unbalance between the capacity of stores and customers that was never experienced by the supermarket chain. The KPI monitoring the allocation of products and the margin were affected by this change. Since some KPIs included also fixes costs, hypermarkets' performances drop significantly.

We faced empty, but expensive, hypermarkets and local shops were assaulted by people! [...] margins considered also fixed costs, and colleagues said they were representing the reality (interviewee 2) anymore

Shipping services increased in cost and management complexity. This aspect affected procurement and delivery to store activities and was caused by a shortage of drivers and transport facilities. The result on lead times was a natural consequence.

Table 2 collects main issues experienced by managers (divided by procurement and distributing), the causes that generate such issues, and the effect on performance measurements.

Case Study: Solutions and Adjustments Implemented by Managers

The previous section reports the six main challenges to the company and their consequent impacts on performance management tools. This section relies on the analysis of collected interviews to show the company's management's solutions to rescue the performance management system and reorganize it into new sense-making considering the emergency.

The solutions implemented by managers are collected into two main areas.

The company's first arrangement to counter the situation was the creation of an emergency committee composed of 20 general managers (including those we interviewed). This group aimed to manage all the ongoing health and organizational emergency dynamics. For our analysis, the emergency committee was expected to use the performance measurement system to set objectives and monitor results. It quickly realized that both of these functions were misaligned with the needs brought about by the pandemic.

Company managers, therefore, decided to structure a new goal-setting system. In regular times, tar-gets were negotiated in a structured process that lasted days and generally took place twice a year. This

Table 2. Main issues experienced by managers (divided into procurement and distributing), causes, and effects on performance measurement

Procurement or Distribution side	Challenge	Causes	Effect on performance measurement
Procurement	Difficulties obtaining non-food items, plastic bags, and other items	Some traditional suppliers were closed due to lock downregulation	Sales performance KPI on some products were affected as well as lead times.
Procurement	Stock-outs of some food products include yeast, flour, lemons, and tomato sauce.	Customers demanded more of some food products due to their changed cooking habits. Demand exceeded supply	Although suppliers of food products were opened during the lockdown, the scarcity of some goods increased the price, extended lead times, and reduced the target for quality. Efficiency KPIs suffered
Procurement	Negotiation power with suppliers reduced. Traditional relationships between suppliers and the supermarket were overthrown, especially in the private label line.	The mismatch between demand and supply caused this change in relationships with suppliers.	The pressure on few-supplier per product was no longer sustainable as well as related efficiency KPIs
Procurement and Distribution	Shipping activities suffered severe delays on both the supply and delivery to stores side.	Increase in delivery demand and shortage of drivers and transport facilities	KPIs on lead times suffered this situation
Distribution	Variability and unpredictability of demand in stores of all products	The quick change in preferences for goods and uncertainty conditions	Algorithms serving load incapable of accurate forecasting
Distribution	of new sales repartition between hypermarkets and local shops	Superstores are generally located in peripheries, while local shops are more present in residential areas.	Repartition between the two sales channels changed forecasts of allocation of products.

pattern proved to be too long and complicated during the emergency period. Therefore, it was decided to make target setting more dynamic by providing daily micro-corrections to targets by a delegated manager. The negotiation and iterative nature of the process was suspended in favour of increasing demand for dynamism.

On the other hand, the performance measurement system reported updates on monitoring the achievement of objectives in a too slow and complicated way. Before being shared, the data had to be reworked by a manual management control system. During the emergency, KPIs were made more dynamic and accessible quickly through automation with ratio spreadsheets. In addition, new KPIs were added to respond to contextual specificities.

Table 3 shows the managers' operational response to the 6 challenges posed by the pandemic. They represent the operational detail of the macro strategies developed by the emergency committee as described above.

It is interesting to note that the managers interviewed stated that they had become aware of the importance of building a more dynamic KPIs system to better respond to the emergency risk as it happened in this case. "It is undoubtedly an emergency," they said, "but I am confident that many protocols will be maintained in the future." "The dynamism of our approach for defining objectives and monitoring success is a factor we will not overlook in the future," says (Interviewee 2) (Interviewee 1). Also, people inside the organization "appreciated the new dynamism of performance measurements" (Interviewee 3).

Table 3. Managers' solutions to the 6 challenges posed by the pandemic on performance measurements

Challenge	Effect on performance measurement	Solution implemented
Difficulties in procuring goods such as non-food goods, plastic bags, etc.	Sales performance KPI on some products were affected as well as lead times.	Sales KPI were updated into new dynamic measurements considering the shortage of suppliers providing that type of non-food products. A constant update was necessary to incorporate information about the pandemic situation
Stock-outs of some food products include yeast, flour, lemons, and tomato sauce.	Although suppliers of food products were opened during the lockdown, the scarcity of some goods increased the price, extended lead times, and reduced the target for quality. Efficiency KPIs suffered	The purchase price was set into a more effective logic instead of efficiency logic. Quality was rebalanced in favour of the effectiveness of supplying some goods.
Negotiation power with suppliers reduced. Traditional relationships between suppliers and the supermarket were overthrown. Especially in the private label line.	The pressure on few-supplier per product was no longer sustainable as well as related efficiency KPIs	Pressure on the few-suppliers policy was relieved, allowing more dynamism and feasibility in managing suppliers.
Shipping activities suffered severe delays on both the supply and delivery to stores side.	KPIs on lead times suffered this situation	Lead times targets were reformulated and adapted to changing shipping market
Variability and unpredictability of demand in stores of all products	Algorithms serving load incapable of accurate forecasting	Algorithms were quickly remodelled in favour of more safety stock, where possible.
new sales repartition between hypermarkets and local shops	Repartition between the two sales channels changed forecasts of allocation of products.	KPI on hypermarkets performances was reshaped to allow more room for unabsorbed fixed costs.

DISCUSSION AND RECOMMENDATIONS

The case study presented in this chapter brings a new perspective into the light. It showed the case of the Italian largest retail group during the Covid-19 pandemic emergency in April 2020. The decision of the government to impose a lockdown of all non-essential business activities compelled citizens to buy goods that they need only from retailers. Like other retailers, the largest supermarket chain in Italy quickly became a significant supplier of any type of goods, from food to non-food ones.

On the other hand, the increase in sales was not sufficiently balanced by easy access to procurement. The performance measurement system suffered under the influence of new pressures from the supply and distribution side. In concrete, the case study results show how managers faced both procurement and distribution challenges in the business. On the procurement side, the company suddenly realized serious difficulties in supplying food (such as yeast, flour, lemons, and tomato) and non-food (such as plastic bags) products. This was due to the increase in demand for some products by customers combined with the closure of traditional suppliers.

Similarly, the negotiation power with suppliers was reduced, and traditional marker partnerships were overthrown due to the mismatch of demand and supply. On the distribution side, on the other hand, variability and unpredictability of demand of all products in stores challenged distribution allocation. This was due to a sudden change in customers' preferences. Furthermore, the balance of the traditional sales between local retailers and hypermarkets was not maintained, with local stores experiencing a significant boost in sales at the expense of hypermarkets. Hypermarkets are typically found on the outskirts and industrial zones, whereas local retailers are typically found near densely populated residential areas. The performance measurement system suffered under the pressure of timely and dynamic data on the company situation during the crisis. KPIs on sales and lead times were affected by procurement challenges. Efficiency KPIs for procurement of some recently rare products suffered under the scarcity of products on the B2B markets that increased purchasing price and lead times while reducing quality. On the other side, algorithms forecasting sales per shop appeared incapable of accurate forecasting. This happened for many products as demand started to follow patterns unseen before. The repartition between the two sales channels (hypermarkets and local shops) changed utterly.

In this context, managers implemented several urgent solutions and adjustments to the performance measurement system. In the first place, sales KPIs were updated into new dynamics measurements considering the shortage of suppliers providing specific types of products. More timely reporting systems were implemented with constant updates to incorporate information about the pandemic situation. Purchase prices were set into a more compelling logic than efficiency as in regular times. Similarly, quality standards had to be slightly rebalanced in favour of some products' availability. The traditional pressure on the 'few suppliers' policies was eased to allow more dynamism and flexibility in finding suppliers. On the distribution side, algorithms were quickly remodelled in favour of more redistribution of local shops allocations and, in general, to allow more safety stock in shops.

Overall, managers stated that they quickly became aware of the importance of building a more dynamic KPIs system to better respond to emergencies. They underlined that the new way of thinking performance measurements could also be maintained in corporate strategy and further implemented in the future.

The results obtained from the case study in this chapter bring exciting insights into the managerial practice during the exception. It shows that management literature on performance measurement in times of emergency (Hohenstein, 2022; Parisi & Bekier, 2022; Rahman et al., 2021) should reflect on the vital need for supply-side chain performance measurement systems (Ivanov, 2020; Ivanov & Das, 2020; Paul & Chowdhury, 2021). In particular, there is a need for managers and management scholars to reflect on the importance of designing dynamic performance monitoring systems in advance. Such dynamism should be expressed in terms of the ability to simultaneously monitor the efficiency and effectiveness of supply chains and the rapidity with which monitoring systems can be adjusted to adapt to unexpected jolts such as the one brought on by the covid-19 pandemic.

CONCLUSION

Performance measurement systems help represent business processes and set objectives (Merchant & der Stede, 2017; Van gorp, 2005). Calculations and metrics (such as KPIs) support the management with relevant information picturing the business situation and dynamics (Chan & Chan, 2004; Parmenter, 2020). In emergencies, such as the one brought by the Covid-19 outbreak, performance management systems are challenged into new challenging scenarios (Hohenstein, 2022). These systems can be insufficient and untimely if their design does not include dynamic elements (Parisi & Bekier, 2022; Rahman et al., 2021).

The aim of the chapter was to uncover and analyse the challenges imposed by the Covid-19 to the retail sector. Furthermore, the chapter aims at depicting some possible solutions that could be implemented by managers in the retails sector to cope with these emerging unexpected difficulties.

This chapter reports the case study conducted in the largest food retailer in Italy during the covid-19 pandemic in April 2020. After the imposition of lockdown of all non-essential businesses by the Italian government in March 2022, Italian People suddenly could only rely on retail shops to source most kinds of goods. Managers of retailers, such as the one analysed in this chapter, experienced a promising increase in sales with mixed feelings. Although the pandemic brought opportunities for the sector, the retail company faced many difficulties in the procurement and distribution of goods. In addition to selecting suppliers and setting contractual conditions, procurement activities ensure products to be delivered to distributing centres. The distribution phase includes those activities meant to allocate and deliver products from distributing centres to shops. The performance monitoring system based on traditional efficiency KPIs was suddenly insufficient to manage the emergency. This was primarily due to a mismatch between demand and supply (especially in non-food products) and distribution forecasting challenges. The mismatch between demand and supply was caused by the fact that sales increased more than availability of products on the procurement side. Some kinds of products, from food to non-food ones, were seriously difficult to procure on the market, while customers increasingly requested them. Consequently, the negotiation power with suppliers was rapidly reduced in favour of suppliers. Traditional market relationships as well as consolidated negotiation positions were overthrown. On the distribution side, variability and unpredictability of demand of all products in stores challenged shops allocation. Local shops outperformed hypermarkets in terms of sales. This was an unexpected effect of the fact that hypermarkets are typically placed on the industrialized outskirts of cities, whereas local shops are typically found near densely populated residential areas.

The performance measurement system presented new difficulties in producing timely and dynamic data on the company situation during the crisis. Procurement challenges affected sales and lead times KPIs. Efficiency KPIs for procurement of products that suddenly became rare, were affected by the scarcity of products whose purchasing prices and lead times were rising while quality declined. Algorithms to allocate products between shops appeared incapable of accurate forecasting.

In this new and challenging scenario, some solutions were set up by the management. They implemented urgent adjustments to the performance measurement system. Sales KPIs were updated with new dynamics measurements that considered the scarcity of specific products and suppliers supplying them. The reporting systems were added with more timely information and constant updates to report about the pandemic situation. Purchase prices were refocused on effectiveness rather than efficiency as more usual in regular times. Quality standards had to be less binding in favour of products' availability. On the distribution side, algorithms had to be reprogrammed in favour of more allocations for local shops and to guarantee more safety stock in shops in general.

The findings obtained from this chapter's case study in the Italian retail sector bring insights into the managerial practice during time of exception. The aim of the chapter was addressed by analysis the practices and the dynamics emerged in response to the challenges brought by the pandemic inside the company. Top managers were listened to gather insights on how the pandemic affected the business and which solutions have been provided to deal with the situation. These findings show that the literature on performance measurement in times of emergency (Hohenstein, 2022; Parisi & Bekier, 2022; Rahman et al., 2021) might reflect on the crucial importance of performance measurement designed for the supply side of values chains (Ivanov, 2020; Ivanov & Das, 2020; Paul & Chowdhury, 2021). Specifically, there is an urgent need for management accounting scholars as well as corporate managers to reflect on the importance of allowing more dynamism in the performance monitoring systems designing process. This awareness should spur to action before a crisis breaks out, so that companies can be ready to cope with it. Such dynamism should be in terms of the ability to simultaneously monitor the efficiency and effectiveness of supply chains. In addition, performance monitoring systems should be ready to rapid adjusted to adapt to unexpected threats such as the ones brought on by the pandemic of Covid-19.

Limitations and Future Development

The present research is limited in the way in which it relies on a single case study. Although the most relevant player in the Italian retail sector was deeply analysed, the need to complete the picture with other competitors' perspectives remains.

This study concentrates on a single country. Italy was the first country and most relevantly hit by the pandemic in its first outbreak in spring 2020. The Italian government had to impose lockdown in Italy before than other countries. However, almost all western countries followed and adopted restrictions to prevent social proximity and to contain the spread of the pandemic. The perspective of this study could be interestingly extended to other countries around the world. The addition of investigations similar to this, conducted in other countries, will certainly complete the frame and return the phenomenon clearer.

The study focused merely on the supply challenges brought by the pandemic in the retail sector. It appears most useful to extend the analysis to costumers' perspectives and attitudes toward services provided by retail shops during times of crisis. Costumers' voice might reveal much of their evaluation of the results achieved by managers in the attempt to contain the threats brought by the pandemic to their company.

REFERENCES

Aberbach, J. D., & Rockman, B. A. (2002). Conducting and Coding Elite Interviews. *PS, Political Science & Politics*, *35*(4), 673–676. doi:10.1017/S1049096502001142

Aguinis, H., & Burgi-Tian, J. (2021). Talent management challenges during COVID-19 and beyond: Performance management to the rescue. *BRQ Business Research Quarterly*, *24*(3), 233–240. doi:10.1177/23409444211009528

Almeida, A., & Azevedo, A. (2016). A multi-perspective performance approach for complex manufacturing environments. *Journal of Innovation Management*, *4*(2), 125–155. doi:10.24840/2183-0606_004.002_0007

Barykin, S. Y., Kapustina, I. V., Kalinina, O. V., Dubolazov, V. A., Esquivel, C. A. N., Alyarovna, N. E., & Sharapaev, P. (2021). The sharing economy and digital logistics in retail chains: Opportunities and threats. *Academy of Strategic Management Journal*, *20*(2), 1–14.

Bazeley, P. (2014). *Qualitative data analysis with nvivo + the coding manual for qualitative researchers*. Sage Publications.

Burgos, D., & Ivanov, D. (2021). Food retail supply chain resilience and the COVID-19 pandemic: A digital twin-based impact analysis and improvement directions. *Transportation Research Part E, Logistics and Transportation Review*, *152*, 1–20. doi:10.1016/j.tre.2021.102412 PMID:34934397

Chan, A. P. C., & Chan, A. P. L. (2004). Key performance indicators for measuring construction success. *Benchmarking*, *11*(2), 203–221. doi:10.1108/14635770410532624

Cowling, M., Brown, R., & Rocha, A. (2020). Did you save some cash for a rainy COVID-19 day? The crisis and SMEs. *International Small Business Journal: Researching Entrepreneurship, 38*(7), 593–604. doi:10.1177/0266242620945102 PMID:35125601

De Vito, A., & Gómez, J.-P. (2020). Estimating the COVID-19 cash crunch: Global evidence and policy. *Journal of Accounting and Public Policy, 39*(2), 1–14. doi:10.1016/j.jaccpubpol.2020.106741

Drever, E. (2006). *Using semi-structured interviews in small-scale research: A teacher's guide*. The SCRE Centre.

Hartmann, N. N., & Lussier, B. (2020). Managing the sales force through the unexpected exogenous COVID-19 crisis. *Industrial Marketing Management, 88*, 101–111. doi:10.1016/j.indmarman.2020.05.005

Hohenstein, N.-O. (2022). Supply chain risk management in the COVID-19 pandemic: strategies and empirical lessons for improving global logistics service providers' performance. *The International Journal of Logistics Management.*

Ivanov, D. (2020). Predicting the impacts of epidemic outbreaks on global supply chains: A simulation-based analysis on the coronavirus outbreak (COVID-19/SARS-CoV-2) case. *Transportation Research Part E, Logistics and Transportation Review, 136*, 1–14. doi:10.1016/j.tre.2020.101922 PMID:32288597

Ivanov, D., & Das, A. (2020). Coronavirus (COVID-19/SARS-CoV-2) and supply chain resilience: A research note. *International Journal of Integrated Supply Management, 13*(1), 90–102. doi:10.1504/IJISM.2020.107780

Kim, J., Kim, J., & Wang, Y. (2021). Uncertainty risks and strategic reaction of restaurant firms amid COVID-19: Evidence from China. *International Journal of Hospitality Management, 92*, 1–21. doi:10.1016/j.ijhm.2020.102752 PMID:33223596

Kim, R. Y. (2020). The Impact of COVID-19 on Consumers: Preparing for Digital Sales. *IEEE Engineering Management Review, 48*(3), 212–218. doi:10.1109/EMR.2020.2990115

Marshall, C., & Rossman, G. B. (2016). Designing Qualitative Research. *Sage (Atlanta, Ga.).*

Merchant, K. A., & der Stede, W. A. (2017). *Management control systems performance measurement, evaluation, and incentives*. Pearson.

O'Dwyer, B. (2004). Qualitative data analysis: illuminating a process for transforming a 'messy' but 'attractive' 'nuisance. In *The real life guide to accounting research* (pp. 391–407). Elsevier. doi:10.1016/B978-008043972-3/50025-6

Parisi, C., & Bekier, J. (2022). Assessing and managing the impact of COVID-19: A study of six European cities participating in a circular economy project. *Accounting, Auditing & Accountability Journal, 35*(1), 97–107. doi:10.1108/AAAJ-08-2020-4837

Parmenter, D. (2020). *Key performance indicators : developing, implementing, and using winning KPIs*. Wiley.

Paul, S. K., & Chowdhury, P. (2021). A production recovery plan in manufacturing supply chains for a high-demand item during COVID-19. *International Journal of Physical Distribution & Logistics Management, 51*(2), 104–125. doi:10.1108/IJPDLM-04-2020-0127

Rahman, T., Moktadir, M. A., & Paul, S. K. (2021). Key performance indicators for a sustainable recovery strategy in health-care supply chains: COVID-19 pandemic perspective. *Journal of Asia Business Studies*.

Robinson, K. (1992). Accounting Numbers As "Inscription": Action At a Distance and the Development of Accounting. *Accounting, Organizations and Society, 17*(7), 685–708. doi:10.1016/0361-3682(92)90019-O

Schmidt, C. (2004). The analysis of semi-structured interviews. A Companion to Qualitative Research (pp. 253–258). Sage.

Smith, J. (1972). *Interviewing in market and social research.* Routledge & Kegan Paul.

Van gorp, J. C. (2005). Using key performance indicators to manage energy costs. *Strategic Planning for Energy and the Environment, 25*(2), 9–25.

Yin, R. K. (1983). *The Case Study Method: An Annotated Bibliography.* Sage.

Yuan, J., Zeng, A. Y., Skibniewski, M. J., & Li, Q. (2009). Selection of performance objectives and key performance indicators in public-private partnership projects to achieve value for money. *Construction Management and Economics, 27*(3), 253–270. doi:10.1080/01446190902748705

ENDNOTES

[1]   The Human Resources department faced new difficulties in managing people during the crisis. In the first place, HR managers had to implement practices to protect workers from the virus. Shift management was deeply influenced by sickness and quarantines as some workers got infected by the Covid-19 virus or some of their familiars were. On the other hand, HR department had to provide philological support to employees who manifested new diseases at work and life. Furthermore, HR managers should deal with complex relations with trade unions in which employees exigencies were to be balanced with business's.

[2]   The IT department of the company had to reorganize all servers in order to allow remote access to employees. They were asked to bring home the company's personal computers in order to continue working from home. In some cases, internet connections were not available to all and the IT service provide external internet providers to employees. However, the most challenging part was to make corporate data on servers available from outside in a secure way. The issue of security while moving 95% (around 1000 people) of the workforce from offices to houses had an important impact on data security. Furthermore, some servers were still physically installed in offices and VPN services had to be quickly implemented.

[3]   The stores had to be equipped with Plexiglas barriers at each checkout. Each store had to be equipped with a hand sanitizing point for customers and shopping carts. New staff members were introduced to support and control compliance with anti-infection regulations at the entrance and inside the stores.

Chapter 8
Analyzing Digital Transformation in Brazilian SMEs

Marcelo Amaral Dionisio
ⓘ https://orcid.org/0000-0001-6346-2307
Pontifical Catholic University of Rio de Janeiro (PUC-Rio), Brazil

ABSTRACT

The COVID-19 pandemic promoted a sudden impact on businesses across the globe, leaving strong concerns about how it will affect SMEs that contribute with 40% of GDP in emerging economies, where they already operate in challenging circumstances due to institutional voids and scarce resources, in a continuous struggle to survive. In this scenario, Brazilian SMEs accelerated their digital transformation (DT) to maintain their economic activity, moving from physical stores to the virtual environment using websites, social networks, and messaging applications, in a context where effective digital inclusion becomes essential, with the effective appropriation of digital technologies. The purpose of this work is to examine in 20 Brazilian SMEs, challenges, strategies, and activities they had faced to deal with this digital transformation. This chapter is expected to fill a gap in literature as studies into SME development through social media are still in the early stages and to be a practical contribution by demonstrating true challenges and results faced in this process.

INTRODUCTION

The COVID-19 pandemic promoted a sudden and violent impact on businesses across the globe, leaving strong concerns about how it will affect SMEs that contribute 40% of GDP in emerging economies, where entrepreneurs already operate in challenging circumstances because of institutional voids and scarce resource environments, in a continuous struggle to survive (M. A. Dionisio, 2021; Ionescu-Somers & Tarnawa, 2020; Klein & Todesco, 2021). In this scenario, many Brazilian SMEs, following a global trend, accelerated their digital transformation to maintain their economic activity, moving from physical stores to the virtual environment using websites, social networks, and messaging applications, in a

DOI: 10.4018/978-1-6684-6762-6.ch008

context where effective digital inclusion becomes essential to the continuity of their businesses (Klein & Todesco, 2021; Priyono & Moin, 2020; Sebrae, 2021).

Digital transformation (DT) is defined as "the initiative of firms to use new capabilities by leveraging digital technologies to transform organizational strategies and operations" (Priyono & Moin, 2020; p.1). Hence, the transformation of SME's business model supported by digital technology has been perceived as a suitable response to the disruptive changes caused by the COVID-19 pandemic, which triggered a race for fast digitalization to adapt to the new market realities including new consumer habits, and new ways to market and sell products, where transactions using technology are practical, easy, flexible, and no longer need, as before, to rely on face to face transactions (Klein & Todesco, 2021; Nguyen, Sukunesan, & Huynh, 2021; Priyono & Moin, 2020; Rizka, Hida, & Dewi, 2021).

What is seen in Brazil is the wide use of social networks (e.g., Instagram, Facebook, and WhatsApp) to promote and directly sell products and services, with the use of bank apps to receive payments (Klein & Todesco, 2021; Sebrae, 2021). But, although companies have been able to successfully adapt and grow with the support of digital technologies, the journey to becoming digital is challenging, most of all for small and medium enterprises (SMEs), especially considering the lack of necessary resources, skills, commitment, and proper understanding of digital opportunities (Matarazzo, Penco, Profumo, & Quaglia, 2021; Priyono & Moin, 2020). To overcome these difficulties entrepreneurs must build various capabilities, requiring a change in management and vision, with the acquisition of new organizational and marketing capabilities to adequately advance in this new and challenging scenario (Matarazzo et al., 2021). Nevertheless, studies into SMEs development through social media are still in the early stages, with few studies analyzing the evolution of SME's management and innovation aspects, especially the adoption process, considering that SMEs face increased difficulty in adopting new technologies along with the urgency to reach sales results (Matarazzo et al., 2021; Nguyen et al., 2021; Roth Cardoso, Dantas Gonçalves, Dambiski Gomes de Carvalho, & Gomes de Carvalho, 2020). Hence, to fill this literature gap, we propose the following research questions:

RQ 1: How does digital transformation change the processes of SMEs?

RQ 2: What are the most important capabilities necessary for the success of DT in SMEs?

RQ 3: How did the emergency adoption of DT help in the development of activities and increase sales?

To address these questions, we utilized a multiple case study approach, considered appropriate for understanding how phenomena develop in an organizational context (Yin, 2014). The research was conducted with 20 Brazilian SMEs that went to DT to promote and sell their products and services, through semi-structured interviews with their founders. Then all cases were analyzed and classified into five groups adapted from a typology proposed by Walley & Taylor (2002) that identifies four types of entrepreneurs: innovative opportunist, visionary, Ad hoc, and maverick. We also included an additional type that we identified as unrealistic to complete our analysis. This work aims to examine the challenges, strategies, and activities these entrepreneurs have faced to deal with this digital transformation. We expect to offer a theoretical contribution considering that studies into SMEs development through social media are still in the early stages, along with a practical contribution by analyzing the effectiveness of the use of social media, by demonstrating true challenges and results in these SMEs faced in this process.

This chapter is structured as follows: we present a brief literature review of the transition from SMEs to DT and dynamic capabilities, followed by a detailed description of our research method, including the description of our cases and their classification, to proceed with a discussion and finalizing with concluding remarks.

THE IMPACT OF COVID-19 IN SMEs

The pandemic of coronavirus imposed business around the world lockdowns that affected companies, especially SMEs (small and medium-sized enterprises) which attributes make them more vulnerable to the effects of this crisis. They generally have scarce financial resources, gaps in specialized knowledge both managerial and technological and lack of human resources which the literature calls the liability of smallness, which means that the smaller the firm, the more vulnerable it is to internal and external events. Some also face a liability of newness, meaning that the youngest companies tend to be more vulnerable than older ones (Klein & Todesco, 2021; Stinchcombe, 1965).

In Brazil, the coronavirus pandemic changed the functioning of 5.3 million SMEs, an equivalent of 31% of the total. Another 10.1 million temporarily stopped activities, according to a survey carried out by Sebrae. As a result of the crisis, SMEs had to lay off on average three employees in a scenario where they usually have from 10 to 49 employees in total (M. A. Dionisio, 2021; Sebrae, 2020). This impact is even worse considering that the financial situation of most companies was already bad before the Covid-19 crisis and that personnel costs appear among the main expenses of most SMEs, impacting directly their living conditions (M. A. Dionisio, 2021; Ionescu-Somers & Tarnawa, 2020; Sebrae, 2020).

DIGITAL TRANSFORMATION IN SMEs

Technologies allow communication between people in different parts of the world and the digitalization of business routines, promoting a cultural change in the way companies provide their services and sell their products (Pereira & Rodrigues, 2021). Along with this transformation, we observe the enormous growth of social media, not only in terms of users but as a consolidated channel to communicate and sell products, with Ad spending projected to reach US$173,988m in 2022, with an estimate growing rate of 9.77% a year, resulting in a projected market volume of US$252,569m by 2026 (Lindsey-Mullikin & Borin, 2017; Statista, 2022).

The difficulties imposed by the pandemic triggered a race for fast digitalization to adapt to the new relation between supply and demand, where SMEs are searching for fast digital adaptation to a new market and consumer demands (Klein & Todesco, 2021; Sebrae, 2021). New business methods became widely used such as the use of social networks (e.g. Facebook, Instagram, WhatsApp) to promote sales, and the use of bank apps to collect payments, where some SMEs paid for the first time for online advertisements, for some of them it was the first time they advertised at all (Klein & Todesco, 2021; Sebrae, 2020, 2021). A study concluded that few businesses were prepared for this sudden digital transformation because it demands changes in the business model, which in practical terms happened abruptly (Pereira & Rodrigues, 2021). The literature claims that to efficiently adapt companies need to develop an adaptive capacity to change strategies and renew core competencies to maintain or obtain competitive advantages, which happens through knowledge creation, dissemination, and implementation (Sirén et al. 2020). So we posit that SMEs must adopt digital technologies, which have a significant impact on their development, and therefore must prepare to obtain the necessary skills to efficiently achieve the results these changes must offer such as reduced costs, improvement of supply chains, and more easily sell products and services (Wysokińska, 2021).

EVALUATING ENTREPRENEURIAL MANAGEMENT IN SMEs

Increased competition and a faster pace of technological change over the years have forced all types of businesses to adapt for survival and growth. This ability to pursue new opportunities while not undermining their existing advantages is called ambidexterity which in turn, is encompassed by a larger framework known as dynamic capabilities that emphasize flexibility and adaptability and their efforts to act strategically (Lampikoski, Westerlund, Rajala, & Möller, 2014; Teece, 2009, 2016).

In SMEs, dynamic capabilities see the owners as the main actor in an organization, responsible to bring about changes in business models, especially in times of uncertainty. Dynamic capabilities can enable a business to move its activities toward high-demand uses, develop new capabilities, and effectively coordinate internal and external resources to address and shape-shifting business environments (Teece, 2009, 2016). Literature has found that SMEs face increased difficulty in adopting new technologies due to the lack of resources, skills, human resources, and proper understanding of digital opportunities. To overcome these difficulties, SMEs must build various capabilities that reside in the entrepreneur. The ability to perceive new digital opportunities will only work efficiently with the development of these capabilities, especially considering the importance of digital technologies as competitive tools for SMEs. Digital technologies provide support for value creation and customer engagement, however, the use of technologies requires change management and a vision based on the acquisition of new managerial capabilities (Matarazzo et al., 2021; Stead & Stead, 2013; Vargo & Lusch, 2004).

An analysis of general management patterns among Brazilian SMEs confirmed this idea, as it revealed significant differences in businesses with higher levels of management dimensions, corroborating the relevance of management to small business outcomes. Concerning efficiency, higher management dimension levels were related to higher innovation and higher improvement levels in most dimensions, reinforcing the need for continuous development of managerial skills among entrepreneurs and SMEs (Roth Cardoso et al., 2020).

RESEARCH METHOD

This work utilizes illustrative case studies resulting from a consulting service to support start-ups encompassing more than 40 SMEs that were having different problems sustaining their business and overcoming the impacts of Covid-19 pandemics. A case study is a research strategy that creates theoretical constructs and propositions, providing rich and empirical descriptions of a phenomenon (Eisenhardt & Graebner, 2007; Yin, 2014). Therefore, data were collected through interviews that occurred exclusively online between October and December 2021. Interviews were conducted with founders and in a few cases with supporting staff, and they lasted on average four hours, split into a maximum of three meetings. The interviews were complemented by the exchange of e-mails and supported by secondary data such as news, websites, social network, and online searches that made it possible to collect empirical information, adding rigor to explore our research. After finishing the consulting process, 20 SMEs were selected because they reflected a necessity to review and improve their digital transformation strategies, which are tightly scoped within the context of existing theory, but the qualitative data would offer valuable insights to build theory based on their empirical evidence (Eisenhardt & Graebner, 2007).

The data analysis adopted an induct-deductive approach where the researcher took a constant iteration between data collection and analysis with the focus on theory development. After analyzing and

Table 1. Summary of cases and classification

Company	Segment	Classification
CAE	Local Crafts	ad hoc
TSA	Environmental services	ad hoc
ERG	Architecture & Design	ad hoc
BOS	Fashion	ad hoc
DIB	Eco Diapers	Maverick
MAR	Sustainable products	Maverick
TAB	Sanitation	Maverick
REC	Recycling	Maverick
BIA	Cultural events	opportunist
INF	Influencer platform	opportunist
LUP	Info Products platform	opportunist
BOL	Child clothes	opportunist
APR	Education 3.0	unrealistic
GER	Recycling	unrealistic
COM	Ecolodge	unrealistic
MAR	Sales platform	unrealistic
PRO	Organic food	visionary
BAZ	Thrift Store	visionary
PAI	Cultural events	visionary
WII	Technology	visionary

identifying each company's problems we classified them based on the typology proposed by Walley & Taylor (2002), which categorized green entrepreneurs into four types: innovative opportunist, visionary, Ad hoc, and maverick. We adapted their typology and included an additional type that we identified as unrealistic to complete our analysis. The final list of cases and their classification is presented in table 1. To protect the identity of the companies we are identifying them by the first three letters of their real name.

Based on Walley & Taylor (2002) we defined ´opportunist' as the entrepreneur who spots a niche or opportunity, influenced mainly by other drivers, such as competition, or even necessity, which is the case considering the demands imposed by lockdowns and other restrictions. The 'visionary´ is the type of entrepreneur who embraces a transformative and long-term orientation, operating at the forefront vision of a new future. The 'maverick' is characterized by a mission-orientated entrepreneur with a focus on friends, networks, and personal experiences with visions to change the world with alternative-style businesses. The 'ad hoc' category is financially motivated and is influenced mostly by personal networks, family, and friends. Finally, the 'unrealistic' entrepreneur has dreams of grandeur and believes that digital transformation is the key to offering extraordinary opportunities and results, but that has no practical application, although he would not accept this point of view.

FINDINGS

Our findings will be presented in groups based on the different classifications proposed. We will then explain our classification and briefly describe each case and its main problems.

Ad Hoc: CAE, TSA, ERG and BOS

These SMEs in general do not take a complete digital transformation. They are characterized as ad hoc, because according to the definition, their key motivation is financial, especially influenced by their networks – co-workers, friends, etc. that claim that the digital world can offer limitless opportunities. CAE is an association of artisans that jointly sell and advertise their products. During the Covid pandemic they needed urgently to increase their sales thus they set up channels on Instagram and Facebook to communicate and sell their products. TSA is an engineering company that offers environmental services that also saw the internet as a way to connect to new customers and communicate their services. Nevertheless, due to the idiosyncrasies of this business, its CEO does not know exactly how to proceed with his digital transformation. He claims that "the decision-makers are still 'old school' so although I feel the need to invest in social media, especially on LinkedIn, I have the feeling I will be connecting with people that will only help me in a few years, but my need is for now!". ERG has an established business of solar panels, but the perspective of building a platform to sell "solar credits" seemed tempted for them. Nevertheless, the idea is not clear and of difficult implementation. They could be almost considered an "unrealistic" type of business, but considering that they plan to complement their revenues, we included them in this ad hoc category. Finally, BOS has a fashion business that produces bags and backpacks and needs to increase its sales. Their CEO claims that "My biggest problem today is lack of time and human resources to help me out" so he believes that a digital transformation could help him to address this issue, even though he does not know exactly how.

Maverick: DIB, MPE, TAB and REC

The 'maverick' is characterized by a mission-orientated entrepreneur with a focus on personal networks, and experiences with visions to change the world with alternative-style businesses. In this case, we selected four social enterprises that aim to combine their business with a purpose and use the digital transformation to increase their sales and connect with target customers, being able to communicate their social impact. These SMEs perceive the digital transformation differently, as they see it as a compliment and support to their business. Nonetheless, they are still dealing with difficulties in better use and effectively exploiting these opportunities, especially considering that some of them have an urgent need to increase sales. DIB produces eco diapers and pads, while MPE produces bags and accessories with used fishnets, generating income for local fishermen and helping the environment. They both see the social networks as a tool to communicate the benefit of their products, in the case of DIB, how to use and in the case of MPE how they positively impact both the environment and their community. The problem with them is that they do not have a previous management background, they are mostly focused on the purpose and the desire to generate social impact. MPE was created by oceanographers, and one of their partners claims that "It scares me! There are many things I need to do, and I don't know how to take advantage of the opportunities that arise". TAB develops ecological sanitation projects for shantytowns and rural communities and aims to use DT to develop quality sales materials and improve their website. One of the partners claims that they "always have the passion for the social impact", but they need urgently to find recurrent sales and define the best sales strategy to consolidate their business. Finally, REC is an incubated startup from a local university from a smaller town in Rio de Janeiro state that also needs to according to its owners "structure our commercial side and expand to Rio de Janeiro (city)" so they also appealed to DT to encourage the population to direct their waste for recycling, their main business.

Opportunist: BIA, INF, LUP, BOL

Opportunists are entrepreneurs who spot an opportunity, influenced mainly by other drivers, to grow their business. In this case, we consider that this opportunity is the use of DT, believed to be the ultimate solution for all their business problems, heavily increased by lockdowns and other restrictions imposed by the Covid-19 pandemic. Their vision and actions are very close to unrealistic, but the character of their goals and in some cases the possibility of success granted them this classification. Both BIA and LUP are in a very incipient stage, with no clear view of how to structure their ideas, and they plan to create a platform to structure and sell their services. The former wants to offer diverse cultural events for her local community (e.g. sports, theater, gastronomy, etc.), and the latter to launch a platform to allow small computer stores to sell online. They have no formal management background and suffer to define their business model, with a lack of focus and segment to implement their ideas. The case of LUP is even more serious as it already spent money to implement its platform, but due to lack of experience, most of it will become sunk investment as it is constantly reviewing its business model. He claims that "opting to start investing to accelerate things was not a good idea, that I now regret, but I believe in my idea and want to move on with my plans". INF has a more structured idea to connect emergent social influencers with SMEs. The idea seems promising, but very opportunistic in itself, worsened but the founder's lack of management skills and her fear of investing in her idea. Finally, BOL is a brick-and-mortar retailer of children's clothes that because of the lockdown decided to focus its sales on Instagram. As their move was too sudden and they disregarded their existing business, results were not as expected.

Unrealistic: APR, GER, COM and MAR

We created this category for the entrepreneur with dreams of grandeur that believes digital transformation is the key to offering extraordinary opportunities and results, but whose ideas, in reality, have no practical application, even though they would not accept this point of view. In the case of APR the founder aims to use his academic experience to launch an education platform with a focus on STEM, which is a good idea, but the concept is not clear, and the beta version is poor as he has no IT experience and no budget to invest accordingly and most of all it is not clear who are going to be his costumers, so in practical terms, APR is on the verge of bankruptcy. His founder declared "We have no more ways to invest, we have debts, but our idea is already applied in Canada in more than 30k people. Our idea has already won an award, so I truly believe in its potential". GER is another case that departure from a valid concept but without adequate business support. The team is very young and inexperienced, which led to a lack of a business plan and a definition of who is and how to approach their customers. It is another case of a business that needs a fast turnaround or will cease to exist shortly. One of the partners said, "We have until March 2022 to structure ourselves or we will think of a new path for each of us". COM is a different case, the founder has an established B&B with an ecological proposal, but she is willing to launch a platform to teach and certify other hotels and B&Bs to become ecological and make a lot of money with that. The reality is that her own business is not fully eco and again her project is based on the possibilities offered by the DT itself without a clear project. Another business that is focused to grow based on the platform concept is MAR, which today is a retail store where its owner wants to build a platform that combines the concept of Uber and Amazon to expand the sales of his products by hiring independent salesmen to sell his actual products and in the future sell pretty much everything in a large marketplace. He believes that the sole existence of the platform will be enough to kick off his business, even though he does not know any details about how to get partners, who are going to be his customers and why would they buy with him instead of on the existing competition that is massive.

Visionary: PRO, BAZ, PAI and WII

We understand that the 'visionary´ has a long-term orientation and the DT is part of a strategy that aims to transform and allow its business to grow. These entrepreneurs are more flexible and open to new ideas and are willing to mix the use of digital tools with traditional approaches such as in-store promotions, use of salesforce, and partnerships. PRO produces and sells soy-based protein with a focus on food conscient consumers. Although he is struggling to create awareness of his products and increase his base of customers, his DT is planned along with a complete strategy based on partnerships with nutritionists, retailers, and chefs along with a sales effort to map potential retailers and distributors, stimulate trial and communicate benefits and usage of his products. During his consulting, he was always open and curious, willing to try different approaches to grow and consolidate his business. BAZ is a thrift Store based in a small city near Rio de Janeiro Capital and with both the DT and a series of partnerships and participation in events (e.g. fairs) has seen her business become a success. Her main problem is her fear of losing control if her business becomes too big, the owner said "I'm afraid the business will grow too much and I am no longer able to implement all my ideas", which she has, and she is planning to create a podcast, deliver some of her products to nursing homes and other institutions that support vulnerable groups, and many others with the clear vision that the social media are tools to help her. PAI develops cultural events and it exists since 2014. Heavily impacted by the COVID-19 pandemic with the decreased number of face-to-face events, the owner decided to turn her business into a service provider, supporting smaller cultural promoters with her market experience. She has a very managerial perspective and along with the power of social media to create awareness of her events, a willingness to search for opportunities to consolidate her business. WII is a tech startup, created in a local university offering solutions and analytics to help cities become smart, resilient, and sustainable. At this moment they are aiming to professionalize all its procedures with the ambition to scale its business. It is another case of a company with a long-term perspective and a more professional vision. One of the partners stated that "We need to become more business-like instead of solely technical, and thus structure our salesforce, develop our business model and define how to measure our impact".

DISCUSSION

These cases, despite their classification, presented SMEs that were heavily impacted by the Covid-19 pandemics and needed to change to survive this serious crisis. Overall, they all implemented a digital strategy that to succeed, needed to be balanced with their realities, and should not be considered a solution on its own. They follow the profile presented by the literature with limited financial resources, gaps in managerial and technological knowledge, and lack of human resources, living both the liability of smallness and liability of newness, implying that to survive they needed to build their dynamic capabilities to face their difficulty in adopting new technologies.

In general, their digital transformation was based mostly on the use of social media (e.g. Facebook, Instagram, WhatsApp) to create awareness, promote and sell their products and services. In most cases, it was their first contact with digital advertising, and overall, most SMEs needed to increase sales very fast. In this scenario, the lack of managerial capability, that would allow them to introduce more competitive strategies and identify better market opportunities has become more clear (M. Dionisio, Pinho, & Macedo, 2020). This lack of management capabilities was concentrated on three main problems within their digital transformation strategies: sales problems, marketing problems, and a platform perspective.

Sales Problems

The main challenges faced by SMEs during the COVID-19 pandemic were the accelerated transition towards more digitalized firms and the digitalization of sales for the firms' survival. But for a positive result, the digitalization of the sales function must include the redesign of its distribution and sales channels from retail and boutique shops to online marketing, and this is where most of the problems were concentrated (Priyono & Moin, 2020). Despite the benefits that digital sales may provide, it is crucial to align digital strategies with a sales plan based on traditional procedures such as an active sales force, sales promotions, and price strategies. This idea that digital sales would offer an increase in sales by itself can be very misleading and compromise the survival of different SMEs. In our cases we see many companies in need to develop their sales strategies. The ad hoc group is the one that better deals with this challenge, as it is clear that DT is either an opportunity or a complement of their existing strategies. In the case of mavericks, they are in their totality a group of social enterprises, so they need urgently to balance their social impact with stronger managerial capabilities, not only in sales but in all areas to correctly define their target customers, sales channels, etc. This is the same problem that opportunist faces, as they see DT as the ultimate solution for their problems. The most impactful case is BOL which completely replaced its retail store with an Instagram store, but due to its structure and location, they have much more potential to sell through its store than through Instagram. They could implement strategies such as delivery and pick up, and heavily communicate to their own and neighboring towns to whom they would much easily provide a quality service. The visionary SMEs have this perspective more clearly, but this is the right moment to develop new capabilities to strengthen their business.

Marketing Problem

The literature identifies five elements in a social media marketing strategy: advertising, sales promotion, public relations, personal selling, and direct marketing (Rizka et al., 2021). Instead, what we observed was the use of social media mostly to display their products and promote sales. This is more evident when we realize that many SMEs demonstrated a huge difficulty to design their ads. They rarely followed an integrated campaign, based on a theme or in a plan, knowing exactly what to communicate and most of all, it was very difficult for them to correctly target their audience, despite the many tools the different systems offer. We observed a general idea that the more people they communicate to the better, not considering that in this way, considering the small amount they were willing to invest (usually the minimum - around US$ 10 a week), they would have their message lost in a world of competitors. Thus

SMEs must know exactly who and where are their customers, to efficiently reach their targets and step by step increase their market growth and penetration. All groups need to improve their marketing skills and refine their marketing strategies if they want to succeed in the long term. We have a very positive case, as BAZ implemented a Christmas campaign for the first time with a structured weekly plan based on four different pieces focused on a narrow selected target in her advertising on both Facebook and Instagram and a strategy that included a sales promotion, a social impact activity, advertising of new products, which she complemented with in-store communication. Results exceeded her target by 20%, a goal she initially found very hard to reach.

Platform Perspective

The recent proliferation of digital platforms had a significant impact on firm strategy across a wide array of industries. Famous examples such as eBay which allows buyers and sellers from very different places to trade with each other, and Airbnb which facilitates transactions among property owners and seekers of short-term accommodations have awakened the creativity of many entrepreneurs to follow this successful trend. Nevertheless, it is imperative to recognize the complexity to implement and coordinating strategies to successfully create and capture value from this model. Platforms are embodied in software and a technological interface, based on four conceptual themes: network effects and implications, platform ecosystem, platforms complements and users, and platform governance, which demonstrates the sophistication of this model (McIntyre, Srinivasan, & Chintakananda, 2021; Rietveld & Schilling, 2021).

Unfortunately, many of our entrepreneurs see the platform model as an alternative to succeed with their DT, leading to plans that seem way beyond their capacity to successfully implement it, especially considering their investments and management capabilities. This is the case of two SMEs in the opportunist group – BIA and LUP and three from the unrealistic group – APR, COM, and MAR. Their main miscalculation, in the case of APR, LUP and BIA concerns the difficulty of a startup with this kind of model, considering their limitations, and in the case of MAR and COM the need to further consolidate their existing business before moving to a platform model. In my opinion, this is a very risky strategy that although may reflect some good ideas, face a very complex context that prevents them to succeed.

CONCLUDING REMARKS

This study observed the impact of fast digital transformation on SMEs in Brazil. We conclude that DT changed processes and in most cases offered an important alternative to increase sales and better engage and communicate with customers, which was very important and necessary due to the new demands imposed by the covid-19 pandemics where customers increased significantly their digital purchases. Nevertheless, it became very clear that management capabilities to overcome their limitations, not only in terms of smallness or newness, but especially in terms of knowledge, financial and human resources are crucial to efficiently allow them to introduce more competitive strategies, and identify better market opportunities. We have seen in our cases that sometimes the DT itself is not enough to increase sales or recover business in times of crisis. Only a well-planned strategy, aligned with the business resources, with a long-term perspective, will draw the path for growth and survival, in this very important segment of business in any society.

REFERENCES

Dionisio, M., Pinho, J. C., & Macedo, I. M. (2020). Resourced-based View and Internationalization in Social Enterprises : An exploratory study from Ashoka's Globalizer in Brazil. In International Marketing Trends (pp. 1–11). IGI Global.

Dionisio, M. A. (2021). The Impact of COVID-19: A Major Crisis or Just Another One? In *Cases on Small Business Economics and Development During Economic Crises* (pp. 207–217). IGI Global. doi:10.4018/978-1-7998-7657-1.ch010

Eisenhardt, K. M., & Graebner, M. (2007). Theory Building From Cases: Opportunities and Challenges. *Academy of Management Journal*, *50*(1), 25–32. doi:10.5465/amj.2007.24160888

Ionescu-Somers, A., & Tarnawa, A. (2020). *Diagnosing COVID-19 Impacts on Entrepreneurship Exploring policy remedies for recovery*. Global Monitor. Retrieved from https://www.gemconsortium.org/reports/covid-impact-report

Klein, V. B., & Todesco, J. L. (2021). COVID-19 crisis and SMEs responses : The role of digital transformation. *Knowledge and Process Management*, *28*(2), 117–133. doi:10.1002/kpm.1660

Lampikoski, T., Westerlund, M., Rajala, R., & Möller, K. (2014). Green innovation games: Value-creation strategies for corporate sustainability. *California Management Review*, *57*(1), 88–116. doi:10.1525/cmr.2014.57.1.88

Lindsey-Mullikin, J., & Borin, N. (2017). Why strategy is key for successful social media sales. *Business Horizons*, *60*(4), 473–482. doi:10.1016/j.bushor.2017.03.005

Matarazzo, M., Penco, L., Profumo, G., & Quaglia, R. (2021). Digital transformation and customer value creation in Made in Italy SMEs : A dynamic capabilities perspective. *Journal of Business Research, 123*(February), 642–656. doi:10.1016/j.jbusres.2020.10.033

McIntyre, D. P., Srinivasan, A., & Chintakananda, A. (2021). The persistence of platforms: The role of network, platform, and complementor attributes. *Long Range Planning*, *54*(5), 101987. doi:10.1016/j.lrp.2020.101987

Nguyen, V.-H., Sukunesan, S., & Huynh, M. (2021). Analyzing Australian SME Instagram Engagement via Web Scraping. *Pacific Asia Journal of the Association for Information Systems*, *13*(2), 11–43. doi:10.17705/1pais.13202

Pereira, G., & Rodrigues, D. A. (2021). Transformação digital em pequenos negócios no contexto da pandemia da COVID-19: uma revisão da literatura. *Revista de Gestão Do Unilasalle*, 1–11.

Priyono, A., & Moin, A. (2020). *Identifying Digital Transformation Paths in the Business Model of SMEs during the COVID-19 Pandemic*. Academic Press.

Rietveld, J., & Schilling, M. A. (2021). Platform Competition: A Systematic and Interdisciplinary Review of the Literature. *Journal of Management*, *47*(6), 1528–1563. doi:10.1177/0149206320969791

Rizka, A., Hida, N., & Dewi, Y. R. (2021). Marketing Strategies Through Instagram to Increase Sales. In BISTIC (Vol. 193, pp. 273–277). Academic Press.

Roth Cardoso, H. H., Dantas Gonçalves, A., Dambiski Gomes de Carvalho, G., & Gomes de Carvalho, H. (2020). Evaluating innovation development among Brazilian micro and small businesses in view of management level: Insights from the local innovation agents program. *Evaluation and Program Planning, 80*(December), 101797. doi:10.1016/j.evalprogplan.2020.101797

Sebrae. (2020). *O impacto da pandemia de coronavírus nos pequenos negócios.* Author.

Sebrae. (2021). *O Impacto da pandemia de coronavírus nos Pequenos Negócios – 13ª edição.* Author.

Sirén, C., Hakala, H., Wincent, J., & Grichnik, D. (2016). Breaking the Routines: Entrepreneurial Orientation, Strategic Learning, Firm Size, and Age. *Long Range Planning.* Advance online publication. doi:10.1016/j.lrp.2016.09.005

Statista. (2022). *Social Media Advertising.* Retrieved February 26, 2022, from https://www.statista.com/outlook/dmo/digital-advertising/social-media-advertising/worldwide

Stead, J. G., & Stead, W. E. (2013). The Coevolution of Sustainable Strategic Management in the Global Marketplace. *Organization & Environment, 26*(2), 162–183. doi:10.1177/1086026613489138

Stinchcombe, A. L. (1965). Social structure and organizations. In Handbook of Organizations. Academic Press.

Teece, D. J. (2009). *Dynamic capabilities and strategic management.* Academic Press.

Teece, D. J. (2016). Dynamic capabilities and entrepreneurial management in large organizations: Toward a theory of the (entrepreneurial) firm. *European Economic Review, 86*, 202–216. doi:10.1016/j.euroecorev.2015.11.006

Vargo, S. L., & Lusch, R. F. (2004). Evolving to a New Dominant Logic. *English, 68*(January), 1–17.

Walley, L. E. E., & Taylor, D. W. (2002). Opportunists, Champions, Mavericks? A Typology of Green Entrepreneurs. *Greener Management International.* doi:10.9774/GLEAF.3062.2002.su.00005

Wysokińska, Z. (2021). A review of the impact of the digital transformation on the global and European economy. *Comparative Economic Research, 24*(3), 75–92. doi:10.18778/1508-2008.24.22

Yin, R. K. (2014). Applied social research methods series: Vol. 5. *Case study research : design and methods.* doi:10.1097/FCH.0b013e31822dda9e

Chapter 9
Dialectics of Self–Movement of Resilient Companies in the Economy and Society Post COVID–19:
Patterns of Organizational Transformations of Networking Interactions

Andrey I. Pilipenko

ⓘD https://orcid.org/0000-0001-9446-345X

The Russian Presidential Academy of National Economy and Public Administration, Russia

Zoya I. Pilipenko

ⓘD https://orcid.org/0000-0001-5734-5673

Bank of Russia, Russia

Olga I. Pilipenko

ⓘD https://orcid.org/0000-0001-5734-5673

The Russian Presidential Academy of National Economy and Public Administration, Russia

ABSTRACT

The COVID-19 global pandemic had a shock effect on all spheres of human activities: technology, society, and economy. They are distinguished by the fact that they are structural integrities capable of self-movement. All systemic changes in the economy before COVID-19 are interpreted in terms of statics and, post pandemic, in dynamics. Self-sufficient companies are the main drivers of modern system formation processes. They form the entire structure of interactions in static economic systems, mediating the mechanism of their self-organization. Their functions of "creative destruction" of organizational interactions mediate the mechanism of self-movement of systems both in statics and in dynamics. A model of the structure formation in the economy by resilient companies is presented as horizontal structure interactions of dialectical pairs and hierarchical structural levels according to the upward and downward causation principles. The mechanism of system self-movement is regulated by the dialectical laws.

DOI: 10.4018/978-1-6684-6762-6.ch009

INTRODUCTION

The COVID-19 global pandemic had a shock effect on all spheres of human activities: in technology, in society, in the economic system, etc. In fact, all of a sudden, a situation was formed that was associated with the end of order and the beginning of chaos against the backdrop of increasing uncertainty, negatively affected the existing networking interaction (Prigogine, and Stengers, 1983; Haken, 1977; Arnold, 1975,1979). As a result, the ongoing changes in man-made systems need to be rethought and theoretically re-understood. The dialectical approach (Hegel, 1892; Schelling, 1993; Marx, 1995; Vernadsky, 1998) and system interpretation (Bertalanffy, 1968; Guckenheimer, 1973; Thom, 1974; Hacken, 1977) of the processes of organizing human activity enabled the authors to form a more or less adequate picture of system formation in the economy. The use of the methodological approaches outlined above made it possible to determine the obvious dialectic of interaction between the economy and self-sufficient companies, which are a dialectical pair in the face of the system and its backbone elements. The search for the laws of their complication (Arthur, 2009, 2013) led the authors to the highlighting tectological principles of the organization of networking interactions in the economic systems (Bogdanov, 1934). The treatment of self-sufficient companies (Manyika, at al., 2021; Economist Impact, 2022) as the backbone elements made it possible to consider them as the main drivers of system formation processes (Schumpeter, 1961), which are based on the patterns of change of networking interactions.

Systemic ideas about the complexity of human-created organizations at the macro level predetermined the need to consider them in the processes of static and dynamic changes (Frisch, 1933; Slutsky, 1937; Schumpeter, 1961; Robinson, 1980; Clark, 2007; Pilipenko, 2021; Khosrow-Pour, 2022). The complication of a static system in the economy was mediated by companies that strengthened its integrity and stability through the multiplication of horizontal and vertical structural relationships. The reverse side of the complication of the economic system's structure became its growing fragility (Minsky, 2008; Taleb, 2007, 2012). It was this characteristic that ultimately predetermined the limit of the complication of the economic system in statics or of its self-organization. In this context, the ability of self-sufficient companies to Schumpeterian "creative destruction" was manifested. They mediated the action of the dialectical laws of unity and struggle of opposites and the transition of quantitative changes into qualitative ones in the processes of self-organization of the economy in statics. Such a theoretical approach allowed the authors to find explanations for the changes in networking interactions that occur in economic systems with the onset of the COVID-19 pandemic. Moreover, the approach of a static economy to its limit state, beyond which uncertainty grows, was noted by such authors as Roger Bootle (2009), Carmen M. Reinhart, and Kenneth S. Rogoff (2009), Branko Milanovic (2019), Eric Lonergan, and Mark Blyth (2020), Klaus, Schwab, and Malleret Thierry (2020); World Economic Forum experts (2020, 2020a) and many others.

The uncertainty of the future economic system, according to the authors, is associated first of all, with new objects of exchange, with its other participants, a change in the quality of exchange processes in the course of creating new networking interactions by self-sufficient companies. This, according to the authors, distinguishes the specifics of constructing the contours of the future economic system in its dynamic state. In other words, self-sufficient companies destroy the structural ties they have created in a static economy and are called upon to form new structures for a dynamic economy, realizing the operation of the dialectical law of negation of negation (Pilipenko, et al., 2022). Moreover, this process was initiated by COVID-19, and while approaching the end of the pandemic, the rate of formation of new structural interactions will only increase.

The issue of singling out resilient companies as backbone elements in the economic system, both in statics and in dynamics, has not only theoretical but also practical significance. It is for this reason that they are presented in the title of the chapter. So far, there are not enough statistical data and the analysis period is short, therefore, it is only possible to substantiate theoretically those characteristics of self-sufficient companies that distinguish them from all other private business organizations (Gjaja, et al., 2020; Feber, et al., 2022). The authors proceeded from theoretical concepts based on dialectical logic, systemic laws, the principles of tectology and the theory of complexity of the economy. This made it possible to conceptually highlight the qualities that should be inherent in companies capable of fulfilling the role of backbone elements of the new post-COVID-19 integrity in the economy. It is about modern large and the largest companies that have managed not only to maintain their market positions in a pandemic, but even improve them in a number of cases. Moreover, if we ignore the market factors of the growing demand for their products, then in the vast majority they turned out to be successful, because their CEOs were able to quickly understand the fundamental changes in the economy, society and technology and quickly get involved in their implementation (Hunt, et al., 2018; Dewar, et al., 2022; Economist Impact, 2022; Khosrow-Pour, 2022). It is about the digitalization of business, the introduction of the principles of "responsible investing" (Environmental, Social, Governance (ESG) principles) (Economist Impact, 2022), about the fundamental changes in the internal structure of the organization on the principles of "diversity – equity – inclusion" (Dixon-Fyle, et al., 2020; Garcia-Alonso, et al., 2020; Novacek, et al., 2021), the formation of the best employer's image for talented employees (Emmett, et al., 2020; Ghose, 2020; Pilipenko, 2021), about the orientation of the top management of companies towards the formation of human-centric foundations of an intra-company organization (Davies, et al., 2019; Dietz, et al., 2020; Leap by McKinsey, 2021) and etc. However, the practical substantiation of the correctness of the theoretical conclusions regarding resilient companies is only waiting in the wings.

Considering all the above, this chapter aims to theoretically rethink the phenomenon of self-sufficient companies in connection with the construction of the networking interactions post COVID-19. The following tasks are subordinated to this aim:

- To determine the functions of resilient companies in the process of complicating the economy in statics, according to the authors, before COVID-19; of destruction of its networking structural interactions during the coronavirus pandemic and of construction of the economic system with dynamic properties in the future;
- To substantiate the role of downwards and upwards causation mechanisms in ensuring the resilience of self-sufficient companies;
- To give a theoretical interpretation of the patterns of organization of networking interactions by these companies both at the intra-company and at the structural level of the economic system as a whole;
- To prove the necessity to understand the business operations of resilient companies in connection with the preparation of conditions for the formation of dynamic properties of the future systemic reality in the economy, society, subject to their transfer to a new technological base.

Theoretically, the authors proved that large and the largest resilient companies should be identified with the drivers of organizational changes in the economy and society in the post-COVID-19 future due to their capability to self-sufficiency. The complex internal structure of self-sufficient companies makes them sustainable, since they are capable of both self-organization through the restructuring of internal structural interactions and self-development due to the construction of structural relationships at the macro level in the process of system formation in the economy. In this context, the self-sufficiency of companies should be associated with their inherent ability to self-propel, either in the form of self-organization or in the form of self-development. Thus, due to internal self-organization, self-sufficient companies quickly adapt their internal structure to the impact of market factors, and by implementing the mechanism of self-development they construct new structural ties that correspond to the dynamic reality post COVID-19. This is how the capacity of resilient companies for Schumpeterian "creative destruction" is realized.

Based on the findings of institutional theory, the authors associated the ability of self-sufficient companies to self-organize with downward causation, and their ability for self-development - with upward causation (Hodgson 1988, 2002). By implementing the downward causation mechanism, self-sufficient companies reorganize the internal structural interactions necessary for successful operation in the context of a break in previous relationships due to the COVID-19 pandemic. And with the help of the upward causation mechanism, resilient companies begin to build horizontal organizational networking interactions adequate to post COVID-19 dynamic reality. Thus, resilient companies are able to structure economic (market) and social network interactions as necessary conditions for constructing systems with dynamic qualities. In this context, the theoretical rethinking of the phenomenon of self-sufficient companies makes it possible to understand the patterns of structuring their networking interactions during the pandemic and after it. If databases and analytical studies on resilient companies in the near future confirm the validity of the above conclusions, then decision makers at the level of top management and government officials will be able to minimize uncertainty in the process of constructing the post-COVID-19 reality.

BACKGROUND

The COVID-19 pandemic has exacerbated the fundamental problems of our time, which urgent solution has been actualized by the uncertainty of the future reality. Without rethinking the features of system formation in the economy, society, and the functions of private business in these processes, it is impossible to predict the order from the chaotic heap of phenomena that accompany the ongoing changes in the reality built before the pandemic. Of particular importance it becomes the emerging phenomenon of self-sufficient large and the largest companies that have managed to maintain their positions in business in spite of economic lockdowns and social distancing due to the pandemic. The rethinking of their new role in constructing the future reality predetermined a return to the issue of the static and dynamic state of systems in the economy and society; of the patterns of their self-movement due to the organization of networking interactions by self-sufficient companies; of their new mission in preparing the conditions for constructing a new dynamic reality after the end of the pandemic.

Many of the questions listed above have been raised in the past by great scientists. Thus, over a century ago J. B. Clark (2007) insisted on the need to separate statics and dynamics in the processes of economic changes. At the beginning of the last century N.D. Kondratiev (1984) emphasized that dynamic economic changes significantly differ from their stationary, static (circular) state. W. White (2009) substantiated a misunderstanding of the patterns of maturing of the large-scale global and economic crisis of 2008-2009 by the fact that a static (equilibrium) paradigm prevailed in macroeconomic theory (Bootle, 2009; Minsky, 2008).

The authors used the findings of those scientists to construct methodological approaches to the interpretation of the special role of self-sufficient companies in the processes of system formation, to highlight their structure-forming functions in organizing networking interactions. It made it possible to determine the resilient companies as drivers for constructing the post-COVID-19 reality as systemic integrities in the economy, society and technology. To form the necessary methodological base the authors attracted the findings of the following researchers: Ludwig von Bertalanffy (1968); R. Thom (1974); J. Guckenheimer (1973); H. Hacken (1977); E.C. Zeeman (1977); V.I. Arnold (1975, 1979); N.D. Kondratiev (1984); K. Anderson, J. Arrow, and D. Pines (1988); R. Hausmann, and M. Gavin (1996); W. Brian Arthur (1997, 1999), and etc. As for dialectical logic, the authors' approach was formed under the influence of the developments of the greatest thinkers, such as: G.W.F. Hegel (1892); A.A. Bogdanov (1934), J. M. Keynes (1936); Joseph A. Schumpeter (1961); D. North (1981, 1996); K. Marx (1995); Ludwig H. von Mises (1998); G.M. Hodgson (2002). It was under the influence of the developments of these scientists that the authors were able to theoretically substantiate the characteristics of the economic system in statics and dynamics, dialectically connect resilient companies with it as its backbone elements and identify the laws of their self-organization and self-development in the process of analyzing changes in structural networking interactions.

The authors deepened the understanding of the dialectics of interaction of the system as the integrity and its structure-forming elements, defining the role of the latter in organizational changes in the structure embedding the mechanism of the system's self-movement (Bogdanov, 1934; Bertalanffy, 1968; Hacken, 1977; Arnold, 1975, 1979). It follows that if these structural networking interactions are organized by self-sufficient companies, then it is they that mediate the operation of the mechanism of self-propulsion of the economic system. This determines their special role in constructing a dynamic system in the economy and society post COVID-19. The authors have built a theoretical proof that these companies have a priority role both in the self-organization of a static economy and in its self-development in a dynamic state. This gave the authors grounds to theoretically justify the legitimacy of considering resilient companies as drivers of all system formation processes post COVID-19.

However, the statement of the fact that self-sufficient companies act as drivers of the system formation of the future dynamic reality is not sufficient for understanding the patterns of changes in structural relationships in the economy in statics and in the economy in dynamics. Only understanding the essence of these changes will make it possible to turn the chaos of phenomena caused by the pandemic into a completely understandable logic of the system formation of the future reality.

However, the statement of the fact that self-sufficient companies act as drivers of the system formation of the future dynamic reality is not sufficient for understanding the patterns of changes in structural relationships in the economy in statics and in dynamics. Only understanding the essence of these changes will make it possible to turn the chaos of phenomena caused by the pandemic into a completely understandable logic of the system formation of the future reality. The authors tried to dialectically approach the understanding of structural changes in the system and to present them as the result of the interaction of the following phenomena as a dialectical pair – integration (cooperation, association, inclusion) and disintegration (differentiation, separation, diversity) (Dixon-Fyle, et al., 2020; Garcia-Alonso, et al., 2020; Novacek, et al., 2021). It should be paid tribute to the genius of the Russian scientist A.A. Bogdanov (1934), who was the first to substantiate tectology as a general organizational science and to determine the universal laws of self-organization of systems.

The authors rethought the processes of system formation in the context of organizational changes in structural networking interactions with the participation of self-sufficient companies and faced the dialectic of the interaction between the phenomena of "inclusion" (integration) and "diversity" (disintegration). It turned out that their interaction in the processes of organizing structural networking interactions was regulated by the three dialectical laws. For a better understanding of the mechanism of self-propulsion of systemic integrity with the participation of self-sufficient companies, the authors presented descriptive models of the operation of the laws of unity and the struggle of opposites, the transition of quantitative changes into qualitative ones and of the negation of negation (Figure 2, 3). In other words, resilient companies building structural networking interactions mediate the action of objective dialectical laws of self-movement of economic and social systems.

The importance of getting answers to questions about the features of the future reality and identifying the drivers of its construction processes is constantly increasing. This is evidenced by the publications of such authors as Klaus Schwab (2016), B. Milanovic (2019), Eric Lonergan, and Mark Blyth (2020), Martin Sandbu (2020), Klaus Schwab, and Thierry Malleret (2020), David Feber, Oskar Lingqvist, Daniel Nordigaarden, and Matthew Seidner (2022), and many others.

So, following the dialectical logic and system laws, the authors have built the following sequence of the material presentation. The study begins with substantiating the significance of self-sufficient companies in the role of drivers of structuring networking interactions in an economic system. Using a systematic approach, the authors define dialectical relationships between the economic system and its structure-forming elements, which functions are performed by resilient companies. Having proved this interdependence, the authors theoretically comprehend the fundamental mission of these companies, which is related to their ability to form the structural connections of the system and thereby mediate the mechanism of its self-organization in a static state. Further, the authors make preliminary remarks about the qualities that these companies should possess and delve into the specifics of the functioning of the self-organization mechanism of economic system in statics involving self-sufficient companies. As such, they construct horizontal and vertical levels of the structure of systemic integrity in statics in the sphere of economy mediating its mechanism of self-organization. As a result, a hierarchy of horizontal and vertical levels appears, built on the basis of upwards causation dependencies. So, on the one hand, the stability of the structural relationships of self-sufficient companies increases, and, on the other hand, the fragility of the structure of the entire economic system in statics grows. Following the dialectical logic, the authors complete the study of the functions of self-sufficient companies as drivers for building the structural links of economic systems with a theoretical substantiation of the specifics of the transformation of the mechanism of their self-organization into the mechanism of their self-destruction. Thus, the continuity of the dialectics of static changes of economic systems is interrupted and their dialectical leap into a dynamic state that denies statics is carried out. The emergence of systems with dynamic characteristics and the acquisition of the quality of integrity and the ability for self-development by them directly depend on self-sufficient companies and their structure-forming abilities. The practical section is devoted to concretizing the theoretical constructions of the authors on the real practice of self-sufficient companies that act as drivers for constructing a post-COVID-19 reality both in the economy and in society.

Organizational Changes in Network Interactions in Economy as System Integrity and the Mechanism of Its Self-Organization

The logic of the presentation of this point of the study is subject to the principle "from the general to the particular". The authors argued as follows. If the question is conceptually raised that self-sufficient companies are drivers of structuring networking interactions in an economic system, then it is necessary to theoretically substantiate the special role of the system's structural connections as a mechanism for its self-organization. If, at the same time, it becomes possible to connect the fundamental mission of self-sufficient companies as backbone elements with their ability to form and complicate structural interactions, it will become clear why the study of the dialectics of the system and its elements begins with an understanding of the patterns of self-movement of the economy as a systemic integrity.

It becomes of fundamental significance the methodological principle of the dialectical connection and interaction of elements in any human-created system, whether in the economy or in society. It turns out that the quality of system integrity arises due to the strengthening of internal structural relationships (networking interactions) of elements among themselves and with the system as a whole. In other words, the formation of structural (stable, constantly recurring, network) internal interactions of the system, the increase in their diversity, their constant repetition and immutability predetermine the system integrity. This quality is manifested in its structural certainty and specific features, which are constantly (cyclically) recreated (renewed) through stable direct and inverse relationships organized according to the causation principle.

As a result, the interpretation of the quality of system integrity logically connects it with the ability of the system to remain in an unchanged form of manifestation. This is the essence of the mechanism of its self-organization. It ensures the stability of the system and mediates the complication of its internal structure interactions due to the multiplication and repetition of cause-and-effect relationships between dialectically interconnected elements. At the same time, the state of systemic stability is always relative, since it is provided by constantly changing structural networking interactions. Nevertheless, a system with the quality of integrity is capable of self-organizing in the process of preserving and multiplying its elements, that mediate the mechanism of cyclic repetition of its internal interactions. It is necessary to highlight the special role of the elements of the system that organize numerous connections that predetermine the structure of the system and, thereby, mediate the action of the self-organization mechanism.

In this context, if the modern economy and society can be represented as systemic entities capable of self-organization, then self-sufficient companies act as their structural elements. It is on them that the quality of structural connections, the stability of the entire system depends, since it is they that mediate the mechanism of its self-organization. So if it could be possible to understand the patterns of organization of the structural interactions of the system by self-sufficient companies, as well as the factors that predetermine their fundamental changes, then it would be possible to minimize the uncertainty of the future systemic reality both in the economy and in the society post the coronavirus pandemic.

From the theoretical point of view, all structural interactions in the economic system are predetermined by the exchange of economic activities and/or of its results. The market exchange itself is brought to life by two dialectically interconnected processes - differentiation and integration of economic activity, which in modern conditions are carried out in companies. According to A.A. Bogdanov (1934), any economic system as the integrity was formed gradually in the process of the optimization of division and cooperation of labor as interrelated aspects of a single process of joint economic activity. At any given moment, these forms of economic activity's organization are mutually dependent on each other in such a way that they could be called the abscissa and ordinate of the economic curve describing the behavior of private firms. Following this logic, the economic exchange represents the result of the integration by the private business of many differentiated economic activities as the base for stable, constantly recurring structural ties in a market economy.

It is with this that the authors associate the dialectics of complication of networking interactions which predetermines the systemic integrity and the mission of self-sufficient companies in their organization.

Fig.1 represents the descriptive model of organizing economic activity starting with its differentiation and integration and finishing with the structural interactions of buyers and sellers as for the exchange of goods (Pilipenko, et al., 2021). So, market exchange, in which diverse firms participate, integrates differentiated activities and predetermines the stability of structural interactions in the market economy. Essentially, in the same way, modern self-sufficient companies mediate the networking interactions in economic systems.

According to Fig. 1, the differentiation of economic activity realizes a positive selection of its specialized types, increasing their diversity. Combining only a part of the various types of specialized economic activity, integration carries out their negative selection. This is how the formation of structural network interactions between companies that carry out the exchange takes place, and the coordination of their market behavior. The importance of companies that form and correct structural interactions in the process of exchange is predetermined by the fact that, thanks to their stability and growing number, the system strengthens its integrity. Moreover, in the case of a system in statics its progress is carried out due to the complication of internal structural relationships by their expanding and strengthening their stability at the horizontal level and the formation of a vertical hierarchy of structural levels. This progress of the economic system due to the complication of its internal structural connections, the authors call the self-organization of the system in its statics. As for companies in general and self-sufficient ones in particular, their fundamental mission in the self-propulsion of systemic integrity in the economy is to mediate the mechanism of its self-organization.

Другими словами, it is in the exchange of economic activity and of its results that modern self-sufficient companies form and complicate structural interactions in the economic system that mediate its self-organization. On this basis, the authors single out self-sufficient companies being backbone elements as drivers of system formation in economy post pandemic. Their main mission is to form the structural networking interactions of the economic system, to mediate the positive and negative selection of certain types of economic activity and to organize dialectical pairs that mediate the exchange of material and non-material goods and services. Fig. 1 presents the logical result of positive and negative selections of differentiated types of economic activity and their results in the form of an organization of dialectical pairs of companies that mediate exchange at the horizontal level of the system structure.

These horizontally located structural links of dialectically interdependent backbone companies mediate the mechanism of self-organization of the economic system. Extrapolating these conclusions to the example of system integrity and their structural elements represented by self-sufficient companies, it can be argued that it is the latter that implement the mechanism of self-organization through the organization of numerous networking interactions within their framework.

Beforehand a number of comments should be made. Structural relationships in the system are distinguished by their constant repetition, stability and immutability. Such a quality of networking interactions can arise only within the framework of dialectical pairs. If self-sufficient (system-forming) companies mediate dialectical (structural) interactions that set in motion the mechanism of self-organization of the system, then they should be subject to the action of dialectical laws.

So, any human-created systemic integrity is capable of self-organization due to the complication of structural connections of dialectically interconnected elements. They form structural dialectically interdependent connections within the system in the form of network of horizontal and vertical structural levels. In their complication, the dialectic of constancy and variability is realized, which strengthens the stability of the structure of the system and at the same time enhances its fragility. This is where the complexity of understanding the mechanism of self-organization of static systems and the role of self-sufficient companies in its realization is manifested. The problem is exacerbated by the fact that the system and its relationships with structure-forming elements change depending on the quality of the system's growth. In a static state, it progresses due to self-organization, i.e. complication of horizontal and vertical structural levels that are built by self-sufficient companies. At the stage of self-organization of static system integrity, resilient companies are subject to the laws of unity and struggle of opposites and the transition of quantitative changes into qualitative ones.

At the same time, the self-movement of human-created systems is realized not only through the self-organization of a static system, but also through its self-development in a state of dynamics. At the same time, self-sufficient companies retain the status of structural elements in any case.

Figure 1. Descriptive model of the interaction of differentiation, integration and exchange of economic activities and their intermediation by backbone companies, which thus organize the horizontal level of structural networking interactions
Source: the authors' development
Note: A_1, A_2,..A_n – backbone companies

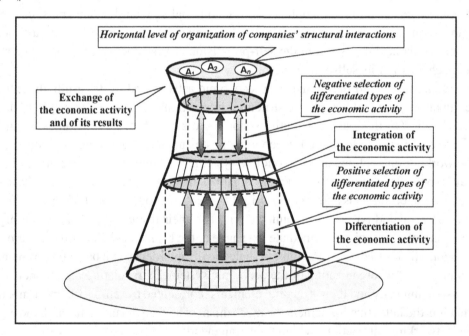

Their mission in the dynamic system becomes more complicated, since they must destroy the old structural interactions under the action of the dialectical law of negation of negation, and organize new horizontal and vertical structural relationships corresponding to the new dynamic reality. The theoretical concept presented by the authors makes it possible to position economic systems in the pre-Covid-19 period as in statics, during the pandemic as moving from statics to dynamics, and post COVID-19 as dynamic ones. In accordance with this, the functions of self-sufficient companies change in each of these periods.

Self-Sufficient Companies in Economic Systems in Statics: Organization of Horizontal and Vertical Structural Levels of Networking Interactions

In this part, the authors focus on the role of self-sufficient companies in the self-organization of economic systems in a static state. That is why the study focuses on the features of the formation of horizontal and vertical levels of the structure of systemic integrity in the economy.

It is necessary to preface the presentation of the material with a number of remarks. Based on their theoretical concept, the authors define self-sufficient companies as structure-forming elements of systemic integrity capable of self-movement. As such, resilient companies are able to form the structural levels of systems and mediate the mechanism of their self-organization in a static state. As self-sufficient companies the authors single out only large and the largest companies. The answer to the question, what caused this choice, lies again in the authors' theoretical understanding of the structure-forming elements of a system capable of self-movement. Based on this, resilient companies must be capable of stable, constantly repeating interactions within the dialectical pairs involved in the exchange. Large companies are more capable of this quality of relationships than small ones. Moreover, in the face of volatile market conditions, such companies must have a certain margin of stability, allowing them to abandon some assets and activities in order to maintain the basis of the business structure.

There is another point that awaits further research. The point is that the self-sufficiency of companies is associated with their ability not only to restructure the internal organization of the business, but also to construct economic and social structural networking interactions external to them. The ESG principles of business organization by modern self-sufficient companies have already been mentioned above. Thus, the presence in them of an internal mechanism of self-organization (through downwards causation) and the ability to self-develop outward (through upwards causation) makes them self-sufficient or resilient. The same qualities distinguish the structure-forming elements of systemic integrity capable of self-propulsion.

These theoretical approaches to the interpretation of self-sufficient companies were put by the authors as the basis for the following reasoning regarding their special status. First, when the economic lockdown and social distancing regimes were imposed by nation states, they negatively affected all spheres of economic activities and private business. The resilient companies have stood out from the crowd during the pandemic, because they have been afloat and not only have not lost their place in the market, but have also succeeded significantly. Second, the reasons for such a unique position of these companies turned out to be related to their active transformation of intra-company structures, with rapid adaptation to new trends in digitalization, business process automation, with the rapid introduction of hybrid models of work with employees, and etc. In essence all this was associated with their ability to quickly rebuild the internal functional structure of the company, taking into account the new external conditions of functioning. Third, these companies turned out to be active in terms of restructuring their organizational interactions with external counterparties and succeeded quite well in this.

The theoretical interpretation of companies with such volatility, both in terms of internal organizational transformations and the formation of external relations with all stakeholders, let the authors suggest that their self-sufficiency is determined by their structural integrity. The latter quality implies their own ability for self-propulsion, both through self-organization and through self-development. The specifics of self-organization of such self-sufficient companies will be discussed in this book in the authors' chapter entitled "Patterns of self-sufficient companies' network interactions reorganization due to the post-COVID-19 reality: dialectics of organizational structures optimization". As for the formation of structural ties in the economic system by such companies, this aspect will be discussed below.

So, the self-organization of economic systems in a static state is realized by complicating structural connections of the self-sufficient companies. At the same time, the horizontal structural level of system integrity is formed by self-sufficient companies connected in dialectical pairs according to the principle of unity and struggle of opposites. The beginning of the organization of the basic horizontal structural level was associated with the commodity-money exchange, in which dialectically related partners participated. This quality of interaction between the exchange participants predetermines the formation of the structure of the economic system, and is functionally designed to ensure its stability, qualitative certainty and resistance to change.

With the advent of money as a stable exchange equivalent, the economic system acquired a structure capable of serving as an internal mechanism for its self-organization. It is set in motion by dialectically interacting self-sufficient companies. A descriptive model of the functioning of the phenomenon described above is presented in Fig. 2. So, the mechanism of self-organization of the economic system in a static state is based on the structural interconnections of dialectically interacting companies that combine both unity and opposites. As the commodity-money exchange deepened, the divergence of interests of partners in market transactions was initiated by an increase in the demand for money as a means of circulation. This significantly hampered the development of real markets (for consumer goods; for investment goods, for labor). The problem was solved in the process of self-organization of the economic system, when the horizontal structural level (real markets), on which the problem of lack of money arose, generated a new structural level, on which money substitutes began to be traded. As a result, the lack of money in the real markets was eliminated.

In other words, the self-organization of the system manifests itself in the generation of a vertical hierarchy of structural levels, in which the lower structures cause the appearance of higher levels-consequences that interact with each other according to the principle of cause-and-effect relationships. As a result, a new level-effect is designed to solve problems that have arisen at the level-cause. This happened with the commodity-money exchange. As the shortage of money in circulation grew, operations with money as a means of payment began to stand out from the structural interactions of companies regarding the commodity-money exchange and the number of companies servicing the money transactions increased. A new structural level was represented by dialectically interconnected operations in the markets for banking loans, for bonds, stocks, and mortgage loans. Companies that mediate transactions in the money market actually solved the problem of the lack of money as a means of circulation in real markets.

Figure 2 represents the model description of self-sufficient companies building both horizontal and vertical structural levels in the system. The logic of the formation of structural levels of vertical hierarchy is predetermined by the needs of the self-sufficient companies on their basic horizontal level of networking interactions. These companies function on real markets, represented by the market for consumer (material) goods and services, the market for investment goods, and by the market for labor. As transactions with deferred payment increase, there is a need for intermediary transactions related to lending borrowers against their obligations to repay debt. The problem of transactions with real goods with delayed payment is depicted by a dashed arrow with index **1** (Figure 2). The increase in this kind of transactions to a critical level becomes the reason for the formation of a vertical structural level represented by money markets. This dependence is depicted by dashed lines with an arrow with index **1** to **A** in square – the reason for the formation of a new level- consequence, represented with **B** in square. The dashed line with index **2**, which returns to the level of real markets, solves the problem of credit support for transactions with real goods and services and restores the broken equivalence in transactions with deferred payment. It is in this connection that all vertical structural levels, organized by the self-sufficient

Figure 2. Descriptive model of self-organization mechanism functioning: formation by resilient companies of horizontal and vertical structural levels of the economic system in statics
Source: the authors' development
Note: A_1, A_2,..A_n – resilient companies

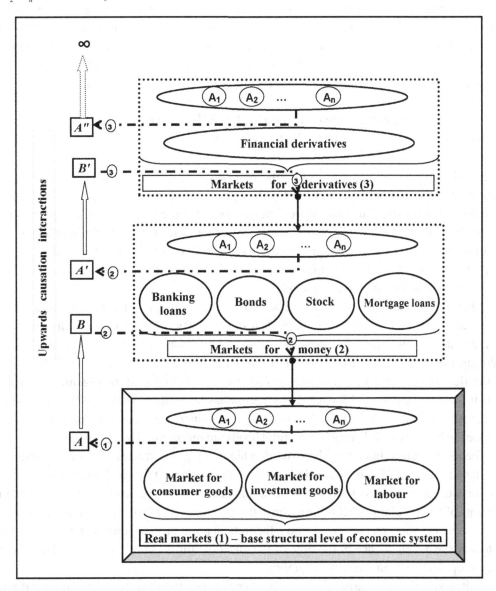

companies, arise. All of them realize the upward causal subordination of higher levels to the solution of problems of lower structural levels of networking interactions. Figure 2 replicated the same logic in the networking interactions between players on money markets and on financial instruments markets. It should be especially noted that the structural ties of self-sufficient companies at any horizontal structural level are regulated by the law of unity and struggle of opposites. But the process of organizing structural ties by self-sufficient companies that mediate the transition from one horizontal structural level to another higher level is regulated by the dialectical law of the transition of quantitative changes into qualitative ones. In fact, this presentation gives an idea of the self-organization of the economic system as a whole, which is realized through the formation of organizational structures by self-sufficient companies in the form of a hierarchical structure in accordance with the upward causation principal.

This is the mechanism of self-organization of the economic system in a static state, set in motion by the structural ties of self-sufficient companies. It is in this connection that the authors define self-sufficient companies as backbone elements and drivers of self-organization processes of static systems. This is of great importance for understanding the factors influencing the behavior of self-sufficient companies during a pandemic, when the economic system has all the features of a static economy.

Self-Sufficient Companies and the Dialectical Jump of Economic Systems from Statics to Dynamics

According to the authors, all economic systems were static on the eve of the coronavirus pandemic. And in this regard, the question arises of what is the role of self-sufficient companies in the next stages of the transformation of structural ties. Specifically, it is about the fact that while self-organization is implemented by building a hierarchy of structural levels, in which each of their higher levels solves the problems of the lower one, then the integrity of the system and its stability are strengthened. But in parallel, its fragility is growing. What does this mean for the system in statics and what role do self-sufficient companies play here as its structural elements?

From a theoretical point of view, it should be assumed that strengthening the structural interactions of a self-organizing system has its limits. Nevertheless, self-sufficient companies as drivers of structure formation remain so even in the conditions of complication of structural ties to the limit of their fragility and during the period of their destruction to the basic horizontal structural level. In other words, with the limitless possibilities of self-sufficient companies to complicate the organizational structures of systems in statics, the potential for self-organization has its limits (Arnold, 1979; Santomero, 1996; Taleb, 2012; Arthur, 2013). The latter are associated with an increase in the structural complexity of the system, since the horizontal and vertical structural levels are represented by interdependent dialectically related resilient companies. In fact, as the structural hierarchy grows the fragility of the entire structure increases many times over (Taleb, 2007). This is explained by the fact that under the new conditions, the stability of network interactions of self-sufficient companies becomes dependent not only on themselves as participants of a particular market transaction at the horizontal level, but also on the stability of many vertical structural network interactions. From a theoretical point of view, this is due to the fact that it is difficult to achieve a coincidence in the time of the onset of "turns" in the dialectical laws themselves: from unity to opposites, from quantity to quality.

As a result, a situation may arise when resilient companies fail to form a new structural level with the help of their structural relationships to solve problems of a lower level in the system. Leaving aside the problem of factors that can lead to the system's collapse (Pilipenko, et al., 2021), it is reasonable to trace the logic of its self-destruction. At the same time, this mechanism will be implemented by the same self-sufficient companies, which in this case will mediate the upwards causation process, causing the destruction of the entire structure of the static system. In other words, instead of erecting a vertical hierarchy according to the principle of upward causation in the process of self-organization, self-sufficient companies mediate downward causation, destroying all structural levels of the system. Self-destruction of the system will occur when the higher structural level becomes the cause of the destruction of the next lower structural level. Moreover, chaos should not be seen in this, since it turns into order if it is interpreted through the prism of the impact of the dialectical law of double negation on the structural ties of self-sufficient companies (left panel of Figure 3). By the way, the authors see an analogy of these events in the destruction of structural ties in the economies caused by the COVID-19 pandemic (Okamoto, 2020). It should be emphasized that it was in these conditions that the importance of the question of who will lead the economy out of collapse during the pandemic and after it has increased (Mendy, 2020)

The authors have built a descriptive model that makes it possible to highlight the specifics of the self-destruction of the system structure in a static state and theoretically raise the question of what exactly the uncertain future will manifest itself in and which players will construct it. So, following the theoretical logic, if the lower structural levels of a static system cannot (for some reasons) solve their problems due to the structural ties of self-sufficient companies at a higher structural level, then unresolved problems will cause a multiplication of the destruction of structural ties and of the system structure as a whole, starting from the above and ending with the base horizontal level (Fig 3, $t_1 - t_2$). This is due to the fact that the transformation of upward causation into downward one unresolved problems of the upper structural level are multiplied because of the unresolved problems of lower structural levels, and all the system structure collapses like a house of cards. At the same time, the destruction of the structural levels of the system and of the structural interconnections of self-sufficient companies as its elements is regulated by the dialectical law of negation of negation. The first denial concerns the destruction of the built-up vertical of structural levels, and the second denial destroys the basic structural level that gave rise to them. So as cause-and-effect relationships reorient the organizational structure of the system from the upward causation principle to downward, both the vertical organizational structure and its basic horizontal structural level are destroyed.

If all structural connections are destroyed, then this means that the system in a static state has passed the point of no return (to the past) and its evolution in the previous state is interrupted. Therefore, its quality must change. That is why the situation of the collapse of the structure of a static system is associated with a dialectical leap from statics to dynamics. At the same time, there can be many options for structuring a dynamic reality, as, for example, in the case of the post-COVID-19 future, and this is shown on the right panel of Figure 3.

Moreover, for each national economy, the features of a dynamic reality will be different. And this choice will depend on the structure-forming elements of the future system. It is about self-sufficient companies and the realization of their potential in the context of constructing a new technological base for the national economy and society; of the formation of new dialectical links between the economy and society; of the implementation of the principles of harmonization of interactions of human-created systems and the Earth's biosphere, and etc. And besides these resilient companies, no one is able to prepare the conditions for structuring a dynamic system with its own mechanism of self-development, which can be mediated only by these dialectically complex, self-sufficient organizations represented by these companies.

Thus the system has lost its former integrity, its vertical and horizontal structures have been destroyed then it turns out that only companies as its structure-forming elements are called upon to mediate the formation of structural ties and dialectical interactions as the future structure of a new dynamic system.

As the main guidelines for the future, it is possible to theoretically substantiate the presence of a few fundamental trends. The new post-COVID-19 reality as a dynamic system both in the economy and the society should be formed on a new technological foundation, which greatly increases the possibilities of self-sufficient companies in organizing qualitatively new networking interactions (Dietz, et al., 2020). In fact, the mass replication of new technological solutions in business operations by self-sufficient com-

Figure 3. Descriptive model of self-destruction of the structure of a system in statics, starting from the upper structural level and ending with the basic horizontal level (t1 – t2) and the beginning of the structure formation of the economic system in dynamics (t2 – t3)

Source: the authors' development

Note: **A (A', A'')** *stands for* **CAUSES***;* **B (B', B'')** *stands for* **CONSEQUENCES**

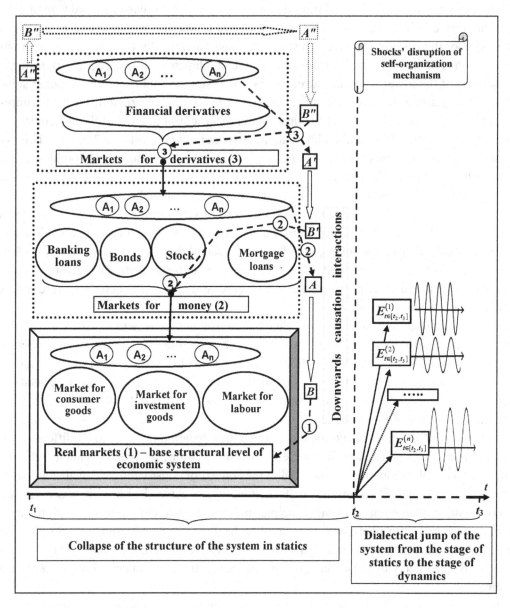

panies is the key to the movement of a dynamic system only in one direction – into the post-COVID-19 future. In addition, the implementation of the dynamic future scenario becomes possible only if the role of a man in the human-created systems in general and in their dynamic state, in particular, is rethought (Davies, et al., 2019; Schwab, et al., 2020). Considering the vast possibilities of the new technological revolution 4.0, there has emerged and is growing the lack of professionals with relevant skills and competencies (Siebel, 2019). Consequently, self-sufficient companies will be forced to solve this problem, which is at the crossroads of education systems and the mechanism of socialization (Taplett, et al., 2019). Taking into account the phenomenon of growing necessity in intellectually autonomous individuals in a dynamic economy, there is an even more difficult problem of choosing the principles for organizing their activities in the economy and society in general, and at the level of self-sufficient companies, in particular (Mazzucato, 2013; Mendy, 2020). And hence it becomes obvious the sharpness of the discussion of the principles of the capital-centric organization of modern society and of its reorientation towards human-centrism (Ziolo, 2021). And then there are a huge number of questions related to the organization of society and the functions of the state in the new realities. In other words, the choice by self-sufficient companies of the trajectory of constructing the future reality will be determined by the specifics in which national communities differ from each other.

EMPIRICAL EVIDENCE

The empirical part of the chapter is aimed at deepening the understanding of the problems of the interaction of the system and its structure-forming elements, i.e. economic system and self-sufficient companies. Throughout the previous discussions, self-sufficient companies appeared as drivers of the processes of structuring interconnections in the system, turning them into more and more stable and durable based on the dialectical principles of unity and opposites. It also deepens one aspect of structure formation with the participation of self-sufficient companies. They form a structure that is the most conservative component of systemic integrity. In other words, everything can and does change, but the structure will be adjusted last. Moreover, it is self-sufficient companies that are called upon to strengthen the static economy by forming a whole vertical hierarchy of structural levels, to destroy it in conditions where ascending causality changes to downward, and to ensure the transformation of a static economy into a dynamic one. In this regard, it is necessary to single out the sphere of intersection of interests of self-sufficient companies and the economic system or society, which predetermines the above mentioned effects. At the same time, if there is no consolidation of interests among the elements and the system, then the economy will not have integrity and the opportunism of self-sufficient companies will not ensure its self-organization and self-development. So the subjective component comes to the fore, which the authors tried to demonstrate using the Lotka–Volterra mathematical model.

Having built the logic of the dialectics of self-movement (self-organization and self-development) of self-sufficient companies, it is advisable to illustrate the theoretical conclusions with the help of mathematical model. The authors turned to the well-known Lotka–Volterra mathematical model (often called «predator–prey» model) (Lotka, 1920; Lotka, 1925; Volterra, 1926; Volterra, 1931). I it is applicable for different processes description in biology, ecology, medicine, in sociology investigations, in history, radio physics, economy, and etc. The variant of this model is considered methodologically in this paragraph.

Based on this model, the authors built a dynamic (constructive) model for reconciling the interests of a dialectical pair, represented by the system as the integrity and its structure-forming elements - self-sufficient companies. To this end, the authors note the following points.

First, they identify A_1, A_2, .., A_n as *resilient companies*, which are shown in Fig. 1 – Fig. 3. Since their number may change over time, the authors introduced into consideration a set A, reflecting this dynamics as a dynamic set. The period of the spread of the COVID-19 pandemic was taken as the time interval $t \in \left[t_1, t_2 \right]$, which caused the collapse of the structure of the system in statics (Fig. 3).

Let $n_1(t)$ be the number of participants in the dynamic set $A_{[t_1, t_2]}$, expressing the sphere of interests of self-sufficient companies, which are structural elements that ensure the integrity of the national system.

Second, the national economy as system integrity, the sphere of interests of which are expressed by $n_2(t)$ of the participants of the dynamic set $B_{[t_1, t_2]}$, constitutes a dialectical pair with its own structural elements - a dynamic set $A_{[t_1, t_2]}$.

In this semantic field, the following system of ordinary differential equations of the first order, resolved with respect to the derivative, appears (1)

$$\left.\begin{array}{l} \dfrac{dn_1}{dt} = \varepsilon_1 n_1 - \alpha_1 n_1 n_2 \\[2mm] \dfrac{dn_2}{dt} = -\varepsilon_2 n_2 + \alpha_2 n_1 n_2 \end{array}\right\}. \tag{1}$$

It should be noted that this model is aggregated, since it does not consider individual self-sufficient companies from different groups of market players in the time interval $t \in [t_1, t_2]$. It only describes their aggregate behavior. So, in the first equation of system (1), the term $\varepsilon_1 n_1$ takes into account the growth of the sphere of interests of the first group of companies. Here ε_1 – is a positive interest growth coefficient, for example, due to the emergence of new representatives of this group of companies. On the other hand, the term $-\alpha_1 n_1 n_2$ characterizes the decrease in their sphere of interest due to the growth of opposites that predetermine the behavior of an integral national system, the sphere of interests of which is expressed by $n_2(t)$ participants. Moreover, in this case, the dynamics of the interest of the second group of companies decreases while there is a reorientation to another market segment. This situation is described by the first term of the second equation $-\varepsilon_2 n_2$. Accordingly, the growth of interest of the integral national system is associated with an increase in the mutual interest of self-sufficient companies and the national system. This is a circumstance that is taken into account by the term $\alpha_2 n_1 n_2$.

The authors do not intend to solve the system of differential equations (1), since human-created systems do not obey the "predator-prey" logic, but strive for a consensus of interests $A_{[t_1, t_2]} \cap B_{[t_1, t_2]}$ at the stage of the coronavirus pandemic, i.e. in conditions of the collapse of the structure of the system in statics (Fig. 3),

Note that in the post-COVID-19 reality, this parity will be significantly higher than 50% $A_{[t_2, t_3]} \cap B_{[t_2, t_3]} > 50\%$. In this case, the parameters $\varepsilon_1, \varepsilon_2, \alpha_1, \alpha_2$ will change accordingly in the time interval related to the post-COVID-19 reality $t \in [t_2, t_3]$.

To study the parity of interests of participants in dialectical pairs, it is necessary to investigate the equilibrium solution of the system of differential equations (1). In this case, the rates of change of $n_1(t)$ and $n_2(t)$ vanish. Since the derivatives on the left-hand sides of system (1) disappear, a system of algebraic equations (2) arises

$$n_1\left(\varepsilon_1 - \alpha_1 n_2\right) = 0$$
$$-n_2\left(\varepsilon_2 - \alpha_2 n_1\right) = 0$$

$$(2)$$

Consider the solutions of the system (2).

The first group of decisions expresses the necessary and sufficient condition for the unity of interests of the dialectical pair: *the first group of self-sufficient companies - national economy as the system integrity*

$$n_2^0 = \frac{\varepsilon_1}{\alpha_1}$$
$$n_1^0 = \frac{\varepsilon_2}{\alpha_2}$$

$$(3)$$

In fact, the unity of interests of dialectical pairs is essentially an abstraction. To complete the picture, it is necessary to take into account the presence of small fluctuations near the unity of interests. Taking into account these small deviations, the system of solutions (3) should be rewritten in the form (4)

$$n_1\left(t\right) = \frac{\varepsilon_2}{\alpha_2} + \nu_1\left(t\right)$$
$$n_2\left(t\right) = \frac{\varepsilon_1}{\alpha_1} + \nu_2\left(t\right)$$

$$(4)$$

where the variables $\nu_1(t)$ and $\nu_2(t)$ should be considered sufficiently small compared to the variables $n_1(t)$ and $n_2(t)$ respectively. This means that they are of the first order of smallness compared to $n_1(t)$ and $n_2(t)$. Note that the rates of change of the variables $\nu_1(t)$ and $\nu_2(t)$, that is, their derivatives, respectively, are equal to the time derivatives of the variables $n_1(t)$ and $n_2(t)$.

Under these conditions, the substitution of expressions (4) into the system of equations (1), after performing a series of transformations, leads to the system of equations (5)

$$\frac{d\nu_1}{dt} = -\varepsilon_2 \frac{\alpha_1}{\alpha_2} \nu_2$$
$$\frac{d\nu_2}{dt} = \varepsilon_1 \frac{\alpha_2}{\alpha_1} \nu_1$$

$$(5)$$

Let us find out what information this system of differential equations carries. To do this, we differentiate with respect to time, for example, the first equation of system (5). In the resulting expression, we substitute the value of the first derivative of the variable $\nu_2(t)$ from the second equation of the system. As a result, we obtain an equation that can be considered as a harmonic oscillator (6)

$$\frac{d^2\nu_1}{dt^2} + \varepsilon_1\varepsilon_2\nu_1 = 0. \tag{6}$$

Indeed, since the coefficient ε_1 and ε_2 are positive, we can introduce the notation $\omega_0^2 = \varepsilon_1\varepsilon_2$. As a result, the well-known equation of a harmonic (or linear) oscillator that oscillates freely (7) is obtained

$$\frac{d^2\nu_1}{dt^2} + \omega_0^2\nu_1 = 0, \tag{7}$$

where $\omega_0 = \dfrac{2\pi}{T}$ – cyclic natural frequency of a linear oscillator, but T – the period of such fluctuations. Obviously, the numerical value of ω_0 is determined by the relation $\omega_0 = \sqrt{\varepsilon_1\varepsilon_2}$.

Now it is easy to find the period T of harmonic oscillations in the agreement of mutual interests of a dialectical pair: *the first group of self-sufficient companies - the second group of national economy as the system integrity*:

$$T = \frac{2\pi}{\omega_0} \quad \Rightarrow \quad T = \frac{2\pi}{\sqrt{\varepsilon_1\varepsilon_2}} \tag{8}$$

Thus, the parity of interests of the system of two groups of self-sufficient companies makes free harmonic oscillations near the unity of interests of the dialectical pair, the period of which is inversely proportional to the square root of the product of the growth-loss coefficients of each component of the dialectical pair. It is important to note that the obtained result (7) or (8) is methodologically very important. He objectively indicates that the excitation of harmonic oscillations in the economic system does not need an external impulse, as was commonly believed, starting with the work (Udny, 1927; Frisch, 1933; Slutsky, 1937). It is endogenous factors that are primarily responsible for the formation of oscillators in economic, technological and social systems. Thus, it is shown how the first group of decisions of system (2) ensures the coordination (parity) of interests within the framework of the law of unity and struggle of opposites.

The second group of solutions to system (2), at first glance, seems quite trivial (9)

$$n_1 = 0; \quad n_2 = 0. \tag{9}$$

However, this decision has a deep methodological meaning. Namely, it testifies to that stage of the operation of the law of unity and struggle of opposites, when there are no common interests and opposing interests prevail. But this means that the law of unity and struggle of opposites on the horizontal structural level of the economic system at the moment t_1 has exhausted itself. The point is that the lower structural level generates the need to form a vertically located new structural level according to the law of the transition of quantitative changes into qualitative ones.

It is advisable to present a graphical illustration of the dynamic model (6) or (7). As is known, the general solution of the second-order linear differential equation (7) has the form (10)

$$\nu_1(t) = C_1 \cos(\omega t) + C_2 \sin(\omega t),$$
(10)

and the general solution of equation (6) can be represented as

$$\nu_1(t) = C_1 \cos\left(\sqrt{\varepsilon_1 \varepsilon_2} t\right) + C_2 \sin\left(\sqrt{\varepsilon_1 \varepsilon_2} t\right),$$
(11)

where C_1 and C_2 arbitrary constants, the value of which is easy to calculate.

Let at the moment $t = 0$ the parity of interests of the buyer-seller system be in an equilibrium state, i.e. $n_1(0) = 0$. Hence it follows that $C_1 = 0$. On the other hand, the system passes through the state of equilibrium at maximum speed, i.e. derivative of equality (11)

$$\frac{d\nu_1}{dt} = C_2 \sqrt{\varepsilon_1 \varepsilon_2} \cos\left(\sqrt{\varepsilon_1 \varepsilon_2} t\right)$$
(12)

at $t = 0$ has the greatest value. In order to simplify the calculation of the constant C_2 we set $\varepsilon_1 = \varepsilon_2 = 1$, and the value of the derivative is taken equal to 0.25. Under these conditions, $C_2 = 0.25$ and is the oscillation amplitude. Let us denote the oscillation amplitude as C.

On Fig. 4 expressions (11) and (12) are presented as functions of dimensionless time, where the amplitude takes the value $C = 0.25$

$$\nu_1\left(\frac{t}{T}\right) = C \sin\left(2\pi \frac{t}{T}\right) \text{ и } \frac{d\nu_1}{dt} = C \cos\left(2\pi \frac{t}{T}\right)$$
(13)

Fig. 4 clearly illustrates the properties of the system of equations (13). Thus, the displacement from the equilibrium position and the speed of the linear oscillator change according to the harmonic law. In this case, the velocity is ahead in phase of the displacement by one-fourth of the oscillation period. To complete the picture, one should construct a phase trajectory defined by equations (13). It is shown in Fig. 5 and, as is easy to see, is symmetrical with respect to the coordinate axes ν_1 and $\frac{d\nu_1}{dt}$. Note that the original system of differential equations (1), adequate to the Lotka–Volterra model, does not have such a symmetry property of phase trajectories.

So, understanding the laws of self-movement of systemic integrity at the stage of their self-organization allows us to identify the moment of the turning point of the ascending and descending processes of causation, which indicate the limiting state of the mechanisms of systemic self-organization. The authors have already mentioned above that these processes are regulated by the laws of unity and struggle of opposites and the transition of quantitative changes into qualitative ones. And the breaks in their dialectics also predetermine the limiting state of static system integrity. The above model gives an idea of

Figure 4. Harmonic oscillations of the self-sufficient companies interests parity and the rate of interest parity change with amplitude **C** *= 0.25 or the case of* $\varepsilon_1 = \varepsilon_2 = 1$ *and dimensionless time*
Source: the authors' development

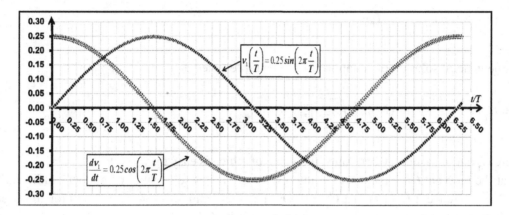

the subjective component in the behavior of self-sustaining companies that mediate self-organization processes and mechanisms of upward and downward causation.

Figure 5. Phase trajectory (phase portrait) of the system of equations (13) on the plane $\left(\nu_1, \dfrac{d\nu_1}{dt}\right)$ *at* $\varepsilon 1$ $= \varepsilon 2 = 1$
Source: the authors' development

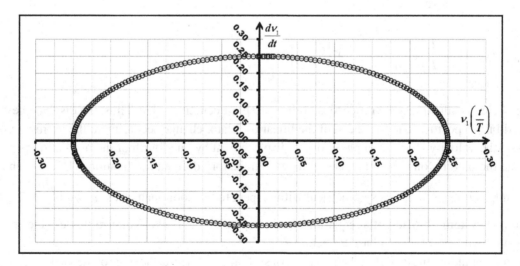

Coincidence or discrepancy of the motivations of self-sufficient companies building organizational interactions in the system makes it possible to differentiate the problems of exhausting the potential of self-organization and determine the motivation of self-sufficient companies in relation to the further trajectory of their organizational structures. This approach is of great importance for understanding these problems by the state, since the coordination of its interests and the motivation of self-sufficient companies predetermines both potential progress and possible regression in the construction of the post-COVID-19 reality.

RESULTS AND DISCUSSION

The authors built a theoretical approach that allowed them to conceptually determine the place of self-sufficient companies in the economic system as its structural elements. This means that the interaction of sustainable companies with systemic integrity in the economy forms a dialectical pair, which is characterized by unity and opposition of participants and of their interests. Moreover, this dialectic of relations is also manifested in the process of constructing by self-sufficient companies of structural links in the system. Being the integrity, the system is capable of both self-organization in a static state and of self-development in dynamics. Resilient companies mediate this ability by realizing the action of the self-movement mechanisms of the economic system in the process of forming structural ties. The dialectic of contradictory actions of such companies lies in the fact that at the stage of self-organization, self-sufficient companies are able to strengthen its integrity by building a hierarchy of structural relationships according to the principle of cause-and-effect relationships. However, as the system in a static state reaches the limits of its complexity, these same companies, using cause-and-effect relationships, destroy the structure they have erected. In fact, a self-organizing system in a static state is predetermined in its complication by the actions of self-sufficient companies. Even the destruction of the structure of a static economy does not detract from their fundamental structure-forming mission. The development of events over the past 2 years confirms the validity of the authors' conclusions: the static economy reaches its limit in the pre-COVID-19 period; in the context of the pandemic, it is gradually losing its former structural ties, which are being replaced by qualitatively different ones, built by self-sufficient companies. In other words, their structure-forming function is realized according to the Schumpeterian scenario of "creative destruction" of the structure of a self-organizing system. Further, instead of broken connections, it is these companies that will erect new structures and structural levels that correspond to the dynamic characteristics of the future reality and mediate the mechanism of its self-development.

However, the most important aspect of the post-COVID-19 dynamic reality associated with the interaction of these companies and the state as a mega-regulator of all processes in the economy remains outside the study. The definition of self-sufficient companies as the main drivers of the system formation of the future reality does not detract from the importance of rethinking the functions of the state in a static economy, and even more so at the stage of its self-development to a dynamic state. Moreover, most likely the relationship between the state as a mega-regulator and self-sufficient companies in the process of constructing the future reality will determine the progress or regression on this path for each national socio-economic system.

As for self-sufficient companies, they are objectively facing the future and are satisfied with the dynamic economy and society. But as for the state, its functions were formed in a static economy at the stage of its self-organization, and it was objectively charged with the duty of institutionalization the stability of the economic system and society (Tanzi, 2011; Mazzucato, 2013). There is no reason for the state to strive for an uncertain future without understanding the specifics of a dynamic economy and society and its own new functions. That is why, as a central element of the institutional structure of the system, the state is more inclined to return the economy and society to the pre-COVID-19 situation. This is evidenced by the forecasts of the world's leading analytical centers. Thus, by the end of 2020, the share of budget expenditures of national states in GDP and the level of their budget deficits were planned at the level of 2019 indicators (IMF, 2021). The volume of public debt of the countries of the world was planned for a gradual reduction. According to experts from PwC and IMF, no major changes in global economic growth are expected until 2027 (Kupelian, et al., 2021). Thus, relatively low average GDP growth rates and a reduction in the share of fiscal spending to the pre-COVID-19 level hardly indicate a fundamental change in the state's understanding of its new functions.

And, meanwhile, the societal crisis persists, social fault lines deepen (Rajan, 2010; Bell, 2022), citizens' distrust of their government, at best, does not change (Keneally, et al., 2020). It turns out that everything is changing, except for the state and its functions. This is also proved by the IMF forecasts: if in 2021 global economic growth was projected at 10% compared to the low base of 2020, then in comparison with the previous period in 2023 it should decrease to 4%, in 2024 – to 3% and in 2025 – to 1%, respectively (IMF, 2020). In other words, the static economy began to falter long before the pandemic: the economic growth rates of the leading countries of the world gradually slowed down, social polarization deepened in national communities, the middle class was shrinking, the quality of healthcare and the education system as public goods were declining. The abstraction of the state from the need to maintain societal integrity was explained by the dominant ideology, according to which the solution of the economic problems of citizens would automatically solve social problems. Even the focus of the state on ensuring financial stability can be considered an atavism of setting the priority of the economy in maintaining the stability of national society. Therefore, it was not surprising that on the eve of the pandemic the pace of economic growth in the global economy began to slow down, predetermined, first of all, by downward dynamics in advanced economies. It was they who first reached the limits of the potential of a static economy.

Despite the dramatic changes caused by the pandemic, nothing has changed in the practice of state regulation at the national level. Such conservatism of the state is quite understandable, since it is due to its main systemic function – to ensure that the organizational structure that has already been formed remains unchanged and stable. In this capacity, the state was called upon to limit the whole variety of structural ties between companies in order to preserve the static system unchanged. Institutionalization of all network connections within the country is the essence of structuring the interactions between the state and economic agents. It is no coincidence that in the context of the pandemic, the nation-states of almost all countries of the world used the most destructive tool in the fight against coronavirus – economic lockdown and social distancing, which destroyed structural ties in the economy and society. Thus, the state has demonstrated its inefficiency as a mega-regulator of the economic and social systems responsible for their integrity.

Moreover, the state overlooked the changed trends in connection with self-sufficient companies that are able to build the organizational ties of the future reality. If nothing changes in interaction with private business, which is forced to quickly respond to new opportunities, then the inconsistency of their future trajectories may worsen: self-sufficient companies will focus on the irreversibility of processes, while the state will focus on restoring the former static economy. There can be no progress in this case, and the extent of the regression will be shown by specific national practice.

Another problem remained outside the interests of the modern state: changing the subordination of the economy and society, the importance of achieving the integrity of society and of solving the problem of the societal crisis. The fundamental nature of the problem of violation of the dialectic of interaction between society and the economy became apparent in connection with the problems, the severity of which began to intensify as the COVID-19 pandemic spread. In principle, there is a logical explanation for this. The fact is that initially humanity faced the problem of ensuring the material conditions for the life of people, which predetermined the priority of the economy in comparison with other structures of national systems. Under these conditions, the state, as their structure-forming beginning, was charged with the obligation to ensure the stability of economic systems with all means at its disposal (including fiscal ones). In this context, it is advisable to quote the following words of the outstanding Russian philosopher N. Berdiaev: «The state exists not to turn earthly life into heaven, but to prevent it from finally turning into hell." (Tanzi, 2011). So, in the indefinite post-COVID future, the political capabilities of the state to restore the integrity of society as the basis for accelerating technological and economic progress will depend on how quickly and far the state moves away from the last line that the most disadvantaged part of the population approached in a pandemic in order to interfere with life on earth finally turn into hell (Pew Research Center, October, 2021).

According to Martin Sandbu «…..things will never be the same. But how they will change is wide open, and policy choices made over the next few years will make a big difference to whether the post-COVID-19 world favor broadly shared prosperity more than the status quo ante….. At rare moments, however, leaders' decisions help reset the course of their societies for a long time. This is such a moment» (Sandbu, 2020). Thus, success or failure in constructing the post-COVID-19 reality will be determined by the structural interactions between the state and self-sufficient companies in each national socio-economic system.

CONCLUSION

Model ideas about the destruction of the organizational structure of the economic system are accompanied by numerous questions about the uncertain future reality. From the point of view of the authors, rethinking the patterns of systemic integrity changes in the economy allows to assume that the reality developed in the pre-COVID-19 period is a static self-organizing model, but the post-COVID-19 period is associated with the construction of a dynamic system capable of self-development. Static systems at the stage of self-organization are regulated by the dialectical laws of the unity and struggle of opposites and the transition of quantitative changes into qualitative ones, which predetermine the complication of the system by generating and resolving the essential problems that arise in their structure. In fact, there would be no self-organization if this mechanism did not contain the dialectic of unity and opposites, changes in the quantity and new quality of the changes that have occurred. The point is that the dialectic of the transition from unity to opposites, and the denial of quantity for the sake of quality, is the essence of the organizational complexity of the system in its static state. All of the above characterizes the state of self-organization of national economic and social systems on the eve of the COVID-19 pandemic. In their bulk, these national system integrities have come to the limit of the potential possibilities of their self-organization mechanism. In this sense, the post-COVID-19 future is uncertain because it is associated with the transformation of a static systemic integrity in the economy and society into dynamic ones. And such an essential transformation of self-sufficient systems from statics to dynamics is carried out by a dialectical leap from the stage of self-organization to the stage of self-development, which begins with the formation of a structure of a new systemic integrity. The main drivers of these processes are self-sufficient companies that were formed at the stage of self-organization of system integrity pre COVID-19.

And in this situation, only resilient self-sufficient companies capable of both self-organization and self-development are prepared to play the role of drivers of organizational restructuring that is adequate to the economic system in dynamics. The authors demonstrate the formation of these new organizational network interactions on the example of self-sufficient companies that, thanks to the downward causation mechanism, change their internal organization, and thanks to the upward causation mechanism, they structure the external environment of their networking interactions.

A new phenomenon in this regard is the increasingly active participation of CEOs of sustainable self-sufficient companies in social relationships (the status of the best employer, an extensive social package for their talented employees, the expanded implementation of ESG principles, human-centric principles, etc.), which concretizes the idea of "the New Normal" in relation to the post-COVID-19 economy and society. The authors prove that self-sufficient companies seem to structure interaction in the market and in social networks during the pandemic and post COVID-19, since the sustainability of the national socio-economic systems of the future will depend not so much on the stability of the economic system, but on the integrity of society and success in eliminating negative consequences of the contemporary societal crisis. In other words, it is self-sufficient companies that are destined for the role of a laboratory of the future post-COVID reality, in which they must test the most acceptable alternative forms of organizational structures and network interactions and which will allow them to form the latest technological base for a self-developing economy and prepare intellectually autonomous individuals who express a desire to live in society post COVID-19 and create for the benefit of its prosperity.

REFERENCES

Anderson, K., Arrow, J., & Pines, D. (Eds.). (1988). *The Economy as an Evolving Complex System.* Addison-Wesley.

Arnold, V.I. (1979). Catastrophe theory. *Nature, 10*, 54-63.

Arnold, V. I. (1975). Critical points of smooth functions. *Proc. of International Congress of Mathematicians, 1*, 19-40.

Arthur, W. B. (2009). *The Nature of Technology: What it Is and How it Evolves.* Free Press.

Arthur, W. B. (2013). *Complexity economics: A different framework for economic thought.* Santa Fe Institute Working Paper. 2013-04-012.

Bell, J. A., & Nuzzo, J. B. (2022). *Global Health Security Index: Advancing Collective Action and Accountability Amid Global Crisis.* Retrieved from: www.GHSIndex.org

von Bertalanffy, L. (1968). General System Theory: Foundations, Development, Applications. University of Alberta.

Bogdanov, A. A. (1934). *Tectology or General Organizational Science.* Conjuncture Institute publishing house.

Bootle, R. (2009). *The Trouble with Markets: Saving Capitalism from Itself.* Nicholas Brealey Publishing.

Clark, J. B. (2007). *Essentials of Economic Theory: As Applied to Modern Problems of Industry and Public Policy*. Ludwig von Mises Institute.

Davies, B., Diemand-Yauman, C., & van Dam, N. (2019). *Competitive advantage with a human dimension: From lifelong learning to lifelong employability. McKinsey Quarterly*.

Dewar, C., Keller, S., & Milhotra, V. (2022). *CEO Excellence: The Six Mindsets That Distinguish the Best Leaders from the Rest*. Scribner.

Dietz, Khan, & Rab. (2020). *How do companies create value from digital ecosystems?* McKinsey & Co.

Dixon-Fyle, Hunt, & Prince. (2020). *Diversity wins: How inclusion matters*. McKinsey & Company.

Impact, E. (2022). *The ESG conundrum: How investors and companies can find common purpose in ESG*. The Economist Group.

Emmett, J., Schrah, G., Schrimper, M., & Wood, A. (2020). *COVID-19 and the employee experience: How leaders can seize the moment. Organization Practice*. McKinsey & Company.

Feber, D., Lingqvist, O., Nordigaarden, D., & Seidner, M. (2022). *2022 and beyond for the packaging industry's CEOs: The priorities for resilience*. McKinsey & Company.

Frisch, R. (1933). Propagation problems and impulse problems in dynamic economics. In *Economic Essays in Honour of Gustav Cassel*. Allen and Unwin.

Garcia-Alonso, J., Krentz, M., Lovich, D., & Mingardon, S. (2020). Diversity, equity, and inclusion still matter in a pandemic. Boston Consulting Group.

Gjaja, Hutchinson, Farber, Brimmer, & Kahn. (2020). *Three Paths to the Future*. Boston Consulting Group Analysis.

Guckenheimer, J. (1973). Bifurcation and catastrophe. Proc. International Sympos. In M. Peixoto (Ed.), *Dynamical Systems*. Academic Press.

Haken, H. (1977). *Synergetics. An Introduction*. Springer-Verlag.

Hausmann, R., & Gavin, M. (1996). *Securing stability and growth in a shock prone region: the policy challenge for Latin America*. Inter-American Development Bank. Working Paper. No. 315. Office of the Chief Economist.

Hegel, G. W. F. (1892). The science of logics. In:The Logic of Hegel (2nd ed.). Oxford University Press.

Hodgson, G. M. (1988). Economics and Institutions: A Manifesto or a Modern Institutional Economics. University of Pennsylvania Press. doi:10.9783/9781512816952

Hodgson, G. M. (2002). Reconstitutive downward causation: social structure and the development of individual agency. In Intersubjectivity in Economics: Agents and Structures. Routledge.

Hunt, Prince, Dixon-Fyle, & Yee. (2018). *Delivering through Diversity*. McKinsey & Company.

IMF. (2020). *The Great Lockdown*. IMF.

IMF. (2021). *Fiscal Monitor: Government Support Is Vital as Countries Race to Vaccinate*. IMF.

Keneally, Brimmer, & Gjaja. (2020). *To Restart Economies, Governments Need a Social Interactions Budget*. BCG.

Keynes, J. M. (1936). *The General Theory of Employment? Interest and Money. The Selected Works*. Harcourt, Brace and Company.

Khosrow-Pour, M. (2022). *Research Anthology on Business Continuity and Navigating Times of Crisis* (Vols. 1–4). Information Resources Management Association.

Kondratiev, N. D. (1984). The Long Wave Cycle (G. Daniels, Trans.). Richardson and Snyder.

Kupelian, B., & Clarry, R. (2021). *Predictions for 2021: From the Great Lockdown to the Great Rebound*. Global Economy Watch. PwC.

Leap by McKinsey. (2021). *2021 global report: The state of new-business building*. McKinsey & Co.

Lonergan, E., & Blyth, M. (2020). *Angrynomics*. Columbia University Press. doi:10.2307/j.ctv13840ch

Lotka, A. J. (1920). Analytical note on certain rhythmic relations in organic systems. *Proceedings of the National Academy of Sciences of the United States of America*, 6(7), 410–415. doi:10.1073/pnas.6.7.410 PMID:16576509

Lotka, A. J. (1925). *Elements of Physical Biology*. Williams & Wilkins.

Malone, T. W. (2018). *Superminds. The Surprising Power of People and Computers Thinking Together*. Oneworld Publications.

Manyika, J., Birshan, M., Smit, S., Woetzel, J., Russell, K., Purcell, L., & Ramaswamy, S. (2021). *Companies in the 21st century. A new look at how corporations impact the economy and households. Discussion paper*. McKinsey Global Institute. Retrieved from: www.mckinsey.com/mgi

Marx, K. (1995). *Capital: A New Abridgement*. Oxford University Press.

Mazzucato, M. (2013). *The Entrepreneurial State: Debunking Public vs. Private Sector Myths*. Anthem Press.

Mendy, Stewart, & VanAkin. (2020). *A leader's guide: Communicating with teams, stakeholders, and communities during COVID-19. Organization Practice*. McKinsey & Company.

Milanovic, B. (2019). Capitalism, Alone: The Future of the System that Rules the World. Harvard University Press. doi:10.4159/9780674242852

Minsky, H. P. (2008). *Stabilizing an Unstable Economy*. McGraw-Hill.

Mises. (1998). *Human Action: A Treatise on Economics*. Yale University Press.

North, D. (1996). *Institutions, Institutional Change and Economic Performance*. Cambridge University Press.

North, D. C. (1981). *Structure and Change in Economic History*. W. W. Norton & Co.

Novacek, Lee, & Krentz. (2021). *It's time to reimagine diversity, equity, and inclusion*. Boston Consulting Group.

Okamoto, G. (2020). Knightmare uncertainty. *IMF Finance & Development, 57*(3).

Pew Research Center. (2021). *Citizens in Advanced Economies Want Significant Changes to Their Political Systems*. Pew Research Center.

Pilipenko, A. I., Pilipenko, Z. A., & Pilipenko, O. I. (2021). Rebuilding a stronger business in the uncertain Post-COVID-19 future: Factor of intellectually autonomous and adequately socialized employees. In M. Ziolo (Ed.), *Adapting and Mitigating Environmental, Social, and Governance Risk in Business. (A volume in the Advances in Business Information Systems and Analytics (ABISA) Book Series)*. IGI Global. doi:10.4018/978-1-7998-6788-3.ch009

Pilipenko, O. I., Pilipenko, Z. A., & Pilipenko, A. I. (2021). Theory of Shocks, COVID-19, and Normative Fundamentals for Policy Responses. IGI Global.

Pilipenko, O. I., Pilipenko, Z. A., & Pilipenko, A. I. (2022). COVID-19 shock and Schumpeterian "creative destruction": Self-enforcing companies and self-development of the future dynamic economy. In M. Khosrow-Pour (Ed.), *Research Anthology on Business Continuity and Navigating Times of Crisis* (Vols. 1–4). Information Resources Management Association. doi:10.4018/978-1-6684-4503-7.ch057

Prigogine, I., & Stengers, I. (1983). *Order Out of Chaos: Man's New Dialogue with Nature*. Bantam Books.

Rajan, R. G. (2010). *Fault Lines: How Hidden Fractures Still Threaten the World Economy*. Princeton University Press.

Reinhart, C. M., & Rogoff, K. S. (2009). *This Time Is Different. Eight Centuries of Financial Folly*. Princeton University Press.

Robinson, J. (1980). Time in economic theory. Kyklos, 33(2), 219–29.

Sandbu, M. (2020). The post-pandemic brave new world. *Finance & Development, 57*(4).

Sandbu, M. (2020). *The Economics of Belonging*. Princeton University Press.

SantomeroA. (1996). *The Regulatory and Public Policy Agenda for Effective Intermediation in Post Socialist Economies*. Available at SSRN: https://ssrn.com/abstract=7913

Schelling. (1993). *System of Transcendental Idealism*. University of Virginia Press.

Schumpeter, J. A. (1961). *The Theory of Economic Development*. Oxford Univ. Press.

Schwab, K. (2016). *The Fourth Industrial Revolution*. Geneva: World Economic Forum.

Schwab, K., & Thierry, M. (2020). *COVID-19: The Great Reset*. World Economic Forum.

Siebel, T. M. (2019). *Digital Transformation: Survive and Thrive in an Era of Mass Extinction*. RosettaBooks.

Slutsky, E. (1937). The summation of random causes as the source of cyclic processes. Econometrica, 5(2), 105–146. doi:10.2307/1907241

Taleb, N. N. (2007). The Black Swan: The Impact of the Highly Improbable. The Random House Publishing Group.

Taleb, N. N. (2012). *Antifragile: Things That Gain from Disorder*. Random House Trade Paperbacks.

Tanzi, V. (2011). *Government versus Markets: The Changing Economic Role of the State*. Syndicate of the Press of the University of Cambridge.

Taplett, F. B., Krentz, M., Dean, J., & Novacek, G. (2019). Diversity is just the first step. Inclusion comes next. Boston Consulting Group.

Thom, R. (1974). Catastrophe theory: its present state and future perspectives. Dynamical Systems-Warwick. Lecture Notes in Mathematics. Math., 468, 366–372.

Udny, Y. G. (1927). *On a method of investigating periodicity* (Vol. 226; D. Series, Trans.). Royal Society.

Vernadsky, W. (1998). The Biosphere. Springer-Verlag Inc. doi:10.1007/978-1-4612-1750-3

Volterra, V. (1926). Fluctuations in the abundance of a species considered mathematically. Nature, 118, 558–560.

Volterra, V. (1931). *Leçons sur la Théorie Mathématique de la Lutte pour la Vie*. Gauthier-Villars.

White, W. (2009). Modern macroeconomics is on the wrong track. Finance & Development, 46(4), 15-18.

Wiener, N. (1930). *Generalized Harmonic Analysis* [Doctoral dissertation]. Acta Mathematica.

World Bank. (2020). *The COVID-19 pandemic: shocks to education and policy responses*. World Bank Report.

World Economic Forum. (2020). *The Future of Nature and Business. New Nature Economy*. Report II. World Economic Forum.

World Economic Forum. (2020a). *Emerging Pathways towards a Post-COVID-19 Reset and Recovery*. Chief Economists Outlook. World Economic Forum.

Zeeman, E. C. (1977). *Catastrophe Theory: Selected Papers*. Addison-Wesley.

Ziolo, M. (Ed.). (2021). Adapting and Mitigating Environmental, Social, and Governance Risk in Business. IGI Global. doi:10.4018/978-1-7998-6788-3

Chapter 10
Teleworking During the Pandemic of COVID–19:
Empirical Study of Its Effects

Sara Elouadi
https://orcid.org/0000-0001-5412-2714
Hassan II University, Morocco

Nariman Elouadi
Univesidad de Almeria España, Spain

ABSTRACT

This research focuses on the practice of teleworking during the COVID-19 pandemic. The objective is to analyze its effects on employees and companies, in particular the creation of the feeling of blurring between private life and professional life. The chapter begins with a theoretical analysis of telework by borrowing the framework of the theory of social regulation and the theory of conventions. Both make it possible to understand and situate the formation and control of the rules established by telework. Then the authors present their questionnaire survey and its main results.

INTRODUCTION

Blurring means the lack of clarity and the inability to distinguish between two spheres. In management, blurring describes the absence of boundaries between private life and professional life. As such, teleworking widely practiced during the Covid-19 crisis is blamed for creating the feeling of blurring among employees. It contributes, in fact, to the loss of the notion of sapatio-temporality of work and leads to its encroachment on personal life. The permeability of the boundaries between family and work can generate, according to many studies, negative and counterproductive emotions, including loneliness, anxiety, guilt and irritability (Mann and Holdsworth, 2003).

It should be noted that telework is not a recent organizational innovation. Literature attributes it to cybernetician Norbert Wiener in 1950 who suggested the use of new communication technologies to

DOI: 10.4018/978-1-6684-6762-6.ch010

work from home. Later, telecommuting experienced a large boom thanks to the possibilities offered by technological progress.

French law defines telework in article 46 of March 22, 2012 as a form of work organization in which the work which is carried out on the premises of the employer is carried out by an employee outside these premises on a regular basis. and voluntary by using TIC within the framework of an employment contract or an amendment thereto.

The health and economic crisis triggered by the Covid-19 pandemic and the physical distancing measures it has made mandatory have forced many companies to urgently switch to teleworking. This mode was, in fact, widely applied during confinement to limit the number of people present in the workplace in accordance with the health protocol. In addition to the preservation of the health of employees, teleworking allows, according to its tenors, to reconcile private life and professional life. It leads to a reduction in the time spent in transport and trips to the workplace and thus improves organizational productivity. Teleworking also allows you to work in a comfortable family environment.

Nevertheless, many studies affirm the existence of harmful effects linked to the distancing mode, including, in particular, blurring and violation of privacy, social isolation, dehumanization of relationships at work and increased mental workload exacerbated by technical problems related to technological tools.

Klein and Ratier (2012, p. 184) explain that although a number of works see in the blurring of private and professional borders a fluidification and a harmonious convergence of uses, most studies focus on the risks that this interference represents for the well-being of employees, both in their life at work and out of work (Jones, 1997).

In an attempt to understand the effects of telework, and the role of teleworking conditions on its perceived effects, we conducted a study with 284 teleworker employees in Morocco and abroad. We then conducted a questionnaire survey to assess the degree of satisfaction of teleworkers and the conditions for exercising remote work.

TELEWORKING THEORETICAL ANALYSIS FRAMEWORK

To analyze teleworking, we mobilized the theory of social regulation and the theory of conventions. They offer an interesting framework for understanding the mechanisms of formation of work and operating rules in organizations.

The Theory of Social Regulation and Teleworking

According to the theory of social regulation founded by the French sociologist Jean-Daniel Reynaud, social regulation constitutes the activity of producing, preserving or modifying the rules of operation. The theory of social regulation finds its origin in the analysis of professional relations in France at the beginning of the 1960s. interests and logics within organizations.

The author's work highlights the existence of three modes of social regulation to produce formal and informal rules. The first mode is called control regulation; it is a question of imposing disciplines and duties operated in general by the leaders and the managers vis-à-vis the employees.

The second mode is called autonomous regulation which aims to preserve the autonomy of operational staff. It is about adapting, transgressing or inventing new operating rules. Like, for example, the rules created by the employees themselves in the workshops. Autonomous regulation makes the rules of the leaders acceptable, because it is impossible to control everything and impose everything from the top down and this is part of the limits of the scientific organization of work and of Taylorism.

The third mode represents joint regulation. It defines the rules resulting from the negotiation between the managers and the performers for the creation of a collective agreement. Control regulation is a main action lever for managers to drive the company's strategy. And guarantee the consistency of practices, to provide the various sites with a common framework for action.

The complementarity between control regulation and autonomous regulation allows the establishment of new work organizations such as autonomous production groups, grouping by projects or work cells. And the implementation of new management methods, namely participatory management or management by objectives.

Joint regulation makes it possible to succeed in the bet of trust and the decentralization of tasks towards the performers by taking into account the mutual interests and the different logics of the employees.

According to Reynaud (1999, p. 20) in the company, what clashes are not only interests, but claims to rules, desires for regulation. But one of the parties holds, in practice, the statement and the execution. The other seeks to promote informal practices, clandestine networks of accomplices: at best, to introduce them into the official organization; at least to shelter them and make them respected. It is convenient to present this meeting as that of two regulations, a regulation of control and an autonomous regulation.

According to the theory of social regulation, telework can then be considered as the result of a social regulation that integrates the actors of the organization and the professional context. Telework is then the result of interactions and confrontations in order to find a balance and common operating rules likely to generate consensus between managers and workers. This theory of social regulation makes it possible, on the one hand, to interpret the use of telework as a new mode of operation. And on the other hand, to frame and control it by bringing it new rules in order to master it in the sense of autonomous regulation and joint regulation of Reynaud (1999).

The Theory of Conventions and Telework

It is at the crossroads of economics and sociology that the theory of conventions finds its essence. Developed in the 1980s, the theory of conventions focuses on the modes of coordination between individuals within organizations. According to this theory, the behaviors of the actors are not dictated solely by rationality but emanate from the harmonization and convergence of individual behaviors in order to face uncertainty.

According to Chatel and Rivaud-Danset (2004), convention is defined as an ambiguous conceptual reference, it can designate a regularity of behavior which can be apprehended as a solution to a coordination problem. Indeed, the convention constitutes a common framework which makes the uncertainty resulting from the action of others bearable, which facilitates coordination operations (Salais, Chatel and Riveau-Danset 1998).

Dupuy (1992) explains, in his work, the extreme difficulty of an individual action away from any reference to a collective, even within the framework of game theory. Favereau (2002) assimilates the economics of conventions to a theory in the sense of contemporary economic theory. According to him, it represents an intellectual construction generated by the behavior of people, in isolation from each other. The first conventionalist works are situated in a radical vision and do not agree to attribute to the conventionalist phenomenon the name "theory". They limit themselves to calling it "Method of inquiry" (Thévenot 1989; Salais, Baverez and Reynaud 1986). The meeting point between the radical vision and the pragmatic vision is, as Raveau (2005) specifies, the concentration of the analysis on the modes of coordination in their plurality and on the justifications provided by the actors for their actions.

The point of divergence between the two visions is the consideration of the individual, in the collective sense and not in the sense individualist, enunciated by the radical vision. The same author specifies that the objective of the economy of conventions is to understand the phenomena of coordination.

In the founding collective text of the school of the economy of conventions there is the hypothesis principle according to which, "the agreement between individuals, even when it is limited to the contract of a commercial exchange, is not possible without a common framework, without a conventionconstitutive", (Dupuy et al. 1989, p. 142).

For Boltanski and Thévenot (1987, 1989, 1991), the convention is an analytical framework from which actors perceive, analyze and solve problems. It allows them to seal agreements. Actors are endowed with the cognitive ability to make connections and agree on generalities.

Convention theory defines organizational actors as sharing systems of representation that contribute to forging rules of interaction. The same authors explain that the convention constitutes a framework of analysis which, while allowing the actors to perceive, analyze and solve the problems, also allows them to seal agreements. This process takes place in a cognitive framework that gives actors the possibility of making connections and agreeing on generalities, under the obligation to respect the principles of justice and provide justifications. The company is not an aggregation of rational individual calculations, according to Gensse (2003, p. 18), the conditions of uncertainty linked to the cognitive inability of individuals to predict the behavior of others, push individuals to develop "procedural rationality.

According to Gomez (1997, p. 61), it is a question of "rationalization" and no longer of rationality in going beyond the model of the "super calculating individual". The actor, to face management problems, will refer to regularities and convictions. The result is good management practices "that is to say practices for which the actors are convinced of the effectiveness" rather than practices "effective in themselves". According to him, the perception of the company as a place of production or a coalition of actors is largely over, the company is considered today as a place of conventions. "It is defined through a convention of effort, that is to say a collective procedure, a set of customs, speeches, sanctions making it possible to solve the problem of uncertainty in the face of the effort to be made", (Gensse 2003, p. 18). In 1976, Herbert Simon introduced the notion of procedural rationality, according to him, it results from an appropriate deliberation in view of the cognitive limits of man.

Deliberation brings together procedures through which humans adapt during decision-making to their own cognitive limits (Quinet 1994, p. 41).

For Boyer and Orléan (1989, p. 239), "if there is a small number of individuals who do not do not conform to the convention, they obtain a utility less than that which they had obtained by following the convention. As such, Amblard (2010, p. 90) explains that submission to the convention has many advantages, on the one hand, it makes it possible to avoid calculations and the justification of decisions "the individual rationalizes his acts by conformity ". On the other hand, it helps to gain recognition from others and integration into the group. Conventional dissent, he said, carries penalties such as lowering the status of the individual in the group, infamy and banishment.

The theory of conventions then offers an interesting framework for understanding the adoption of teleworking by companies. According to Gomez (1994), the convention is characterized by four properties, the first is that the convention emerges in a situation of radical uncertainty. Teleworking imposed by the epidemic and distancing is therefore a conventional response accepted by companies during confinement in order to preserve the health of employees and continue the activity.

Rational mimicry constitutes the second property of the convention. Telecommuting is widely adopted by companies and it continues to exist. It is not only a mimetic practice but its recurrence and regularity indicates the presence of a reflection of rationalization.

The third property removes the character of constraint from the convention insofar as the actors follow it with freedom. Telework is seen as a solution to preserve business continuity while protecting employees. However, companies have adopted teleworking deliberately by considering the practices of others in a conventionalist and non-prescriptive framework.

The fourth property indicates that the convention provides meaning to actors in the face of ambiguity and helps to make a decision. Similarly, it can be said that telework as a conventional practice has enabled managers and decision-makers to provide a healthy alternative to continue working despite the imperatives of distancing.

LITERATURE REVIEW

The COVID-19 crisis has disrupted working methods for almost a year. The confinement imposed to fight the epidemic has forced millions of people to stay at home and forced company managers to react quickly in this unprecedented context. Organizations have resorted to the only means available to them to maintain their activity: teleworking.

The main characteristic of telework is that it is a situation in which an employee works from home at least part of the time (Sullivan, 2003). This particular form of work has become the daily life of millions of people, emblematic of current changes in the conception of work and the workplace (Bailey and Kurland, 2002). There is a strong link between teleworking and organizational and managerial changes (Taskin, 2006), it underlines the role of the e-leader in the management of management teams (Seeley, 2006) and gives full meaning to managerial steering.

The new managerial paradigm linked to telework has a strong impact on employee engagement by promoting the notions of autonomy, development and personal fulfillment (Laloux, 2019). Indeed, the managerial relationship being called into question by the organizational context imposed by teleworking, managerial practices must be adapted to this specific work relationship in which the role of the hierarchical superior must be analyzed (Deffayet, 2002). Vayre, a specialist in organizational psychology, insists that teleworking is a change that companies must support by rethinking social relations and training their managers for this change. This leads us to question the managerial practices it induces and therefore its impact on job satisfaction.

The literature that studies the link between space and identity is abundant and mainly revolves around three levels: the individual, the work and the organization. At the individual level, several studies show, for example, that having a personal and customizable workspace reflects a way of existing (Byron and Laurence, 2015; Donis, 2015). Therefore, when teleworking is accompanied by flex-desk practices that materialize in non-territorial spaces, this directly questions the way of defining oneself as a worker (Elsbach, 2003; Hirst, 2011, Costas, 2012; Brown, 2015). In fact, the house could represent a space where it is possible to be yourself. Furthermore, other studies show that the different places where work is carried out reconfigure the relationship to space. (Felstead, et al., 2005; Tietze and Nadin, 2011; Wapshott and Mallett, 2012) and (Richardson et McKenna, 2014). Then, we find a second part of the literature which establishes the link between space and identity through the notion of "identity work" which reflects the way in which identity is defined by work.

(Antoine, 2018). It mainly contains studies that describe how flexwork questions the professional identity of a manager or a mobile worker, for example

(Brown and O'Hara, 2003; Richardson, 2010; Costas, 2013; Collins et al., 2016). On the contrary, the survey by Baldry and Barnes (2012) shows how the introduction of open space in a university is perceived as a degradation of physical working conditions, but also as an erosion of the fundamental functions of research and teaching and an attack on the professional status of academic work

Finally, several studies focus more on the organizational level and establish the link between the use of flexwork practices and the degree of identification with the organization (Thatcher and Zhu, 2006; Golden, 2007). For example, a context of reduced face-to-face exchanges combined with non-territorial spaces would lead to greater dis-identification but also to greater isolation. (Golden, 2007; Hirst, 2011; Pyöriä, 2011; Costas, 2013). More recently, several studies have proposed approaching this link between identity and flexwork as a process, a collective dynamic at work, rather than as causal links between individuals and practices, thus showing the ability of actors to define themselves through configurable spaces (Richardson and McKenna, 2014; Stang-Våland and Georg, 2018). Finally, beyond the spatial dimension of work, other research highlights the way in which the discourse that accompanies the implementation of spatial and temporal flexibility practices tends to define a new way of thinking about the relationship to work.

For example, offering a Smartphone (Hislop and Axtell, 2011; Cavazotte et al., 2014), configuring non-territorial spaces limited in number (Donis, 2015), offering greater autonomy in working time (Kelliher and Anderson, 2010; Seitz and Rigotti, 2018) or even establishing a type of management based on trust (Antoine, 2018) are all markers that trace the outlines of flexible work, carried out autonomously and controlled according to the results. Some postulate that this new world of work would give rise to new management techniques aimed at controlling the subjectivity of workers by defining a flexible and results-oriented individual as an entrepreneur (Seitz and Rigotti, 2018).

However, in this particularly unstable environment linked to COVID 19 and which has imposed remote working, employee satisfaction is a determining factor within organizations regardless of the nature of their activity.

The work of CEFRIO[1], (2001) and Tremblay, (2001) had already shown that the productivity and the quality of work were maintained and even improved. More recently, a survey by Indeed (Wolfe, 2019), conducted with more than 500 employees and 500 employers in various sectors, showed that 96% of organizations that had a regular telework policy and practice found that teleworking did not had no impact on productivity, and 65% had even seen an increase in productivity.

Among the disadvantages of telework, there is a risk of isolation and exclusion from important decisions in the organization (Tremblay, 2013, 2006)

According to a study by the Directorate for the Animation of Research, Studies and Statistics (DARES, the statistical service of the Ministry of Labor), published in November 2019, only 3% of French people had teleworked regularly until then (in least once a week).

The ANACT "National Agency for the Improvement of Working Conditions" survey through a questionnaire posted on the ANACT website from March 8 to May 10, 2020, to which 8,675 people in a telework situation in the context of confinement. concludes that a quarter of French employees, i.e. more than 5 million people, carried out their activity remotely during confinement. This is almost eight times more than before the health crisis. Nearly half of the people questioned thus had the feeling of working more than usual, which was reflected in particular by an increase in their fatigue. The results show an increase in working time materialized in particular by the reduction in break times and the increase in hourly amplitude.

A recent study by Registry et al. (2022) on a sample of 3771 Canadian teleworkers showed that teleworking has generated additional constraints such as the interdependence of tasks and professional isolation. These requests had negative consequences on telecommuting performance by increasing the frequency of perceived stress. However, administrative support plays a moderating role for isolation at work.

THE EMPIRICAL RESEARCH METHODOLOGY

This section focuses on the data collection methodology, the objectives of the empirical study and the presentation of the results of our statistical study on the effects of teleworking and the evaluation of its psychological and organizational impacts.

To analyze the effects of telework, we conducted a study with 284 teleworkers in Morocco and abroad. We then conducted a questionnaire survey between April and June 2021 to assess the degree of satisfaction of teleworkers and the conditions for exercising remote work.

Descriptive Statistics

We note from the results obtained from our survey that the majority of respondents are female teleworkers, namely 54.80% of respondents. On the other hand, 55.60% of respondents represent teleworkers with a baccalaureate level + 5, the most common level among respondents. 27% of respondents have a license and the others are divided between the doctorate and the baccalaureate level.

Our results show that the practice of telework varies greatly from one sector to another and from one service to another. It is in intellectually intensive services such as education that we recorded the most teleworkers among our sample. In our study, teaching and education dominated with a percentage of 29%, against 21% for sales and marketing. And about 50% of teleworkers are divided between other services, namely: 18.5% finance service; 8.5% human resources management service. 15.7% for the information and computer system.

We see here that the teleworkers surveyed represent a variety of functions and positions held. These differences can no doubt be explained at least in part by the nature of the tasks to be performed: indeed, in knowledge-intensive sectors, a large number of highly skilled jobs can be carried out remotely, using a laptop and an internet connection. Similarly, in many non-market services, there are jobs for which physical presence in the workplace is an important attribute. Activities for human health and social action, for example. In what follows, we present the questions of our survey and the answers collected.

How Do You Manage Your Working Hours?

Employees were asked about their ability to manage working time. A large majority of respondents, a percentage of 56.8%, claim to manage teleworking in the same way as face-to-face, respecting normal working hours. While, 22.2% of respondents chose to have the freedom to work when they want. However, 21% of employees find it difficult to manage remote work.

How Would You Rate Your Satisfaction with Teleworking?

We also asked respondents about their level of satisfaction with working from home. This question is used to calculate the Employee Satisfaction Score, the equivalent of the Customer Satisfaction Score. The results confirm that 75% of employees are satisfied with teleworking. This is a clear indication that employees have found a work pace that suits their needs in terms of organization, time management and stress. This statement is reinforced by the responses on the propensity to recommend telework to colleagues.

On a Scale of 1 to 5, Would You Recommend This Way of Working to Your Colleagues?

We asked the respondents to present their answers on a scale of 1 to 5. As such, the majority of the employees questioned, i.e. nearly 75%, give a score of 3 to 5 to the propensity to recommend telework. However, in-depth statistical analysis of the data shows that the degree of satisfaction is positively correlated with the allocation of technical means to facilitate teleworking. In other words, the companies of satisfied teleworkers have already put in place the necessary tools to facilitate working from home.

What are the Positive Impacts of Telework on the Psychology of Teleworkers?

In general, the results of our study show the existence of positive impacts on the psychological state of workers, the choice of answers was not exclusive and each respondent has the right to choose several impacts. Our study shows that teleworkers mostly feel less tired and stressed and more productive and efficient.

What are the Negative Impacts of Telework on the Psychology of Teleworkers?

Telework was imposed in a health emergency situation, and therefore dictated, sometimes, without the allocation of the necessary means and without the psychological and organizational support of employees. This has led, in some cases, to negative impacts such as increased mental workload, lack of concentration, lower morale, stress, deterioration of relationships with colleagues and demotivation. According to our survey, the most noticed effects among respondents are the increase in working time and difficulty concentrating.

Do Teleworkers Have a Well-Equipped Space Dedicated to Work at Home?

The urgent and massive deployment of telework has transformed the private sphere into a place of professional productivity. If the employee does not have a space dedicated to work at home, this can aggravate stress and lead to musculoskeletal disorders. According to our study, 55.2% of respondents have a space equipped for teleworking compared to 44.8% who suffer from the lack of a space adapted to their professional activity.

Do Teleworkers Succeed in Separating Their Professional and Private Lives?

This is, unquestionably, the most notorious negative effect of teleworking. The absence of a boundary between work and family constitutes a major risk, likely to compromise the psychosocial health of the worker and his organizational productivity. The results of our study show that 57.3% of employees succeed in separating their personal life from their professional life. On the other hand, 42.7% of the employees questioned note an alteration and an imbalance between family and work.

Are Teleworkers Satisfied with the IT and Technological Tools Made Available to Them?

The computer tool facilitates the management of work from home and makes it possible to maintain communication with colleagues and managers. The results of our study show overall satisfaction with the technological means. In fact, nearly 65% of employees surveyed say they are satisfied with the work tools made available to them, 19% say they are neutral. And more than 16% say they are dissatisfied with the technical devices.

Are Telemeetings as Productive as Physical Meetings?

The physical presence of employees in the workplace inevitably creates social interactions and facilitates the management of disagreements and conflicts. However, the physical distance imposed by telemeetings dehumanizes social relations and can lead to misunderstandings and frustrations.

Many of our employees surveyed said that participation in telemeetings is less productive than physical meetings, i.e. a percentage of 68.5% and only nearly 31% are satisfied with virtual meetings.

Do Employees Want to Continue Teleworking Beyond the COVID-19 Crisis?

The answer to this question is unequivocal, the majority of employees (52.4%) wish to continue in teleworking mode beyond the Covid-19 crisis.

In the current sanitary conditions, teleworking is destined to become firmly anchored in managerial practices. Our employees seem to find in the distanciel a good compromise to improve the balance and the flexibility between the private life and the professional life.

LINEAR REGRESSION RESULTS

We carried out a linear regression, with the explanatory variable "the degree of recommendation of teleworking to colleagues" and the explanatory variable "the possession at home of a space dedicated to teleworking".

We selected the potential adjustment variables among all the variables collected in such a way that there are less than 20% of respondents with missing data or variables with less than 5% missing values. The adjustment variable "the possession at home of a space dedicated to teleworking" was defined a priori according to data from the literature. The other potential adjustment variables were introduced into a LASSO (Least Absolute Shrinkage and Selection Operation) penalized regression model. The

Table 1. Descriptive statistics of the quantitative variable

	Average (standard deviation)	Median [Q25-75]	Min	max	n
degree of recommendation of teleworking to colleagues	3.36 (1.25)	3.00 [3.00; 4.00]	1.00	5.00	248

Table 2. Descriptive statistics of the qualitative variable

		n (%)
possession at home of a space dedicated to teleworking	Yes	137 (55%)
	No	111 (45%)

penalty coefficient (lambda) was chosen so that it provides an estimation error less than one standard deviation of the minimum error obtained by cross-validation 10 times, while being as parsimonious as possible. No variable had a coefficient different from 0 with this lambda coefficient.

As the distribution of residuals does not follow a normal distribution, we calculated confidence intervals and p-values by bootstrap (1000 iterations).

Table 3. Univariate analyzes

		Average (standard deviation)	Median [Q25-75]	Min	max	n	P	test
possession at home of a space dedicated to teleworking	Yes	3.74 (±1.12)	4.00 [3.00 - 5.00]	1.00	5.00	137	<0.001	Welch
	Non	2.90 (±1.26)	3.00 [2.00 - 4.00]	1.00	5.00	111	-	-

Table 4. Linear regression

		Coefficients	P
possession at home of a space dedicated to teleworking	No vs Yes	-0.836 [-1.13; -0.499]	<0.001

At the 5% risk, there is a statistically significant relationship between "the degree of recommendation of telework to colleagues" and "the possession at home of a space dedicated to telework".

Figure 1. Possession at home of a space dedicated to teleworking

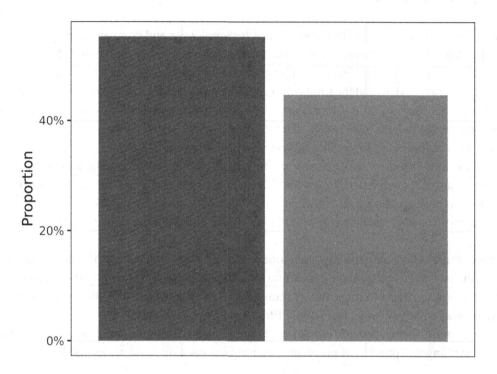

Figure 2. Crossing of the variable possession at home of a space dedicated to teleworking and degree of recommendation of teleworking to colleagues

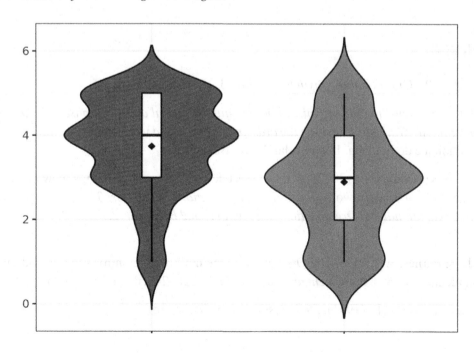

RESULTS AND DISCUSSION

If remote work is a provider of many opportunities for employees and companies, it must, however, be kept in mind that it can generate risks and abuses such as blurring, social isolation and increased mental load of employees. According to Tremblay, Chevrier and Di Loreto (2006, p. 4), the members of the entourage do not always understand the limits of the teleworker and allow themselves to formulate requests for availability that they would not formulate if the person was not working not at home. Conversely for the entourage, the parents, the friends, the fact of seeing the teleworker working a few hours on the weekend can encourage them to say that this one is always working.

Companies must therefore adopt a new organizational strategy by training their managers in the psychosocial constraints and risks of telework. Managers must therefore set the rules of availability and disconnection to preserve the privacy of their employees without forgetting the right to a break during the working day. It is also necessary to provide assistance and listening units to support employees in difficulty.

Teleworkers are called upon to adopt operational and regulatory measures with their family members to avoid intrusions and improve their concentration and productivity. Informing those around you and establishing morning rituals to mark the working day seem to be effective solutions for improving the congruence between private and professional life (Dumas and Ruiller, 2014).

Companies must, finally, provide employees with the means and equipment necessary to effectively manage teleworking and provide, if necessary, training or coaching sessions for the least equipped employees.

In accordance with the work of Klein and Ratier (2012), three levers make it possible to adapt teleworking and avoid the risks of interference for employees: Information and Communication Technologies (ICT) and the definition of operating rules by human resources departments; self-regulation in the learning phase of new uses of time and space related to ICT; and the organization of teleworked activities to better organize their working time.

REFERENCES

Amblard, M. (2010). *La rationalité - mythes et réalité*. L'Harmattan.

Antoine, M. (2018). *Unveiling the organisational identity: A spatial approach based on the office. The case of ORES Picardy Wallonia transition towards an activity-based workspace* (Doctoral dissertation). Université catholique de Louvain, Louvain-la-Neuve, Belgique.

Bailey, D. E., & Kurland, N. B. (2002). A review of telework research: Findings, new directions, and lessons for the study of modern work. *Journal of Organizational Behavior: The International Journal of Industrial, Occupational and Organizational Psychology and Behavior, 23*(4), 383–400. doi:10.1002/job.144

Baldry, C. J., & Barnes, A. (2012). The Open-plan Academy: Space, Control and the Undermining of Professional Identity. *Work, Employment and Society, 26*(2), 228–245. doi:10.1177/0950017011432917

Boltanski, L., & Thévenot, L. (1991). *De la justification*. Gallimard.

Boyer, R., & Orléan, A. (1989). Les transformations des conventions salariales entre théorie et histoire. *Revista Economica, 42*(2), 233–272.

Brown, B., & O'Hara, K. (2003). Place as a practical concern of mobile workers. *Environment & Planning A, 35*(9), 1565–1587. doi:10.1068/a34231

Byron, K., & Laurence, G. A. (2015). Diplomas, photos, and tchotchkes as symbolic self-representations: Understanding employees' individual use of symbols. *Academy of Management Journal, 58*(1), 298–323. doi:10.5465/amj.2012.0932

Cavazotte, F., Lemos, A. H., & Villadsen, K. (2014). Corporate smart phones: Professionals' conscious engagement in escalating work connectivity. *New Technology, Work and Employment, 29*(1), 72–87. doi:10.1111/ntwe.12022

Cefrio. (2001). *Le télétravail: articuler qualité de vie et performance.* Cefrio.

Chatel, E., & Rivaud-Danset, D. (2004). L'économie des conventions: une lecture critique à partir de la philosophie pragmatiste de John Dewey. *Revue de philosophie économique, 13*(1), 49-76.

Collins, A. M., Hislop, D., & Cartwright, S. (2016). Social support in the workplace between teleworkers, office-based colleagues and supervisors. *New Technology, Work and Employment, 31*(2), 161–175. doi:10.1111/ntwe.12065

Costas, J. (2013). Problematizing mobility: A metaphor of stickiness, non-places and the kinetic elite. *Organization Studies, 34*(10), 1467–1485. doi:10.1177/0170840613495324

Deffayet, S. (2002). Nouvelles Technologies de l'Information et de la Communication (NTIC) et contrôle dans la relation managériale. *Recherches Sociologiques, 33*(1), 27–48.

Donis, C., Perret, V., & Taskin, L. (2017). *Space, Place, and Scale: Critical Reflections on the New Spatial Turn in Organization Studies.* Academic Press.

Dumas, M., & Ruiller, C. (2014). Le télétravail: Les risques d'un outil de gestion des frontières entre vie personnelle et vie professionnelle? *Management Avenir*, (8), 71–95. doi:10.3917/mav.074.0071

Dupuy, J. P. (1992). *Libéralisme et justice sociale: le sacrifice et l'envie.* Hachette.

Dupuy, J. P., Eymard-Duvernay, F., Favereau, O., Salais, R., & Thévenot, L. (1989). Economie des conventions. *Revista Economica, 40*(2), 329–359.

Elsbach, K. D. (2003). Relating physical environment to self-categorizations: Identity threat and affirmation in a non-territorial office space. *Administrative Science Quarterly, 48*(4), 622–654. doi:10.2307/3556639

Favereau, O. (2002). Conventions and regulation. In R. Boyer & Y. Saillard (Eds.), *Régulation theory: the state of the art* (pp. 312–319). Routlege.

Felstead, A., Jewson, N., & Walters, S. (2005). The shifting locations of work: New statistical evidence on the spaces and places of employment. *Work, Employment and Society, 19*(2), 415–431. doi:10.1177/0950017005053186

Gensse, P. (2003). Introduction générale. In M. Amblard (Ed.), *Conventions & management*. De Boeck Supérieur.

Golden, T. (2007). Co-workers who telework and the impact on those in the office: Understanding the implications of virtual work for co-worker satisfaction and turnover intentions. *Human Relations*, *60*(11), 1641–1667. doi:10.1177/0018726707084303

Hirst, A. (2011). Settlers, vagrants and mutual indifference: Unintended consequences of hot-desking. *Journal of Organizational Change Management*, *24*(6), 767–788. doi:10.1108/09534811111175742

Hislop, D., & Axtell, C. (2011). Mobile phones during work and non-work time: A case study of mobile, non-managerial workers. *Information and Organization*, *21*(1), 41–56. doi:10.1016/j.infoandorg.2011.01.001

Jones, M. (1997). Out of the office, out of control. *Psychology Today*, *30*(2).

Kelliher, C., & Anderson, D. (2010). Doing more with less? Flexible working practices and the intensification of work. *Human Relations*, *63*(1), 83–106. doi:10.1177/0018726709349199

Klein, T., & Ratier, D. (2012). L'impact des TIC sur les conditions de travail. Centred'Analyse Stratégique, La documentation française, Rapports et documents, n° 49, 328 p.

Laloux, F. (2019). *Reinventing Organizations*. Diatenio.

Mann, S., & Holdsworth, L. (2003). The psychological impact of teleworking: Stress, emotions and health. *New Technology, Work and Employment*, *18*(3), 196–211. doi:10.1111/1468-005X.00121

Pyöriä, P. (2011). Managing telework: Risks, fears and rules. *Management Research Review*, *34*(4), 386–399. doi:10.1108/01409171111117843

Quinet, C. (1994). Herbert Simon et la rationalité. *Revue française d'économie, 9*(1), 133-181.

Registre, J. F. R., Danthine, É., Ouellet, A. M., Cachat-Rosset, G., & Saba, T. (2022). Effet du télétravail sur la santé psychologique et la performance des travailleurs durant la pandémie de la COVID-19. *Psychologie du Travail et des Organisations*.

Reynaud, J.-D. (1991). Pour une sociologie de la régulation sociale. *Sociologie et Sociétés*, *23*(2), 13–26. doi:10.7202/001632ar

Richardson, J. (2010). Managing flexworkers: Holding on and letting go. *Journal of Management Development*, *29*(2), 137–147. doi:10.1108/02621711011019279

Richardson, J., & McKenna, S. (2014). Reordering spatial and social relations: A case study of professional and managerial flexworkers. *British Journal of Management*, *25*(4), 724–736. doi:10.1111/1467-8551.12017

Salais, R., Baverez, N., Reynaud, B. (1986). *L'invention du chômage*. Presses Universitaires de France Raveau.

Salais, R., Chatel, E., & Riveau-Danset, D. (1998). *Institutions et conventions, la réflexivité de l'action économique*. Raison Pratique, École des Hautes Études en Sciences Sociales. doi:10.4000/books.editionsehess.10492

Seitz, J., & Rigotti, T. (2018). How do differing degrees of working-time autonomy and overtime affect worker well-being? A multilevel approach using data from the German Socio-Economic Panel (SOEP). *German Journal of Human Resource Management*, *32*(3-4), 177–194. doi:10.1177/2397002218780630

Sullivan, C. (2003). What's in a name? Definitions and conceptualisations of teleworking and homeworking. *New Technology, Work and Employment*, *18*(3), 158–165. doi:10.1111/1468-005X.00118

Taskin, L. (2006). Télétravail: Les enjeux de la déspatialisation pour le Management Humain. *Revue Interventions économiques. Papers in Political Economy*, (34).

Thatcher, S. M., & Zhu, X. (2006). Changing identities in a changing workplace: Identification, identity enactment, self-verification, and telecommuting. *Academy of Management Review*, *31*(4), 1076–1088. doi:10.5465/amr.2006.22528174

Tietze, S., & Nadin, S. (2011). The psychological contract and the transition from office-based to home-based work'. *Human Resource Management Journal*, *21*(3), 318–334. doi:10.1111/j.1748-8583.2010.00137.x

Tremblay, D. G. (2001). Le télétravail: Les avantages et inconvénients pour les individus et les défis de gestion des RH. La GRH dans la société de l'information.

Tremblay, D.-G., Chevrier, C., & Et Di Loreto, M. (2006). Le télétravail à domicile: Meilleure conciliation emploi-famille ou source d'envahissement de la vie privée? *Revue Interventions Economiques*, *34*(34), 1–16. doi:10.4000/interventionseconomiques.689

Våland, M. S., & Georg, S. (2018). Spacing identity: Unfolding social and spatial-material entanglements of identity performance. *Scandinavian Journal of Management*, *34*(2), 193–204. doi:10.1016/j.scaman.2018.04.002

Wapshott, R., & Mallett, O. (2012). The spatial implications of homeworking: A Lefebvrian approach to the rewards and challenges of home-based work. *Organization*, *19*(1), 63–79. doi:10.1177/1350508411405376

Wolfe, P. (2019). Télétravail: 62% des employeurs canadiens permettent cette pratique. *Infopresse*, 18-19.

ENDNOTE

[1]   Francophone Center for the Computerization of Organizations.

Chapter 11
Innovative Digital Transformation Strategies of Large Suppliers for Mexican Corner Stores During a Pandemic:
Challenges and Opportunities

Regina G. Diaz
https://orcid.org/0000-0002-4025-0691
EGADE Business School, Mexico

Raul F. Montalvo
EGADE Business School, Mexico

ABSTRACT

With the pandemic, digital transformation (DT) was accelerated, and consumers adopted new consumption patterns. Therefore, suppliers had to adapt their business models quickly. This study aims to understand the strategies of large suppliers on Mexican corner stores (CS) during the pandemic and show the perception of CS about these DT strategies. Many digital platform initiatives that were developed by both the government and large suppliers are introduced in this chapter. Additionally, interviews with large suppliers' executives were consulted to clarify their activities that were developed in favor of CS. By conducting 20 interviews with CS, the authors found their perception of large suppliers' DT actions. Findings reveal that the lack of training, investment, and incentives are key factors for the entire virtuous cycle to be fulfilled.

DOI: 10.4018/978-1-6684-6762-6.ch011

INTRODUCTION

The global COVID-19 pandemic has disrupted the traditional life model for both companies and people. Experts predict that once the world overcomes this trance, economic, and social activities will no longer be as they were known. The virus, among other things, has accelerated the adoption of the digitization of economic activities and new ways of conducting things.

Previous studies have been developed on the pandemic impact on small businesses, emphasizing that COVID-19 stay-at-home policies had a major impact on small businesses, especially hard hit are businesses reliant on physical space businesses (Mandviwall & Flanagan, 2021). Some other studies have analyzed the digital platforms developed by health services during the pandemic (Dennis et al., 2020). There is a gap in this type of analysis between small- and medium-sized enterprises (SME), and the corner store´s (CS) situation during a pandemic or a related context of this level. In some countries the CSs are of great importance because they were the front desks for large suppliers during the pandemic Therefore, large suppliers made great efforts to support them.

In Mexico, 2,227,058 establishments belong to the commerce sector, of which 998,120 businesses (44.81%) were under the subsector of retail commerce of groceries, food, beverages, ice, and tobacco (INEGI, 2019). For most, CSs represent much more than a place of purchase since besides being a convenience place for purchasing implies security and trust. Since March 2020, when the pandemic was declared in Mexico, the government has promoted initiatives, such as keeping a healthy distance and staying home (Secretaria de Salud, 2020). Simultaneously, they promoted many initiatives to help local businesses (International Labour Organization [ILO], 2021). Despite these efforts, around 300,000 CSs in Mexico closed last year because of the economic damage caused by the COVID-19 pandemic (Ochoa, 2021).

In this analysis we analyze the innovative strategies of large suppliers in Mexican CS during the pandemic while we consider this as a contribution to the literature, since we identify the lack of incentives as a key factor for the whole virtuous cycle to be fulfilled. Therefore, on the one hand side an objective of this chapter is to show the strategies of large suppliers in Mexican CS during the pandemic, but also together with this to understand the perception of the CS about these digital transformation (DT) strategies. Finally, this chapter identifies the benefits that the end customer obtains from this DT strategies.

BACKGROUND

It is important to mention that, recent studies show that 40% of all technology spending at a global level has been invested in DT, with enterprises spending over $2 trillion in 2019. Moreover, 52% of companies plan to cut or delay investments because of COVID-19, whereas only 9% make those cuts in DT projects (Appio et al., 2021). Accordingly, most business-to-business (B2B) companies have started their DT projects to ensure their competitiveness in the market. The sales team is making its own effort in contributing to the productivity gains of the company: since the 1980s, sales researchers have been particularly concerned with the implementation of digital technologies in the form of customer relationship management systems or sales force automation (Wengler et al., 2021).

Providing a comprehensive definition of DT is complex because it is a multifaceted and multidimensional phenomenon that affects organizations at different levels and forms (Appio et al., 2021). DT is defined as transformation "concerned with the changes digital technologies can bring about in company's business model, products, or organizational structures" (Nadkarni & Prügl, 2021); it is perhaps the most pervasive managerial challenge for incumbent firms of the last and coming decades. The term "digital transformation" is primarily discussed in the research domain of information systems and increasingly in sales; it encompasses profound organizational and societal changes (Wengler et al., 2021).

Business digitalization began with the democratization of technology and the implementation of the Internet as a tool for everyday use. Note that several signs indicate that the digital economy is transforming the traditional economy (Fernández et al., 2021). The technological transformation is a fact that accompanies the advent of the digital society or the network society—the type of society in which information and communication technologies play a fundamental role. Today's society is undergoing a constant technological transformation that involves changes in all areas, especially in terms of labor and the business world. According to several authors, we are at the beginning of the Fourth Industrial Revolution (Fernández et al., 2021).

Artificial intelligence is the greatest technological transformation of the information society, placing society at the gates of the Fourth Industrial Revolution. The datafication of business, that is, the use of Big Data to build customer loyalty and especially user-generated data to predict customer behavior, is a growing trend in the business world (Fernández et al., 2021). However, digital possibilities should come together with skilled employees and executives to reveal its transformative power. Thus, DT requires both technology and people (Nadkarni & Prügl, 2021). Creating a digital workplace is not about emails and social media nor integrating digital technologies; it is about transforming personal, team, and organizational performance (Dressler & Paunovic, 2021).

The main purpose of DT is to redesign the organizational business by introducing digital technologies and achieving benefits, such as productivity improvements, cost reductions, and innovation (Ulas, 2019). Digitalization of businesses has grown recently. Across sectors, firms of all sizes are increasingly equipping their staff with digital tools, although smaller firms do so more slowly, whereas some sectors do so more quickly (OECD iLibrary, 2021).

Digital technologies are radically changing how business is conducted, and many small businesses must more fully engage with the trend toward digitization (Chan et al., 2020).

Small and Medium Enterprise

Globally, small firms are important drivers of economic growth and prosperity. In particular, SMEs are critical for national economies because they contribute to innovation, job creation, and economic growth (Chan et al., 2020). Not all SMEs have the capacity to undertake this transformation. The smaller the firms, the less likely they are to adopt new digital practices, and the more likely they are to limit uptake to basic services. Overall, SME digitalization is strongly related to the way value is created within the firm and the sector in which it operates (OECD iLibrary, 2021).

Studies have focused less attention on SME's DT in developing countries, which contrasts to developed countries because of economic, political, social and cultural differences and legal aspects (Rassool & Dissanayake, 2019). A single market mistake may be a temporary setback for a large firm, but it results to the failure of a small firm. Therefore, small firms must accurately identify and evaluate opportunities (Chan et al., 2020).

The COVID-19 crisis has heightened the importance of SME digitalization and served as an accelerator. Firms have moved operations online and implemented smart working solutions to remain in business during lockdown and overcome disruptions in supply chains, with online platforms playing an instrumental role in connecting users to new markets, suppliers, or resources (OECD iLibrary, 2021). The pandemic is a major crisis for small businesses. DT offers a lifeline for some small businesses (Mandviwalla & Flanagan, 2021). The current pandemic has accelerated the race for DT, also known as "Industry 4.0" or "Society 5.0," which changes the structures of how organizations can create value by digitally obtaining insights from their customers' behavior and by restructuring supply chains (Klein & Todesco, 2021).

Results from previous studies on small business´ DT in the context of the pandemic (Mandviwalla & Flanagan, 2021) illustrate how small businesses can engage, sell, and deliver using technology and the factors influencing the transformation process (Mandviwalla & Flanagan, 2021). Larson et al. (2005) determined significantly greater use of relational exchange and electronic communication media with large suppliers than small suppliers. The needs of SMEs in the DT process can vary. It must privatize the content by using the size of enterprise, sector, and SME. Meanwhile, electronic operation adopts other business processes, such as supply, manufacturing, marketing, sale, finance, accounting, human resources, and new technology. Digitization requires radical changes in terms of not only strategy but also culture within the company (Ulas, 2019). Priyono et al. (2020) stated that SMEs follow three different major paths toward a digitalized firm: accelerating digitalization, digitalizing sales functions, and finding digital partners to reach the market. The decision to select one of the three DT paths is determined by the existing digital maturity level, the learning culture, and the history of digital technology adoption, among others. (Priyono et al., 2020).

Previous studies have emphasized the major impact of COVID-19 stay-at-home policies on small businesses. The following businesses reliant on physical space are especially hit: a wine store in which the customer walks in, browses, and then completes the purchase; a bridal store that offers planning, browsing, and a changing room; a hair salon offering unique services in social atmosphere; pet stores wherein animals are dropped off for some services; boutique personal care product manufacturer that sells in flea markets; and a therapist or a music instructor that requires private one-on-one interaction (Mandviwalla & Flanagan, 2021). In Mexico, the health emergency has affected firms in some way, and SMEs are no exception. Many of these companies were looking for financial relief to survive in the coming months, and through solidarity, they may be able to thrive (Mercado Solidario, 2021). With the limitations presented by the contingency of COVID-19, the active hours of the stores have been reduced considerably. This year's projections indicate that revenue in this format could be reduced by up to 25%, but small businesses are resilient (The Coca-Cola Company, 2020).

SMEs must take a holistic view of the internal DT, including the implementation of measures that far exceed the technical aspects (Stich et al., 2020).

Chan et al.'s (2020) work on technology-driven innovation in small firms provides some recommendations for small firms on using digital technologies to drive innovation. The first two recommendations relate to opportunity recognition, the next one to opportunity development, and the final two to opportunity evaluation: (1) monitor how core technologies and markets are changing and identify new business opportunities; (2) clarify business concepts; (3) identify and access external partners and resources to implement solutions; (4) evaluate the solutions and implement best designs and practices; and (5) stay agile.

DT and Business Models

In the last decade, management and organizational scholars have paid increasing attention to the inter-connections between DT and innovation management (Appio et al., 2021). In the analysis of leading businesses, it is found that companies with a cohesive plan for integrating the digital and physical components of operations can successfully transform their business models (Berman, 2012). Research at the intersection between DT and innovation management is still scattered and lacks a unified perspective and overarching framework that can inform future theoretical and empirical studies. This is due to the conceptual vagueness characterizing DT and the embryonic development stage of scholarly research into this fascinating topic, which has dramatic practical implications (Appio et al., 2021)

Research at the crossroads of DT and innovation management is still in its infancy, but it is gaining momentum, thus entering an era that can pave the way to new insights and deeper understandings. From a mere descriptive perspective, the topic has been experiencing a phase of exponential growth only since 2017 (Appio et al., 2021). Challenges to integrating DT into the business model arise. For example, the concept of DT has gained immense attention during the past few years, and it is a topic of concern for conventional organizations. DT refers to the alteration of the business models using innovative and technological processes that lead to immense changes in the behavior of society and the consumer. The increased use of technological innovations within various industries has transformed the behavior and use of organizations, market structures, and individuals' attitudes. However, the companies have also observed several challenges while combining DTs in their business models (Sundaram et al., 2020).

Technology adoption strategies are directly connected to the issues of business model transformation and the interplay between path dependence, strategic flexibility, and many business modules involved. The business-level perspective of technology adoption inside Industry 4.0 recognizes the importance of redesigning operating processes in the transition, which can take different pathways, from being dominated by demand pull (high servitization level), to being dominated by technology push (high DT level) (Dressler & Paunovic, 2021). The choice of strategy and the success of DT depends on various factors, such as the firms' existing digital capabilities, learning culture, history of digital technology adoption, and ability to develop with supporting parties (Priyono et al., 2020).

Consumer Market

It is important also to highlight the evolution of the consumption market considering all these new contexts. Within the framework of the changes that characterize the digital revolution in the information society, the use of Big Data is presented as the most important challenge and innovation of recent years. The use of massive data, which are only accessible to the largest companies, is seen as an effective tool for building customer loyalty by using data generated by the customers themselves to predict their behavior as consumers (Fernández et al., 2021). Products and services, information, and customer engagement can be reshaped using the new mobility, interactivity, and information access capabilities. The challenge then is monetizing these new customer value propositions (Berman, 2012).

In today's increasingly digital world, even companies in primarily physical industries will not start their DT journey from "zero." Instead, most organizations are already finding ways to use digital information by providing interactive websites, improving customer service, or enhancing customer experiences. Similarly, they are creating basic operating capabilities, such as online channels or digital supply chain tracking. From this starting point, a company's strategic approach to transformation typically follows one of the three paths:

Path 1: Create and integrate digital operations first. Then, address the customer value proposition to achieve full transformation.

Path 2: Enhance, extend, or reshape the customer value propositions with digital content, insight and engagement. Then focus on integrating digital operations.

Path 3: Build a new set of capabilities around the transformed customer value proposition and operating model in lock-step (Berman, 2012).

B2B selling and sales processes are being challenged by major disruptions brought about by advanced selling technologies, artificial intelligence, machine learning, and new digital working environments. Several studies have shown that using digital tools and technologies in B2B sales increases revenue, profitability, effectiveness, and understanding of the customers' needs. A recent commercial study by Bages-Amat et al. (2020) showed that the COVID-19 pandemic has also changed buying and selling, with 70%–80% of decision-makers preferring to make purchases remotely or using self-service (Mattila et al., 2021).

Digital platforms spark practitioner and researcher interest through their ability to transform how customers, suppliers, and other participants interact. Importantly, on digital platforms, users' roles can become blurred, allowing a user to be both a customer and a seller. The success of a digital platform depends on the size of its user base and especially the number of attractive users the platform can attract, highlighting the vital role of sales and marketing (Mattila et al., 2021).

Consumers have become technology savvy and use interactive tools and gain instant knowledge about the product and compare it with the other variants, based on which they decide whom to trust and then buy accordingly. With the emergence of the Internet, people are exploiting the Internet while managing their socialization, household, shopping, and entertainment needs (Sundaram et al., 2020).

COVID-19 Pandemic in Mexico

On March 11, 2020, the World Health Organization (WHO) Director-General declared COVID-19 as a pandemic (WHO, 2020). However, the Mexican Agreement declared the disease an epidemic generated by the SARS-CoV2 virus (COVID-19) as a health emergency on March 30, 2020, due to force majeure published by the General Health Council (ILO, 2021).

The immediate main action that Mexico followed was the so-called "National Day of Healthy Distance," which lasted from March 23 to April 30, 2020 (Secretaria de Salud, 2020). Despite all the efforts of the government and citizens, to date, Mexico has produced the following COVID-19 figures: a cumulative total of 330,757 deaths and an estimate of 5,710,174 confirmed cases (CentroGeo–GeoInt-DataLab, 2021).

The official campaign to contain the pandemic is as follows:

In Mexico and in the world, we face an unprecedented challenge. COVID-19 is very contagious and spreads throughout the country. The only way to contain it is for all of us to stay home. If we do, we will all protect ourselves from disease. We must be responsible, leaving only if it is strictly necessary, taking safe distance measures. The virus does not discriminate age or social status. Let us be in solidarity and together we will move forward. Stay at home. (Secretaria de Salud, 2021)

Community Mobility Reports provide insights into what has changed in response to policies aimed at combating COVID-19. Mexican Mobility trends for places like grocery markets, food warehouses, farmers markets, specialty food stores, drug stores, and pharmacies have increased to 26% during the last 6 weeks—baseline Aug. 27 until Oct. 08 (Google, 2021).

Government Actions to Support Micro-Business

In the context of the health emergency, a series of measures were developed to protect family income, production, and employment, and guarantee supplies: (1) credits to support family micro-businesses and self-employed workers despite the effects caused by COVID-19; and (2) "Mercado Solidario" (Coordinación de Estrategia Digital Nacional de la Oficina de la Presidencia de la República–Medidas, 2021). In "Mercado Solidario," these businesses can be supported through local consumption at home and in advance (Mercado Solidario, 2021). On the *Juntos por el Trabajo* platform, a stamp is available for companies to download and let their customers know that if they consume locally, the company will preserve their sources of employment (ILO, 2021).

Other previous research has also agreed that government is a key factor in SMEs' DT success. The government also has a role to play in stimulating DT of SMEs. The proposed government interventions include evaluating how the current legal and regulatory framework enhances the DT (Ulas, 2019). European SMEs are the ideal target to explore the research scope due to several initiatives released by the European Commission in enhancing SMEs' digital capabilities. For instance, the innovation voucher stimulates collaboration between SMEs and research centers to develop and/or improve their digital advancements. It allows cross-fertilization skills and spurs innovations (Scuotto et al., 2021). In Germany, competence centers have existed since 2015 to give SMEs a holistic approach to digitization and quickly identify simple potentials. The centers support the companies in taking the first steps toward an independent digitally networked enterprise (Stich et al., 2020).

In Mexico, the Central Bank (Banco de México) developed a platform called CoDi® to facilitate payment and collection transactions through electronic transfers quickly, safely and efficiently using mobile phones. It is a 24 × 7 scheme, most importantly, at no cost! CoDi® uses the technology of Quick Response codes and Near Field Communication codes to facilitate cashless transactions among businesses and users (Banco de México, 2021).

As a reliable example to promoting this initiative, Citibanamex, PepsiCo Alimentos México, and Amigo PAQ have formed an unprecedented alliance to promote financial inclusion in order to benefit more than 800,000 storekeepers by equipping them with digital financial tools. Thanks to this initiative, which invites people to work "without trash in small stores" through a cashless ecosystem, small businesses can use the electronic payment method CoDi® offered by Banco de México in the Citibanamex application Mobile or Transfer® (Pepsico-CoDi, 2020).

Large Suppliers' Efforts and Strategies

For many years, brands have exhibited a strong presence. In a survey of grocery stores in Mexico City, merchants confirmed that Coca-Cola, Pepsi, Bimbo, Modelo, Lala, Alpura, Philip Morris, and Nestlé supply most of their inventory (Pallares, 2013). CS are a key element for large suppliers. As an example, a large supplier has mentioned: "Miscellanies of the colony, these places where it is possible to find what we need, because our storekeeper and brand taster know us perfectly well." (The Coca-Cola Company, 2020).

But, how is it that large suppliers envision the DT strategies for the CSs? There are different approaches depending on the company. The following four initiatives exemplifies the view of some companies, for example:

1. **PepsiCo**: For them, the benefits of digitalization for CSs are?
   a. They can increase their sales up to 30%.
   b. They obtain greater security and efficiency in handling their boxes.
   c. They become more competitive by using digital tools.
   d. Obtain and offer payment and collection models at no cost.
   e. They can expand their portfolio of services.
   f. They have access to more advanced products like digital loans (PepsiCo, 2021).
2. **The Coca-Cola Company** is accompanied by some private industry initiatives, such as "My Safe Store," which seeks to promote small local businesses and provide confidence and security to storekeepers to keep their stores open. Merchants have not stopped, they know that keeping their business running is essential to keep their environments running in a relatively normal order" (The Coca-Cola Company, 2020). Like this project, which includes Kellogg, Mars, Mondelez México, and PepsiCo, hand in hand with Concanaco and Coparmex, the Mexican Coca-Cola Industry has joined and created other projects. Through communication campaigns and protection tactics at the point of sale, it has given storekeeper tools to keep their businesses running (The Coca-Cola Company, 2020).
3. **Grupo Bimbo** affirmed, "We are a 100% Mexican company, of people committed to our country and its people. We were born here 75 years ago, and in these difficult times we want to contribute our grain of flour so that together we overcome the crisis due to the impact of COVID-19" (Grupo Bimbo, 2020).
4. **Grupo Modelo** launched a platform for small stores with home delivery. The company indicated that about 15,000 CSs and 3,000 Modeloramas will be established to avoid going out in the face of the coronavirus contingency (Redaccion de Negocios, 2020).

So, for the large suppliers some of the most significant pillars of DT have been driven by innovation accelerators. Among other solutions, DT includes Internet of Things, robotics, 3D printing, artificial intelligence, augmented and virtual reality, new generation, security, simulation, horizontal/lateral software integration, cyber security, blockchain, nanotechnology, cloud computing, and Big Data (Ulas, 2019). With this in mind, the authors rely on interviews conducted by the EGADE Business School with two notable people representing the large supplier sector. Both interviews can be found on YouTube.

In an interview with Isaías Martínez, Senior Vice President of Sales at PepsiCo entitled *"They expose trends in operations, logistics and supply chain"* conducted by the EGADE Business School in October 12, 2021, Isaías Martinez stated that the pandemic has given rise to a dramatic way of doing business. Three key factors were mentioned: (1) adaptability, which requires a model of flexibility; (2) capacity to adopt new technological models; and (3) a deep change of mindset of everyone within the company, or stakeholders had to be more human-centric.

At the beginning of the COVID-19 pandemic, customer consumption patterns changed dramatically, and panic buying changed the volume of purchases and the mix of products that were in demand. Before the pandemic, planning models were rigorous. The rapid change with the pandemic was a matter of days; the planning and algorithms stopped working. Supply chains collapsed due to restrictions on circulation. Before the pandemic, large meetings were held to define the sales algorithms; however, during the pandemic, communications were conducted via Zoom or WhatsApp meetings, using mobiles to bring teams closer and understand customer needs. The communication and planning were performed in real time (EGADE Business School, 2021).

Enterprise resource planning stopped working as usual, and new technologies were developed to support a more agile process. Direct sales models to small stores could no longer be planned as before; they were forced to use technology. Moreover, most people have a smartphone that has an interface to take orders in real time store by store. This model was planned to be developed in the company for 2 years, and with the pandemic, it had to be completed in 8 or 9 months. Not only did it have to be fast, but via remote, the technology adoption process required designing technology that was intuitive to facilitate learning (EGADE Business School, 2021).

Thanks to technology, geo-segmentation analyses were carried out to define contagion areas, avoid them, change routes, and prepare salespeople. With artificial intelligence algorithms, the information from the stores was analyzed to know where they were growing and where they were falling. The information was used to predict which ones will close during the pandemic depending on which products they stopped buying. Thus, the products and displays from stores that will expire can be removed to give way to products that can survive. "Win with the winner" was the name of the strategy (EGADE Business School, 2021).

Last August 17, 2021, during an interview from EGADE Business School with Oriol Bonaclocha, President of Mondeléz México titled "Adaptab*ility to change, key to transforming businesses in the face of COVID-19,*" Oriol Bonaclocha said that the reality was that Mondelez had to change in two aspects: the way of operating the business and the leadership styles. During the first 20 weeks of the pandemic, weekly monitoring was carried out to understand what was happening to the consumer, tensions, and his life and time.

The pandemic disrupted businesses. In these times, consumer empowerment has been achieved. End customers choose what they want to consume, when they want it, how they consume it, and where they want to do it. Digitization has occurred both in consumption and purchase. Companies have had to adapt. The consumer consumes media, like webinars. Therefore, companies have had to generate content to promote the consumption of their products (EGADE Business School, 2021).

Digital transformation is not an option, you cannot decide whether to do it or not. You have to digitize, the question is how fast you can do it. I see digitalization at three levels: (1) how we operate within the organization, (2) how we transform the business into digital, with the use of machine learning to know in real time how what the business is doing, and (3) how to create the digital layer with consumers and with retail. For example, the conversational commerce tools where you can buy, order and receive by WhatsApp. There all the incentives work, it's easy for the consumer, it's easy for the company, it's easy for the supplier and the system is totally aligned with incentives so that everything works correctly. (Oriol Bonaclocha, EGADE Business School, 2021)

Moreover, he commented on the barriers in this DT process:

I believe that we are not providing the necessary incentives. There is a transformation that is taking place in the entire implementation of CoDi®, in retail. To avoid the handling of cash, in order to really move forward, create a series of elements that are better in traceability, in ease, in documentation in everything. Well, the adoption of CoDi® is being pushed, in the trade, but I think that not all the elements are aligned yet. We are asking a corner store to help us and pay us with CoDi®, but we don't have the incentives for consumers to pay in CoDi®. Nobody receives money with CoDi®. Thus, we are not helping the whole system work. Therefore, I think that sometimes we see the systems, we don't see them in an integral way. (Oriol Bonaclocha, EGADE Business School, 2021)

Platforms Developed in Response to the Pandemic

According to the Asociación Nacional de Tiendas de Autoservicio y Departamentales (ANTAD), the digital channel of SMEs in Mexico has strengthened in the first half of 2021, because their Internet sales grew by 100%. Moreover, 6 out of 10 SMEs continue to sell online, confirming a stabilization of this trend that emerged because of the pandemic (Hernández, 2021). Many digital platforms were developed during the pandemic to help CS maintain their sales and help final customers obtain the products they needed. Some of them are mentioned in the following.

At least 8 out of 10 Internet users already make purchases through the Internet, and given the confinement measures caused by the pandemic, the average expenditure per person rose from 207 to 259 pesos, according to a study by Nielsen Mexico, which is why many businesses were immersed in digitization to continue operating (EF Branded Media, 2020).

- **Wabi2you.** Wabipay uses the following taglines: "If you are a store, warehouse or kiosk and want to start receiving online orders with Wabi for free, join us!" Also, payment methods are offered. It added, "using debit or credit card, or using available funds on the e-wallet, or any points you may have on the payment platform" (Wabi2you, 2021).
- **Tiendita cerca.** The little store on the corner at the door of your house (TIENDITA CERCA, 2021).
- **Kiwi.** Kiwi "accepts card payments." Users can "learn about all the benefits of being part of Kiwi to make remote payments with the lowest commission in the market" (Kiwi Mexico, 2021).
- **Mandamelo**. The private initiative and Concanaco and ANTAD both launched digital applications. "Mándamelo," a platform developed by a group of young engineers from the Autonomous University of Mexico (UNAM), works through Facebook and WhatsApp Messenger chats, so the application must be downloaded, and no commission will be charged (Sanchez, 2020). Small businesses reactivate their economy by making remote payments via WhatsApp safely without commissions and at no cost to the business. Sales are deposited on the next day. (Concanaco Servytur, 2020).

The founder and CEO of MIT Mercadotecnia, Ideas y Tecnología, Juan Carlos Viramontes, pointed out that this tool will empower stores and receive remote payments in due course. He explained that this platform does not generate additional costs for storekeepers: "For the storekeeper there is no cost, each order is increased by 10 pesos that are paid by the customer, but for the storekeeper he has no investment in technology, or in monthly income, or in bank commissions (De la Rosa & Ochoa, 2020).

Understanding the Other Side of the Coin: Interviews with CSs

Since for a country like Mexico the business model of the CS has a tradition and has been along the history one of the most important channels of purchase for many Mexicans above all in terms of convenience. For most Mexicans, CS represent much more than a place of purchase, although currently, other distribution models exists. However, until now, none has managed to emulate the closeness and familiarity of the CS fully (The Coca-Cola Company, 2020). Therefore, Mexico provides a context where CSs are an important topic of analysis during a pandemic.

To carry out our analysis, we took on the task of conducting interviews with convenience stores managers in Atizapán de Zaragoza, a municipality of the State of Mexico. In 2020, the population in Atizapán de Zaragoza was 523,674 inhabitants. According to data from the 2019 Economic Census, the economic sectors that concentrated the most economical units in this municipality were retail trade (8,661 units), other services except government activities (2,850 units), and temporary accommodation and food and beverage preparation services (2,103 units). Appendix 1, Table 5 shows descriptive characteristics of the study participants.

This study focused only on analyzing the impact of DT and the influence of the technological process of large suppliers over CSs; thus, the authors restrict the focus to stores buying their products directly from large suppliers. Focusing on such stores only reduced the heterogeneity in the sample along this dimension, enabling a stricter examination of the variation in the meaning of services provided by suppliers and suppliers' platforms.

To select participants, this study used the following criteria: (1) they had opened before the pandemic started; (2) they had established a relationship with large vendors before the pandemic; (3) they were able to remain open during the pandemic; and (4) they are still open. To increase the diversity of our sample, this study includes male and female main employees in varied locations. Appendix 1 provides information about the stores: their name, the avenue or street where they are located, the type of location, the number of employees, and gender of main employee. The authors have carried out a pre-interview observation to select stores suitable for the study and identified whether the stores had refrigerators or merchandise displays from large suppliers. With this in mind, 20 CS employees were interviewed. This agrees with previous phonographic studies that have shown that theoretical saturation is typically achieved between 15 and 20 participants (Angel, 2018; Sandberg, 2000; Tight, 2016; Wright et al., 2007).

Data Collection

Interview Design

Semi-structured interviews were performed ($n = 20$) for data collection, as this method enables participants to capture their own perspectives and meanings (Angel, 2018; Kvale, 2007). The interviews investigated understanding of DT and the influence of technological processes of large suppliers through four open-ended questions:

1. What kind of technology do you use?
2. What were your initial motivations for using technology in your store?
3. How have you developed with customers since the start of the pandemic until today?
4. How has the technological process of the suppliers influenced the development of your store? Why?

The Interview Process

A total of 20 interviews were conducted face-to-face with CS employees. The first author conducted all the interviews and transcribed each interview in Spanish. Data collection occurred on October 2021; this involved visiting CS by foot. The interviews ranged in duration from 10 to 12 minutes.

Data Analysis and Results

Data analysis followed the constant comparison method of Glaser and Strauss (1999). As we reviewed the data chronologically, we identified general understandings of digital technology, and we categorized statements for and against its use. Table 1 shows the results of this analysis. The authors tried understanding the main changes since the pandemic began and achieved that purpose regarding customer service provided by the CS. Table 1 shows the opinions for or against its use of technology. Figure 1 shows the results graphically.

Storekeepers were asked about their relationship with large suppliers, and interviewers described the services provided, based on trust and mutual benefit. Table 2 presents the illustrative examples.

When asked about how the technological process of the suppliers had influenced the development of their store, most of them answered "nothing." Therefore, we focused on understanding more specific details about the reasons and feelings they have about the platforms developed by the suppliers during the pandemic. Figure 2 exhibits CS opinions on large suppliers' platforms.

Most of them said, "We do not use supplier platforms because the sales volume is very low."

Some stores that sell cigarettes affirmed, "We only order cigarettes online, and it takes a day for the product to arrive."

Meanwhile, the person responsible for the merchandise stated, "If I use Bimbo platforms, I will have to keep track of their inventories, expiration dates and report them to the supplier."

"I feel annoyed. I think that is the job of the suppliers, for that service they earn a salary. I'm not going to do their job."

The identified problem is that despite the innovative DT strategies of large suppliers on CSs, they remained the same as before the pandemic. Figure 3 represents the ecosystem during the pandemic.

Results, Reflections and Recommendations

Customer Service

In many cases, DT results in customer alignment and consequently improves efficiency. However, if competitors also undergo a similar transformation to interact with customers in new and better ways, the organization could lose market share and sales. Thus, a DT needs to be carried out continuously to ensure that the company's value delivery to customers is better than that of its competitors (Priyono et al., 2020). In the new digital marketplace, consumers are using mobile and interactive tools to become instant experts on product and service offerings; they also used their relative merits as they decide who to trust, where to make their purchases, and what to buy. Simultaneously, businesses are undertaking their own DTs, rethinking what customers value most, and creating operating models that take advantage of new possibilities for competitive differentiation (Berman, 2012).

Table 1. Identifying general understanding of digital technology

Digital Technology	Representative Statements about Motivations for Using (Or Not) Digital Technology in the Store
Point of sale system	*In favor...*
	It is easier to make the check out because I no longer have to learn the prices of all products.
	It makes the job easier because the prices are already uploaded into the system and it avoids making sales records by hand.
	It prevents me from labeling products.
	My employer wanted to install it to have more control over sales.
	It avoids me doing inventory counts by hand because I register the merchandise when it arrives and when it is sold, I register the exit. Before, I counted down everything and if I committed a mistake, I had to start over again.'
	Against...
	I do the inventory by hand. I prepare daily cash closings. With the results, I place the order to the suppliers. It does not work online because just like WhatsApp is out today, I prefer to do it by hand.
Security cameras	*In favor...*
	They are necessary, they make us feel more secure.
	My boss wanted to install them so he could see the store from home
	Against...
	The marketplace has its security camera system
Payment terminal	*In favor...*
	Due to the sale of alcoholic beverages, it is better to have a credit card terminal
	Against...
	Sales amounts are insignificant, so I only receive cash
	Bank commissions are very high and the client does not want to pay them
	The bank's system makes many mistakes and clarification take several days.
WhatsApp	*In favor...*
	Since the pandemic started, we have received orders by WhatsApp, motorbike delivery man takes merchandise to clients' homes
	We accept orders from neighbors by WhatsApp. Due to the pandemic, they didn't want to go out of their homes, so we delivered by foot.
	Against...
	I do not receive orders by WhatsApp, only by phone. At the end of the day, I deliver merchandise to four seniors, in my car.
	We don't receive orders by phone, or by WhatsApp. No home delivery.

Undoubtfully, digital technology was a success factor for CS during the pandemic. The convenience and popularity of WhatsApp, in addition to the willingness of storekeepers to provide home delivery service, allow customer service to be constant and successful. According to the most recent study on the habits of Internet users in Mexico (2019), prepared by the Internet.mx Association, Mexico has 82.7 million users. Of these Internet users, almost 77 million have WhatsApp, accounting for 93% (Gaceta UNAM, 2020).

Figure 1. Opinions for or against each use of technology

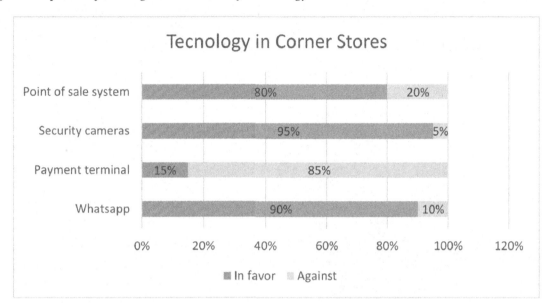

Technology Process of Suppliers

Despite great efforts by large suppliers to develop digital platforms, employees at CS showed no interest in using them. Furthermore, some of them refuse to become involved with technology platforms as it would represent more work for them.

Table 2. Identifying services provided by large suppliers

Services Provided by Suppliers	Illustrative Examples
Pre-sale service	Pre-sales staff come to make a list the day before and the distributor leaves the products the next day.
	If I am not in the store, they write to me via WhatsApp so I can order what I need.
Direct sale	Direct sales providers leave the needed product, and we pay them immediately.
	Suppliers arrive and check what is needed and the suppliers provide them. We must always have the same number of pieces.
Date of expiry	Deliverymen review expiration dates and are responsible for inventory management.
	They must come to see if products expire. Bimbo collects and distributes on the same day. Lala, Pepsi, Coca, they check what is expired, and the next day they supply you with what you asked for.
	The supplier comes and checks the products and what will expire is taken away.
Consignment	Consignment providers conduct inventory control and product replenishment.
	It is easy because the supplier says how much product is missing and they replenish the product.
	Providers already have their assigned days, twice a week, they come and replenish the missing.

Figure 2. CS' opinions on large suppliers' platforms

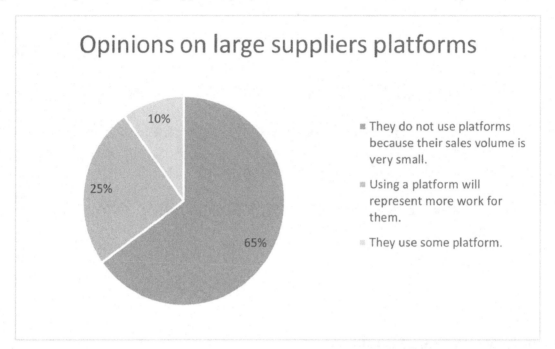

What is Missing?

Previous studies have determined key factors against DT adoption in SMEs: obstacles in adopting DT are budget deficiencies of SMEs, impossibility of investment due to high investments and operational costs, inability to understand Internet technologies, inconvenience for sector, data security, privacy concern, technological developments, insufficient information regarding digital standards, unawareness of the benefits of digitization, connection problems, and lack of qualified employment (Ulas, 2019). SMEs in developing countries, such as Sri Lanka, face a lack of sound telecommunications infrastructure, absence of knowledgeable and qualified personnel, lack of Internet accessibility, limited credit card and bank accounts, and low PC ownership (Rassool & Dissanayake, 2019). Especially, medium-sized companies

Figure 3. Corner store ecosystem during COVID-19 pandemic

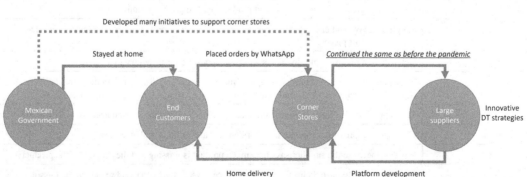

Table 3. Comparison between CS and large suppliers

		Low	High
Corner Stores	Digital transformation		
	Training		
	Investment		
	Incentives		
Large suppliers			Digital transformation
			Training
			Investment
			Incentives

have limited resources to plan and implement digitization projects. In addition to financial and time resources, they often lack the expertise and know-how (Stich et al., 2020).

The authors present a comparison between CS and large suppliers about DT and the main opportunities to achieve it in Table 3.

Training

Although platforms developed by large providers are user-friendly and intuitive, providers could offer training and support to store personnel regarding digital payment methods and the use of platforms. SMEs' lack of customized tools and a misalignment between the digital tools' functionalities—provided by large technology companies—and SME businesses requirements are reported as additional difficulties (Klein & Todesco, 2021).

Previous studies have also achieved similar results. We can assert that the ability of SMEs to innovate depends on employees with appropriate digital capabilities to maximize the use of digital technologies (Scuotto et al., 2021). The main DT technologies are heterogeneous and always evolving, thus requiring new knowledge and skills. A high level of business domain knowledge and leadership capabilities are also required. This creates a never-ending resilient cycle of learning, responding, monitoring, and forecasting new knowledge constructs necessary to keep delivering value in a digital economy (Klein & Todesco, 2021). To do so, policymakers could use the present study and conceptual representations to develop and strengthen further the information technology (IT) related support agenda for "DT of SMEs," especially the smaller ones. This could be completed through customized training programs and support and coaching initiatives, among others. However, this includes an in-depth investigation of items found in two clusters concerning *attitude and behavior* regarding IT and the development of *relational capital* (Pelletier & Cloutier, 2019).

Investment

Analysts suggest that small firms are risk-averse and reluctant to make major investments in technology and people (Larson et al., 2005). As demonstrated, a successful and consistent DT requires investing not only in IT artifacts and infrastructure (e.g., hardware, software, and networks) but also in strategic, intellectual, structural, formal and informal, social, and cultural dimensions (Pelletier & Cloutier, 2019).

Table 4. Pros and cons of this opportunity

	Pros	Cons
Training	Friendly Platforms developed by large suppliers	Many providers, each one with a different Digital Platform
Investment	Affordable Internet	Storekeeper use Internet for different purposes
Incentives	Inventory control	Requires more work for the storekeeper

Individual digital capabilities support SME growth, but developing those capabilities in a small company with a lack of financial resources is still a challenge (Scuotto et al., 2021). Although many SMEs have increasingly realized that the Internet is a key to success, they still do not have a website that can be viewed on a smartphone in many cases. SMEs use the Internet for various purposes. Most SMEs use it to find out general information relating to the business, customer emails, online banking, paying bills, ordering supplies, and paying taxes online (Ulas, 2019).

Still, the specific challenges for SMEs must be emphasized. Knowledge constructs for DT need to be as simple as possible because SMEs lack internal expertise or financial constraints to access specialized external professionals. Additionally, the delay on return over investment that digital technologies may have can be a problem for SMEs, such as the roadmap to create value from such heterogeneous technology convergence (Klein & Todesco, 2021).

Incentives

According to large suppliers, "incentives are needed to make the whole system work" (EGADE Business School, 2021, 32 m and 27 s). The government can also offer incentives for small businesses investing in electronic communication media (Larson et al., 2005). Moreover, the government may incentivize SMEs to embark on the DT process and e-commerce-related assistance through government agencies already established to assist SMEs (Ulas, 2019). For example, CoDi® will be useful only if the CS has a smartphone and Internet service, which saves the store owner an outlay of money.

Through this research, the authors found pros and cons of these key factors. Table 4 shows these findings.

FUTURE RESEARCH DIRECTIONS

This analysis aims to be an initial and different approach to analyze opportunity areas for both large suppliers and Convenience Stores while implementing and sharing DT initiatives. However, there are many important areas for future research. First, although interviews were conducted in Mexico, different states or towns can be studied. Second, CSs that are still open are part of this study; if stores that closed during the pandemic were included, we may obtain different results. This research is limited by the number of publications on SMEs' responses to COVID-19 crisis, which is hampered by the effects of pandemic on many researchers and universities' routines (Klein & Todesco, 2021).

According to Azhari et al., the model for the DT includes eight dimensions of digitization: strategy, leadership, products, operations, culture, people, governance, and technology (Ulas, 2019). The authors suggest that future research should evaluate CS's DT under this framework. Moreover, the next steps would be to automate processes, document buying patterns, measure trends, and develop consumption correlations. Moreover, researchers must pursue the efficient inventory management, zero waste, and efficient use of resources. In this research, we mentioned the actions carried out by large suppliers and by the federal government to support small stores. Although the purpose of the interviews was to know the store's relationship with suppliers, no store employee mentioned any government initiative, which may be material for another future research. The CoDi® initiative developed by the Bank of Mexico is greatly expected to promote financial inclusion and the traceability of transactions, thus leaving the door open for future research in Mexican small businesses like CS.

Stich et al. (2020) explored measures for a successful DT of SMEs and showed the universal digitization measures for SMEs relevant in this context. Especially, two services are critical to shape SMEs digital strategy and transformation roadmap: the potential analysis and the design workshop. Within these services, we use the Acatech Industry 4.0 Maturity Index (Stich et al., 2020).

This maturity index explains four steps to create high business value by implementing measures to see what happens in a company (visibility), understand why something happens (transparency), forecast what will happen (ability to forecast), and self-optimize the whole production system (adaptability). These services are built on each other. In the potential analysis, project experts and company's employees create the order processing. In this workshop, the foundation for every next step is built. Hence, it influences the transformation culture because employees become involved. Using a questionnaire, the authors determined the level of maturity. After building the process and discussing several company issues, the result were analyzed. With methods like systematic media break analysis, gap analysis, and problem tree, relevant digitization potentials can be identified. In the next step, we design by considering each weakness and potential of the future DT roadmap. This roadmap defines different measures to face each weakness and raise each potential (Stich et al., 2020).

CONCLUSION

DT was already an ongoing paradigm shift in our society before the pandemic, where organizations started to migrate from analog-based production process to a digital-based value creation process, based on a data culture and customer-to-business data stream (Klein & Todesco, 2021). Small firms are drivers of economic growth and social well-being, but they often struggle to find and retain human talent, access financial capital, form external alliances, and scale their businesses (Chan et al., 2020). The fact Classic business models have been disappearing and substituted for business models, which are flexible, changeable instantly, have real time responses to consumers' habits, and are knowledge-based (Ulas, 2019).

The following is the central question addressed in this study: How do CS perceive the DT strategies of large suppliers during a pandemic? Based on the views of a sample of 20 CSs, this study concludes that the main tool during the pandemic was WhatsApp, along with home delivery service provided by CS. This also shows that not only did large suppliers develop platforms for CS, but also they completely changed their process to satisfy CS's needs. However, CS did not perceive it that way. Other implications of this article are that incentives, training on digital platforms, and the investment needed to make them work are necessary.

Although DT starts with digital technologies, the more important issue is how companies make their way through this new digital world (Volberda et al., 2021).

REFERENCES

Angel, P., Jenkins, A., & Stephens, A. (2018). Understanding entrepreneurial success: A phenomeno-graphic approach. *International Small Business Journal, 36*(6), 611–636. doi:10.1177/0266242618768662

Appio, F., Frattini, F., Petruzzelli, A. & Neirotti, P. (2021). Digital Transformation and Innovation Management: A Synthesis of Existing Research and an Agenda for Future Studies. *Journal of Product Innovation Management, 38*(1), 4-20.

Banco de México. (2021). *Información sobre CoDi® Cobro Digital.* https://www.banxico.org.mx/sistemas-de-pago/codi-cobro-digital-banco-me.html

Berman, S. J. (2012). Digital transformation: Opportunities to create new business models. *Strategy and Leadership, 40*(2), 16–24. doi:10.1108/10878571211209314

Branded Media, E. F. (2020). *Las tienditas mexicanas recurrieron a la innovación digital.* https://www.elfinanciero.com.mx/mundo-empresa/las-tienditas-mexicanas-recurrieron-a-la-innovacion-digital/

CentroGeo-GeoInt-DataLab. (2021). *Covid-19 México Actualizado 22-02-2022.* https://datos.covid-19.conacyt.mx/

Chan, Y., Krishnamurthy, R., & Desjardins, C. (2020). Technology-Driven Innovation in Small Firms. *MIS Quarterly Executive, 19*(1), 1. doi:10.17705/2msqe.00024

Concanaco Servytur. (2020). *¿Qué es Mándamelo?* https://www.concanaco.com.mx/que-es-mandamelo/

Coordinación de Estrategia Digital Nacional de la Oficina de la Presidencia de la República - Medidas. (2021). *COVID-19 Medidas Económicas.* https://www.gob.mx/covid19medidaseconomicas

Creswell, J. W. (2007). Five Qualitative Approaches to Inquiry. In Qualitative Inquiry & Research Design. Choosing among five approaches (pp. 68-72). Sage Publications Inc.

DataMéxico. (2020) *Unidades económicas según sector económico en 2019.* https://datamexico.org/es/profile/geo/atizapan-de-zaragoza

De la Rosa, E., & Ochoa, C. (2020). *Antad y Concanaco lanzan "Mándamelo", plataforma digital para 'tienditas'.* https://www.milenio.com/negocios/mandamelo-plataforma-digital-antad-concanaco-tienditas

Dennis, A., Antino, K., Rahimi, M., & Ayabakan, S. (2020). User reactions to COVID-19 screening chatbots from reputable providers. *Journal of the American Medical Informatics Association: JAMIA, 27*(11), 1727–1731. doi:10.1093/jamia/ocaa167 PMID:32984890

Dressler, M., & Paunovic, I. (2021). Sensing Technologies, Roles and Technology Adoption Strategies for Digital Transformation of Grape Harvesting in SME Wineries. *Journal of Open Innovation, 7*(2), 123. doi:10.3390/joitmc7020123

EGADE Business School. (2021). *Adaptabilidad al cambio, clave para transformar los negocios frente a COVID-19.* https://egade.tec.mx/es/blog/adaptabilidad-al-cambio-clave-para-transformar-los-negocios-frente-covid-19

EGADE Business School. (2021). *Exponen tendencias en operaciones, logística y cadena de suministro.* https://egade.tec.mx/es/blog/exponen-tendencias-en-operaciones-logistica-y-cadena-de-suministro

EGADE Business School. (2021). *EGADE Future Forum - Reinvención del negocio en un entorno desafiante* [Video]. Youtube. https://www.youtube.com/watch?v=JBFYGU9cWrk&t=3447s

EGADE Business School. (2021). *EGADE Future Forum: Tendencias en Operaciones, Logísitca y Cadena de Suministro* [Video]. Youtube. https://www.youtube.com/watch?v=zPUJ5wcPDMk&t=1111s

Fernández-Rovira, C., Álvarez, J., Molleví, G., & Nicolas-Sans, R. (2021). The digital transformation of business. Towards the datafication of the relationship with customers. *Technological Forecasting and Social Change, 162*, 120339. doi:10.1016/j.techfore.2020.120339

Gaceta, U. N. A. M. (2020). *Mexicanos usan hasta 4 horas su WhatsApp.* https://www.fundacionunam.org.mx/unam-al-dia/mexicanos-usan-hasta-4-horas-su-whatsapp/

Glaser, B., & Strauss, A. (1999). *The Discovery off rounded theory: Strategies for qualitative research.* Aldine Publishing.

Google. (2021). *Informes de Movilidad Local sobre el COVID-19, 2021.* https://www.google.com/covid19/mobility/

Grupo Bimbo. (2020). *Bimbo Contingo.* https://bimbocontingo.com/

Hernández, V. (2021). *GS1 México y AMVO confirman el músculo digital de las pymes.* https://retailers.mx/gs1-mexico-y-amvo-confirman-el-musculo-digital-de-las-pymes/

ILO. (2021). *Country policy responses.* https://www.ilo.org/global/topics/coronavirus/regional-country/country-responses/lang--en/index.htm#MX

Instituto Nacional de Estadística. Geografía e Informática. (2021). *Censos Económicos 2019.* https://www.inegi.org.mx/default.html

Kiwi México. (2021). *Acepta pagos a distancia.* https://conkiwi.com/luchacovid/tienditacerca?utm_source=tiendita_cerca&utm_medium=organico&utm_=

Klein, V. B., & Todesco, J. L. (2021). COVID-19 crisis and SMEs responses: The Role of Digital Transformation. *Knowledge and Process Management, 28*(2), 117–133. doi:10.1002/kpm.1660

Kvale, S. (2007) Doing Interviews. London: Sage.

Larson, P., Carr, P., & Dhariwal, K. (2005). SCM Involving Small Versus Large Suppliers: Relational Exchange and Electronic Communication Media. *The Journal of Supply Chain Management, 41*(1), 18–29. doi:10.1111/j.1745-493X.2005.tb00181.x

Mandviwalla, M., & Flanagan, R. (2021). Small business digital transformation in the context of the pandemic. *European Journal of Information Systems, 30*(4), 359–375. doi:10.1080/0960085X.2021.1891004

Mattila, M., Yrjölä, M., & Hautamäki, P. (2021). Digital transformation of business-to-business sales: What needs to be unlearned? *Journal of Personal Selling & Sales Management, 41*(2), 113–129. doi:10.1080/08853134.2021.1916396

Mercado Solidario. (2021). *Mercado Solidario*. https://mercadosolidario.gob.mx/

Nadkarni, S., & Prügl, R. (2021). Digital transformation: A review, synthesis and opportunities for future research. *Management Review Quarterly*, *71*(2), 233–341. doi:10.100711301-020-00185-7

Ochoa, C. (2021). *Más de 100 mil tienditas han logrado reabrir este año, pero con otros giros: Anpec*. https://www.milenio.com/negocios/tienditas-logran-reabrir-2021-giros-anpec

OECD iLibrary. (2021). *The Digital Transformation of SMEs*. https://www.oecd-ilibrary.org/sites/bdb9256a-en/index.html?itemId=/content/publication/bdb9256a-en

Pallares, M. A. (2013). *Tienditas, una mina para 8 empresas*. https://www.elfinanciero.com.mx/archivo/tienditas-una-mina-para-empresas-1/

Pelletier, C., & Cloutier, L. M. (2019). Conceptualising Digital Transformation in SMEs: An Ecosystemic perspective. *Journal of Small Business and Enterprise Development*, *26*, 855–876.

PepsiCo. (2021). *Seis maneras de apoyar a las tienditas con la digitalización*. https://www.pepsico.com.mx/noticias/historias/seis-beneficios-de-impulsar-la-inclusion-digital-de-las-tienditas

PepsiCo-CoDi. (2020). *Citibanamex, PepsiCo y Amigo PAQ impulsan la inclusión financiera digital de tienditas a través de CoDi®*. https://www.pepsico.com.mx/noticias/boletines-de-prensa/citibanamex-pepsico-y-amigo-paq-impulsan-inclusion-financiera-de-tienditas

Priyono, A., Moin, A., & Putri, V.N.A.O. (2020). Identifying Digital Transformation Paths in the Business Model of SMEs during the COVID-19 Pandemic. *Journal of Open Innovation*, *6*, 104.

Rassool, R., & Dissanayake, R. (2019). Digital Transformation for Small & Medium Enterprises: With Special focus on Sri Lankan Context as an Emerging Economy. *International Journal of Business and Management Review*, *7*(4), 59–76.

Redacción Negocios. (2020). *Grupo Modelo lanza plataforma de tienditas con servicio a domicilio*. https://www.milenio.com/negocios/coronavirus-grupo-modelo-lanza-plataforma-abastecer-despensa

Sánchez, S. (2020*). Concanaco y Antad lanzan 'Mándamelo', una plataforma de venta en línea para las 'tienditas'*. https://www.forbes.com.mx/negocios-concanaco-y-antad-lanzan-mandamelo-una-plataforma-en-linea-para-las-tienditas/

Sandberg, J. (2005). How do we justify knowledge produced within interpretive approaches? *Organizational Research Methods*, *8*(1), 41–68.

Scuotto, V., Nicotra, M., Del Giudice, M., Krueger, N., & Gregori, G. L. (2021). A microfoundational perspective on SMEs' growth in the digital transformation era. *Journal of Business Research*, *129*, 382–392.

Secretaria de Salud. (2020). *Jornada Nacional de Sana Distancia*. https://www.gob.mx/cms/uploads/attachment/file/541687/Jornada_Nacional_de_Sana_Distancia.pdf

Secretaría de Salud. (2021). *Quédate en casa*. https://coronavirus.gob.mx/quedate-en-casa/

Stich, V., Zeller, V., Hicking, J., & Kraut, A. (2020). Measures for a successful digital transformation of SMEs. *Procedia CIRP*, *93*, 286–291.

Sundaram, R., Sharma, R. & Shakya, A. (2020). Digital Transformation of Business Models: A Systematic Review of Impact on Revenue and Supply Chain. *International Journal of Management*, *11*(5), 9-21.

The Coca-Cola Company. (2020). *Hablemos de tienditas*. https://www.coca-colamexico.com.mx/noticias/comunidad/hablemos-de-tienditas

Tiendita Cerca. (2021). *La tienda de la esquina en la puerta de tu casa*. https://www.tienditacerca.com/

Tight, M. (2016). Phenomenography: The development and application of an innovative research design in higher education research. *International Journal of Social Research Methodology*, *19*(3), 319–338.

Ulas, D. (2019). Digital Transformation Process and SMEs. *Procedia Computer Science*, *158*, 662–671.

Wabi2you. (2021). *WABI*. https://www.wabicasa.com/

Wengler, S., Hildmann, G., & Vossebein, U. (2021). Digital transformation in sales as an evolving process. *Journal of Business and Industrial Marketing*, *36*(4), 599–614.

WHO. (2020). *Director-general's opening remarks at the media briefing on COVID-19*. https://www.who.int/dg/speeches/detail/who-director-general-s-opening-remarks-at-the-media-briefing-on-covid-19

Wiklund, J., & Shepherd, D. (2003). Aspiring for, and achieving growth: The moderating role of resources and opportunities. *Journal of Management Studies*, *40*(8), 1919–1941.

Wright, A., Murray, J. P., & Geale, P. (2007). A phenomenographic study of what it means to supervise doctoral students. *Academy of Management Learning & Education*, *6*(4), 458–474.

ADDITIONAL READING

Amankwah-Amoah, J., Khan, Z., & Wood, G. (2021). COVID-19 and business failures: The paradoxes of experience, scale, and scope for theory and practice. *European Management Journal*, *39*(2, I-2), 179–184. doi:10.1016/j.emj.2020.09.002

Carmine, S., Andriopoulos, C., Gotsi, M., Härtel, C. E. J., Krzeminska, A., Mafico, N., Pradies, C., Raza, H., Raza-Ullah, T., Schrage, S., Sharma, G., Slawinski, N., Stadtler, L., Tunarosa, A., Winther-Hansen, C., & Keller, J. (2021). A Paradox Approach to Organizational Tensions During the Pandemic Crisis. *Journal of Management Inquiry*, *30*(2), 138–153. doi:10.1177/1056492620986863

Crupi, A., Del Sarto, N., Di Minin, A., Gregori, G. L., Lepore, D., Marinelli, L., & Spigarelli, F. (2020). The digital transformation of SMEs – a new knowledge broker called the digital innovation hub. *Journal of Knowledge Management*, *24*(6), 1263–1288. doi:10.1108/JKM-11-2019-0623

Gao, S., Lim, M. K., & Qiao, R. (2021). Identifying critical failure factors of green supply chain management in China's SMEs with a hierarchical cause–effect model. *Environment, Development and Sustainability*.

Gaskill, L. R., Auken, H. E., & Manning, R. A. (1993). A Factor Analytic Study of the Perceived Causes of Small Business Failure. *Journal of Small Business Management*, *31*, 18.

Hinterhuber, A., & Nilles, M. (2021). Digital transformation, the Holy Grail and the disruption of business models. *Business Horizons*.

Matarazzo, M., Penco, L., Profumo, G., & Quaglia, R. (2021). Digital Transformation and Customer Value Creation in Made in Italy SMEs: A dynamic capabilities perspective. *Journal of Business Research, 123*, 642–656. doi:10.1016/j.jbusres.2020.10.033

Nguyen, T. (2021). Digital Transformation: Opportunities and Challenges for Leaders in the Emerging Countries in Response to Covid-19 Pandemic. Emerging Science Journal, 5.

Pelletier, C., & Cloutier, L. M. (2019). Challenges of Digital Transformation in SMEs: Exploration of IT-Related Perceptions in a Service Ecosystem. *Proceedings of the 52nd Hawaii International Conference on System Sciences*, 4967-4976. 10.24251/HICSS.2019.597

Volberda, H., Khanagha, S., Baden-Fuller, C., Mihalache, O., & Birkinshaw, J. (2021). Strategizing in a digital world: Overcoming cognitive barriers, reconfiguring routines and introducing new organizational forms. *Long Range Planning, 54*(5), I-5. doi:10.1016/j.lrp.2021.102110

APPENDIX

Table 5. Descriptive characteristics of study participants

Name of the Store	Avenue/Street	Location	Employees (Number)	Main Employee Gender
Abarrotes "La Glorieta"	Mar de Molucas	Roundabout	3	M
Abarrotes Ceci	Mar de Molucas	Side-street	2	F
Abarrotes Don Jorge	Oceáno Pacífico	Main Street	3	M
Abarrotes El Padrino	Oceáno Pacífico	Main Street	3	M
Abarrotes Manolo	Mar Brillante	Side-street	2	M
Abarrotes y vinos La Rosita	Oceáno Pacífico	Main Street	4	F
Abarrotes, vinos y licores La Higienica	Oceáno Índico	Roundabout	3	M
Abts "La Hormiga"	Oceáno Antártico	Roundabout	2	F
ChavaLu	Oceáno Antártico	Roundabout	2	F
Dimaso	Oceáno Pacífico	Main Street	3	F
La Bodeguita de Don Mateo	Oceáno Antártico	Roundabout	2	M
La Lupita	Atizapán Centro	Marketplace	2	F
La mejor tienda	Oceáno Pacífico	Main Street	2	M
Miscelanea "El Pentágono"	Oceáno Pacífico	Main Street	2	F
Miscelanea "Yayuco"	Mar de Andaman	Side-street	2	F
Miscelanea Chita	Av. Hidalgo	Main Street	2	F
Miscelanea La Rosa de Oro	Av. Adolfo Lopez Mateos	Side-street	3	F
Miscelanea Yessica	Oceáno Pacífico	Main Street	2	F
Miscelanea Zafiro	Zafiro	Main Street	2	F
Razo	Oceáno Antártico	Side-street	2	F
M: male; F: female;				

Chapter 12
Significance of the COVID–19 Pandemic on the Tourism Business in Nigeria:
Perspectives From Airports, Hotels, and Recreational Centres

Olukemi Adedokun Fagbolu
National Open University of Nigeria, Nigeria

Kikelomo Aminat Abdulkadir
Kwara State University, Malete, Nigeria

ABSTRACT

This chapter explores the effects of the COVID-19 pandemic on tourism business. This exploratory research adopts a structured questionnaire and purposive sampling method to gather primary data from the respondents at the study organization. Data collected are presented on tables and further analyzed using descriptive statistics through PSPP analytical free software tool comprising means (M) and simple percentages. The outcomes of the study reveal that the COVID-19 pandemic has a negative significance on the tourism industry.

INTRODUCTION

Tourism has become a way of exploring new sites, meeting friends, visitors and business ventures. As such, tourism business has been making significant contributions to local and foreign exchange earnings of many countries of the world (Fagbolu, 2021). However, the era of COVID-19 pandemic disrupts the business as a result of domestic, regional and foreign lockdowns. The outbreak of the Delta variant and Omicron variant further pose serious threat to the business and the industry at large extensively (Gössling, Scott & Hall, 2020; Martínez et al., 2020). Even though not everyone the tourists meet during their movement from the generating areas to destinations can contact the virus. Possibly, they stand a

DOI: 10.4018/978-1-6684-6762-6.ch012

chance to play a remarkable role in transferring the virus between themselves, co travelers and tourism business owners.

Authors (Kreiner & Ram, 2020; Marinko et al., 2021; Vikrant & Sidharth, 2021; Yeh, 2021) have examined impacts of COVID-19 on tourism industry but unable to investigate the impacts on particular sectors of the industry. As a result, the focus of this chapter in an exploratory perspective is to explore the impact of the pandemic on the tourism business particularly airport, hotel and recreational centre. Literature are retrieved and from JSTOR, Emerald, Pro-Quest and Google Scholar search engines for literature review. The study conducts a survey to collect data from the respondents in order to discover the extent of effects of the pandemic on the tourism industry. The findings of the research are further presented and analyzed to achieve the purpose of this chapter.

OUTBREAK OF CORONAVIRUS PANDEMIC

Coronavirus was initially identified in 1937 by the researchers. Meanwhile, coronavirus disease outbreak first occurred in Wuhan, China in 2019. Researchers opine that the virus transmits from the respiratory system through fluids. Hence, it is named COVID-19 by the experts typically affecting the respiratory tract. The symptoms are categorized into mild and severe symptoms including cough, sneezing, cold, fever and difficulty in breathing. Others comprise a sore throat, fatigue, diarrhea, muscle pain, loss of taste and vomiting. Children with the disease have mild or without symptoms. Those with a higher risk of severe its symptoms include pregnant women, older adults and people with underlying medical conditions such as cancer, lung and heart challenges, high blood pressure and diabetes (Guan et al., 2020; Liu et al., 2020).

In March 2020, World Health Organization (WHO) proclaimed it a pandemic due to the rapid spread of the disease worldwide. The organization disclose that transmission may occur when an individual sneezes or coughs without covering their mouth, thereby, discharging droplets containing the virus into the air. As a result, someone can contact through physical contact with a person who has the infection, touching a surface that contains the virus with hands, then touching mouth, nose, eyes, or handshakes with the same hand (Gössling, Scott & Hall, 2020; Moorthy et al., 2020).

The virus progresses as well as severe complications affecting body systems causing failure of multiple organs. The disease has since then responsible for millions of infections and death across the globe. Several measures are mapped out to curb the spread in order to reduce the risk of infection. The measures include regular washing of hands with soap under running water, application of hand sanitizers, wearing of nose mask and social distancing. Other measures entail self-isolation, establishment of public isolation centers, tests, vaccination and domestic, international and global lockdowns. In order to cushion the hard effect of the lockdowns on people, several governments distribute several palliatives are to their citizens. The outbreak of Delta and Omicron variants in 2021 further triggered the extent of the pandemic as the world was relaxing from the global lockdown. The effect in no doubt affect global movement, thereby disrupt local, domestic and international tourism businesses.

TOURISM BUSINESS IN PRE COVID-19 PANDEMIC ERA

Prior to the Covid-19 pandemic, globally, tourism is one of the significant industries. The significant contribution and value of tourism industry is very high for each nation. It is an industry known for a vast flexible and elastic value chain due to its business specific nature of offering tourism products for the consumption of travelers and tourists (Kaushal & Srivastava, 2021). The industry operates through a wide network of related industries and inter connected as well as other ancillary industries offering tourism products for the travelers and tourists for different purposes. The broad tourism and niche products comprise of travel and tour services like hotel reservation and booking, local, domestic and international transportation, foods & beverages; tourism destinations and attractions.

Tourism brings benefits and advantages and contributes in the overall growth and development of the economy of a country and also in progress of the society and social structure of a country.

It also helps and motivates in preserving of natural resources (McKee & Stuckler, 2020). The industry is one of the top sources known for creating about 10% employment and gross domestic product (GDP) across the globe.

Therefore, it has become a critical factor for economic growth in many countries (Yeh, 2021).

Several factors serve as driver of growth in the sector before the pandemic. The drivers include desires and needs, income growth, availability of leisure periods, suitable transportation facilities, better communication networks, level of growth of business events and dealings, attractiveness

Significantly, the industry is driven by tourists who are the consumer and primary segment with the desire to visit places for different purposes (Khalid, Okafor & Burzynska, 2021). It is also driven by the progress and development in its value chain industries in providing more facilities, services and convenience to its segment to make travel and tourism more desirable, easy and attractive.

TOURISM BUSINESS DURING COVID-19 PANDEMIC ERA

Research so far has shown that pandemic has been a major set –back on tourism industry. COVID-19 pandemic leads to significant uncertainty and chaotic conditions virtually in every sector of the industry (Rogerson & Rogerson, 2020; Siagla, 2020). The tourism industry has experienced sharply falling revenues. It is one of the economic sectors most severely affected by the disease outbreak. The shock cause negative effects on both the supply and demand. On supply issues, every sector of the business such as accommodation, transportation, catering, tourist destinations and attractions, meetings, incentives, conferences and exhibition (MICE) are closed down (Del Valle, 2020). On the demand side, customers are unable to enjoy tourism products as result of lockdowns leading to closures of borders, accommodation, catering outfits, other recreational facilities, fear of infections and restricted movement (Foo et al., 2021; Uğur & Akbıyık, 2020; Zenker & Kock, 2020). Primarily, this chapter further explores the effect of COVID-19 on tourism business.

Research Objective

In a bid to investigate the impact of the pandemic, the main objective of this study is

1.   To explore the impact of Covid-19 pandemic on the tourism industry.

Table 1. Arbitrary level and descriptive rating for the study

Arbitrary Level	Descriptive Rating
1.00 - 1.80	Strongly Disagree
1.81 - 2.61	Disagree
2.62 - 3.42	Neither Disagree nor Agree
3.43 - 4.23	Agree
4.24 - 5.00	Strongly Agree

Source: Field Survey, 2021.

Research Question

1. To what extent does covid-19 affect the tourism sectors in the tourism industry?

A structured questionnaire is administered to the respondents. The survey on a Five-Point Likert Scale entailing Strongly Agree (SA), Agree (A), Neither Agree nor Disagree (N), Disagree (D) and Strongly Disagree (SD). It comprises two (2) sections which are respondents' profile section and close ended section. A purposive sampling method is adopted to gather primary data from sixty (60) respondents in some selected tourism organizations entailing an international airport, a hotel, and a recreational center. This exploratory research presents data collected on tables and further employs PSPP analytical free software tool comprising means (M) and simple percentages. The following descriptive statistics stated on Table 1 below are employed to interpret the outcomes:

The profiles of the respondents are hereby presented below on Table 2.

Table 2 shows the distribution of respondents based on gender 23 of the respondents representing 38.3% were male while 37 of the respondents were female representing 61.7%. From the analysis above, it is apparent that female respondents were found to be more in number than male respondents. Considering their age, the age range depict that 14 respondents (22.3%) fall within 20-25 range, 26 respondents (43.3%) are within 26-30 years of age, 15 respondents (25%) are between 31-40 years, 5 respondents (8.4%) represent 41-50 years while none of the respondents fall within age 46 and above. The distribution of respondents based on organization location portrays that 60 of the respondents representing 100% were in an urban environment while none of the respondent operates in the rural area. The table further shows the distribution of respondents based on the type of organization. 20 of the respondents representing 33.3% are from public organization while 40 of the respondents representing 66.7% are from private tourism organization.

Progressively, the Table 3 below presents the outcomes of the research question stated above.

The Table 3 reveals that the respondents agree to all appreciative inquiries as the mean of the responses are above 3.42. The respondents agree that there have been extremely low occupancy rates ($M = 3.53$). The same way, the respondents agree that there have been limitations in food related activities and strongly agree there has been uncertainty and fear in the costumer and there have been decline in accommodation reservation due to COVID-19 pandemic having mean ($M = 3.55, 4.55$ and 4.78) respectively. The respondents agree there has been staff shortage due to social distancing ($M = 3.79$). The organizations strongly agree that they are facing difficulty in paying staff due to sharp drop in sales and income having ($M = 4.66$). The respondents agree that many people under estimate the diseases and its effect on

Table 2. The frequency and percentage distribution of the respondents

Items	Categories	Frequency (F)	Percentage (%)
Gender	Male	23	38.3
	Female	37	61.7
Total		**60**	**100.0**
Age	20-25 26-30 31-40 41-45 46 and above	14 26 15 5 -	23.3 43.3 25 8.4 -
Total		**60**	**100**
Location of Organization	Urban Rural	60 -	60 -
Total		**60**	**100**
Type of Organization	Public Private	20 40	33.3 66.7
Total		**60**	**100**

Source: Field Survey, 2021.

tourism industry ($M = 3.89$). The same way the respondents strongly agree that Covid-19 pandemic has hindered performance in the tourists' attractions in the industry ($M = 4.85$). The respondents agree that they feel financial stress due to COVID-19 ($M = 3.75$). Meanwhile, they strongly agree that they expect that tourism businesses and organizations will go back to new normal ($M = 4.58$). Overall, the table

Table 3. Effects of COVID-19 pandemic on tourism industry

S/N	Label	N	Mean	Rating Level
1	There have been extremely low occupancy rates	60	3.53	Agree
2	There have been limitations in food related activities	60	3.55	Agree
3	There has been uncertainty and fear in the customer	60	4.55	Strongly Agree
4	There have been decline in accommodation reservation due to COVID-19 pandemic	60	4.78	Strongly Agree
5	There has been staff shortage due to social distancing	60	3.79	Agree
6	There has been difficulty in paying staff due to sharp drop in sales and income	60	4.66	Strongly Agree
7	Many people under estimate the diseases and its effect on tourism industry	60	3.89	Agree
8	Covid-19 pandemic has hindered performance in the tourists' attractions	60	4.85	Strongly Agree
9	I feel financial stress due to COVID -19	60	3.75	Agree
10	I expect organisation to go back normal	60	4.58	Strongly Agree
Weighted Average			**4.19**	**Agree**

Source: Field Survey, 2021.

shows a calculated weighted average mean (*M*) of (mean = 4.19) which means the respondents agree to all the inquiries. This is an implication that covid-19 negatively affect tourism industry.

CONCLUSION

This research investigates effect of Covid-19 pandemic on tourism industry. The findings depict that Covid-19 has a negative impact on the industry. There are extremely low occupancy rates as a result of low catering related activities and accommodation reservation and booking in the accommodation sector of the industry. By extension, the organizations are short staffed due to social distancing measure while it is difficult to pay staff. As many underestimates the effect and the extent of covid-19 on the business, it has posed a negative effect on the industry at large. Nevertheless, it is expected that there will be a new normal tourism business in due course. As a result, the destination management organizations (DMO) need to encourage the tourism business operators in providing basic amenities to combat the rate at which people contact the disease.

REFERENCES

Correa-Martínez, L., Kampmeier, S., Kümpers, P., Schwierzeck, V., Hennies, M., Hafezi, W., & Mellmann, A. (2020). A pandemic in times of global tourism: Superspreading and exportation of COVID-19 cases from a ski area in Austria. *Journal of Clinical Microbiology, 58*(6), 1–3. doi:10.1128/JCM.00588-20 PMID:32245833

Del Valle, A. S. (2020). *The tourism industry and the impact of Covid-19, scenarios and proposals.* Global Journey Consulting.

Fagbolu, A. O. (2021). The reasons for failure of tourism small and medium scale enterprises (TSMEs) and possible strategies for restraining the failure. *Global Scientific Journals, 9,* 576–580.

Foo, L. P., Chin, M. Y., Tan, K. L., & Phuah, K. T. (2021). The impact of COVID-19 on tourism industry in Malaysia. *Current Issues in Tourism, 24*(19), 2735–2739. doi:10.1080/13683500.2020.1777951

Gössling, S., Scott, D., & Hall, C. M. (2020). Pandemics, tourism and global change: A rapid assessment of COVID-19. *Journal of Sustainable Tourism, 29*(1), 1–20. doi:10.1080/09669582.2020.1758708

Guan, H., Okely, A. D., Aguilar-Farias, N., del Pozo Cruz, B., Draper, C. E., El Hamdouchi, A., Florindo, A. A., Jáuregui, A., Katzmarzyk, P. T., Kontsevaya, A., Löf, M., Park, W., Reilly, J. J., Sharma, D., Tremblay, M. S., & Veldman, S. L. (2020). Promoting healthy movement behaviours among children during the COVID-19 pandemic. *The Lancet. Child & Adolescent Health, 4*(6), 416–418. doi:10.1016/S2352-4642(20)30131-0 PMID:32458805

Kaushal, V., & Srivastava, S. (2021). Hospitality and tourism industry amid COVID-19 pandemic: Perspectives on challenges and learnings from India. *International Journal of Hospitality Management, 92,* 102707. doi:10.1016/j.ijhm.2020.102707 PMID:33024348

Khalid, U., Okafor, L. E., & Burzynska, K. (2021). Does the size of the tourism sector influence the economic policy response to the COVID-19 pandemic? *Current Issues in Tourism*, *24*(19), 2801–2820. doi:10.1080/13683500.2021.1874311

Kreiner, N. C., & Ram, Y. (2020). National tourism strategies during the Covid-19 pandemic. *Annals of Tourism Research*, *103076*. Advance online publication. doi:10.1016/j.annals.2020.103076 PMID:33100431

Liu, J. J., Bao, Y., Huang, X., Shi, J., & Lu, L. (2020). Mental health considerations for children quarantined because of COVID-19. *The Lancet Child & Adolescent Health*, *4*, 347–349. doi:10.1016/S2352-4642(20)30096

Marinko, Š., Domingo, R. S., & Małgorzata, P. (2021). Impact of COVID-19 on the travel and tourism industry. *Technological Forecasting and Social Change*, *163*, 1–14. doi:10.1016/j.techfore.2020.120469

McKee, M., & Stuckler, D. (2020). If the world fails to protect the economy, COVID-19 will damage health not just now but also in the future. *Nature Medicine*, *26*(5), 640–642. doi:10.103841591-020-0863-y PMID:32273610

Moorthy, V., Restrepo, A. M. H., Preziosi, M. P., & Swaminathan, S. (2020). Data sharing for novel coronavirus (COVID-19). *Bulletin of the World Health Organization*, *98*(3), 150. doi:10.2471/BLT.20.251561 PMID:32132744

Rogerson, C. M., & Rogerson, J. M. (2020). COVID-19 tourism impacts in South Africa: Government and industry responses. *Geo Journal of Tourism and Geosites*, *31*(3), 1083–1091. doi:10.30892/gtg.31321-544

Sigala, M. (2020). Tourism and COVID-19: Impacts and implications for advancing and resetting industry and research. *Journal of Business Research*, *117*, 312–321. doi:10.1016/j.jbusres.2020.06.015 PMID:32546875

Uğur, N. G., & Akbıyık, A. (2020). Impacts of COVID-19 on global tourism industry: A cross-regional comparison. *Tourism Management Perspectives*, *36*, 100744. doi:10.1016/j.tmp.2020.100744 PMID:32923356

Vikrant, K., & Sidharth, S. (2021). Hospitality and tourism industry amid COVID-19 pandemic: Perspectives on challenges and learnings from India. *International Journal of Hospitality Management*, *92*, 1–9. doi:10.1016/j.ijhm.2020.102707 PMID:33024348

Yeh, S. S. (2021). Tourism recovery strategy against COVID-19 pandemic. *Tourism Recreation Research*, *46*(2), 188–194. doi:10.1080/02508281.2020.1805933

Zenker, S., & Kock, F. (2020). The coronavirus pandemic–A critical discussion of a tourism research agenda. *Tourism Management*, *81*, 104164. doi:10.1016/j.tourman.2020.104164 PMID:32518437

Chapter 13
COVID–19 Welcomes a New Variable That Influences Consumer Behavior:
Anxiety

Alicia Blanco

iD https://orcid.org/0000-0002-8509-7993
Rey Juan Carlos University, Spain

Gabriel Cachón-Rodríguez
Rey Juan Carlos University, Spain

Ana Cruz-Suárez
Rey Juan Carlos University, Spain

Cristina Del-Castillo-Feito
Rey Juan Carlos University, Spain

ABSTRACT

COVID-19 has generated a context full of questions about the effects of mental health in the economic or social sphere. Significant changes in consumer behavior have been investigated. As consumers reduced their purchases in physical establishments and increased online purchases, retailers took measures to minimize health risks, but also to retain consumers. The objective of this research is to identify the intellectual structure of the research field on anxiety and consumption, including the main lines of research in the area, the sources of knowledge, and the connection points that are helping to spread this knowledge. To do this, this research uses a bibliometric methodology based on co-citations. This research concludes that academics must incorporate anxiety in their models and that companies must take this variable into account in the design of their business strategies. We have to legitimize anxiety as one more variable influences on consumer behavior.

DOI: 10.4018/978-1-6684-6762-6.ch013

INTRODUCTION

Millions of people around the world have mental health problems and 1 out of 4 will suffer from this issue throughout their lives (Word Health Organization, 2021). Due to the borders´ and workplace´s closing, family balancing or the increase in unemployment rates, employees´ daily stress reached record levels in 2020, increasing the number of people suffering from anxiety from 38% in 2019 to 43% in 2020 (Gallup, 2021). Covid-19 revealed a disease which already existed, but strongly increased the numbers, since in 2020 53 million depressive disorders as well as 76 million anxiety diagnosis more were identified (Santomauro et al., 2021).

Covid-19 has generated a context full of questions regarding the effects that mental health might have on the economic and social environment (Baker et al., 2020; Díez-Martín et al., 2022; Guttman & Lev, 2021). Considering that legitimacy relates to social acceptance (Díez-Martín et al., 2021), we can consider that Covid-19 has legitimated a disease about which people did not speak openly, and which is now appearing in television programs, newspapers and even is recognized by athletes, singers of famous individuals. As a result of Covid-19, many research papers have focused on the changes that the pandemic has caused on consumers´ behavior (Payne et al., 2021; Yang et al., 2020). For example, due to the pandemic, consumers reduced the purchases made in physical stores and increased their online purchases, thus, retailers developed initiatives to minimize health risks as well as to earn customers´ loyalty (Payne et al., 2021).

When consumers experiment anxiety, it is more likely for them to become risk averse (Cachón-Rodríguez et al., 2019) and to evaluate external stimulus as imminent dangers (Lerner & Keltner, 2001). Anxiety arises from a personality feature linked with the individual´s self-concept which cause behavioral changes (Cachón-Rodríguez et al., 2021). It is a generalized imbalance sensation which rises from concern, stress about what will happen in the future (Turner et al., 1989). This emotional state can appear due to internal or external processes and is the result of the combination of stress, threats´ perceptions, even though the threat might not be real (Stephan et al., 1999). Anxiety can motivate individuals to behave in an uncomfortable manner or increase its efficacy by influencing in proactive behaviors (Stephan et al., 1999). When the anxiety level is high individuals suffering from it can experiment panic attacks (Omar et al., 2021). Just the thought of experimenting a panic attack can cause the individual to flee from any behavior or situation that can trigger it (Aafjes-van Doorn et al., 2019). These behaviors have the ability to modify consumers´ purchase behavior, for example, enhancing the purchases motivated by panic (Islam et al., 2021).

The increase in mental health diseases as well as the effect over consumers behavior has attracted academics´ attention, resulting in an increase of the research within this field. Under this scenario, the objective of this research is to identify the intellectual structure of the anxiety and consumption research field, including the main research lines within the area, the knowledge sources, and the connection points which are enhancing the dissemination of this knowledge. For this purpose, within this research, a citation-based bibliometric methodology will be applied (Small, 1973). Bibliometric methods seek to analyze theoretical fundaments in a specific field as well as authors and documents networks within the same line of thought (Zupic & Cater, 2015). This methodology is based on quantitative analysis methods which minimize the issued related to the subjective qualitative reviews. Through the application of bibliometric analysis, this work contributes to the development of the anxiety and consumption research field through the identification of the main research areas and knowledge dissemination routes.

Following the introduction, the next section describes the methodology, justifies the use of co-citation, and specifies the origin of the considered data. Next, we focus on answering questions regarding the intellectual structure of the research field. Finally, the last section analyzes the obtained results and indicates the identified limitations.

SAMPLE AND METHODOLOGY

For this research, we apply the bibliometric analysis to correctly identify and visualize the intellectual structure of the anxiety and consumption research field. Bibliometric methods enable the understanding of the origin and growth of a specific discipline. It is also applied to complete and increase the scope of the results achieved using more traditional techniques to review the literature (Ramos-Rodríguez & Ruiz-Navarro, 2004). Bibliometric methods allow researchers to evaluate the impact of publications, a science map, to reveal the structure and the dynamics of the knowledge areas (Zupic & Cater, 2015).

Within the existing bibliometric techniques, this research applies co-citation analysis. The co-citation analysis is the most validated and applied bibliometric method (Zupic & Cater, 2015). A co-citation is defined as the frequency with which two units are cited together (Small, 1973). It is a dynamic approach, which shows the number of times that two references appear together. When two papers are cited together, it is probable that they share similar content, and thus, their influence on the research field in stronger.

Unlike citation counting, co-citation analysis identifies networks of interconnections as well as schools of thought or paradigm shifts (Zupic & Cater, 2015). The co-citation analysis can identify the intellectual structure of a specific research field and answer questions such as: Which are the main research areas, trends, and the knowledge dissemination forms of an area? Is there any research rea which has a higher acceptance?

Nowadays, the co-citation analysis can be developed through any of the multiple scientific visualization software, each one of them with their advantages and disadvantages: SciMAT (Cobo Martín, 2012), CiteSpace (Chen, Ibekwe-SanJuan, & Hou, 2010), VOSviewer (Van Eck & Waltman, 2010) o CitNet (Van Eck & Waltman, 2014). All these tools have their own strengths and weakness. For this research, we have applied CiteSpace, which is a scientific visualization and detection software based on Java that shows the analysis of the critical changes that take place in a research area (Chen, 2006). CiteSpace can analyze the topic´s evolution through a time division option, as well as to reduce the data information, filter a network´s nodes through a prune algorithm, discover the intermediation centrality, articles that set trends and the main tipping points (Moral-Muñoz et al., 2019). This tool has been previously applied in the corporate research area to analyze consumer dissatisfaction (Pascual-Nebreda et al., 2021) or organizational legitimacy (Díez-Martín et al., 2021).

For the construction of the data base, research papers published in the main Web of Science (WoS) collection were selected. This selection was based on research papers including the "anxiety" and "consum*" terms in their title, abstract of keywords. The term "consum*" was used to include every word which contained the root, but with a different termination (for example, consumer, consumption). In addition, we filtered by the "Business Economics" research area, since we wanted to specifically analyze the knowledge generation within this context, beyond other contexts such as health science.

The number papers in WoS before the application of the knowledge area filter was 9,847, from which 1,866 were from Psychiatry, 1,433 from Neurosciences Neurology, 1,067 from Psychology and 1,067 from Substance abuse. Once we filtered by the "Business Economics" knowledge area, the number of valid

Figure 1. Evolution of publications - WoS
Source: Web of Science (2022).

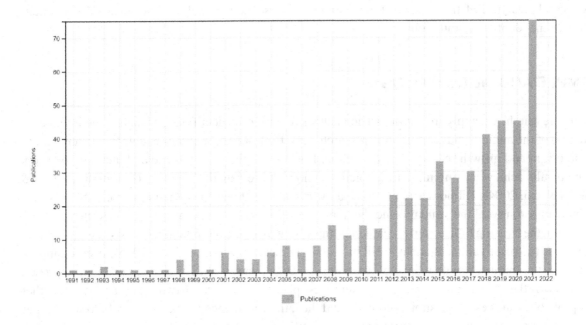

articles were 485, considering the period from 1991 (first published paper) to January 31st of 2022. As it can be seen on Figure 1, the number of publications related to anxiety and consumption significantly increases during Covid, since publication during 2021 exploded.

Moreover, the number of citations has increased in this period (Figure 2). The evolution of the figure of citations shows a stable growth in the number of citations until 2018. As of 2018, and also as a consequence of the notable increase in publications, the citations of articles that analyze anxiety in the field of Business Economics increase a lot compared to previous years.

To obtain the results, we used the following parameters in CiteSpace: (a) Timeslice = from 1991 to 2022 (slice length = 1 year); (b) Term source = title/abstract/author keywords/keywords plus; (c) Node type = cited reference; (d) Selection criteria = g-index (k = 25). It refers to the way to sample records to compose the final networks. These parameters show a sufficiently cohesive network, where the Modularity Q is equal to 0.95 and the Silhouette 0.96. The anxiety and consumption research field are divided in several research clusters formed by similar research, but sufficiently different from other clusters.

RESULTS

Title Publications and Authors

First, the scientific journals which have published more papers regarding anxiety and consumption are presented (Table 1). The two journals with highest number of publications are indexed in the first positions within the Journal Citation Report, since they appear in the first quartile (Q1). This fact shows the interest that relevant journals have on the presented topic.

Figure 2. Evolution of citations - Wos
Source: Web of Science (2022).

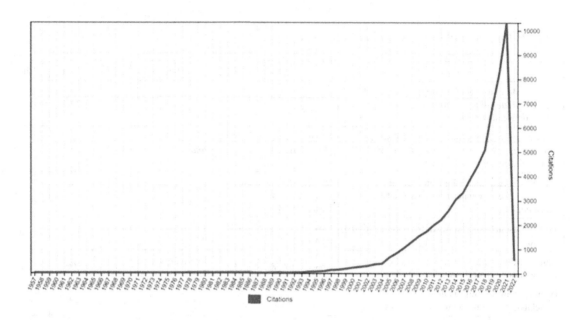

Table 1. Top-ten title publication about anxiety and consumer

Publication Title	Impact Factor 2020	Record Count	%
Journal of Consumer Research	7.000 (Q1)	24	4.948%
Journal of Business Research	7.555 (Q1)	22	4.536%
Psychology Marketing	2.939 (Q3)	22	4.536%
Journal of Consumer Psychology	3.330 (Q3)	16	3.299%
Journal of Retailing and Consumer Services	7.135 (Q1)	16	3.299%
European Journal of Marketing	4.647 (Q2)	13	2.680%
Journal of Consumer Affairs	2.131 (Q4)	11	2.268%
Advances in Consumer Research	-	10	2.062%
Journal of Consumer Behaviour	3.280 (Q3)	10	2.062%
Young Consumers	-	10	2.062%
Q: Category Quartile – JCR Category: Business			

Source: Own elaboration by Web of Science (2022).

Second, we have analyzed the data from the top ten more coted authors (Table 2). The papers from Dahholkar y Bagozzi (2002) y Meuter et al. (2005) which include anxiety to explain technological acceptance models are highlighted. We should take into consideration that the publication date of these articles, is generally at the beginning of the 21st century, when the technological evolution and the e-commerce were at their starting point. Therefore, it is important to analyze the current research lines and potential clusters since they will definitely show that Covid has led interest towards and even legitimized the study of anxiety.

Table 2. Top-ten authors, journal and citations

Title	Authors	Source Title	Year	Citations
An attitudinal model of technology-based self-service: Moderating effects of consumer traits and situational factors	Dabholkar, P.A. & Bagozzi, R.P.	*Journal of the Academy of Marketing Science*	2002	869
Choosing among alternative service delivery modes: An investigation of customer trial of self-service technologies	Meuter, M.L., Bitner, M.J., Ostrom, A.L. & Brown, S.W.	*Journal of Marketing*	2005	701
The influence of technology anxiety on consumer use and experiences with self-service technologies	Meuter, M.L., Ostrom, A.L., Bitner, M.J. & Roundtree, R.	*Journal of Business Research*	2003	453
Word-of-mouth communications: A motivational analysis	Sundaram, D.S., Mitra, K. & Webster, C.	*Advances in Consumer Research*	1998	418
Money attitudes, credit card use, and compulsive buying among American college students	Roberts, J.A. & Jones, E.	*Journal of Consumer Affairs*	2001	256
Demographic and motivation variables associated with Internet usage activities	Teo, T.S.H.	*Internet Research*	2001	233
The Digitization of Healthcare: Boundary Risks, Emotion, and Consumer Willingness to Disclose Personal Health Information	Anderson, C.L. & Agarwal, R.	*Information Systems Research*	2011	229
Factors affecting purchase intention on mobile shopping web sites	Lu, H-P. & Su, P.	*Internet Research*	2009	217
The urge to splurge: A terror management account of materialism and consumer behavior	Arndt, J., Solomon, S., Kasser, T. & Sheldon, K.M.	*Journal of Consumer Psychology*	2004	217
Form versus function: How the intensities of specific emotions evoked in functional versus hedonic trade-offs mediate product preferences	Chitturi, R., Raghunathan, R. & Mahajan, V.	*Journal of Marketing Research*	2007	213

CLUSTERS

Cluster analysis provides a general understanding about the anxiety and consumption research from 1991 to 2022. Each cluster represents a research line related to the anxiety and consumption theme (Figure 3). The main research areas within this context are presented in Table 3. The network is divided in 4 main groups (from #1 al #4). The selected clusters are those holding a Silhoutte (internal cohesion measure of the cluster) value over 0.7 (Chen et al., 2010).

The obtained results show that anxiety influences consumption through how we accept ourselves as well as how we are influenced by others, since the pressure for behave on a certain manner is present (Cluster #1). Anxiety has generated panic buying behavior, for example, when consumers emptied the supermarket shelves during a catastrophe (Cluster #2). Anxiety also influences technological acceptance, for example, the adaptation to teleworking, the increase in online purchases, the dependence on electronic devices or the emergence of issued such as the cyberchondria (Cluster #3). Finally, the perceived risk provokes anxiety on consumers which react in different manners (Cluster #4)

Figure 3. Cluster´ structure. Period: 1991 – 2022
Source: Our elaboration.

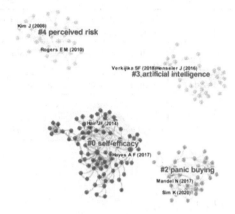

Table 3. Clusters and research questions

Cluster ID	Size	Silhoutte	Mean Year	Label	Research question
#1	83	0.964	2014	Ideal self-efficacy	Do we accept ourselves? Are we influences by what others say?
#2	40	0.934	2018	Panic buying	In from of a crisis (such as Covid), what generates a panic buying?
#3	36	0.928	2017	Technology anxiety	How does technology affect our mental health?
#4	32	0.990	2010	Perceived risk	How does consumption react in front of risk situations?

In conclusion, the results also show which authors have been the main knowledge disseminators within this knowledge area (Table 4). In the two first positions we identify two publications related to research methodology, since most of the research papers have developed empirical analysis. Regarding the other authors, we can confirm that they have focused mainly on explaining the consumer behavior related to technology, taking into consideration the effects that it generated on anxiety levels.

COVID, ANXIETY AND CONSUMPTION

Considering that Covid emerged at the end of 2019, we have also analyzed the research network from 2020 to 2022. The purpose is to test the direct effect of anxiety over consumer behavior during this period. First, the total change on the clusters´ structure can be confirmed (Figure 4). During this period, terms such as covid, coronavirus or mortality related with trips and tourism emerge with high interest levels.

Table 4. Top four intellectual turning point. Period 1991-2022

Centrality	Author	Year	Source
0.06	Hayes, A.F.	2017	Partial, conditional, and moderated moderated mediation: Quantification, inference, and interpretation
0.08	Hair, J.F., Black, B., Black, W.C., & Babin, B.J.	2014	Multivariate Data Analysis. 7th Edition, Pearson Education, Upper Saddle River.
0.03	Rogers, E. M.	2010	Diffusion of Innovations, 4th Edition.
0.02	Celik, H.	2011	Influence of social norms, perceived playfulness and online shopping anxiety on customers' adoption of online retail shopping: An empirical study in the Turkish context. *International Journal of Retail & Distribution Management*

Figure 4. Cluster´ structure. Period 2020-2022
Source: Our elaboration

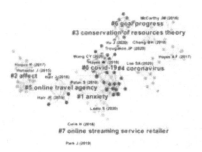

IMPLICATIONS

Consumers with anxiety are more likely to act with risk aversion and to evaluate external stimuli as imminent dangers (Lerner & Keltner, 2001). Anxiety is a generalized sense of imbalance arising from feelings of unease, tension, worry, or apprehension about what might happen (Turner et al., 1989; Stephan & Stephan, 1985). Anxiety is the combined result of stress and the perception of a threat from a negative outcome, even if the threat is not real (Stephan et al., 1999). When the level of anxiety is high, panic attacks can occur (Omar et al., 2021). The mere fact of fearing a panic attack causes the person to avoid behaviours or situations that can trigger it (Aafjes-van Doorn et al., 2019), so anxiety can influence the fact of going shopping or not.

Duan and Zhu (2020), Sheth (2020) and Díez et al. (2022) have shown how the uncertainty generated by Covid-19 influences consumer behaviour. Arumugam (2020) demonstrated how anxiety of an infectious deadly virus can increased anxiety. Yang et al. (2020) or Meyer (2020) determine that Covid welcome new variables because consumers' experiences have changed. In this context, the increase in mental health diseases as well as the effect over consumers behavior has attracted academics´ attention, resulting in an increase of the research within this field.

This research organized a growing research line knowledge through the application of co-citation analysis (Moral-Muñoz et al., 2019). The evolution of the knowledge regarding anxiety and consumption is presented, where the interest that academics have shown has enables the better understanding about the influence that perceived risk has on anxiety and consumption; the effect of society over individual perceptions and subsequent behaviors; the influence that technology has on anxiety and consumption, and finally, anxiety as an antecedent of panic buying.

Research on this field highlights the changes that mental health generates on consumer behavior. Before the development of this research, there was a lack of understanding on the anxiety and consumption knowledge field. Therefore, the first theoretical contribution of this paper is to examine the area of activity around which anxiety and purchase processes are spinning. This purpose is achieved through the integration of a bibliometric analysis on the knowledge field. Second, this cluster model provides evidence such as the fact that anxiety is an element which goes beyond clinical effects but that it is also related to the social sciences area. For example, through how market psychological factors such as individual self-concept or social identification affect purchase intention. Third, the obtained results suggest that anxiety has restructures purchase behavioral models and the need to analyze new variables related to technological innovation which traditionally have not caught enough attention in the field, such as lack of control, perceived risk, cyberchondria or rumination, which means that anxiety is associated to technological factors like online purchases, cyber security, facial recognition, or contactless payments.

In addition, several practical implications can be suggested by this research. First, this study provides a deeper understanding which could help public and private organizations to identify what motivations and factors can produce an effect on consumers anxiety towards their purchase intention. Second, organizations can take advantage of these contributions to identify which factors could reduce the anxiety effect on consumer behavior to decrease their efforts in the purchase process. Moreover, with teleworking and the increase in online purchases, enterprises should improve the quality and layout of the inline stores to make them more user friendly, and thus reduce the purchase perceived risk, for example, providing clear information on how to use the different online channels or the use of secure payment methods in the purchase transactions. New academics can also use the contributions of this research to enlarge the existing research lines or identifying new ones.

Finally, from this research, several future research lines which have not yet been covered by academics have been identified. For example, are there any variables which could reduce consumers anxiety level during the purchase process? Companies with more hygiene, security, sustainability or more legitimated, reduce the consumer anxiety? Can psychographic variables such as age or gender vary perceived anxiety level in the purchase process? Are there differences between perceived anxiety in online purchase processes and offline ones?

REFERENCES

Aafjes-van Doorn, K., Zilcha-Mano, S., Graham, K., Caldari, A., Barber, J. P., Chambless, D. L., & Milrod, B. (2019). The Role of Safety Behaviors in Panic Disorder Treatment: Self-Regulation or Self-Defeat? *Journal of Contemporary Psychotherapy*, *49*(4), 203–212. doi:10.100710879-019-09432-9

Arumugam, T. (2020). Caring for Your Mental Health during MCO. *News Straits Times*. https://www.nst.com.my/news/nation/2020/03/578414/caring-your-mental-health-during-mco

Baker, S., Farrokhnia, R.A., Meyer, S., Pagel, M., & Yannelis, C. (2020). *How Does Household Spending Respond to an Epidemic? Consumption During the 2020 COVID-19 Pandemic*. doi:10.3386/w26949

Cachón-Rodríguez, G., Prado-Román, C., & Zúñiga-Vicente, J. Á. (2019). The relationship between identification and loyalty in a public university: Are there differences between (the perceptions) professors and graduates? *European Research on Management and Business Economics, 25*(3), 122–128. doi:10.1016/j.iedeen.2019.04.005

Cachón-Rodríguez, G., Prado-Román, C., & Blanco-González, A. (2021). The relationship between corporate identity and university loyalty: The moderating effect of brand identification in managing an institutional crisis. *Journal of Contingencies and Crisis Management, 29*(3), 265–280. doi:10.1111/1468-5973.12342

Chen, C. (2006). CiteSpace II: Detecting and visualizing emerging trends and transient patterns in scientific literature. *Journal of the American Society for Information Science and Technology, 57*(3), 359–377. doi:10.1002/asi.20317

Chen, C., Ibekwe-SanJuan, F., & Hou, J. (2010). The structure and dynamics of co-citation clusters: A multiple-perspective co-citation analysis. *Journal of the American Society for Information Science and Technology, 61*(7), 1386–1409. doi:10.1002/asi.21309

Cobo Martín, J. M. (2012). *Scimat, herramienta software para el análisis de la evolución del conocimiento científico: Propuesta de una metodología de evaluación* (Tesis Doctoral). Universidad de Granada, Granada.

Dabholkar, P. A., & Bagozzi, R. P. (2002). An attitudinal model of technology-based self-service: Moderating effects of consumer traits and situational factors. *Journal of the Academy of Marketing Science, 30*(3), 184–201. doi:10.1177/0092070302303001

Díez-Martín, F., Blanco-González, A., & Díez-de-Castro, E. (2021). Measuring a scientifically multifaceted concept. The jungle of organizational legitimacy. *European Research on Management and Business Economics, 27*(1), 100131. doi:10.1016/j.iedeen.2020.10.001

Díez-Martín, F., Miotto, G., & Cachón-Rodríguez, G. (2022). Organizational legitimacy perception: Gender and uncertainty as bias for evaluation criteria. *Journal of Business Research, 139*, 426–436. doi:10.1016/j.jbusres.2021.09.073

Duan, L., & Zhu, G. (2020). Psychological interventions for people affected by the COVID-19 epidemic. *The Lancet. Psychiatry, 7*(4), 300–302. doi:10.1016/S2215-0366(20)30073-0 PMID:32085840

Gallup. (2021). *State of the Global Workplace: 2021 Report.* https://www.gallup.com/workplace/349484/state-of-the-global-workplace.aspx

Guttman, N., & Lev, E. (2021). Ethical Issues in COVID-19 Communication to Mitigate the Pandemic: Dilemmas and Practical Implications. *Health Communication, 36*(1), 116–123. doi:10.1080/10410236.2020.1847439 PMID:33191801

Islam, T., Pitafi, A. H., Arya, V., Wang, Y., Akhtar, N., Mubarik, S., & Xiaobei, L. (2021). Panic buying in the COVID-19 pandemic: A multi-country examination. *Journal of Retailing and Consumer Services, 59*, 102357. doi:10.1016/j.jretconser.2020.102357

Lerner, J., & Keltner, D. (2001). Fear, anger, and risk. *Journal of Personality and Social Psychology*, *81*(1), 146–159. doi:10.1037/0022-3514.81.1.146 PMID:11474720

Dabholkar, P. A. (1996). Consumer evaluations of new technology-based self-service options: An investigation of alternative models of service quality. *International Journal of Research in Marketing*, *13*(1), 29–51. doi:10.1016/0167-8116(95)00027-5

Meyer, S. (2020). *Understanding the Covid-19 effect on online shopping behaviour.* BigCommerce. https://www.bigcommerce.com/blog/covid-19 ecommerce/#conclusion

Moral-Munoz, J. A., López-Herrera, A. G., Herrera-Viedma, E., & Cobo, M. J. (2019). Science mapping analysis software tools: A review. In Springer handbook of science and technology indicators. Springer. doi:10.1007/978-3-030-02511-3_7

Omar, N. A., Nazri, M. A., Ali, M. H., & Alam, S. S. (2021). The panic buying behavior of consumers during the COVID-19 pandemic: Examining the influences of uncertainty, perceptions of severity, perceptions of scarcity, and anxiety. *Journal of Retailing and Consumer Services*, *62*, 102600. doi:10.1016/j.jretconser.2021.102600

Payne, G., Blanco-González, A., Miotto, G., & Del-Castillo, C. (2021). Consumer Ethicality Perception and Legitimacy: Competitive Advantages in COVID-19 Crisis. *The American Behavioral Scientist*. Advance online publication. doi:10.1177/00027642211016515

Ramos-Rodríguez, A.-R., & Ruíz-Navarro, J. (2004). Changes in the intellectual structure of strategic management research: A bibliometric study of the Strategic management journal, 1980–2000. *Strategic Management Journal*, *25*(10), 981–1004. doi:10.1002mj.397

Santomauro, D. F., Mantilla Herrera, A. M., Shadid, J., Zheng, P., Ashbaugh, C., Pigott, D. M., Abbafati, C., Adolph, C., Amlag, J. O., Aravkin, A. Y., Bang-Jensen, B. L., Bertolacci, G. J., Bloom, S. S., Castellano, R., Castro, E., Chakrabarti, S., Chattopadhyay, J., Cogen, R. M., Collins, J. K., ... Ferrari, A. J. (2021). Articles Global prevalence and burden of depressive and anxiety disorders in 204 countries and territories in 2020 due to the COVID-19 pandemic. *Lancet*, *398*(10312), 1700–1712. doi:10.1016/S0140-6736(21)02143-7 PMID:34634250

Sheth, J. (2020). Impact of Covid-19 on consumer behavior: Will the old habits return or die? *Journal of Business Research*, *117*, 280–283. doi:10.1016/j.jbusres.2020.05.059 PMID:32536735

Small, H. (1973). Co-citation in the scientific literature: A new measure of the relationship between two documents. *Journal of the American Society for Information Science*, *24*(4), 265–269. doi:10.1002/asi.4630240406

Stephan, W., & Stephan, C. W. (1985). Intergroup Anxiety. *The Journal of Social Issues*, *41*(3), 157–175. doi:10.1111/j.1540-4560.1985.tb01134.x

Stephan, W., Stephan, C. W., & Gudykunst, W. B. (1999). Anxiety in intergroup relations: A comparison of anxiety/uncertainty management theory and integrated threat theory. *International Journal of Intercultural Relations*, *23*(4), 613–628. doi:10.1016/S0147-1767(99)00012-7

Turner, S. M., Beidel, D. C., Dancu, C. V., & Stanley, M. A. (1989). An empirically derived inventory to measure social fears and anxiety: The Social Phobia and Anxiety Inventory. *Psychological Assessment, 1*(1), 35–40. doi:10.1037/1040-3590.1.1.35

Van Eck, N. J., & Waltman, L. (2014). CitNetExplorer: A new software tool for analyzing and visualizing citation networks. *Journal of Informetrics, 8*(4), 802–823. doi:10.1016/j.joi.2014.07.006

Yang, K., Kim, J., Min, J., & Hernandez-Calderon, A. (2020). Effects of retailers' service quality and legitimacy on behavioral intention: The role of emotions during COVID-19. *Service Industries Journal, 41*(1-2), 84–106. doi:10.1080/02642069.2020.1863373

Zupic, I., & Cater, T. (2015). Bibliometric methods in management and organization. *Organizational Research Methods, 18*(3), 429–472. doi:10.1177/1094428114562629

Word Health Organization. (2021). www.who.int

KEY TERMS AND DEFINITIONS

Anxiety: It is a generalized imbalance sensation which rises from concern, stress about what will happen in the future.

Bibliometric Methods: Methods to review the literature. These methods permit to understanding of the origin, future and growth of a specific discipline.

Co-Citation Analysis: Type of bibliometric methods that identifies networks of interconnections between authors.

Ideal Self-Efficacy: How we accept ourselves as well as how we are influenced by others, since the pressure for behave on a certain manner is present.

Legitimacy: It is a fundamental element of strategic management that refers to the social acceptance of the actions carried out by the organization.

Panic Buying Behavior: When consumers emptied the supermarket shelves during a catastrophe.

Chapter 14
Fast-Paced Technology Evolution Faced by Operators With the Needs Emerging From Work Model Changes and General Information Access for Customers

Carlos Silva
NOS Inovação, Portugal

Joana Coutinho Sousa
iD https://orcid.org/0000-0002-6418-2312
NOS Inovação, Portugal

Nuno Cid Ponte
NOS Inovação, Portugal

Nuno Martins
iD https://orcid.org/0000-0002-4509-2493
NOS Inovação, Portugal

Nuno Miguel Felizardo
NOS Inovação, Portugal

João Miguel Ferreira
NOS Inovação, Portugal

ABSTRACT

This chapter presents insights about how NOS Inovação has reshaped their teams to get a more horizontal and holistic overview about their services (from development to operations) and how this change has positively impacted the development of new services targeting internet personalisation. Furthermore, this chapter also describes the NOS vision about Industry 5.0, where digital transition is a key enabler and presents a critical role in the future.

INTRODUCTION

Covid-19 brought to the surface the urgent need for a faster transition to digitalization. This transition

DOI: 10.4018/978-1-6684-6762-6.ch014

also showed that the way we see digital tools and the way we work were key players in this transition.

The need to promote digital inclusion, to ensure that everyone had access to telecommunication services and to maintain continuity of everyday social, educational, and economic interactions and leaving no one excluded, was a big challenge.

The importance of the telecommunications networks, their resilience and scalability as well as their role in helping get more people online and its responsibility in developing better connectivity were also very well reflected in this time of crisis.

This dramatic change has occurred pushing not only the digital literacy and skills for all, but also the way teams were working. The remote working demands, a more and more agile mindset to build multi-disciplinary teams to get a holistic approach about telecom services, products and network, sustained in transversal service quality KPIs ensuring that the industry was able to respond faster to the customer's needs in the digital world.

This chapter presents insights about how NOS Inovação has reshaped their teams to get a more horizontal and holistic overview about their services (from Development to Operations) and how this change has positively impacted the development of new services targeting Internet personalization. Furthermore, this chapter also describes NOS' vision about Industry 5.0, where digital transition is a key enabler and presents a critical role in the future.

BACKGROUND

The evolution of society has been dominated by industrial revolutions which have changed the face of the modern world (Figure 1). The first revolution (Industry 1.0 - Mechanization) occurred in 1780 with the introduction of industrial production equipment driven by water and steam power. Approximately, one century afterwards (1870), the world witnessed to the second revolution (Industry 2.0 - electrification) where mass production was possible due to the electrical energy and assembly lines. In 1970, the automated production due to the rise of electronics, telecommunications and computers led to the third revolution (Industry 3.0 - Automation). The fourth revolution started with the use of cyber-physical systems (CPS) on connected devices to automated processes, and the development of technologies such as Big Data, Internet-of-Things (IoT), 3D printing and Artificial Intelligence (AI).

The IoT is a network over which the CPS connects to the Internet in an auditable and secure manner. On the other hand, a smart society will use a combination of cyber-physical systems and humans with support from intelligence and automation.

Since its introduction in 2011, Industry 4.0 – Digitalization has led to rediscovered growth and transformation in technology. Although with potential to create high impact, Industry 4.0 was only accelerated in 2020 due to the COVID-19 pandemic crisis.

COVID-19 brought to the surface the urgent need for a faster transition to digitalization. This transition also showed that the way digital was seen, and the way people were working, were key players in this transition. And because of that, the fifth revolution (Industry 5.0 – Personalization) started (Sarfraz, Z, 2021).

According to European Commission (European Commission, 2022), Industry 5.0 "shifts the focus from the shareholder value to stakeholder value and reinforces the role and the contribution of industry to society" as illustrated in the following Figure 2.

Figure 1. Industrial revolutions

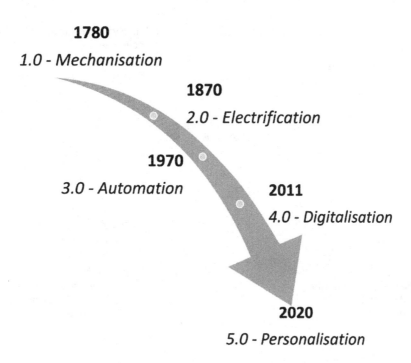

As depicted by Esben H. Østergaard, CEO at REInvest Robotics: "By placing humans back at the center of industrial production, Industry 5.0 gives consumers the products they want and gives workers jobs that are more meaningful."

Industry 5.0 brings in this 'human' touch. Resilience (business resilience and cyber resilience), sustainability and environment concerns, circular economy, the place of people in a future of work with more human-machine collaboration and human-centric solutions.

This way, the personalization of broadband services is very important following the concept of "The Internet of Me: Creating a Personalized Broadband Experience"

The Importance of the Internet

During the pandemic crisis, the Internet providers were faced with several changes due to the increase in digital traffic, as illustrated in the Figure 3. With the increase of mobile downloads of several online platforms, the need for a resilient and fast infrastructure like 5G or enhanced WiFi technologies, such as WiFi6, became the evident demand from the market for a robust and personalized broadband service (Jonathan, 2020).

WiFi6 Technology

WiFi AX, rebranded WiFi6 by the WiFi Alliance (Wi-Fi Alliance 2018) is the latest advancement in a path of continuous innovation. This standard builds on the strengths of 802.11ac while providing more

Figure 2. The 3 pillars of industry 5.0 according to the EC – human-centric, resilient, and sustainable

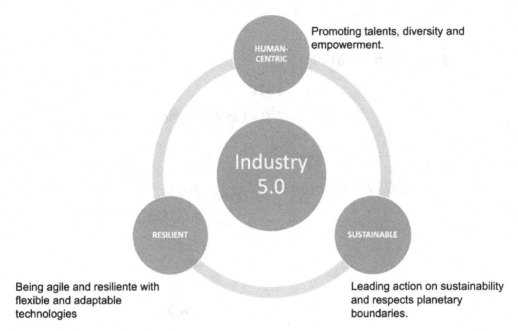

speed, flexibility, and dimensionality. This allows for more speed and capacity on new and existing next-generation networks.

This technology is characterized by (CISCO, 2021):

- Denser modulation using 1024 QAM, enabling a speed climb of more than 35%.
- OFDMA-based programming to reduce overhead and latency
- Robust, high definition signaling for better performance with significantly lower RSSI.
- Better planning and longer device battery life like TWT (Target Wake Time).

Figure 3. Internet traffic increase at major peering exchanges. Adopted by (Jonathan, 2020)

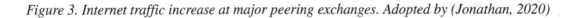
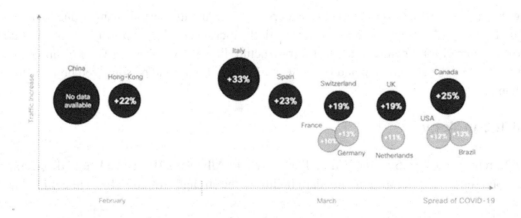

Figure 4. WiFi evolution

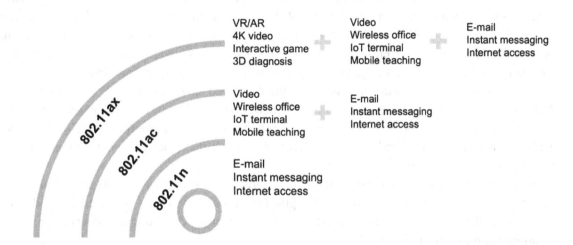

Thus, WiFi6 allows access points to support more clients in dense environments and provides a better experience in typical wireless LAN networks. It also makes the performance of advanced applications such as 4K and 8K video, high-density and high-definition collaboration applications, fully wireless offices, and further leverage of IoT more predictable. This new standard will propel WiFi into the future, following the growth of wireless technologies. This is well illustrated in Figure 4.

Over the last two decades a massive transformation was observed and the evolution of WiFi technologies as well as new WiFi generations have been deployed in very fast pace. As an example, today we're on the WiFi6 generation, at the same time the WiFi7 is almost ready for deployment, bringing even more performance, lower latencies and a better WiFi spectrum management, positioning the internet as the main service in customer services (Net Centrality is now real).

Mesh WiFi

Wireless signals degrade with distance, when passing through walls made of common construction materials. This attenuation is particularly dramatic if the walls are brick, stone or metal foil (common in insulation in newer homes). The wireless signal corresponding to the WiFi 11ac and 11ax standard degrades even more rapidly with distance since it uses the 5GHz spectrum as compared to the 2.4GHz spectrum used by earlier, slower versions of the standard (Wi-Fi EasyMesh).

As the consumer is using increasingly more bandwidth-hungry WiFi devices at more places in the home, the approach taken by the more capable routers is to use more powerful hardware in the router, driving the WiFi signal to more places in the home (the full power approach). This has some drawbacks of course, more powerful hardware means using more radio chains (antennas) with signal processing (MIMO) and higher-power amplifiers to generate a stronger signal. The increase in range that can be achieved this way is incremental but will drive upwards power and complexity. As distance increases, the rate of performance of the WiFi signal is lower, and expensive increases in signal power and parallel transmissions, provide marginal WiFi performance at distance (G. R. Hiertz et al, 2010).

Besides the fact that WiFi generations are being every time more efficient and with coverage optimization, the mesh solution (Chunming, 2014) provides the capability to use WiFi solutions in a multi node (although a demoting expression because it is associated with less "smart" devices, let's call them: extenders), this class of WiFi products unite to create a mesh network to coordinate with each other to increase the WiFi range. Current mesh routing protocols are designed to provide sustained traffic and connection between mesh nodes, ensuring that that the information reaches the internet gateway.

The WiFi signal is forwarded across the optimally placed extenders around the home to reach all client devices. With enough extenders, the WiFi signal will need to travel less between extenders, or from the last extender to the final client device. By shortening the distance that the WiFi transmissions needs to travel, this solution reduces the degradation of the WiFi signal, allowing for higher data rates throughout the entire home

With a single router, the WiFi performance at different places in the home will wildly vary based on the placement of the router, and sources of degradation around the home. In the case of a distributed WiFi system, the signal can take several paths to get to the client device, and the system can be optimized to choose the most effective path.

Structure of the Chapter

The topics previously discussed are clearly enablers to the Personalisation (Industry 5.0). Although they have been applied as individual components to provide faster Internet and more bandwidth at the customer's home, they need to be as a holistic approach in order to change the current telecom paradigm not only in terms of technology but also in terms of new business models and way of working. The personalization pushes the final user to the center. This is particularly critical to collect key data to know more and better the final user and, consequently, to provide customized broadband services. Although not covered by the Chapter, 5G technology has shown that currently mature network technology is already available in the market, but telecom operators are not fully leverage its potential. The Era of Internet Things is already over, and Internet of People is now rising. In order to address this new concept, bring all technology as an integrated way and whole solution is mandatory to create smart environments and smart products and services. However, to achieve this main goal, develop technology is not enough, and teams shall re-structure and built as high-performance teams' concept in terms of multidisciplinary and cross function. This will give companies the ability of addressing the user's pains and market's needs in a better and faster way. Following this thought, this chapter presents a potential technological approach aiming at the Internet of People, leveraged by the most advanced broadband technology. The chapter presents some insights about how NOS sees a Smart Environment through a Smart Router product. For that, the Chapter is divided into three sections:

- Introduction section, where a briefly resume about the content is provided.
- Background section where technological components are discussed as individual. These technologies are considered key enablers to build the Smart Environment.
- The Smart Router section, where a conceptual overview about Smart Router is presented and then each component that contributes is also explained and discussed.
- New Ways of Working Models section briefly discussed how NOS has structured teams to get the necessary holistic approach.

Figure 5. Internet add-value for NOS ecosystem

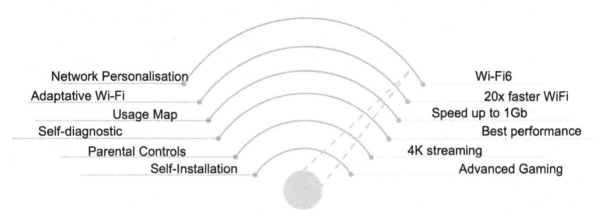

- Future Research Work section where some highlights about some challenges and issues already identified and not covered by the proposed solution are explained.
- Conclusion section gives the main highlights of the chapter.

THE SMART ROUTER

NOS Inovação as a telecommunication company was presented with several challenges during the pandemic crisis. Most of them were already explained in the previous section. However, the company has recognized these challenges as an opportunity, not only for improving its infrastructure, evolving to a more robust and resilient ground for a stable service, but also for a better understanding of their customers, particularly the residential market customers, and what they want from their service provider. This was particularly key considering the diversity of the customers. If in the one hand, some customers only want to have a good broadband service to work in terms of Internet stability, other customers demand more powerful connections in terms of stability, more speed, more bandwidth and better performance.

To address these profiling challenges, some actions were done in different branches.

Firstly, the company understood that in order to have a good knowledge about their customers and what they are in terms of data, products and services, the way of working needed to change. A transversal and holistic approach, with the customer at the center, was necessary.

Secondly and using customer's data, NOS identified the power of data to deliver a personalized broadband service according to the customer needs as well giving the opportunity to personalize their own service. Lastly, to respond to market demands, advanced WiFi such as WiFi6 and the use of advanced Machine Learning techniques were critical. The Figure 5 highlights the Internet add-value based on WiFi6 technology.

Based on these premises, teams were re-created in order to have a more cross-functional and diverse, allowing a holistic overview of the services, and a new broadband ecosystem was designed to ensure the following features: personalized service and smart internet. The following Figure 6 illustrated how these NOS Broadband ecosystem consists of.

Figure 6. NOS smart router ecosystem

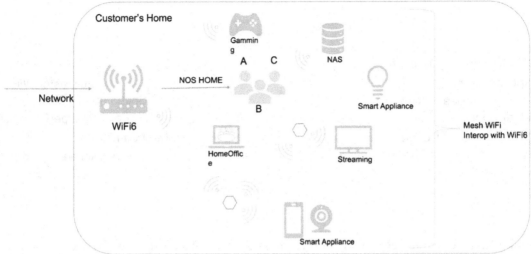

The Personalized Broadband Service

Personalized broadband service is a complex area but one that NOS Inovação has been exploring as part of their work to engage more and more with their customers. Modern algorithms and AI systems based on data about network infrastructure, home gateways (HGW) and customer behavior give companies the ability to personalize services in a more sophisticated way.

Although some telecom companies have addressed this matter in terms of personalized prices or more recently broadband speeds prices personalized for customer's homes (Backer, 2020), NOS Inovação believes that the personalization is beyond price or speed: it will also cover bandwidth considering the typology of customer's home, density in terms of number of connected devices at home and customers profile (is it a gamer? Is it an Internet advanced user? Is it a regular/normal Internet user?).

To address this holistic approach centered in personalization, the authors identified key technical points to investigate and implement:

1. The first step was changing the way of how the company performed troubleshooting.

If before COVID-19 pandemic crisis, NOS took a more passive role, waiting for customer's contacts; after the pandemic, NOS realized that proactive troubleshooting was more efficient in terms of cost and a better path to engage customers since they feel closer to the service provider.

The proactive troubleshooting has been executed into two different environments:

a. From outside to customer's home
b. Inside customer's home:
    i. At the HGW (Home Gate Way) equipment
    ii. From the HGW equipment to connected devices

This work will only focus on Inside the customer's home, where different tools were developed and implemented, and they will be briefly described in the section Smart Troubleshooting.

2.   The second step was to bring the customer to the center, as Industry 5.0 demands.

If before pandemic, the company didn't clearly profile their customers based on their behavior in terms of how they use the broadband service, after pandemic and in order to optimize the network infrastructure to answer the market demands, customers' profiles revealed to be a key point both for technical issues and personalization. To do that, the authors implemented a QoS strategy (Hussain, 2022) to create profiles without infringing on any legal or privacy issues. How the company designs it will be further discussed in Section Smart Profiling.

3.   Based on 2), the authors realized that speed was not the most important feature for the customer. The optimization of bandwidth as well as the IoT behavior were also important (Qualcomm, 2020). Considering this knowledge, the authors implemented a solution for a smart Quality of Experience (QoE) KPI (Guha, 2022), and a predictive behavioral IoT system was explored (Gadde, 2022). All these points will be described in Smart Quality of Experience.

4.   With the pandemic, digital literacy and skills increase; however, if on the one hand this was very important to the digital transition, on counterpoint, cyberattacks also started growing exponentially. Thus, security concerns will be very important to protect customers, particularly in IoT ecosystems. This issue was also explored by the authors and will be further developed in Smart Security (Walker, 2014).

All these points are components developed to design what the authors call the Smart Internet.

The Smart Internet

The Smart Internet consists of an architecture to deliver personalized broadband services. This architecture aims at providing a set of services, as presented before, to better understand the customer's needs and, consequently, to automatically adapt the service accordingly.

Although this architecture is implemented into the HGW, it is fully transparent to the customer through NOS digital endpoints. In these apps, customers can see what the company is offering in terms of services and be able to personalize its own service. The following sections discuss further these features.

Smart Troubleshooting

As previously presented, troubleshooting is performed in two different environments: from outside the customer's home, and inside customer's home. In this chapter, the authors will focus on the second one: inside customer's home.

In pre-pandemic the troubleshoot efforts were more self-contained to each network element. No correlation or crosschecking KPIs were done, mostly due to the lack of analytics platforms and management protocols scalable to do it.

Analytics tools, such as Kibana (Elastic, 2022), enabled having a centralized platform that collects and processes access networks data. With data correlation and data processing using well known thresholds on top of all KPIs it is now easier to identify affected devices, the ones mitigated and the ones that are in a failure scenario.

This platform was also useful to collect data from which some ML (Machine Learning) algorithms have been developed to predict anomalies and, consequently, to take actions based on those predictions. From access network, such as DOCSIS impaired devices, to wrong behavior of Wi-Fi and voice services related to the router are some examples of ML algorithms outputs being used.

Troubleshooting from HGW Equipment to Connected Devices

The solution presented above can be used not only for troubleshooting network elements, where HGW equipment is included. Connected devices need to be part of the analytics solution, since degradation and bad experience of the broadband service could also occur in the connection between HGW and connected devices.

To address these issues, the authors have designed a solution in order to monitor the quality of the connection between HGW and all connected devices and, if necessary, to execute actions to improve it. This solution consists of the following features:

- Status of the connection
- Connection dropouts
- Measuring quality connection KPIs, such as speed and latency
- WiFi band and WiFi mode connection between device and HGW
- Coverage and steering failures
- Data/bandwidth consumption

Such tool requires probing periodically with a short interval to guarantee that the analytics platform has significant samples to predict and act with the best decision to solve customer problems.

This tool will provide opportunities to create personalized offers and services taking into consideration the broadband service needs per customer:

- Identify the best profile
- Create a guaranteed coverage offer
- Suggest traffic prioritization based on services used by the customer (example: remote work, gaming, streaming)

On top of the approach described above in order to measure stability and performance of the access network, NOS Inovação has developed a software client in the HGWs with RIPE SW probes. This type of approach enables to use public data set to monitor the network quality from CPE perspective across type and use same data for benchmarking with the RIPE community probes/operators.

Ripe Atlas

Ripe Atlas (Ripe Atlas, 2022) is a global, open, and innovative project from Ripe Network Coordination Centre (Ripe NCC) which aims to create the world largest Internet measurement network platform, consisting of thousands of measurement devices (probes) that measure Internet connectivity in real time. This tool has been used by NOS Inovação to get network key performance indicators (KPIs) and

Table 1. Collected parameters in Ripe Atlas

24 hours	Data for each measurement from the last 24 hours, counting from the current hour the user queries the data
Measurements	Measurement results starting from 1 January 2020
Probes	Information regarding probes
Samples	1% sample of recent measurement results
Yesterday	Measurement results for the full day immediately prior.

connection stability and latency. Correlation between those KPIs and the ones from access network provides the company with ability to create a holistic and transversal powerful tool to react fast without user perception and assuring a better user experience.

To do that, the authors started having a first grasp of the data available, creating a dashboard able to track and compare six different measures for each Portuguese probe registered on Ripe Atlas. To create this flow, a methodology was followed:

1.   Data collection and Data Preparation

The initial data was retrieved from the public dataset by Ripe and analyzed using Google Cloud Platform (GCP) through Big Query. Raw data was divided as followed:

Afterwards, one new feature was created in order to allow a deeper analysis of the existing data: District. District was based on districts' latitude and longitude, having a total of 20 districts (18 continental plus Azores and Madeira).

The field tags have information regarding the technology of probes (ipv4 and ipv6). It also contains data about CMTS, which play an important role on the geographical analysis. Several queries were created to gather information from the public dataset. The idea behind these queries was to add the measure's table all the information regarding the previous day, performing a joint query between *probes_portugal* and *yesterday*.

2.   Data Exploration and Measures

Through the collected data, dashboards were created allowing teams to have a global perspective about the dataset. Teams can see probes' location and data on the specification of the existing probes – HGW generation, system ipv4 vs. system ipv6, different status and its evolution throughout a defined timeframe. These dashboards also provide more detailed information regarding the probe, as illustrated in the following Figure 7.

These dashboards show the average packets sent by each probe, the average packages received and the average loss rate for each probe (on the date range specified). The gauges showing the minimum, average and maximum roundtrip time (rtt) for each probe gives a first approach on whether that probe is having good or poor performances. There are also five different charts detailed by company, probe, type of technology (ipv4 and ipv6), HGW generation and the distribution of eventual errors in the selected timeframe.

Figure 7. Dashboards with collected measures

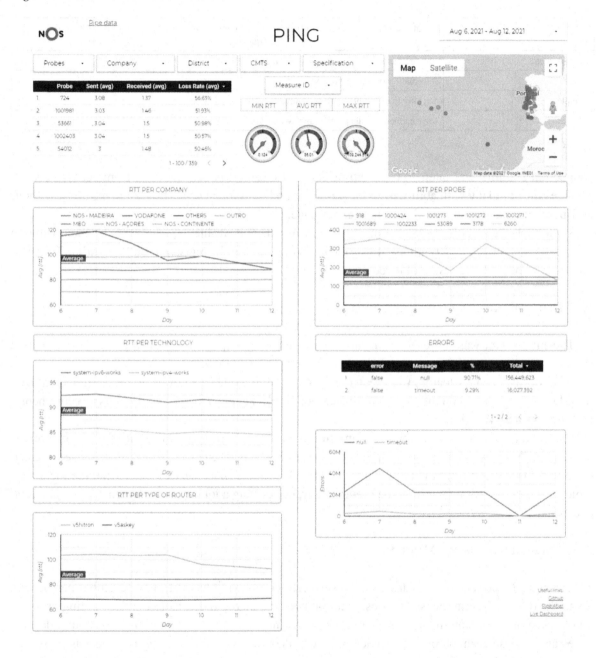

Besides the fact this kind of probes cannot be deployed for the hole installed base, it can be used to have a geographical dispersion. This approach enables us to observe different quality metrics in the whole country and promote focused detailed analysis in certain areas of the country, promoting a better resolution time in the customer experience.

Table 2. Traffic parameterization, where access category 3 is the most relevant and 0 is less relevant

Access Category	Name	Description
0	BE	Best Effort
1	BK	Background
2	VI	Video
3	VO	Voice

Smart Customer Profiling

The home environment has changed drastically since March 2020, where the lockdowns imposed to people and companies a new way of working and living, and all in the same physical space.

Residential networks were not dimensioned to have such intense and simultaneous use of a whole family with different needs. Homeworking, homeschool, online activities, gaming, etc. were already a reality but not at the same time inside customers' homes.

This became a challenge for telecom operators that had to respond fast to this suddenly change. One of the challenges is to attend different user's needs in terms of traffic priority inside the residential network, where collaborative work applications concurred with other type of traffic like gaming, streaming and so on.

The access control features gained relevance in this type of scenarios, but they are a shortcoming to the user's needs. Thus, a more powerful solution was required to handle with the traffic priority inside the customer's home network, where the homeworking tools can have more priority than others, for example.

The NOS solution to this challenge was to implement a QoS mechanism that takes in consideration the:

- Application type
- User QoS profile
- Schedule
- Network (SSID)

Since Wi-Fi is a shared media access network, the challenge was to have the right priority to the intended user/application. To address it, the 802.11e was used to classify the traffic in terms of priority and parameterization in accordance with Table 2.

Based on this parameterization, several applications are mapped in the respective Access Categories according to their type, following the example in the table below:

The above mapping will be available to the customer from which HGW will assign to the users the respective QoS profiles. These QoS profiles can be applied accordingly to a schedule based on the day of the week or the day period. Also, the rules can be applied to different Wi-Fi Networks (SSIDs) existing at customer's home.

In Figure 8, we can find the architecture used to the solution. The traffic sent by user to the residential network enters, via Data Plane, in the HGW where it is analysed by the Application Recognition Module, then the rules configured in the QoS Profile Module are taken in consideration so that the Data Classifier Module can mark the traffic and sent it back to the Residential Network.

Table 3. Application type mapped in Access Categories

Application type examples	Access Category
WhatsApp; Messenger; Teams; Zoom; Webex; Gaming	3
Youtube: Netflix; Amazon; Disney; Prime Video	2
Trackers; Analytics	1
Http; Https; snmp; igmp; dns; ipsec; ntp; SIP	0

Figure 8. QoS profiling architecture

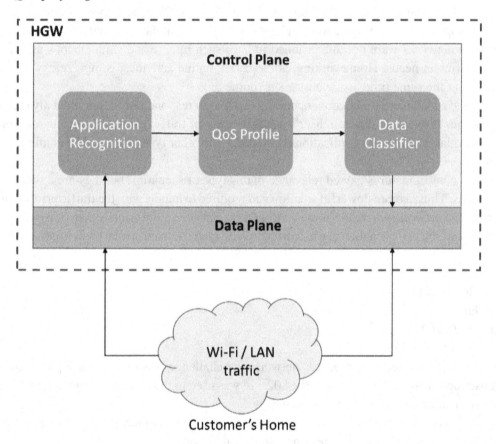

To guaranty net neutrality, the QoS mechanism will only be used inside the residential network and all traffic sent to the Internet will not be marked by the gateway when passing through the WAN port.

Smart Quality of Experience

Smart Monitoring the Quality of Broadband Bandwidth

Based on the technological service described in the previous sections (Smart Customer Profiling), it's possible to better understand the customer's needs and, consequently, to provide a personalized broadband service.

If on the one hand Internet speed was important for certain profiles, on the other hand, the quality of service for a specific application type was even more important for a significant number of customers. Taking into consideration this knowledge, NOS team addressed it into two different branches:

1. Providing a robust mesh WiFi technology
2. Implementing smart algorithms to identify and monitor the localization of mesh WiFi hardware to optimize the bandwidth to the typology of customer's home.

Delivering WiFi6 HGW with Mesh WiFi, NOS supplies the customers with a smarter Internet with the maximum stability and bandwidth. Using WiFi6 associate with Mesh solution, it will be possible deliver WiFi covering all customers homes as a plug-and-play service, ensuring the maximum number of extenders adequate to each customer's home.

With the pandemic crisis, self-installation concept has grown exponentially; however, this prompted rethinking how technical validations could be performed in order to proactively identify issues throughout the customer's life cycle. One approach that the team designed to address this challenge was to correlate the needed bandwidth with the location of mesh WiFi hardware. To do that, the team implemented an algorithm that uses history data from all extenders and connected devices to evaluate the bandwidth quality. With this algorithm, issues with either the quality of bandwidth, extenders not adequality installed or need to install even more extenders are proactively identified. If the team identifies that bad quality of bandwidth comes from a low number of installed extenders, sales teams proactively contact the customer explaining the situation and presenting more sophisticated solutions. If the team identifies that the problem resides in poorly positioned extenders, operational teams contact the customers to support them in this process.

The following Figure 9 gives a highlighted view on how teams see all this information:

Smart IoT Ecosystem

The concept of smart home behavior is considered by the authors more than to proactively check the broadband services. It also consists of providing customer with a smart solution to manage their IoT ecosystem at home.

The management of IoT devices is not limited to integrating their devices and push actions to a mobile app. It should include the collection of information about the connected devices, such as software versions, updates, security, among other KPIs, providing the user with value information in a format of alarms, alerts or warnings. Examples of these messages are: "A new software release for your connected device X was delivered. Do you want to update?" or "The device Y presents poor protection. Do you need support to improve it?" or even "Your device Z is disconnected".

These types of messages help customers to manage their connected devices and use then in a continuously and smoothly way.

Figure 9. Smart bandwidth dashboard

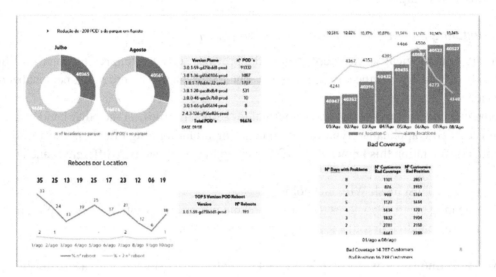

To address this feature, authors are working in smart algorithms able to identify what the "normal" pattern is in terms of customer IoT ecosystem. This includes to know the number and type of connected devices installed at home but also to know that new installations or some disconnections shall be considered as "normal" behavioral. Messages are triggered based on what is not normal patterns. To make this possible, several use-cases, were designed based on what a normal IoT pattern is. These use-cases allow team to implement and test the algorithms as well as to improve them in terms of performance and accuracy.

Smart Security

At the end of 2017, NOS had launched a study in Portugal aiming at assessing attitudes and behaviors regarding Internet use and evaluating satisfaction with Internet Accesses Macro and Micro. 670 online interviews were carried out, targeting residents in the Portuguese territory, from 15 to 64 years old, internet users, whether they have internet access (fixed or mobile). The collection period took place between 10 and 21 November 2017. The sample size corresponds to an Error Margin of +/- 3.79%, for a Confidence Interval of 95%. The study was focused on the usage of WiFi access and the corresponding concerns on several areas such as: e-mail, social network access, information search, chats, home-banking and online purchases. In all instances, security was in the top 3 of the users' concerns.

With the COVID-19 pandemic, this concern was emphasized even more with the increase of cyberattacks that world is witnessing. Considering this, NOS team have been developing security services that will be integrated in the NOS NET service. These security services focus on home network, combining the best practices of applications designed with the availability of a set of features for the mitigation of cyberattacks. Thus, the solution is focused on customer's premises and the protection is thought to be smart and simple.

The developed service support features such as: active traffic monitoring & detection, automatic attack mitigations, availability guarantee, mitigation policies tuned to customers applications, metrics & alerts, mitigation flow logs and cyberattack rapid response support. The cyberattack mitigation is designed to be always-on in terms of monitoring and analyzing. This is done through smart algorithms and filters before to consider an anomaly. For that, data from traffic behavior, consumed bandwidth per period and protocols normally used by the customer are analyzed to classify the attack. This flow allows to reduce the false positives and make the mitigations actions more effective and helpful for the customer.

The final goal is providing a scalable and secure IoT framework based on smart auto-discover, smart interoperability and smart cybersecurity.

NEW WAYS OF WORKING MODELS

As previously discussed, the COVID-19 pandemic clearly demonstrated that the way the teams were working, and the way that companies saw their customers demanded a dramatic change in order to be more in tune with the new conditions in the market.

Since several years ago, agile manifest was more and more adopted by many companies, particularly the ones with business focus on software. However, in most cases, agile manifest was badly interpreted and agile frameworks such as Scrum, Kaban, DevOps, Sigma, among others were incorrectly used by teams and companies. This was clearly reflected during the pandemic in which teams were not really agile and didn't have a holistic overview about broadband services. The working model issue led to several challenges particularly the ones related to fix problems with the service, compromising the quality of customer support.

To develop and implement the personalized broadband services as described, network teams were reshaped in terms of skillset, roles, and mindset. The targeted diversity brought more value to the product development and customer's support. The reshaping completely broke with silos, prompting more collaboration and cooperation among teams. The way teams were built has had a positive impact not only on the implementation of the best practices of agile frameworks (giving teams with more capacity to deliver and respond faster) but also to provide teams with a transversal and holistic overview of the services (from outside network infrastructure to customer support). This new capability is illustrated in the following Figure 10.

Although changes are not always well accepted by humans, getting evidence that NPS has drastically increased after those changes showed to the the teams that this reshaping had high positive impact whatever the working model was: at the office, remote or hybrid.

The authors cannot state what the future of the working models will be, but authors can clearly state that the most important key point learnings by the described changes is that diversity and focus are very important to deliver services with high quality, allowing a faster and better engagement of customers.

FUTURE RESEARCH DIRECTIONS

The chapter shares some insights about how COVID-19 pandemic impacted the working model of teams and the development of personalized broadband services.

All the developments and changes were done based on information available about NOS' customers, their needs and market demands. Indeed, data revealed to be a powerful tool to better know the customer; however, some challenges related to privacy need to be addressed. If on the one hand the development of personalized services demands data analytics, on the other, companies need to carefully select which

Figure 10. The holistic overview

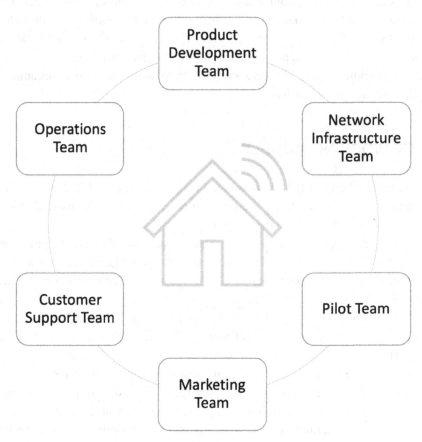

type of data should be collected to ensure the customer's privacy. In this chapter, the collected date was related to network and connected devices parameters; however, in some cases such as smart security services the collected data wasn't enough to create good features for the algorithm. Even so, this aspect could be complemented with more HGW metrics such as reboots, led behavior, or internet stability. The authors believe that adding this information could help in improving the robustness of the algorithms.

As previously stated, the authors are not in the position of discussing the future of working models: will it be fully remote? Will it be fully onsite? Will it be hybrid? Companies are currently testing several approaches in order to find the best fit to the business but also the best working balance to their workers; however, it should be very interesting to analyze how agile frameworks will be also evolved following the new ways of the testing working models.

CONCLUSION

COVID-19 crisis accelerated the transition for digital transformation, known as Industry 4.0. Industry from several sectors faced many challenges, such as new ways of working and customers' needs and pains more exposed. Both streams prompted or rather demanded from companies drastic changes in how teams work and how to develop and deliver services.

Furthermore, the importance of telecommunications networks, their resilience and scalability as well as their role in helping more people online and its responsibility in developing better connectivity were also very well reflected in this time of crisis.

This chapter discussed how NOS Inovação has addressed some of the COVID-19 pandemic challenges in terms of the way teams started working and the way to develop and deliver services to customers targeting the personalization.

With this in mind, all implemented changes have shown the power of data, as a useful tool for development of personalized services. At NOS Inovação, this was reflected into the development of a Smart Internet ecosystem leveraged by the most advanced technologies, such as WiFi6 and AI-models for behavioral prediction. This personalized broadband ecosystem includes a smart router, smart troubleshooting, smart IoT ecosystem and smart security. The key points of this development were 1) to push the customer to the center of the analytics and data exploration, 2) to provide smart personalized broadband services and support according to customer's needs, and 3) to give teams with a holistic overview about the provided services.

Sharing these insights, the authors considered that these may be accelerators for Industry 5.0 with the expectation of increasing innovations in the field, changing the markets and customer's lives.

REFERENCES

CISCO. (2021). *O que é o Wi-Fi 6? Wi-Fi da próxima geração?* https://www.cisco.com/c/pt_pt/products/wireless/what-is-wi-fi-6.html

Everything you need to know about 5G (Qualcomm 2020). (n.d.). https://www.qualcomm.com/5g/what-is-5g

Gadde, N., Jakkali, B., Siddamallaih, H., & Babu, R. (2022). Quality of experience aware network selection model for service provisioning in heterogeneous network. *International Journal of Electrical & Computer Engineering, 12*(2).

Guha Roy, D., Mahato, B., De, D., & Srirama, S. N. (2022). Quality of experience aware recommendation system with IoT data filtration for handshaking among users using MQTT-SN protocol. *Journal of Ambient Intelligence and Humanized Computing*, 1–16.

Hiertz, G. R., Denteneer, D., Max, S., Taori, R., Cardona, J., Berlemann, L., & Walke, B. (2010). IEEE 802.11s: The WLAN Mesh Standard. *IEEE Wireless Communications, 17*(1), 104–111. doi:10.1109/MWC.2010.5416357

How adaptive WiFi can solve your WFH woes. (2020). https://www.plume.com/homepass/blog/how-adaptive-wifi-can-solve-your-wfh-woes/

Hussain, M., Ahmed, N., Ahmed, M., Iqubal, Z., & Sarma, N. (2022). QoS Provisioning in Wireless Mesh Networks: A Survey. *Wireless Personal Communications, 122*(1), 157–195.

Jonathan Davidson. (2020). *Global Traffic Spikes. No Panic at the Cisco!* https://blogs.cisco.com/news/global-traffic-spikes-no-panic-at-the-cisco

Renda, A., Schwaag Serger, S., & Tataj, D. (2022). *Industry 5.0, a transformative vision for Europe: governing systemic transformations towards a sustainable industry.* https://data.europa.eu/doi/10.2777/17322

Rong, C., Zhao, G., & Yan, L. (2014). *Erdal Cayirci, Hongbing Cheng.* Wireless Network Security. doi:10.1016/B978-0-12-416689-9.00010-1

Sarfraz, Z., Sarfraz, A., Iftikar, H. M., & Akhund, R. (2021). Is COVID-19 pushing us to the Fifth Industrial Revolution (Society 5.0)? *Pakistan Journal of Medical Sciences, 37*(2), 591–594. https://doi.org/10.12669/pjms.37.2.3387

Walker, J. (2014). *Internet Security.* doi:10.1016/B978-0-12-416689-9.00007-1

What is Ripe Atlas? (2022). https://atlas.ripe.net/about/

Wi-Fi Alliance. (2018). *Wi-Fi Alliance® introduces Wi-Fi 6.* https://www.wi-fi.org/news-events/newsroom/wi-fi-alliance-introduces-wi-fi-6

Wi-Fi EasyMesh (Wi-Fi Alliance). (n.d.). https://www.wi-fi.org/discover-wi-fi/wi-fi-easymesh

KEY TERMS AND DEFINITIONS

AI: Artificial intelligence.
GCP: Google cloud platform.
HGW: Home gateway.
KPIs: Key performance indicators.
ML: Machine learning.
QoE: Quality of experience.
QoS: Quality of service.
RTT: Roundtrip time.
SSID: Service set identifier.
WAN: Wide area network.
Wi-Fi: Wireless fidelity.

Chapter 15

Augmented Reality as an Efficient Marketing Strategy in a New Consumption Model During the COVID-19 Pandemic

Gerardo Reyes Ruiz

iD https://orcid.org/0000-0003-0212-2952

Centro de Estudios Superiores Navales (CESNAV), Mexico

ABSTRACT

The technology known as augmented reality (AR) adds virtual elements to a real physical environment observed through a screen of a mobile device. This innovative and relatively new technology can be used and adapted to other applications that in turn generate new consumption habits. The main objective of these applications is to surprise the consumer and get their full attention and interest. In other words, an AR-based consumer environment will, first of all, arouse the customer's desire to purchase and, subsequently, will motivate him to own a product that he has already viewed through an application, generally through a mobile device with access to internet, new and innovative as AR is. This new approach to consumption allows innovative and efficient marketing strategies because it depends on the way a product or service is displayed beyond the traditional forms such as a window display in a store, a commercial on television, a catalog with images 2D or the box that contains the product.

INTRODUCTION

In recent decades there have been extremely important changes both in people's consumption and in the field of so-called new technologies (Singh et al. 2021). On the one hand, we have witnessed that some brands have gradually been positioning their products in markets that are becoming more competitive every day and, on the other hand, new technologies have shown vertiginous advances, which have allowed the creation, precisely, of new consumer markets (Grubor and Milovanov 2017). With the appearance of the internet, our life underwent more than evident changes, however, it has been the new technologies,

DOI: 10.4018/978-1-6684-6762-6.ch015

which by making use of data transmission, currently allow us to have a more comfortable, pleasant, and, safe life. In other words, our daily lives have also been transformed by the proliferation of new technologies, particularly after experiencing the COVID19 pandemic (Sharma and Bashir 2020; He, Zhang and Li, 2021). Let's see some examples, there are currently countless establishments around the world that allow you to make purchases of all kinds of products or services, from the comfort and safety of home, just with a telephone connected to the Internet or with access to a data plan (Reyes, Olmos and Hernández, 2016; Forecast GMDT 2019). There are also currently countless establishments that focus on or have the service of bringing purchases, which are generally carried out through a mobile device with Internet access, to the door of the home (Bulearca and Tamarjan, 2010). In the same way, and also with a smartphone connected to the Internet, you can make multiple payments for services, bank cards, money transfers, etc. from the comfort and safety of the home: of course, banking institutions have been facilitators and promoters of these changes in order, among other things, to create a more comfortable and secure life for us (Shaikh and Karjaluoto, 2015; Fenu and Pau, 2015). These examples serve to establish that the contemporary human being has become a co-dependent entity of new technologies, regardless of whether any technological innovation satisfies any of their specific needs. That is to say, the life that touched us in the 21st century is, by far, more bearable than the life of just 100 years ago. Without a doubt, this is due to the leaps and bounds with which science and technology have advanced (Lee and Daiute, 2019). Therefore, the benefits of technological advances for contemporary human beings are also more than evident.

We are currently immersed in a world of information (Hugill, 2016). Surely, this is due, to a large extent, to the fact that the approach and knowledge of new technologies are becoming easier and more accessible to all people. However, these technological changes are becoming faster and it is clear that the interaction between technology and human beings has changed drastically over time (Elsobeihi and Abu Naser, 2017). In other words, there is so much information that is handled today that contemporary human beings must quickly assimilate a large number of technological developments instead of adapting them to their needs. As a consequence of this interaction, it can be said that the current dynamics of product or service markets have led us, among other things, to be immersed in a global society with cutting-edge technologies (Ameen, Hosany and Tarhini, 2021). Similarly, the current marketing trends have also had to adapt to the imminent technological changes, since currently, it is not enough to implement marketing strategies that only focus on showing a product on the window of a store or through from any other conventional media such as television, radio, social networks, some magazines and/or printed catalogs (Rust, 2020). That is, how the products or services are presented and sold to the final consumer has gradually changed over time (Willman-Iivarinen, 2017; Nurul et al, 2016; Lee, Cheng and Shih, 2010). However, an important factor to consider is that current marketing strategies, which have survived a globalized world and have been able to adapt to technological advances, depend largely on the purchasing habits of the people who live in a country (Pang, Keh and Peng, 2009).

The great impact of the use of the internet and its adoption through new technologies has also transformed the way people interact: communications are now more impersonal but faster, more efficient, and safer. The response of the new technologies was evident at the beginning and through the COVID19 pandemic worldwide (Toussaert, 2021; Lee and Trimi, 2021). In this context, the efficiency of mobile devices, and in particular smartphones (Yesilyurt and Yalman, 2016), has reached a level of dependency for people that is currently a necessary and indispensable product with which people communicate or may well be able to shop online and not so much in a comfortable way but rather in a safe way (Agrebi and Jallais, 2015). Furthermore, mobile devices, and particularly through social networks, have become an extremely important and sensitive means of introducing and/or disseminating a product or service more efficiently and dynamically (Lindsey-Mullikin and Borin, 2017; Dolega, Rowe and Branagan, 2020). The many uses of these innovative applications have not been ignored by companies looking for new and innovative ways to sell their products or services.

Of course, large and even medium-sized companies have not been and cannot be indifferent to technological advances, marketing trends, and, obviously, new sales strategies, particularly those carried out online (Yu, 2012). Companies that invest in new technologies to publicize their products, expand their market, and even position some of their products must be very clear about the sales strategies they will use to achieve their goal (Wijayanto, Soeaidy and Rochmah, 2014). Otherwise, it is very likely that they will incur unnecessary expenses or that their products will not be well received by consumers. Undoubtedly, a primary objective in the sales process for a product or service is precise to arouse the consumer's desire to purchase. In this context, the new sales strategies must consider the entire consumer process, because they need to identify how many and which goods are demanded by their consumers so that the finished product or service is to their liking and they intend to buy it. (Agmeka, Wathoni and Santoso, 2019). It is also important that these sales strategies identify the main needs of your consumers; from how to reach them, through the profitability of the product and even knowing if the final product or service can be paid for by the consumer or if it is of their total interest (Schwarz and Tan, 2021).

The latest generations of consumers have witnessed vertiginous changes both in the so-called new technologies and in consumption habits and forms of payment for some products (Dibrova, 2016). Scientific and technological development, as well as technology transfer, have contributed to multiple advances, which have supported new sales strategies (Ramli, 2017; Stonehouse and Snowdon, 2007; Shukla et al, 2017; Khan et al, 2014). These new sales strategies have been developed to present to consumers, in a much more accessible and attractive way, a finished product or service that is already on the market, that is about to be introduced in a new market segment or that its innovation will allow it to create, precisely, a new consumer market (Jagpal and Spiegel, 2011). However, new technologies, seen as a process of innovation, in no way can be considered as a synonym for business growth and progress, that is, over time the companies that managed to survive these rapid technological developments had to face these imminent changes and, consequently, adapt their products or services, with new sales strategies, to markets that are more competitive every day (Rice, 2013). On the other hand, the companies that were unable to adapt or did not know how to understand these multiple technological changes and that, unfortunately, could not adopt the new sales strategies, found themselves in the painful need to withdraw some of their products or services from the market, even some companies with a long tradition in the market had to close their operations temporarily or permanently (Bai and Tian, 2020).

As mentioned above, new technologies, particularly those adapted to the internet, played a leading role, globally, during the COVID19 pandemic (Sipior, 2020; Park, Choi and Ko, 2020). In this stage of crisis, multiple applications emerged that allowed people to stay in communication through videoconferences (Zoom, Google Meet, Cisco Webex Meetings, Skype, among others), make all kinds of purchases (both products and services) from the comfort of your home (Amazon, Chedraui, Costco, The Green Corner, Superama, Petco, OfficeMax, Postmates, Delivery.com, etc.) and some of these applications have become very popular because they bring these purchases to the door of the home (Uber Eats, Rappi, Didi Food, DoorDash, GrubHub, etc.), perform all kinds of banking transactions with a smartphone (Paypal, Venmo, Google Wallet, Payoneer, etc.), hire a streaming service (Netflix, Amazon Prime, Disney +, HBO, Tubi, Discovery, etc.). In this context, the sale and purchase of products and services made through the internet (e-commerce) had, and continues to have, considerable growth throughout the world.

Undoubtedly, this behavior of consumers was favored because they avoided, as far as possible, getting infected and/or suffering from the symptoms of COVID19 by having direct contact with another person (Kalgotra, Gupta and Sharda, 2021). In other words, the internet has become the best ally; became the default shopping channel. What has become clear is that new technologies are an extremely important factor so that people do not risk the most valuable thing they have, their lives. In this world scenario, consumers had to learn to use numerous applications, generally through a mobile device, to satisfy their basic needs through online purchases (Anvari and Norouzi, 2016).

For its part, e-commerce or internet commerce is known as that commerce that is carried out electronically, where the purchase and sale of products or services are carried out through the internet (Shambhu and Prasanna, 2021; Phillips, 2016; OECD, 2019; Kutz, 2016). However, e-commerce is not limited only to the internet, since it can also be done through intranets (Turban et al. 2018) and neither is e-commerce limited to the purchase or sale of products or services since you can also transport, trade data, goods, information, communication, among others (Radovilsky, 2015). In this way, e-commerce has become a very popular sales channel that offers products or services to customers in a new way. This channel, which is now a large world market, originated with the sale of electronic devices and small products, which could have been easily transferred between the seller and the buyer. This is how Amazon, the most popular e-commerce provider, started its online business selling books (Buchanan and McMenemy, 2012). Consequently, offering goods that exist only in electronic form, such as software, was an even more natural process. Therefore, the rapid growth of this online sales channel resulted in a greater diversity of products to be sold through the Internet. In modern times, there are countless products or services, even large items like furniture or cars, that can be bought or sold in online stores. In this dynamic, most likely the only thing that changes is the shipping method to deliver the product to the customer. Undoubtedly, some important factors that influenced this rapid expansion of e-commerce have been: 1) a low barrier to entry of financing for distributors; 2) explosive growth of mobile devices; 3) a clear expansion of social networks; 4) a disproportionate growth of users on the world wide web and; 5) easy access to the internet (Cabot, 2018).

Now let's see some data related to e-commerce worldwide: The increase in internet users has been an important factor for the growth of e-commerce worldwide since based on the figures reported by Internet World Stats (2021) internet users went from 3,696 million (with a global penetration rate of 49.5%) in December 2015 to 5,053 million (with a global penetration rate of 64.2%) in December 2020. This growth in global connectivity by the Internet is positive for the e-commerce industry because all new users are potential customers to buy through the Internet. For its part, the number of e-commerce buyers in the world went from 1,520 million in 2016 to 2,050 million in 2020 (Statista, 2021), which represented a variation of 34.9% for this period. Without a doubt, e-commerce is a representation of how digital transactions continue to shape the behavior and purchasing practices of people around the world. In this context, online retail sales in the world went from 1,845 billion USD in 2016 to 4,206 billion USD in 2020 (Statista, 2021), which represented a variation of 128% during the 2016-2020 period. In other words, in five years the monetary figures associated with this type of e-commerce increased by five-eighths worldwide. This implies that the growth of sales through e-commerce is also associated with an increase in the number of Internet users, who appreciate the benefits of making purchases online compared to traditional media.

E-commerce has changed the way people shop. This type of commerce has changed the way companies carry out their processes from how they design, produce, deliver their products or services to the way consumers trust suppliers (Laudon and Laudon, 2019). Without a doubt, e-commerce is here to stay, especially in times of pandemics such as the current COVID19 (Kissler et al, 2020). According to Digital 2021: Global Digital Overview (Hootsuite, 2021), consumers in the world made, through e-commerce during 2020, approximately 347 billion purchases, which is equivalent to 44.5% of purchases worldwide. Furthermore, during the COVID19 pandemic in 2020, the total value of the global B2C (Business-to-Consumer) e-commerce market was approximately US$2.44 trillion (Hootsuite 2021). As a consequence of this dynamic in B2C e-commerce around the world, the use of road transport for the distribution of products has also increased (Huang, Savelsbergh and Zhao, 2018). However, this sales success was due, in addition to COVID19, to how a product or service was presented.

BACKGROUND

New technologies based on the provision of information and the generation of knowledge are more than a fad. These tools are increasingly accessible to all people, who can obtain many benefits from their use, for example in marketing applications. The purpose of marketing is to serve as a platform for companies to promote their products and increase their sales. In this context, new technologies represent innovative and efficient strategies to present the finished product in the most attractive way possible, using enticing media capable of generating people's desire to have the product in their hands. Many people would like to see a toy in action, learn how it works, and be aware of its main features before buying it or opening its package. In the case of clothing, trying on garments in different colors and different kinds of matching accessories while they are still in their boxes instead of waiting until a mirror is available to confirm whether these articles are to one's liking would also be desirable. Flat images are not enough to stimulate people's excitement or desire to own the product; therefore, firms deploy innovative and efficient marketing strategies to cater to people's desires and, consequently, increase their sales considerably or grow the preference for their products among the audience.

Multiple scientific and technological advances support the use of new marketing strategies (Ramli, 2017; Shukla et al, 2017). When the goal is to present potential clients with a finished product, already for sale in the market or about to enter a new market segment (Grubor and Milovanov, 2017), current marketing strategies focus on accessibility in addition to allure (Jagpal and Spiegel, 2011). Scientific and technological change is evident also in this area, and clearly, the interaction between technology and human beings changes all the time. Nowadays, human beings must quickly assimilate large amounts of information presented by new technologies, but these technologies have not been fully adapted to the requirements and needs of human beings. On the other hand, studies on marketing strategies have shown that, over time, how products are presented and sold to the consumer has also changed (Willman-Iivarinen, 2017). As a consequence, adopting a marketing strategy limited to displaying a specific product on a counter or to other conventional media such as television, radio, magazines, newspapers, or print catalogs fall short of its task. It is also important to mention that certain marketing strategies, besides adapting to technological advances, depend to a great extent on people's buying habits (Pang, Keh, and Peng, 2009).

The use of the internet has revolutionized how people interact: communications are now faster and more efficient, but they are also more impersonal. At the same time, the development of mobile devices has reached a level of dependence for human beings; that is, it is a necessary and almost indispensable item for people to communicate or purchase online (Agrebi and Jallais, 2015). Mobile devices have become an extremely important and efficient means of introducing and disseminating a product innovatively and dynamically. Enticing the desire of the potential consumer to buy is undoubtedly one of the main objectives of the complex process of commercializing any product. It is also important for the distributor to identify the main needs of potential clients (Wijayanto, Soeaidy, and Rochmah, 2014). In this regard, we consider that establishing an innovative consumption environment requires swift, direct, and efficient interaction with the potential client, all of which can be accomplished using Augmented Reality (AR) (Zendjebil et al, 2008; Baratali et al, 2016). This new technology responds immediately to data transmission (depending on the data transmission rate) and interacts directly with a consumer using a mobile device, and is also efficient because it can display features and information specific to the product being viewed in real-time (Orlosky, Kiyokawa and Takemura, 2017). AR is a relatively new technology that allows for the addition of virtual reality to a real environment (Riobó Iglesias et al, 2015; Abdoli-Sejzi, 2015). This extraordinary quality makes AR an innovative and efficient tool to discover new uses and forms and, in particular, to create new consumer habits or trends (Pantano and Servidio, 2012; Alkhamisi and Monowar, 2013).

The main goal of AR is to surprise the client and focus their undivided attention and interest in the product that the client is examining via this new technology (Ooi and Yazdanifard, 2015). Therefore, AR could be an ideal way to stir up the consumer's desire and motivate them to purchase the product displayed in an app (usually on a mobile device). Even though this new approach allows for the creation of an innovative marketing strategy and the technology is well known, many companies have not yet applied it, and even fewer dare to develop an app specifically designed for one of their products. Undoubtedly, this is due to the high cost of implementing this technology, although this might not always be the case. For their part, Rana and Davoud (2016) found that companies committed to innovation have better opportunities to achieve higher sales levels. By creating and implementing new technologies, firms envision new technological horizons and support the progress of their environment. AR provides a special visual and creative interaction in which the product is presented in novel ways that can result in an important increase in sales (Holcombe, 2009). This novel and innovative marketing strategy capitalize on known information on how to attract consumer attention. This premise is mainly because the interaction with the client via the visualization provided by an AR-based app and accessed from any mobile device represents a change in the way in which advertising is currently known, involving a new consumption environment or new consumption habits.

Consumers have multiple options within the same product line, which allows the firm to create preferences for a particular brand in the client's mind (Kumar and E. M. Steenkamp, 2007) and, gradually, to increase trust and loyalty (Rubio, Villaseñor and Oubiña, 2015). In this context, it is important to ask the following question: Why does a consumer choose a certain product? The answer is not trivial since multiple factors are involved in a person's purchase decision (Lian et al, 2015). One of these factors, which justifies the preference and success of one product in comparison with another, is the potential consumer's perception of the product. This abstract concept can motivate the consumer and produce certain perceptions and emotions associated with the product during its presentation (Otubanjo, 2013; Manzur et al, 2011; Aghekyan-Simonian et al, 2012).

As an example of the above, a private brand product (usually differentiated) is often preferred over an own-brand product (Tih and Lee, 2013; Katrijn, 2012; Gala and Patil, 2013). However, the sales of private brand products decreased significantly over the past decade, mainly due to the proliferation and preference of the consumer for their brands (Kakkos, Trivellas and Sdrolia, 2015; Cuneo et al, 2015). This behavior was due, firstly, to the high quality achieved by own brands and, secondly, to technological breakthroughs that supported the quality increase (Calvo-Porral and Lévy-Manginb, 2017). A private brand product entails important aspects such as innovation, high advertising costs, and, above all, continuous investment in R and D. In this regard, it makes sense to highlight the advantage of presenting a specific product using new technology, in our case RA, which has the advantage of showing the product in a more interesting and novel way, even without taking product quality into account (Guo, Wang and Wei, 2018).

Such product perception can in no way be taken lightly; the preference for a product or brand can take place because the client has had a pleasant experience with the product or because the client has positive attitudes, sometimes based on comments by other clients concerning a certain product (Winchester and Romaniuk, 2008; Webber, 2011; Wan-I, Cheng and Shih, 2017). However, Wang, Yeh, and Liao (2013) showed that the perception of a product varies considerably from one region to another. Nevertheless, image-based product perception is also dependent on how it is presented to the consumer. In sum, AR is an innovative marketing strategy that presents a product, regardless of its qualities and characteristics, in a new, economic, and efficient way aimed at creating new consumption habits or trends.

MAIN FOCUS OF THE CHAPTER

Issues, Controversies, Problems

Mobile internet traffic is a huge and inescapable phenomenon, almost all transactions carried out globally could be carried out through a mobile network (social network services, e-commerce, banking, etc.), that is to say, almost all aspects of our daily lives can be easily done just by using a mobile device. In this universe of online transactions, and because consumers differ so much, it's hard to know which elements of a product work best and which should be dropped or improved. However, the quality information associated with a product is necessary and important for consumers to value it and better understand the products they wish to buy (Nor Asshidin, Abidin and Borhan, 2016). Therefore, this information is a preponderant factor for consumers to decide whether they prefer online products (Lin et al, 2018). Of course, the decision that the online consumer makes is very important to the success of the sale (Sharma, Mahajan and Rana, 2019). In this sense, consumers generally see photographs of the products they are looking for on the internet in a static and boring way (see Figure 1). In addition, if they need to know more information about the product of their interest, then they have to click on multiple links to learn more about the product they are analyzing. Figure 1 shows the traditional way of presenting a product, which can be through an internet page or interactive catalogs with static designs that do not use objects focused on a better perception of the product by the consumer. With the use of an App, a hologram of the finished product can be presented in specific places where the said product could not usually be placed. For example, through AR, the aim is to surprise the customer and obtain his full attention and interest: one of the main objectives, and perhaps the most important, of the sale of products with the use of these new technologies is to amaze and impress to the customer to then motivate him to purchase the final product, which he previously viewed through an App (generally with a mobile phone).

The present study proposes a new and innovative marketing strategy based on the technology known as AR. It allows the user to view a finished product available in a department store as a virtual presence on a mobile device (Honkamaa, Jäppinen and Woodward, 2007). Two AR-based systems are described below to highlight the potential and scope of this innovative marketing strategy:

1. A marketing strategy based on AR catalogs or magazines.

Figure 1. A traditional example of internet sales
Source: Blacksip (2021).

2.   Product location strategy using AR.

These two systems provide an accessible format to interact with the client. Additionally, these systems can be quickly adapted to product quality, that is, they can be provided with a software update service and an extra service focused on technical support, for this innovative marketing strategy to be acquired by the largest number of interested companies given its low price. Another advantage of this proposal is that AR allows for the efficient and dynamic combination of the marketing strategy with other technologies, social networks, and multiple virtual applications focused on mobile devices. Therefore, this novel approach can help firms to present any product in a novel and original way (Mekni and Lemieux, 2014). This marketing strategy should be oriented toward the mass consumer market, mainly because a large number of products are offered in a traditional way (radio, television, print media). Independently of their sales strategy, which drives the use of new technologies as a strategic precursor and competitive differentiator, firms must be prepared to surpass their business objectives by taking advantage of new marketing strategies (Nor Asshidin, Abidin and Borhan, 2016; Miyazaki, Grewal and Goodstein, 2005).

SOLUTIONS AND RECOMMENDATIONS

Information Systems

Information systems are codes built to help people make decisions in an easy, accessible, and fast way. These decisions are applied to different areas ranging from the acquisition of knowledge, medicine, and tourism to others that include the areas applied to the sale and purchase of products and, consequently, the offering of products to consumers (commonly referred to as marketing). There are examples of systems that give this type of facility to consumers by the way they offer products and services, such as the selection of places in a cinema, theater, auditorium, where their options also contain the date or time. Other types of marketing systems can be flight or bus travel reservations, and marketing is also oriented towards everyday actions: offering the consumer products and services through the Internet, catalogs, magazines, or simply on a shelf. To carry out marketing actions, it is necessary to advance more and more with the inclusion of avant-garde technological elements to the sales systems to improve sales strategies, and therefore it is necessary to build information systems.

Method

The technology known as AR supports the development of applications that take into account the diversity of clients visiting stores; these clients will have heterogeneous and changing characteristics in terms of age, schooling, occupation, and interests, among others. Many companies seek to provide an easy, friendly, and adequate sales service to their multiple clients, who will consequently refer the business to their contacts and justify their preference. It is also clear that the world has been invaded by mobile devices, a very important reason to add new marketing elements to the products offered in stores. For that reason, innovative and avant-garde technological resources must be created in such a way that clients can appreciate and use them. The hardware and software of these technological resources must be widely accepted and used on an everyday basis, such as a mobile device or smartphone.

For their part, information systems use accurately compiled codes to support people in making their decisions conveniently, easily, and quickly. These decisions refer to different areas, from knowledge acquisition, medicine, and tourism to applications focused on the sale and purchase of products and the offering and presentation of products to consumers, that is, regular marketing practices. To create innovative marketing actions, it is necessary to increase the avant-garde technological elements used in sales systems. Therefore, it is necessary to build inventive information systems; as Cornford and Shaikh (2013) argue, our capacity to choose will be improved by optimizing information resources, an essential part of the invention and improvement of information and communication technologies. This type of system accelerated their evolution when they were combined with features such as mobility, big data for business applications, and cloud computing (Laudon and Laudon, 2019).

As a consequence, new technologies must use the internet and mobile devices to meet the foremost requirements of users, for example, potential customers. Rabbi and Ullah (2013) have defined AR as a technology using which the visualization of a real environment is added computer-generated visual elements in a device. This definition of AR entails that the customer is not guided through a fantasy but presented with virtual objects superposed to their physical reality. Despite the availability of technological resources using RA, the use of these tools in the field of marketing is still underexploited. For that purpose, these new systems are proposed as a tool to help sellers to display a product to their potential customers in the way that they intend; the essentials of the product must be established to determine what to show to the customer, and the product is then presented using multimedia elements. The AR-based design is shown below.

Design of a System Based on AR

In the design phase, the behavior of the population under study is considered and a solution is proposed, the latter must consider improvements to the two systems pre-established in this document. These improvements should address aspects such as speed of response, the economy of resources, efficiency, effectiveness, and visually attractive design. In this context, the following two types of systems are considered:

1. Systems using product catalogs that can be displayed using AR in stores. This type of system is intended to purchase a product more attractive to a potential customer. A similar system is used in online sales; the RA system is activated when the "trigger" marker is detected by the smartphone or webcam. The use of technology has allowed online sales systems to increase their statistics; thus, they can be very promising in marketing.
2. Systems based on RA and focused on marketing (Product location systems using AR). The design of these systems must follow certain criteria, but in general, all of them must have similar benefits, such as the following:
    a. Their design should be visually attractive.
    b. They must contain multimedia elements so that any user can understand and retain the product's features, and their purchase decision is facilitated.
    c. The information provided must be easy to process.

The full development and reliable operation of these tools require many basic technologies, but for simplicity, and according to Pressman (2014), they could be developed in the following phases:

a. Analysis of the requirements of the RA-based system.
b. Formulate the abstract and physical design so that software coding and creation can in time take place.
c. Preparation of files, identification, and creation of test data.
d. Finally, software testing and integration.

RESULTS AND DISCUSSION

This section presents the design of two marketing systems based on AR, which, as already mentioned, can take different forms depending on the target audience. The first refers to "Marketing systems in catalogs, shelves, or magazines," and the second to "Product location systems using AR." Additionally, the necessary elements involved in both systems are:

Hardware: 1) Camera. Most mobile devices have a built-in camera that can be used to "trigger" the AR software. 2) Screen. It showcases the image of the product, generally in 3D, using the device with which the AR-based system interacts. Thus, the screen superimposes the AR elements using 3D images and presents a virtual tour; this environment is returned as a query result. The screen of a mobile device is normally used for this purpose. 3) Audio. This accessory is also included in mobile devices and computers, which are used to complement the AR with sound (in most cases using a Podcast).

Bookmarks: The data associated with these 2D images, also called reference images, is easily extracted due to their predefined shape and color features (Uchiyama and Marchand, 2012). The AR is triggered by these elements when the mobile device detects them via its camera.

3D Images: These elements have a realistic appearance, and their X, Y, and Z coordinates produce models that overlap the RA to simulate physical reality.

Virtual Tour: This specialized software application creates paths based on (usually panoramic) images for the user to travel through a virtual environment to a specific place by simply pressing the arrow keys.

Software: The software used to create the AR should be aimed at solving these types of problems. This is because RA-based applications work by association; in the two systems dealt with in this article, the AR will be associated with the bookmark to show the 3D images and reproduce the simultaneous audio recording.

1. *Marketing System in Catalogs, Shelves, or Magazines*

The marketing of a product using the innovative presentation described in the present article has very important implications. To discuss these implications, we will analyze two everyday situations experienced in any consumer store: 1) A customer walks through the corridors of a department store and spends most of their time learning about the functionality of a product or how a product fits him or her. 2) A customer enters a department store, and he or she is handed an AR catalog; the client uses their mobile device and scans the catalog to find out all the features and information of any product of their interest. In the second situation, the client is offered the best possible situation to choose any product they would like, both because of the information presented and because of the speed and novelty with which the information was provided—this experience goes beyond that of a customer satisfied with their purchase. This marketing strategy can also be implemented via websites.

The firm's website can be adapted so that its clients can interact with the AR from any place in the world: the webcam identifies the bookmark and displays an overlaid image on the computer screen, which is instantly downloaded from an existing ad-hoc website. The main idea of this marketing strategy is to place an image or a code next to each product shown to the clients on the website. These codes or images can be scanned using a webcam or a mobile device, which will allow the client to view all the additional information associated with the selected product, presented as close to reality as possible. In other words, when the code is detected by a camera on the website, all types of virtual information such as images, audio, videos, 3D models, or external links to other websites are superimposed on the screen. This same innovation can also be implemented in product packages, wraps, or boxes. Undoubtedly, this AR-based marketing strategy provides a dynamic interaction between the product and the client; this interaction shall result in higher product expectations and, of course, a more critical assessment.

If the business does not have a website, it can use a visually attractive catalog including product images and a scannable code as bookmarks (Uchiyama and Marchand, 2012; Denso Wave Incorporated, 2015) to trigger the 3D product representation using an AR app and the camera on a mobile device or display product-specific information from a multimedia file (Reyes, Olmos, and Hernández, 2016). In this context, it is important to highlight that the superimposed image is a key element that should draw the consumer's full attention. This image, whether presented on a website or in a catalog, should be attractive to the client, represent the contents of the product package and their use, indicate whether the product is in stock, track the location of the sale, request customer data, provide a purchase button, and ask the client to provide a product evaluation (Kaufmann, 2002). An important advantage of such

Figure 2. Marketing system using AR-based product catalogs
Source: Prepared by the authors.

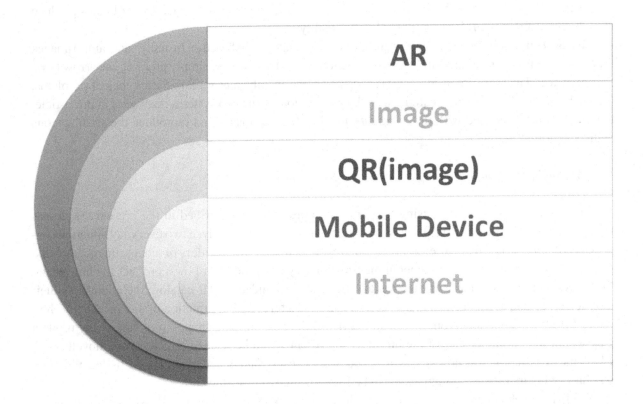

a catalog is that it can be available at any strategic area of the store or in certain areas where superior quality products are offered.

On the other hand, Agrebi and Jallais (2015) reported on a direct relationship between the perceived ease of use of a product and people's intentions to use their smartphones to buy the product. Moreover, innovations can be more attractive when using a mobile device to view an AR-based product catalog in 3D. Thus, the goal of the sales system is to encourage people to perceive the purchase of a utilitarian product as a hedonistic experience. This innovative marketing strategy can motivate an increasing number of firms to introduce or present their products in this way. All the requirements presented in Figure 2 must be met to implement this system for the first time.

Figure 2 implies that a system of this nature must take into account all the elements considered in that figure. At the same time, these elements must contemplate, in the first instance, how the product to be promoted must be determined and, subsequently, gather some data concerning the model to be used; among the data that can be considered are the benefits, the price, the website and/or its operation, etc. Once all these criteria have been defined, then it is possible to transform (combine) the data into "advertisements". All this is done with the perspective of selling the finished product in an easier, more attractive, and more dynamic way (see Figure 3).

Figure 3. Data overlaid by AR
Source: Prepared by the authors.

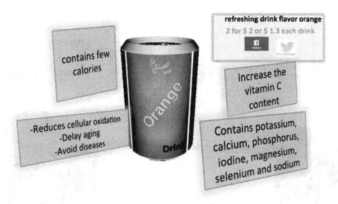

Once the product's highlight features and information to be displayed in the system are determined, a product catalog is created and displayed on the shelves or in strategic areas of stores (see Figure 4).

When the catalog has been designed and produced, the product is presented in a three-dimensional model, including the previously selected multimedia elements, such as sound, in addition to product information or a link to the product website (see Figure 5). In other words, the presentation of the products can be shown in three dimensions in a mobile device. Audio and movement add allure to the experience, and customers are provided with thorough product specifications. Finally, the three-dimensional product model, its information, and its characteristics are added to the catalog. During this last phase, the product is presented using the AR system, and the client can access the data stored in a repository via the internet using a mobile device (see Figure 6).

2. AR-Based Product Location System

A product search system based on AR is created using software specific for the creation of these virtual environments. These programs should also support the design of 3D images, virtual tours, and audio and animation playback. In addition, the creation or implementation of these systems should consider the use of mobile technologies for the user to run the AR app in small portable devices (smartphones or tablets). Mobile devices contain the necessary components to appreciate AR, that is, high-resolution cameras and screens, GPS, wireless connectivity, and radio links, among others (Woodward et al, 2007). The purpose of the system described in this section is to locate the products displayed in a store. The system takes into account the arrangement of the products on shelves and whether they are classified by area, use, purpose, or brand. In addition to the location of the product, the RA system provides the shelf number and product availability, its coordinates, geometry, or any other piece of information of interest for the client. Once the needs of the system have been defined, the cost-benefit of a marketing strategy using a system of this nature can be determined. An important goal of marketing is that the strategy be as flexible as possible (De Pablos Heredero et al, 2012) so that it can be adapted to the requirements of a sales-oriented system. Kendall and Kendall (2011) have proposed that the initial condition for an AR-based system to meet all of these requirements is to conduct a thorough analysis of the system's requirements. This analysis should be focused on optimal functionality for the user to interact with the

Figure 4. AR-based product catalog
Source: Prepared by the authors.

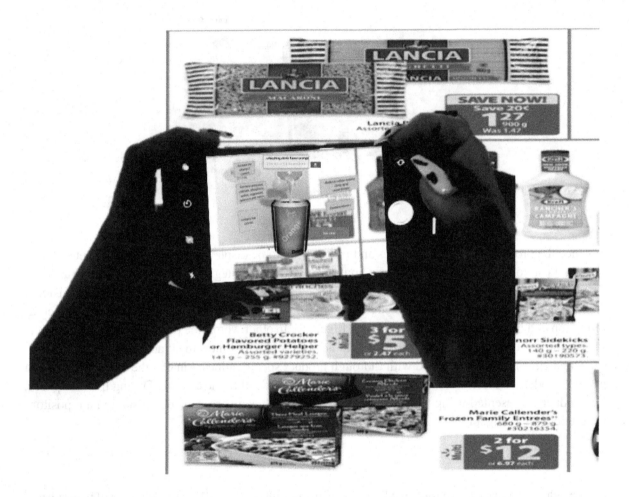

program and the virtual environment easily and independently. In other words, the actor would be the client, and the actions of the system would reveal how the application is connected to the AR environment and how the location, query, and purchase of one or more products is performed (see Figure 7).

Cost-Benefit

Another important aspect to analyze in terms of the requirements of an AR system is its cost-benefit trade-off, that is, a measure of the profits in economic terms. In addition to economic gain, aspects such as the preferences of the clients for specific stores, the latest innovations, and state-of-the-art technologies are other elements of this analysis. Undoubtedly, some of these aspects improve the clients' perception of certain products, and they are a response to very specific events in their daily lives. Although intangible, these aspects represent a considerable transformation value in terms of marketing. Therefore, the metrics of some systems are focused on the performance of individuals, the quality of the information media (flexibility, reliability, and ease of use), and the quality of the information supplied by the media

Figure 5. Product with 3D design
Source: Prepared by the authors.

(comprehensible, complete, relevant, and timely); the scope of these metrics ranges from the usage of the information system to user satisfaction (Bravo, Santana and Rodon, 2015).

The design of this system takes into account the same aspects as in the case of catalogs, shown in Figure 1, except that the concept of the catalog is in this case location. Another important feature to incorporate into these systems is intuitive and easy-to-use interface improvement features capable of producing reliable and intelligible results to increase the use of the systems in marketing. The product location system must consider, at least, the following stages:

1. The query is entered into a mobile device on which the software has been installed. The AR is triggered at the moment when the client is in front of the screen of the mobile device. After detecting the customer's face, the screen indicates that the AR system has been initialized and is ready to continue. During this stage of the experience, physical reality is shown next to whatever is in front of the camera, and the digital scene acquires a realistic tone. Subsequently, the next stage of the experience is triggered, and a dialog box appears for the client to type what they are looking for

Figure 6. The product was presented using an AR-based catalog
Source: Prepared by the authors.

(see Figure 8). If the user fails to write the desired product correctly, the system displays a list of similar products.

2. Once the system has been given a search word, the screen displays a three-dimensional image of the store presented as a virtual tour (see Figure 9). In addition to its novelty, the virtual tour provides the client with an easy and pleasant way to locate any product of their interest inside the store. Thus, the client is provided an overview of the physical space of the store so that they can tour the different areas or departments, and their desire to purchase is increased.

3. When the system displays the AR-based virtual tour, the user is presented with a preview of the store to locate the shelves using position keys. Additionally, this scenario allows the client to move virtually to anywhere they wish to be. As the client tours the store, they visualize the store and listen to instructions to easily locate any product (see Figure 10).

Figure 7. AR-based search system
Source: Prepared by the authors.

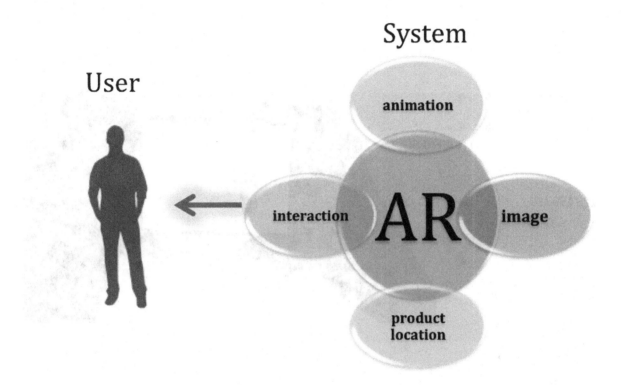

As can be appreciated, RA-based search systems could be used for many different purposes. For example, the product location system can be tailored to different types of stores, and the AR environment can be adapted to the different types of potential customers; overlapping images displaying specifications and attractive designs will motivate the customer to purchase an article. Public places such as museums can also use this technology: the different areas can be displayed in three dimensions as a virtual tour. Similarly, an eco-tourism park can be presented to visitors as a virtual tour to increase their interest, excitement, and motivation to visit all the areas in the park. Archaeological sites, stadiums, or any other type of touristic or public venue could also present their signaling as AR elements, as opposed to traditional unidirectional signaling (a static and dull way to convey information), whereas AR-based systems are dynamic, interactive, and intuitive. Additionally, RA-based systems using virtual multimedia tools can be complemented with messages to gain the client's attention or to provide them with detailed explanations. The present article has highlighted the novelty, innovative nature, and efficiency of AR. AR can be used for different purposes, and its systems can provide classified results for detailed queries based on different entry parameters. It is important to mention that the central idea of this second system is to generate, through the motivation of users, clear expectations of use through new marketing options. This confirms that RA is a technology capable of discovering multiple uses, forms, and habits of consumption. In other words, AR allows and facilitates the creation of a novel and efficient marketing strategy to show any product to a specific segment of customers.

Figure 8. The initial screen of an AR-based product search system
Source: Prepared by the authors.

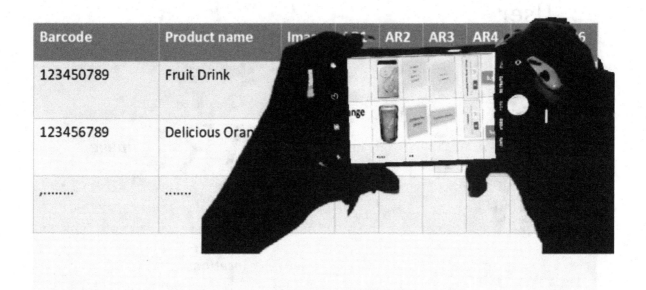

Evaluation of the Marketing System Based on AR

The marketing system, made with the new AR technology, was validated by a series of questions that were asked to various people in some shopping centers. People were randomly selected until they made up the statistically significant sample size[1] (384 people), which was calculated using simple random sampling and without the knowledge of the total population (Cochran, 2017). In this test, a series of questions was asked to evaluate both the presentation and the search for a product through AR. This evaluation contains questions with dichotomous answers (the questions were implemented with JavaScript events performed on the SDK platform), which served as input so that, through the SDK platform, the score obtained for each section or section of questions is displayed.

After the randomly selected people had the opportunity and experience to learn about the AR-based marketing system, a survey was applied to them. The purpose of this survey was to know three evaluation parameters, consistent with the objective of this research and whose concept implies that people evaluate and know a product through a system based on AR: presentation, novelty, and ease of use. Likewise, the level of knowledge retention was contrasted concerning the mentioned variables, which was carried out by comparing the two ways in which people appreciated a product, that is, with and without AR. Table 1 contains the responses of the people selected and surveyed regarding 1) the score given to the presentation of a product through the AR-based marketing system; 2) what was your assessment of the novelty of a product through an AR-based marketing system and; 3) how accessible or complicated they found the management of the AR-based marketing system. Finally, all the selected people were asked if

Figure 9. AR-based 3D store
Source: Prepared by the authors.

the AR-based marketing system motivated them to buy the product shown and the result was that 91% (that is, 9 out of 10 people) answered that the new way of Appreciating and looking for a product in the store motivated them to buy that product.

FUTURE RESEARCH DIRECTIONS

The new technologies, more than being fashionable, are increasingly closer to people, who by making use of them obtain various benefits; An example is the sale of products online, which makes use of other technologies to make its products better known and, in this way, increase sales. In addition, these technologies seek ways to make the product more attractive, through multimedia files, to generate in

Figure 10. AR-based virtual tour
Source: Prepared by the authors.

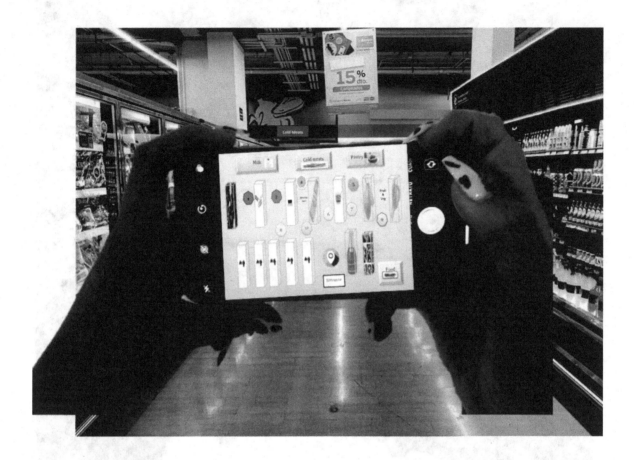

people the desire to have it in their hands. How many times have people dreamed of observing the details (such as the colors, dimensions, their music, their operation, their movements, etc.) of their favorite toys before buying them, or the items in operation before opening them, they even wanted to see the clothes in various colors and try on decorations without removing them from the wrapper. This was generally done after purchasing the product, that is, until the moment the person appreciated the product when they tried it on in front of a mirror and saw if that product was to their liking. Since flat images do not

Table 1. Results for the AR-based marketing system

Concept	with AR	without AR
Presentation	91.3%	33%
Novelty	96.4	37.5
Easy to use	94.8	73.6
Motivation	91%	60%

Source: Prepared by the authors.

stimulate emotion and desire to own the product, companies are increasingly using new sales strategies to make people's wishes come true, thereby increasing people's preference for the product. their products, which will be reflected in an increase in their sales.

Currently, the world is invaded by mobile devices, according to data from Hootsuite (2021) in January 2021, there were 5.22 billion people with a mobile phone, which represented a penetration level of 66.6% worldwide. Likewise, the level of penetration of social networks was 53.6% (4.2 billion people in the world). This is a great reason to add new technological elements to the products offered on the web pages; elements that encourage the consumer to enter a world of avant-garde buying and selling and, for this reason, new and innovative technological resources must be generated so that users can use them quickly. In addition, these technological resources must be designed, built, and sold with software that is used daily. Furthermore, these technological resources must be essential in those programs that are used with devices that are used very frequently by the user, in this case, the so-called mobile devices.

Taking into account that computer systems have evolved since factors such as the mobile platform, the growing use of big data for business and the enormous use of cloud computing (Laundon and Laudon 2019) have been added to them, it is necessary to look for technologies that make more effective use of the internet and mobile devices that are up to the requirements of consumers. To be at the forefront of these sales issues, our ability to choose must be improved by using information resources that are, in large part, the invention and improvement of information and communication technologies, that is, of those systems that involve new technologies with characteristics and capabilities in information management.

Although technological resources and tools that use QR codes have already been developed, it is necessary to introduce more of these resources in the area of e-commerce, for this new system are proposed that help consumers and sellers to show what you want to express yourself with the display of a product. In other words, the abstract of a product must be extracted to know how to show it to the consumer, which, without a doubt, can be achieved with fairly accessible elements, such as multimedia elements. In this context, and to continue to use QR code technology, it is proposed to use multilevel QR codes (see Figure 11). These multilevel codes contain multiple layers of information, which can independently function as a simple QR code. Among the multiple advantages of using multilevel QR codes, the following stand out: increase the use of information with a single code, encrypt multiple information channels, use multiple apps simultaneously, can be used as multiple security codes, intertwine information, reduce the use of simple QR codes, motivate the creation, adaptation, and use of new technologies, among others. In addition, with the use of these multilevel codes, new sales strategies would be generated.

The information that is added to the product image, using a multilevel QR code, can be information that is downloaded from a website (text, images, sound, video or multimedia files, augmented or virtual reality, etc.) and/or contain from a 3D presentation of the product its correct use, its construction through a manual or video, the location of sale, stock in the store, the contact email, a purchase button, set aside the product, track the purchase or shipment, among others. On the other hand, this type of new technology allows connection with others that, together, can achieve a new shopping experience for the consumer. For example, the shopping experience through mobile commerce (m-commerce), which includes information services (Google, yellow pages, the cloud, etc.), multiple transactions, location-based services (such as the reception of discounts, coupons in a local store, taxis, etc.), support services, emergency services, entertainment, etc. All these aspects can be carried out in real-time, which will depend, logically, only on the speed at which the data is transmitted. In this context, products that associate a multilevel QR code can be an important component for this type of commerce, since when using these codes, the camera of the mobile device would be used as an interaction device. Therefore,

Figure 11. Multi-level QR codes
Source: Prepared by the authors.

and through this simple mechanism, the user could view with a mobile device all the information found on the Internet and associated with the product viewed.

CONCLUSION

Continuous technological innovation allows for ever newer ways to empower consumers to evaluate products. A closer and more detailed look at the product and its operation or details enables the consumer to make a more critical and objective decision. Moreover, these novel ways to evaluate products by using current technology allow firms to promote any type of product. In this context, a novel, innovative, and efficient AR-based approach to marketing can be used to create a space of interaction between human intuition and a real-virtual environment where the user can examine goods; the virtual element is achieved using real 3D objects that present information interactively and dynamically. The user, a potential client, is shown the most outstanding features of the product to motivate their purchase. On the other hand, AR is a highly flexible technological tool that can be used efficiently to display a product already for sale.

The virtual environment (images) is added to the physical space where the product is presented on a website, in an interactive catalog, or in the product envelope itself, where it can be linked to additional information stored in one or more websites. Such information could be used to support a product's marketing strategy, for example, by adding a purchase button, indicating where the product can be acquired, providing a link to product documentation, showcasing a 3D product presentation, or requesting consumer information such as an email address to send them promotional materials or surveys. AR creates different virtual scenarios to potentiate the customers' interest in a given product. It can be used as advertising media and easily adapted to specific factors such as the country or region, shopping habits, age, gender, and the behavior of certain clients in groups. These client characteristics, to name a few, are of utmost importance to be taken into account by firms that intend to sell their products. This strategy will undoubtedly promote the use of new technologies and address new ways of presenting, choosing, and purchasing a product. By adopting AR as a sales strategy, the products will be promoted in a novel way.

This marketing strategy seeks to generate emotions in the consumer at the moment of the purchase, increase their satisfaction, and reassure their purchase decision. Nowadays, many consumers are increasingly interested in seeing the product directly and being better informed about its features. Moreover, as a result of the increased access to information made possible by technology, customers are increasingly aware of environmental issues when purchasing a product. Humanity, and in particular the users of new technologies, is in a stage of transition. On the one hand, new technologies are increasingly necessary (not to say obligatory) for customers, as they are indispensable for showing and knowing more in detail the characteristics of a product. At the same time, companies are looking to be more innovative, so they are looking for the newest and most interesting (but not necessarily expensive) technologies to present and promote their products to customers. Translated with www.DeepL.com/Translator (free version). We are probably facing an imminent cultural change in which products will no longer be purchased via traditional channels, which can be polluting, invasive, or even toxic, but via new technologies. This new culture is already creating, defining, and shaping dynamic, innovative, and efficient markets, such as online sales and automated sales points.

The advantages for firms opting for any of the marketing strategies presented in this article will undoubtedly be many, but above all, they will charge the client's perspective on their products. Consumers will inevitably learn about products and compare them with alternatives, and such evaluation can be substantially different if the products are presented to clients differently. This advantage could certainly be favorable in the case of products already in the market, which would be selected due to the innovative way in which they are being presented to clients. Specifically, some of the advantages for these companies will be: encourage the use, dissemination, and creation of new technologies; greater convenience when purchasing their products; highlighting the most important product features and providing relevant information to increase the potential customer's knowledge of their products; building and enhancing product image; customizing their products; supporting their market positioning; building and maintaining customer loyalty; increasing the quality of their products and services, and motivating innovation.

REFERENCES

Abdoli-Sejzi, A. (2015). Augmented Reality and Virtual Learning Environment. *Journal of Applied Sciences Research, 11*(8), 1–5.

Aghekyan-Simonian, M., Forsythe, S., Suk Kwon, W., & Chattaraman, V. (2012). The role of product brand image and online store image on perceived risks and online purchase intentions for apparel. *Journal of Retailing and Consumer Services, 19*(3), 325–331. doi:10.1016/j.jretconser.2012.03.006

Agmeka, F., Wathoni, R. N., & Santoso, A. S. (2019). The Influence of Discount Framing towards Brand Reputation and Brand Image on Purchase Intention and Actual Behaviour in e-commerce. *Procedia Computer Science, 161*, 851–858. doi:10.1016/j.procs.2019.11.192

Agrebi, S., & Jallais, J. (2015). Explain the intention to use smartphones for mobile shopping. *Journal of Retailing and Consumer Services*, *22*, 16–23. doi:10.1016/j.jretconser.2014.09.003

Alkhamisi, A. O., & Muhammad, M. M. (2013). Rise of Augmented Reality: Current and Future Application Areas. *International Journal of Internet and Distributed Systems*, *1*(04), 25–34. doi:10.4236/ijids.2013.14005

Ameen, N., Hosany, S., & Tarhini, A. (2021). Consumer interaction with cutting-edge technologies: Implications for future research. *Computers in Human Behavior*, *120*, 106761. Advance online publication. doi:10.1016/j.chb.2021.106761

Anvari, R. D., & Norouzi, D. (2016). The impact of e-commerce and R&D on economic development in some selected countries. *Procedia: Social and Behavioral Sciences*, *229*, 354–362. doi:10.1016/j.sbspro.2016.07.146

Bai, Q., & Tian, S. (2020). Innovate or die: Corporate innovation and bankruptcy forecasts. *Journal of Empirical Finance*, *59*, 88–108. doi:10.1016/j.jempfin.2020.09.002

Baratali, E. (2016). Effective of Augmented Reality (AR) in marketing communication; a case study on brand interactive advertising. *International Journal of Management and Applied Science*, *2*(4), 133–137.

Blacksip. (2021). Recovered from https://blacksip.com

Bravo, E. R., Santana, M., & Rodon, J. (2015). Information systems and performance: The role of technology, the task, and the individual. *Journal Behaviour & Information Technology*, *1*(3), 247–260. doi:10.1080/0144929X.2014.934287

Buchanan, S., & McMenemy, D. (2012). Digital service analysis and design: The role of process modeling. *International Journal of Information Management*, *32*(3), 251–256. doi:10.1016/j.ijinfomgt.2011.11.008

Bulearca, M., & Tamarjan, D. (2010). Augmented Reality: A Sustainable Marketing Tool? *Global Business and Management Research*, *2*(2-3), 237–252.

Cabot, J. (2018). WordPress: A Content Management System to Democratize Publishing. *IEEE Software*, *35*(3), 89–92. doi:10.1109/MS.2018.2141016

Calvo-Porral, C., & Lévy-Manginb, J. (2017). Store brands' purchase intention: Examining the role of perceived quality. *European Research on Management and Business Economics*, *23*(2), 90–95. doi:10.1016/j.iedeen.2016.10.001

Cochran, W. G. (2017). *Sampling Techniques* (3rd ed.). John Wiley & Sons.

Cornford, T., & Shaikh, M. (2013). Introduction to Information Systems. In *Undergraduate study in Economics, Management, Finance and the Social Sciences*. University of London.

Cuneo, A., Milberg, S. J., Benavente, J. M., & Palacios-Fenech, J. (2015). The growth of private label brands: A worldwide phenomenon? *Journal of International Marketing*, *23*(1), 72–90. doi:10.1509/jim.14.0036

De Pablos Heredero, C. (2012). *Organización y transformación de los sistemas de información en la empresa*. ESIC Editorial.

Denso Wave Incorporated. (2021). Retrieved from http://www.qrcode.com

Dibrova, A. (2016). Virtual currency: New step in monetary development. *Procedia: Social and Behavioral Sciences, 229*, 42–49. doi:10.1016/j.sbspro.2016.07.112

Dolega, L., Rowe, F., & Branagan, E. (2020). Going digital? The impact of social media marketing on retail website traffic, orders, and sales. *Journal of Retailing and Consumer Services, 60*, 102501. Advance online publication. doi:10.1016/j.jretconser.2021.102501

Elsobeihi, M. M., & Abu Naser, S. S. (2017). Effects of Mobile Technology on Human Relationships. *International Journal of Engineering and Information Systems, 1*(5), 110–125.

Fenu, G., & Pau, P. L. (2015). An Analysis of Features and Tendencies in Mobile Banking Apps. *Procedia Computer Science, 56*, 26–33. doi:10.1016/j.procs.2015.07.177

Forecast, G. M. D. T. (2019). *Cisco visual networking index: global mobile data traffic forecast update, 2017-2022.* Retrieved from https://www.cisco.com/c/en/us/solutions/service-provider/visualnetworking-index-vni/index.html

Gala, D., & Patil, R. D. (2013). Consumer Attitude towards Private Labels in Comparison To National Brands International. *Journal of Business and Management Invention, 2*(5), 12–18.

Grubor, A., & Milovanov, O. (2017). Brand strategies in the era of sustainability. *Interdisciplinary Description of Complex Systems, 15*(1), 78–88. doi:10.7906/indecs.15.1.6

Guo, B., Wang, J., & Wei, S. X. (2018). R&D spending, strategic position and firm performance. *Frontiers of Business Research in China, 12*(1), 1–19. doi:10.118611782-018-0037-7

He, W., Zhang, Z. J., & Li, W. (2021). Information technology solutions, challenges, and suggestions for tackling the COVID-19 pandemic. *International Journal of Information Management, 57*, 102287. Advance online publication. doi:10.1016/j.ijinfomgt.2020.102287 PMID:33318721

Holcombe, R. G. (2009). Product differentiation and economic progress. *The Quarterly Journal of Austrian Economics, 12*(1), 17–35.

Honkamaa, P., Jäppinen, J., & Woodward, Ch. (2007). *A Lightweight Approach for Augmented Reality on Camera Phones using 2D Images to Simulate in 3D.* VTT Technical Research Centre of Finland. doi:10.1145/1329469.1329490

Hootsuite. (2021). *Digital 2021: A global digital overview.* Retrieved from https://datareportal.com/reports/digital-2021-global-overview-report

Huang, Y., Savelsbergh, M., & Zhao, L. (2018). Designing logistics systems for home delivery in densely populated urban area. *Transportation Research Part B: Methodological, 115*, 95–125. doi:10.1016/j.trb.2018.07.006

Hugill, P. J. (2016). The Power of Knowledge: How Information and Technology Made the Modern World. *Journal of Historical Geography, 52*, 123–124. doi:10.1016/j.jhg.2015.06.007

Internet World Stats. (2021). Retrieved from https://www.internetworldstats.com/emarketing.htm

Jagpal, S., & Spiegel, M. (2011). Free samples, profits, and welfare: The effect of market structures and behavioral modes. *Journal of Business Research*, *64*(2), 213–219. doi:10.1016/j.jbusres.2010.02.001

Kakkos, N., Trivellas, P., & Sdrolias, L. (2015). Identifying Drivers of Purchase Intention for Private Label Brands. Preliminary Evidence from Greek Consumers. *Procedia: Social and Behavioral Sciences*, *175*(12), 522–528. doi:10.1016/j.sbspro.2015.01.1232

Kalgotra, P., Gupta, A., & Sharda, R. (2021). Pandemic information support lifecycle: Evidence from the evolution of mobile apps during COVID-19. *Journal of Business Research*, *134*, 540–559. doi:10.1016/j.jbusres.2021.06.002 PMID:34565948

Katrijn, G. (2012). New Products: The Antidote to Private Label Growth? *JMR, Journal of Marketing Research*, *49*(3), 408–423. doi:10.1509/jmr.10.0183

Kaufmann, H. (2002). Construct 3D: An augmented reality application for mathematics and geometry education. *Proc. 10th ACM International Conference on Multimedia*, 656-657.

Kendall, K. E., & Kendall, J. E. (2011). *Systems Analysis and Design* (8th ed.). Pearson Education, Inc.

Khan, R. T. (2014). Synthesis of Constructs for Modeling Consumers' Understanding and Perception of Eco-Labels. *Sustainability*, *6*(4), 2176–2200. doi:10.3390u6042176

Kissler, S. M., Tedijanto, C., Goldstein, E., Grad, Y. H., & Lipsitch, M. (2020). Projecting the transmission dynamics of SARS-CoV-2 through the post-pandemic period. *Science*, *368*(6493), 860–868. doi:10.1126cience.abb5793 PMID:32291278

Kumar, N., & Steenkamp, E. M. J. B. (2007). Private Label Strategy-How to Meet the Store Brand Challenge. Harvard Business School Press.

Kutz, M. (2016). *Introduction to e-commerce: Combining business and information technology*. bookboon.com Ltd.

Laudon, K. C., & Laudon, J. P. (2019). *Management Information Systems Managing the Digital Firm* (16th ed.). Pearson Education Limited.

Lee, C. D., & Daiute, C. (2019). Introduction to Developmental Digital Technologies in Human History, Culture, and Well-Being. *Human Development*, *62*(1-2), 5–13. doi:10.1159/000496072

Lee, S. M., & Trimi, S. (2021). Convergence Innovation in the Digital Age and in the COVID-19 Pandemic Crisis. *Journal of Business Research*, *123*, 14–22. doi:10.1016/j.jbusres.2020.09.041 PMID:33012897

Lee, W.-I., Cheng, S.-Y., & Shih, Y.-T. (2010). Effects among product attributes, involvement, word-of-mouth, and purchase intention in online shopping. *Asia Pacific Management Review*, *22*(4), 223–229. doi:10.1016/j.apmrv.2017.07.007

Lian, F., & ... . (2015). Monetary and Image Influences on the Purchase Decision of Private Label Products in Malaysia. *Journal of Advanced Management Science*, *3*(4), 312–318.

Lin, X., Featherman, M., Brooks, S. L., & Hajli, N. (2018). Exploring gender differences in online consumer purchase decision making: An online product presentation perspective. *Information Systems Frontiers*, *21*(5), 1187–1201. doi:10.100710796-018-9831-1

Lindsey-Mullikin, J., & Borin, N. (2017). Why strategy is key for successful social media sales. *Business Horizons*, *60*(4), 473–482. doi:10.1016/j.bushor.2017.03.005

Manzur, E., Olavarrieta, S., Hidalgo, P., Farías, P., & Uribe, R. (2011). Store brand and national brand promotion attitudes antecedents. *Journal of Business Research*, *64*(3), 286–291. doi:10.1016/j.jbusres.2009.11.014

Mekni, M., & Lemieux, A. (2014). Augmented reality: Applications, challenges, and future trends. *Applied Computational Science Proceedings of the 13th International Conference on Applied Computer and Applied Computational Science*, 23-25.

Miyazaki, A. D., Grewal, D., & Goodstein, R. C. (2005). The effect of multiple extrinsic cues on quality perceptions: A matter of consistency. *The Journal of Consumer Research*, *32*(1), 146–153. doi:10.1086/429606

Nor Asshidin, N. H., Abidin, N., & Borhan, H. B. (2016). Consumer Attitude and Uniqueness towards International Products. *Procedia Economics and Finance*, *35*, 632–638. doi:10.1016/S2212-5671(16)00077-0

Nurul, A. H. (2016). The Relationship of Attitude, Subjective Norm and Website Usability on Consumer Intention to Purchase Online: An Evidence of Malaysian Youth. *Procedia Economics and Finance*, *35*, 493–502. doi:10.1016/S2212-5671(16)00061-7

OECD. (2019). *Unpacking E-commerce: Business models, trends and policies*. OECD Publishing. Retrieved from https://www.oecd-ilibrary.org/science-and-technology/unpacking-e-commerce_23561431-en

Ooi, J., & Yazdanifard, R. (2015). The Review of the Effectivity of the Augmented Reality Experiential Marketing Tool in Customer Engagement. *Global Journal of Management and Business Research: EMarketing*, *15*(8), 12–17.

Orlosky, J., Kiyokawa, K., & Takemura, H. (2017). Virtual and Augmented Reality on the 5G highway. *Journal of Information Processing*, *25*(0), 133–141. doi:10.2197/ipsjjip.25.133

Otubanjo, O. (2013). A Discourse Approach to Brand Leadership Management. *International Journal of Marketing Studies*, *5*(2), 131–137. doi:10.5539/ijms.v5n2p131

Pang, J., Keh, H. T., & Peng, S. (2009). Effects of advertising strategy on consumer-brand relationships: A brand love perspective. *Frontiers of Business Research in China*, *3*(4), 599–620. doi:10.100711782-009-0029-8

Pantano, E., & Rocco, S. (2012). Modeling innovative points of sales through virtual and immersive technologies. *Journal of Retailing and Consumer Services*, *19*(3), 279–286. doi:10.1016/j.jretconser.2012.02.002

Park, S., Choi, G. J., & Ko, H. (2020). Information technology-based tracing strategy in response to COVID-19 in South Korea-privacy controversies. *Journal of the American Medical Association*, *323*(21), 2129–2130. doi:10.1001/jama.2020.6602 PMID:32324202

Phillips, J. (2016). *Ecommerce Analytics. Analyze and Improve the Impact of Your Digital Strategy*. Pearson Education, Inc.

Pressman, R. S. (2014). *Software engineering. a practitioner's approach*. Edit. McGraw Hill.

Rabbi, I., & Ullah, S. (2013). A survey on augmented reality challenges and tracking. *Acta Graphica*, *24*(1-2), 29–46. https://hrcak.srce.hr/102430

Radovilsky, Z. (2015). *Business Models for E-Commerce*. Cognella Academic Publishing.

Ramli, N. S. (2017). A review of marketing strategies from the European chocolate industry. *Journal of Global Entrepreneurship Research*, *7*(10), 1–17. doi:10.118640497-017-0068-0

Rana, D. A. & Davoud, N. (2016). The impact of e-commerce and R&D on economic development in some selected countries. *Procedia-Social and Behavioral Sciences, 229*, 354-362. doi:10.1016/j.sbspro.2016.07.146

Reyes, G., Olmos, S., & Hernández, M. (2016). Private Label Sales through Catalogs with Augmented Reality. In Handbook of Research on Strategic Retailing of Private Label Products in a Recovering Economy. IGI Global.

Rice, A. L. (2013). *The Enterprise and Its Environment: A System Theory of Management Organization*. Psychology Press. doi:10.4324/9781315013756

Riobó, I. J. (2015). *TecsMedia: Análisis de tendencias: Realidad Aumentada y Realidad Virtual*. Instituto Tecnológico de Aragón. Retrieved from https://www.aragon.es/documents/20127/674325/Estudio%20Prospectiva%20Analisis%20de%20tendencias%20RA%20y%20RV%20con%20formato.pdf/45cb187d-55a4-9577-a0ce-476fa0ed1b06

Rubio, N., Villaseñor, N., & Oubiña, J. (2015). Consumer identification with store brands: Differences between consumers according to their brand loyalty. *Business Research Quarterly*, *18*(2), 111–126. doi:10.1016/j.brq.2014.03.004

Rust, R. T. (2020). The future of marketing. *International Journal of Research in Marketing*, *37*(1), 15–26. doi:10.1016/j.ijresmar.2019.08.002

Schwarz, J. A., & Tan, B. (2021). Optimal sales and production rollover strategies under capacity constraints. *European Journal of Operational Research*, *294*(2), 507–524. doi:10.1016/j.ejor.2021.01.040

Shaikh, A. A., & Karjaluoto, H. (2015). Mobile banking adoption: A literature review. *Telematics and Informatics*, *32*(1), 129–142. doi:10.1016/j.tele.2014.05.003

Shambhu, N. S., & Prasanna, S. (2021). Influence of conditional holoentropy-based feature selection on automatic recommendation system in the E-commerce sector. *Journal of King Saud University-Computer and Information Sciences*. Advance online publication. doi:10.1016/j.jksuci.2020.12.022

Sharma, S., Mahajan, S., & Rana, V. (2019). A semantic framework for e-commerce search engine optimization. *International Journal of Information Technology*, *11*(1), 31–36. doi:10.100741870-018-0232-y

Sharma, T., & Bashir, M. (2020). Use of apps in the COVID-19 response and the loss of privacy protection. *Nature Medicine*, *26*(8), 1165–1175. doi:10.103841591-020-0928-y PMID:32457443

Shukla, M., Dos Santos, R., Fong, A., & Lu, C.-T. (2017). DERIV: Distributed brand perception tracking framework. *Journal of Big Data*, *4*(17), 1–23. doi:10.1109/ICMLA.2016.0069

Singh, U. S. (2021). A study on the revolution of consumer relationships as a combination of human interactions and digital transformations. *Materials Today: Proceedings*. Advance online publication. doi:10.1016/j.matpr.2021.05.578

Sipior, J. C. (2020). Considerations for development and use of AI in response to COVID- 19. *International Journal of Information Management, 55*, 102170. Advance online publication. doi:10.1016/j.ijinfomgt.2020.102170 PMID:32836632

Statista. (2021). Retrieved from https://www.statista.com

Stonehouse, G., & Snowdon, B. (2007). Competitive Advantage Revisited: Michael Porter on Strategy and Competitiveness. *Journal of Management Inquiry, 16*(3), 256–273. doi:10.1177/1056492607306333

Tih, S., & Lee, K. H. (2013). Perceptions and Predictors of Consumers' Purchase Intentions for Store Brands: Evidence from Malaysia. *Asian Journal of Business and Accounting, 6*(2), 105–136.

Toussaert, S. (2021). Upping uptake of COVID contact tracing apps. *Nature Human Behaviour, 5*(2), 183–184. doi:10.103841562-021-01048-1 PMID:33479504

Turban, E. (2018). *Electronic Commerce 2018. A Managerial and Social Networks Perspective* (9th ed.). Springer Nature. doi:10.1007/978-3-319-58715-8

Uchiyama, H., & Marchand, E. (2012). Object detection and pose tracking for augmented reality: recent approaches. *18th Korea-Japan Joint Workshop on Frontiers of Computer Vision (FCV)*.

Wan-I, L., Cheng, S.-Y., & Shih, Y.-T. (2017). Effects among product attributes, involvement, word-of-mouth, and purchase intention in online shopping. *Asia Pacific Management Review, 22*(4), 223–229. doi:10.1016/j.apmrv.2017.07.007

Wang, Y.-S., Yeh, C.-H., & Liao, Y.-W. (2013). What drives purchase intention in the context of online content services? The moderating role of ethical self-efficacy for online piracy. *International Journal of Information Management, 33*(1), 199–208. doi:10.1016/j.ijinfomgt.2012.09.004

Webber, S. S. (2011). Dual organizational identification impacting client satisfaction and word of mouth loyalty. *Journal of Business Research, 64*(2), 119–125. doi:10.1016/j.jbusres.2010.02.005

Wijayanto, I. H., Soeaidy, M. S., & Rochmah, S. (2014). Tourism Based on the Model of Strategic Place Triangle (A Case Study in Wisata Bahari Lamongan). *Journal of Indonesian Tourism and Development Studies, 2*(3), 114–119. doi:10.21776/ub.jitode.2014.002.03.04

Willman-Iivarinen, H. (2017). The future of consumer decision making. *European Journal of Futures Research, 5*(14), 1–12. doi:10.100740309-017-0125-5

Winchester, M., & Romaniuk, J. (2008). Negative brand beliefs and brand usage. *International Journal of Market Research, 50*(3), 355–375. doi:10.1177/147078530805000306

Woodward, C., & ... . (2007). Virtual and augmented reality in the Digital building project. *International Journal of Design Sciences and Technology, 14*(1), 23–40.

Yesilyurt, M., & Yalman, Y. (2016). Security threats on mobile devices and their effects: Estimations for the future. *International Journal of Security and Its Applications*, *10*(2), 13–26. doi:10.14257/ijsia.2016.10.2.02

Yu, S. J. (2012). The dynamic competitive recommendation algorithm in social network services. *Information Sciences*, *187*, 1–14. doi:10.1016/j.ins.2011.10.020

Zendjebil, I. M. (2008). Outdoor Augmented Reality: State of the Art and Issues. *10th ACM/IEEE Virtual Reality International Conference (VRIC 2008)*, 177-187.

ENDNOTE

[1]   The total sample size was calculated with 95% confidence, 5% error and 50% homogeneity.

Chapter 16

The Readiness of Higher Education Academic Staff in Cyprus for Shifting the Instructional Delivery Mode From Face-to-Face to Emergency Remote Teaching

George Yiapanas
🆔 https://orcid.org/0000-0002-3725-4122
University of Roehampton, UK

Maria Constantinou
University of Roehampton, UK

Elena Marcoulli
Ministry of Education, Culture, Sport, and Youth (CY), Cyprus

ABSTRACT

The COVID-19 pandemic outbreak is considered one of the most serious crises. It affected the education industry causing huge complications and high levels of uncertainty. The pandemic crisis led governments worldwide to rapidly proceed into mandatory emergency measures to restrict physical interactions between people and prevent the virus from spreading extensively. One of the measures was the immediate closure of universities. This unpleasant action hit hard and interrupted education at every rank. To maintain its educational continuity, the Cyprus Government responded immediately to the emerging educational needs, driving higher education institutions to terminate all conventional courses and turn to online education. This chapter aims to evaluate the readiness of the academic staff in high education institutions in Cyprus for shifting the instructional mode from face-to-face to emergency remote teaching (ERT). Methodologically, the research adopted the quantitative approach, collecting data from academics (n=146) in the higher education institutions in Cyprus.

DOI: 10.4018/978-1-6684-6762-6.ch016

INTRODUCTION

Currently, higher education institutions are struggling to adapt to the digital era of the 21st century, creating new innovative ways to transfer knowledge to their students with the support of technology and online learning systems. Within this new digital educational environment, academics are required to gain or improve a variety of digital competencies (Traxler, 2018). The Covid-19 pandemic outbreak unexpectedly forced universities around the world to entirely cancel face-to-face teaching and deliver online lectures and services (Schneider and Council, 2021; Barbierato et al., 2021). This led the higher education sector into adopting immediate online learning strategies and implementing an emergency remote teaching strategy to maintain continuity (Danchikov et al., 2021; Shohel, 2022). Remote education became the only alternative (Hodges et al., 2020). This new scenario, and driven transition from traditional face-to-face teaching to remote teaching, caught numerous institutions and their personnel unprepared and lacking digital competence (Schneider and Council, 2021; Subekti, 2021).

In an attempt to *"flatten the curve"* of the Covid-19 pandemic, educators were required to rapidly readjust and adapt their pedagogy, teaching methods and techniques to a remote learning environment (Mohmmed et al., 2020; Tackie, 2022). Additionally, the gap in digital awareness and effective usage of online tools, given that academics largely use technology as an auxiliary and optional learning instrument, generated an extra challenge in their effort to overcome this crisis (Liguori and Winkler, 2020; Anthony and Noel, 2021).

Several studies have been conducted, examining the Covid-19 pandemic impact on the educational system in various countries, however, limited knowledge exists related to the higher education in Cyprus, and how they managed to respond to this challenge. This research provides a critical reflection of Cyprus higher education institutions academics' digital experiences and delineates the challenges they experienced during the Covid-19 crisis, due to the transition from on-campus teaching to emergency remote teaching, forcing them to develop effective online classes (Nisiforou, Kosmas and Vrasidas, 2021; Barbierato et al., 2021). Consequently, this chapter aims to examine their experiences, competencies, and attitudes toward emergency remote teaching during the Covid-19 outbreak. Additionally, it analyses their experience and perception regarding their overall personal development in the new digital environment.

Research Aim

Flowing from the above, the aim of this book chapter is to evaluate the readiness of the academic staff in high education institutions in Cyprus for shifting the instructional mode from face-to-face to emergency remote teaching during the Covid-19 pandemic outbreak and recognise whether they obtained new digital skills and pedagogy strategies to overcome these challenges.

Significance of the Study

The paradigm of Cyprus as a particular field of study, due to its unique characteristics, can be used as a pilot study for countries aiming to acquire precise and reliable data consistently. Throughout this study, one can acknowledge the challenging elements that academic staff in higher education institutions in Cyprus had to confront during the transition towards the online teaching environment due to the Covid-19 pandemic outbreak. Furthermore, the different types of online education techniques and strategies may be evaluated, to delineate their pros and cons, which may allow a deeper viewpoint on this type of learning. The findings of this research can provide invaluable insight for small-size education industries and draw explicit theoretical and practical conclusions towards scholarly advancement and managerial implementation in the context of improving the online teaching setting by implementing pre-existing theories, well-established practices, emerging strategies, and valid techniques.

THEORETICAL FRAMEWORK

Higher education institutions are struggling in a dynamic environment, turning to industry-business practices to survive and achieve their goals and strategic targets (Melanthiou, Thrassou, and Vrontis, 2017). Thus, educational systems have undergone significant changes throughout the years to incorporate current educational ideas and improve their learning outcomes. The main goal of any educational system is to develop the necessary skills, enhance critical thinking, and build strong moral principles (Howells, 2018). The above-mentioned objectives cannot be met without the active involvement of teachers/educators, who are the cornerstone of any educational system. They motivate, advise, teach, listen, consult, and serve as role models for the students. Teachers' abilities and skills to perform well in this crucial role are linked to their level of motivation and readiness (Biggs and Tang, 2011).

Education in the 21st Century

During the previous decade, education evolved drastically, either because of the changes and advancements in learning technology and the various techniques or due to the societal and global shifts that created new education trends (Meletiou-Mavrotheris, Mavrou, and Rebelo, 2021). Traditional classroom teaching is probably unable to fulfil the needs of this new technological environment. The introduction of the internet had a major influence on how knowledge was transferred (Johnson et al., 2016). Technology tools, like the online classroom, the video conferencing, the digital whiteboards, the networks and learning communities, provide unlimited possibilities in teaching and learning, while the teacher-student relationship is shifting, into a more interactive and engaged relationship (Samaniego-Erazo, Esteve-González and Vaca, 2015; Rinekso and Muslim, 2020).

A distinctive feature of the digital era is the widespread use of communication technologies in our everyday activities with the use of the internet. In just thirty years, the internet completely altered communication networks and technology forecasts. The robust pace at which technological and economic advancements are changing has set the bar high for greater demands on the educational systems (Freeman, Becker and Cummins, 2017). This technological evolution has shaped a dynamic reality in education, presenting innovative ways to spread knowledge to students clearly and pleasantly. Academics are expected to regularly upgrade their pedagogical skills and knowledge regarding their teaching subject and integrate technology into their teaching strategy, by developing necessary digital competencies that match the digitalization of the 21st century (Spante et al., 2018). In most disciplines and at all levels of education, distance learning education has rapidly become a common approach. Nowadays, distance learning has significantly advanced into an efficient way of learning, by applying various pedagogical techniques through digital technologies (Picciano, 2017).

Many universities offer a variety of quality distance learning programs, enabling students to study at their place, pace, and time (Carey, 2016). With the help of the internet and technology, students can enrol on various online courses, have qualified tutors offering online teaching, and obtain degrees on the same scale as face-to-face conventional degrees (Aithal and Aithal, 2016). Nevertheless, sceptics are expressing their concerns about the quality of the online courses offered by universities, citing poorer success rates particularly among students of downgraded groups, and lack of teacher-student engagement for a deeper understanding of the courses (Baum and McPherson, 2019).

Distance Learning Education

As technology, and thus educational technology, continues to advance, distance teaching has become increasingly popular (Spante et al., 2018). Through this educational technology advancement and development, new challenges and opportunities naturally arise. Over the past twenty years, distance teaching education has been growing rapidly (Lay et al., 2020). Distance learning education involves skills that can be taught and assessed face-to-face, developing expertise in several areas (Salehi, Shojaee and Sattar, 2015; Kentnor, 2015). In contrast with traditional teaching, in which academics interact with a number of students who are concentrated simultaneously within the same area and time, in distance education, the academic and the student are separately, and the information can be "consumed" even at different times (Srivastava, 2019). Berg and Simonson (2016) refer to distance learning as an educational process and system in which all or a significant proportion of teaching is carried out by someone, or something, removed in space and time from the learner. This process requires an internet connection, and it is supported by technological devices such as computers, laptops, smartphones, tablets, etc. (Burns, 2011; Chang and Windeatt, 2016). As a result, students receive tutoring from the comfort of their own space, rather than travelling to the campus (Schneider and Council, 2021; Subekti, 2021).

Connected to distance learning, three types of online learning are frequently used: '*synchronous*', '*asynchronous*' and '*hybrid*' (Perveen, 2016). Synchronous teaching requires the engagement of all students at the same time (Kebede and Bhattacharya, 2022). The educator/learner interaction occurs in real-time, through online learning systems, sharing instructional content and ideas. Simultaneous engagement can be achieved either by being in the same space or by being interconnected through a network that allows audio and/or video conferencing while in addition there is the possibility of exchanging files and data (Rinekso and Muslim, 2020). On the contrary, asynchronous learning is considered a more adaptable method since it does not require students and educators to simultaneously participate and engage. Instead, students may set their education schedule and gather training material accordingly (Kebede and Bhattacharya, 2022). Asynchronous learning is a self-guided method that can be applied with the help of emails, lecture notes, correspondence courses, and tutoring sessions. It is considered a more flexible and affordable learning type (Yamagata-Lynch, 2014). Additionally, hybrid courses, also known as blended learning courses, involve learning environments that enable students and educators to interact both in person and online (Barbierato et al., 2021). Hybrid courses are a blend of synchronous and asynchronous methods, enabling students to autonomously study and learn at their own time and pace, at the same time interact in real-time with the educator and other students (Bhadri and Patil, 2022).

Pros and Cons of Distance Learning

Based on the data collected and the research conducted over the past years, numerous advantages, and benefits, as well as obstacles and challenges exist in distance learning education (Mahlangu, 2018; Danchikov et al., 2021).

Distance learning education provides equal opportunities for lifelong and quality education to everyone, expanding the classroom boundaries to anywhere and at any time (Carey, 2016; Saykili, 2018). In many cases, it facilitates wider participation and equivalent access to higher education institutions, enabling students to choose programs and receive support according to their preferences (Behera, 2013). It is considered a flexible method of learning, in which students participate according to their schedule, through virtual classes anywhere and anytime, themselves defining the preferable place and time that learning occurs (Martin and Trang, 2018). Moreover, this flexibility is associated with individualisation, as it provides students with the ability for personalised education according to their requirements (Cooke, Lane and Taylor, 2018), and offers the possibility of choosing their study methods and strategies (Baum and McPherson, 2019). Consequently, distance learning creates a student-centered environment, emphasising the pace (Berg and Simonson, 2016). Through the students' active participation in the learning process, the educational autonomy is reinforced, enhancing this way their critical thinking and the "learn how to learn" ability (Smith and Darvas, 2017). As a result, the students' stress limit is lower while the learning experience is elevated (Al-Azawei, Parslow and Lundqvist, 2016).

Distance learning education strengthens the knowledge quality and the student approach since each course is developed within a controlled environment and applies specific pedagogical guidelines and concepts (Iberahim, 2021). Moreover, it is observed that distance learning education promotes the active participation of a specific segment of students who tend to be shy and low profile, as it allows them to study with alternative methods (Smith and Darvas, 2017; Jurs and Kulberga, 2021). In conclusion, distance education may provide students with essential knowledge, expertise, abilities, and skills to satisfy the diverse requirements of a fast-evolving, modern, digital society (Pakhomova et al., 2021).

On the other hand, distance learning education excludes several soft skills from the learning process, such as communication, creativity, social interaction, etc. Students lack direct connection with the rest of the academic community and in engaging with other students (Al-Qahtani and Higgins, 2013). Danchikov et al. (2021) acknowledge that distance learning is not easily and effectively applied to all disciplines. For instance, it can be applied in various social studies, however, in educational fields, such as medical and pharmaceutical, where practical skills development is an essential educational element, it is difficult to be applied.

Questions are raised by researchers concerning the quality and adequacy of knowledge gained through distance education. Despite the vast increase of higher education institutions offering these types of programs, it is considered that this method of learning cannot match or reach the quality of education offered in traditional face-to-face courses (Baum and McPherson, 2019). The academics' role in an online learning environment is limited, as they mainly focus on tutoring and managing the course content and material. Due to the lack of physical interaction, it is difficult for them to efficiently motivate and engage their students (Van de Vord and Pogue, 2012; Abaci et al., 2021). Academics also experience difficulties in designing their lectures, and in providing quality feedback to their students (Al-Azawei, Parslow and Lundqvist, 2016). Furthermore, it is evidenced that a high drop-out percentage exists in distance learning courses, at least higher than in traditional education, since students often have technology issues, they fail to manage their study time properly, they are unable to remain engaged, and many more (Xu and Jaggars, 2011; Danchikov et al., 2021).

To develop and offer distance learning courses, a significant investment in infrastructure and innovative technology is required, and afterward, also in maintenance, human resources, etc. (Appiah and Van Tonder, 2018). Academics are obliged to constantly improve their skills and knowledge to be able to effectively utilise new technology and adapt to technological advancements (Grytsenko, 2022). Numerous factors may challenge distance learning courses, or even lead to failure, such as the stakeholder's ignorance about online pedagogy, the absence of technical provisions for digital education, the number of newly registered students, the school's admission criteria, the tuition fees, the course duration, the constrain of financial aid, the educators' prejudice towards online degrees, etc. (Kentnor, 2015).

Regardless of the above drawbacks, distance learning is becoming very popular, and constantly increasing its numbers. Higher education institutions invest in such programs, hoping to attract more students. Nonetheless, distance learning does not intend to replace traditional, face-to-face education (Carey, 2016).

Distance Learning in Higher Education Institutions

School curricula have recognised distance learning as an important method of producing knowledge and skills (Baum and McPherson, 2019). Even though this method became very popular during the Covid-19 pandemic outbreak, it is not a recent concept for higher education institutions (Aithal and Aithal, 2016). The necessity of distance learning in higher education institutions came as a result of the limited capacity of traditional classrooms, and of the time-limitation of working adults. Online learning was officially established in Y1971 in the United Kingdom by the Open University, where advanced technological media were used for delivering off-campus postgraduate courses. After that, many other higher education institutions adopted online education (Simonson, Zvacek, and Smaldino, 2019).

Over the last decade, the distance learning concept in higher education institutions has demonstrated substantial growth (Traxler, 2018). Higher education institutions implemented distance education to increase their student numbers without needing to accommodate them on campus (Baum and McPherson, 2019). Moreover, via these programs, they can promote continuous learning and lifelong education (Palvia et al., 2018). Individuals such as full-time employees or people living in isolated areas for whom it is difficult to attend face-to-face conventional programs, benefit the most from the existence of distance learning programs (Berg and Simonson, 2016).

Most higher education institutions utilise both synchronous and asynchronous methods for their online courses, with the implementation of the relevant technology and tools. Students have access to their online classrooms, teaching material, assignments, files, etc., through a learning management system (Kapsargina, Shmeleva and Olentsova, 2019). These systems can efficiently monitor each student's progress, as well as assist them in terms of communication, material access, etc. (Sariyalcinkaya, Altun and Erümit, 2022). It is proven that technology is an essential element of the quality of distance learning education, therefore, higher education institutions constantly adjust their services and content within this scope (Means, Bakia and Murphy, 2014). They improve quality through creative techniques to enhance their students' motives, engagement, and interaction, but also through the development of their teaching staff to upgrade their communication and teaching skills within the online environment (Danchikov et al., 2021).

Transformation to Emergency Remote Teaching [ERT]

In contrast to distance learning education which is planned from the beginning and designed in a way that supports a long-term teaching environment, Emergency Remote Teaching [ERT] is a temporary shift to alternative education, that mainly occurs due to specific crisis conditions (Hodges et al., 2020; Anthony and Noel, 2021). It involves the utilisation of entirely remote teaching methods that might rather be delivered face-to-face or as blended, and that will reverse once the crisis has abated (Mohmmed et al., 2020). The primary goal is not to re-create a robust learning environment, but rather to provide short-term and quick access to learning material and teaching support and remain available to students during an emergency or a crisis (Bozkurt and Sharma, 2020).

Considering that this change occurs without a warning and the implementation must be instantaneous, shifting education from a conventional mode to online teaching, generates a set of challenges, thus, needs to be designed and planned very well (Hodges et al., 2020). To make ERT work, institutions and academics need to take the reins in developing plans in advance and prepare themselves with the requisite skills and tools in a fast manner for this shift (Huber and Helm, 2020). An ERT should take into consideration elements such as technical facilities, modality, pacing, pedagogy, communication, evaluation, the student-to-teacher ratio, the student's role, the teacher's role, the sources of feedback, etc. (Means, Bakia and Murphy, 2014; Hodges et al., 2020; Tackie, 2022).

To shift from face-to-face mode to ERT, institutions employ some of the main components and technological tools they use in their distance learning courses. Nevertheless, the transformation is achieved over a two-phase process, involving the curriculum and content transformation, circulation and delivery, and the academics' development (Kapsargina, Shmeleva and Olentsova, 2019; Mohmmed et al., 2020).

Curriculum and Content Transformation, Circulation, and Delivery

Online education is built on an extensive variety of technology tools. Teachers need to engage in innovative methods to gain effective and quality education (Tackie, 2022). When developing a distance learning program, institutions apply a formal standardised process to build the curriculum and the content, to ensure and maintain quality and at the same time, comply with a series of pedagogical guidelines (Appiah and Van Tonder, 2018). In ERT the curriculum and course content is temporarily converted to an online form. The teaching material is circulated to students via Learning Management Systems [LMS]. These systems support streamlining the learning process by providing a central location for students to access teaching material online and for teachers to develop their content (Kapsargina, Shmeleva and Olentsova, 2019). Primarily, an LMS helps academics design and manage online courses, create and integrate course materials, conduct customised tests, quizzes and assessments, articulate learning goals and track studying progress (Gamage, Ayres and Behrend, 2022). The content is delivered through virtual classrooms, as in a distance learning context. However, when engaging ERT, institutions often utilise a variety of temporary tools and collaboration apps, that allow them to stay organised and have online conversations and meetings (Grytsenko, 2022).

The Academics' Role during Emergency Remote Teaching

Academics are a key element in education, and contribute to fulfilling the students' satisfaction, affect their participation and encourage them to engage. Conventional teaching is a straightforward process, in which academics need to develop specific pedagogical skills and prepare themselves before the lecture (Mohmmed et al., 2020). On the other hand, distance learning teaching comes with a variety of challenges regarding student engagement, technology awareness, content adaptation, connection issues, and many more (Beaunoyer, Dupéré and Guitton, 2020; Tackie, 2022). Combining all the above with the unique attributes of ERT creates even more challenges and increases the risk of failing. The academic's role in implementing ERT is vital. Shifting the instructional delivery mode in a limited time generates risks, and academics need to understand, evaluate and resolve several issues to achieve their teaching objectives (Hodges et al., 2020).

Implementing ERT requires academics to transform their content, familiarise themselves with technology, gain experience with online lectures, find ways to keep their students engaged, administer secure evaluation and maintain modality, pace and communication (Taladriz, 2019; Bozkurt and Sharma, 2020). These are actions and practices that, although familiar to those who teach in distance learning programs, are still for the majority of academics a scenario that finds them unprepared (Mohmmed et al., 2020).

Industry Research Context - Higher Education in Cyprus

Higher education in Cyprus is regulated and controlled by the Ministry of Education, Culture, Sport and Youth [MOEC]. In particular, MOEC is assigned to implement educational regulations and strategies, educational management, and budgeting preparation (Tsiakkiros and Pashiardis, 2002). The Department of Higher Education is the "competent authority" within the Ministry as regards all divisions and matters directly connected to higher education in Cyprus. It aims to create and maintain the necessary conditions to deliver high-quality education within a regulated and controlled framework (Karageorgos, 2021).

The Government policy regarding higher education in Cyprus aims to fulfil the local requirements of education and establish the country as a regional educational and research centre for multinational academics and students (Tsiakkiros and Pashiardis, 2002). The higher education system is shaped by the European Higher Education Area, as defined by the Bologna Progress (Ministry of Education, Culture, Sport and Youth, 2020). The higher education landscape consists of public and private universities and tertiary education institutes. Common key values, such as academic freedom and student's union independence, are adopted, with a primary objective to improve student mobility and facilitate employability (Office of the Law Commissioner, 2014).

Distance Learning in Higher Education in Cyprus

Even though face-to-face conventional education is mostly preferred in Cyprus, over the past years, higher education institutions offer a substantial number of distance learning courses (KPMG, 2020). Since Y2006, several universities in Cyprus offer high-quality distance learning courses in various fields and disciplines. The Open University of Cyprus, which was established in Y2006, became the first public university in Cyprus offering exclusively distance learning programs, and at the same time an educational model that works as a paradigm for other universities offering distance learning courses. Cyprus' higher education system managed to create a modern and creative academic framework, enabling higher education institutions to provide high-quality distance learning courses that meet the international requirements (Cyprus Ministry of Education, Culture, Sport and Youth, 2012).

The Cyprus Agency of Quality Assurance and Accreditation [CYQAA] is the authority responsible to safeguard the higher education procedures and processes, as formed by the Bologna Progress (Dakowska, 2019). CYQAA's duties are to maintain quality and promote the continuous improvement and development of higher education. The Agency specifies the basic principles for institutions that wish to deliver distance learning programs. These programs must apply pedagogical techniques through digital technologies, explicitly fulfil the course learning objectives, and define precise standards and measurable evaluation methods (Koutselini, 2019). In addition, these courses must be taught in such a way that students have an active role, remain engaged throughout the process, and gain the necessary knowledge and skills (Jurs and Kulberga, 2021).

Emerging Strategy in Cyprus during the COVID-19 Pandemic Outbreak

The Covid-19 pandemic outbreak is considered one of the most serious health catastrophes, and a major global crisis, with most industries facing tremendous issues and high levels of uncertainty. This led governments around the world to rapidly proceed into mandatory emergency measures, to restrict physical interactions between people, to prevent the virus from spreading on a large scale. One of the measures was the immediate closure of schools and universities. This unpleasant action hit hard and interrupted education at every rank (Bozkurt et al., 2020). According to UNESCO, more than 1.5 billion students worldwide have been affected by the school or university closures due to the Covid-19 crisis. This resulted in the unprecedented challenge for educational institutions to rapidly shift all courses online, placing them under great pressure (Abaci et al., 2021).

In March 2020, the Cyprus Government responded immediately to the emerging educational needs that followed the Covid-19 crisis, in order to maintain its educational continuity. More specifically, the MOEC forced all higher education institutions to immediately cancel all face-to-face sessions, including laboratories and other educational activities and shift to ERT (Nisiforou, Kosmas and Vrasidas, 2021). According to MOEC's mapping of the educational field, fifty-three thousand two hundred sixty-two [53.262] students were studying in Cyprus for the academic year 2019-2020, in all public and private higher and tertiary institutions (Ministry of Education, Culture, Sport and Youth, 2022). Consequently, institutions have been forced to rapidly switch all their programs to distance learning and implement ERT, utilising a variety of education systems and teaching technologies and strategies (Basilaia and Kvavadze, 2020). Additionally, each institution was instructed to manage its final examination process remotely, via oral exams, portfolios, open-book papers, online monitored exams, etc. (Kafa and Pashiardis, 2020). Most institutions implemented their strategies relying on the existing resources, processes and procedures of their distance learning programs, to transform the conventional face-to-face programs into ERT.

All strategies were driven by the need to maintain the students' equity and inclusion combined with the ability to ensure that education is designed and implemented in a way that satisfies a range of pedagogical processes and does not amplify any existing academic and social disparities (Nisiforou, Kosmas and Vrasidas, 2021). These measures required a high level of self-directed learning and studying abilities by the students, aided by novel teaching, learning, and mentoring techniques by teachers (Bozkurt and Sharma, 2020). Moreover, safeguarding the quality of life was also a critical aspect during the implementation of ERT (Hadjicharalambous, Demetriou and Erotocritou, 2021; Demetriou, Keramioti and Hadjicharalambous, 2021). As this caught most higher education institutions and academics unprepared, the challenge they had to confront in a short time was huge. All academics were compelled to drastically convert their teaching methods and material into digital, so they could continue their educational work through virtual learning environments without decreasing the required pedagogical quality (Subekti, 2021).

METHOD

Methodologically, the research adopted the quantitative approach, collecting primary data from academics in the higher education institutions in Cyprus. Participants were invited to complete an online survey, demonstrating their experience during the transition to ERT. The questionnaire was designed, and the data were collected using an online survey instrument, circulated via email as a direct link. The use of an online survey had a major advantage during the Covid-19 pandemic outbreak. Participation was voluntary and uncompensated. The response rate was high, yielding one hundred sixty [160] responses over fourteen [14] days beginning May 9, 2021 [during the period in which all higher educational institutions applied ERT]. Submissions that were not fully complete were deleted from the study sample.

Following the identification of the participants, they were approached through an invitation letter in the form of informed consent. The letter introduced the researchers, presented the aim of the research study, informed the potential participants about confidentiality issues and how the researchers would preserve their anonymity, and how data and information would be gathered and used. Finally, the letter explained the nature of their involvement and the estimated time needed in case they agreed to participate. The researchers were aware of and abided by any ethical code that governs this study. They recognised the importance of ethics and the responsibility towards the people involved in the research process. This research has taken into consideration the abovementioned considerations to lessen any possible ethical risks and issues.

The analysis was based on one hundred and \forty-six [n=146] random responses from academics employed in higher education institutions in Cyprus. The majority of the participants were female [70%]. On average, 74% of the participants were up to thirty-nine [39] years old, while 59% of them had a teaching experience of over four [4] years. Additionally, 84% of the respondents held a postgraduate degree (Table 1).

The survey was divided into six [6] sections, with clear guidelines for their completion. Questions were assessed on a five-point Likert scale and took an average of twelve [12] minutes to complete. The first four [4] questions in section A asked participants about their demographics, teaching experience and education level. Next, respondents were given three [3] questions in Section B, examining the level of their digital awareness and competence. Academics were then asked to evaluate the challenges they faced during the ERT with six [6] questions in Section C, while in Section D they were requested to identify the delivery approach/type. This section contained two [2] questions. In Section E, academics were invited to identify elements related to the curriculum and content transformation and were given five [5] options to select from. The final section, Section F, included seven [7] questions asking participants to assess their professional development after implementing ERT.

RESEARCH FINDINGS

Overall, the academic staff demonstrates high awareness, competence, and familiarity with the significance and importance that technology has in the ERT environment. However, still, the transition from the conventional form of teaching to ERT was a challenging task (Table 2).

Technology tools such as the online classroom, video conferencing, digital whiteboards, etc., provide unlimited possibilities in teaching and learning (Samaniego-Erazo, Esteve-González and Vaca, 2015; Rinekso and Muslim, 2020). This is proven and highly reflected in the case of Cyprus, with respondents affirming [84%] that it maximises the teaching and learning process. Nevertheless, it is revealed that the academic staff was familiar with using the technology [73%]. The fact that remote teaching comes with a variety of risks, was also validated in this study, with the majority of the participants [63%] stating that shifting from conventional face-to-face teaching to ERT was certainly very challenging.

Table 1. Academics demographics

Demographics	Percentage [%]	Academics [n=146]
Gender		
Male	30	44
Female	70	102
Age | years		
20-30	29	42
30-39	45	66
40-49	19	28
50 +	7	10
Teaching experience | years		
0-1	16	24
2-3	25	36
4-6	30	44
7-9	14	20
10 +	15	22
Education		
Bachelor's degree	16	24
Master's degree	62	90
PhD	22	32

Implementing ERT under those unique and demanding circumstances was not easy, and the academics' role was vital for its success (Hodges et al., 2020). Remote teaching comes with a range of challenges concerning student engagement, curriculum and content transformation, connection issues, and many more (Mohmmed et al., 2020; Tackie, 2022). The data analysis revealed that during ERT these challenges had an impact on the examined context (Table 3).

Although staff development and skills are considered a fundamental element during ERT, in the case of Cyprus this challenge was assessed equally over the evaluation scale, with the majority [67%] of the participants highlighting the opposite. Considering that academics were familiar and confident with distance teaching before the specific crisis [see Table 6], this might have produced a different view. In

Table 2. Digital awareness and competence of academics

	Strongly agree	Agree	Nor agree or disagree	Disagree	Strongly disagree
	%	%	%	%	%
Technology tools maximise the teaching and learning process	41	43	11	5	0
Familiar with using technology during ERT	37	36	23	4	0
The transition from face-to-face to ERT was challenging	29	34	27	10	0

Table 3. Challenges during ERT

	Always	Often	Sometimes	Rarely	Never
	%	%	%	%	%
Academic staff development, skills	14	19	27	22	18
Teaching process, modality, pace, and communicatio	35	27	22	8	8
Curriculum and content transformation	9	27	42	18	4
Difficulties with technology and systems	6	24	46	19	5
Keeping students engaged	11	49	30	10	0
Administering secure evaluation	16	28	25	21	10

contrast, the teaching process, modality, pace and communication were a great concern in higher education in Cyprus, with participants [62%] stating that this was a challenging issue during ERT. Transforming the curriculum and content [69%], and possible difficulties with technology and systems [70%], were both evaluated by participants as a routine challenge, and not something that created problems. It seems that, again, their familiarity with distance education, helped them minimise these risks. On the other hand, student engagement was considered an important task and at the same time, a critical challenge. Participants, often [49%], or sometimes [30%] faced problems in keeping the class active and alive. Finally, securing the quality and validity of the final examination process remotely, via oral exams, portfolios, open-book papers, online monitored exams, etc., was considered by participants as a critical factor, however, once again assessed consistently over the valuation range. The answers may vary, due to the different approaches and evaluation methods each academic selected (Huber and Helm, 2020).

Another key factor once switching to ERT is the use of a learning management system to provide a central online location for students to access teaching material, to enable academics to deliver the content, and provide a variety of collaboration tools to host online meetings, conversations and lectures (Grytsenko, 2022; Gamage, Ayres and Behrend, 2022). In the specific research context, the institutions and academics employed all three types of learning approaches (Table 4).

The data analysis revealed that academics in higher education in Cyprus took great advantage of the use of LMS software and virtual classrooms. More than 75% of the participants, stated that they used LMS to design and manage their courses, create and integrate their material, conduct quizzes and assessments, articulate learning goals and track studying progress. Interestingly, the majority of the

Table 4. Shift to ERT: Using LMS and specific learning approaches

	Always	Often	Sometimes	Rarely	Never
	%	%	%	%	%
Learning Management System [LMS]	51	25	10	12	2
			Percentage [%]	Academics [n=146]	
Adopted the synchronous distance learning approach			58	85	
Adopted the asynchronous distance learning approach			15	22	
Adopted the hybrid distance learning approach			27	39	

Table 5. Curriculum and content transformation

	Percentage [%]	Academics [n=146]
Curriculum included *[Participants were able to select more than one option]*		
Live lectures through virtual classes	85	124 academics
Frequent online quizzes	56	82 academics
Topics presented by students online	38	56 academics
Assignments to work in small groups online	44	64 academics
Live sessions / online tutoring	37	54 academics

participants employed the synchronous distance learning approach [58%], using a virtual classroom as their main tool to interact with their students in real-time, while a small number [15%] adopted the asynchronous approach, with pre-recorded lectures to give a more autonomous environment to students. In addition, some academics [27%] preferred blended learning, allowing students to study and learn at their own time and pace, while at the same time interacting in real-time. The rationale for choosing the suitable approach lies in the course type, content, and teaching attitude (Barbierato et al., 2021; Kebede and Bhattacharya, 2022).

In ERT the curriculum and course content is temporarily converted to an online form, with institutions applying a formal standardised process to ensure quality and to comply with a range of pedagogical guidelines (Appiah and Van Tonder, 2018). Academics are required to drastically convert their teaching methods and material into digital, to continue their educational work through a distance learning environment without decreasing the required pedagogical quality (Subekti, 2021). Even though curriculum and content transformation are considered a critical ERT success factor, carrying a variety of challenges and risks, academics in the examined context evaluated this as a routine task [69% - see Table 3 above] and developed their curriculum based on a range of alternatives (Table 5).

According to the data analysis, the great majority of academics [85%] adopted the synchronous distance learning approach [also verified in Table 4], conducting live lectures through virtual classes. Additionally, to keep students active and engaged, they carried out frequent online quizzes [56%], they requested students to present specific topics online [38%] and they gave assignments to work in small groups online [44%]. Furthermore, a small number of academics [37%] offered online sessions for tutoring and student support. The asynchronous distance learning approach requires online tutoring to assist students and keep them engaged (Kebede and Bhattacharya, 2022).

All the above components are critical, and it is imperative to be taken into consideration when evaluating the performance of ERT. However, the readiness of the academic staff to implement such a demanding task is an equally important success factor (Hodges et al., 2020). Considering that emergency teaching occurs without warning, and actions are instant, shifting education from a conventional mode increases the responsibility associated with the academic staff. They need to take the reins in developing plans in advance and be ready for this shift (Huber and Helm, 2020). The academics' readiness in the examined context was assessed, taking into consideration their previous and current experience with online teaching, and their confidence in using online teaching and evaluation tools and pedagogical methods. Lastly,

Table 6. Academics' readiness and professional development

	Extensive previous experience	Some previous experience	No previous experience	
	%	%	%	
Experience with online teaching before the Covid-19 pandemic outbreak	10	51	39	

	Very confident	Confident enough	Confident	A little confident	Not confident
	%	%	%	%	%
Teaching online before ERT	40	24	10	7	19
Teaching online after ERT	46	20	18	13	3
Using online tools to transform curriculum and content after ERT	32	15	29	20	4
Evaluating, giving feedback and online support after ERT	17	34	18	24	7

	More effective	The same	Less effective
	%	%	%
How effective was the shift from face-to-face mode to ERT, in developing their digital skills	58	34	8
How effective was ERT compared to the traditional face-to-face teaching	27	28	45

academics were evaluated based on a personal reflection statement regarding the effectiveness of ERT on their digital skills (Table 6).

Most academics [61%] stated they had previous experience with online teaching before the implementation of ERT, something that certainly helped them overcome possible risks and challenges. The data analysis shows that academics gained confidence in online teaching after ERT implementation. The majority of academics [74%] felt confident and ready to teach online, and this number grew bigger [84%] after ERT. Additionally, it is apparent that the use of ERT has improved and strengthened the pedagogical skills and competencies of the academic staff. A great majority of them can use online tools to transform the curriculum and content [76%] and are familiar with ways to evaluate, give feedback and support students effectively and constructively [69%]. These elements reflect the individual positioning concerning the effectiveness that the shift from face-to-face mode to ERT had in developing their digital skills. Although academics were familiar with online teaching and confident to shift to ERT, still the majority of them [58%] gained further digital skills.

Finally, in an attempt to assess and evaluate the effectiveness of ERT compared to the traditional face-to-face teaching mode, respondents appeared to be sceptical and concerned. ERT maintains education during crisis conditions (Hodges et al., 2020), however, the academics in the specific research context strongly believe that the pedagogical outcome is less effective [45%] than, or at least the same [28%] as, in conventional education.

Catalexis

The findings indicate that the vast majority of the academic staff in higher education in Cyprus, acknowledge that the utilisation of technology tools has a significant impact, provides unlimited possibilities, and maximises the teaching and learning process during ERT. Furthermore, they appreciate that such a demanding task comes with a range of challenges such as transforming the curriculum and content, maintaining student engagement, keeping communication effective, resolving connection issues, administering evaluation processes, etc. Consequently, these challenges have a direct impact on pedagogical quality.

To resolve implementation risks and challenges, and minimise possible issues while shifting towards ERT, the academic staff took full advantage of the possibilities of a learning management system, to deliver the content, provide a central online location for students for accessing teaching material, and host online meetings, conversations and lectures. Most academics adopted either the synchronous distance learning or the blended learning approach. The curriculum and course content was adapted to an online digital form, applying a formal process to ensure quality and to comply with a range of pedagogical guidelines. The majority of academics conducted live lectures through virtual classes and kept their students engaged and active with frequent online quizzes, online presentations by students, small group assignments, and other interactive activities. Additionally, they offered online sessions for tutoring and student support.

It is evidenced that the academic staff in the higher education institutions in Cyprus demonstrates high awareness and familiarity with the significance that technology has in ERT, particularly on how to resolve challenges, and on how to ensure the required quality in distance education. Undoubtedly, their previous experience with online teaching helped them overcome the aforementioned risks and challenges. Regardless of their prior experience and high confidence in online teaching, still, ERT has strengthened their pedagogical skills and competencies. Through this experience, they managed to improve their digital skills, enhance their ability to use online tools to transform the curriculum and content, and familiarise themselves with techniques and methods to evaluate, give feedback and support students effectively and constructively.

Despite the sudden nature of this crisis due to the Covid-19 pandemic outbreak, this study shows that academics in higher education in Cyprus were aware of the challenging environment of ERT. It appears that they were ready and competent to provide stability in higher education. They employed synchronous and hybrid teaching methods through the use of learning management systems, and adopted a variety of tools, techniques, and pedagogical methods, to transfer knowledge and engage students. Their experience in the higher education ecosystem, their prior knowledge in distance teaching, and their awareness of possible challenges enabled them to efficiently implement ERT, to maintain continuity in higher education.

However, it is revealed that although ERT secures and supports education during periods of crisis, remote teaching is still less effective than face-to-face conventional teaching in terms of pedagogical outcomes.

RECOMMENDATIONS

Undoubtedly, institutions are currently going through a period of uncertainty that threatens their sustainability. They are struggling to generate innovative ideas and solutions to maintain attractiveness and competitiveness, and continue providing high-quality education, despite the challenges they are facing.

Additionally, crises occur, forcing them to implement emergency plans to continue providing education through emergency remote teaching. Any occurring changes in the education ecosystem, certainly affect academics as well. To make remote teaching work, institutions and academics are recommended to take the reins on developing strategies in advance and prepare themselves with the requisite skills and competencies to preserve their readiness for shifting between teaching methods and approaches in a fast manner for change. These strategies should take into consideration elements such as technical facilities, module content, modality, pedagogy, teaching and communication methods, evaluation procedures, etc. (Hodges et al., 2020). A standardised framework on emergency remote teaching, with specific guidelines, pedagogical approaches, and methods, can evidently minimise the risks and challenges that come with instantaneous shifts.

In the post-pandemic era and as the higher education landscape continues to be confronted with challenges, uncertainty and opportunities, academics are recommended to further develop their skills in remote teaching approaches (Anthony and Noel, 2021). Moreover, current global and social shifts create new education trends; hence, higher education institutions should invest in new technological environments to expand their prospects in teaching and learning, moving into a more interactive and engaging teaching environment.

CONCLUSION AND PRACTICAL IMPLICATIONS

The Covid-19 pandemic outbreak unexpectedly forced higher education to cancel all face-to-face courses and deliver online lectures and services. This led institutions to adopt immediate online learning strategies and implement an emergency remote teaching approach to maintain continuity. This book chapter aims to evaluate the readiness of the academic staff in high education institutions in Cyprus for shifting the instructional mode from face-to-face to emergency remote teaching during the Covid-19 pandemic outbreak and recognise whether they obtained new digital skills and pedagogy strategies to overcome these challenges.

In terms of context and input, the academic staff in higher education institutions in Cyprus demonstrates high awareness, competence, and familiarity with the significance and importance that technology has in the ERT landscape, mainly on how to minimise and resolve challenges and risks, and on how to ensure the required pedagogical quality in distance education. It is evidenced that the vast majority of academics were ready to implement ERT strategies due to their experience in distance teaching and their expertise with online teaching tools.

The research has several practical implications. In general, it presents a variety of actions that can be implemented as a response to remote teaching. ERT that entered our lives with the Covid-19 pandemic outbreak, provided an understanding of the academics' role in distance education. The findings of this research present valuable information relating to the key challenges in remote teaching and offer academics in higher education recommendations on how to implement ERT. It has been revealed that academics should not only develop their teaching skills and competencies to maintain their readiness for such unforeseen events in the future but also increase the digital awareness that will enable them to retain their efficiency and effectiveness during routine education cycles. The use of technology in higher education is inevitable and distance education may become a vital sustainability component in the education ecosystem.

The findings of this research certainly help to improve the business of education. The Covid-19 crisis marked the first mass attempt of ERT in education. Institutions should utilise these experiences, delineate the several risks and challenges, and prepare a detailed systematised framework for any future crises, including those elements that satisfy the pedagogical requirements of the broad educational system. Since variables such as technology access, academics' role, curriculum and content, educational goals, etc. constantly change, this dynamic process should not only involve and consider the institutions and their academics but also integrate every other stakeholder involved in remote education.

Additionally, the findings of this study provide the foundation for general application/adaptation. Practitioners [institutions and educators] in other education stages can apply or adopt several of the study's elements to assess their readiness in emergencies and crises.

Finally, regulators and policy-makers may evaluate the findings of this study, assess the readiness of the academics in higher education institutions and develop guidelines and processes for enhancing remote teaching. Establishing a standardised National Emergency Remote Teaching plan, will minimise future risks and challenges and protect pedagogy.

RESEARCH LIMITATIONS

Even though this study contributes in several ways, some limitations exist and need to be identified. First, the research was conducted during the response to the Covid-19 crisis in 2020. At a time when people were experiencing unprecedented situations and intensely emotional and psychological alternations. Uncertainty and fear may have influenced their decisions and answers, as well as how they experienced the implementation of ERT.

The second limitation is inherent to the very nature of the method and the instrument that has been employed, which, as with all methodologies, carries some limitations. The study adopted the quantitative research approach and gathered information through an online survey. Even though quantitative research receives more responses and gathers data faster, still there is always the possibility that contributors may misunderstand the questions and give incorrect answers that undermine the survey results. Moreover, the fact that the research adopted the Likert five scale may have failed to measure the true attitudes of respondents. Their answers could be influenced by the previous questions, or they may heavily focus on one response side, avoiding choosing the extreme options on the scale and remaining neutral.

Lastly, this study involved a relatively small sample size, and this lessens its power and complicates the prospect of generalising the results. However, although the study sample may not represent the general population, still the findings reveal a clear overview of the research problem and provide practical insights.

FURTHER RESEARCH DIRECTIONS

This book chapter provides the groundwork for assessing the readiness of academics in higher education in Cyprus. The research findings create the urge for re-examining the readiness of the academic staff in higher education institutions in Cyprus, in a post-covid environment, in order to compare the results and draw valuable conclusions. Additionally, researchers may conduct analogous studies in higher education in Cyprus involving other stakeholders such as students, administrative staff, etc., to evaluate their readiness for shifting the instructional mode from face-to-face to emergency remote teaching during the Covid-19 pandemic outbreak and identify whether they obtained specific skills to overcome this challenge. The results of such studies can be part of a general assessment of the readiness of higher education in Cyprus to respond to emergencies.

Finally, similar studies may be conducted in other education stages [i.e., primary, and secondary education] to examine the characteristics, challenges, and risks from the interruption of education due to the Covid-19 pandemic outbreak and delineate the educators' readiness and response to ERT.

REFERENCES

Abaci, S., Robertson, J., Linklater, H., & McNeill, F. (2021). Supporting school teachers' rapid engagement with online education. *Educational Technology Research and Development*, *69*(1), 29–34. doi:10.100711423-020-09839-5 PMID:33052183

Aithal, P., & Aithal, S. (2016). Impact of on-line education on higher education system. *International Journal of Engineering Research and Modern Education*, *1*(1), 225–235.

Al-Azawei, A., Parslow, P., & Lundqvist, K. (2016). Barriers and opportunities of e-learning implementation in Iraq: A case of public universities. *The International Review of Research in Open and Distributed Learning*, *17*(5), 126–146. doi:10.19173/irrodl.v17i5.2501

Al-Qahtani, A., & Higgins, S. (2013). Effects of traditional, blended and e-learning on students' achievement in higher education. *Journal of Computer Assisted Learning*, *29*(3), 220–234. doi:10.1111/j.1365-2729.2012.00490.x

Anthony, B. Jnr, & Noel, S. (2021). Examining the adoption of emergency remote teaching and virtual learning during and after COVID-19 pandemic. *International Journal of Educational Management*, *35*(6), 1136–1150. doi:10.1108/IJEM-08-2020-0370

Appiah, M., & Van Tonder, F. (2018). E-Assessment in Higher Education: A Review. *International Journal of Business Management and Economic Research*, *9*(6), 1454–1460.

Barbierato, E., Campanile, L., Gribaudo, M., Iacono, M., Mastroianni, M., & Nacchia, S. (2021). Performance evaluation for the design of a hybrid cloud-based distance synchronous and asynchronous learning architecture. *Simulation Modelling Practice and Theory*, *109*, 102303. doi:10.1016/j.simpat.2021.102303

Basilaia, G., & Kvavadze, D. (2020). Transition to online education in schools during a SARS-CoV-2 coronavirus (COVID-19) pandemic in Georgia. *Pedagogical Research*, *5*(4), 1–9. doi:10.29333/pr/7937

Baum, S., & McPherson, M. (2019). The human factor: The promise & limits of online education. *Daedalus*, *148*(4), 235–254. doi:10.1162/daed_a_01769

Beaunoyer, E., Dupéré, S., & Guitton, M. J. (2020). COVID-19 and digital inequalities: Reciprocal impacts and mitigation strategies. *Computers in Human Behavior*, *111*, 106424. doi:10.1016/j.chb.2020.106424 PMID:32398890

Behera, S. (2013). E-and M-Learning: A comparative study. *International Journal on New Trends in Education and Their Implications*, *4*(3), 65–78.

Berg, G., & Simonson, M. (2016). *Distance learning*. Encyclopedia Britannica.

Bhadri, G. N., & Patil, L. R. (2022). Blended Learning: An Effective Approach for Online Teaching and Learning. *Journal of Engineering Education Transformations*, *35*, 53–60.

Biggs, J., & Tang, C. (2011). *Teaching for quality learning at university* (4th ed.). McGraw-Hill.

Bozkurt, A., & Sharma, R. (2020). Emergency remote teaching in a time of global crisis due to CoronaVirus pandemic. *Asian Journal of Distance Education*, *15*(1), i–vi.

Bozkurt, A., Jung, I., Xiao, J., Vladimirschi, V., Schuwer, R., Egorov, G., Lambert, S., Al-Freih, M., Pete, J., Olcott, D. Jr, & Rodes, V. (2020). A global outlook to the interruption of education due to COVID-19 pandemic: Navigating in a time of uncertainty and crisis. *Asian Journal of Distance Education*, *15*(1), 1–126.

Burns, M. (2011). *Distance education for teacher training: modes, models, and methods*. Education Development Center-EDC.

Carey, K. (2016). *The end of college: Creating the future of learning and the university of everywhere*. Riverhead Books.

Chang, H., & Windeatt, S. (2016). Developing collaborative learning practices in an online language course. *Computer Assisted Language Learning*, *29*(8), 1271–1286. doi:10.1080/09588221.2016.1274331

Cooke, H., Lane, A., & Taylor, P. (2018) Open by degrees: a case of flexibility or personalization? In Enhancing Education Through Open Degree Programs and Prior Learning Assessment. IGI Global. doi:10.4018/978-1-5225-5255-0.ch008

Cyprus Ministry of Education, Culture, Sport and Youth. (2012). Higher Education in Cyprus. Department of Higher and Tertiary Education, MOEC: Nicosia: PIO

Dakowska, D. (2019). *Decentring European higher education governance: The construction of expertise in the Bologna Process*. Routledge. doi:10.4324/9781351209557-5

Danchikov, E. A., Prodanova, N. A., Kovalenko, Y. N., & Bondarenko, T. G. (2021). Using different approaches to organizing distance learning during the COVID-19 pandemic: Opportunities and disadvantages. *Linguistics and Culture Review*, *5*(S1), 587–595. doi:10.21744/lingcure.v5nS1.1444

Demetriou, L., Keramioti, L., & Hadjicharalambous, D. (2021). Examining the Relationship between Distance Learning Processes and University Students' Anxiety in Times of COVID-19. *European Journal of Social Sciences Studies*, *6*(2), 123–141. doi:10.46827/ejsss.v6i2.1012

Freeman, A., Becker, S., & Cummins, M. (2017). *The NMC/CoSN Horizon Report*. The New Media Consortium and Consortium for School Networking.

Gamage, S. H., Ayres, J. R., & Behrend, M. B. (2022). A systematic review on trends in using Moodle for teaching and learning. *International Journal of STEM Education*, *9*(1), 1–24. doi:10.118640594-021-00323-x PMID:35096513

Grytsenko, I., Borysenko, N., Sydorenko, N., Vashchuk, V., & Valuieva, I. (2022). Higher education institution: Distance learning and modern communicative opportunities. *Review of Education, 10*(1), e3318. doi:10.1002/rev3.3318

Hadjicharalambous, D., Demetriou, L., & Erotocritou, K. (2021). Exploring the quality of life and psychological symptoms of university students in Cyprus during the Covid-19 pandemic. *Journal of Social Science Research, 17*, 2321–1091.

Hodges, C., Moore, S., Lockee, B., & Trust, T. B. A. (2020). The difference between emergency remote teaching and online learning. *EDUCAUSE Review, 27*(1), 1–9.

Howells, K. (2018). *The future of education and skills: education 2030: the future we want, OECD*. DES.

Huber, S. G., & Helm, C. (2020). COVID-19 and schooling: Evaluation, assessment and accountability in times of crises-reacting quickly to explore key issues for policy, practice and research with the school barometer. *Educational Assessment, Evaluation and Accountability, 32*(2), 237–270. doi:10.100711092-020-09322-y PMID:32837626

Iberahim, H. (2021). Designing online and distance learning: Aid pedagogical approach for creative and critical thinking course. *The Insight Journal.*

Johnson, A., Jacovina, M., Russell, D., & Soto, C. (2016). Challenges and solutions when using technologies in the classroom. In *Adaptive Educational Technologies for Literacy Instructions.l* (pp. 13–30). Routledge. doi:10.4324/9781315647500-2

Jurs, P., & Kulberga, I. (2021). Pedagogical challenges in Distance Learning during COVID-19 conditions–Experience of Latvia. *World Journal on Educational Technology: Current Issues, 13*(4), 947–955. doi:10.18844/wjet.v13i4.6278

Kafa, A., & Pashiardis, P. (2020). *Coping with the Global Pandemic COVID-19 Through the Lenses of the Cyprus Education System*. CCEAM.

Kapsargina, S., Shmeleva, Z., & Olentsova, J. (2019). *The use of LMS-MOODLE in the implementation of a point-rating system of evaluation in the discipline "Foreign language"*. 19th International Multidisciplinary Scientific GeoConference SGEM.

Karageorgos, C., Kriemadis, A., Travlos, A., & Kokaridas, D. (2021). Planning and Implementing Total Quality Management In Education: The Case Of Cyprus. *International Journal of Educational Management and Innovation, 2*(1), 1–12. doi:10.12928/ijemi.v2i1.2627

Kebede, A., & Bhattacharya, S. (2022) Student Engagement Awareness Dashboard for Asynchronous E-learning Environment. ICT Systems and Sustainability, 737-749. doi:10.1007/978-981-16-5987-4_74

Kentnor, H. (2015). Distance education and the evolution of online learning in the United States. *Curriculum and Teaching Dialogue, 17*(1), 21-34.

Koutselini, M. (2019). *Strengthening Institutions for Quality Assurance - Seminar on Quality Assurance of Distance Learning (E-Learning) Programs of Study*. Cyprus Ministry of Education, Culture, Sport and Youth.

KPMG. (2020). *Cyprus Education sector - Trends, challenges and opportunities*. KPMG Limited.

Lay, C., Allman, B., Cutri, R., & Kimmons, R. (2020) Examining a Decade of Research in Online Teacher Professional Development. Frontiers in Education, 5, 167.

Liguori, E., & Winkler, C. (2020). From offline to online: Challenges and opportunities for entrepreneurship education following the COVID-19 pandemic. *Sage (Atlanta, Ga.)*, *3*(4), 346–351. doi:10.1177/2515127420916738

Mahlangu, V. (2018). *The good, the bad, and the ugly of distance learning in higher education*. Trends in E-learning. doi:10.5772/intechopen.75702

Martin, S., & Trang, M. (2018). Creating Personalized Learning Using Aggregated Data from Students' Online Conversational Interactions in Customized Groups. Learning Engineering for Online Education, 144-165.

Means, B., Bakia, M., & Murphy, R. (2014). *What research tells us about where, when and how*. Routledge. doi:10.4324/9780203095959

Melanthiou, Y., Thrassou, A., & Vrontis, D. (2017). A value-based transcription of student choices into higher education branding practices. *Global Business and Economics Review*, *19*(2), 121–136. doi:10.1504/GBER.2017.082574

Meletiou-Mavrotheris, M., Mavrou, K., & Rebelo, P. V. (2021). The Role of Learning and Communication Technologies in Online Courses' Design and Delivery: A Cross-National Study of Faculty Perceptions and Practices. *Frontiers in Education*, *11*, 1–17. doi:10.3389/feduc.2021.558676

Ministry of Education, Culture, Sports and Youth. (2020). *Annual Report 2020*. Republic of Cyprus.

Ministry of Education, Culture, Sports, and Youth. (2022). *Higher Education Statistics*. Republic of Cyprus.

Mohmmed, A. O., Khidhir, B. A., Nazeer, A., & Vijayan, V. J. (2020). Emergency remote teaching during Coronavirus pandemic: The current trend and future directive at Middle East College Oman. *Innovative Infrastructure Solutions*, *5*(3), 1–11. doi:10.100741062-020-00326-7

Nisiforou, E. A., Kosmas, P., & Vrasidas, C. (2021). Emergency remote teaching during Covid-19 pandemic: Lessons learned from Cyprus. *Educational Media International*, *58*(2), 1–7. doi:10.1080/09523987.2021.1930484

Office of the Law Commissioner. (2014). *The Institutions of Tertiary Education Laws 1996 To 2013*. Printing Office of The Republic of Cyprus.

Pakhomova, T. O., Komova, O. S., Belia, V. V., Yivzhenko, Y. V., & Demidko, E. V. (2021). Transformation of the pedagogical process in higher education during the quarantine. *Linguistics and Culture Review*, *5*(S2), 215–230. doi:10.21744/lingcure.v5nS2.1341

Palvia, S., Aeron, P., Gupta, P., Mahapatra, D., Parida, R., Rosner, R., & Sindhi, S. (2018). Online education: Worldwide status, challenges, trends, and implications. *Journal of Global Information Technology Management*, *21*(4), 233–241. doi:10.1080/1097198X.2018.1542262

Perveen, A. (2016). Synchronous and asynchronous e-language learning: A case study of virtual university of Pakistan. *Open Praxis*, *8*(1), 21–39. doi:10.5944/openpraxis.8.1.212

Picciano, A. (2017). Theories and frameworks for online education: Seeking an integrated model. *Online Learning*, *21*(3), 166–190. doi:10.24059/olj.v21i3.1225

Rinekso, A. and Muslim, A. (2020) Synchronous online discussion: Teaching English in higher education amidst the covid-19 pandemic. *Journal of English Educators Society, 5*(2), 155-162.

Salehi, H., Shojaee, M., & Sattar, S. (2015). Using E-Learning and ICT courses in educational environment: A review. *English Language Teaching*, *8*(1), 63–70.

Samaniego-Erazo, G., Esteve-González, V., & Vaca, B. (2015). Teaching and Learning in digital worlds: strategies and issues in higher education. In M. B. Mercè Gisbert (Ed.), *Teaching and Learning in Digital World: Strategies and Issues in Higher Education* (pp. 129–136). Publicacions Universitat Rovira.

Sariyalcinkaya, A. D., Altun, E., & Erümit, A. K. (2022). Managing Distance Learning Systematically: The Change of the LMS and Virtual Classroom Paradigm. In *Handbook of Research on Managing and Designing Online Courses in Synchronous and Asynchronous Environments* (pp. 352–379). IGI Global. doi:10.4018/978-1-7998-8701-0.ch018

Saykili, A. (2018). Distance education: Definitions, generations and key concepts and future directions. *International Journal of Contemporary Educational Research*, *5*(1), 2–17.

Schneider, S. L., & Council, M. L. (2021). Distance learning in the era of COVID-19. *Archives of Dermatological Research*, *313*(5), 389–390. doi:10.100700403-020-02088-9 PMID:32385691

Shohel, M. M. C., Shams, S., Ashrafuzzaman, M., Alam, A. S., Al Mamun, M. A., & Kabir, M. M. (2022). Emergency remote teaching and learning: Digital competencies and pedagogical transformation in resource-constrained contexts. In *Handbook of Research on Asian Perspectives of the Educational Impact of COVID-19* (pp. 175–200). IGI Global. doi:10.4018/978-1-7998-8402-6.ch011

Simonson, M., Zvacek, S., & Smaldino, S. (2019). *Teaching and Learning at a Distance: Foundations of Distance Education* (7th ed.). IAP Information Age Publishing.

Smith, V., & Darvas, J. (2017). Encouraging Student Autonomy through Higher Order Thinking Skills. *Journal of Institutional Research*, *6*(1), 29–34. doi:10.9743/JIR.2017.5

Spante, M., Hashemi, S., Lundin, M., & Algers, A. (2018) Digital competence and digital literacy in higher education research: Systematic review of concept use. Cogent Education, 5(1).

Srivastava, P. (2019). Advantages & disadvantages of e-education & e-learning. *Journal of Retail Marketing & Distribution Management*, *2*(3), 22–27.

Subekti, A. (2021). Covid-19-triggered online learning implementation: Pre-service English teachers' beliefs. *Metathesis: Journal of English Language, Literature, and Teaching*, *4*(3), 232–248. doi:10.31002/metathesis.v4i3.2591

Tackie, H. N. (2022). (Dis)Connected: Establishing Social Presence and Intimacy in Teacher-Student Relationships During Emergency Remote Learning. *AERA Open*, *8*. Advance online publication. doi:10.1177/23328584211069525

Taladriz, C. C. (2019) Technology to empower relationships, interactions and emotions in the classroom. *2019 IEEE Global Engineering Education Conference*, 1493-1498. 10.1109/EDUCON.2019.8725076

Traxler, J. (2018). Distance learning-Predictions and possibilities. *Education Sciences*, *8*(1), 35. doi:10.3390/educsci8010035

Tsiakkiros, A., & Pashiardis, P. (2002). Strategic planning and education: The case of Cyprus. *International Journal of Educational Management*, *16*(1), 6–17. doi:10.1108/09513540210415505

Van de Vord, R., & Pogue, K. (2012). Teaching time investment: Does online really take more time than face-to-face? *International Review of Research in Open and Distributed Learning*, *13*(3), 132–146. doi:10.19173/irrodl.v13i3.1190

Xu, D., & Jaggars, S. (2011). The effectiveness of distance education across Virginia's community colleges: Evidence from introductory college-level math and English courses. *Educational Evaluation and Policy Analysis*, *33*(3), 360–377. doi:10.3102/0162373711413814

Yamagata-Lynch, L. C. (2014). Blending Online Asynchronous and Synchronous Learning. *International Review of Research in Open and Distributed Learning*, *15*(2), 189–212. doi:10.19173/irrodl.v15i2.1778

Chapter 17

The COVID-19 Pandemic and How Brazilian Organizations Faced Its Challenges:
From Remote Employee Behavior to Innovation Using Agile Management

Bruno Luiz Bucci Bandeira
Pontifícia Universidade Católica de São Paulo, Brazil

Caio Eduardo Doná Araújo
Pontifícia Universidade Católica de São Paulo, Brazil

Jonas William Barros Godoy
Pontifícia Universidade Católica de São Paulo, Brazil

João Pinheiro de Barros Neto
iD https://orcid.org/0000-0002-5680-6658
Pontifícia Universidade Católica de São Paulo, Brazil

ABSTRACT

The COVID-19 pandemic brought many challenges to people, organizations, and governments, and businesses were impacted by social isolation measures and falling consumption. To cope with this situation, it was not only necessary to send the workforce out of offices into remote working or telecommuting, but it was also imperative to innovate to retain customers. In this context, this exploratory study was elaborated to better understand teleworking, workers' behavior, and the usefulness of agile management methods to innovate and help companies stay competitive in the Brazilian scenario. The chapter discusses the results of three surveys conducted during the most critical period of the pandemic, which showed that working from home, despite its great economic and social advantages, needs the companies' attention to employees' potential health problems, and that companies that adopted agile management earlier were able to adapt and innovate faster to overcome the challenges imposed by the pandemic.

DOI: 10.4018/978-1-6684-6762-6.ch017

INTRODUCTION

Given the scenario imposed by the SARS-COV-2 pandemic, popularly known as Coronavirus in 2020, several sectors of the global economy were forced to review their work models, making several adjustments to overcome the sudden urgent challenges to minimize as much as possible the negative impacts generated by the sanitary security measures around the world.

After the WHO (World Health Organization) had declared the outbreak of the new coronavirus pandemic, which is a local epidemic that spreads across countries and continents (WHO, 2020), one of the actions taken by Brazilian states and municipalities in March 2020 was social isolation, which according to the Ministry of Health aims to ensure the maintenance of health services (Brazil, 2020).

These actions limited the circulation of people on the streets and non-essential services had to close their doors for months. This restriction made companies face several changes and uncertainties, such as the fact that many of them were forced to adopt the remote work model (Picchi, 2020).

The context of changes and uncertainties in the business environment intensified during the COVID-19 period of social isolation in Brazil in 2020, where companies were unable to open their doors for months due to state and local government decrees passed in order to prevent a collapse in the country's health system.

Moreover, due to the exponential advance of technology and market dynamism, companies need to adapt more quickly to changes and trends to remain innovative and competitive in order to provide better experiences for consumers.

In Brazil, the adoption of teleworking gained strength in mid-March 2020 following the measures imposed by municipal and federal governments. The adoption of this model was followed by the most diverse sectors of society, with emphasis on the service and education sectors.

According to research conducted by the Institute of Management Foundation (Fundação Instituto de Administração, FIA) between April 14 and 29, 2020 on large, medium, and small Brazilian companies, 94% of these organizations stated that employees' performance working remotely met or exceeded their expectations. However, about 70% of these companies reported that they intend to terminate or partially maintain this work model when the pandemic ends (Lazaretti, 2020).

The difficulties encountered in the compulsory implementation of remote work ranged from regulatory issues in markets such as the financial, where bank secrecy is very important, to the shortage of equipment acquisition such as notebooks and peripheral devices. (Saraiva & Boas, 2020).

As months passed, with technological issues mitigated and the health agencies predicting the extension of social isolation, various aspects related to human relationships began to receive more attention.

In this scenario of rapid change, uncertainty, and the need for quick answers, it becomes necessary to perform flawless process management because in a fast-paced business environment filled with uncertainty and change, project management can feel more like running an obstacle course. People have to run to overcome internal and external challenges by changing direction frequently. But acting quickly to keep projects aligned with shifting business priorities does not mean acting hastily. What companies need, especially their project and process management teams, is agility (Chin, 2004).

Considering this situation, the objective of this study is to identify and understand the key factors that influenced the adaptation and productivity by adopting teleworking and agile project management, as well as the behaviors of people who started working remotely due to the COVID-19 pandemic.

BACKGROUND

Teleworking

According to Chahad (2002), until the late 1970s, the traditional work model was based on searching for employment and financial stability. A new rationale emerged from the competition between global markets, giving rise to new ways of working.

Over the last decades, technological advances in the most diverse fields of knowledge, together with global markets interconnectivity, have provided various industries with a level of competitiveness never seen before.

Thus, Lima and Soares (2014) point out that several organizations, in order to maintain and expand their productive capabilities, resort to available technologies to attract and retain talent that is often physically distant from the organization.

Meanwhile, however, the difficulties arising from the digital work model transcend the technological universe and permeate human relationships. Levasseur (2013) highlights that some of the challenges of remote work or telecommuting are building trust relationships among team members and overcoming social distancing.

The option of working remotely or telecommuting gives workers, among other possibilities, the opportunity to access previously unviable labor markets, closer geographic proximity to their families, and the chance of performing several other activities due to the elimination of commute time.

Among the disadvantages of remote work, social isolation can lead to the loss of organizational culture and the onset of psychological illnesses (Estrada, 2010).

From an organizational point of view, some of the advantages of adopting a remote work model are the reduction and eventually the elimination of costs related to facilities and the possibility of hiring professionals worldwide (Johns & Gratton, 2013).

The work from home model is characterized by the performance of professional activities in the worker's home environment, who may or may not depend on the use of technology.

According to Mendonça (2010) the nomenclature "home office" should only refer to the residential environment. He also reinforces the fact that work activities have a greater or lesser degree of flexibility in starting and ending times.

In several locations around the globe, teleworking has established as an effective work model and is considered to be in line with technological advances so as to be widely adopted over the coming decades (Rasmussen & Corbett, 2008; Ward & Shabha, 2001).

Before we entered the 21st century, Mello (1999) already stated that working from home gives employees more flexibility in terms of routine and schedules, and this favorable point has led diverse companies to adopt the model as a way to retain talents. This becomes even more valid in a post-pandemic context.

For Duarte (2005) working from home has become more effective, both from the organizational point of view and from the workers' point of view, because they are able to maximize their production potential without using a different physical space, thus reducing organizational costs.

Telecommuting did not emerge during the pandemic, the coronavirus only accelerated or forced its adoption, so much so that Raghuram et al. (1998) pointed out that the success of virtual work depends on workers' resilience in this change of work model, in such a way that distance is no longer an obstacle for the employee-employer relationship.

Raghuram et al. (2001) propose a division in the relationship between worker and employer into two categories: structural and relational. In structural relations we have to consider work independence, which is the autonomy generated by technological advances that have allowed workers to perform their activities and interactions with other organization members online without generating production losses. In this category is also included the clarity of appraisal criteria, fundamental to maintain the rights and responsibilities of workers in both face-to-face and remote modalities (Kurland & Egan, 1999).

In the relational category we mention interpersonal and organizational trust that is related to the trust process established between workers and employers. It refers to employees' sense of belonging to the organization. For Baumeister & Leary (1995) as well as for Raghuram et al. (2001) this feeling is what maintains the employee's desire to remain in the organization.

According to Ferreira Júnior (2000), cost reduction can be highlighted as a benefit of this work-from-home model. This advantage benefits not only the worker but also the employer since there is a reduction of expenses related to commuting and to the company's office spaces.

The increase in productivity is explained by the increase in autonomy, thus increasing the workers' sense of self-confidence regarding their abilities.

The increase in productivity is also related to working environments and working hours, since tele-commuting enables employees to start their workday when they feel a higher level of disposition.

Among the disadvantages, Rosenfield and Alves (2011) highlight the replacement of face-to-face human relations with distance relationships, reinforcing the isolation of the worker and occasionally leading to damages mainly associated with mental health.

Fontoura and Reis (2022) discuss the increase in domestic and family violence against women during the pandemic due to the adoption of teleworking and the role of the employer in these situations.

Contact reduction with the organizational environment results in, among other things, the reduction of feedback from managers and ends up influencing the learning process, promotions, and dismissals, living up to the popular saying "out of sight, out of mind". Therefore, working from home has its pros and cons, like everything in life.

Agile Management

Drucker (1976), a visionary management guru, already pointed out in the 1970s that the new reality of companies and their demands require a review of policies that worked well during the last century, and going further, there is a need for a paradigm shift in organizations and in individuals. The author also warned that managers would have to learn to build and manage innovative organizations, that is, learn to construct and manage a human group capable of foreseeing what is coming, of transforming ideas into technology, products, and processes, willing and able to agree with the new.

One of the first industries that felt the need for a paradigm shift was software development. For a long time, this industry was ruled by a paradigm of industrial beliefs and views, such as Taylorism, where workers are not trusted to do their jobs with intelligence, autonomy, and creativity, but are expected to perform pre-defined jobs designed and planned by senior management. To grasp the idea, the industrial paradigm was getting the software development industry in a serious crisis, where only 10-20% of software projects were successful (Verheyen, 2013).

After a few years, new ideas started to emerge by observing the flaws of the industrial paradigm in the software development industry, so in February 2001 seventeen software development leaders met in Utah, United States and discussed their views on different methods and paths they were following to

Table 1. Twelve principles and four values of agile software

Principles
    1. Our highest priority is to satisfy the customer through early and continuous delivery of valuable software.
    2. Welcome changing requirements, even late in development. Agile processes harness change for the customer's competitive advantage.
    3. Deliver working software frequently, from a couple of weeks to a couple of months, with a preference to the shorter timescale.
    4. Businesspeople and developers must work together daily throughout the project.
    5. Build projects around motivated individuals. Give them the environment and support they need and trust them to get the job done.
    6. The most efficient and effective method of conveying information to and within a development team is face-to-face conversation.
    7. Working software is the primary measure of progress.
    8. Agile processes promote sustainable development. The sponsors, developers, and users should be able to maintain a constant pace indefinitely.
    9. Continuous attention to technical excellence and good design enhances agility.
    10. Simplicity--the art of maximizing the amount of work not done--is essential.
    11. The best architectures, requirements, and designs emerge from self-organizing teams.
    12. At regular intervals, the team reflects on how to become more effective, then tunes and adjusts its behavior accordingly.
Values
    • Individuals and interactions over processes and tools
    • Working software over comprehensive documentation
    • Customer collaboration over contract negotiation.
    • Responding to change over following a plan.

Source: Beck, et al (2001).

achieve better results. Each one used a different methodology, for example Scrum, eXtreme Programming, Crystal, and each one followed their own paradigm. The result of the common principles, beliefs and thoughts of these leaders and their methods was called Agile and was published as the Manifesto for Agile Software Development (Beck, et al., 2001).

Agile is not a process, method, or practice, but the collection of principles that Agile Software Development methods have in common, that is, Agile refers to the thinking and convictions expressed in the manifesto for agile software development. Agile project management is a set of principles, values, and practices that assist teams to deliver valuable products and services in a challenging environment, which results in a higher success rate when managing projects in uncertain environments due to agility. Agility is the ability to balance flexibility and stability and to both create and respond to change in order to be successful in a turbulent business environment. (Highsmith, 2004). The Manifesto for Agile software development has twelve principles, which are presented in Table 1.

Guimarães and Santos (2022) show that agile management is a current and useful option even in civil construction, a significant sector in the global industry scenario which undergoes constant transformations that increasingly demand alternatives to generate competitive advantages and present both flexibilities to react quickly to changes in the market and adaptability to respond to the challenges of the COVID-19 pandemic. The authors conclude that agile management has a high potential for development in the market, offering important benefits, such as short execution time, high quality standard of the final product, and low rate of losses and waste generated. The principles of agile project management are divided into two categories, as shown in Table 2.

Innovation is the process by which novel ideas become reality. Thus, an innovative company is one that stimulates and channels efforts to transform an idea into a product, a process, a company, or a technology, that is, the company's capacity for innovation is proportional to the effort of the stimulus it makes to transform an idea into reality (Barbieri, 2009).

Table 2. Categories and principles of agile project management

	Principle
	Deliver value to the customer.
Clients and Products	Employ iterative, feature-based deliverables.
	Pursue technical excellence.
	Encourage exploration.
Management	Form adaptive teams (self-organized and self-disciplined).
	Simplify.

Source: Benassi & Amaral, 2007.

Innovation and its applications in organizations and its impacts on commerce, competitive business management and the economic structure are increasing, which come from the disruptive innovations emerging mainly in information and communication technologies. This is due to the unprecedented combination of knowledge that was being developed relatively independently until recently, but that now converge thanks to the internet and cloud computing, including artificial intelligence, quantum computing, Internet of Things, big data, blockchain, robotics, virtual reality, technologies that have been converging in what we call industry 4.0 and Industrial Internet (Tigre, 2019).

Innovation can be classified as radical and incremental. Radical innovation is the development of a new product, process, or technology to break established patterns, originating new markets; on the other hand, incremental innovation is considered the introduction of some improvement in an already existing product, not originating new markets (Dosi et al, 1988).

Incremental innovation is most frequent in agile models and some of its benefits are increased efficiency and productivity, cost reduction, increased quality, and changes that broaden the applications of a product or process. Nevertheless, the innovation process is fraught with uncertainties, given that problem solutions and their consequences are unknown (Dosi et al., 1988).

Martarello (2021) studied and analyzed an informal productive business, whose practice improvement was conducted based on technological resources. The findings showed that process innovation enabled a greater productive efficiency, as well as health, safety, and hygiene in the workplace, since it has reduced costs and manufacturing time; and it has eliminated unnecessary procedures, besides promoting improvement of the ability of adapting to different customer demands.

In view of the above, agile management accelerates the introduction of innovations, which are essential to overcome market challenges and keep organizations competitive and meeting their customers' needs.

Worker's Behavior during the Pandemic

Chiavenato (2014) explains that people spend most of their time organizing a workplace that composes their habitual grounds and that the work environment is characterized by physical and material conditions as well as psychological and social conditions. Both are closely related.

However, the COVID-19 pandemic brought great challenges for people management, from a shift to a work-from-home model to mental health problems and even the coexistence of different generations of workers, a remarkable characteristic of the workforce in this second decade of the 21st century.

In this context, companies all over the world have adopted preventive measures and provided the necessary assistance to reduce COVID-19 transmission. This situation is somewhat atypical and thus required a differentiated response.

A closer look reveals how automated the lives of many people were, that is, the week began, the week ended, and on most occasions, there was no time to value what was really important, but the pandemic caused by the invisible enemy, COVID-19, led many to reflect about family, work, economy, health, and fear (Soares, 2020).

At the center of this health crisis, employees also experience fast-paced changes that result in different workdays for those who managed to keep their jobs. Distance, teleworking, and family with young or older children, a husband or wife, are now also part of the work schedule completely.

The point is that this change in most people's lives has brought about a new understanding of the family, as in the case of an employee whose wife was raising his young son and now, he is directly participating in his upbringing, seeing his son discovering the things of life and getting used to always eating at home.

On the other hand, this change of habits is also leading certain people of different generations with various disorders such as depression, stress, anxiety, weight gain, to an aggressive sanitizing behavior due to the fear of contracting this disease.

There are still people who are participating in massive clandestine parties because they cannot stand isolation or social distancing, risking transmitting the virus to others or getting sick.

Currently, companies are living a historical moment since their workforce is made up of remnants of Baby Boomers (born between 1946 and 1964), managers from Generation X (born between 1965 and 1980) and Y (born between 1981 and 1997); and they will also have to deal with the newcomers from Generation Z (born as of 1998) who are entering the labor market. This could mean new knowledge (valuable to competitiveness) coming into the organization, as well as clashes of ideas between generations (Grubb, 2018).

Thus, it is important to understand how each generation has been dealing with the challenges in work relationships imposed by the COVID-19 pandemic, for organizations to define more assertive, efficient, and effective support strategies and actions best suited to the characteristics of their workforce.

METHODS

This is an exploratory study (Futi & Bumba, 2021). The technical procedures used were bibliographical research and three surveys (Aarons, 2020), that is, there was also direct questioning by means of questionnaires to those people whose behavior was desired to be known.

The data collection instruments used were three distinct questionnaires prepared in Google Forms©, given its practicality during the entire research journey: development, distribution, response, and data compilation.

The questionnaires contained closed and open questions in relation to their objectives and were always subdivided into three sections: Research Acceptance Agreement, Sociodemographic information about the respondent and the organization, and finally Questions about the topic (teleworking, agile management and innovation, and behavior during the pandemic).

The concept of sampling according to Mattar (2012) comes from the collection of data from the surveyed population providing relevant information about the general population. In non-probability sampling, the selection of the elements of the population to compose the sample depends at least partially on the judgment of the researcher or interviewer.

In line with this, the questionnaires were sent from the social networks LinkedIn, WhatsApp, and Facebook of the researchers; therefore, non-probability sampling was used given the difficulty of data collection during the pandemic.

Respondents were asked to share the form to generate the snowball effect, that is, a form of sociocultural research that requires the use of a set of procedures and norms that enable the organization and production of knowledge to reach as many people as possible. Snowball sampling is a non-probability sampling technique used in social research, where the initial participants of a study indicate new participants who, in turn, indicate other participants and so on, until the proposed objective is reached (Vinuto, 2014).

To analyze the data obtained we used quantitative methods (Alexandre, 2021) that generated statistics (averages, percentages, etc.) with the use of Microsoft Excel©. The statistical method according to Gil (2019, p.17) "is based on the application of the statistical theory of probability and constitutes an important aid for research in social sciences".

To analyze the answers to open-ended questions, that is, qualitative data, qualitative tools were used (Américo, 2021), such as discourse analysis, content analysis and the aid of the so-called word cloud, which is nothing more than a digital graph that shows the degree of frequency of words in a text. To this end, we used the Word Cloud Generator, a free application available on the Internet, which creates word clouds in fonts of various sizes, indicating words that are more relevant and those that are less relevant in the context of this study.

We will detail each of the surveys and their specific characteristics in the following sub-items, while analyzing the collected data.

Data Analysis on Telecommuting

The questionnaire was available for respondents between September 17, 2020, and October 8, 2020, for financial and technology professionals residing in the city of Sao Paulo since these are the areas where the researchers work.

During the period when the questionnaire was open, it received 72 responses, despite reaching more than 1,000 users on both platforms; however, only 68 questionnaires/respondents were considered valid.

It is worth noting that a portion of the public approached decided not to participate in the survey under the pretext of reprisal by the organization where they work, even after being informed of the anonymity of their answers, and another portion simply did not express their opinion.

Among the public interviewed, 94% said they were working from home, which is a very high rate. Table 3 shows the amount of overtime hours reported during the remote work mode, remembering that work hours are limited in Brazil to eight hours per day (working more than that is considered overtime).

Therefore, as the Brazilian law allows for a maximum of two hours of overtime per day, that is, up to ten hours of overtime per week, according to the survey data, 40% of telecommuters exceed the legal daily limit of two hours of overtime. Table 4 presents the reasons why these workers extrapolate their working hours.

Among the main reasons that lead to overtime, the increase of activities and the excess of meetings or calls stand out, representing 72% of the total pointed out by the interviewees as the main reason.

It is worth noting that overtime due to distractions at home corresponds to only 11% of the total interviewees, which seems to indicate that the company itself needs to be more disciplined when adopt-

Table 3. Amount of overtime worked by telecommuters

No overtime	1 up to 2 hours	More than 2 and up to 5 hours	More than 5 hours
36%	24%	22%	18%

Source: research (2020).

ing this type of work. This probably comes from the insecurity of managers regarding the control of the working day and, especially, regarding the maintenance of employee productivity.

Among the respondents who work from home, 75% said that there was an increase in productivity when adopting this model, that is, the vast majority noticed that they produced more than in the company, despite working overtime.

Among the main reasons pointed out by the respondents that increased productivity (open question), the most important was the increase in focus and concentration, but the following were also mentioned a lot: time, silence, environment, and reduced commuting. These reasons allow us to infer that a quiet and welcoming environment, such as the worker's home free of distractions, contributes to the increase of focus and concentration, and that although at home there are other types of distractions, these did not interfere significantly.

The main challenges reported by the interviewees are workload increase causing the extension of the workday, often taking over leisure time. Other difficulties faced are associated with family matters. The division of the residential environment with family members also working remotely and with children in school hours triggered a series of momentary difficulties reported by the respondents, such as excessive noise and even conflicts of interest in the case of families working in competing companies.

The main benefit highlighted by teleworkers is commuting time, which often represented more than three hours a day. This time was automatically transformed into more time with the family and quality of life, enabling the respondents to perform a series of activities related to well-being, studies, and leisure. It is important to consider that one of the significant problems in big Brazilian cities is traffic and the poor quality of public transportation.

Respondents highlighted that some negative aspects of this work modality were a greater feeling of loneliness, loss of focus, and increased number of activities. The feeling of loneliness seems to be associated with the reduction of interactions with co-workers and the increased time confined in the work environment at home. Some other negative points reported deserve more attention, such as the increase in residential expenses like electricity and internet bills, often not even partially subsidized by the organization where they work, and the increase in sedentary lifestyles.

The approval for the permanent adoption of telework is showed in Table 5. It indicates that the favorability rate for the definitive institution of teleworking is higher than 70% for respondents over 30 years of age. For respondents between the ages 18 and 25 and between ages 26 and 30 the adoption rate is

Table 4. Main reason for overtime

Increase of activities	Excessive meetings	System slowdowns	Distractions at home
38%	34%	17%	11%

Source: research (2020).

Table 5. Teleworking approval rate

Age (years)	18-25	26-30	31-40	41-50	< 51
Percentage	60%	40%	81%	80%	71%

Source: research (2020).

60% and 40% respectively. The group with the lowest favorability (highest resistance) was the 26 to 30 age group and the resistance to permanent teleworking adoption was reported as being associated with a greater need for interaction with other individuals.

The research participants who are managers informed that some of the biggest challenges for the adoption of telecommuting are the monitoring and discipline of the team regarding work schedules and delivery of activities. Another aspect highlighted by them was workers' emotional imbalance, often due to family, social or professional issues.

This same group of managers pointed out that the main reasons to definitively implement telecommuting are the increase in productivity and quality of delivery of the worker. However, for about 60% of the responding managers, the ideal situation would be a hybrid work model with on-site work twice a week.

The adoption of a hybrid model, according to the managerial respondents, helps perpetuate the organization's culture, as well as contributes to greater interaction among the workers.

Data Analysis on Agile Management and Innovation

The form that contained the questions about agile management and innovation during the COVID-19 pandemic remained available during September and October 2020, obtaining 50 (fifty) valid questionnaires. Regarding the gender of the respondents, there were 31 male (62%) and 19 female (38%) participants, and all of them were working in their respective organizations when they answered the questionnaire on a telecommuting or non-telecommuting basis. Table 6 presents the distribution of respondents by company segment.

The vast majority of respondents, 74%, reported working in companies that use agile methodologies on a daily basis, which indicates the dissemination of these methodologies in organizations. Among the three largest sectors represented in the survey, more than half use them. The technology sector applies agile methodologies the most (94.12%), followed by the financial sector (83.33%) and retail (62.5%).

Table 6. Company's sector of the respondents

Sector	Percentage	Sector	Percentage
Technology	34%	Consulting	4%
Financial	24%	Insurance	4%
Retail	16%	Marketing	4%
Health	6%	Education	2%
Food	6%	Did not inform	0%

Source: research (2020).

Table 7. Agile management time of use by the sectors that mostly use it

Sector	Less than 1 year	From 1 year up to 5 years	More than 5 years
Financial	30%	50%	20%
Technology	50%	37,5%	12,5%
Retail	60%	40%	

Source: research (2020).

The respondents who work in organizations that use agile methodologies on a regular basis indicated that 43.24% of the companies started using them less than 1 year ago, 45.95% of the companies have been using the methodologies from 1 to 5 years, while 10.81% have been using agile management for more than 5 years. This allows us to infer that it is still a recent methodology.

Table 7 shows that the sector that has been using agile methodologies the longest is the financial sector. Twenty percent of the financial organizations in the sample have been using agile methods for more than 5 years and 50% from 1 to 5 years, followed by the technology sector companies with 12.5% of usage for more than 5 years and 37.5% from 1 to 5 years. Finally, sixty percent of the companies in the retail sector have been using the methodologies for less than 1 year.

It is pointed out that the vast majority of organizations (92%) had to adapt their processes, products, or services during the quarantine period.

Ninety-seven point three percent (97.3%) of the respondents who work in companies that use agile methodologies on a daily basis felt that agile project management helped their organizations to adapt better to the quarantine period.

It is noteworthy that all respondents felt that agile project management helped the companies they work for to create innovative products, processes, or service solutions during the quarantine period.

It can be seen, after analyzing the answers to closed questions, that the technology sector uses agile project management extensively and has been using this method for the longest time.

It can also be observed that the financial sector follows the technology sector in terms of agile project management time of use, followed by the retail sector, where more than half companies have been using agile for less than a year but are already reaping satisfactory results when it comes to adaptation and innovation.

The respondents were asked to freely give an example of a process, product, or service that the company adapted during the quarantine and how agile management helped in this adaptation. The answers were organized in alphabetical order in Table 8. This question did not require a mandatory answer.

The respondents were also asked to give an example of innovation in the company's processes, products, or services in which the use of agile methodologies had an influence. The answers are presented in Table 9.

It can be observed, by analyzing the answers to the open-ended questions, that the companies faced two major challenges. The first one concerns the fluidity, transparency, and organization of internal processes related to different areas. The second challenge, on the other hand, refers to the speed in which the customers' priorities and demands changed and the solutions to meet them had to emerge quickly.

Regarding the first challenge, the interaction between the different areas of the companies was hindered as employees were working remotely and some of the previously mentioned values of the agile model, highlighting the value: "People and interactions more than processes and tools" (Beck, et. al.,

Table 8. Adaptations made during the pandemic using agile methods

The expertise that used to be done in person is now done remotely.
Online scheduling.
Communication app for reaching employees in a different way than just marketing e-mail.
Communities/squads performing rituals remotely.
Digital Signature for financial transactions.
Customer Service, simpler solutions for customers.
Customer Service (two answers).
Increase in online classes.
Teleworking in teams of companies that would hardly accept this kind of work.
Teleworking, organized ceremonies, and structured Product Canvas. All gave transparency to the company.
Intensified use of Jira to meet demands from other areas and internally.
Release of system updates (two responses).
Permission to work from home for all employees.
We needed to offer new services and adapt some, so agile helped with that.
Promotion of online events.

Source: research (2020).

2001) forced organizations to develop solutions for the efficient collaboration between employees and the different areas involved in their processes; for example, the use of collaboration tools and the creation of periodic meetings to discuss problem solutions and promote continuous improvement.

With reference to the second challenge, the concern about health has made people prefer digital products and services in a short period of time. The category of customer-focused principles: delivering value to the customer, iterative feature-based delivery, and the pursuit of technical excellence (Highsmith, 2004) made companies think of innovative products that add value to their customers. Analyzing the open answers we noticed the creation of online classes, creation of apps for various purposes involving products and services.

Worker Behavior Data Analysis

The questionnaires were available in September 2020 and 247 valid responses were collected. The participants who answered the questionnaire had to be working from home. Table 6 shows the presence of four generations representatives in the sample, which are the ones that currently make up the labor market.

Table 9. Innovations made using agile methodologies

Service app (two answers).
Electronic signature of contracts.
CarDelivery Webmotors, *Troca+Troco* (change your car and receive money) Webmotors.
Integrated communities between technology and business ending the waterfall model.
Development of new services (two answers).
Facilitation of new clients because of the agile processes.
It was created a new feature in the app, which enabled the client to see the situation of the claim/policy
Virtual reality goggles.
Online courses platform.
Digital Business and Investment Platform. Focus on their UX to offer confidence and information to the customer in order to contract financial products online.

Source: research (2020).

Table 10. Distribution of participants by generation

Baby Boomers	X	Y	Z	Total
5,75%	28,74%	60,92%	4,60%	100%

Source: research (2020).

As can be seen in Table 10, only 25.5%, i.e., 63 respondents did not develop any illness, all other respondents had some disorder during the pandemic. The most frequently mentioned disorders were anxiety (49.4%), weight gain (41.3%), and stress (34.4%). This question accepted more than one answer.

Table 11. Disorders developed during the pandemic

Disorder	Percentage	Disorder	Percentage
Anxiety	49,39%	Sleep Disorders	27,53%
Stress	34,41%	Panic syndrome	2,43%
Weight gain	41,30%	Depression	7,29%
Rotins Breaking	23,89%	Burnout syndrome	0,40%
Loss of appetite	4,86%	No disorder	25,41%

Source: research (2020).

The data clearly show the strong consequences of isolation measures on the health of workers, that is, it is not only about the disease caused by the virus, but also about the impacts of disease prevention measures.

Depression affected 7.3% of respondents, of which 67% are female, twice as many as male respondents.

The respondents mostly stated (87%) that during the pandemic period they did not go to clandestine parties, but the remaining 13% reported attending such events.

Segmenting the participants who confessed to attending parties during the pandemic by region, it is observed that 61% of those who were in clandestine parties were from the state of São Paulo, 30% were from the capital, and 9% were from the coast.

Sixty four percent of the respondents said that they did not contract the virus, 31% could not give an opinion and 5% said that they did. However, the disorders and health problems indirectly caused by the pandemic, i.e., social isolation measures, reached 75% of the sample (Table 11).

The fact that people do not know whether they have contracted the virus or not (many people are asymptomatic) can be a triggering factor for anxiety, and 66% of the respondents stated that they could perform some kind of physical activity indoors, even if only partially (35%), but 34% have not been successful in performing any kind of physical activity at home.

Table 12 shows the measures taken by the respondents in the pandemic. 59.9% of them implemented social isolation, 98% hand hygiene, 98.8% used alcohol-based sanitizer, and 98.4% wore face masks, while only one person said that was not adopting any type of measure. More than one answer was accepted for this question.

Table 12. Measures taken to face the pandemic

Measures	%	Measures	%
Social isolation	59,92%	Wear face masks	98,38%
Hand hygiene	97,98	Use of alcohol-based sanitizer	98,79%
Personal hygiene (shower)	79,76	No measure	0,4%
Keeping distance	70,85	Vitamin D	0,4%
Food hygiene	69,23%	Face Shield	0,4%

Source: research (2020).

These data show a high level of awareness and engagement of the participants with prevention procedures, an auspicious finding, despite the fact that 13%, as pointed out earlier, confessed having participated in parties even though they were forbidden.

When asked about the return to normal life after vaccination, 73% of the respondents said that they believe it is positive to continue wearing masks, which seems to have become a habit, a situation to be confirmed when we return to a life considered normal.

The results show that the pandemic aggravated and strongly impacted people's health in many ways and indicate that from now on organizations should rethink their human resource management practices in order to seek proactive actions to care for the physical and mental health of their employees.

DISCUSSION

Tooze (2021) conducted a comprehensive analysis of what he termed "the coronavirus crisis." He addressed not only the crisis' impact on the world economy and geopolitics, but also its effects on science, the environment, education, culture, and individual behavior. Tooze mainly emphasized the pandemic's negative outcomes, such as closed factories, lost jobs, and widened social gaps due to remote work and learning. Humanity will likely take long to overcome such nefarious legacy.

Our data showed that, despite its social ills, the pandemic has also enabled solutions and alternatives in some way. As with all crises, adversity often brings learning opportunities and positive change. Remote work, for example, used to spark fear among managers due to insecurity around the control of productivity. With the pandemic, organizations—especially human resources (HR) departments—had no alternative but to implement remote work immediately. Within weeks, white-collar employees started working from home. Two years later, organizations and HR departments have seen a leap in people management policies, guidelines, and practices.

Much has been said about the capacity of Agile methods to transform work by bringing innovation and advancements faster and at lower costs. However, the Agile method is often implemented in a rushed, flawed manner, resulting in nervous customers, dissatisfied employees, and compromised managers (Rigby, Elk & Berez, 2020). Our study indicated that, in terms of innovation and adaptation during the pandemic, companies with a more mature application of the Agile method outperformed companies that had implemented it recently. These results suggest that the Agile method cannot be adopted merely as a trend. Instead, it must be implemented safely, step by step, so companies can avoid implementation failures arising from haste and obtain increasingly better results.

As for employee behavior, the pandemic has transformed people's routine, work, behavior, and, of course, human relations (Harari, 2020). Our study corroborates that people quickly adapted to new hygiene habits, but they have not yet been able to cope well with social isolation and their own feelings and emotions. A huge opportunity lies ahead for organizations to help their employees, regardless of which generation they are part of, to reflect on life, work, and social interaction. Our data indicated that people need more than just financial aid to set up their home offices. They also need psychological support in this moment of transition, in order to enhance gains at work (increased productivity, flexibility, autonomy, more time with family) and gains for society (less traffic, less urban pollution, social awareness). A possible imbalance between personal and professional life must be considered, since employees working remotely may have trouble managing time (as we have seen) and may exceed working hours. In this sense, it is worth investing in the development of time management skills and technologies that limit or prevent the accumulation of overtime.

SOLUTIONS AND RECOMMENDATIONS

It was verified, both through the literature and survey data, that the development and acceptance of remote work goes beyond the technological field and mostly permeates human relationships.

During the first weeks of confinement imposed by sanitary protocols, the most diverse labor organizations placed a greater focus on technological needs in order to provide in a short period of time all the necessary tools to continue their operations.

The workers that participated in the research stated that sharing the environment with other residents triggered momentary difficulties associated with household activities and the need for attention, mainly involving children and elderly people. Young workers asserted that the feeling of loneliness associated with reduced interactions was the main disadvantage of this work model.

As a counterpoint, such negative aspects are minimized when compared to the reduction of workers' commuting time to their jobs, resulting in a longer period for leisure, family, and personal development.

For managers, besides having to deal with the psychological aspects of the workers, partly affected by the imposed distance, the biggest challenge is related to the follow-up of the teams, which often results in an excessive volume of calls and conferences. In this case, manager training to lead in this new work model can bring good results and solve this difficulty.

The adoption of agile methodologies empowered organizations to face the challenges of the COVID-19 pandemic more robustly, so companies that do not yet make use of these methodologies may equip themselves to achieve relevant innovations and productivity increase since the survey results indicated that there are many benefits for organizations.

It was observed that the working-from-home model offers benefits for organizations, workers, and the entire society in several fields, from the reduction of pollutants in the atmosphere due to the lower volume of daily commuting to more time available for workers to perform activities related to leisure, well-being, or family; however, there are also some risks to workers' health.

In this sense, it is suggested that organizations seek to adopt and disseminate this work model that brings social and economic benefits without neglecting the adverse consequences to workers.

FUTURE RESEARCH DIRECTIONS

This is an exploratory study that brought several insights and greater familiarity with the issues studied, in order to make them more explicit and suggest further studies, the sample selection was non-probabilistic.

In view of the foregoing considerations, it is not possible to generalize the data, however, it is understood that this method is simple, fast, and allows us to obtain answers from a very broad spectrum of respondent profiles and in no way invalidates the results obtained; notwithstanding we recognize that other studies along the same lines are needed, but with more significant samples.

Lockdown has affected most companies, forcing them to adapt their products, processes, and services to new market dynamics and customer priorities have been redefined. The digitalization process has been accelerated with internal solutions such as teleworking, and with external ones, such as digital solutions for customers.

After we analyzed the survey results, it can be concluded that companies that have been using agile project management for more than a year have been able to adapt better and faster to new customer requirements by creating innovative solutions to satisfy their needs and have managed to keep their internal processes efficient.

Companies that have been using agile project management for less than a year or started using it during the quarantine reaped satisfactory results, but they were at a competitive disadvantage compared to those organizations that had been using these methodologies for a longer time.

Therefore, we suggest studies about how agile methodologies can be even more positive to overcome challenges, ensuring better customer satisfaction with greater competitiveness and efficiency of internal processes.

Employees working remotely not only suffered from psychological problems such as depression or anxiety, but also from weight gain. In fact, research indicates that perhaps the biggest problem to be faced by companies and HR is not only the virus itself, now that vaccines already exist, but the way our society is dealing with new demands of lockdown, homeschooling, social isolation, social distancing and spending the entire day with the people you share a house with, which requires further research because these are sensitive topics.

Thus, the results of the study suggest the need for companies to research new and diverse initiatives to help all people with anxious and depressive symptoms caused by the adoption of social isolation, especially remote employees, by offering employees solidarity and support.

It was observed that after some time, teleworking can be harmful to workers' health, causing psychological and physical problems resulting from the excessive lack of activities related to body and mind. These issues are also worthy of further study.

In view of the results, an interesting line of research is also suggested about a probable and viable work mode that would be hybrid. In such a mode, working remotely would be performed as part of a typical working day.

Such a measure could bring all the benefits mentioned, besides keeping the organizational culture and human relations strong, mitigating possible health problems both in psychological and physical aspects, but only future research will be able to effectively confirm this hypothesis.

As mentioned before, one of the first sectors to realize the need for a paradigm shift was software development and this fact was reflected in the study, that is why research into the application of agile methods in different industries is extremely promising.

Each generation of workers has its own characteristics, has suffered and is overcoming the challenges of the COVID-19 pandemic in their own way, therefore, there is a need for a thorough adjustment of generations in the organizational environment (balance); that is, companies' human resources areas can specifically research each generation in order to become a strong protagonist in a way of empowering managers to deal with their work team, technologies, and the encounter of generations, meeting an increasingly diverse labor market.

Moreover, it is understood that this type of study should be repeated throughout the pandemic and after its end by the companies to check the situation of their employees and direct more specific actions to each case.

CONCLUSION

We conclude, therefore, that the adoption of telecommuting improves the worker's performance, increasing productivity and reducing costs for the organization, and it should gain more prominence over the next few years, as long as companies do not neglect the human side of the issue.

In view of the above, by adopting a teleworking model the people management area can offer ample possibilities for improvement in work relations, quality of life and productivity, because employees working remotely not only suffered from psychological problems such as depression or anxiety, but also from weight gain.

Thus, we can think of support groups on the companies' intranet social networks and prevention programs, conversations with psychologists, guidance, tips to overcome and get past this phase, and many other relevant contents to promote workers' well-being and mental health.

The results of the study also suggest the need for companies to adopt initiatives related to agile management methodologies in order to assist the implementation of innovative solutions in a systematic way by offering their employees and customers appropriate solutions with adequate timeliness.

REFERENCES

Aarons, H. (2020). *A practical introduction to survey design: a beginner's guide*. SAGE Publications Ltd.

Alexandre, A. F. (2021). *Metodologia científica: princípios e fundamentos*. Blucher. doi:10.5151/9786555062229

Américo, B. (2021). *Método De Pesquisa Qualitativa: Analisando fora da caixa a Prática de Pesquisar Organizações*. Alta Books.

Barbieri, J. C., & Álvares, A. (2009). *Gestão de ideias para inovação contínua*. Bookman.

Baumeister, R. & Leary, M. (1995). The Need to Belong: desire for interpersonal attachments as a fundamental human motivation. *Psychological Bulletin, 3*(117), 497-529.

Beck, K. (2022). *Manifesto para Desenvolvimento Ágil de Software*. https://agilemanifesto.org/iso/ptbr/manifesto.html

Benassi, J. L., & Amaral, D. C. (2007). Gerenciamento ágil de projetos aplicados ao desenvolvimento de produto físico. *Anais Simpósio de Engenharia de Produção*. https://simpep.feb.unesp.br/anterior.php?evento=1

Brasil, Ministério da Saúde. (2020). *Brasil confirma primeiro caso da doença*. https://www.saude.gov.br/noticias/agencia-saude/46435-brasil-confirma-primeiro-caso-de-novo-coronavirus

Chahad, J. P. Z. (2002). As modalidades especiais de contratos de trabalho e o emprego flexível no Brasil. *RDT- Revista de Direito do Trabalho, 28*(106), 76-95.

Chiavenato, I. (2014). *Gestão de pessoas: o novo papel dos recursos humanos nas organizações*. Manole.

Chin, G. L. (2004). *Agile project management: how to succeed in the face of changing project requirements*. Amacon.

Dosi, G., Freeman, C., Nelson, R., Silverberg, G., & Soete, L. (1988). *Technical change and economic theory*. Printer Publisher Limited.

Drucker, P. F. (1976). *Uma era de descontinuidade*. Zahar.

Duarte, J. B. (2005). *O trabalho no domicílio do empregado: controle da jornada e responsabilidade pelo custeio dos equipamentos envolvidos*. https://migalhas.uol.com.br/depeso/12333/o-trabalho-no-domicilio-do-empregado--controle-da-jornada-e-responsabilidade

Estrada, M. M. (2010). Realidade do teletrabalho no Brasil e nos tribunais brasileiros. *Revista Direito e Liberdade*, 193-116.

Ferreira Júnior, J. C. (2000). Telecommuting: o paradigma de um novo estilo de trabalho. *Revista de Administração de Empresas*, 8-17.

Fontoura, I. H. N. da, & Reis, S. d. S. (2022). As consequências da modalidade home office às mulheres vítimas de violência doméstica e familiar e o papel do empregador. In *Anais da III Jornada de Desenvolvimento e Políticas Públicas*. Criciúma: Universidade do Extremo Sul Catarinense.

Futi & Bumba. (2021). *Metodologia de elaboração de trabalhos científicos: uma abordagem de acordo com as normas APA e ABNT*. Curitiba: CRV.

Gil, A. C. (2019). *Métodos e Técnicas de Pesquisa Social* (7th ed.). Atlas.

Grubb, V. M. (2018). *Conflito de gerações: desafios e estratégias para gerenciar quatro gerações no ambiente de trabalho*. Autêntica Business.

Guimarães, T. d. C., & Santos, B. S. M. (2022). Metodologias ágeis na construção civil: estudo de caso da construção modular off site aplicada no hospital m'boi mirim em São Paulo / agile methodologies in civil construction: a case study of offsite modular construction applied at hospital M'boi Mirin in São Paulo:.*BJD - Brazilian Journal of Development, 8*(1). doi:10.34117/bjdv8n1-143

Harari, Y. N. (2020). *Notas sobre a pandemia: e breves lições para o mundo pós-coronavírus*. Companhia das Letras.

Highsmith, J. (2004). *Agile project management: creating innovative products*. Addison-Wesley.

Johns, T., & Gratton, L. (2013). The Third Wave of Virtual Work. *Harvard Business Review*. https://hbr.org/2013/01/the-third-wave-of-virtual-work

Kurland, N. B., & Egana, T. D. (1999). Telecommuting: justice and control in the virtual organization. *Organization Science*, 500-513. https://www.jstor.org/sTable/2640368

Lazaretti, B. (2020). *94% das firmas aprovam home office, mas 70% vão encerrar ou manter em parte*. https://economia.uol.com.br/noticias/redacao/2020/07/28/94-das-empresas-aprovam-home-office-mas-75-nao-o-manterao-apos-pandemia.htm

Levasseur, R. E. (2012, April). People skills: Leading virtual teams - a change management perspective. *Interfaces*, *42*(2), 213–216. doi:10.1287/inte.1120.0634

Lima, M. A., & Soares, A. d. (May 2014). O secretário executivo e a tecnologia da informação: um estudo sobre a utilização de recursos tecnológicos pelos profissionais da cidade de Belém/PA. *Revista de Gestão e Secretariado*, *5*(2), 138-157. https://www.revistagesec.org.br/secretariado/article/view/254

Martarello, R. de A., & Ferro, D. (2021). Entrepreneurship and innovation in informal productive enterprises: Development of process innovation in a floral arrangement company. *Iberoamerican Journal of Entrepreneurship and Small Business, 11*(1). doi:10.14211/ibjesb.e1985

Mattar, F. N. (2012). *Pesquisa de Marketing: edição compacta*. Atlas.

Mello, A. (1999). *Teletrabalho (telework): o trabalho em qualquer lugar e em qualquer hora*. Qualitymark.

Mendonça, M. (2010). *A inclusão dos home offices no setor residencial no município de São Paulo*. Tese de Doutorado: Curso de Tecnologia da Arquitetura, Faculdade de Arquitetura e Urbanismo, Universidade de São Paulo. São Paulo. Accessed Sep. 2021, available at https://www.teses.usp.br/teses/disponiveis/16/16132/tde-25112010-145910/pt-br.php

OMS, Organização Mundial da Saúde. (2020). *OMS declara emergência de saúde pública de importância internacional por surto de novo coronavírus*. Fonte: OPAS Organização Pan-Americana de Saúde: https://www.paho.org/pt/news/30-1-2020-who-declares-public-health-emergency-novel-coronavirus

Picchi, F. (2020). *Home office forçado vai mudar a forma como trabalhamos nas empresas*. Época Negócios Online. https://epocanegocios.globo.com/colunas/Enxuga-Ai/noticia/2020/04/home-office-forcado-vai-mudar-forma-como-trabalhamos-nas-empresas.html

Raghuram, S. (1998). Telework: managing distances in a connected world. *Strategy Business*. https://www.strategy-business.com/article/9530?gko=f82ad

Raghuram, S. (2001). Factors contributing to virtual work adjustment. *Journal of Management*, 383-405. https://www.researchgate.net/publication/228751940_Factors_contributing_to_virtual_work_adjustment

Rasmussen, E., & Corbett, G. (2008). Why Isn't Teleworking Working? *New Zealand Journal of Employment Relations*, 20-32. http://www.nzjournal.org/33(2)Rasmussen.pdf

Rigby, D., Elk, S., & Berez, S. (2020). *Ágil do jeito certo: transformação sem caos*. Benvirá.

Rosenfield, C. L., & Alves, D. A. (2011). Autonomia e trabalho informacional: o teletrabalho. *Dados*, *54*(1), 207-233. https://www.scielo.br/scielo.php?script=sci_arttext&pid=S0011-52582011000100006&lng= en&nrm=iso

Saraiva, A., & Boas, B. V. (2020). Com quarentena e dólar, notebook tem maior alta de preço em 7 anos. *Valor Econômico Online*. https://valor.globo.com/empresas/noticia/2020/07/20/com-quarentena-e-dolar-notebook-tem-maior-alta-de-preco-em-7-anos.ghtml

Soares, F. (2020). Pandemia expõe as fragilidades do nosso sistema de avaliação. *Revista Educação Online*. RFM. Accessed 24 Jan. 2022, available at https://revistaeducacao.com.br/2020/11/03/avaliacao-chico-soares/

Tigre, P. B. (2019). *Gestão da inovação: uma abordagem estratégica, organizacional e de gestão de conhecimento*. Atlas.

Verheyen, G. (2019). Scrum: a pocket guide. Hertogenbosch: Van Haren Publishing.

Vinuto, J. (2014). A amostragem em bola de neve na pesquisa qualitativa: um debate em aberto. *Temáticas*, 203–220.

Ward, N., & Shaba, G. (2001). Teleworking: an assessment of sociopsychological factors. *Facilities*, *19*(1), 61-71. https://www.emerald.com/insight/content/doi/10.1108/02632770110362811/full/html

Chapter 18
Innovations in the Service Industry During the COVID-19 Pandemic:
The Case of Japan

Mitsunori Hirogaki
ⓘ https://orcid.org/0000-0002-0215-2011
Kyushu University, Japan

ABSTRACT

This chapter investigates the impact of the COVID-19 pandemic on the Japanese service sector and the resulting innovations to manage and respond to the difficult situation. Specifically, this study illustrates how e-commerce is emerging as a leading channel for retailers, examines the ethical awareness of both businesses and consumers, and studies the new business models resulting from this trend. Based on several case studies, this study examines the service sector's response to a series of disasters, the cultural background of consumers, and age-long corporate cultures. Additionally, the future direction of innovation in Japan's service sector is discussed and forecasted.

INTRODUCTION

The COVID-19 pandemic had a serious impact on both human lives and the society and economy worldwide. The various recommendations and measures introduced by governments across the world to prevent the spread of the infection had adversely affected the service sectors.

On November 16, 2021, Japan officially recorded 13,700 infections and 146 deaths per million population (Worldometer, 2021). The economy was severely crippled during this time. A government survey reported that Japan's Gross Domestic Product (GDP) shrank by 27.8% during April–June 2020 compared with that during April–June 2019. This was the worst economic loss experienced in the past 50 years. The service sector accounted for nearly 60% of this loss because the country had been inten-

DOI: 10.4018/978-1-6684-6762-6.ch018

sively investing in the service sector in preparation for the 2020 Summer Olympics and Paralympics and trying to attract s many foreign tourists to Japan but failed because of the immigration restrictions.

The plight of the service sector in several countries was similar owing to government recommendations and measures undertaken to curb the pandemic(Aldrich and Yoshida,2020; Konishi, et al., 2021; Shanka & Menebo,2022). However, the policy characteristics in Japan was exceptional. While the national government declared a state of emergency in response to the pandemic, this was sheer recommendations only to the service sector; thus, there are no legal restrictions(Aldrich and Yoshida,2020; Konishi, et al., 2021).

Therefore, the service sector was not subject to legal restrictions such as lockdown and business hour restrictions practiced and imposed in other countries. The service sector rather engaged in voluntary industry initiatives to combat the infection(Konishi, et al., 2021).

Consumers were also receptive to these nonlegal measures and cooperated through self-restraint(Wakashima, et. al, 2020). Ironically, the so-called go-to travel campaign by the national government in cooperation with the travel industries was a great success(Ochi, 2021; Anzai and Nishiura, 2021). Consumers practiced minimum health protocols during this campaign, which contributed significantly to the dwindling travel industries and the regional economy(Ochi, 2021).

Consumers' cooperation went to the extent that there were a few instances of hoarding in the retail sector. Fortunately, there was no reported massive hoarding(Konishi, et al., 2021).

Few studies have attempted to understand the impact of the pandemic and other imperative factors that act as a blueprint for navigating businesses to the future. Therefore, this chapter uses numerous case studies to analyze the impact of the pandemic, empirically examines how it has been an engine of innovation in the service sector, and studies the characteristics of these innovations. This study leads to a foundation in forecasting through the changes in the service sector and provides analytical inputs to academicians, business practitioners, and policymakers.

This chapter is presented as follows. First, Section 1 briefly summarizes the outbreak and course of the COVID-19 pandemic in Japan. Next, Section 2 presents unique examples of the so-called hoarding behavior in Japan that occurred during the outbreak of the pandemic. Section 3 presents examples of e-commerce developments related to the retailing of food and daily necessities that occurred during the pandemic. Section 4 introduces a new form of purchasing, called "supportive purchasing," that emerged from the ethical awareness of businesses and consumers. Section 5 presents the conclusion.

THE SUMMARY OF THE PANDEMIC IN JAPAN: 2020–2022

Outbreak Course of the Pandemic

The first case of COVID-19 infection in Japan was confirmed on January 16, 2020, in a resident of Kanagawa Prefecture who had returned from Wuhan, China (Wakashima, et. al, 2020; Nihon Housou Kyoukai, 2020). The first confirmed death occurred on February 14, 2020. Subsequently, a second outbreak occurred in travelers and returnees from Europe and the United States.

Moreover, the cruise ship *Diamond Princess* departed Yokohama Port on January 20, 2020, stopping at Kagoshima, Hong Kong, Vietnam, Taiwan, and Okinawa, before returning to Yokohama Port on February 3, 2020. During the voyage, a passenger who disembarked in Hong Kong on January 25 began coughing on January 19–23, developed fever on January 30, and was confirmed to be positive for the new coronavirus on February 1. On February 5, the test results confirmed that the passenger was positive for COVID-19. Consequently, 14-day quarantine of the cruise ship was enforced at 7:00 a.m. on the same day. As of February 18, 2020, there were 531 confirmed cases, including 65 crew members and 466 passengers (14.3% of the total number of passengers on board as of February 5). A total of 2,404 samples were tested and 542 samples were positive (22.5%)(National Institute of Infectious Diseases, 2020).

Consumer Product Hoarding 2020 in Japan

In Japan, because of the psychological effect resulting from the health crisis, consumers hoarded products such as surgical masks and toilet tissue papers during the early part of the pandemic in 2020. According to a survey by the Consumer Affairs Agency, since March 2020, prices of food and daily necessities rose by 25%–30%. This resulted in panic buying and supply shortages. Moreover, false and misleading information on food and daily necessities had rapidly spread at almost the same time as in the United States and Sweden (Sakamoto et al, 2021).

In early February 2020, masks were reportedly sold out and were difficult to obtain at retail stores (Konishi et al., 2020). Thus, from late March, the government imposed a ban on the resale of masks.

Subsequently, there were cases of fake news from social media platforms: on February 27 and 28, 2020, samples of false information uploaded on Twitter, a popular social media platform in Japan, read: "masks and toilet tissue papers are made of the same raw materials, therefore, a serious shortage of toilet tissue papers will occur." Besides, "most toilet tissue papers are manufactured in China and since it is difficult for China to export to Japan because of the pandemic. Toilet tissue papers will likewise be in short supply." However, all toilet papers were being manufactured domestically, and thus, this information was an outright falsehood. The national and regional governments, as well as toilet tissue paper manufacturers announced that they have sufficient stocks for all Japanese and there are no shortages at all (Komori, 2021). Nevertheless, for psychological reasons, consumer hoarding continued, and therefore, these products remained in short supply and out of stock nationwide until early April 2020 when the majority began to adjust to the situation (Komori, 2021).

Interestingly, a survey by the Ministry of Internal Affairs and Communications (2021) showed that only 6.2% of those surveyed respondents believed the fake news circulated on various social media platforms. Besides, a survey by Toriumi and Lim (2021) showed that the magnitude of fake news dissemination was not significant. Surprisingly, however, those who engaged in hoarding behavior believed that the others must have been tricked into hoarding by the fake news. While they did not believe the fake news, theyacted defensively by hoarding, thus distorting the supplies of masks and toilet tissue papers.

A survey conducted by Miyaki (2021) supported the earlier result. Even during this period of panic over hoarding of some products, 90.7% of respondents indicated that they were trying to conserve the consumption of these two products, and 89.9% of respondents indicated that they did not want to focus their consumption solely on their own interests. (Miyaki, 2021).

Ministry of Internal Affairs and Communications (Ministry of Internal Affairs and Communications, 2021), Fukunaga (2020), and Ishibashi and Sekiya (2021) conducted follow-up studies on this issue.

The Increasing Online Grocery Business and Related Businesses

Online Grocery During the Pandemic

According to Nikkei MJ(2020a), more than 15% of the respondents availed online groceries in 2020, which is above the 10% average of the five years prior to 2019.

The increase in online grocery sales corroborate the aforementioned percentages, according to a Nikkei MJ(2020b) report. As cited, Tokyu Store, which operates supermarkets in the Tokyo suburbs and nearby prefectures, reportedly witnessed a 30% increase in online grocery sales from March to December 2020 compared with that in 2019, and a 15% increase in the number of online grocery services availments. Additionally, the payment per customer per transaction also increased by approximately 1,000 yen from the previous year(Nikkei MJ,2020b).

Japan's largest retailer Aeon Group operating Aeon Net Super partnered with Ocado Solution (Ocado Group, UK) in November 2019 to run an online grocery based on Ocado's technology. 2023 in the suburbs of the Tokyo metropolitan area, the largest in Japan. Aeon Net Super, with a total floor space of 43,070 square meters, plans to open a Customer Fulfillment Center (CFC) to overcome the difficulty in meeting demand due to a 60% year-on-year increase in order volume caused by the 2020 pandemic. However, it was also because online grocery sales had continued to expand by 20% per year over the past several years before the pandemic (Hirogaki,2021).

Online grocery succeeded in attracting the elderly population during the pandemic, which had long been a challenging task for online grocery retailers.

According to a survey conducted by the Distribution Economics Institute of Japan (2021) of online grocery retailers operating in the Tokyo Metropolitan Area, the older age groups were more active in availing online grocery services from April to May 2020. The consumption among the elderly sharply increased up to 192% (from 2019 data) among those in their 60s and more than doubled to as high as 210% among those in their 70s and older. In contrast, among the 30s, the consumption was 134% higher than the 2019 consumption, and among the 40s, the consumption was 130% higher than the previous year. In contrast to the 30- and 40-year-olds, whose use of online grocery has slowed since the summer of 2020, the elderly population had a comparatively higher growth than in the previous year, with those aged 70 and older continuously using the services at nearly twice that in the previous year.

Mobile Supermarket Services

Seven-Eleven Japan has been providing mobile supermarkets mainly in suburban food desert areas since 2011. As of May 2021, "Seven Anshin Otodokebin" (English name: Seven-Eleven's delivery) provided food supplements in 38 prefectures (about 80% of all prefectures) (Ryutsuu biz, 2021). The company sells approximately 150 items, including food and daily necessities, through light trucks equipped with sales equipment. The service responds to customer needs to avoid congestion, but originally targeted the elderly who lack mobility or had physical difficulties in going shopping.

These mobile supermarkets are mainly located in food deserts, which are areas where residents are inconvenienced in purchasing daily necessities and groceries (e.g., in areas where supermarkets and public transport services have been withdrawn or where the aging population has lost the means to travel to the supermarkets). The company has been conducting business in well-populated areas and is continually growing its business.

After the outbreak of the pandemic, the business expanded tremendously because of its social distance and ability to shop. According to Daiamond (2021), by 2020, the company had expanded in all regions of Japan, with an additional 671 stores and total sales of 12.14 billion yen. This is in comparison to 515 stores and total sales of 10.7 billion yen in 2019 before the pandemic, which shows a 30% increase in the number of stores and a 13% increase in total sales. The daily sales per outlet also grew from approximately 91,000 yen before the pandemic to approximately 107,000 yen. Furthermore, the number of customers visiting and spending per customer also increased, with an average of 50–60 people using each unit per day, and the average spending per customer was about 2,000 yen. This was due to an increase in the number of visitors who were willing to avoid using retail stores and to the fact that people who used to shop for the elderly, such as children of the elderly, were no longer able to do so, owing to mobility limitations caused by emergency restrictions or the risk of infection.

The expansion of these online grocery and mobile retail store businesses is based on the widespread recognition that retail stores are a basic infrastructure that supports people's daily lives, which was triggered by the earthquake and tsunami in Japan in 2011. As Ishikawa (2021) described, this recognition had led to various pre-pandemic preparations on the part of the government, the public, and retailers.

CHANGES IN THE RELATIONSHIP BETWEEN BUSINESSES AND CONSUMERS

Socially Ethical Conduct by Businesses

Miyazu (2021) described how, during the COVID-19 pandemic, companies were required to show sympathy and commitment to the consumers' burden. Similar to consumers voluntarily restricting their behavior, corporations were also required to be willing to restrict themselves and contribute something to the consumers and society.

The following are cases of this phenomenon:

After the first state of emergency was declared, major cell phone companies provided schoolchildren with free additional data capacity for studying from home.

For customers who could not go to the bank due to the state of emergency, major banks drastically reduced the fees related to online banking(Miyazu, 2021).

Major cram schools provided free learning content to all children who had to stay at home. Similarly, many publishers and game makers offered free online manga, games, and other entertainment-related products(Miyazu, 2021).

A consumer electronics manufacturer, SHARP, temporarily suspended its production line for consumer electronics and manufactured masks instead. Similarly, Toyota manufactured face shields and donated to medical organizations(Ministry of Economy, Trade and Industry, 2020; Nikkei, 2020b; Nakajima, 2020).

The Apa Hotel chain willingly accepted patients with mild symptoms and not accepted by hospitals owing to the capacity limitation (Nishinippon, 2021). Those infected by the the novel coronavirus were stigmatized, and the acceptance of infected people for quarantine was a risk that could lead to damage to the hotel's brand image (Bloomberg,2021).

SOCIALLY ETHICAL CONDUCT BY CONSUMERS: OUEN PURCHARGING (OUEN-SYOUHI)

Ouen purcharging (in Japanese, *Ouen-Syouhi*) is the compassion-led purchase of products or services to support people, companies, and communities. An example of Ouen purcharging is buying milk to support farmers during the forced school-closing period under the emergency of the COVID-19 pandemic. This would augment farmers' income at a time when they are unable to sell milk. Other examples included Furusato-nouzei (Hometown Tax Payments), a prepayment of some taxes to the city of one's choice and getting free goods in return; and voluntary consumption in support of entertainment personalities affected by the pandemic.

In a study(DoHouse,2020), consumers were interviewed about what supportive consumption means to them. The respondents described what they considered supportive consumption as follows:

"For me, Ouen is emergency support consumption which is actually born out of love. I owe Miyagi Prefecture a high sense of gratitude because I lived there for 28 years." (Female respondent, aged 30, bought local rice of Miyagi Prefecture as Ouen consumption.)

"For me, Ouen consumption is a strong statement of will. I think that by daring to buy something for a special reason, the message of 'I'm interested in it,' 'I like it,' or 'I'm paying attention to it' is more easily conveyed to the creator or seller."(Female respondent, aged 50, bought a concert ticket as Ouen consumption.).

"For me, Ouen consumption is about helping each other. Even if you can't move to the place you want to help something, you can indirectly show your support by buying things, and if you can prevent a company from going bankrupt, that would be great." (Female respondent, aged 50, bought Fukubukuro (a bag containing several goods))

Miyazu (2022) stated that, in Japan, the restriction of shopping and other behavior after the declaration of the state of emergency in April 2020 has brought a significant change in consumer recognition. Miyazu (2022) also stated that changes in consumer sentiment have been occurring long before and contributed to the change owing to factors such as the 911 terrorism act in 2001, the market crash in 2008 (known as "Re-i-man shock" in Japanese language), and the most significant impact of the Great East Japan Earthquake in 2011.

According to Noguchi et al (2021), people began valuing their security and relationships because their daily lives suddenly became extraordinary owing to the massive earthquake and tsunami, and they experienced the fear of losing people close to them and their homes. This led consumers to place more value on family-oriented living, and many people considered getting married within five years, and increased intention to live with their parents or near their workplace (Kuwayama et al. 2013). In terms of consumption activities, ethical consumption (supportive consumption) and supportive consumption with the intention of supporting disaster-stricken areas was popular (Ishizuka 2012).

Since the declaration of the state of emergency, some areas of Japan, mainly in the fishing and agro-industry sectors, have suffered significant economic losses. This was especially true in areas with strong ties to tourism and the food service industry, such as those with high-end food products. Under these circumstances, consumers' purchasing behavior, known as "support consumption," flourished(Markezine,2020).

Consumers actively purchased products to economically support the region that had suffered economic losses. According to a survey conducted by Miyaki (2021), before the declaration of the state of emergency, 67.6% male and 79.6% female respondents were willing to help by purchasing goods and services from businesses that were suffering from the effects of the novel coronavirus.

According to Stanislawski et al. (2015), after the Great East Japan Earthquake of March 11, 2011, the media called the actions by businesses and consumers to support the Tohoku region through ethical consumption as "support consumption. Watanabe (2014) stated that after the Great East Japan Earthquake, there was a mood of self-restraint in anticipation of graduation and entrance ceremonies, and thus, a "cheering consumption" movement emerged, in which people actively purchased products from the affected areas to support reconstruction efforts.

Crowdfunding has played a major role in this support consumption (Tashiro, 2020). For example, since the early 1980s, the Hida region (an old name for a part of Gifu Prefecture) is known as a region that produces Hida beef, a premium brand. Restaurants and sales outlets serving this brand of beef have contributed greatly to tourism in Gifu Prefecture up to the pre-pandemic period. Since the declaration of the state of emergency, there has been a sharp decline in the number of tourists and a drop in the demand for high-quality beef from restaurants. Thus, producers in the region faced grave business crisis. Therefore, through CAMPFIRE (one of the largest crowdfunding sites in Japan), a crowdfunding campaign was conducted to appeal for the maintenance of Hida beef production while giving away Hida beef to be consumed in restaurants and tourist attractions as a gift in return. Thus, between April 29, 2020 at 7:00 pm and May 10, 2020 at 23:59 pm, the support amounted to 114,370,014 yen, the number of supporters totaled 10,002 people, which was over 11 times the initial donation target (Tashiro, 2020). The local government and banks supported this crowdfunding, which led to its smooth operation.

CONCLUSION

This chapter addressed the changes in businesses in Japan during the COVID-19 pandemic.

Although the service sector was severely affected by the pandemic and imposition of the recommendatory government restrictions, they could innovate to adapt to the new normal.

A key success factor is that in the decades before the pandemic, the service sector had already experienced a series of serious disasters and established various response mechanisms. These responses were integrated into the cultural psyche of every Japanese consumer and their changing perceptions caused by the series of disasters. The success of the service sector in its pandemic response can be argued to be an extension of those earlier experiences and efforts.

Based on several case studies, the chapter examined the service sector's response to a series of disasters, the cultural background of consumers, and age-long corporate cultures. Additionally, the future direction of innovation in Japan's service sector was discussed and forecast.

As of March 2022, while the pandemic has not yet been fully contained, the Japanese government lifted almost all mandatory restrictions in the same month(Kyodo News, 2022). This means that basic health protocols or the new normal that affect the business environment were re-adjusted, i.e., social distancing was eased significantly at this point. Further research is needed to evaluate existing innovations in the social service sector, i.e. online grocery, online tourism, door-to-door deliveries, the like., whether these innovations will develop some more or gradually disappear as the sector goes back to the traditional model.

ACKNOWLEDGMENT

This research was partially supported by the Japan Society for the Promotion of Science (JSPS) KAKENHI [Grant Numbers 20K01989].

REFERENCES

Aldrich, D. P., & Yoshida, T. (2020). How Japan stumbled into a pandemic miracle. *Current History (New York, N.Y.)*, *119*(818), 217–221. doi:10.1525/curh.2020.119.818.217

Anzai, A., & Nishiura, H. (2021). "Go To Travel" campaign and travel-associated coronavirus disease 2019 cases: A descriptive analysis, July–August 2020. *Journal of Clinical Medicine*, *10*(3), 398. doi:10.3390/jcm10030398 PMID:33494315

Bloomberg. (2021). https://www.bloomberg.co.jp/news/articles/2021-12-08/R3RS5ST0AFB401

Diamond. (2021). *Tokushimaru's Present and Future.* https://diamond-rm.net/management/74592/

Distribution Economics Institute of Japan. (2021). *Internet supermarkets growing dramatically under Covid-19.* https://www.dei.or.jp/aboutdei/column/20210215

DoHouse. (2020). *The thought behind Ouen purcharging, "What is Ouen purcharging for you?"* https://www.dohouse.co.jp/kikulab/?p=14285

Fukunaga, H. (2020). Toilet paper rumors and hoarding induced by the spread of coronavirus infections. *The NHK Monthly Report on Broadcast Research*, *70*(7), 2–24.

Hirogaki, M. (2021). Online Consumer Behaviors Trigger Drastic Distribution Changes: The Case of Japan. In Impact of Globalization and Advanced Technologies on Online Business Models (pp. 303-321). IGI Global.

Ishibashi, M., & Sekiya, N. (2021). Exploratory Study on the Spread of Rumors and Psychological Factors Related to COVID-19. *Japanese Journal of Risk Analysis*, *31*(2), 123–132.

Ishikawa, T.(2012). Emergency mobile supply of goods in the regional retail channel: case studies and challenges. *The Journal of Marketing and Distribution*, *2012*(499), 22-29.

Ishizuka, Y. (2012). *Changes in consumption trends due to the Great East Japan Earthquake. Macroeconomic Analysis Project.* The Asia Pacific Research Institute.

Komori, M. (2020). The toilet paper fiasco triggered by social networking sites. *Kokumin Seikatsu*, *99*, 4-5.

Konishi, Y., Saito, T., Ishikawa, T., Kanai, H., & Igei, N. (2021). How did Japan cope with COVID-19? Big data and purchasing behavior. *Asian Economic Papers*, *20*(1), 146–167.

Kuwayama, M., Ariu, T., Kato, M., & Sugita, J. (2013). Analysis of Consumer Attitudes, Values, and Behavior after the Great East Japan Earthquake from a CSR Perspective. *Journal of Japan Society for Business Ethics Study*, *20*, 129–146.

Kyodo News. (2022). *Japan formally decides to end COVID-19 quasi-emergency next week.* https://english.kyodonews.net/news/2022/03/bc188041dee7-panel-oks-japan-ending-covid-19-quasi-emergency-next-week.html

Markezine. (2020). https://markezine.jp/article/detail/34347

Ministry of Economy, Trade and Industry. (2020). https://www.meti.go.jp/covid-19/mask.html

Ministry of Internal Affairs and Communications. (2020). *Report on Information Distribution Survey on New Coronavirus Infections.* https://www.soumu.go.jp/menu_news/s-news/01kiban18_01000082.html

Miyaki, Y. (2011). Growing awareness of "ethical consumption" in the wake of the earthquake. *Life Design Report*, (200), 38-40.

Miyaki, Y.(2020). The Corona Disaster and Attitudes toward Sustainable Consumption Behavior: From the New Coronavirus Awareness Survey and the Post-Earthquake Survey. *Life Design Report 2020.*

Miyazu, K. (2022) Corporate Marketing IT Strategy with Consideration of Consumer Sentiment During COVID-19 Pandemic. *St. Andrew's University Economic and Business Review*, *63*(3).

Nakajima, O. (2020). Masks depleted and skyrocketing due to spread of new corona infection. *The Journal of New Product Liability*, (5), 85-92.

National Institute of Infectious Diseases. (2020). *Field Briefing: Diamond Princess COVID-19 Cases.* https://www.niid.go.jp/niid/en/2019-ncov-e/9407-covid-dp-fe-01.html(accessed 21 March 2022,)

Nihon Housou Kyoukai. (2020, Jan. 16). *NHK News Web.* Author.

Nikkei, M.J. (2020a). *The goal is not to be unmanned, but to add value by saving supermarkets and people.* Academic Press.

Nikkei, M. J. (2020b). Tokyu Store, DX, and Synops are collaborating to make the store a test site for ordering and and reduce the burden of back-office. Academic Press.

Nikkei. (2020). https://www.nikkei.com/article/DGXMZO56173900Y0A220C2EA5000/

Nishinippon. (2020). *APA Hotel to accept infected patients.* https://www.nishinippon.co.jp/item/o/597779/

Noguchi, H., Sano, S., Kitakaze, Y., & Aoki, Y. (2012). One Year After 3.11, Exploring Changes in Consumer Sentiment: From Survey Data. *Marketing Journal*, *31*(4), 4–21.

Ochi, Y.(2021) Tourism and Economy Recovery Initiatives-Go To Travel Campaign Project in Japan. *Journal of Leisure and Tourism*, (8), 75-84.

Ryutu Biz. (2021). https://www.ryutsuu.biz/strategy/n051843.html

Sakamoto, M., Matsuda, J., & Inakura, N. (2021) *Hoarding behavior during the COVID-19 pandemic and Consumer Trouble - Implications for Consumer Education.* Research Discussion Paper, International Consumer Policy Research Center (ICPRC).

Shanka, M. S., & Menebo, M. M. (2022). When and How Trust in Government Leads to Compliance with COVID-19 Precautionary Measures. *Journal of Business Research*, *139*, 1275–1283. doi:10.1016/j. jbusres.2021.10.036

Stanislawski, S., Ohira, S., & Sonobe, Y. (2015). Consuming to help—Post-disaster consumption in Japan. *Asia-Pacific Advances in Consumer Research*, *11*, 76–79.

Tashiro, T. (2020). We got 100 million yen! Hida beef at home project" with Corona's marketing of local products. *Economic Monthly Report, 87*, 2-8. https://www.think-t.gr.jp/pdf/award_01.pdf

Toriumi, F., & Lim, D. (2021). Information Sharing During the Pandemic. *Yokokan Rengo Conference*. https://www.jstage.jst.go.jp/article/oukan/2021/0/2021_A-4-4/_pdf/-char/ja

Wakashima, K., Asai, K., Kobayashi, D., Koiwa, K., Kamoshida, S., & Sakuraba, M. (2020). The Japanese version of the Fear of COVID-19 scale: Reliability, validity, and relation to coping behavior. *PLoS One*, *15*(11), e0241958.

Watanabe, T. (2014). Chins Up! Discovery of Ethical Consumption after the Great Earthquake in Northeastern Japan. *Tokyo Keizai Law Review*, *26*, 311–342.

Worldometers. (2021). *COVID-19 coronavirus pandemic*. https://www.worldometers.info/coronavirus/

Chapter 19
Turning a Crisis Into an Opportunity:
Innovation During the Pandemic

Francesca Bonetti
London College of Fashion, UK

Alessandra Vecchi
ⓘ https://orcid.org/0000-0003-3449-7927
London College of Fashion, UK

ABSTRACT

The impact of the COVID-19 pandemic has not been uniform across industries. In some, we have witnessed a remarkable degree of innovation which has seen the establishment of a vast array of business models. By contrast, in others innovation has been rather slack. These conflicting trends raise the questions of whether the COVID-19 pandemic has accelerated the demise of certain industries or hastened the emergence of others. By coupling the crisis management literature with organizational learning theory and by relying on 23 in-depth interviews, the chapter provides a taxonomy of the various types of innovation responses to the existing crisis and disruption. The taxonomy is instrumental to gain a better understanding of how companies across countries and industry sectors respond to disruption by innovating and the valuable lessons that can be drawn from this experience.

INTRODUCTION

The COVID-19 pandemic has had severe repercussions from an economic and social point of view, having a detrimental effect for production, exports and supply chains for most industries. Within this context of unprecedented change, this chapter analyses the process of adjustment adopted by a vast array of industries in response to the pandemic. The recent COVID-19 crisis has radically revolutionized and transformed the business environment. This ranges from the way firms react to this suddenly needed transformation by shortcutting the way they provide their products and services (Lee and Trimi, 2021),

DOI: 10.4018/978-1-6684-6762-6.ch019

how they can transform their supply chain infrastructures to adapt their products (Samson, 2020), and to how they enhance and extend their service and performance capacity according to disruptive market demands (Sharma et al., 2020). Overall, these developments have led firms in the industry to fundamentally change the ways they "do business", in particular the ways they organize and conduct activities across the firm and the industry with customers, vendors, partners and other stakeholders. In this very dynamic context, it becomes an imperative for companies to reinvent themselves by often introducing innovative products or novel business models and by utilizing their existing resources and capabilities as well as combining them with new ones (George et al., 2020). For example, L'Oreal promptly pivoted to produce hand sanitizer in short supply and freely distributed it to hospitals, pharmacies, care homes, and food stores.

However, while the majority of the academic articles published so far on the COVID-19 crisis mostly focuses on either supply chain disruptions (Sharma et al., 2020; Samson, 2020), internal organizational disruptions (Carnevale and Hatak, 2020) or the impact of the crisis on customers (Hall et al., 2020), our work embraces a more holistic approach by focusing on a cross-national and cross-sectorial comparison of those innovation strategies that ultimately might as well yield to growth opportunities. In particular, since crises are defined largely by uncertainty, we couple approaches from grand challenges (George et al., 2016), the crisis management literature (Boersma et al., 2022) with organizational learning theory (Bundy et al., 2016; James et al., 2011) to gain a better understanding of how companies across countries and industry sectors respond to disruption by innovating, and the valuable lessons that can be drawn from this experience.

Research Aim

By drawing on the relevant literature, the purpose of this study, therefore, is to develop a taxonomy that allows to classify the different types of innovation responses towards crisis and disruption. The proposed taxonomy is instrumental to develop a set of valuable lessons that can have a broader applicability, beyond the COVID-19 crisis.

Research Significance

The impact of the C19 pandemic has not been uniform across industries (George et al., 2020). In some, including education we have seen a remarkable rate of innovation which has seen the establishment of a vast array of business models (Cooper, 2021). By contrast, in others such as in the tourism and hospitality industry innovation has been rather slack (Lai & Wong, 2021). These conflicting trends raise the questions of whether the C19 pandemic has accelerated the demise of certain industries or hastened the emergence of others? This chapter endorses the view that while the pandemic has tested the agility and the resilience of firms, it has also forced us to question the assumptions underlying established theoretical framework that drive managerial decisions along with managerial practice.

Chapter Structure

This chapter comprises five sections. While the next section provides the theoretical foundations for our work by highlighting the relevant theories, namely a brief overview of the literature on crisis management and organizational learning theory, the third section of the chapter describes the methodology adopted.

The fourth section describe the findings. The final section provides the conclusion by highlighting the original contribution of our work, the managerial and the policy implications stemming from our findings, their limitations along with directions for future research.

LITERATURE REVIEW

Grand Challenges and Ensuing Organizational Responses

According to George et al. (2016), grand challenges require the coordinated and sustained effort from multiple and diverse stakeholders toward a clearly articulated problem or goal. Solutions typically involve changes in individual and societal behaviours, changes to how actions are organized and implemented, and progress in technologies and tools to solve these problems. Thus, the tackling of grand challenges could be fundamentally characterized as an organizational problem. To this end the authors separate the studies into two broad themes: (1) studies that provide management insights on how global problems can be tackled; and (2) studies that identify mechanisms and contexts by which grand challenges affect organizations and institutions such as business environments. Within this taxonomy, given our focus on organizational adjustment (Williams et al., 2019) our research falls into the latter category.

Within nowadays' business environment complexity and volatility and given the recursive nature of grand challenges (Clemente et al., 2017), it becomes of pivotal importance to fully understand the implications stemming from organizational responses. Organization scholars increasingly advocate for research that addresses grand challenges, noting that "*the fundamental principles underlying a grand challenge are the pursuit of bold ideas and the adoption of less conventional approaches to tackling large, unresolved problems*" (Colquitt & George, 2011, p. 432). An environmental shock, such as the COVID-19 pandemic, is an unanticipated and disruptive change in the firm's external environment (Meyer et al., 1990). It is severe and affects specific organizations (Brege & Brandes, 1993), industrial segments (Sheppard & Chowdhury, 2005) and entire economies (Singh & Yip, 2000).

Crises Management

How companies respond to such changes in their external environment has become an increasingly relevant matter. Ecological theory (Hannan & Freeman, 1977, 1984) provides a helpful angle, arguing that organizations exhibit inertial tendencies, which can be attributed to four different internal constraints: political factions supportive of vested interests, organizational history that might prevent consideration of alternative strategies, investment in plant, equipment and specialized personnel, and limits on information received by decision-makers. Organizations that fail to respond to the changing environment, or respond in an inappropriate fashion, may be susceptible to failure.

At a systemic level, resilience has been defined as the "*capacity [...] to proactively adapt to and recover from disturbances that are perceived within the system to fall outside the range of normal and expected disturbance*" (Boin et al., 2010, p. 9). According to Dentoni et al. (2020), resilience can be interpreted through two dimensions. First, the amount of disturbance a system can absorb while remaining within the same balancing state, and second, the degree to which the system is capable of self-organization, learning, and adaptation. The field of ecology has focused mostly on the first dimension - the capacity to *absorb* disturbances. From an ecology perspective, this "absorbing" capacity of the system can be measured in terms of the persistence of the relationships within a system (Holling, 1973). The second dimension of resilience was established in the early 2000s when social scientists engaged in multidisciplinary work with ecologists in developing the so-called adaptive ecosystem management perspective (Berkes et al., 2003). From this perspective, resilience can be observed as a capacity to *adapt* to disturbances (Norberg & Cumming, 2006). This adaptive capacity takes place as actors engage in a "*recombination of evolved structures and processes*" in response to external changes (Folke, 2006, p. 259). This perspective suggests that organizations need to learn and change in anticipation of disturbances (Berkes et al., 2003; Kinzig et al., 2006).

Furthermore, when dealing with external shocks, companies must above all develop or activate dynamic capabilities with which they can adapt their resource base to the changes in the external environment (Teece et al., 1997; Eisenhardt & Martin, 2000; Peteraf et al., 2013). In this line, the dynamic capability approach is a useful lens that allows to provide guidance on how managers can keep the business afloat when dealing with uncertainty and volatility (Teece, 2007). Companies must be able to develop capabilities to respond to rapidly evolving market conditions (Lin & Wu, 2014). Within dynamic capabilities, ambidexterity plays a crucial role (Mei, 2014). Companies frequently attempt to gain a competitive advantage in their market through innovation that requires both exploration to tap new opportunities and exploitation to enhance existing capabilities. The ability to excel at these conflicting modes of innovation is termed organisational ambidexterity (Andriopolous & Lewis, 2009).

Crisis and disaster management models are recognized as significant in organizational disasters and crises studies. Within the crisis process, Bundy et al. (2016)'s literature review highlights three core stages: pre-crisis prevention, crisis management and post-crisis outcomes stages.

Organizational Learning

But do organizations learn from crises? And if they do, how? These questions have been an ongoing debate among scholars for over two decades (Ghaderi & Paraskevas, 2021). This debate has focused on the pessimist versus optimist perspective, inquiring into whether organizations are capable of learning from a crisis (e.g., Zhou et al., 2018) and on the individual versus organizational perspective towards identifying the learning agents (e.g., Stemn et al., 2018). There is a quite well established consensus that organizational crises are conducive to the process of intensive organizational knowledge acquisition. Crises also trigger organizational changes that otherwise would have not taken place. Therefore, shaping the ability of an organization to learn from a crisis is an important antecedent for its capability to cope with future crises.

By matching up the crisis management and organizational learning stages, and focusing on the within-organization dynamics of managing risk and complexity, James et al. (2011) and Lampel et al. (2009) highlighted the role of top management to react to crises and either frame them as threats, thus being more limited in their efforts, or as opportunities to be more open and flexible towards change in an emergency situation, learning from it and developing organizational capabilities (Bartsch et al., 2020). Here, the authors stressed the importance of moving beyond the status quo to generate new competitive advantage hence learning from a crisis situation (Bundy et al., 2016; Hunt el al., 1999). Organizational learning is considered an important element of crisis handling (Pearson and Clair, 1998). An organization's ability to change behaviour in response to an experience or changes (e.g., a crisis) is defined adaptive organizational learning (Glynn et al., 1994). As James et al. (2011) stressed, there is a need to investigate organizational extraordinary performance and positive change and opportunities for organizations to flourish following a crisis. Nonetheless, a considerable part of the literature on strategic management has highlighted that incumbents often fail due to their dominant position, market share, and established way of operating which lead to avoiding risk, instead of focusing on innovation (Christensen, 2015; Schumpeter, 1947; Tellis, 2013). In these regards, the organizational learning literature defines competitive inertia as the level of activity that an organization exhibits when altering its competitive stance in areas such as new product, pricing, advertising, service introductions, or market scope (Hunt, 1999; Miller and Chen, 1994). The theory highlights drivers to inertia, where Miller and Chen (1994) claimed that good past performance contributes to competitive inertia leading to stagnation in products, policies and methods that often underlies inadequate adaptation to a changing environment. Instead, a diversity of markets discourages it, leading to organizational evolution. Crisis is thought to play a key role in initiating change (James et al., 2011). The organizational learning theory on the notion of inertia therefore provides a valuable lens for this research, where organizational responses in dealing with crises can determine success and future crises.

Theoretical Lens

Despite the increasing adoption of crisis management theories to assess how companies learn from crises and risks, the theoretical models that currently exist (e.g., Brockner and James, 2008) are not fully specified, but tend to be conceptual and generic (James et al., 2011). In particular, there is an opportunity to gain a deeper understanding of managerial perspective on innovation responses and processes to COVID-19 as a disruptive event and across different sectors, which this work aims to fulfil.

METHODOLOGY

By relying on extensive semi-structured interviews, we explore the innovation actions and strategies implemented in response to the current COVID-19 crisis. The respondents were selected with a purposive sampling technique (Yin, 2017). The 23 interviews are overall representative of a taxonomy of different responses, involving: potential and temporality regarding COVID-19 crisis (i.e. temporary changes dependent on crisis; long-term changes independent of crisis) and degree of innovation of product/ service and market/ consumer segment (i.e. existing product and market; new product and market). The selected firms offer a wealth of diversity since they tend to operate in different industries (e.g. hospitality, automotive, fashion and creative industries, e-commerce, education) across a variety of countries (e.g. US, Italy, UK, Germany, Denmark, France, Spain, China). The 23 interviews followed a structured research protocol, where themes for discussion were informed by the literature on crises management, product innovation and organizational learning theory, and were formulated to understand changes in the firms related to COVID-19 crisis and temporality of effects on the firm along with the main lessons learnt.

Interview respondents were recruited from the research team's contacts and invited to participate through e-mail, LinkedIn and telephone calls. In-depth interviews were conducted with 23 senior informants who were deemed as knowledgeable about the companies' relevant innovation activities. This allowed the development of a close dialogue (Clark, 1998) with practitioners who had relevant expertise and depth of involvement, thus enabling rich analysis (Patton, 2002) to understand the phenomena under investigation. Interviews were conducted from spring 2020 to early 2021, recorded and transcribed.

The primary data collected through the interviews was then triangulated and complemented by secondary data, in the form of media reports and company documentation. The interviews and the secondary data collected were then analyzed following established qualitative analysis principles of thematic analysis, using the research protocol to guide the data coding (Guest et al., 2012; Miles et al., 2014) in order to identify possible patterns in the firms' innovation responses to the COVID-19 crisis. Coding labels were revised as data collection and analysis proceeded iteratively, and conducting a back-and-forth examination of theory and data (Spiggle 1994). This rigorous interpretive process continued until data saturation meant no new themes were emerging from the analysis. We conducted members check with 3 senior informants, through an ongoing dialogue with the participants via sharing results, consulting and running workshops. This resulted in the provision of additional reflections and insights about how our findings might apply to their circumstances. Our analytical process ultimately led to the development of a taxonomy that allows to classify the different types of innovation responses towards crisis and disruption.

RESULTS AND DISCUSSION

Findings showed that the response of the most proactive organizations has been shaped by some of their distinctive resources that make them adaptive survivors. These are namely the *widespread creativity*, the *contagious enthusiasm* that swipe through the industry, and the *emotional attachment* to the businesses since some of them are family businesses that often own heritage brands. Many of the organizations investigated showed *resourcefulness,* being able to turn a crisis into a viable opportunity, *ambidexterity* by exploring new opportunities capitalizing on their existing core capabilities and know-how. *Promptness* as they were able to seize the relevant opportunities in a timely manner, *pragmatism* and *flexibility* as they were able to strategize and implement change within the time constraints imposed by the crisis. Thus, our findings show the ability of successful organizations to develop new capabilities (Bartsch et al., 2020) that have allowed them to learn from a crisis situation (Bundy et al., 2016; Hunt el al., 1999). In this section we provide a classification of the various types of innovation responses to the existing crisis and disruption, derived from our analysis as depicted in Table 1 below. These responses are classified according to the temporality of changes depending on COVID-19 crisis, and degree of innovation of product/ service and market/ consumer segment. This classification will then allow us to draw valuable lessons that organizations across countries and industry sectors can learn from each other, and that can help build competitive advantage and resilience beyond the COVID-19 crisis.

Temporary Changes Depending on COVID-19 Crisis, Existing Products

Several firms adapting to crisis through temporary and ad-hoc solutions emerged. This involved prompt, short-term changes to the ways of operating, with only minor changes to existing products or services. Examples involved flexible hospital solutions and hotels and schools temporary converted into isolation hospitals to treat COVID-19 affected patients. In a rapid search for more beds, the Manager of Ayre Gran Hotel Colón in Madrid, Spain, explains that *"our hotel has been repurposed to fight the pandemic. We have offered our hotel beds and facilities for nursing staff, vulnerable populations and anyone fighting the spread of coronavirus."* Along similar lines, prompt agility was manifested by Air Dolomiti. Their Vice President stressed that, despite the airline sector's fixed ways of operating which make it hard to implement agile solutions, *"Especially during pandemic times, agility has become a key concept for*

Table 1. Classification of innovation responses to COVID-19 crisis

Temporality depending on COVID-19 crisis Innovation product/ market	Temporary depending on COVID-19 crisis	Long-term changes independent of COVID-19 crisis
Existing product (and existing/ new market/ customer segment)	• Ayre Gran Hotel Colón, turning hotel facilities into hospital solutions • Barbieri, providing flexible hospital solutions • Air Dolomiti, providing special flight routes during pandemic	• Deliveroo Essentials, food delivery from supermarkets • Gousto, partnering with local supermarkets and farmers • LogMeIn, extending online meeting and education provision • Cisco Webex, enhancing software versions • TooGoodToGo, empowering restaurants' takeaway services • OmniLabs, providing telepresence robots • Anthropology, expanding into home design and loungewear • Alibaba, livestreaming latest collection with celebrities • Amazon, adapting supply chain to serve higher demands • Lamborghini, creating an app for car customization and interaction with customer service • Oysho, extending into sports line and providing fitness classes
New product (and existing/ new market/ customer segment)	• Miroglio, producing gowns and masks • Ferrari, producing ventilators • Luxottica, producing medical eyewear • Bosch Healthcare, using viral testing devices in tents • Kinderheldin, providing midwife services online • Distillerie Mazzari, producing hand sanitizers	• Gousto, setting up Table for One Million event • Balenciaga, debuting new runway format customized video game • Airbnb, creating virtual experiences in a set of contexts • Lululemon, providing a virtual reality mirror to practice yoga and check postures at home

airways." They started running more national flights, following restrictions on international travels leading to preferences of tourists to travel within Italy. Their CEO commented that *"In those days [of pandemic] it is not anymore a plus to be adaptable, but it is becoming a requirement to survive in the industry. Our recovery strategy is a fresh approach in targeting a new set of inflated destinations".* According to him, *"The fear brought by the pandemic implied a repositioning of the image by communicating a sense of safety."* This was implemented by offering "COVID-free" flights where passengers had to be tested before boarding. These temporary reactions show the flexibility and agility of the top management to pivot and solve a problem caused by market disruption (Zhou et al., 2018; Bundy et al., 2016; Hunt el al., 1999), especially in contexts in which existing products and services are not utilized due to an emergency situation.

Temporary Changes Depending on COVID-19 Crisis, New Products and Customer Segments

Another cluster of firms emerged to reply to crisis by adapting their solutions in a temporary way, by shifting into new product or service solutions, hence targeting a new customer base and / or a new market. This involves a swift response of companies to learn by the crisis and promptly adapt their solutions. Several informants shared the view that this reaction could be related to marketing and brand promotion, to generate PR and media interest and gain publicity for the company, involving a short-term, visible initiative, as opposed to a long-term benefit for the community as a whole. This differs from the development of long-term dynamic capabilities to respond to rapidly evolving market conditions (Lin & Wu, 2014). Independently of this, many respondents agreed that this short-term, rapid solution showed reactive responses to manage the pandemic crisis and leading to the development of organizational capabilities (Bartsch et al., 2020).

Examples include fashion companies starting to produce medical gowns and gloves to assist medical staff dealing with the emergency, cosmetics companies starting to produce hand sanitizers and lotions, and eyewear companies providing medical eyewear. Italian company Distillerie Mazzari producing food alcohol represents a valid example of how the supply chain was adapted to the pandemic. The company reacted to the pandemic by shifting its production to a new product, namely it opened a new production line, using the existing machinery, to *"Produce products dedicated to sanitation, including hand sanitizer and cleaner for surfaces using the alcohol we used originally for our main products"*, their Manager of Alcohol Department explained. The company created a joint venture with another company responsible for packing and distributing the final product. This allowed Distillerie Mazzali to quickly pivot to the new market needs, thanks to the ability to collaborate with other businesses and outsourcing the capabilities needed (i.e., for distribution and packaging), thus showing the prompt reaction of top management to see opportunities in the crisis and learn from it by being flexible in outsourcing needed skills (Bartsch et al., 2020; Bundy et al., 2016; Hunt el al., 1999). The top management could also see the potential in their response to the COVID crisis beyond the immediate terms, as they state that *"The tendency to wash and sanitize hands and surfaces more often will remain anyway because, once we have the vaccine for COVID-19, it cannot be excluded that there will not be some other infections that can affect us. Our attention to hygiene will stay high"* (Manager of Alcohol Department). This evidences the company's strategic thinking and ability to jump onto opportunities (James et al., 2011).

Furthermore, adaptation of existing services into new operational contexts emerged being another area where organizations showed proactive attitude to face the crisis. The German motherhood care company Kinderheldin started offering midwife services online instead of home visits, thus showing flexibility turning an existing service to supply for customer needs during the pandemic. The CEO of Kinderheldin states that *"Figuring out that German health insurances where willing to finance online health-services, we reached over 400 new clients for our digital midwife classes within 3 days."* This is a remarkable pragmatic change that the company has undertaken to react to market changes by showing resourcefulness. While the service provision is likely to go back to what they offered prior to the pandemic emergency, some degrees of blended delivery of health service might remain.

Long-Term Changes, Existing Products

Findings revealed that in many cases a key success factor consisted in firms applying a long-term transformation of their product or service offering, in terms of adapting their existing business model to better serve an existing market and reach out to a broader range of customers within that market segment. Consider, Italian brand and manufacturer of luxury sports cars Lamborghini that responded to the pandemic crisis by launching an invitation-only app allowing customers to *"Configure their own vehicle, constantly monitoring the work-in-progress, which can be thought of as a collaboration in the designing process"* explains their Head of Product. This prompt reaction has allowed the company to pivot to an online offer of their service, without losing the co-creation aspect between the brand and the consumer, also allowing them to expand their data collection. The interviewee goes on explaining that *"the app gives the possibility to configure the car, be in contact with the dealer and the company, share content such as videos, photos during the production phase until delivery. In this way we can profile customers, know their history."* These changes are likely to stay long-term, as consumers' habits are likely to change and become more technology oriented and expect higher levels of services from companies. Therefore, Lamborghini showed the capability to adapt to external shocks and learn from them (Folke, 2006).

To fight crisis stagnation of many industries, especially hospitality where many activities were not allowed during the pandemic crisis, a strong spirit of creative adaptation emerged from several organizations. For example, UK company Gousto providing subscription-based fresh food and recipes box delivery partnered up with local supermarkets through the initiative "Food Finder" allowing customers during lockdown to shop online at local supermarkets through an app powered by Gousto. Gousto also expanded their services by partnering up with local farmers to supply for the rapidly increased demand for recipe boxes, as their Acquisition and Retention Director explains, *"with lockdown measures being imposed, we suddenly saw a sharp increase of our customers' demand, and new customers wanting to join in too. As we could not expand our supply chain facilities so promptly, we partnered up with local farmers to serve more customers, and at the same time that gave the possibility to farmers to use our facilities and infrastructures to help distribute their products"*. This pragmatic response shows the ability of the most proactive businesses to partner up and join forces with other players to help expand one's customer base or innovate the existing business model to face sudden changes (Eisenhardt & Martin, 2000; Peteraf et al., 2013).

Within this cluster, several apparel companies started to collaborate with designers and expand their offering into home design and new loungewear products, as the lockdown forced people to spend more time at home. Several fashion retailers expanded their online channels, by offering further delivery and return options, and better ways of visualizing products online and interact with the brand's customer care teams. In China, Little Red Book, Weibo, and Taobao have been livestreaming their latest collections, making them shoppable with Chinese influencers. As Alibaba's Relationships Director comments, *"We think livestreaming is very important. Currently, around 60 percent of our livestreaming audience is from lower-tier cities."* This shopping channel therefore helps businesses in China expand and reach a broader customer base, using celebrities and shows formats to provide entertainment and connect with their customers during the lockdown phase. As these trends towards online shopping and engagement are likely to remain post pandemic, due to the crisis triggering societal trend changes, those companies that have been embracing innovation have shown dynamic capabilities to adapt their resources due to changes in the external environment (Eisenhardt & Martin, 2000; Peteraf et al., 2013), thanks to a visionary and highly responsive top management and internal organization capabilities (James et al., 2011; Lampel et al., 2009).

Long-Term Changes, New Products and Customer Segments

Few cases emerged of firms who disrupted their ways of thinking and operating, expanding into new products or services to reach a new customer base, and with long-term changes that are likely to stay post pandemic. This cluster of "true innovators" emerged from a creative response of the organization to the crisis (James et al., 2011), and included the organizations' ability to adapt functional core processes

(Bartsch et al., 2020; Boin et al., 2010). Here, strong innovation embracement and an agile, flexible approach characterized the company (Bartsch et al., 2020), by forcing it to think outside the existing customer base and product offering. This involved the provision of online parties and experiences, and online events. Consider, for instance, online marketplace for lodging Airbnb, that during the pandemic could not see their business of home rentals progress as usual. They quickly pivoted and started *"Offering online experiences, which are hosted on Zoom and that can be done completely remotely at home. Registered participants can join on their desktop, tablet, or mobile device."* Says their Director of Communications. Participants can choose from a range of online experiences, *"Live interactive sessions, conducted over Zoom by guides around the world, for small groups of "tourists" stuck at home"* explains their Director. *"Over the course of an hour or two"*, he goes on telling, *"The hosts dive into a wide range of artistic, cultural, musical, culinary, and athletic topics: "Dance Like a K-pop Star," presented live by a guide in South Korea; "Cooking with a Moroccan Family," from Marrakesh; "Tokyo Anime and Subcultures," from Japan."* This has shown the agility and resilience of the company, proactively adapting to external shocks (Boin et al., 2010; Berkes et al., 2003) through changes that are likely to stay post pandemic, since consumer trends have been changed. The new format of online experiences represents in fact an inexpensive way to carry users away from their physical locations that is likely to stay, and be merged to in-person experiences, post pandemic.

Several fashion brands embraced new ways of delivering their catwalk shows during the fashion weeks, going virtual to find new way to engage their audience. Luxury fashion brand Balenciaga, for example, debuted a novel runway show format thorough a customized video game where guests could register (with a long queue), to then interact with avatars wearing the Fall 2021 collection. *"If there is one thing that this Pandemic has given to us"* Comments CEO of innovation studio Kinestry, *"that accelerated growth of digital experiences. Balenciaga took the first dive into the metaverse by presenting their collection in a virtual world game. And now, their breaking the gaming industry by partnering with Fortnite to create a digital collection of in-game wearables for your Fortnite characters."* This shows an attempt to deliver a new format in the midst of the pandemic, showing fast adaptability of companies (Dentoni et al., 2020) when entire fashion runway seasons were forced to cancel, and involving a set of stakeholders to interact with the new collection. This tendency to move to the online, metaverse world is likely to stay post pandemic, involving fashion shows and virtual spaces to "hang out" and experience brands, due to changed society trends and the advantages of online experiences.

Overview of Main Findings and Achieving the Research Aim

Our in-depth interviews with senior informants from organizations spanning across an array of industries and countries allowed us to develop a detailed taxonomy that classifies the different types of innovation responses towards crisis and disruption, thus achieving the research aim. In particular, our data analysis reveals a classification of responses around temporality of changes depending on COVID-19 crisis, and degree of innovation of product/ service and market/ consumer segment. Our taxonomy can be summarized around the following four clusters:

1. Companies implementing prompt, short-term changes to the ways of operating related to COVID-19 crisis, applying minor adaptations of existing products and services through ad-hoc solutions.
2. Companies introducing temporary changes related to COVID-19 crisis by shifting into new product or service solutions to target a new customer base and / or a new market.

3. Companies applying a long-term transformation of their product or service offering, in terms of adapting their existing business model to better serve an existing market and reach out to a broader range of customers within that market segment.
4. Companies disrupting their ways of thinking and operating, expanding into new products or services to reach a new customer segment, and with long-term changes that are likely to stay post pandemic.

Overall, our findings showed that some industries are more proactive than other in innovating to respond to the COVID-19 crisis. The technology and healthcare industries stoop up significantly as they both had to cope with the sanitary emergency. Other sectors such as the hospitality and the fashion industry also showed remarkable creativity in coming up with rather unexpected solutions to keep their business afloat. Moreover, our data shows that company size is not playing a major role on how firms engaged with innovation, but top management vision and overall organization capabilities, together with the promptness to team up and collaborate with other organizations, were key to survive and ultimately lead to innovation.

This classification has then allowed to develop a set of valuable lessons that organizations across countries and industry sectors can learn from each other, and that can help build competitive advantage and resilience whose implications can be far reaching, well beyond the COVID-19 crisis. These lessons are outlined in the managerial implications section below, as well as in the theoretical implications stemming from the findings.

CONCLUSIONS, IMPLICATIONS, LIMITATIONS AND FUTURE RESEARCH AREAS

The recent COVID-19 crisis has suddenly changed the way organizations across industries "do business", acting as a catalyst for change. This has shown different behavioral responses of organizations across industries. In this scenario, adaptability, development of new skills, merging competences and unique strengths have emerged as key elements of success. Although various studies have been conducted on how the COVID-19 pandemic has disrupted organizations across industries focusing on specific aspects, our work provides a more holistic approach, conducting a cross-national and cross-sectorial comparison of organizations' innovation strategies. Our aim was to develop a taxonomy classifying innovation responses towards COVID-19 crisis and disruption, with the view of providing valuable lessons that could have had wider applicability and could help businesses innovate beyond the COVID-19 crisis. We therefore contribute a classification of key responses in the form of a taxonomy around change temporality, types of products/ services and segments targeted, as presented in the above section.

Theoretical Implications

Our classification of the various types of firms' innovation responses to the existing crisis and disruption, largely depending on top management commitment to deal with disruption, provides valuable insights to risk and crisis management and wider implications for organizational innovation and growth. In line with James et al. (2011) and Lampel et al. (2009), a strong commitment from top management to react to crisis, and the resources available to deal with it, including overall change embracement across the organization and capabilities (Bartsch et al., 2020), are needed for the management of the responses to the crisis. These aspects in turn influence the capability of firms to collaborate with other businesses to exploit know-how and resources available. Whilst strategically engaging with partners, maintaining alignment with the overall brand image and identity emerged to be of pivotal importance. In particular, our findings revealed that the adaptive behavior of firms does not depend exclusively on their size and degree of establishment. In other words, in contrast with the literature (Miller and Chen, 1994; Tellis, 2003) some of the most reactive firms emerged being incumbents with established market share. Accordingly, our findings revealed that the flexibility and promptness of organizations to learn from crises and adapt to them, is what drives success (Stemn et al., 2018; Glynn et al., 1994; James et al., 2011). Our work therefore contributes to the strategic management literature, especially concerning grand challenges, crisis management and organizational learning.

Managerial Implications

Our work contributes a framework for managing crisis and business growth and innovation. The framework, drawing from the different initiatives undertaken by the firms clustered according to their innovation response, is instrumental to explicate a set of lessons that can be valuable to managers and practitioners from a variety of different industries. In a time in which businesses more than ever need to innovate to survive and thrive through crises and the rapid pace of market change, our study provides recommendations to managers on how to deal with crises in the future, and how to innovate to respond to disruption.

In particular, key lessons emerging from our study include that success from embracing the crisis calls for managers to encourage and nurture a mind-set and practice that are open to intensive experimentation, including multiple trial and error iterations infused with action learning. In turn, this demands a high degree of resilience within the organization. As our findings show, embedding learning via experimentation, action learning cycles, resilience and an entrepreneurial mind-set is the critical point of departure if the potential successes and benefits of embracing the crisis are to be attained. Our findings highlight the key role of top management to embrace innovation, and then diffuse it across the organizations. Therefore, a leadership team that is strongly open to respond to crises, ad who in turn can effectively communicate decisions, and the rationale for the same, to employees across the organization, emerged as a fundamental aspect to thrive competitive advantage. Another key lesson concerns the importance of collaborating across industries, maximizing resources and know-how to face prompt shifts in the market (e.g., Gousto collaborating with local farmers and supermarkets to supply for increasing demand for local products; Balenciaga collaborating with the gaming industry to showcase their catwalk shows online in an immersive and interactive way). Finally, being able to foresee what market trends are likely to stay from disruption generated from a crisis, and which ones are more likely to be temporary, is fundamental for managers to make important decisions on how to pivot and which investments to make. Although foreseeing the future is not possible, joining forces across industries and a solid knowledge of the target segment, emerged to be key to future proof businesses.

Limitations and Future Research Directions

While our work provides valuable insights that contribute to the existing literature and provide managerial recommendations, it is recognized that is has some limitations. Our data collection involved one interview per firm. While participants were carefully selected based on their role and expertise, as well as availability, to provide valuable insights on the issues investigated, several interviews across various internal (and external) stakeholders would have contributed to obtain a richer, more critical view on the phenomena. Furthermore, we collected data at one specific point in time, when the COVID-19 crisis had outburst. This highlights the opportunity for a a longitudinal study to understand the challenges and opportunities deriving from the adopted behaviors of the organizations, hence how that impacted organizational performance. In this direction, future research could tease out organizational responses to crises to understand whether it is part of organizational characteristics (i.e., being prone to change) or a COVID-19 specific organizational tactic. Finally, future research could investigate whether a firm builds up a reputation for strong vs. poor crisis management, and whether that impacts external reputation and internal employee confidence in the tactical decisions.

REFERENCES

Andriopoulos, C., & Lewis, M. W. (2009). Exploitation-exploration tensions and organizational ambidexterity: Managing paradoxes of innovation. *Organization Science*, *20*(4), 696–717. doi:10.1287/orsc.1080.0406

Bartsch, S., Weber, E., Büttgen, M., & Huber, A. (2020). Leadership matters in crisis-induced digital transformation: How to lead service employees effectively during the COVID-19 pandemic. *Journal of Service Management*, *32*(1), 71–85. doi:10.1108/JOSM-05-2020-0160

Berkes, F., Colding, J., & Folke, C. (Eds.). (2003). *Navigating Social–Ecological Systems: Building Resilience for Complexity and Change*. Cambridge University Press.

Boersma, K., Büscher, M., & Fonio, C. (2022). Crisis management, surveillance, and digital ethics in the COVID-19 era. *Journal of Contingencies and Crisis Management*, *30*(1), 2–9. doi:10.1111/1468-5973.12398

Boin, A., Kuipers, S., & Overdijk, W. (2013). Leadership in times of crisis: A framework for assessment. *International Review of Public Administration*, *18*(1), 79–91. doi:10.1080/12294659.2013.10805241

Brege, S., & Brandes, O. (1993). The successful double turnaround of ASEA and ABB—Twenty lessons. *Strategic Change*, *2*(4), 185–205. doi:10.1002/jsc.4240020403

Brockner, J., & James, E. H. (2008). Toward an understanding of when executives see crisis as opportunity. *The Journal of Applied Behavioral Science*, *44*(1), 94–115. doi:10.1177/0021886307313824

Bundy, J., Pfarrer, M. D., Short, C. E., & Timothy Coombs, W. (2016). Crises and crisis management: Integration, interpretation, and research development. *Journal of Management*, *43*(6), 1661–1692. doi:10.1177/0149206316680030

Carnevale, J. B., & Hatak, I. (2020). Employee adjustment and well-being in the era of COVID-19: Implications for human resource management. *Journal of Business Research*, *116*, 183–187. doi:10.1016/j.jbusres.2020.05.037 PMID:32501303

Christensen, C. M., Raynor, M., & McDonald, R. (2015). What is Disruptive Innovation. *Harvard Business Review*, *93*(12), 44–53. PMID:17183796

Clark, A. M. (1988). The qualitative-quantitative debate: Moving from positivism and confrontation to post-positivism and reconciliation. *Journal of Advanced Nursing*, *27*(6), 1242–1249. doi:10.1046/j.1365-2648.1998.00651.x PMID:9663876

Clemente, M., Durand, R., & Roulet, T. (2017). The recursive nature of institutional change: An Annales School perspective. *Journal of Management Inquiry*, *26*(1), 17–31. doi:10.1177/1056492616656408

Colquitt, J. A., & George, G. (2011). 'Publishing in AMJ – part 1: Topic choice'. *Academy of Management Journal*, *54*(3), 432–435. doi:10.5465/amj.2011.61965960

Cooper, R. G. (2021). Accelerating innovation: Some lessons from the pandemic. *Journal of Product Innovation Management*, *38*(2), 221–232. doi:10.1111/jpim.12565 PMID:33821086

Dentoni, D., Pinkse, J., & Lubberink, R. (2021). Linking sustainable business models to socio-ecological resilience through cross-sector partnerships: A complex adaptive systems view. *Business & Society*, *60*(5), 1216–1252. doi:10.1177/0007650320935015

Eisenhardt, K. M., & Martin, J. A. (2000). Dynamic capabilities: What are they? *Strategic Management Journal*, *21*(10-11), 1105–1121. doi:10.1002/1097-0266(200010/11)21:10/11<1105::AID-SMJ133>3.0.CO;2-E

Folke, C. (2006). Resilience: The emergence of a perspective for social–ecological systems analyses. *Global Environmental Change*, *16*(3), 253–267. doi:10.1016/j.gloenvcha.2006.04.002

George, G., Howard-Grenville, J., Joshi, A., & Tihanyi, L. (2016). Understanding and tackling societal grand challenges through management research. *Academy of Management Journal*, *59*(6), 1880–1895. doi:10.5465/amj.2016.4007

George, G., Lakhani, K., & Puranam, P. (2020). What has changed? The impact of Covid pandemic on the technology and innovation management research agenda. *Journal of Management Studies*, *57*(8), 1754–1758. doi:10.1111/joms.12634

Ghaderi, Z., & Paraskevas, A. (2021). Approaching Organizational Learning through Crisis Management. In *Organizational Learning in Hospitality and Tourism Crisis Management*. De Gruyter Publishing.

Glynn, S. M., & Denise Muth, K. (1994). Reading and writing to learn science: Achieving scientific literacy. *Journal of Research in Science Teaching*, *31*(9), 1057–1073. doi:10.1002/tea.3660310915

Guest, G., MacQueen, K. M., & Namey, E. E. (2012). *Applied Thematic Analysis*. Sage. doi:10.4135/9781483384436

Hall, M. C., Prayag, G., Fieger, P., & Dyason, D. (2020). Beyond panic buying: Consumption displacement and COVID-19. *Journal of Service Management*, *32*(1), 113–128. doi:10.1108/JOSM-05-2020-0151

Hannan, M. T., & Freeman, J. (1977). The population ecology of organizations. *American Journal of Sociology*, *82*(5), 929–964. doi:10.1086/226424

Hannan, M. T., & Freeman, J. (1984). Structural inertia and organizational change. *American Sociological Review*, *49*(2), 149–164. doi:10.2307/2095567

Holling, C. S. (1973). Resilience and stability of ecological systems. *Annual Review of Ecology and Systematics*, *4*(1), 1–23. doi:10.1146/annurev.es.04.110173.000245

Hunt, J. G., Boal, K. B., & Dodge, G. E. (1999). The effects of visionary and crisis-responsive charisma on followers: An experimental examination of two kinds of charismatic leadership. *The Leadership Quarterly*, *10*(3), 423–448. doi:10.1016/S1048-9843(99)00027-2

James, E. H., Wooten, L. P., & Dushek, K. (2011). Crisis management: Informing a new leadership research agenda. *The Academy of Management Annals*, *5*(1), 455–493. doi:10.5465/19416520.2011.589594

Kinzig, A. P., Ryan, P., Etienne, M., Elmqvist, T., Allison, H. E., & Walker, B. H. (2006). Resilience and regime shifts: Assessing cascading effects. *Ecology and Society*, *11*(1), 20. doi:10.5751/ES-01678-110120

Lai, I. K. W., & Wong, J. W. C. (2020). Comparing crisis management practices in the hotel industry between initial and pandemic stages of COVID-19. *International Journal of Contemporary Hospitality Management*, *32*(10), 3135–3156. doi:10.1108/IJCHM-04-2020-0325

Lampel, J., Shamsie, J., & Shapira, Z. (2009). Experiencing the improbable: Rare events and organizational learning. *Organization Science*, *20*(5), 835–845. doi:10.1287/orsc.1090.0479

Lee, S. M., & Trimi, S. (2021). Convergence innovation in the digital age and in the COVID-19 pandemic crisis. *Journal of Business Research*, *123*, 14–22. doi:10.1016/j.jbusres.2020.09.041 PMID:33012897

Lin, Y., & Wu, L. Y. (2014). Exploring the role of dynamic capabilities in firm performance under the resource-based view framework. *Journal of Business Research*, *67*(3), 407–413. doi:10.1016/j.jbusres.2012.12.019

McKinsey & Co. (2020). *The State of Fashion 2021 BOF McKinsey & Co*. https://www.mckinsey.com/industries/retail/our-insights/state-of-fashion

Mei, M. Q. (2014). Learning to innovate: The role of ambidexterity, standard, and decision process. Frederiksberg: Copenhagen Business School (CBS).

Meyer, A. D., Brooks, G. R., & Goes, J. B. (1990). Environmental jolts and industry revolutions: Organizational responses to discontinuous change. *Strategic Management Journal*, 93–110.

Miles, M. B., Huberman, A. M., & Saldaña, J. (2014). *Qualitative Data Analysis: A Methods Sourcebook*. Sage.

Miller, D., & Chen, M.-J. (1994). Sources and consequences of competitive inertia: A study of the US airline industry. *Administrative Science Quarterly*, *39*(1), 1–23. doi:10.2307/2393492

Norberg, J., & Cumming, G. S. (2006). *Complexity Theory for a Sustainable Future*. Columbia University Press.

Patton, M. (2014). *Qualitative Research & Evaluation Methods*. Sage.

Pearson, C. M., & Clair, J. A. (1998). Reframing crisis management. *Academy of Management Review*, *23*(1), 59–76. doi:10.2307/259099

Peteraf, M., Di Stefano, G., & Verona, G. (2013). The elephant in the room of dynamic capabilities: Bringing two diverging conversations together. *Strategic Management Journal, 34*(12), 1389–1410. doi:10.1002mj.2078

Samson, D. (2020). Operations/supply chain management in a new world context. *Operations Management Research, 13*(1), 1–3. doi:10.100712063-020-00157-w

Schumpeter, J. A. (1947). The creative response in economic history. *The Journal of Economic History, 7*(2), 149–159. doi:10.1017/S0022050700054279

Sharma, P., Leung, T. Y., Kingshott, R. P. J., Davcik, N. S., & Cardinali, S. (2020). Managing uncertainty during a global pandemic: An international business perspective. *Journal of Business Research, 116*, 188–192. doi:10.1016/j.jbusres.2020.05.026 PMID:32501304

Sheppard, J. P., & Chowdhury, S. D. (2005). Riding the wrong wave: Organizational failure as a failed turnaround. *Long Range Planning, 38*(3), 239–260. doi:10.1016/j.lrp.2005.03.009

Singh, K., & Yip, G. S. (2000). Strategic lessons from the Asian crisis. *Long Range Planning, 33*(5), 706–729. doi:10.1016/S0024-6301(00)00078-9

Spiggle, S. (1994). Analysis and interpretation of in qualitative data in consumer research. *The Journal of Consumer Research, 21*(3), 491–503. doi:10.1086/209413

Stemn, E., Bofinger, C., Cliff, D., & Hassall, M. E. (2018). Failure to learn from safety incidents: Status, challenges and opportunities. *Safety Science, 101*, 313–325. doi:10.1016/j.ssci.2017.09.018

Teece, D. J. (2007). Explicating dynamic capabilities: The nature and microfoundations of (sustainable) enterprise performance. *Strategic Management Journal, 28*(13), 1319–1350. doi:10.1002mj.640

Teece, D. J., Pisano, G., & Shuen, A. (1997). Dynamic capabilities and strategic management. *Strategic Management Journal, 18*(7), 509–533. doi:10.1002/(SICI)1097-0266(199708)18:7<509::AID-SMJ882>3.0.CO;2-Z

Tellis, G. J. (2013). Unrelenting Innovation: How to Build a Culture for Market Dominance. John Wiley & Sons.

Williams, A., Whiteman, G., & Kennedy, S. (2021). Cross-scale systemic resilience: Implications for organization studies. *Business & Society, 60*(1), 95–124. doi:10.1177/0007650319825870

Yin, R. K. (2017). *Case Study Research and Applications: Design and Methods.* Sage.

Zhou, S., Battaglia, M., & Frey, M. (2018). Organizational learning through disasters: A multi-utility company's experience. *Disaster Prevention and Management, 27*(2), 243–254. doi:10.1108/DPM-11-2017-0290

Chapter 20
Sustainability Issues and Livelihood Coping Strategies in the COVID–19 Pandemic

Md. Shafiqul Islam

State University of Bangladesh, Bangladesh

ABSTRACT

The COVID-19 pandemic in Bangladesh tells us that economic activities and alternative livelihoods have been disturbed. There are challenges in the areas of equitable distribution of resources and providing economic support to the disadvantaged groups (cash and kind support, food supports, social safety net). This research explores the short term livelihood coping strategies to respond to and recover from COVID-19 with a special focus on socio-demography, socio-economy, food security, and health aspect. As the crisis develops, future rounds of representative monitoring data on the same respondents will help us understand the evolving impacts and potential recovery.

INTRODUCTION

Onset of early 2020, the COVID-19 enthralled the globe suddenly (Nagel, 2020 cited in Sohel et al., 2021) and many people on this earth affected by the virulent virus (Adhikari et al., 2020). At first the Coronavirus was recognized in Bangladesh on 8 March 2020 and spread over the country. The Government of Bangladesh declared first time strict lockdown during the period of 26 March to 30 may 2020 (Hamadani et al., 2020). The COVID-19 pandemic affects livelihood of marginalized people especially in Bangladesh. It has been led to preeminent levels of mental health shocks such as sleep problems, depressive issues, and post-traumatic stress symptoms. It is well known to all that China is the first country where COVID-19 caused pandemic situation in the world. The affected people suffered by severe acute respiratory syndrome coronavirus 2 (SARS-CoV-2). The more consequences of pandemic, the negative impact on livelihood of the pandemic that resulted in an unprecedented lockdown of daily life and economic activities might account for part of the mental health problems in participants whose earning capacities are declining. The COVID-19 pandemic began as a livelihood crisis but has in time

DOI: 10.4018/978-1-6684-6762-6.ch020

triggered a grave and unfolding economic crisis with particular concerns for the poor and vulnerable. Very low-income people have been the quickest and hardest hit in their daily lives including economic crisis, health crisis, especially those living in urban and peri-urban areas and working in the informal sector. The necessity of factual evidence cannot be over-emphasized for effective policy response to the poverty moments of the contagion. The socioeconomic impact of the COVID-19 should be reduced for which a proactive management approach should be followed, health policies should be taken by considering social detriments of health, employment opportunity, awareness and public private partnership network and linkages should be strengthen to combat pandemic situations like COVID-19 among mass population. In this regard there is immense needs of both national, and international collaboration for charity funding and more investment in health sector of the state. The country especially Bangladesh declared lockdown at the national level in the middle of March 2020, which caused huge hardship and negative impact on the marginalized livelihoods of the nation, grasping poor people who lives on hand to mouth. Huge number of household livelihood was affected by the COVID-19 outbreak. The loss of livelihood activities are immeasurable and the impact was high to extreme. It means that the marginalized people turned into more marginalized and fall into the category of hardcore poor due to COVID-19. Several studies investigated different dimension of health wellbeing and other consequences such as economic growth, poverty, income loss, mental depression (Janssen et al., 2021; Guo et al., 2020; Niles et al.,2020; prime et al., 2020). The study aims to look at the direct impact of COVID-19 on livelihoods of the marginalized people and their household welfare, by understanding all sorts of shocks including economic shocks of the poor and vulnerable people are facing, what coping mechanisms they are using and whether there are systematic variations among different demographic and occupational groups. The study eventually deployed to analyze not only livelihoods and coping during the COVID-19 crisis and lockdown but included an added effort on repossession crescendos. The study was conducted with the key purpose of to know the livelihood impacts and explore livelihood coping strategies during COVID-19 pandemic situation and post lockdown crisis. Hence, this study evaluate these effects, at least in the short-term. It indicates that they have divers option for coping strategies that have lower likelihood of longer-term detrimental impacts on the household. It is recognized that the financial coping strategies available to rural households are able to rely upon their personal incomes and savings to a much greater extent than urban slum households. A substantial number of households of whom, in contrast, have been forced to rely upon borrowing money from different sources. Recent statistics of the International Labour Organization (2021) revealed that because of the Coronavirus pandemic, fifty percent of the global workforce may lose their livelihoods, as 1.6 billion workers in the informal economy are at immediate risk of losing their income source. The ongoing pandemic will not only affect the national economy but also the financial status of millions of families in Bangladesh. The marginalized people including rickshaw-pullers, day-laborers, domestic workers, transport workers, street vendors, and construction laborers become jobless due to COVID-19 lock down. It indicates that they are the worst sufferers of this outbreak. The lockdown created economic hardship for the low and middle income people. They lived in psychological anxiety, stress, and fear even hunger by losing their jobs and income (Mandal et al., 2021). The immense negative impacts are multidimensional that gives stress on the livelihood of the vulnerable communities during the endemic crisis. Additionally, it gave birth of an unprecedented lockdown of daily life and economic activities dwindling earning capacities. The more devastating exposure of the pandemic through the media propagate more mental health problems as individuals may feel intense empathic concern and distress witnessing or constantly hearing about other people's painful struggles with the coronavirus (Egger et al., 2020). There is immense need of study on the sustainable coping strategies to cope with the pandemic situations for appropriate policy measures. Few studies on pandemic issue reported two types of coping, i.e., general coping style and practical coping behaviors. Coping style represents the cognitive and behavioral patterns to manage particular external or internal demands appraised as taxing or even exceeding the resources of individuals, which has not yet been studied in relation to livelihood problems in the context of the COVID-19 pandemic of Bangladesh. There is no enough secondary evidence and available study or literatures that can exhibit the exposure related to shock and stresses during the COVID-19 outbreak (Chowdhury et al., 2020). Livelihood defined as the bridging efforts of the capabilities, assets (both material and social assets) and activities essential for a means of living (Chambers and Conway, 1992 cited in Eneyew, 2012). Livelihood assets essentially contributes to the vulnerable situation to lead their livelihood strategies (Chambers and Conway, 1992). The ambiguity in sustainability parameters, present complex social-environmental relationship, optimize the complicated realistic problems (Govindan et. al., 2015c cited in Ansari & Kant, 2017). Coping is a short term response to an emergency or immediate needs and is understood to be adaptational activity that involves effort. It is tied up with the immediate success and very short term, indeed who have little option they employ coping to survive. This short term adjustments are not either economically or environmentally sustainable (Wechsler, 1995). Coping strategies are mainly emotion and problem oriented (Tuncay et al., 2008). Coping response intended to fade the physical, emotional and psychological shocks that is linked stresses (Snyder, 1999). Coping impart changing cognitive, behavioral and emotional efforts to manage shocks and stresses or exceeding the resources of the individual (Lazarus, 1984). Coping strategies with the livelihood and stresses have not been studied extensively. Hossain (2021) reported that practical coping behaviors are the ways in which people are likely to behave in a pandemic. The COVID-19 pandemic began as a livelihood crisis but has in time triggered a grave and unfolding economic crisis with particular concerns for the poor and vulnerable. World Bank noted (2021), highlights the ridiculous interest rates that often accompany loans from moneylenders to cope with short-term emergency costs. According to CPD report (2020) out of 60.8 million working people, 14 million people get their monthly salary from employers, 10 million workers are day laborers and the remaining 27 million are self-employed. The Asian Development Bank (2020) assumed that Bangladesh will reduce $3 billion GDP and cuts for around 9 million individuals. After reviewing all the relevant studies a gap was found about the impact of COVID-19 on the vulnerable population. The most effective coping strategies were in relation to financial, administrative and employment cuts opts by $ 1.14 billion and 2, 01,106 individuals separately followed by agribusiness ($637 million, 4, 58,000 individuals), the travel industry ($510 million, 50,000 people), development and utilities ($ 400 million, 1.18 million people) and transport administration (Shammi et al., 2021). Paul et al. (2021) suggested the governments increase public health spending to tackle the virus. As per International Labour Organization (2021), 50 percent of the global workforce may lose their livelihoods. Islam et al., (2020) mentioned that COVID-19 could create an increase poverty. The pandemic will affect the national economy and financial status of millions families in Bangladesh. The COVID lockdown hit hard low and middle income people who have lost their jobs and income sources that ultimately resulted in psychological anxiety, stress, and fear of death from hunger (Mandal et al., 2021). Food availability at household level in urban poor or daily wage earners are extremely challenged due to COVID-19 and discontinuation of livelihood activities. In addition to this there are vulnerable groups who don't have sufficient food at their household and need immediate food assistance. All these vulnerable groups are not covered by safety net programs and life becoming extremely vulnerable (Khan and Mamun, 2020). The COVID-19 pandemic crisis has directed to a harsh predicament. The state experienced the worst economic crisis to manage livelihoods sustenance, health well-being and social safety net. World Bank noted (2021), highlights the exorbitant rates of interest that often accompany loans from moneylenders to cope with short-term emergency costs. Islam (2021) reported that construction indutries terminated their employees and cartailed festival bonus and reduced salary during pandemic situations. There is no complete study on the livelihood coping strategies of the marginalized people during lockdown and post COVID-19 situations. Thus the study will explore all gaps and coping strategies of the marginalized people. Several studies at national and international level tried to elicit the impacts of COVID-19 and its consequences on the economic growth, poverty, health risks, mental disorder and household income loss (Otache et al., 2020; Niles et al., 2020; Phillipson et al.,2020; prime et al., 2020; Kramer and Kramer, 2020; Beland et al., 2020). Several Sustainable Development Goals (SDGs) are interlinked with this study that focus on clean water and sanitation (SDG 6), poor economic development and the lack of decent jobs (SDG 8), inequality in coping (SDG 10), no poverty (SDG 1) and food insecurity (SDG 2). This research is also elicit the answer of the some questions including i) What are the impacts of COVID-19 on livelihood of marginalized people? and ii) How and at what extent they cope COVID-19 situation effectively?.

OBJECTIVE

The central aim of the study was to identify COVID-19 impacts and analyze the choice of livelihood coping strategies in the study area. The study aimed to look at the immediate impact of COVID-19 on livelihoods and household welfare, by understanding the kind of economic shocks the poor and vulnerable people are facing, what coping mechanisms they are using to survive. The specific objectives of this study were to:

- know the impact of COVID-19 on livelihood
- explore the coping strategies with the devastating situation
- elicit the livelihood status during pre and post lockdown situation

METHODOLOGY

This study conducted in Dhaka city targeting a lower income group of people (mostly daily income earners) in Mirpur area of Dhaka city (Figure1). The people of the study area usually have limited access to the income during pandemic situations at lock down period. This is the first and the most recent research response to COVID-19 initiative, in which the study employed survey on urban households people in Mirpur area of Dhaka city to understand the impacts of COVID-19 on the livelihoods of these people, how they were coping with the crisis, and what kind of support they needed to recover from this crisis. In addition to that focus group discussions, key informant's interview and case studies were carried out in getting qualitative information. Considering the impact of current livelihood lockdown for the rising curve of COVID-19 in Mirpur, Dhaka city. A total of 124 respondents were selected for individual interview using semi-structure questionnaire to understand the coping strategy during COVID-19 outbreak in Bangladesh. The study also collected expert suggestions, and cross-validation of 5 FGDs participants, 8 KIIs for getting insights at depth and perceptions from a different group of people.

Figure 1. Study area (affected by COVID-19 in Dhaka city)
Source: corona.gov.bd

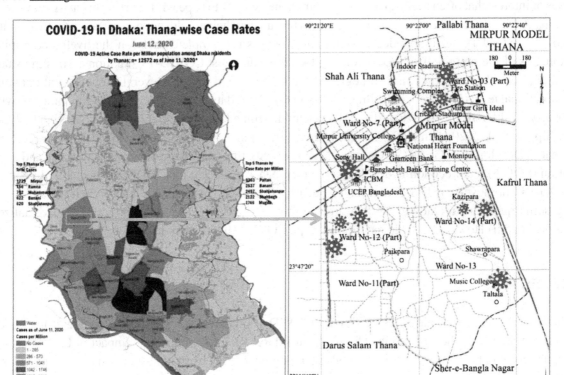

Data were analyzed using Microsoft Excel with data entry and data output. All statistical data outputs presented by table, graph and chart.

RESULTS AND DISCUSSIONS

Sources of Income before Lockdown

It was found that around 15 percent respondents earned from self-employment (small business) followed by from foreign remittance, private job and casual labor (daily or irregular), pension, assistance from other, farming own or leased land and had no source of income before the lockdown announced by government (figure 2) respectively. Respondents mentioned that the income has been drastically reduced during lockdown period and COVID-19 pandemic situation. Similarly, a study reported that the income of the people in Dhaka city dramatically declined during the outbreak of COVID-19 and lockdown (Sohel et al., 2021).

Figure 2. Before the lockdown announced by government family's main source of income
Source: Field survey, 2021

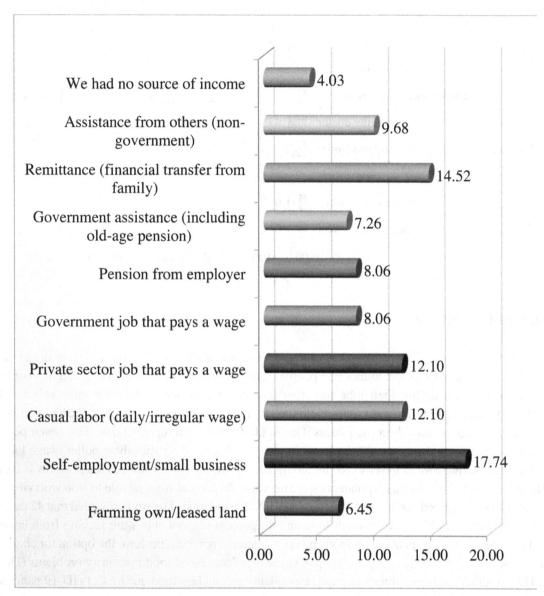

Information Sources used to Learn about the COVID-19

The vulnerable people learnt more about the COVID-19 and it's symptom from local practitioners. It was found that around 55 percent respondents know about COVID-19 from the traditional medicine practitioner followed by the government health officials and local health workers to gather more information on COVID-19 respectively (figure 3).

Figure 3. Sources used to learn about the COVID-19 in the past 7 days
Source: Field survey, 2021

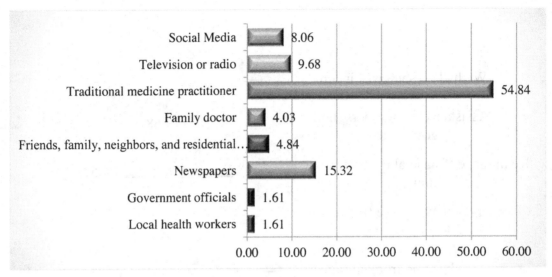

Impacts of COVID-19

COVID-19 affects badly the livelihood of almost half of the global work force living in urban areas especially the marginalized and vulnerable people. Many low and middle-income group of people of Bangladesh have already lost their jobs and other income sources due to the substantial effect of the COVID-19 pandemic. Low-income groups including day laborers and garment workers are badly-affected as they instantaneously have become jobless. One study from Kenya reported that sixty seven percent respondents encountered income shocks (Kansiime et al., 2021). Most Rickshaw puller, wage laborer don't have any savings. Most lower-class, including those working garment factories in slums is facing the same fate. Forty six percent respondents were nervous, 26 percent were unable to stop worrying and 24 percent were depressed and hopeless during COVID-19 pandemic. The study revealed that 42 percent respondents were not able to eat enough food and 40 percent respondents were lacking from enough food, 11 percent didn't have choice on food and only 7 percent respondents have the option for choosing food. A research showed that nearly ninety percent respondents faced food insecurity problems (Das et al., 2020). Another study mentioned that the respondents getting less food during COVID-19 pandemic situation (Sohel et al., 2021). More than 43 percent respondents lost their job, 26 percent respondents lost income and 16 percent were unable to access healthcare facilities in pandemic crisis. Matin et al., (2020) reported that in Kenya, some individual respondents having experience on income shocks. A study mentioned that lockdown and COVID-19 pandemic caused significantly the unemployment (McGann et al., 2020). Highly price of product, Inexplicable medical cost, Food shortage, food insecurity, unexpected expenses, job interrupted, job crisis, low salary, communication incompatibility, inefficiency of work, Lack of facilities, fear of income, stress and anxiety, feeling bore, living cost, income, unemployment are the common impacts of COVID-19. Almost similar experience gained by the people from Ethiopia, Nigeria and Malawi during COVID-19 pandemic (Rahman and Matin, 2020).

Figure 4. COVID-19 Impact on Mental Health Treatment Access

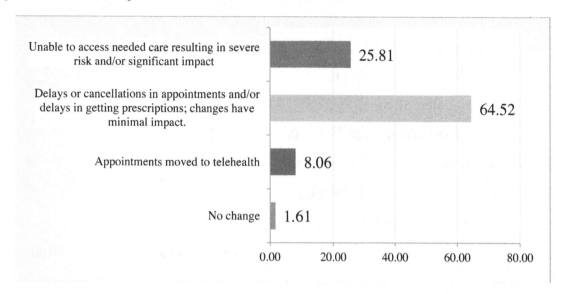

65 percent of the respondents were need to delay or cancellation in appointments and 26 percent of the respondents were unable to access healthcare resulting in server risks and 2 percent respondents who don't have no impact on their mental health (figure 4)

Coping Strategies of the Respondents

A wide array of coping strategies applied by the respondents for their livelihood. Respondents used their savings followed by seeking support from relatives and friends. It was mentioned by the respondents that who have strong kinship and social bondage are in good position. Similarly Ayral (2018) emphasized on the importance of social bondage and kinship during crisis. Eventually they took loan from money lenders, Samity, clubs, NGOs and Bank. Similarly a study reported that the respondents taking loan is also one of the coping mechanism in lockdown situation (Sohel et al., 2021). Another study showed that respondents use their savings for consumption in urban and rural areas of Bangladesh (Martin et al., 2020). Additionally they sold their belongings (furniture, cycle, rickshaw, motorbike. electronic devices, and jewelry) to cope with pandemic situation. More than thirty one percent respondents reported that authority reduce working hours, 19.35 percent business income reduced, 13.71 percent quitted their job, 12.10 percent respondents were performing job from home and 10.48 percent lost their job respectively. It was found that a set of coping strategies are practicing by the respondents of which 45 percent respondents sleep more followed by searching new work or business, meditation, physical exercise, consuming stress and working more respectively (Figure 5). Only 10.48 percent respondents were not initiated coping strategies. It was mentioned by the respondents that they have adjusted several coping strategies for food, economic hardship at the time of no income during pandemic and lockdown.

The results revealed that (31.45%) of the respondents perform their job at workplace but with the reduced hours and only 10.48 percent of the respondents lost their job respectively (Figure 6).

The result explored that majority respondents had multiple answer for sometimes and rest of the respondents had multiple answer for always coping strategy on devastating situations (figure 7).

Figure 5. Coping strategies

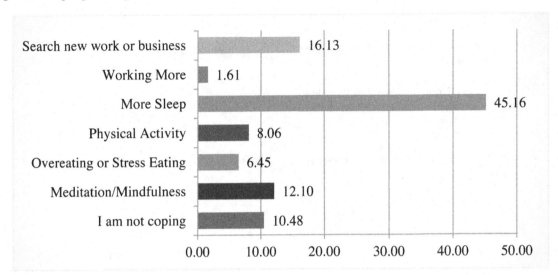

Coping with Meals and Food

Ten percent respondents changed their diet (lowering intake of rich food, decreasing fish, milk, meat consuming days), fifteen percent respondents compromised with the meal quality and quantity (switching from fine rice to coarse rice). Five percent coped with the meals from three times to two times. And also most of the respondents cut off morning and afternoon snacks from their daily diet. Around 42 percent of the respondents are sometimes not enough to eat, 39.52 percent of the respondents have not enough food and only 7 percent respondents have enough food to eat (figure 8). Respondents said that adult

Figure 6. Employment/business/job status changed since the COVID-19 pandemic

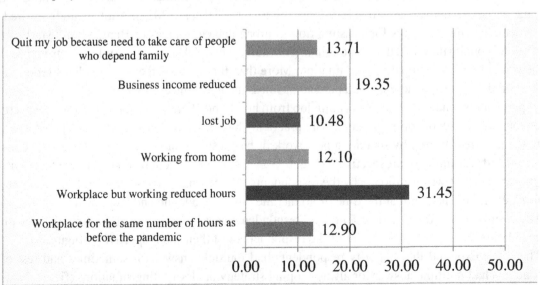

Figure 7. Coping Strategies with the Devastating Situation

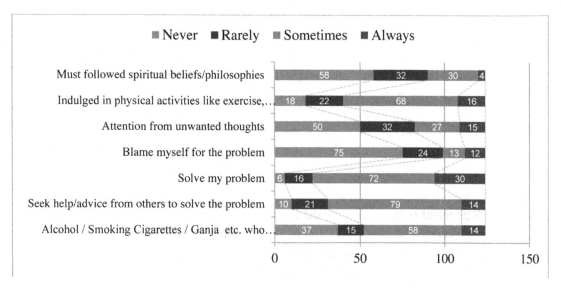

person scarify their own food and feed the kids (European Food Safety Authority, 2020 cited in Sohel et al., 2021). According to Ruszczyk et al., (2020) the respondents from small cities consuming less food and sacrifice the quality of the food. Another study described that the people restrict from food due to affordability and limited access to the market (Bene et al., 2015). Taylor (2020) pointed that pandemic showing the existing inequalities among the urban dwellers in Bangladesh.

Figure 8. Getting enough food to eat

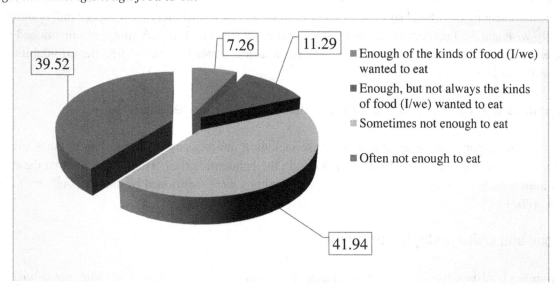

Figure 9. Sources of free food during pandemic situation

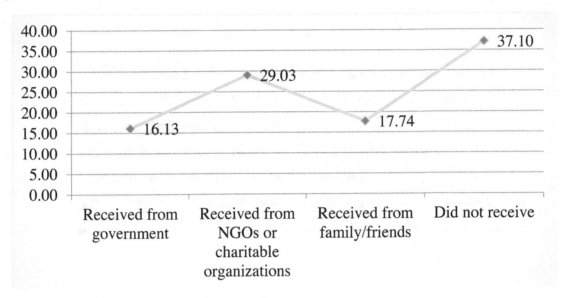

37 percent of the majority respondents did not obtain free food from any sources. Twenty nine percent respondents from NGOs followed by family friends and only 16 percent of the respondents received free food from government (Figure 9).

Housing and Other Facilities

People lost their jobs and left Dhaka city & rental house toward rural village to cope with the extra cost of livelihood expenditure. Few of them who continued jobs/business they shifted their family to rural home in managing livelihood style. 35 percent respondents used kitchen or living space individually or family wise and 3.23 percent shared both living space, kitchen and toilet. A study also mentioned that the essential associate costs in urban living such as housing, water and fuel restrict the affordability of the urban dwellers (Satterthwaite, 2004).

Adjustment in Clothes, Dress, Ornaments and Other Necessities

Most of the respondents reduced new purchase including unnecessary wearing clothes, fancy goods, ornaments, jewelry items and electronic devices in the pandemic crisis. They also cut down the extra and unnecessary ceremonial expenditure. Similar findings were mentioned by another study by Sohel et al., (2021).

Social and Cultural Coping Strategies

Within the hardship, the respondents restricted their social movement, long travelling, not to visiting friends and relatives, avoiding different family occasion (birthday, marriage day) religious practices (Prayers, Friday prayers not going to the mosque, mandir or church). The enjoyed no cultural events (folksongs, Baisakhi fair) physically and celebrated festivals (Eid, Christmas, Puja) in restricted ways.

It was mentioned by the respondents they were restricted in movement and several social and cultural activities due to lockdown. Dollman (2018) reported that less physical activity lead towards many diseases especially in the crisis.

Employers Coping Strategy

The small scale entrepreneurs survived by taking out loans, which have now totaled a substantial sum. They paid their employees for two months, and then reduced pay and finally cut them off with unpaid vacations.

CONCLUSION AND RECOMMENDATIONS

It is clear that the COVID-19 pandemic and lockdown disturbed people's way of thinking, activities and livelihoods globally. Mostly it hampered the lives of developing countries such as Bangladesh. The study also gives us few hope of coping initiatives such as spending savings, taking loan, getting support from relatives and others, customizing expenditure, consuming less, shifting occupations and avoiding ceremonial activities. COVID-19 pandemic in Bangladesh tells us that economic activities and alternative livelihoods have been emerging. There are challenges in areas of equitable distribution of resources and providing economic support to the disadvantageous groups (cash and kind support, food supports, social safety net). This research some early insights into coping strategies of livelihood during COVID-19, with a special focus on socio-demography, socio-economy, food security and health aspect. As the crisis develops, future rounds of representative monitoring data on the same respondents will help understand the evolving impacts and potential recovery. The findings presented here indicate socioeconomic impacts both at the lower and middle class family with important variation across areas and gender, largely due to the different nature of occupations affected by this crisis. The following recommendations were made for the community, further research and policy implications:

- Provision of subsidies for the underprivileged people with essential government assistance
- Easy access to the business grants (seed money, grants distributions and payments modalities for beneficiaries).
- Government, autonomous institution, private company and NGOs should create safe employment for lower and middle class people.
- Effective use of gloves, sanitizers, hand wash, keeping social distance and discouraging gatherings that are unnecessary
- Creating new job with longer-term consequences for poverty, food security, and future earnings for vulnerable people
- An assessment process could help the government and policymakers to judge the public perceptions to deal with the COVID-19 pandemic especially for lower-middle-income people
- Strategic assessment of COVID-19 pandemic in Bangladesh for comparative lockdown scenario analysis, public perception and management for sustainability.
- The study is also suggested for more specific research on the assessment of the livelihood status of the vulnerable people before and after lockdown period of the marginalized people in the slum and rural areas.

REFERENCES

Adhikari, S.P., Meng, S., Wu, Y., Mao, Y., Ye, R., Wang, Q., Sun, C., Sylvia, S., Rozelle, S., Raat, H., & Zhou, H. (2020). *A literature review of 2019 Novel Coronavirus during the early outbreak period: Epidemiology, causes, clinical manifestation and diagnosis, prevention and control.* Academic Press.

Ansari, Z. N., & Kant, R. (2017). A state-of-art literature review reflecting 15 years of focus on sustainable supply chain management. *Journal of Cleaner Production, 142,* 2524–2543. doi:10.1016/j.jclepro.2016.11.023

Aryal, R. (2018). Kinship as a social capital in rural development: An anthropological perspective. *Dhaulagiri, 12,* 88–97. doi:10.3126/dsaj.v12i0.22184

Asian Development Bank. (2021). *In the Spotlight.* https://www.adb.org/countries /bangladesh/main

Béland, L.P., Brodeur, A., & Wright, T. (2020). *The short-term economic consequences of Covid-19: exposure to disease, remote work and government response.* Academic Press.

Béné, C., Waid, J., Jackson-deGraffenried, M., Begum, A., Chowdhury, M., Skarin, V., Rahman, A., Islam, N., Mamnun, N., Mainuddin, K., & Amin, S.M.A. (2015). Impact of climate-related shocks and stresses on nutrition and food security in selected areas of rural Bangladesh. *Dhaka World Food Programme, 3.*

Chambers, R., & Conway, G. (1992). *Sustainable rural livelihoods: practical concepts for the 21st century.* Institute of Development Studies.

Chowdhury, R., Luhar, S., Khan, N., Choudhury, S. R., Matin, I., & Franco, O. H. (2020). Long-term strategies to control COVID-19 in low and middle-income countries: An options overview of community-based, non-pharmacological interventions. *European Journal of Epidemiology, 35*(8), 743–748. doi:10.100710654-020-00660-1 PMID:32656618

CPD. (2020). *Dealing with COVID-19.* https://cpd.org.bd/dealing-with-covid-19/

Das, S., Rasul, M. G., Hossain, M. S., Khan, A. R., Alam, M. A., Ahmed, T., & Clemens, J. D. (2020). Acute food insecurity and short-term coping strategies of urban and rural households of Bangladesh during the lockdown period of COVID-19 pandemic of 2020: Report of a cross-sectional survey. *BMJ Open, 10*(12), e043365. doi:10.1136/bmjopen-2020-043365 PMID:33310813

Dollman, J. (2018). Social and environmental influences on physical activity behaviours. *International Journal of Environmental Research and Public Health, 15*(1), 169. doi:10.3390/ijerph15010169 PMID:29361761

Egger, D., Miguel, E., Warren, S. S., Shenoy, A., Collins, E., Karlan, D., Parkerson, D., Mobarak, A. M., Fink, G., Udry, C., Walker, M., Haushofer, J., Larreboure, M., Athey, S., Lopez-Pena, P., Benhachmi, S., Humphreys, M., Lowe, L., Meriggi, N. F., ... Vernot, C. (2021). Falling living standards during the COVID-19 crisis: Quantitative evidence from nine developing countries. *Science Advances, 7*(6), eabe0997. doi:10.1126ciadv.abe0997 PMID:33547077

Eneyew, A., & Bekele, W. (2012). Determinants of livelihood strategies in Wolaita, southern Ethiopia. *Agricultural Research and Reviews, 1*(5), 153–161.

Govindan, K., Jafarian, A., & Nourbakhsh, V. (2015). Bi-objective integrating sustainable order allocation and sustainable supply chain network strategic design with stochastic demand using a novel robust hybrid multi-objective metaheuristic. *Computers & Operations Research*, *62*, 112–130. doi:10.1016/j.cor.2014.12.014

Guo, J., Feng, X. L., Wang, X. H., & van IJzendoorn, M. H. (2020). Coping with COVID-19: Exposure to COVID-19 and negative impact on livelihood predict elevated mental health problems in Chinese adults. *International Journal of Environmental Research and Public Health*, *17*(11), 3857. doi:10.3390/ijerph17113857 PMID:32485859

Hamadani, J. D., Hasan, M. I., Baldi, A. J., Hossain, S. J., Shiraji, S., Bhuiyan, M. S. A., Mehrin, S. F., Fisher, J., Tofail, F., Tipu, S. M. U., Grantham-McGregor, S., Biggs, B.-A., Braat, S., & Pasricha, S.-R. (2020). Immediate impact of stay-at-home orders to control COVID-19 transmission on socioeconomic conditions, food insecurity, mental health, and intimate partner violence in Bangladeshi women and their families: An interrupted time series. *The Lancet. Global Health*, *8*(11), e1380–e1389. doi:10.1016/S2214-109X(20)30366-1 PMID:32857955

Hossain, M. I. (2021). COVID-19 Impacts on Employment and Livelihood of Marginal People in Bangladesh: Lessons Learned and Way Forward. *South Asian Survey*, *28*(1), 57–71. doi:10.1177/0971523121995072

Islam, M. S. (2021). COVID-19 and the construction industries in Dhaka, Bangladesh. *Academic Letters*, *193*(6), 3971. Advance online publication. doi:10.20935/AL3971

Islam, S., Islam, R., Mannan, F., Rahman, S., & Islam, T. (2020). COVID-19 pandemic: An analysis of the healthcare, social and economic challenges in Bangladesh. *Progress in Disaster Science*, *8*, 100135. doi:10.1016/j.pdisas.2020.100135 PMID:34173450

Janssens, W., Pradhan, M., de Groot, R., Sidze, E., Donfouet, H. P. P., & Abajobir, A. (2021). The short-term economic effects of COVID-19 on low-income households in rural Kenya: An analysis using weekly financial household data. *World Development*, *138*, 105280. doi:10.1016/j.worlddev.2020.105280

Kansiime, M. K., Tambo, J. A., Mugambi, I., Bundi, M., Kara, A., & Owuor, C. (2021). COVID-19 implications on household income and food security in Kenya and Uganda: Findings from a rapid assessment. *World Development*, *137*, 105199. doi:10.1016/j.worlddev.2020.105199 PMID:32982018

Khan, K. S., Mamun, M. A., Griffiths, M. D., & Ullah, I. (2020). The mental health impact of the COVID-19 pandemic across different cohorts. *International Journal of Mental Health and Addiction*, 1–7. PMID:32837440

Kramer, A., & Kramer, K. Z. (2020). The potential impact of the Covid-19 pandemic on occupational status, work from home, and occupational mobility. *Journal of Vocational Behavior*, *119*, 103442. doi:10.1016/j.jvb.2020.103442 PMID:32390661

Lazarus, R. S., & Folkman, S. (1984). *Stress, appraisal, and coping*. Springer publishing company.

Mandal, S. C., Boidya, P., Haque, M. I. M., Hossain, A., Shams, Z., & Mamun, A. A. (2021). The impact of the COVID-19 pandemic on fish consumption and household food security in Dhaka city, Bangladesh. *Global Food Security*, *29*, 100526. doi:10.1016/j.gfs.2021.100526 PMID:35155095

Martin, A., Markhvida, M., Hallegatte, S., & Walsh, B. (2020). Socio-economic impacts of COVID-19 on household consumption and poverty. *Economics of Disasters and Climate Change*, *4*(3), 453–479. doi:10.100741885-020-00070-3 PMID:32838120

McGann, M., Murphy, M. P., & Whelan, N. (2020). Workfare redux? Pandemic unemployment, labour activation and the lessons of post-crisis welfare reform in Ireland. *The International Journal of Sociology and Social Policy*, *40*(9/10), 963–978. doi:10.1108/IJSSP-07-2020-0343

Monitor, I.L.O. (2020). *COVID-19 and the world of work. Updated estimates and analysis*. ILO.

Nagel, L. (2020). The influence of the COVID-19 pandemic on the digital transformation of work. *The International Journal of Sociology and Social Policy*, *40*(9/10), 861–875. doi:10.1108/IJSSP-07-2020-0323

Niles, M. T., Bertmann, F., Belarmino, E. H., Wentworth, T., Biehl, E., & Neff, R. (2020). The early food insecurity impacts of COVID-19. *Nutrients*, *12*(7), 2096. doi:10.3390/nu12072096 PMID:32679788

Otache, I. (2020). The effects of the Covid-19 Pandemic on the Nigeria's economy and possible coping strategies. *Asian Journal of Social Sciences and Management Studies*, *7*(3), 173–179. doi:10.20448/journal.500.2020.73.173.179

Paul, A., Nath, T. K., Mahanta, J., Sultana, N. N., Kayes, A. I., Noon, S. J., Jabed, M. A., Podder, S., & Paul, S. (2021). Psychological and livelihood impacts of COVID-19 on Bangladeshi lower income people. *Asia-Pacific Journal of Public Health*, *33*(1), 100–108. doi:10.1177/1010539520977304 PMID:33289393

Phillipson, J., Gorton, M., Turner, R., Shucksmith, M., Aitken-McDermott, K., Areal, F., Cowie, P., Hubbard, C., Maioli, S., McAreavey, R., Souza-Monteiro, D., Newbery, R., Panzone, L., Rowe, F., & Shortall, S. (2020). The COVID-19 pandemic and its implications for rural economies. *Sustainability*, *12*(10), 3973. doi:10.3390u12103973

Prime, H., Wade, M., & Browne, D. T. (2020). Risk and resilience in family well-being during the COVID-19 pandemic. *The American Psychologist*, *75*(5), 631–643. doi:10.1037/amp0000660 PMID:32437181

Rahman, H. Z., & Matin, I. (2020). *Livelihoods, coping, and support during COVID-19 crisis*. BRAC Institute of Governance and Development.

Ruszczyk, H. A., Rahman, M. F., Bracken, L. J., & Sudha, S. (2021). Contextualizing the COVID-19 pandemic's impact on food security in two small cities in Bangladesh. *Environment and Urbanization*, *33*(1), 239–254. doi:10.1177/0956247820965156 PMID:34253941

Satterthwaite, D. (2004). *The under-estimation of urban poverty in low and middle-income nations* (Vol. 14). Iied.

Shammi, M., Bodrud-Doza, M., Islam, A. R. M. T., & Rahman, M. M. (2021). Strategic assessment of COVID-19 pandemic in Bangladesh: Comparative lockdown scenario analysis, public perception, and management for sustainability. *Environment, Development and Sustainability*, *23*(4), 6148–6191. doi:10.100710668-020-00867-y PMID:32837281

Snyder, C. R. (Ed.). (1999). *Coping: The psychology of what works*. Oxford University Press. doi:10.1093/med:psych/9780195119343.001.0001

Sohel, M. S., Hossain, B., Alam, M. K., Shi, G., Shabbir, R., Sifullah, M. K., & Mamy, M. M. B. (2021). COVID-19 induced impact on informal migrants in Bangladesh: A qualitative study. *The International Journal of Sociology and Social Policy.*

Taylor, J. (2020). How Dhaka's urban poor are dealing with Covid-19. *Urban Matters, 1.*

Tuncay, T., Musabak, I., Gok, D. E., & Kutlu, M. (2008). The relationship between anxiety, coping strategies and characteristics of patients with diabetes. *Health and Quality of Life Outcomes*, *6*(1), 1–9. doi:10.1186/1477-7525-6-79 PMID:18851745

Wechsler, B. (1995). Coping and coping strategies: A behavioural view. *Applied Animal Behaviour Science*, *43*(2), 123–134. doi:10.1016/0168-1591(95)00557-9

World Bank. (2021). *The World Bank in Bangladesh.* https://www.worldbank.org/ en/ country/bangladesh/overview

Chapter 21

Estimating the Impact of COVID–19 on the Future of the Tourism Sector:
Implications on Tourism and Sustainability Post Pandemic

Viana Imad Hassan

https://orcid.org/0000-0002-7372-5059

Rushford Business School, Switzerland

Georges Bellos

Lebanese International University, Lebanon

ABSTRACT

The tourism sector is a wide-ranging industry that provides myriad job opportunities worldwide, especially for countries whose economies depends on tourism, like Greece, Spain, and Lebanon. However, the COVID-19 pandemic has tremendously affected this sector. To better understand the post-COVID-19 situation on tourism, the research is mainly based on different sources (articles, papers, reports, and statistics based on the UNWTO, WTO, WHO, etc.) collected through secondary and primary data interpretation. The methodology has been adapted accordingly to collect data from expert interviews and semi-structured surveys following Saunders et al. As a result, this study aims to gather information about the post-COVID-19 impact on the tourism sector through exploring sustainable tourism as one of the solutions for the speedy recovery of the industry in terms of recovery. The main findings presented in this research have shown that domestic tourism will be more sustainable until international tourism gets back on its feet.

DOI: 10.4018/978-1-6684-6762-6.ch021

INTRODUCTION

Huang et al. (2020) point out that the Coronavirus disease 2019 (COVID-19) is an infectious disease caused by the coronavirus 2 that causes extreme acute respiratory syndrome (SARS-CoV-2). The first case of COVID-19 was discovered in Wuhan China in November 2019. As such, and after that the disease was deemed as a world pandemic and as a highly contagious disease, it has propagated extremely quickly (Huang et al., 2020). The total cases reported of COVID-19 worldwide, according to the World Health Organization (WHO), casualties reached about 4 Million (WHO, 2020, 2021).

This pandemic spreads primarily through the direct contact of an infected person who shows the virus symptoms like coughing, and sneezing. In addition to that, COVID-19 virus lives up to 72 hours on objects and surfaces so by touching these surfaces and objects anyone could get infected (WHO, 2020, 2021). As the globe is facing an unprecedented global health, social and economic emergency with the COVID-19 pandemic, travel and tourism are of the most affected industries cancelled flights, hotels and other hospitality businesses, forced to shut down, and travel bans put in place in practically all nations around the world (Poeta & Maragall, 2021).

Furthermore, the tourism industry has experienced tremendous deficits, due to the pandemic, with no chances for immediate recovery, as the UNWTO (2020a, b, c, d) statistics attest. They refer to the terrible effects of the pandemic left on the industry, namely through the global deficit of 900 bn USD. This worldwide loss of revenue for 2020, was a major blow for the economies of countries highly dependent on tourism as their related businesses also suffered greatly. The shock has an effect on both the demand (constraints on freedom of movement, border closures, and visitors' fear of virus) and supply (closure of accommodation and catering establishments as well as leisure and entertainment facilities used for tourism) sides (Ugur & Akbıyık, 2020).

Moreover, the pandemic's impact on global GDP growth is enormous. The COVID-19 economic crisis is the worst since World War II ended. And the World War I Spanish Flu, the pandemic that decimated 50 million people is also important not to forget. According to the World Economic Outlook Report the global economy contracted by 3.5% in 2020 (World Economic Forum, 2020a, b). In the following months, the COVID-19 pandemic may reach a peak and settle, but the already inflected damage will persist for a longer duration. Thus, countries will need to take short, medium, and long-term actions to curb these severe economic damages (Rogoff, 2020).

However, incomes have been lowered as a result of their respective countries' governments' mitigating initiatives. The work-from-home directive, as well as the restriction of public meetings, the closing of eateries, and the early evening curfew, have resulted in shortened working hours, with certain organizations, particularly MSMEs with erratic cash flows, being forced to lay off personnel, at least, they should be required to take unpaid leave for an unknown period of time. Consequently, incomes have decreased, putting downward pressure on consumer spending (World Health Organization, 2020). Besides that, several recommendations were suggested to avoid the spread of COVID-19 virus: wearing facemasks, washing hands, social distancing, etc. Yet, due to this pandemic, the recovery of the tourism industry worldwide will take some time. In this research a qualitative method was used through conducting interviews and disseminating a google forms survey via WhatsApp, in order to study post COVID-19, tourism and sustainability (cf. Hall, et al., 2015; Kamran, 2020; Woyo, 2021). Our method was drafted from Sargeant (2012).

LITERATURE REVIEW

Tourism and Sustainability

Tourism contributes directly and indirectly to all the planned goals for a better future. It helps in enhancing the sustainability of the economic growth, the flora and fauna resources, the consumption and the production (Kuhlman & Farrington, 2020; Hall, et al., 2015; James et al., 2015). Sustainable tourism involves the optimal use of minimizing the negative impacts of tourism on economic, socio-cultural, and ecological pillars and maximizing the benefits of it on the local communities, national economies, and on the conservation of nature (Pascariu, 2009; Kamran, 2020). Sustainable tourism development surrounds Tourism central's focus depending on sustaining the natural and man-made resources in a destination when traveling to it (McKercher, 1993; Kamran, 2020; UNWTO, 2021).

According to the UNWTO, achieving sustainable tourism is a continuous process that needs a constant supervision of its impacts on an attraction (UNWTO, 2020a, b, c, d). In addition, it maintains a high level of tourist satisfaction and ensures a delightful experience for the tourists meanwhile raising the awareness and knowledge about sustainability issues (UNWTO, 2021). Richards stated that sustainable tourism develops quickly by taking into consideration the current accommodation capacity, the local population, and the environment (see: UNWTO, 2021).

Figure 1 shows the different types of tourism which consider it as sustainable tourism such as responsible tourism, alternative tourism, eco-tourism, environmentally friendly tourism, minimum impact tourism, and soft tourism which help in preserving and sustaining tourism. Yet, according to UNBC (United Nations Brundtland Commission), sustainability is when meeting the needs of the present without compromising future generations' ability to meet their own needs (Kamran, 2020; McChesney, 1991). Moreover, the University of Alberta added a new definition for sustainability: It's the act of living within the constraints of available physical, environmental, and cultural resources in such a way that the living systems in which humans are situated can survive indefinitely (Kamran, 2020).

Figure 2 shows the three essential pillars that are society, economy, and environment of sustainability. Environment pillar is everything related to the quality of air, water and the preservation of these resources with sustainability. Society pillar focuses on issues like education, health, justice, and communities with the help of sustainability. Finally, the last pillar is economy that holds job creation, mobility, government incentives; business profits all are monitored by sustainability (Ben-Eli, 2018). Figure 3 explains this in more details (see: UNWTO, 2021).

Tourism and Infectious Diseases

Earlier studies have determined that many diseases have affected the tourism industry, such as H1N1, HIV, AIDS, SARS, Ebola, Zika viruses, and lately, COVID-19, which suspended tourism activities worldwide (Kumudumali, 2020). Literature explored how previous diseases affected tourism. Kumudumali, (2020) studied how Malaria, Yellow Fever, Dengue, and Ebola impacted tourist arrivals in affected countries, which showed a significant decline in these arrivals especially the Malaria affected countries leaded to 47% fewer tourist arrivals. Kumudumali, (2020) also said that the study of SARS disease showed an effect on Asia tourist arrivals while Avian Flu disease (H1 N1, H5 N1 etc.) study showed no effect on the Asia tourist arrivals. As for the case of COVID-19 countries are implementing to travel bans, quarantines, and curfews. According to the UNWTO the effect of COVID-19 is like no

Figure 1. The different categories of sustainable tourism (see: Kamran, 2020)

other previous disease or pandemic on the sector, in terms of recovery or sanitation measures (UNWTO, 2020a, b, c, d). Besides, this previous experience has shown little evidence on predicting the effects of the Coronavirus epidemic on tourism (Bilgin, et al., 2020). However, many specialists are now observing for effective planning and development for the sustainability of the tourism sector, leading to the endurance of an excellent experience for both tourists and the host community after this black stage of COVID-19 (Dastgerdi, et al., 2020).

Figure 4 shows the international tourist arrivals worldwide and how it was affected by several factors in various countries. In 2003 the SARS virus led tourist arrivals to decrease to -0.4% (-3m). As for the arrival of tourists in 2009 decreased to -4% (-37m) because of the economic recession (Rogoff, 2020). Whereas, between 2019-2020 when the COVID-19 appeared tourism sector stopped and lost too many visitors, the decrease in visitor's number showed between -20% (-290) and -30% (-440) which was the

Figure 2. The pillars of sustainability (Kamran, 2020)

largest loss in all times (Huang et al., 2020). This indicates that Coronavirus pandemic had the biggest impact on the tourism sector than any other factor (see: UNWTO, 2020a, b, c, d, 2021).

Figure 3. Links of the three spheres of sustainable development on Tourism (see: UNWTO, 2021)

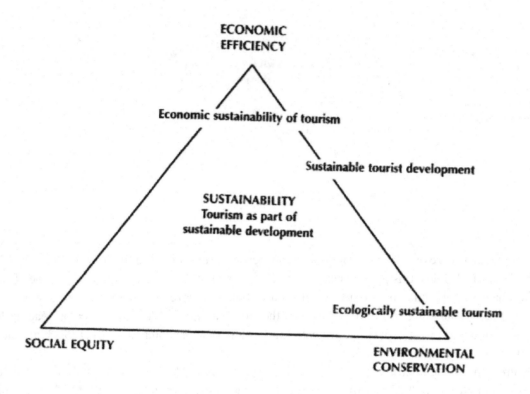

Figure 4. International tourist arrivals 2000-2020. (Davitt, 2020)

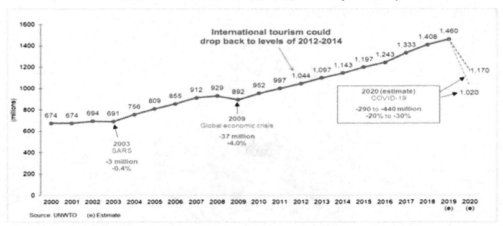

COVID-19 and Tourism

In December 2019, COVID-19 first appeared in Wuhan, China and began to spread worldwide, leading to many death cases worldwide and a large decrease in tourist arrivals, taking into account the various lockdown measures, airport closures, or travel cancelations (Jones & Comfort, 2020). So, if an infected person coughs or sneezes, the virus spreads mainly by saliva droplets or nasal discharge (Huang et al., 2020; WHO, 2020, 2021). Inger Anderson stated that even though COVID-19 has a positive impact on the environment, it improves air quality. COVID-19 also negatively impacts three main sustainable factors: environment, society, and economy since it increased a massive number of medical wastes, led to human distress, and caused the economic recession in most countries (Jones & Comfort, 2020).

Because of COVID-19 tourists stopped traveling so airports stopped functioning, host communities' economy dropped; since many countries' economy depends only on tourism, and as such, many people lost their jobs, leading to decreased quality of life. Therefore, tourism-dependent countries will feel the negative impacts of this pandemic crisis much longer than any other community. UNCTAD (United Nations Conference on Trade and Development) estimated that if foreign tourist arrivals fell by 66%, global GDP losses due to the tourism crisis could lead to 2.8 percent of global GDP (USD 1.2 trillion), with the effects most severe in countries like Croatia (potential GDP drop of 8%), Portugal (6%), Morocco (4%), Greece (4%), Ireland (3%), and Spain (3%). If foreign tourist flows are halted for a year, this could amount to a drop of 4.2 percent of global GDP (USD 3.3 trillion) (OECD, 2020a, b).

Post COVID-19 and Tourism Sustainability

In the Post COVID-19 era tourism will be transformed. Sanitation orders will be strongly obligatory, some tourism businesses will see their economy shrinking, forcing them to turn towards local consumer's market. The World Tourism and Travel Council (WTTC) stated that travelers shifted to focusing on traveling domestically or going to outdoor destinations (WTTC, 2020a, b). Business travelers are somehow a hope for hotels and airlines revenue which will help in shifting the crisis phase (Behsudi, 2020). Planes with 6 ft between seats, resorts with fewer guests and larger dining rooms, restaurants and bars selling luxury products to socially isolated customers – fewer clients; more space; higher rent; more expensive (Lapointe, 2020). Decrease in the demand market will certainly diminish the tourism sector and increase the prices. After the pandemic it is going to be hard for all countries. Regular rules will still be applied until then as increased sanitization, regulations on capacity reduction, and social distancing all may significantly affect the industry's profitability and increase charges. We believe that non-price strategies can be helpful to change customers' perception of products (Assaf & Scuderi, 2020).

One of the effective recovery strategies for tourism organizations in the post-viral world might be allowing the people with coronavirus antibodies travel freely (Woyo, 2021). Airlines, hotels, and spas can provide them with a variety of discounts and packages. It is possible that a small percentage of the healed individuals may need therapy, implying that certain special incentives will be available for certain types of travelers. After all, one critical problem will remain: how to tell the difference between those who have been healed and those who have transmitted COVID-19 and are immune? Any opportunists will almost certainly try to cheat in order to be included in this community of post-viral coronavirus-free visitors. In this case, technology can be useful, just as it is in the battle against the coronavirus.

In Prague, for example, two Uber drivers were among the first persons diagnosed with COVID-19 in early March 2020, both of whom were in serious state (Uber, 2020a). Moreover, thanks to the Uber app, all of their latest trips could be tracked down and their customers checked for coronavirus, where Smart quarantine and tracing are already used in many countries to keep an eye on the spread of CO-VID-19 (Uber, 2020b). So, in China they invented the quarantine tracking bracelet that is given to all new comers, and is connected to the smartphone and any violation of regulations it will be reported directly to the authorities (Hoque, et al., 2020). The code shows a green color which means the Traveler is risk-free, yellow means there could be a mild exposure and risk needing a one-week self-quarantine, and red means there is an immediate exposure and a two-week quarantine is required (cf. Hoque, et al., 2020; Huang et al., 2020).

As in some countries technology is costly for some travelers and citizens so for example, in India they use a quarantine ink hand stamp that contains an expiry date (Strielkowski, 2020). Tourism is not expected to recover worldwide until 2030 even with the help of vaccines it will take time for it to roll out so business stakeholders started to take actions to restore what has been lost by putting several priorities that include (OECD, 2020a, b) restoring traveler's confidence, promotion of domestic tourism and its safety for travel; developing sustainable tourism; to rebuild a strong connection between countries; capacity planning; and giving travelers the tiniest information and detail about his travel (OECD, 2020a, b). Youness (2017) and Lacanilao Arnould (2018) discuss some trends in business including sustainability, as a potential solution for the industry to consider recovery, and explain this clearly.

Impact of COVID-19 on the Socio-Economic Domain

COVID-19 has impacted negatively on the economy of the countries worldwide, especially on Lebanon's economy since many tourism sectors gone bankrupt and dismissed a very big number of employees who depended on their work for living (Rogoff, 2020; UNWTO, 2020a, b, c, d). Organizations that rely on social contacts, such as entertainment and tourism, are suffering greatly, with millions of citizens losing their positions. Layoffs, lower earnings, and increased instability have caused users to pay less, resulting in more business closures and mass unemployment. People were forced to work from home when it's possible, workplace closings have hampered supply chains and reduced productivity (Rogoff, 2020)

This epidemic has afflicted people of all ages of civilization. However, it is especially harmful to vulnerable socioeconomic groups such as the poor, the elderly, individuals with disabilities, adolescents, native communities, and ethnic minorities (Huang et al., 2020). Those without a residence or shelter, such as migrants, refugees, or displaced people, will face significant problems during and after the crisis. This could happen in a variety of ways, such as having limited mobility or fewer career prospects (cf. Huang et al., 2020). To stop the spread, authorities have closed borders. Further precautions include travel prohibitions and the banning of athletic events and certain crowded places. Furthermore, in many places around the world, policies such as preventing the use of local transportation and public venues, such as dining, shopping malls, and public sights, are in place (OECD, 2020a, b). The issue is particularly catastrophic in the hospitality and worldwide travel industries, particularly airlines, cruise lines, casinos, and hotels, which are experiencing a 90% drop-in commercial activity (Mofijur, et al., 2020). Altinay & Paraskevas (2008) also discussed issues pertaoning to the industry.

A study was shown about the tourism industry in China is the most affected, as tourists are unable to visit the country due to the virus. Hotels, airlines, and cruise ships were all shut down. As a result of the virus's continued spread, the effect on China's GDP is growing. As seen in this sense, the tourism industry is facing unimaginable threats (see: Hoque, et al., 2020). The COVID-19 raises a global health warning, creating healthcare insecurity and affecting the economic collapse of activities. Because of the rapid spread of coronavirus, several countries have suspended travel and commerce with China (Hoque, et al., 2020).

METHODOLOGY

For this study, the use of qualitative data allows the author to go deeper into the subject, since the questionnaire consists of open-ended, thus gathering information that is more relevant to the study and offer a better insight about the sustainability of tourism after COVID-19 (Sargeant, 2012; Sigala, 2019). The questionnaire was addressed to residents and employees in the tourism sector, conducted by 'Google Form' (Sargeant, 2012; Sigala, 2020). The selection of this method allows the researcher to view the answers provided by the participants and to analyze the data in an excel sheet. Saunders et al (2019) helped us design the data collection strategies.

The questionnaire was divided into two parts, based on the literature review: (1) Tourism and Sustainability, and (2) Tourism and Covid-19. The first part of questionnaire covered the tourism and sustainability criteria which was sent for the tourism industry staff (Ben-Eli, 2018). It includes several questions such as '*Will tourism be more sustainable as pre Covid-19?*' The second part about tourism and COVID 19 that will help to understand the future of the industry post pandemic. The questions include: (1) *Will tourism be sustainable again*? (2) *Which tourism will be more dominant (domestic/international)*? (3) *Is the public sector helping in sustaining tourism in Lebanon*? We refer to Figure 5 and to Saunders et al. (2019) for our research design, in explaining the best research method we used.

FINDINGS, ANALYSIS AND RESULTS

Findings from our Data Collection

The age groups of the participants, which mainly comprised students, tourism industry staff, and others, noted that 60% of our respondents were between 18-25 years old, and 24.5% of them were between 26-33 years old, while 15.1% above 34 years of age. For the employment status, it was revealed that 47% of them were are students, followed by a 32% of airport staff, 15% who don't work in the tourism sector, while, the remaining 6% of them were travel agent participants.

Accordingly, *tourism will continue to be sustainable after the pandemic ends* since the results showed 68% of them agreed, while 32% of them were unsure *relating to tourism sustainability post COVID-19*. As such, we see that 62% of our respondents expect that *domestic tourism will be dominant after CO-VID-19* and 38% believe that *international tourism will dominate post pandemic*. Proportionally, both results seems to agree with regards to what enhances tourism sustainability (see: Ben-Eli, 2018)

All tourism sectors abided the rules and regulations in that the countries'' respective ministries of tourism had set and all the measures it has taken, and according to the answers received by the participants, a large variety of answers were that COVID-19 safety measures were *regular hand washing* at 57%, while the rest of the responses were divided among *social distancing, avoiding touching your face, covering your mouth and nose when coughing and sneezing,* and *staying at home if you feel unwell,* as well as *avoiding any unnecessary travel*. Other precautions were taken in many different tourism sectors

Figure 5. Saunders's research onion (see: Saunders et al., 2019:130)

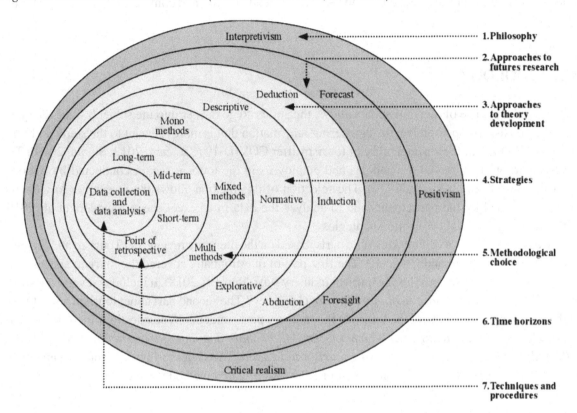

as social distancing 21%, the lockdown process 11% did a little improvement in the country, and for the vaccination 11% of participants responded to this answer but still it's moving slowly according to Figure 6.

In Figure 7, the variation of precautions taken by the tourist to safely travel vary from one respondent to another. The most effective precautions taken are the usual sanitary ones: hand washing, sanitizing, not touching your face with unwashed hands 66% responses, followed by the PCR response 15%, vaccination 13%, and just mask without any other precautions answer 6%.

Depending on this figure many participants think that their travel life will see an conservative change after the ending of COVID-19 crisis 45%, some expect it to change a lot 21%, whereas, a big number of participants think their travel considerations will slightly change 30%, 4% said it will not change at all, and none of them responded to the answer not sure about what to expect. This is show in Figure 8.

As demonstrated in Figure 9, 70% of the participants answered that economic, environment, and social which are tourism sustainability pillars all were affected by COVID-19, 19% said it influenced the economy of the Lebanon, 6% answered that it impacted the social life, and finally only 5% responded to the effect of this virus on the environment (cf. Rogoff, 2020).

The practical findings of the study for a single country, as well need to be considered, so we will discuss briefly what is the case in terms of Lebanon. Some secondary data was recently analyzed through comparing our findings to recent research conducted in the Eastern Mediterranean in term of sustainable tourism development (STD). The authors also bring forth arguments from the existing literature that all environmental activities (hiking, biking etc.) also to some extend help contribute to STD that

Figure 6.

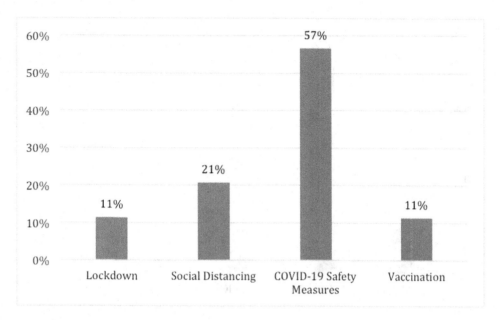

were discussed by Hassan et al. (2021) when they discussed about transportation towards sustainability research article, whose case was Lebanon. According to them transportation is of paramount importance for STD, and at the same time, according to literature, eco-tourism has been since awhile practiced, like hiking, biking, and so on, as Mheidle (2020) discussed.

Both researches have hinted the devastating effects of the coronavirus pandemic and how in Lebanon the industry attempts to restructure itself. So, in terms of analyzing comparatively some secondary data,

Figure 7. Safety precautions for travel

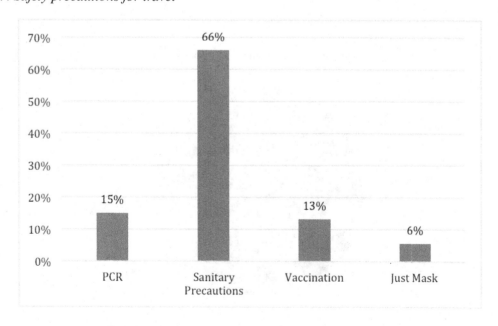

Figure 8.

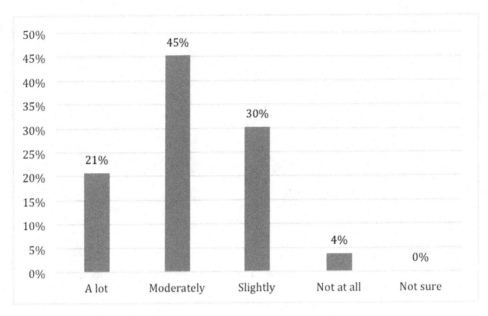

many researchers agree that the pandemic has deeply affected the industry, and lost close to a trillion USD due to the successive lockdowns (see: UNWTO, 2020a, b, c, d; 2021).

As only 20% of participants were optimistic about the tourism sustainability future after the ending of the pandemic, and 80% knew that it not be the same ever again as before. Accordingly, the results of Figure 10 could depict for us a dire picture of our industry's recovery in its current state, yet the UNWTO seems more optimistic (UNWTO, 2020a, b, c, d) in the long run, because now indeed, the figures don't lie.

Figure 9.

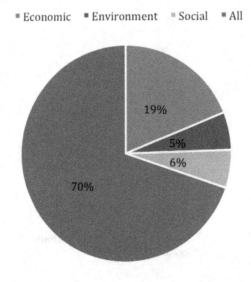

Figure 10. Sustainability of tourism post COVID-19 (see: Woyo, 2021)

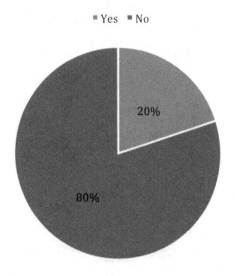

The three answers concerning tourism is essential for life, restoring traveler' confidence, and ecotourism have the same stable percentage of participants' answers which is 27% each. Whereas, the answer maintaining capacity measures contained 18% of respondent's answers. We see these responses in the results depicted in Figure 10, yet it seems that they tell us that as the same number of the respondents' answers tell us that *'tourism is essential for life', 'restoring traveler' confidence', and 'ecotourism'* are of equal importance for enhancing the sector's recovery (Woyo, 2021).

Figure 11. Tourism play a vital role in society

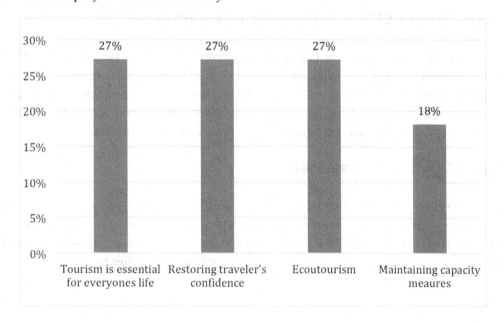

Figure 12. Government's duty tasks

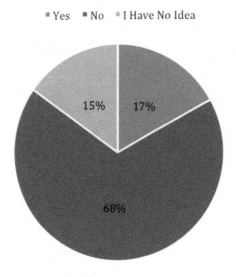

Based on Figure 12, 68% said that the government is not doing its job to ensure the safety and the sustainability of tourism with the current pandemic situation, while 17% said yes about the governments' job fulfillments and took participation in sustaining tourism industry. Whereas the remaining 15% hadn't any idea about the subject. (Sargeant, 2012; Sigala, 2019, Woyo, 2021)

From Figure 13, we gather that 10% of respondents answered that the government have developed new infrastructure for the sustainability of tourism, 40% said that it helped only in setting the rules, regulations and precautions, in addition, the other 50% of them checked the others option box (see: Woyo, 2021).

Data Analysis

Precautions Taken for COVID-19 Pandemic during Travel

For traveling precautions and rules have been placed to secure the safety and security of all people traveling between countries or inside a country. The results of the data collected have shown that the safety measures are the most suitable regulations set for protecting the community; which are sanitization, face mask, hand washing, social distancing, and temperature taking. In addition, vaccination is enhancing tourism to prosper again. Figures 5 and 6 remind us of these major precautions taken.

Tourism Post COVID-19 Sustainability

The results of the study showed that tourism will not be sustainable directly after the coronavirus pandemic ends, but it will definitely get back to normal over a period of time, as experts claim will occur not before 2025 (Huang et al., 2020, UNEWTO, 2020a, b). This is since the major problems that Rogoff (2020) discussed about need to be resolved, and any economic recovery after major (global) recessions take time.

Figure 13. Lebanese government assist in tourism sustainability

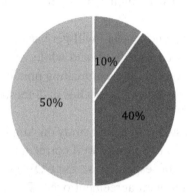

- By Developing New Infrastructure
- Adding Precaution Labels in Everytourism Sector
- Others

Government's Role in Tourism Sustainability

Based on the questionnaire's answer the government didn't do its job in taking control over planning, developing, and sustaining tourism during and after COVID-19. Respondents answered that the government have rarely developed any new infrastructure for the sustainability of tourism. In addition, it helped only in setting the rules, regulations and precautions. (cf. Woyo, 2021).

Results

Finally, after analyzing the statistics that has been done; the majority of vaccinated people will travel internationally but still take the precautions. The other small group of travelers who took the vaccine will move freely without any fear from the virus. Finally, a very slight group of participants will not travel at all even after being vaccinated and will continue to be scared from COVID-19.

The results of the survey and interviews showed that tourism sustainability will be seen after the end of COVID-19. But currently precautions will continuously be taken until vaccination will be given to every citizen (UNWTO, 2020b). However, even when vaccination will be distributed many individuals will still take precautions while traveling because of the fear they lived, and a big amount of them will travel without being afraid of anything (UNWTO, 2020b). Moreover, travel has stopped during the pandemic and lockdowns and many airline companies have lost nearly everything they've built but even with that airplane transportation continued to be the most transport used during the pandemic. In addition, every tourism sector is focusing on domestic tourism till now and planning on the development and forecasting the future of tourism in Lebanon with the governments' help. Some people would go by van or mobile vehicle, which makes sense considering that they are much more self-dependent (see: UNWTO, 2020b). International travel will however revive, led not only by knowledgeable backpackers and independent travelers moving at their own pace and seeing how the experience unfolds, but also by working-class people all over the world looking for relatives back home and leisure time to relax (Fallows et al., 2021).

The 4 interviews showed that the tourism industry will revive, and tourism organizations all over the globe laid off a huge number of employees. Airports stopped functioning as before, multiple airlines closed and stopped operating to specific countries. In addition, Lebanon's restriction rules stated that transit or arrival visitors needed a PCR test four days pre-departure date (UNWTO, 2020b). Moreover, some business travelers who couldn't attend online conferences only personally traveled abroad during COVID, also people who were far from their families in Lebanon got back for a visit and reunion (UNWTO, 2020b).

However, travel will prosper again and tourism will get back as soon as possible, people will continue to travel because curiosity can't be wiped out, and while vaccination campaigns will help revive the sector, we need to be traveling, experiencing and making predictions for better or worse (UNWTO, 2020a, b, c, d) The future of the future of the industry lies in domestic tourism, ecotourism and sustainable tourism, following UNWTO (2021).

Our research methodology was tested with a pilot study on August 2nd, 2021. Cronbach alpha results show to ne 0.89, so the questions seem to be fairly well correlated, yet based on the responses, we see that questions 1 and 5 agree in terms of responses, so the COVID 19 pandemic affected the industry, and that it tends towards virtualization with agreement over 57%. The question 2, fully agreed by the respondents confirms that the sector suffered severe deficits (UNWTO, 2020a, b, c, d).

Questions 3 and 6 shows the same results as well, as a majority agreed (over 85%) confirm that the industry relied on WHO recommended safety measures, and that indeed domestic tourism is booming. Question 7, at over 83% demonstrated that sustainability and ecotourism are key for the industry to explore. Questions 9 and 10 show that half of the respondents agreed to the fact somehow, that luxury tourism will be considered o change to wellness tourism due to COVID 19, and that countries indeed need to preserve the sector as many countries GDP activities nearly entirely depend on tourism. While for both questions the remaining 50%, are between the responses who re not sure, or disagree (of which only 12.5% of them disagree).

Questions 4 and 8 show a tendency of more responses of the respondents disagreeing over those agreeing, so only 14.29% agree that international tourism will no longer be the trend for economic recovery. 57.14% consider this to be maybe the case, while, 28.57% disagree. While, 28.57% agree that mass tourism will no longer be considered as a revenue within this decade, and, 14.29% are neutral, whereas 57.14% disagree.

CONCLUSION

The tourism industry is passing through difficult times due COVID-19. The non-sustainability in tourism practices didn't help the explanation for property living worldwide (see: UNWTO, 2020b). The pandemic has nearly brought the worldwide tourism industry to a halt. All stakeholders within the industry should work along to form the sufficiently resilient industry to alter the crisis (see: UNWTO, 2021). Supporting the studies conducted to know the tourism industry in the context of COVID-19.

Through the researcher's framework, an argument was stated, that with the assistance of the resilient approach from governments, market players, and the involvement of native communities goes to be vastly vital during this journey, because the restrictions on international travel may keep longer than anticipated. Such improvements will benefit not only the tourism industry's bottom line, but also provide opportunities for less-developed tourism destinations to expand (UNWTO, 2020b). Large-scale tourism players will benefit from a boost in order to thrive in the aftermath of a pandemic. Nonetheless, by working in accordance with our resilience-based system, small-scale players will ultimately prevail and ensure societal well-being while also promoting tourism sustainability (UNWTO, 2021).

COVID-19 resulted negatively on socio-cultural, economic and psychological impacts on stakeholders, and tourism sectors. In order to examine how the COVID-19 pandemic affected tourism industry and what future will it hold, an in-person questionnaire as well as an online survey were conducted asking Lebanese residents and tourism sector staff about their opinion and knowledge of tourism sustainability post pandemic (cf. UNWTO, 2021). The participants were divided by age and professional status the more they have information about tourism and work there, the more the answers to the questionnaire questions are clear and contain more content (see: OECD, 2020a, b).

Going through the analysis of the results obtained, the resentment present in the responses of the respondents implies that tourism will continue to be sustainable after COVID-19 ends with the help of vaccination. In addition, domestic tourism is now more important than international due to many rules and regulations that have been set during COVID-19 restrictions (UNWTO, 2020b). Therefore, hope is still present for the tourism industry (see: OECD, 2020a, b; UNWTO, 2020a, b, c, d; World Economic Forum, 2020a, b; WTTC, 2020a, b; WHO, 2012).

Figure 14 agrees with our research question, *that indeed the Covid 19 has impacted on the future of the tourism sector*. The majority of the respondents agreed, while only a minority has disagreed. This confirms that as the totality of the respondents agreed that the sector suffered tremendous deficits, thus in this case, we can agree on the link between the pandemic and the tourism sector.

We recommend, for Lebanon, the enhancement of domestic, eco-tourism and sustainable tourism as a first step in the recovery for the sector, as according to many experts, luxury tourism and mass tourism still need time to recover from the pandemic. Other steps later on can be considered, but the industry needs to bet back on its feet first. We definitely need more thorough researches in estimating how this relationship can be studies, as within our scope we went for qualitative methodologies, due to our scope limitation. Yet, mixed methods approaches using action research definitely are key to detect (a) problem(s) that need(s) imminent resolution and to effectively propose a solution to resolve it/them.

REFERENCES

Altinay, L., & Paraskevas, A. A. (2008). *Planning Research in Hospitality and Tourism*. Elsevier Ltd.

Assaf, A., & Scuderi, R. (2020). COVID-19 and the recovery of the tourism industry. *Tourism Economics*, *26*(5), 731–733. doi:10.1177/1354816620933712

Behsudi, A. (2020). Wish you were here: Tourism-dependent economies are among those harmed the most by the pandemic. *Finance & Development*. Retrieved from: https://www.imf.org/external/pubs/ft/fandd/2020/12/pdf/impact-of-the-pandemic-on-tourism-behsudi.pdf

Ben-Eli, M. U. (2018). Sustainability: Definition and five core principles, a systems prespective. *Sustainability Science*, *13*(5), 1337–1343. doi:10.100711625-018-0564-3

Bilgin, M. H., Demir, E., Doker, A. C., & Karabulut, G. (2020). *How pandamics affect tourism: International evidence*. PMC.

Figure 14. Results of the survey proving the validity of our main research question

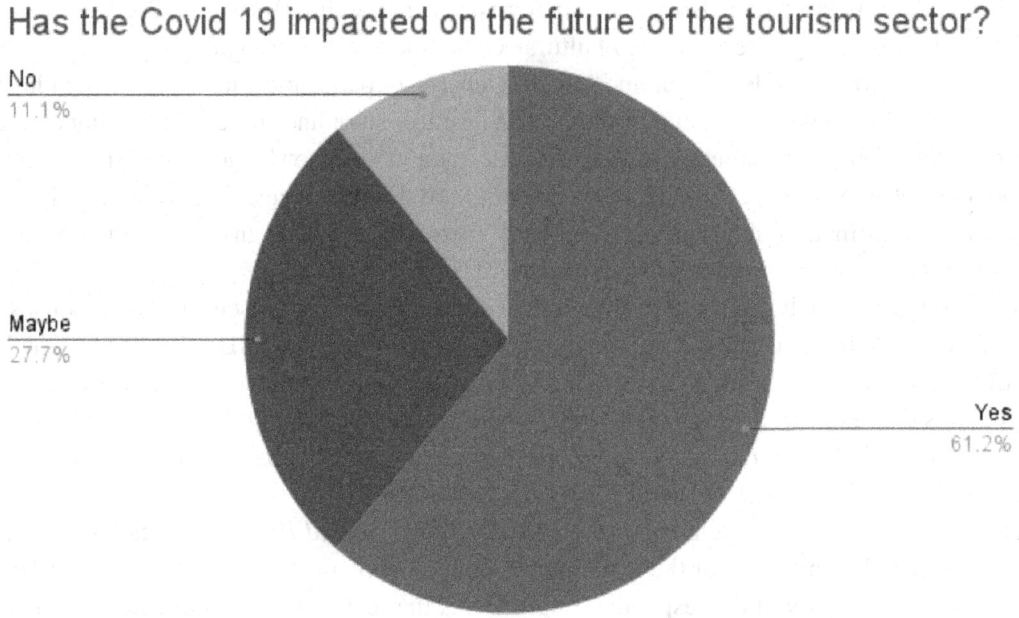

Has the Covid 19 impacted on the future of the tourism sector?

No 11.1%
Maybe 27.7%
Yes 61.2%

Dastgerdi, A. S., De Luca, G., & Francini, C. (2020). *Reforming Housing Policies for the Sustainability of Historic*. MDPI.

Davitt, D. (2020). *UN World Tourism Organisation says "five to seven years" of growth could be lost through COVID-19*. Retrieved from: https://www.moodiedavittreport.com/un-world-tourism-organisation-says-five-to-seven-years-of-growth-could-be-lost-through-covid-19/

Fallows, J. W., Iyer, P., Potts, R., Becker, E., Crabtree, J., & de Juniac, A. (2021). The Future of Travel After the Coronavirus Pandemic: Travel and tourism will be changed forever. We asked seven leading thinkers for their predictions. *FP Insider*. Retrieved from: https://foreignpolicy.com/2020/06/13/travel-tourism-coronavirus-pandemic-future/

Hall, C. M., Gossling, S., & Scott, D. (2015). *The Routledge Handbook of Tourism and Sustainability*. Routledge. doi:10.4324/9780203072332

Hassan, V., Bellos, G. S. G., & Fawaz, R. (2021). Transportation twowards tourism sustainility: Case study of Lebanon. *Athens Journal of Tourism*, *8*(1), 177–192. doi:10.30958/ajt.8-3-3

Hoque, A., Shikha, F. A., Hasanat, M. W., Arif, I., & Hamid, P. D. (2020). The Effect of Coronavirus (COVID-19) in the Tourism Industry in China. *Asian Journal of Multidisciplinary Studies*, *3*(1).

Huang, C., Wang, Y., Li, X., Ren, L., Zhao, J., Hu, Y., Zhang, L., Fan, G., Xu, J., Gu, X., Cheng, Z., Yu, T., Xia, J., Wei, Y., Wu, W., Xie, X., Yin, W., Li, H., Liu, M., ... Cao, B. (2020). Clinical features of patients infected with 2019 novel coronavirus in Wuhan, China. *Lancet*, *395*(10223), 395. doi:10.1016/S0140-6736(20)30183-5 PMID:31986264

James, P., Magee, L., Scerri, A., & Steger, M. B. (2015). *Urban Sustainability in Theory and Practice: Circles of Sustainability*. Routledge.

Jones, P., & Comfort, D. (2020). A commentary on the COVID-19 crisis, sustainability and the. service industries. *Journal of Public Affairs*, *40*(2), 1–5. doi:10.1002/pa.2164 PMID:32837318

Kamran, M. (2020). *Global Sustainability Overview and Role of Policy Instruments for Sustainable Tourism Management in Pakistan* [PhD Thesis]. Faculty of Geography and Tourism, Rovira I Virgili University, Tarragona, Spain.

Kuhlman, T., & Farrington, J. (2010). What is Sustainability? *Sustainability*, *2*(11), 3436–3448. doi:10.3390u2113436

Kumudumali, S. H. (2020). *Impact of COVID-19 on Tourism Industry: A Review*. Munich Personal RePEc Archive (MPRA). MPRA Paper No. 102834. Retrieved from: https://mpra.ub.uni-muenchen.de/102834/

Lacanilao Arnould, P. (2018). *What is Sustainable Tourism & Why is it Important?* Retrieved from https://visit.org/blog/en/what-is-sustainable-tourism/#:~:text=Definition%20of%20Sustainable%20Tourism%20Sustainable%20tourism%20is%20a,Unfortunately,%20most%20people%20do%20not%20travel%20this%20way

Lapointe, D. (2020). Reconnecting tourism after COVID-19: The paradox of alterity in tourism areas. *Tourism Geographies*, *22*(3), 633–638. doi:10.1080/14616688.2020.1762115

McChesney, I.-G. (1991). *The Brundtland Report and sustainable development in New Zealand. Information Paper, 25*. Centre for Resource Management Lincoln University and University of Canterbury.

McKercher, B. (1993). The unrecognized threat to tourism: Can tourism survive 'sustainability'? *Tourism Management*, *14*(2), 131–136. doi:10.1016/0261-5177(93)90046-N

Mheidle, R. A. (2020). *The impact of hiking on sustainable development in Moukhtara*. A Graduation Project Submitted in partial fulfillment of the requirements for the License Degree in Tourism Management, presented at the Lebanese University, Beirut.

Levy Yeyati, E., & Filippini, F. (2021). *Social and economic impact of COVID-19*. Brookings Global Working Paper #158 Global Economy and Development program at Brookings. Retrieved from https://www.brookings.edu/research/social-and-economic-impact-of-covid-19/

Mofijur, M., Rizwanul Fattah, I. M., Asraful Alam, M., Saiful Islam, A. B. M., Chyuan Ong, H., Ashrafur Rahman, S. M., Najafi, G., Ahmed, S. F., Uddin Alhaz, M., & Mahliaa, T. M. I. (2020). Impact of COVID-19 on the social, economic, environmental and energy domains: Lessons learnt from a global pandemic. *Sustain Prod Consum.*, *26*, 343–359. doi:10.1016/j.spc.2020.10.016 PMID:33072833

OECD. (2020a). *Rebuilding tourism for the future: COVID-19 policy responses and recovery*. Retrieved from OECD: https://www.oecd.org/coronavirus/policy-responses/rebuilding-tourism-for-the-future-covid-19-policy-responses-and-recovery-bced9859/

OECD. (2020b). *OECD Policy Responses to Coronavirus (COVID-19): Tourism Policy Responses to the coronavirus (COVID-19)*. Retrieved from: https://www.oecd.org/coronavirus/policy-responses/tourism-policy-responses-to-the-coronavirus-covid-19-6466aa20/

Pascariu, G. C. (2009). The Relationship Between Tourism And Sustainable Development In The European Context. *Annals of Faculty of Economics, University of Oradea, Faculty of Economics*, *1*(1), 293–298.

Poeta, C., & Maragall, J. (2021). *Glossary Of Tourism Terms.* World Tourism Organization. Retrieved from: https://www.unwto.org/glossary-tourism-terms

Price, H. J., & Murnan, J. (2004). Research Limitations and the Necessity of Reporting Them. *American Journal of Health Education*, *35*(2), 66–67. doi:10.1080/19325037.2004.10603611

Rogoff, K. (2020). *Mapping the COVID-19 Recession.* Retrieved from: https://www.project-syndicate.org/commentary/mapping-covid19-global-recession-worst-in-150-years-by-kenneth-rogoff-2020-04

Sargeant, J. (2012). Qualitative Research Part II: Participants, Analysis, and Quality Assurance. *Journal of Graduate Medical Education*, *4*(1), 1–3. doi:10.4300/JGME-D-11-00307.1 PMID:23451297

Saunders, M. N. K., Lewis, P., & Thornhill, A. (2019). *Research Methods for Business Students* (8th ed.). Pearson.

Sigala, M. (2020). Tourism and COVID-19: Impacts and implications for aadvanncing and resetting industry and reasearch. *Journal of Business Research*, *117*, 11. doi:10.1016/j.jbusres.2020.06.015 PMID:32546875

Strielkowski, W. (2020). *International Tourism and COVID-19: Recovery Strategies.* doi:10.20944/preprints202003.0445.v1

Sustainability. (2021). Retrieved from Academic Impact: https://academicimpact.un.org/content/sustainability.

Uber. (2020a). *Supporting you during the Coronavirus.* https://www.uber.com/en-HK/blog/supporting-you-during-coronavirus-v1/

Uber. (2020b). *An update on COVID-19 financial assistance.* Retrieved from: https://www.uber.com/en-HK/blog/supporting-you-during-coronavirus/

Ugur, N. G., & Akbıyık, A., (2020). Impacts of COVID-19 on global tourism industry: A cross-regional comparison. *Tourism Management Perspectives*, 36.

UNWTO. (2020a). *International tourism growth continues to outpace the global economy.* Retrieved from: https://www.unwto.org/international-tourism-growth-continues-to-outpace-the-economy

UNWTO. (2020b). *COVID-19 Related Travel Restrictions: A Global Review for Tourism.* Retrieved from https://webunwto.s3.eu-west1.amazonaws.com/s3fspublic/2020-04/TravelRestrictions - 28 April.pdf

UNWTO. (2020c). *World Tourism Organization Underscores Tourism's Importance for COVID-19 Recovery in Audience with the King of Spain.* Retrieved from https://www.unwto.org/news/unwto-underscores-tourisms-importance-for-covid-19-recovery-in-meeting-with-the-king-of-spain

UNWTO. (2020d). *Impact assessment of the covid-19 outbreak on international tourism.* Retrieved from: https://www.unwto.org/impact-assessment-of-the-covid-19-outbreak-on-international-tourism

UNWTO. (2021). *Sustainable Development*. Retrieved from: https://www.unwto.org/sustainable-development

WHO. (2020). *The COVID 19 global pandemic*. Parliamentary Budget Office.

WHO. (2021). *Coronavirus*. World Health Organization. Retrieved from: https://www.who.int/health-topics/coronavirus#tab=tab_1

Wikipedia/Sustainability. (2021). Retrieved from Sustainability: https://en.wikipedia.org/wiki/Sustainability

Woyo, E. (2021). The Sustainability of Using Domestic Tourism as a Post-COVID-19 Recovery Strategy in Distressed Destination. In *Information and Communication Technologies in Tourism 2021* (p. 489). Naminia: Conference Paper. 10.1007/978-3-030-65785-7_46

World Economic Forum. (2020a). *Latin America and Caribbean Travel & Tourism Competitiveness Landscape Report: Assessing Regional Opportunities and Challenges in the Context of COVID-19*. Retrieved from: https://www.weforum.org/reports/latin-america-and-caribbean-travel-tourism-competitiveness-landscape-report-in-the-context-of-covid-19

World Economic Forum. (2020b). *Blogs and Opinions*. Retrieved from: https://reports.weforum.org/travel-and-tourism-competitiveness-report-2019/blogs-and-opinions/

WTTC. (2020a). *The World Travel & Tourism Council (WTTC) represents the Travel & Tourism sector globally*. Retrieved from https://wttc.org/en-gb/COVID-19/Global-Protocols-for-the-New-Normal

WTTC. (2020b). *WTTC unveils "Safe Travels" – new global protocols to restart the Travel & Tourism sector*. Retrieved from https://wttc.org/News-Article/WTTC-unveils-Safe-Travels-new-global-protocols-to-restart-the-Travel-Tourism-sector

Chapter 22
Perspective for a Digital Teaching Method:
A Case Study About Secondary Schools During the COVID–19 Era in the Algarve Region

Ana Pego

https://orcid.org/0000-0002-4161-7301
Nova University of Lisbon, Portugal

ABSTRACT

Currently, the use of information and communication technologies (ICT) in the various sectors of the economy faces the challenge of improving specialization and competitiveness; it also promotes the ability to deal with decision-making processes in education and the possibility of "trying out" new ways of being with others in school. The aim of the chapter is to investigate how teachers deal with the new forms of teaching methodology based on online teaching during the era of COVID-19 in secondary schools in the Algarve region, based on the following research question: What are teachers' perceptions regarding the impact of the use of digital technologies and platforms on students? To test the research question, an electronic questionnaire was sent to teachers in randomly selected schools in the Algarve region between July 1 and July 15, 2020. The results show that, according to teachers' perceptions, some students were willing to use new digital methods to allow more networking, and on the other hand, other students had difficulties in learning and applying knowledge.

INTRODUCTION

The pandemic COVID -19 triggered a sweeping, sudden and dramatic digital transformation in society. The pandemic forced us to make an extraordinary digital leap in our daily lives and practices, including our children and their education (Iivari, 2020, p. 4). The new economy is facing new social changes based on information and communication technologies (ICT) and a global information society (Cabugueira,

DOI: 10.4018/978-1-6684-6762-6.ch022

2001, p. 313). The technological evolution evidenced in the last decades has enabled a convergence of people, organizations and working methods, which has resulted from the increase of communication and the optimization of technological means in organizations (Pego, 2014). Page & Matos (2017, p. 41) define the use of ICT and information systems (IS) with digital knowledge and innovation and information as a crucial factor in organizational development. The evaluation of the use of ICT is the consequence of optimizing the resources available to users in organizations and promotes the benefits of proximity through communication. This relationship of proximity allows the study of the phenomenon of digital education and the consequences for the educational system. The aim is to identify a collaborative learning system in which the transmission of knowledge is built socially with technologies (Rodrigues & Costa, 2019), that is, to identify questions that allow answering the challenges for institutions and teachers caused by technological changes (Arends, 2008, p. 499). Digital education and the implications for learning are similar to the intelligent

Management capacity of an organization. This means that this close relationship between teachers and digital systems can produce positive externalities associated with the ability to acquire crucial knowledge and skills for users. The use of IS in secondary schools has become an important issue due to the need to use distance learning solutions in the COVID - 19 post-March 2020 era. The education system based on intelligent knowledge has also been a challenge for secondary schools. Teachers have been faced with new opportunities to work virtually and in some cases regularly with students. However, it is important to analyze the impact of digital adaptation on learning and the teaching process itself. The purpose of this research is to describe the remote digital solutions used by secondary schools in the Algarve region between March 2020 and July 2020, and to present the positive and negative aspects from the teachers' point of view in relation to the students. The article is divided into six parts. The first part is an introduction to the research article. The second part presents digital education; the third part presents the case of Portugal from the educational perspective after March 2020; the fourth part presents the methodology; the fifth part presents the results and the sixth part presents the conclusions and further developments.

BACKGROUND

The aim of this study is to analyse digital literacy and the Portuguese case study on first look education. Two main points are presented, digital education in Europe and civic education in Portugal.

The Digital Education

His morning session is just the beginning of a long day of virtual lessons. Every few hours he cheques back in from home or his university office. Long after he's gone to sleep, students will continue to post messages on the course discussion board and send him e-mails dropping off assignments, asking about their grades or just saying hello. Mr. Grenci has been teaching here for nearly 20 years, but this is his first semester teaching online. He quickly discovered what has become conventional wisdom at many universities: it takes more time to teach in a virtual classroom than in a regular one (Reeves, 2003:5).

The unprecedented digital transformation of the global economy and society is likely to increase both the complexity of the modern world and the speed of change, largely due to increased connectivity and better educated people worldwide. These two elements - complexity and speed of change - mean that linking education to the trends shaping the world we live in has never been more urgent (OCDE,

Figure 1. Students who use the Internet at school for learning purposes – at least once a week
Source: European Commission (2019, p. 40)

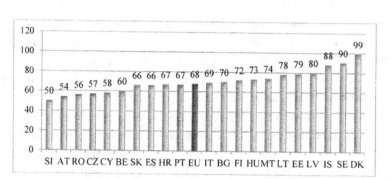

2019:13). Digital education has become popular with the digital economy. The term "digital economy" has been used extensively in recent years to describe the workings of the U.S. economy that are connected to ICT. Digital literacy has been popularised by the digital economy and is associated with three main factors: Network effects, changes in the business cycle and more efficient business methods (L'Hoest, R., 2001:44). Online education has been proving its effectiveness for more than 10 years. The effect of online education is explained by the increasing availability of education by reducing the cost of obtaining information (Maymina, 2018:35). Figure 1 describes the use of the internet in schools for learning purposes at least once a week.

From the students' point of view, it should be noted that Portugal occupies a middle position compared to the EU. It is also important to point out that the Northern European countries are those where more students use the Internet for learning purposes. The use of ICT in the classroom depends largely on teachers' experience with digital technologies. Teachers are crucial in ensuring that young learners can properly develop and acquire the necessary knowledge and skills. It is recognized that curricula should promote innovative teaching and learning methods to meet the needs of society. This can be achieved by integrating the use of ICT in the curriculum which encourages the use of ICT by both teachers and learners (EC, 2019:45).

Figure 2 provides an overview of the intensity of teachers' use of digital technologies in the classroom over a 12-month period. The results show that on average 15% of students in Europe have teachers who use ICT in more than 75% of their lessons. In the same study by EC (2019, pp. 48-49), the main barriers to the use of digital technologies are:

1. equipment-related barriers: Insufficient number of computers; insufficient number of tablets provided by the school; insufficient number of laptops/notebooks; insufficient number of computers with Internet access; insufficient number of interactive whiteboards; school computers that are outdated and/or in need of repair; insufficient Internet bandwidth or speed;

2. pedagogical barriers: Insufficient teacher skills; insufficient technical support for teachers; insufficient pedagogical support for teachers; lack of appropriate content/materials for teaching; lack of content in local language; difficulties in integrating ICT into the curriculum; and lack of pedagogical models for using ICT in learning;

Figure 2. Intensity of use of ICT in lessons by teachers over 12 months (in % of students, country and EU level, 2017-18, at secondary level)
Source: European Commission (2019:47)

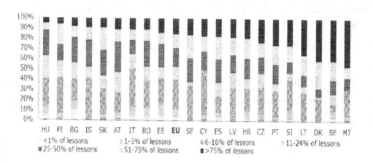

3. attitudinal barriers: Parental resistance; teacher resistance; lack of teacher interest; no or unclear benefits of using ICT in teaching; and that the use of ICT in teaching and learning is not aspired to in schools.

The digital economy and its application in the education system are one of the most important issues in education today (Gomes & Costa, 2010; Pamboukian & Kanaane, 2020; Pego, 2019). Their applicability and impact on achieving results between peers, as well as their adaptability to the evolution of digital education, form the conceptual framework of collaborative work in education, based on a common strategy of collaboration between peers, but also in proximity between users in the context of knowledge sharing. A digital cluster in education can be illustrated in the following Figure 3:

Figure 3. The digital cluster
Source: adopted by the author

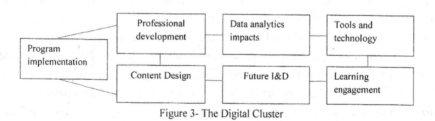

Figure 3- The Digital Cluster

Commitment to a new work methodology in schools should be related to the other variables shown in Figure 3. In line with the OCDE, it is necessary for students and teachers to move in the same direction to take advantage of digital learning. It is important to emphasize in schools a connection within the digital cluster to students and professional benefits. The digital economy and its applications in schools is a long process, although some statements have already been made in the direction of E@D (distance education). The best way to identify the educational perspective is to analyze the participation of students in schools (Levin, 2000). Some authors, such as Barroso (2003); Azevedo (2000); Rodrigues

(2012); Rodrigues and Silva (2016), describe the historical perspective and public policies related to the Portuguese educational system and human capital (Carrasqueira, 2016). However, few authors have described the pedagogical perspective and the use of teaching methods to achieve positive educational outcomes. Participation in schools with secondary students is one way to understand their life perspectives. According to OCDE (2019), the future of education is based on: 1) the need to better prepare education for on-going changes in the economic, social, and technological spheres; 2) understanding how education can influence the complexity and speed of change, based on the promotion of knowledge and decision-making processes. In addition, student engagement and motivation are related to the learning environment, learning time and climate of discipline, student well-being, curriculum and instruction, and teacher practice time (OCDE, 2019). In this sense, education and motivation are interrelated and form a good "marriage" to engage individuals in both school and life.

The Case of Portugal COVID 19

Face à suspensão das atividades letivas presenciais, iniciada em 16 de março de 2020, decorrente da situação epidemiológica, as escolas equacionam os modos de ensinar e de aprender no contexto de um Plano de E@D, com o objetivo de assegurar que todos os alunos continuassem a aprender a partir das suas casas. (Ministério da Educação, 2020, p.5).

In light of the new Portuguese government perspective on education after March 2020 to June 2020, COVID 19 era for education, it is important to describe how educational policies and student participants have been implemented. Student participation in secondary education during this period took place at two levels, one at home and one at school. Educational policies during this period focused on active participation with ICTs and digital platforms for inclusive secondary education. Although, according to the Ministério de Educação (2020), information on best digital practices was not carried out in schools, students had no previous digital training and in some cases teachers' digital practices were lacking. As digital (educational) technology advances, education itself changes, and with it, the nature of teachers' work changes in different places: in the classroom (e.g., from instructor to facilitator), outside the classroom (e.g., in lesson preparation), and in collaboration with other teachers-in short, a whole metamorphosis of teachers' work emerges as they work and teach with digital technology (Trouche et al., 2020, p. 1).

The impact of government interventions in schools after this period has not been identified, and interventions for future years have not been tested with teachers and students. The goal of achieving a remote digital solution in schools has important implications for students, teachers, and families. There is a lack of information on this topic for this period, although the Digital Transition Plan (PTD) was born out of the need to align the digital competencies of school stakeholders, but also out of the need for pedagogical continuity and social interaction to match the relationship between digital distance solutions and schools, as well as other sectors of the economy.

A CASE STUDY ABOUT DIGITAL TEACHING AT SECONDARY SCHOOLS DURING COVID 19 ERA IN THE ALGARVE REGION

This chapter focuses on secondary school education in the Algarve region. The research presented in this chapter will provide valuable insights into students' education and use of ICT and teachers' perceptions of their use. It will also highlight the consequences for students of using digital technologies.

Methodology

An essential first step in surveying the knowledge base of a field, or in our case a concept, is to conduct a literature review that identifies not only the conceptual aspects but also the main publication channels (Korhonen et al., 2018). The aim of the article was to investigate teachers' perceptions of how students interact with the new distance learning solutions based on online classes during COVID - 19 ERA in 2020 middle schools. The research question was: what are teachers' perceptions about the impact of using digital technologies and platforms on students?

The research was conducted in a traditional narrative review fashion that involved an arbitrary mapping of existing intellectual output. To this end, the author searched secondary sources covering the education and technology system in Portugal and in the EU. The mitigation of analytical rigour in this case allowed us to capture a broader perspective of the topic under study, as the author conducted a review of the literature on this point with a different scope, including regional/local and in languages other than English, i.e. Portuguese. The author also studied important reports published by public institutions and organisations related to COVID -19 ERA. The literature analysed was identified by searching electronic databases (Google Scholar, also Web of Science) and library resources. Articles in the electronic databases were searched using keyword combinations (e.g., "methodology," "use of technology in education," "platforms in education"). In the Web of Science database, the subject and title field were used. No additional philtres were used (publication years, categories, document types). The criterion for selecting a particular publication for review was closely related to the problem under study, which the author correctly reviewed, i.e., the publication was related to remote digital solutions and digital platforms in education.

In order to examine the research question of how teachers perceive the impact of the use of digital technologies and platforms on students, a quantitative analysis was conducted using a survey. a quantitative analysis was conducted using an online questionnaire. The questionnaire was anonymous and sent to teachers of randomly selected schools in the Algarve region between July 1 and July 15, 2020. A total of 100 questionnaires were sent out and 70 questionnaires were answered (70% of the answers are considered relevant) in order to capture teachers' experiences during the period April 2020 to June 2020. The questionnaires asked about teachers' experiences of using technology for online teaching, the platform used and their views on students' perceptions of online teaching, the type of technology used and their expectations for the next academic year. The participants are from secondary schools and teach in regular and professional courses. Most participants have a BSc (70%), a Masters (15%) and a PhD (5%). They teach in the fields of tourism, business, arts and sciences.

Results

Emerging technologies in education, as defined by Veletsianos (2010), are those that are "not yet fully understood" and "not yet fully or maturely explored" (15). Not only the technologies, but also the practices, subjectivities, and pedagogies associated with them are characterized by this "not-yet" (Collier and Ross, forthcoming) (Noyes et al., 2020, p. 600). Based on the initial research question, it is possible to discuss whether there is a perception of teachers about students using technology during the outbreak (March to July 2020). The responses were conclusive, the balance was positive and in line with teachers' perceptions. However, there is a need to improve digital distance learning and provide students with additional information to develop assignments. In fact, there was a lack of information, which I would like to call a "roadmap for digital learning", where the procedures for online teaching should be presented. Each school used the platforms on which the procedures for online teaching were to be presented as technologies. Some important results are shown:

1. The results showed that there is a difference between the technologies used and the process used to deliver the lessons. Table 1 shows the digital process in online teaching and the percentage of each digital resource.

Table 1. The digital process

Platforms	Online classes	Technologies
Classroom- 83.1% Moodle- 11,3% Other (Edmodo, email, drawing software) - 4,2% Virtual school- 1,4%	Google meet- 64, 3% Email- 15, 7% Zoom-7, 1% Hangout- 5,7% Whatsapp-2, 9% Virtual school - 2,9% Moodle – 1,4%	Laptop- 73, 2% PC- 24% Tablet- 1,49% Smartphone - 1,4%

The results show that the platforms used are mainly the classroom and Moodle, that online teaching takes place via Zoom and Google Meet, and that teachers are more likely to use laptops for teaching.

2. Another discussion is the fact that schools are not consistent in the type of technology used and resources for online teaching also vary. In fact, a number of difficulties in completing online assignments were mentioned by teachers in this questionnaire. According to the teachers, students experienced psychological, technical and methodological difficulties.

   a. Technical difficulties - the Internet was not flexible enough, computers were not prepared for online teaching; few students have technologies or they are distributed among all family members; some students used smartphones instead of other types of technologies; other difficulties mentioned were related to accessing Google form platforms and knowing how to use an eLearning platform.

   b. Psychological/methodological difficulties - there is a unanimous opinion that online teaching has a negative impact on students. According to the teachers, students feel sad and unmotivated because they do not achieve all the objectives and have difficulties in understanding the tasks because they are not autonomous in using the digital educational resources. In other words, some students do not feel comfortable in online courses because they cannot complete all the assignments in time due to technical difficulties and lack of digital literacy.

3. In another way, some students do not understand what is asked because the teacher does not respond within a short time (via email or WhatsApp) when asked to explain something, and some students feel that the time to do something is short. According to the teachers, some other difficulties were highlighted by the students such as the lack of direct interaction between students and teachers; therefore, in some subjects, the teacher did not do any work because the subject was practical, not enough instructions were given on how to do the work, and too many tasks were given by the teachers. .

4. The problems associated with this type of digital distance education are mainly related to the students' ability to understand how to use digital technology to complete the assignments on time, organization, and following the teachers' instructions. Although teachers feel that in some cases students do not have the knowledge to approach online teaching positively, there is a lack of technical problems and a lack of autonomy. Teachers believe that the relationship between students and teachers needs to be improved in order for this type of learning to be more beneficial.

5. According to the questionnaire, teachers think that the digital technology used for this type of learning is good (33%), although they had some difficulties related to the platforms (41%), the digital platforms are important to connect teachers/students/ and others (33%), the use of TIC was not entirely positive for students (14%), as some difficulties were shown (71.8%).

6. From the teachers' point of view, collaborative learning systems (CLS) promote positive interaction between pairs, help to learn how platforms work, are a complementary way to do some tasks, allow working from home, facilitate the connection between teachers and students, are a powerful tool for learning in a different way and sharing documents, make students more organized, more focused and motivated, It promotes digital knowledge in different areas of life, It is a tool for digital distance learning but not a substitute for face-to-face teaching, It avoids risks in school (COVID 19), It helps in pandemic situations, and They are a consequence of the digital age, even though it can have a negative impact on people because there is no equality of access.

7. Teachers were asked about the next school year and they think that the learning process should be mixed (50.7%) instead of completely digital (5.6%) or in school (43.7%). They also think that the methodology used by the school was positive for the learning process (90.1%).

8. In relation to the original research question and the literature, the results showed that there is a positive expectation of distance learning system for teachers. Moreover, it is possible that PTD has contributed to better use of digital distance learning systems by students and teachers and better learning process in schools. Also, the actions taken in schools during the collapse contributed to a deep analysis of the digital distance education system in Portugal.

FUTURE RESEARCH DIRECTIONS

There is evidence of a positive impact on students following the use of information technology at COVID -19. With the latest data, research shows the possibility of changing patterns in education and school management. Consequently, it is possible to see how schools have adopted a new strategy that is COVID 19 down.

It is important that schools, students and teachers have a positive perception that the use of ICT contributes to a positive level of knowledge associated with digital methods. On the other hand, digital education and its performance will contribute to deep interconnectedness between couples in the long run. The author proposes a new digital education model based on the needs of students and teachers that has a positive impact on education. The Portuguese government started to address this issue in 2020/2021, when students started to use computers provided by Education Ministry. In the long term, it is expected that classes will have a higher percentage of digital education and the contribution to this achievement will be accepted by the scientific community.

CONCLUSION

The research conducted by the author on this topic is up to date and is considered one of the first studies on secondary schools in Portugal. The educational system based on digital platforms and its applicability to secondary education in the Algarve region is considered relevant, since a new learning process is taking place based on the digital distance system. Although it has positive and negative aspects for the teachers interviewed for this study. In accordance with the results and the initial research question (What impact do teachers believe the use of digital technologies and platforms has on students?), it can be concluded that teachers believe that the balance is positive, although there are negative aspects for student learning, such as lack of knowledge in the use of e-learning platforms and the ability to complete many tasks in a short time. Moreover, teachers believe that in the long run, it is possible to improve some platforms towards higher academic benefits. Indeed, there is still a long way to go to improve digital distance teaching and learning in secondary schools in the Algarve. Teachers agree that this type of digital learning could be a way to teach in times of pandemic. Nevertheless, they felt that the period between March and July 2020 was an experience with positive aspects, as I mentioned earlier. Some limitations in conducting this research were the fact that some teachers were not interested in completing the questionnaire and the short time available to conduct it. Further developments can be made to conduct the same study in other regions, which can contribute positively to the implementation of PTD in Portugal. The study will help other researchers to understand and draw conclusions about the positive impact of digital education in secondary schools and will help economic and social actors to act in the field of education.

REFERENCES

Arends, R. (2008). Aprender a ensinar (7th ed.). McGraw Hill Edition.

Azevedo, J. (2000). *O ensino secundário na Europa*. Edições Asa.

Barroso, J. (2003). Organização e regulação do ensino básico e secundário, em Portugal: Sentidos de uma evolução. *Educação & Sociedade, 24*(82), 63–92. doi:10.1590/S0101-73302003000100004

Cabugueira, A. C. C. M. (2001). A nova economia e a educação. *Gestao e Desenvolvimento*, (10), 305–318. doi:10.7559/gestaoedesenvolvimento.2001.76

Carrasqueira, H. (2016). *Economia e educação*. Working paper, ESGHT-UAlg.

European Commission (EC). (2019). *2nd survey of schools: ICT in Education. Objective 1: Benchmark progress in ICT in schools*. Final report. Luxemburg: Publication Office of the European Union.

Gomes, M. J., & Costa, F. A. (2010). A Escola e a agenda digital europeia. *Educação, Formação & Tecnologias*, *3*(1), 1-5.

Iivari, N., Sharma, S., & Ventä-Olkkonen, L. (2020). Digital transformation of everyday life–How COVID-19 pandemic transformed the basic education of the young generation and why information management research should care? *International Journal of Information Management*, *55*, 102183.

Korhonen, J., Nuur, C., Feldmann, A., & Birkie, S. E. (2018). Circular economy as an essentially contested concept. *Journal of Cleaner Production*, *175*, 544–552. doi:10.1016/j.jclepro.2017.12.111

L'Hoest, R. (2001). The European dimension of the digital economy. *Inter Economics*, *36*(1), 44–50. doi:10.1007/BF02927909

Levin, B. (2000). Putting students at the centre in education reform. *Journal of Educational Change*, *1*(2), 155–172. doi:10.1023/A:1010024225888

Maymina, E., Puzynya, T., & Egozaryan, V. (2018). Digital economy in education: Perspectives and development perspectives. *Revista ESPACIOS*, *39*(38), 30.

Ministério da Educação (ME). (2020). *Orientações para a Recuperação e Consolidação das Aprendizagens ao Longo do Ano Letivo de 2020/2021*. Ministério da Educação.

Noyes, J. A., Welch, P. M., Johnson, J. W., & Carbonneau, K. J. (2020). A systematic review of digital badges in health care education. *Medical Education*, *54*(7), 600–615.

OECD. (2019). *Trends Shaping Education 2019*. OECD Publishing.

Pamboukian, S., & Kanaane, R. (2020). Práticas docentes na educação superior tecnológica: A formação de competências demandadas dos profissionais na economia digital. *Revista Educação -. UNG-Ser*, *15*(2), 32–47.

Pego, A. (2014). *Sistemas e tecnologias de informação no turismo em espaço rural: estudo da região Algarve* [Dissertação de Mestrado]. Lisboa: Universidade Aberta.

Pego, A. C. H. C. D. (2019). Os sistemas colaborativos na Educação: Os valores pedagógicos e educacionais. *Desenvolvimento e Sociedade*, *4*(7), 31-36. https://www.researchgate.net/profile/Ana-Pego/publication/338232231_Os_sistemas_colaborativos_na_Educacao_Os_valores_pedagogicos_e_educacionais/links/5e09efe44585159aa4a5d7dd/Os-sistemas-colaborativos-na-Educacao-Os-valores-pedagogicos-e-educacionais.pdf

Pego, A. C. H. C. D., & de Matos, M. D. R. A. (2017). O impacto dos sistemas e tecnologias de informação no turismo em espaço rural na região do Algarve. *Dos Algarves: A Multidisciplinary e-Journal*, (25), 39-59. http://dosalgarves.com/index.php/dosalgarves/article/view/5

Reeves, T. C. (2003). Storms clouds on the digital education horizon. *Journal of Computing in Higher Education*, *15*(1), 3.

Rodrigues, A. R. P., & Costa, W. L. (2019, February). Percepções sobre os processos de ensino e aprendizagem do ensino superior. Simpósio, (7).

Rodrigues, M. D. L. (2012). Os desafios da política de educação no século XXI. *Sociologia, problemas e práticas*, (68), 171-176.

Rodrigues, M. D. L., & Silva, P. A. (2016). A constituição e as políticas públicas em Portugal. *Sociologia, Problemas e Práticas*, 13-22.

Trouche, L., Rocha, K., Gueudet, G., & Pepin, B. (2020). Transition to digital resources as a critical process in teachers' trajectories: The case of Anna's documentation work. *ZDM*, 1-15.

Chapter 23
The Circular Agriculture Products During COVID–19:
A Portuguese Analysis

Ana Pego
https://orcid.org/0000-0002-4161-7301
Nova University of Lisbon, Portugal

ABSTRACT

The agricultural sector was one of the most important sectors in the economy during COVID-19. The potential of agriculture and the needs of consumers were the main factors in changing the way agriculture supplied the market. Circular products in agriculture were important due to the fact that consumer needs changed during COVID-19. This chapter shows which products have been more important to consumers and how the market has changed to improve the strategy in this sector. Therefore, the perspective of producers to supply the market is the main point of this chapter, as it shows that there is an adjustment in the type of products and services, and therefore, this research will help to understand the circular economy in the agricultural sector during COVID-19.

INTRODUCTION

The pandemic COVID -19 has led to historic changes in the norms of our society and the way people interact with each other (Galanakis, C. M. et al., 2021). The importance of the agricultural sector increased after COVID -19. Many countries had adapted their production to the needs of consumers. In fact, the agricultural sector was one of the first to take a step forward. The circular business model and the agricultural sector gave the market the opportunity to reduce the COVID -19 impact on families and organizations and the ability of producers to develop a new strategy in the market (Timuş, A., 2020). In this paper, we have discussed the potential of the circular economy sector during the pandemic, highlighting the Portuguese market. Few studies have promoted the agricultural sector during and after the pandemic COVID -19 (Ibn-Mohammed, T., 2020, Lal, R. et al., 2020; Palahí, M. et al., 2020). Indeed,

DOI: 10.4018/978-1-6684-6762-6.ch023

consumers and producers have adopted a new challenging attitude towards new forms in the market. In this regard, organic products have played an important role in changing consumer needs.

Decision making within organizations and its impact on the market pose a new challenge for agricultural products. Producers have had to adopt new forms of resilience in order to compete and collaborate with the agricultural industry. Therefore, the increase in the agricultural market for organic products is one of the main achievements of the pandemic.

In order to discuss the market for circular economy in Portugal, the research question is: what types of circular economy products were important during the pandemic? To answer the question, a qualitative methodology was applied, based on the analysis of data from statistical national sources, such as INE, and international sources (EUROSTAT and European Commission), as well as academic papers. The results showed a positive impact on the consumption of organic products during the pandemic, a new business model for the agricultural industry.

This paper is divided into four main sections. The first provides an introduction to the research; the second examines the concept of the European circular economy market, the Portuguese circular economy and the Portuguese agricultural market; the third explains the methodology and results; the fourth points out future research directions and conclusions.

BACKGROUND

The aim of this study is to analyse how the circular economy in agriculture has changed the market strategy in terms of consumer needs. In this section, the circular economy and the agricultural sector are characterised. An overview of the European market and the prospects of the circular economy to increase sustainability based on circular business models is provided.

The Circular European Agriculture Market

"By modifying current practices much can be done in terms of improving the productivity of many food and agricultural production systems. Productivity will need to continue to increase in the future to ensure sufficient supply of food and other agricultural products. However, this must be done while limiting the expansion of agricultural land as well as safeguarding and enhancing the environment. This is the core of the transformation necessary for sustainability in food and agriculture systems. Efficiency in productivity has, in the past, been mostly expressed in terms of yield (kg per hectare of production) but future productivity increase should consider more dimensions. Water and energy-smart production systems will become increasingly important as water scarcity increases and as agriculture will need to seek ways to reduce emission of greenhouse gas. This will also have an effect on the use of fertilizers and other agricultural inputs." (Food and Agriculture Organization of the United Nations, n.d.)

Accordingly, with FAO (n.d.) sustainable agriculture is based on the increase in productivity, employment and value addition in food system, protecting and enhance natural resources, improving livelihoods and foster inclusive economic growth, enhance the resilience of people, communities and ecosystems, and adopted governance to the new challenges. Lorencowicz et al., (2014:9) discusses sustainable agriculture as a condition for the survival of mankind. The use of circular economy in agriculture has been a highlight in a worldwide context. One such example has recently been pointed by the World Economic Forum, as one of the 'Shaping the Future of Food' initiatives to develop sustainable, efficient, and nutritious food systems in the agricultural sector (Barros et al., 2020:2). The same authors point out that, to achieve a zero-waste production, the agro-industry is taking initiatives to change processes in the field. However, recycling practices and circular economy are only possible from actions created by top management; this means a new way of improving specific solutions and techniques for soil improvement, mitigating aspects of climate change and, at the same time, working with food security solutions. The importance is to achieve a level of sustainable food production in the field, sustainable practices are required at the production stage and one of these practices is to incorporate the circular economy into the cooperative agro-industrial system (ex: Agrocycle. For circular economy project[1]).

Small farmers who grow vegetables and fruits are particularly affected by labour shortages and lack of outlets, as many restaurants and farmers' markets have closed. Demand for fresh fruits and vegetables is also decreasing, as many people are increasingly consuming highly processed products that have a longer shelf life out of concern for possible supply chain disruptions. This could lead to an increase in diabetes and other diet-related non-communicable diseases, which are risk factors for mortality COVID -19 (Altieri and Nicholls, 2020).

A different view of the food system (food safety, food security and sustainable food) in COVID -19 was presented by Giudice et al. (2020). The author reflects on the market's ability to improve the food system and its resilience to competition towards a circular economy. The food system brings together all policy makers and is the wake-up call for a new economic model that puts social well-being and environmental sustainability at the heart of economic recovery in the EU. This means that production, consumption and waste work together towards a sustainable solution: Localised food systems reduce waste and benefit nutrients; combining local and seasonal elements in short supply chains reduces storage and transport, better balances supply and demand, creates more transparency and traceability, and contributes to waste reduction; policy makers should continue to incentivise the reduced use of plastics and prioritise more durable or recyclable materials such as paper, aluminium, steel and glass, even if these materials do not entirely prevent the accumulation of unwanted metal ions through repeated recycling.

Evidence shows that the consumption of cereals, vegetables and milk has a positive trend (Figure 1). The trade balance is also having a positive impact (Figure 2), which will contribute to encouraging productivity. In line with the World Economic Forum, the future of food is based on the following propositions: environmental footprint, integration of agriculture, value chain efficiency, nutrition and health, food and technology innovation, and demographic change and demand. The agricultural potential in Europe confirms the will to improve the balance of trade, which will lead to an increase in agricultural products. Therefore, in line with Figure 2, this trend is expected to be confirmed in the period COVID -19.

Future projects in agriculture will be based on circular economy. This represents a step forward in reducing, reusing and restoring new products towards a low-waste economy. However, circular consumption is also linked to the ability of the agricultural industry to create new products or reuse some products to sell at lower prices.

The Portuguese Agriculture Circular Economy

"On average across the EU-27 in 2016, each person generated 158 kg of food waste"

Eurostat, 2020

Figure 1.

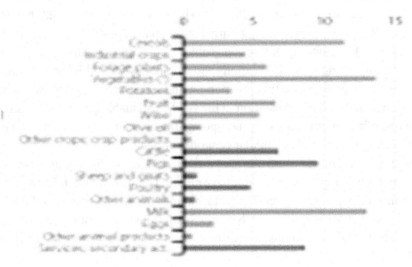

The evolution of Portuguese agriculture before and after joining European Community is well documented in books, book chapters, reports and studies from the 1980s, 1990s and the beginning of this century (Lorencowicz et al., 2014).

The interesting mosaic about agriculture in Portugal was described by Firmino (1999:84). According to the author, there are six main regions with a particular landscape. Certain sub-regions can be adapted to this map and practice agriculture in Portugal. The same author points out some spatial planning problems related to the capacity of agricultural cultivation, the use of land for agricultural production for recreational purposes and for housing, economic problems due to conflicts betweenadvocates of "development" and "conservationists", and social conflicts between newcomers and the rural popula-

Figure 2.

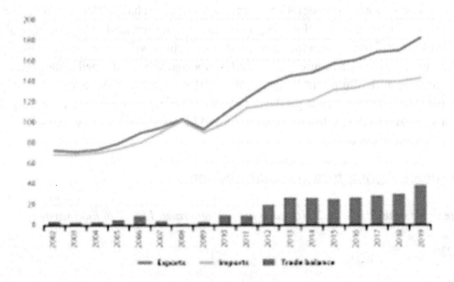

tion. More recently, agricultural projects under Portugal2020 have introduced a new form of agricultural settlement based on specialization and competition.

According to ICEP, agriculture has the following competitive advantages: Soil and climate conditions that favor the production of high quality, differentiated fruits and vegetables that are part of the Mediterranean diet emerging in the EU; competitive production costs; excellent track record in foreign investment; increasing technological modernisation and scientific research practices. According to the same report, the main agricultural export products are wine, olive oil, fruit and tomato concentrate.

"The term circular economy has both a linguistic and a descriptive meaning. Linguistically it is an antonym of a linear economy" Murray et al. (2017:371).

The impact of climate change on agriculture and its implications for food security is a challenging issue (Ozcariz-Fermoselle et al., 2019). According to Pego (2020), the circular economy is one of the biggest challenges for Europe. It is considered as the biggest step for European economies as it represents a new production methodology in the sectors. The circular economy offers the possibility to see its internal qualitative steps as historical paradigms of human economic activity. The challenge is to create new products that can be reused.

To achieve these goals, companies need to innovate in product design and the associated revenue model, using both social and institutional innovations to compete and collaborate. (Barros, 2020; Pego, 2020) discusses the concept of the circular economy, which emerged from the concept of changing behavior, products, and the supply chain. The nonlinear economy and its ability to provide new products based on well-being and ecosystem encompasses the concept of circular economy. The circular economy is a closed system within organizations that allows the reuse of resources to promote new products.

In the study published by Oliveira et al (2020) on circular economy and agriculture, it was found that:

-Strengths: society is dynamic and computerized, leading to more volatile cities; many actions related to CE have already been carried out and recognized, in the field of food production and consumption; the rapprochement between producer and consumer is also consistent with the principles of a social and solitary economy associated with urban and community agriculture. The identification and promotion of transformation actions are fundamental to promote new fronts that can spread the concept of circular economy in the economy.

Weakness: the lack of indicators to measure the circular economy in an economy and the performance of ongoing actions, especially given the diversity and complexity of a country. Such efforts to formulate indicators are the goal of recent research by CE, but still with sectoral focus from case studies; that Portugal still has few projects and partnerships with other countries that take into account the environmental aspect.

- Opportunities: The adoption of CE in the European field, especially with the EU Action Plan for the Circular Economy, with guidelines aimed at stimulating the transition of European companies and consumers to a system where resources are used in a more sustainable way; as financial support, there are European programs aimed at the destination of resources through prices, funds and financing; It is estimated that CE and the technological revolution will allow an annual increase in resource productivity of up to 3% for European economies, which would mean 0.6 trillion euros per year by 2030; possibility of benchmarking with other countries such as Holland, Scotland, Luxembourg, Denmark and Finland, which have adopted strategies, timetables and national action plans to accelerate the transition to CE .

- Threats: the dynamization of CE in Portugal, i.e. the dependence on the import of inputs and energy, especially fossil fuels, which represent more than 70% of imports (Pego, 2020); the need to develop materials and technologies oriented to renewable sources, with the sustainable use of raw materials essential to the country's economy is becoming evident; Competition with international markets, such as the Asian one, also brings implications when materials and products with lower costs, lower quality and longevity are introduced into the system, which goes against the concepts of eco-design and circular economy; the reduction of historical and emotional connections to products, a fact intentionally cited by experts in interviews, leads to an increasing acceleration of global production and consumption; in contrast, over the last two decades there has also been a growing consumer interest in purchasing ethical products linked to fair trade and ecological footprints;

The same author points out that Action Plan for the Circular Economy in Portugal is considered the main representative of a movement that ranges from the articulation of ministries to a comprehensive promotion and discussion with society, workshops and different types of meetings to achieve engagement between public power, educational institutions and society. It includes national actions of a cross-cutting nature that relate to ministerial activities, sectoral agendas - mainly in the most intensive sectors of resource use and export - and local agendas that need to be adapted to the socio-economic characteristics of each region. The tools available for the promotion and implementation of the actions include: the circulars identifying and overcoming the obstacles to the CE; the alignment of the environmental criteria in the operational programs in Portugal; and the approach to the need for monitoring indicators.

The promotion of Circular Economy is a very important and topical issue, fundamental to ensure environmental sustainability and to strengthen the priority of reconciling environmental protection with the needs of consumers and the agri-food industry.

In 2018, FIPA[2] established with APA - Portuguese Environment Agency a Circular Agreement, aiming at institutional collaboration within the process of transition to the circular economy, considering concrete forms of cooperation and coordination. The main points for the circular transition challenge (2019-2023) are:

1. promotion of the concepts of circular economy and Eco design of the food and beverage packaging;
2. Identification of barriers to recyclability and circularity of packaging;
3. Information and provision of technicians from companies in the sector with decision support tools;
4. promotion of clarification of concepts and definitions for support for environmental communication and guidance on the use of harmonized and/or certified environmental claims;
5. defending compliance with the goals set out in the European Directive on waste, as well as for the scope of actions set out in the European Plastics Strategy;
6. support for the implementation of a Deposit-Refund System (SDR) approved by the competent authorities and managed by the industry.

"Every year, one million tons of food go to waste in Portugal".

One of the studies presented by Pego (2020) (a) reports on the circular economy in Portugal and its impact on organizations. The circular economy in Portugal is based on two macro policies: products and consumers. Both aim to be in the market to promote positive externalities based on innovation and R&D products. The balance point in between is the self-regulatory framework, where consumers benefit

Figure 3.

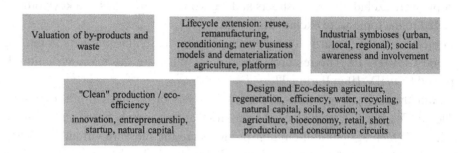

from long-lasting products and the product benefits from utilities, which ultimately benefit consumers' needs. The aim is to support activities where the environmental impact can be reduced; the reduction of single-use packaging and plastics in the transport, storage, display and marketing of products through the reuse of sustainable products; the promotion of the adoption of a basic principle of sustainability, the circular economy and an economy of sharing; the promotion of a sustainable culture through education and implementation of environmental values. The latest data for Portuguese organizations using CE show that growth in many economic sectors has contributed positively to new business models in terms of new products, research and development and investment.

Some points need to be highlighted: the capacity of the Portuguese economy to become one of the largest circular economy production in Europe, the transformation of production and the link between circular economy, consumption and production. This triangle is indeed the beginning of a new era in the Portuguese market. The management process and the value for the circular economy can be achieved if there is a willingness to change the patterns.

THE PORTUGUESE CIRCULAR AGRICULTURE PRODUCTS DURING COVID 19

This chapter focuses on the circular economy products that had an impact on consumers in COVID -19. The research presented in this chapter will provide valuable insights into consumer typology and changing patterns in consumer needs. It will also show the impact of the changing patterns on the market and their influence on circular farm products.

Methodology

The methodology was based on the relevant scientific literature, using three databases, namely Web of Science (WoS), Scopus and ScienceDirect (SD); other relevant data from INE (Portuguese National Institute), EUROSTAT, FAO, Portuguese National Public Bodies, as well as IFAP and Ministério da Agricultura were evaluated.

There was no initial time limit for the search period (only by the initial coverage of the databases). The final time limit was the date on which the search was conducted, i.e. July 2021.

The search of the databases selected research and review articles that were available in English and Portuguese. Three types of philtres were used to select the documents to be reviewed, namely -.

Exclusion of duplicates: all duplicate documents were excluded; titles: all titles were read and articles unrelated to the topic were excluded; and, abstracts and keywords: all abstracts and keywords were read and articles unrelated to the topic were excluded.

The research objective of this paper is to study the agricultural circular products in the Portuguese market in the period COVID -19. The research question is: What are the main agricultural circular products in the period COVID -19 in Portugal?

In order to answer the research questions, a content analysis of the agricultural circular products market was conducted. The research strategy can be classified as a case study based on documented data.

Questions such as "Which agricultural circular products are the most important?", "Why do local markets play an important role in this process?" and "What should be the environmental and social changes?" - from this analysis, conclusions can be drawn about the agricultural circular products in Portugal during COVID -19 and the trends after COVID -19. The question is whether it is a challenge to create a new value chain with agricultural circular products and what impact this has on consumer needs.

Results

"COVID-19 is raising consumer awareness of the relationship between nutrition and health. Consumers are buying more organic and healthy foods as they look to boost their personal immunity" (Specialty Food, 2020)

The analysis of the Portuguese agricultural circular market showed low participation, which means that few organizations participate in this type of market strategy.

Despite the fact that the Portuguese market is a new challenge, it is important to develop some management strategies based on market needs and competitiveness. During the pandemic period (2020-2021), the demand for organic and sustainable food increases as consumers seek healthier options to boost their immunity due to the coronavirus crisis. The market is changing towards a new consumer perception and appreciation of natural foods. Some examples in the Portuguese market are presented: Fruta Feia (cooperative that recycles fruits and vegetables that would otherwise be wasted); PROVE - "promover e vender" (promote and sell).

Fruta Feia Co-operative aims mainly to channel that part of the wasted fruits and vegetables to consumers who do not judge the quality by its appearance, thus fighting market inefficiency and creating a movement that can change consumption patterns and that can create a market for to the so-called "ugly fruit". A market that generates value and fights not only this waste, but also the unnecessary waste of resources used in their production (water, energy and soil) (Fruta Feia, 2022).

PROVE is an inter-territorial co-operation project between eight Local Action Groups located around Portugal that provide continuity to the experience and methodology developed as part of the IC EQUAL initiative, which is intended to resolve issues related to the marketing of local products and to take advantage of the proximity of producers and consumers in peri-urban areas (Prove, n.d.).

Examination of the data from these two organizations proves that Portuguese consumers have adopted a new consumption pattern based on natural agricultural products. The pandemic was responsible for a new sales approach. The online sales and the improved capacity of these organizations, a new challenge in the market, lead us to conclude the products that are appreciated by consumers during COVID -19; fruits and vegetables are the main products. On the other hand, it is important to analyze the market strategy, especially online sales as a business model to improve sales in conjunction with the concept of agricultural cooperative.

The natural concept and the sale of a mixture of vegetables and fruits in a wooden box were important factors to improve the connection with the market. Another distinctive feature was the fact that the products came from local farmers, which was important for the improvement and development of the local economy.

The Portuguese circular products in the period COVID -19 brought a new market perspective and consumers could show a renewed interest in "local" food supply chains. In fact, interest in "local food" was already present before the pandemic, as people believed that these foods offered economic, social, environmental, and health benefits; during the pandemic, consumers also expressed a desire to support the economic recovery of local small and medium-sized enterprises (SMEs); the pandemic forced people to make significant changes in their daily lifestyles, and these changes may continue in the long term. Staying at home all day in a previously hectic, globalized society has tested people's resilience and made them question their priorities.

In summary, the key achievements of the circular economy, local markets and their resilience, low waste, healthy food systems, healthy cooking and short supply chains are the products of the circular economy.

FUTURE RESEARCH DIRECTIONS

As countries across the globe are tackling the devastating impacts of the COVID-19 pandemic, it is clear that our approach to food production and, more generally, our relationship with natural and human-modified ecosystems will be fundamental in preventing the next pandemic – as will the global community's ability to safeguard human, animal and environmental health (Food and Agriculture Organization of the United Nations)

There is evidence of a positive impact on consumer behavior regarding agricultural products (COVID -19). With the latest data, research shows the possibility of a change in consumption patterns and management organization. Consequently, it is possible to see how organizations have adopted a new strategy in the market based on local producers and consumer needs.

This research compares the agricultural products in Europe and consumption in the years COVID -19. Its significance shows the needs of consumers in this period and the ability of the organization in the market. The significance of this study is a step forward to rethink the business methods in organizations. Finally, it is possible to describe the ability of companies to change their value creation and value chain. The authors propose a new business model for circular agricultural products based on a new market perspective of consumer needs.

Furthermore, according to Giudice et al. (2020), it is necessary to transform food production through localized supply chains and improved packaging; to steer consumption towards sustainable choices through a mix of taxation and education policies; to focus on and invest in the transformation of non-edible food waste into energy and materials through green chemistry and biorefineries. A deep and holistic discussion is developing about how sustainable the current food system is and how prepared it is for the shock that the pandemic COVID -19 represents.

CONCLUSION

This chapter deals with the consumption of agricultural circular products produced in Portugal during the period COVID -19. Small and medium enterprises in Portugal are dealing with a new marketing concept for circular agricultural products. Local producers have been shown to have a privileged position in the market during the pandemic. Consumers prefer fresh and natural products from local farmers who have improved the local economy. In addition, online purchasing from small farmers has been introduced to improve their competitiveness, as well as a business model based on recirculating products from vegetables and fruits. The market is changing towards healthy patterns and sustainable production, with vegetables and fruits being the main production successes.

In summary, circular products in agriculture offer new market strategies, low waste, eco-design and eco-production, are based on healthy patterns and represent the future of sustainable production. Circular practices appear to have the potential for a win-win solution that simultaneously improves sustainability throughout the value chain (from production to consumption and beyond) and increases its resilience through the adoption of localized supply chains that minimize waste and further promote sustainable production and consumption (Giudice et al., 2020).

REFERENCES

Altieri, M. A., & Nicholls, C. I. (2020). Agroecology and the reconstruction of a post-COVID-19 agriculture. *The Journal of Peasant Studies*, *47*(5), 881–898. doi:10.1080/03066150.2020.1782891

Barros, M. V., Salvador, R., de Francisco, A. C., & Piekarski, C. M. (2020). Mapping of research lines on circular economy practices in agriculture: From waste to energy. *Renewable & Sustainable Energy Reviews*, *131*, 109958. doi:10.1016/j.rser.2020.109958

Economy: A 10-point Action Plan to create a circular bioeconomy devoted to sustainable wellbeing. (n.d.). *The Solutions Journal, 11*(2).

Eurostat. (2020). *Agriculture, Forestry and Fisheries Statistical book.* https://www.gpp.pt/images/Estatisticas_e_analises/Estatisticas/AgricolasEstruturais_Producao/AgricultureForestryFisheryStatistics_2020_Edition2020.pdf

FeiaF. (2022). https://frutafeia.pt/

Firmino, A. (1999). Agriculture and landscape in Portugal. *Landscape and Urban Planning*, *46*(1-3), 83–91. doi:10.1016/S0169-2046(99)00049-3

Food and Agriculture Organization of the United Nations. (2020). *Preventing the next global pandemic: sustainability and the One Health approach.* Retrieved from https://www.fao.org/sustainability/success-stories/detail/en/c/1300674/

Food and Agriculture Organization of the United Nations. (n.d.). *Sustainable Food and Agriculture*. Retrieved from https://www.fao.org/sustainability/background/en

Galanakis, C. M., Rizou, M., Aldawoud, T. M., Ucak, I., & Rowan, N. J. (2021). Innovations and technology disruptions in the food sector within the COVID-19 pandemic and post-lockdown era. *Trends in Food Science & Technology, 110*, 193–200. doi:10.1016/j.tifs.2021.02.002

Giudice, F., Caferra, R., & Morone, P. (2020). COVID-19, the Food System and the Circular Economy: Challenges and Opportunities. *Sustainability, 12*(19), 7939. doi:10.3390u12197939

Ibn-Mohammed, T., Mustapha, K. B., Godsell, J. M., Adamu, Z., Babatunde, K. A., Akintade, D. D., ... Koh, S. C. L. (2020). A critical review of the impacts of COVID-19 on the global economy and ecosystems and opportunities for circular economy strategies. *Resources, Conservation and Recycling,* 105169.

Lal, R., Brevik, E. C., Dawson, L., Field, D., Glaser, B., Hartemink, A. E., Hatano, R., Lascelles, B., Monger, C., Scholten, T., Singh, B. R., Spiegel, H., Terribile, F., Basile, A., Zhang, Y., Horn, R., Kosaki, T., & Sánchez, L. B. R. (2020). Managing soils for recovering from the COVID-19 pandemic. *Soil Systems, 4*(3), 46. doi:10.3390oilsystems4030046

Lorencowicz, E., Baptista, F., Silva, L. L., & Marques da Silva, J. R. (2014). *Sustainable agriculture–Poland and Portugal*. Academic Press.

Murray, A., Skene, K., & Haynes, K. (2017). The circular economy: An interdisciplinary exploration of the concept and application in a global context. *Journal of Business Ethics, 140*(3), 369–380. doi:10.100710551-015-2693-2

Oliveira, F. R. D., Santos, R. F. D., França, S. L. B., & Rangel, L. A. D. (2020). Strategies and challenges for the circular economy: A case study in Portugal and a panorama for Brazil. *Brazilian Archives of Biology and Technology, 63*, 63. doi:10.1590/1678-4324-2020180646

Ozcariz-Fermoselle, M. V., de Vega-Luttmann, G., de Jesús Lugo-Monter, F., Galhano, C., & Arce-Cervantes, O. (2019). Promoting Circular Economy Through Sustainable Agriculture in Hidalgo: Recycling of Agro-Industrial Waste in Production of High Nutritional Native Mushrooms. In *Climate Change-Resilient Agriculture and Agroforestry* (pp. 455–469). Springer. doi:10.1007/978-3-319-75004-0_26

Palahí, M., Pantsar, M., Costanza, R., Kubiszewski, I., Potočnik, J., Stuchtey, M., ... Dixson-Declève, S. (2020). *Investing in Nature to Transform the Post COVID-19*. Academic Press.

Pego, A. (2020a). New Challenges for the Tourism Sector in the Algarve Region Based on Evaluation of the Circular Economy. In Strategic Business Models to Support Demand, Supply, and Destination Management in the Tourism and Hospitality Industry (pp. 185-199). IGI Global. doi:10.4018/978-1-5225-9936-4.ch010

Pego, A. C. (2020b). Circularity in Portugal: Features of New Business Challenges. In Networked Business Models in the Circular Economy (pp. 224-240). IGI Global.

Prove. (n.d.). *PROVE-Promoting and Selling*. Retrieved from http://www.prove.com.pt/www/english.T9.php

Specialty Food. (2020). *Organic and sustainable foods receive "coronavirus boost".* Retrieved from https://www.specialityfoodmagazine.com/news/organic-and-sustainable-foods-receive-coronavirus-boost

Timuş, A. (2020). Circular agriculture development in the post-COVID-19 era. Competitiveness and sustainable development, 2, 14-14.

KEY TERMS AND DEFINITIONS

Agriculture Sector: Where it is produced agriculture products.

Circular Economy: A nonlinear economy where it is creating value added in goods. The importance of the circular economy is based on the concept of recycling, reduction and reuse material and creating new products assuming that consumers have new needs.

Consumers: Economic agent acting in the market with a purpose of consuming.

Market: A place where consumers and producers interact based on a price for a specific good.

Strategy: Reaching management goals in short, medium, or long runs. Organizations position themselves in their market to achieve goals and objectives.

ENDNOTES

[1]   http://www.agrocycle.eu/ (2018), consulted in 10/06/2021.

[2]   FIFA- Federação da Indústria Portuguese agro-alimentar.

Chapter 24
Evaluation of Supply Chain Performance Using the Balanced Scorecard Approach During the COVID–19 Pandemic:
A Case Study of Js General Hospital

Doni Maryono
Muhammadiyah University of Sidoarjo, Indonesia

Rita Ambarwati
Muhammadiyah University of Sidoarjo, Indonesia

ABSTRACT

The pandemic has an impact on almost all sectors of people's lives, both in the economic, political, and socio-cultural sectors. The government has implemented large-scale social restrictions (PSBB) as an effort to stop the spread of the COVID-19 virus. With the PSBB, it causes disruption to the hospital supply chain management. As a step to anticipate the hospital's impact on the PSBB, the hospital needs to evaluate the performance of supply chain management. The purpose of this chapter is to describe the performance evaluation of hospital supply chain management using a balanced scorecard approach. A new finding from this study is to measure the performance of hospitals experiencing various disruptions in their supply chain management caused by the COVID-19 pandemic with a balanced scorecard. The author concludes that measurements with the balanced scorecard approach can provide information about the performance of hospital supply chain management broadly in areas experiencing disruption due to the COVID-19 pandemic.

INTRODUCTION

In the operational implementation of the company's organization, for the control function, information is

DOI: 10.4018/978-1-6684-6762-6.ch024

needed about how it is performing. (Solihin, 2009) says managers will not be able to plan, organize, lead, and control effectively if they do not have adequate information. Information is a source of knowledge and understanding of a person on a problem that is needed to make a correct decision. The leaders or managers who will perform the control function. As explained that in their informational role, managers continue to look for information that contains the performance of their units, managers' senses scan the unit's internal activities and their environment, Mintzberg in (Raymond & Schell, 2011). From the information obtained, it is known that the performance has been effective and efficient or not. (Solihin, 2014) said the goal to be achieved through controlling is the availability of tools for managers to direct and motivate their subordinates so that they can work towards organizational goals and provide feedback to managers on how well their subordinates are performing. Managers need to make corrections if their performance is low but if it is according to the planned standards then the company's operations are good and maintained to achieve the company's goals that have been set.

The company is a business organization which is an open system. Barnard in (Solihin, 2009) said that the organization as an open system like any other open system that will get influence from the environment. The company's environment will provide various inputs to the organization, so the company must always adapt itself to the development of the company's environment in order to maintain its sustainability. Grant in (Solihin, 2009) said that the general environment of the company consists of various factors such as social values, education level, politics, economy, law, demography, natural resource environment, technology. On the legal side, in 2020 the government issued a large-scale social restriction (PSBB) regulation to control the ongoing pandemic so that it does not spread further. The existence of this government policy has an impact on the nets of almost all companies. Disturbances that occur in the supply chain in the form of demand fluctuations and changes in the length of the order (lead time) are operational disturbances that commonly occur in the supply chain. Supply Chain Management is the management of the activities of procuring goods and services, converting them into semi-finished goods and final products, as well as delivery through the distribution system (Haizer & Render, 2010).

Strategic planning allows companies to anticipate conditions that are always changing, and provide a road map and direction to go and how to achieve it (Jauch & Glueck, 2004). Strategic planning is an important management tool that can help organizations perform their duties better, facilitate strategy development and implementation, and make organizations more sensitive to customer and market needs (Obeng & Ugboro, 2008). Strategic planning (strategic planning) is vital for the organization in maintaining its survival (Wheelen & Hunger, 2004).

Hospital is an entity that is engaged in the treatment and care of people who need health services. As a General Hospital company, it also implements a strategy related to the supply chain. With the PSBB imposed by the government, the supply chain of General Hospitals is also likely to experience disruptions like other companies. As an anticipatory step, General Hospitals against the impact of this PSBB, General Hospitals need to evaluate their supply chain performance, so as to get an overview of the company's supply chain performance during this PSBB. (Fahmi, 2016) said to avoid problems arising in uncertain situations, managers should conduct research first, to seek as much information as possible and use several decision-making methods that are most appropriate for each problem condition. To evaluate the supply chain performance of General Hospitals, several approaches can be used, including the Balanced Scorecard. Luis and Biromo (Gultom, 2009) say that the definition of the Balanced Scorecard is a performance management tool that can help organizations translate their vision and strategy into action by utilizing a set of financial and non-financial indicators, all of which are intertwined in a causal relationship. result. The Balanced Scorecard is a suitable tool for evaluating and designing operations strategy (Dodangh, Majid, & Nasehifar, 2010). Thus, to evaluate supply chain performance at a General Hospital, it can be done with the Balanced Scorecard approach.

From this urgency, it is necessary to analyze the performance of the supply chain at the General Hospital using the Balanced Scorecard approach. From the results of this evaluation, company leaders will get information on whether the company has a good performance in the current situation of the PSBB. Based on this information, the RSU can make corrections if its supply chain management performance shows that it does not meet the established standards.

LITERATURE REVIEW

Supply Chain Management

The supply chain is all stages involved directly or indirectly in meeting the demands of producers, suppliers, transporters, warehouses, retailers and end consumers (Chopra & Peter, 2007). Supply Chain Management (SCM) is a method, tool or approach to supply chain management (Pujawan, 2005). Supply Chain Management (SCM) is the integration of material and service procurement activities, conversion into semi-finished goods and final products, and delivery to customers (Haizer & Render, 2010). According to (Mulyadi, 2001) performance is the success of team personnel, or organizational units in realizing the strategic goals that have been set previously with the expected behavior.

There is a flow that occurs in supply chain activities, namely the flow of materials, information, and money (Chopra & Peter, 2007). The material in question is goods that can be in the form of raw goods, semi-finished goods or finished products, or services for companies engaged in services. Information is data that has been processed, and money is a medium of exchange that is issued to ensure the smooth flow of materials and information. The goal of SCM is to manage and improve the flow of materials from point of origin to point of delivery as well as information feedback from end consumers at the minimum possible cost. The flow of information is well integrated and transparent from the supplier to the end consumer.

According to Tjiptono (2014), "The distribution channel is a set of organizational participants who perform all the functions needed to deliver the product/service from the seller to the final buyer." Meanwhile, according to (Studies et al., 2018) Distribution or place is the process of distributing goods and services from producers to target consumers. From distribution channels to consumer product markets, intermediaries who directly deal with consumers are retailers or retailers.

The government as the regulator must be able to ensure that the entire food supply chain continues to run smoothly and without interruption. The food supply chain must continue to run with a new supply chain strategy in the conditions of covid 19. The continuity of the smooth distribution process without obstacles can avoid a shortage of goods so that there are no price spikes due to insufficient or even non-existent stock of goods. Besides these factors can also avoid the hoarding of goods by some speculators who want to take advantage.

Pandemic Corona Virus Disease 2019 (Covid 19)

Corona Virus Disease tahun 2019 atau COVID-19merupakan penyakit menular yang disebabkan oleh coronavirus jenis baru. Coronavirus (CoV) adalah keluarga besar dari virus yang bisa menyebabkan berbagai gejala ringan hingga berat. Dari segi gejalanya, keluarga virus ini seringkali menyerang di sistem pernapasan manusia. Setidaknya, terdapat dua jenis coronavirus yang juga pernah menyerang masyarakat Indonesia dan kasus penyebarannya cukup tinggi, yakni East Respiratory Syndrome Coronavirus (SARS-CoV) dan Severe Acute Respiratory Syndrome Coronavirus (SARS-CoV). Dan akhir-akhir ini, muncul coronavirus baru yang dinamakan dengan penyakit COVID-19. Menurut WHO (2020) berdasarkan panduan Surveilans Global, definisi COVID-19 dapat diklasifikasikan menjadi tiga bagian yakni:

1. Suspected case
2. Pprobable case or probable case
3. Confirmed cases or patients who have been proven positive through laboratory tests.

Meanwhile in Indonesia Based on the Ministry of Health of the Republic of Indonesia (2020) the definition of the classification of COVID-19 cases is divided into:

1. patients under surveillance or PdP
2. people in monitoring or OdP
3. people without symptoms or OTG

To stop the spread of the virus, the government has made various efforts. Among them are carrying out large-scale social restrictions (PSBB), instructions to always wear masks, always wash hands, keep a distance from one person to another.

Government Policy during the Pandemic Period according to the 1945 Constitution of the Republic of Indonesia

The policy regarding Large-Scale Social Restrictions (PSBB) in Indonesia was first implemented on April 10, 2020 in Jakarta, followed by several other regions in Indonesia. There are several regulations related to the implementation of the PSBB. These include Government Regulation (PP) Number 21 of 2020 concerning Large-Scale Social Restrictions in the Context of Accelerating the Handling of Corona Virus Disease 2019 (COVID-19), Minister of Health Regulation (Permenkes) Number 9 of 2020 concerning Guidelines for Large-Scale Social Restrictions in the Context of Accelerating Handling Corona Virus Disease 2019 (COVID-19), as well as Government Regulation in Lieu of Law (Perpu) Number 1 of 2020 concerning State Financial Policy and Financial System Stability for Handling the 2019 Corona Virus Disease Pandemic and/or in Facing Dangerous Threats National Economy and/or Financial System Stability.

In terms of the mechanism for the application of PSBB, it is stated in Government Regulation Number 21 of 2020 in Article 2, namely:

1. With the approval of the minister who administers government affairs in the health sector, the Regional Government may impose Large-Scale Social Restrictions or restrictions on the movement of people and goods for a particular province or regency/city.
2. Large-Scale Social Restrictions as referred to in paragraph (1) must be based on epidemiological considerations, magnitude of threat, effectiveness, resource support, operational technical, political, economic, social, cultural, defense and security considerations.

Minister of health regulation Number 9 of 2020 contained in Article 2, namely to be able to establish Large-Scale Social Restrictions, a province/district/city area must meet the following criteria: the number of cases and/or number of deaths due to disease increases and spreads significantly and rapidly to several regions; and There is an epidemiological link with similar events in other regions or countries.

Article 4 paragraph (1) Government Regulation Number 21 of 2020:

1. Large-Scale Social Restrictions at least include:
   a. school holidays and workplace
   b. restrictions on religious activities and/or
   c. restrictions on activities in public places or facilities.

Law Number 6 of 2018 concerning Health Quarantine in Article 59 paragraph (3), namely: yaitu:

1. Large-Scale Social Restrictions as referred to in paragraph (1) shall at least include:
   a. school and workplace holidays
   b. restrictions on religious activities

Impact of Large-Scale Social Restrictions on Supply Chain Management Activities

The results of Hadiwardoyo's research (2020) show that what is needed is the right policy, both in terms of location, time and procedure. If the PSBB can guarantee a break in the chain of transmission of Covid-19, then do it properly, and in the shortest possible time. Prolonged restrictions, or changing locations because they are not in sync, risk exceeding the survival capabilities of individuals and business entities. If that happens, then the rescue cannot be carried out, and the losses will be even greater both economically and socially.

We can see this in the various steps taken by the government both at the central and regional levels by recommending or urging the public to limit activities in certain sectors, including pressing the public to postpone activities that invite a lot of people. person. On the other hand, this condition almost stops aspects of daily life, trade and other economic activities (Thorik, 2020)

These impacts also revolve in several sectors of people's lives. Both in the economic, political, and socio-cultural sectors.

since the pandemic that occurred in the international region, the economy of every affected country has experienced a slump.

Dito (2020) stated that the economic and trade sectors that had the biggest impact due to COVID-19 were the economic and trade sectors. Where the implementation of the PSBB causes the state and regional economies to weaken. Even Indonesia's export sector also experienced a weakening. Likewise, investors who seem reluctant to invest because they are in a difficult economic phase. The prospects for world and Indonesian economic growth in 2020 are potentially lower if the Covid-19 outbreak continues to spread, triggering the implementation of stricter restrictions or social distancing policies by various countries, and global financial market pressures continue due to high uncertainty (Michael, 2020).

The determination of the PSBB policy creates supply disruptions and distribution delays which can have an impact on scarcity and price increases (Ariani et al., 2012).

Balanced Scorecard

Definition of Balanced Scorecard

The Balanced Scorecard is a business performance measurement concept that balances the measurement of the performance of a business organization which has been considered too inclined to financial performance. Before the emergence of the balanced scorecard concept, what is commonly used in companies so far is the traditional performance measurement that only focuses on the financial sector.

It is quite realized today that the measurement of financial performance used by many companies to measure executive performance is no longer adequate, so the concept of the "Balanced Scorecard" was born. The balanced scorecard is a business performance measurement concept introduced by Robert S. Kaplan and David P Norton. The Balanced Scorecard consists of two words, namely the scorecard and balanced. A score card is a card used to record a person's performance score. The word balanced is intended to show that personnel performance is measured in a balanced way from two aspects: financial and non-financial, short-term and long-term, internal and external. From this definition, Mulyadi (2001) argues that in a simple sense the Balanced Scorecard is a scorecard used to measure performance by taking into account the balance of financial and non-financial, long-term and short-term, internal and external.

Luis and Biromo (Gultom, 2009) say that the definition of the Balanced Scorecard is a performance management tool that can help organizations translate their vision and strategy into action by utilizing a set of financial and non-financial indicators, all of which are intertwined in a cause and effect relationship result.

Advantages of Balanced Scorecard

In its development, BSC has helped many companies to successfully achieve their goals. BSC has several advantages that traditional strategic management systems do not have. Traditional management strategies only measure organizational performance from the financial side and focus more on measuring things that are tangible, but business development demands to change the view that intangible things also play a role in organizational progress. BSC answers these needs through a contemporary strategic management system, which consists of four perspectives, namely: finance, customers, internal business processes and learning and growth.

The advantage of the BSC approach in the strategic planning system (Mulyadi, 2001) is that it is able to produce strategic plans, which have the following characteristics:

1. Comprehensive
2. Coherent
3. Balanced
4. measurable

The benefits of the Balanced Scorecard for companies according to Kaplan and Norton (2000) are as follows:

1. The Balanced Scorecard integrates the company's strategy and vision to achieve short-term and long-term goals.

2.   The Balanced Scorecard allows managers to see the business in financial and non-financial perspectives (customers, internal business processes, and learn and grow)

3.   The Balanced Scorecard allows managers to assess what they have invested in the development of human resources, systems and procedures for improving the company's performance in the future.

Perspectives in the Balanced Scorecard

The perspectives in the BSC are as follows:

1.   Financial Perspective

BSC uses financial performance benchmarks such as net income and ROI, because these benchmarks are generally used in companies to determine profit. Financial benchmarks alone cannot describe the causes that make changes in wealth created by companies or organizations (Mulyadi and Setyawan, 2000).

The Balanced Scorecard is a performance measurement method in which there is a balance between financial and non-financial to direct the company's performance towards success. BSC can explain further about the achievement of the vision that plays a role in realizing the increase in wealth (Mulyadi and Setyawan, 2000) as follows:

a.   Increased satisfied customers thereby increasing profits (through increased revenue).

b.   Increased productivity and commitment of employees so as to increase profits (through increased cost effectiveness).

c.   Increasing the company's ability to generate financial returns by reducing the capital used or investing in projects that generate high returns.

In the Balanced Scorecard, financial measurement has two important roles, where the first is that all perspectives depend on the financial measurement that shows the implementation of the planned strategy and the second is that it will give impetus to the other 3 perspectives about the targets to be achieved in achieving the goals. organization goals.

According to Kaplan and Norton (2004), the business cycle is divided into 3 stages, namely:

a.   Growth

The growth stage is the initial stage in the business life cycle. At this stage the company tries to use its resources to increase its business growth. In addition, the company will invest as much as possible, increase new products, build production facilities, increase operating capabilities, seize market share, and create distribution networks. In this stage, the company will most likely always be in a state of loss, because at this stage the company focuses on investing in investments that will be enjoyed in the long term.

b.   Sustain

Is the second stage where the company is still investing and reinvesting by signaling the best rate of return. At this stage the company still has a good attraction for investors to invest their capital. At this stage, the company must be able to maintain its market share and must pay attention to better product quality and service so that it will gradually experience growth from year to year.

Financial goals at this stage are usually more profit-oriented. Objectives related to profitability can be expressed using measures related to operating profit. To get good profitability, of course, managers must work hard to maximize the income generated from capital investment, while for business units that already have autonomy, they are asked not only to manage the income stream, but also the level of capital investment that has been invested in the business unit concerned. Other benchmarks that are often used at this stage, such as ROI, profit margin, and operating ratio.

c.   Harvest

This stage is the stage of maturity for a company, because at this stage the company is just reaping from the investments made in the previous stages, what must be done at this stage is that the company no longer invests, but only keeps the company running well.

2.   Customer Perspective

In the customer perspective, the company needs to first determine the market segments and customers that are the targets for the organization or business entity. Furthermore, managers must determine the best measuring tool to measure the performance of each operating unit in an effort to achieve its financial targets. Furthermore, if a business unit wants to achieve superior financial performance in the long term, they must create and present a new product/service of better value to their customers (Kaplan, and Norton, 1996).

The product is said to be of value if the benefits received by the product are higher than the cost (if the product performance is closer to or even exceeding what is expected and perceived by the customer). The company is limited to satisfying potential customers so it is necessary to segment the market to serve in the best way based on existing capabilities and resources.

There are 2 groups of measurements in the customer perspective, namely:

a.   Icore measurement group

This measurement group is used to measure how the company meets customer needs in achieving satisfaction, maintaining, obtaining, and seizing the targeted market share.

Within the core measurement group, we recognize five benchmarks, namely:

i.   Market Share: This measurement reflects the company's share of the overall market, which includes: the number of customers, the number of sales, and the volume of sales units.
ii.   Customer Retention: Measures the level at which a company can maintain a relationship with consumers.
iii. Customer Acquisition (customer acquisition); measures the degree to which a business unit is able to attract new customers or win new business.
iv.   Customer Satisfaction: Assessing the level of customer satisfaction related to specific performance criteria in the value proposition.

v. Customer Profitability: measuring the profits obtained by the company from selling products or services to consumers.

b. Customer value proposition

This measurement group is used to find out how companies measure the value of the market they control and the potential market they might be able to enter. This measurement group can also describe performance drivers regarding what the company must provide to achieve high levels of satisfaction, loyalty, retention, and customer acquisition. Value proposition describes the attributes presented by the company in the products/services that are sold to create customer loyalty and satisfaction.

The customer value measurement group consists of:

i. Product/service attributes, which include: function, price, and product quality.
ii. Relationships with customers, which include: distribution of products to customers, including responses from the company, delivery times, and how customers feel after buying products/services from the company concerned.
iii. Image and reputation, which describe the intangible factors for the company to attract customers to relate to the company, or buy the product.

3. Internal Business Process Perspective

The internal business process perspective presents critical processes that enable business units to provide a value proposition that is able to attract and retain customers in the desired market segment and satisfy the expectations of shareholders through financial returns (Simon, 1999).

Each company has a unique set of value creation processes for its customers. In general, Kaplan and Norton (1996) divide it into 3 basic principles, namely:

a. Innovation Process

The innovation process is the most important part in the whole production process. But there are also companies that put innovation beyond the production process. The innovation process itself consists of two components, namely: identifying customer desires, and carrying out a product design process that is in accordance with customer desires. If the innovation results from the company are not in accordance with the wishes of the customer, the product will not receive a positive response from the customer, so it does not provide additional income for the company and even the company has to incur investment costs in the research and development process.

b. Operation Process

The operating process is an activity carried out by the company, starting from the time the order is received from the customer until the product is sent to the customer. The operation process emphasizes the delivery of products to customers in an efficient and timely manner. This process has, in fact, become the main focus of the performance measurement systems of most organizations.

c.   Post-Sales Service

As for the after-sales service referred to here, it can be in the form of a warranty, replacement for damaged products, etc. The company can measure whether its efforts in after-sales service have met customer expectations, using benchmarks that are quality, cost, and time as carried out in the operating process. For cycle time, companies can use the measurement of the time from when a customer complaint is received until the complaint is resolved.

The following is a picture of the internal business process perspective:

4.   Learning and Growth Perspective

This perspective provides the infrastructure for achieving the previous three perspectives, and for generating long-term growth and improvement.

It is important for a business entity when investing not only in equipment to produce products/services, but also investing in infrastructure, namely: human resources, systems and procedures. Benchmarks of financial performance, customers, and internal business processes can reveal large gaps between existing capabilities of people, systems and procedures. To minimize this gap, a business entity must invest in the form of reskilling employees, namely: improving the ability of systems and information technology, as well as rearranging existing procedures.

The learning and growth perspective includes 3 principles of capability related to the company's internal conditions, namely:

a.   Worker Capability

The ability of workers is part of the contribution of workers to the company. In relation to the capabilities of workers, there are 3 things that must be considered by management:

i.   Worker satisfaction

Worker satisfaction is a precondition for increasing productivity, responsibility, quality, and service to consumers. Elements that can be measured in employee satisfaction are employee involvement in making decisions, recognition, access to information, encouragement to work creatively, and to use initiative, as well as support from superiors.

ii.   Worker Retention

Employee retention is the ability to retain the best workers in the company. Where we know workers are a long term investment for the company. So, the absence of a worker who is not due to the company's wishes is a loss in the intellectual capital of the company. Employee retention is measured by the percentage of turnover in the company.

iii.   Worker Productivity

Worker productivity is the result of the overall effect of improving skills and morale, innovation, internal processes, and customer satisfaction. The goal is to relate the output produced by workers to the number of workers who are supposed to produce that output.

b.   Information System Capability

The benchmarks for information system capabilities are the level of availability of information, the level of accuracy of the information available, and the time period for obtaining the required information.

c.   Organizational Climate

What drives the emergence of motivation, and empowerment is important to create workers who take the initiative. The benchmark for this is the number of suggestions given by workers.

Here is a picture of a learning and growth perspective:

From the four perspectives, there is a causal relationship which is a description of the objectives and measurements of each perspective. The relationship between various strategic objectives that are generated in strategic planning with the Balanced Scorecard framework promises to increase the company's ability to produce financial performance. This capability is indispensable for companies entering a competitive business environment.

The following is an image that explains the causal relationship of the four perspectives in the Balanced Scorecard::

Balanced Scorecard Steps

The Balanced Scorecard steps include four new management processes. This approach combines long-term strategic goals with short-term events. The four processes according to (Kaplan and Norton, 1996) include::

1.   Translating the company's vision, mission and strategy

To determine performance measures, the organization's vision is described in terms of goals and objectives. Vision is a description of the conditions that will be realized by the company in the future. Goals are also one of the foundations for formulating strategies to make them happen. In the strategic planning process, these goals are then elaborated into strategic objectives with measures of achievement.

2.   Communicating and linking the various strategic objectives and measures of the balanced scorecard

This can be done by showing each employee what the company is doing to achieve what the shareholders and consumers want. It aims to achieve good employee performance.

3.   Planning, setting goals, aligning various business plan initiatives

Allows organizations to integrate their business plans and financial plans. The balanced scorecard as a basis for allocating resources and managing which ones are more important to prioritize, will move towards the long-term goals of the company as a whole.

4.   Improve Feedback and strategic learning

This fourth process will provide strategic learning to the company. With the balanced scorecard as the center of the company's system, the company monitors what the company has produced in the short term.

Implementation of the Balanced Scorecard

Organisasi Organizations really need to implement the Balanced Sorecard as a set of multi-dimensional performance measures. This reflects the need to measure all areas of performance that are critical to organizational success.

(Tunggal, 2011) Four perspectives are considered in the BSC, namely:

1.   Financial perspective, related to how to serve the shareholders. Measurements of cash flow, return on capital, sales and income growth are usually used for a particular financial perspective.
2.   Customer perspective, related to the level of customer satisfaction. In general, the measurement of this perspective includes matters relating to the level of damage, timeliness of delivery, warranty support, product development and other things that come from direct input from customers and are associated with specific company activities.
3.   The perspective of internal business processes, namely the perspective related to the main competencies and operational areas. Internal business processes are generally measured through productivity, cycle time, quality, various cost measurements and other related indicators.
4.   Learning and growth perspective, which is a perspective related to continuous improvement and value creation. Measurement is usually emphasized on aspects related to organizational innovation and learning, such as: technology leadership, product development cycle times, operational process improvement, and others.

DISSCUSION

Linking Hospital Supply Chain Management Performance with Performance Measurement Using the Balanced Scorecard

In the context of COVID-19, a skilled organization is an organization that is skilled in acquiring, creating, transferring knowledge about COVID-19, and modifying hospital behavior that reflects new knowledge and insights to maintain business continuity and prepare for the new normal.

Such rapid changes during the COVID-19 pandemic demand a quick response from top managers regarding the direction of the hospital's business continuity so that it does not collapse in the midst of the pandemic. To produce a fast and appropriate response requires the existence of a comprehensive database and accurate evaluation of the field conditions related to supply chain management and those affecting it.

The supply chain has been disrupted due to the ongoing COVID-19 pandemic. Actors in the supply chain have limited activities to avoid contracting COVID-19, distribution of drugs and medical devices has been hampered due to the PSBB, patients as end consumers of hospital services are also afraid to come to the hospital. Patients who suffer from pain that can still be endured will not go to the hospital to seek help, but will endure the pain first. Patients with only emergency cases speculated that they had ruled out the risk of contracting COVID-19, and finally they came to the hospital to seek help.

From a business point of view, the conditions due to the COVID-19 pandemic have changed everything. Hospital income will decrease because hospital service users as the main source of hospital income decline. Service to patients has also decreased because the implementation of procedures related to handling patients during the pandemic disrupts services, causing patient dissatisfaction with the services provided. In addition, the public's perception of the hospital as a place of service for COVID-19 sufferers has resulted in patients being afraid to visit the hospital. As a result of decreased patient visits, the level of hospital bed occupancy will also decrease. Disrupted hospital services will increase patient care time in the hospital.

The changes that occur require hospital entities to learn about what is happening, so that they can survive or even continue to benefit when the COVID-19 pandemic is running.

Changes in the internal and external environment of hospital entities, which in the perspective of hospital supply chain management are disruptions to supply chain activities, namely on the side of actors, products or information. The disruption that occurs disrupts the performance of the hospital's supply chain management. Disruption to supply chain performance requires hospital entities to evaluate, one of which is done with a balanced score card approach.

Using the Balanced scorecard to measure the performance of hospital supply chain management will result in measurements in 4 perspectives, namely:

1. Financial perspective provides information on measurement results regarding Net Profit Margin (NPM), ROI (Return on Investment), Economic Ratios, Efficiency Ratios, Effectiveness Ratios
2. Customer Perspective (Customer Perspective) provides information on measurement results regarding Customer Satisfaction Level, Consumer Profitability Level, Customer Retention/Retention Ability, Customer Acquisition Ability
3. The Internal Business Process Perspective provides information on measurement results from BOR (Bed Occupancy Rate or Bed Use), BTO (Bed Turn Over Rate or Bed Turnover), GDR (Gross Death Rate), NDR (Net Death Rate), ALOS (Average Legth of Stay), TOI (Turn Over Internal)
4. Learning and Growth Perspective (Learn and Growth / Infrastructure Perspective) provides information on the measurement results of Employee Productivity, Employee Turnover, Employee Satisfaction.

FUTURE RESEARCH DIRECTIONS

Research on evaluating the performance of hospital supply chain management during a pandemic needs to be done a lot because supply chain changes will continue to adapt to changes caused by the ongoing pandemic. As a follow-up to the evaluation of supply chain performance, there is a need for research on changes in hospital supply chain management strategies so as to get the right strategy regarding supply chain management during the COVID-19.

CONCLUSION

The COVID-19 pandemic has resulted in disruptions to hospital supply chain management activities. Evaluation must be carried out to obtain information on the level of effectiveness and efficiency of hospital supply chain management performance, which becomes a benchmark in determining the hospital's strategy so that it can continue to survive and even make a profit. Evaluation of hospital supply chain management performance using a balanced scorecard approach can provide balanced performance information between financial and non-financial, between internal and external hospital entities.

REFERENCES

Chopra, S., & Peter, M. (2007). *Supply chain management, strategy planning & operation* (3rd ed.). Pearson Prentice Hall. doi:10.1007/978-3-8349-9320-5_22

Dito. (2020). *Dampak pandemi Covid-19 terhadap perekonomian Indonesia.* Jurnal Benefita. Universitas Sumatera Utara.

Dodangh, J., Majid, M., & Nasehifar, V. (2010). Ranking of strategic plans in balanced scorecard by using electric method. *International Journal of Innovation, Management and Technology.*

Fahmi, I. (2016). *Teori dan paraktik pengambilan keputusan kualitatif dan kuantitatif.* Rajawali Pers.

Gultom, D. R. (2009). *Pengukuran kinerja perusahaan dengan balanced scorecard: studi kasus pada perusahaan perkebunan negara III (Persero) Medan.* Universitas Sumatra Utara.

Hadiwardoyo, W. (2020). Kerugian ekonomi nasional akibat PSBB. *Jurnal of Business and Entrepreneurship, 2.*

Haizer, J., & Render, B. (2010). *Manajemen operasi.* Salemba Empat.

Jauch, L. R., & Glueck, W. F. (2004). *Strategic management and business policy* (9th ed.). McGraw-Hill.

Kaplan, R. S., & dan Norton, D. P. (2000). Balance scorecard, menerapkan strategi menjadi aksi. Terjemahan. Penerbit Erlangga.

Kaplan, R. S., & Norton, D. P. (2004). *Strategy maps: convert intangible assets into tangible outcomes.* Harvard Business School Press.

Kementrian Kesehatan Republik Indonesia. (2020). *Peraturan menteri kesehatan republik indonesia nomor 9 tahun 2020 tentang pedoman pembatasan sosial berskala besar dalam rangka percepatan penanganan corona virus disease 2019 (covid-19).* Author.

Kemenkes, R. I., McLeod, J. R., & Schell, G. P. (2011). *Sistem informasi manajemen.* Salemba Empat.

Michael, H. (2020). *Dampak coronavirus terhadap ekonomi global. Bank indonesia.* https://www.bi.go.id/id/publikasi/ekonomi-keuangan-kerjasama-

Mulyadi, & Setyawan, J. (2000). *Sistem perencanaan dan pengenalian manajemen* (2nd ed.). Jakarta: Salemba Empat.

Mulyadi. (2001). *Balanced scorecard alat manajemen kontemporer untuk memperlipatgandakan kinerja keuangan perusahaan.* Jakarta: Salemba Empat.

Obeng, K., & Ugboro, I. (2008). Effective strategic planning in public transit systems. *Transportation Research, 44*(3), 420–439. doi:10.1016/j.tre.2006.10.008

Pujawan, I. N. (2005). *Supply chain management.* Surabaya: Gundawidya.

Solihin, I. (2009). *Pengantar manajemen.* Erlangga.

Solihin, I. (2014). *Pengantar bisnis.* Erlangga.

Studies, C., Cv, O., & Abadi, K. (2018). Analisis saluran distribusi kayu (studi kasus di cv. Karya abadi, Manado). *Jurnal EMBA: Jurnal Riset Ekonomi, Manajemen. Bisnis Dan Akuntansi, 6.* Advance online publication. doi:10.35794/emba.v6i3.20444

Thorik, S. H. (2020). Efektivitas pembatasan sosial berskala besar di indonesia dalam penanggulangan pandemi covid-19. *Jurnal: Hukum dan Keadilan, 4*(1).

Tjiptono, F. (2014). *Pemasaran jasa – prinsip, penerapan, dan penelitian.* Andi Offset.

Tunggal, A. W. (2011). *Pokok-pokok performance measurement dan balanced scorecard.* Harvindo.

Wheelen, T. L., & Hunger, D. J. (2004). *Concepts in strategic management and business policy.* Prentice Hall.

Yulianti, A. (2020). *Knowledge management: learning organization di rs seri VIII.* http://mutupelay-anankeschatan.net/sample-levels/19-headline/3437-keberlangsungan-usaha-rs-di-masa-covid-19-apakah-akan-menuju-new- normal-perspektif-learning-organization

Chapter 25
Dynamics of Economic Sectors and Human Mobility Before and During COVID–19:
The Portuguese–Specific Context

Vítor João Pereira Domingues Martinho

Agricultural School (ESAV) and CERNAS-IPV Research Centre, Polytechnic Institute of Viseu (IPV), Viseu, Portugal

ABSTRACT

Considering the specific scenario of the Portuguese framework, it seems interesting to perform a research focused in this context. In fact, the Portuguese economic crisis after 2010/2011 created serious socioeconomic difficulties to the country, but in the recent years, the situation performed significant improvements. This new shock brought to the Portuguese society, again, new challenges and the need of new supports for the policies design by the public institutions and government. In this way, the objective of this research is to assess the Portuguese economic dynamics and, from here, discuss potential impacts from the COVID-19 frameworks, considering data disaggregated at regional and municipal level. For that, it considered the developments from the new economic geography, namely those related with the agglomeration processes and circular and cumulative phenomena. As main conclusions, with the social confinement, a greater economic impact around the Lisbon municipalities than in the north is expected.

INTRODUCTION

The dynamics and location of economic activity may be explained by several approaches, where the New Economic Geography (NEG) has its place (Branco et al., 2016). The NEG considers increasing returns to scale at firm level, market size and transport costs to explain why the population and the business sector tend to agglomerate around big poles, such as cities, regions or countries (Krugman, 1996). These agglomeration processes are self-reinforced through circular and cumulative phenomena (Krugman, 2007), because the companies concentrate where there are more population (market size) to save

DOI: 10.4018/978-1-6684-6762-6.ch025

transport costs and the population concentrate in places with more companies (more jobs) and higher real wages (Goto & Minamimura, 2019). The public policies are claimed to promote more balanced growths (Chatti et al., 2019). In fact, the NEG highlighted the importance of the space concept for the economic explanations (Krugman, 1998a) and brought the geographical dimensions for the economic theory (Krugman, 1998b). However, the NEG after these years continues as an approach with, still, great potential to be explored (Fujita & Krugman, 2004) in several dimensions (Krugman, 2011). More balanced relationships between the transport costs and the innovation may play a relevant role to promote a more sustainable development (Gonzalez-Val & Pueyo, 2019).

The developments from the NEG have been considered for the explanation of several economic agglomeration processes around the world (Kim & McCann, 2020), since the Thailand (Bui & Preechametta, 2019) and Asian integration (Gopalan et al., 2020) until the European context (Commendatore et al., 2020). The European Union integration context is a particular framework that motivates the scientific community to apply the NEG approaches in the assessment of potential scenarios. The Asian evolution process is another interesting context that aroused curiosity for specific cases, as that related with the relationships among China and Pakistan (Imran et al., 2020) or the specific Chinese framework (Jin et al., 2020), with their particularities (Li et al., 2019). In a sectorial perspective, the NEG developments have been considered for the location explanations of the several sectors, since the industry until some agricultural productions, where it is possible the spatial relocation (Csonka & Fertő, 2019), passing through the production of knowledge (Hinzmann et al., 2019) or Dutch disease (Morales, 2020). The NEG approaches were, also, considered in other assessments, as the implications of the housing prices in the urban contexts (Pengfei et al., 2019), logistics activities in Brazil (Rocha & Perobelli, 2020), Portuguese transport strategies (Teixeira, 2006), capital movement management (Wiberg, 2020) and creation of urban poles in an integrated and multifactorial growth process (Yi & Yao, 2019).

Considered the framework described before, the aim of this study is to analyse the Portuguese economic dynamics and, from this scenario, discuss likely impacts from the Covid-19 contexts, considering data disaggregated at regional and municipal level. For that, it was considered the developments from the New Economic Geography, namely those related with the agglomeration phenomena and increasing returns to scale (in the base of the circular and cumulative processes).

LITERATURE REVIEW

The Covid-19 pandemic has had several consequences (Zuev & Hannam, 2021), including economic (Quintino & Ferreira, 2021), in Portugal as has been happening all over the world (Camoes et al., 2021). The health, social and economic implications from the pandemic have affected asymmetrically the sectors and the regions, depending on their vulnerabilities to the more impacted activities. For the example, the tourism sector was one of the most affected economic activity (Martinho, 2021), particularly in regions more dependent on this source of income, as is the case in some contexts of the Azores Archipelago (Couto et al., 2020). These new paradigms created unemployment with consequences for the women, older people and with less qualifications (Lopes et al., 2021). The pandemic also brought heightened concerns about old challenges (Rodrigues et al., 2021) and threats (Sara et al., 2021). In addition, the impact of the Covid-19 cases on the economic variables depends on the structure of the population, health records, population mobility and the structure of the society (Sannigrahi et al., 2020).

In these new frameworks for the different dimensions of the society, including in the agrifood sector (Skalkos et al., 2021), consumer and business confidence (Teresiene et al., 2021) and rural communities (Pato, 2020), the several institutions, specifically the municipalities, have a particular role to support the populations, including increasing resilience and skills to deal with the new realities (da Silva, 2021), during and after the Covid-19 (Sabat et al., 2020).

The mobility of persons, namely to their jobs, in more populated municipalities, such as those around Lisbon, for example, have contributed to spread the contagions (da Costa & da Costa, 2020).

These scenarios brought pressures for the health and economic systems (Melenotte et al., 2020) and will bring challenges to find balanced commitments between the economic growth goals, the rules from the European Union and international institutions and the public expenditure (Illario et al., 2020).

MATERIAL AND METHODS

It was considered statistical information from the Statistics Portugal (INE, 2020d) for the Portuguese Mainland context, disaggregated at NUTS 2 and municipality level and over the period 2011-2018, related with the number of employees (staff serving companies) and the number of companies in each one economic sector.

These data were analysed through pairwise correlation matrices and panel data regressions, following the procedures proposed by Stata (2020).

Considering these data and results, the logarithm of employees at municipal level was predicted, taking into account the following steps: obtain the weight of the number of employees in each sector, over the total municipal economy; find the weight average of the number of employees in each sector over the total municipal economy; multiplication of these averages by the respective elasticities to obtain a global elasticity; multiplication of these global elasticities by the respective annual average logarithms, in each region; sum of these values to obtain the logarithm of employees predicted at municipal level.

DATA ANALYSIS

In this section, following the New Economic Geography developments, will be analysed statistical information obtained from the Statistics Portugal (INE, 2020d) for the Portuguese Mainland context, disaggregated at NUTS 2 level and over the period 2011-2018, related with the number of employees (staff serving companies) and the number of companies in each one economic sector (figures 1a, 1b, and 1c), as well as, data associated with the passengers and goods transported.

Figures 1a, 1b, and 1c reveal that, in general, the North and Lisbon Metropolitan Area regions are where there are more companies and employees, followed by the Centre region. Looking for the context of each one economic sector, associated with these two variables (employees and companies), figures 1a, 1b, and 1c show that the agricultural and fishing sector (agriculture, animal production, hunting, forestry and fishing) has more companies and employees in the North and Centre regions followed by the Alentejo. A similar pattern is verified for the extractive industries. The manufacturing industries have clearly higher values, for these variables, in the North region. The electricity, gas, steam, hot and cold water and cold air sector has more companies, in the more recent years, in the North and Centre regions, but has more employees around Lisbon. The water collection, treatment and distribution; sanitation, waste management and depollution sector has more companies in the North, but more employees around Lisbon. The construction sector is stronger, for the number of companies, in the North followed by the Centre and after the municipalities around Lisbon, but for the number of employees the Lisbon Metropolitan Area region wins to the Centre region (the North region maintain the leadership). For the wholesale and retail trade; repair of motor vehicles and motorcycles, the pattern is similar to that described for the construction sector. For the sectors related with the transport and storage; accommodation, catering and similar; information and communication activities; and real estate activities, the Lisbon Metropolitan Area region seems to have leadership (namely in the more recent years) that, in general, is more clear for the number of employees. A similar pattern of the municipalities around Lisbon leadership for these variables, with exceptions namely for the education and health sectors where the North region has more companies, is verified for the following sectors: consulting, scientific, technical and similar activities; administrative and support service activities; artistic, show, sports and recreational activities; and other service activities. These data show a clear agglomeration of companies and employees around two poles of development, Oporto (North region) and Lisbon (Lisbon Metropolitan Area region), with Lisbon in the leadership. In turn, the companies located around Lisbon are bigger in terms average number of employees.

Figure 2 presents that the municipalities around Lisbon has more passengers transported by road and by land, but this difference is lower with the North region when considered the passengers-Kilometre, showing that, in general, in the North the passengers travel more kilometres. In turn, the weight of goods in national transport of heavy goods vehicles is higher in the Centre region followed by the North.

Exploring the data for the number of companies and employees in growth rates (tables 1a, 1b, and 1c) and in percentage of each sector in the total economy (table 2 and 3) it is possible to obtain other interesting outputs and insights.

Tables 1a, 1b, and 1c show that the agriculture, animal production, hunting, forestry and fishing sector and the electricity, gas, steam, hot and cold water and cold air sector is where there was, in average (over the period considered), higher growth rates in the number of companies and employees. On the other hand, the services activities present, in general, positive average growth rates, exception for the wholesale and retail trade; repair of motor vehicles and motorcycles sector and the education sector, where the average growth rates mostly negatives (as happens with the number of companies for the transport and storage sector). In terms of regional evolution, the Algarve is the region with higher growth rates, in average (over the period considered and across the several economic sectors).

The wholesale and retail trade; repair of motor vehicles and motorcycles sector and the administrative and support service activities sector are the economic activities with high average (over the period considered) weight in the total regional economy for the number of companies in all regions, around 20% and 12% in average, respectively (table 2). Other sector with relatively high importance, in terms of number of companies, is the agriculture, animal production, hunting, forestry and fishing for the North (around 11% in average), Centre (around 11% in average) and Alentejo (around 23% in average) regions. In the Algarve another sector with relatively great importance are the accommodation, catering and similar activities (17% in average) and in the Lisbon Metropolitan Area are the consulting, scientific, technical and similar activities (14% in average).

For the number of employees (table 3), the wholesale and retail trade; repair of motor vehicles and motorcycles sector is that, in all regions, with high average (over the period considered) weight in the total regional economy (around 20% in average). In the North and Centre regions the manufacturing industries and the construction sectors appear, also, with relatively great importance, around 30% and 10%, respectively. In the Alentejo the relatively high weight is for the agriculture, animal production,

Figure 1a. Evolution of the number of companies and employees, over the period 2011-2018 and across the Portuguese Mainland NUTS 2, for the several economic sectors

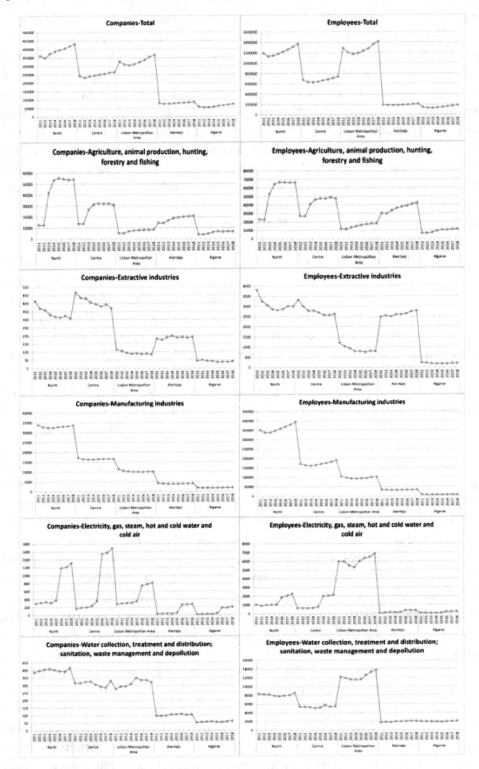

Figure 1b. Evolution of the number of companies and employees, over the period 2011-2018 and across the Portuguese Mainland NUTS 2, for the several economic sectors (Continuation)

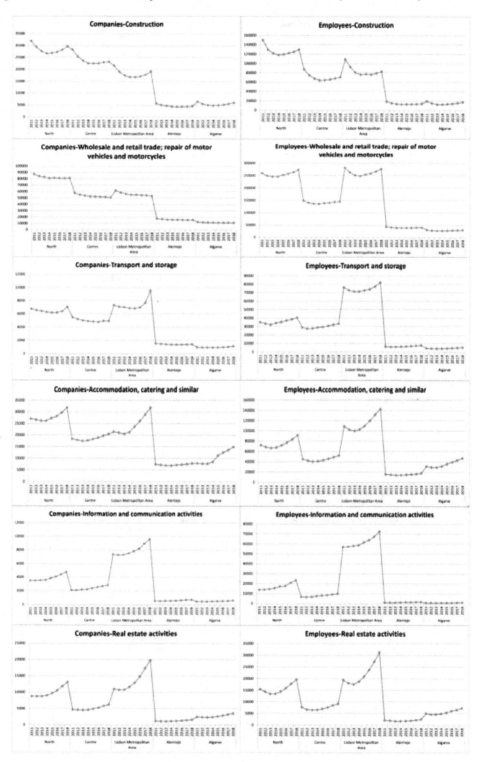

Figure 1c. Evolution of the number of companies and employees, over the period 2011-2018 and across the Portuguese Mainland NUTS 2, for the several economic sectors (Continuation)

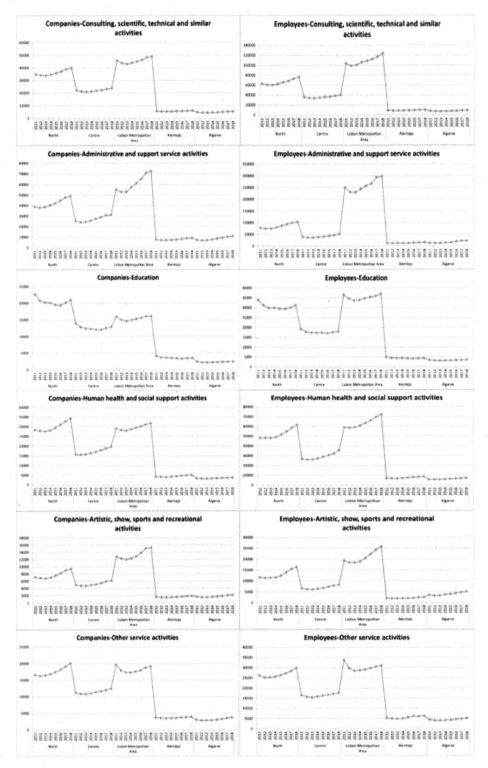

Figure 2. Passengers (number) and goods (tons) transported over the period 2011-2018 and across the Portuguese Mainland NUTS 2

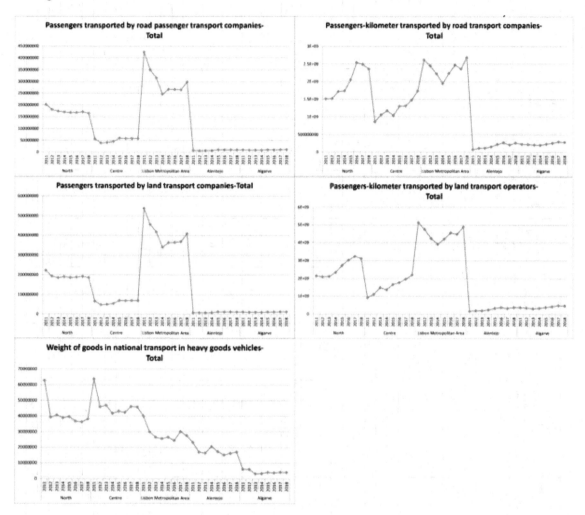

hunting, forestry and fishing sector and for the manufacturing industries. In Algarve and around Lisbon, the sectors with great relevance are the accommodation, catering and similar activities (more average percentage for Algarve) and the administrative and support service activities (more average percentage for the Lisbon Metropolitan Area).

RESULTS FOR PAIRWISE CORRELATION MATRIX AND PANEL DATA

The results presented in the tables 4, 5 and 6 were obtained with the statistical information available in Statistics Portugal (INE, 2020d) and through the procedures proposed by Stata (2020).

Table 4 shows that there are strong, positive a statistically significant relationships between the total number of companies and the number of companies in the several economic sectors, exception for the following sectors where the relationships are weaker (around 0.5): agriculture, animal production, hunt-

Table 1a. Number of companies and employees in growth rates (%), over the period 2011-2018 and across the Portuguese Mainland NUTS 2, for the several economic sectors

		Companies-Total	Employees-Total	Companies-Agriculture, animal production, hunting, forestry and fishing	Employees-Agriculture, animal production, hunting, forestry and fishing	Companies-Extractive industries	Employees-Extractive industries	Companies-Manufacturing industries	Employees-Manufacturing industries	Companies-Electricity, gas, steam, hot and cold water and cold air	Employees-Electricity, Electricity, gas, steam, hot and cold water and cold air	Companies-Water collection, distribution; sanitation, waste management and depollution	Employees-Water collection, treatment and distribution; sanitation, waste management and depollution	Companies-Construction	Employees-Construction
North	2012	-3.42	-5.27	-0.37	-2.20	-10.87	-14.79	-3.29	-4.05	8.50	-13.00	3.12	-1.22	-7.97	-13.87
North	2013	7.36	1.31	234.04	133.70	-2.44	-5.61	-0.75	0.03	5.02	10.47	2.27	-0.70	-5.94	-5.66
North	2014	3.26	2.68	27.18	22.22	-8.33	-6.89	-0.11	2.86	-6.27	0.39	0.74	-3.09	-3.35	-2.89
North	2015	2.58	3.70	3.68	3.35	-3.64	-1.37	1.21	3.30	20.70	2.36	-1.71	-2.07	0.66	1.05
North	2016	2.23	3.54	-1.58	-0.60	-1.57	1.67	0.61	2.91	213.72	78.39	-1.99	2.03	1.55	2.59
North	2017	3.10	4.01	-1.28	-0.20	3.51	5.28	0.66	3.17	1.77	10.12	-0.76	1.34	3.27	1.93
North	2018	3.10	4.30	0.41	0.24	-4.94	-0.63	1.04	3.17	8.18	11.10	6.14	6.35	5.20	4.04
Centre	2012	-4.47	-6.14	-0.68	-1.35	-7.28	-10.05	-4.39	-3.99	22.01	1.75	0.00	-0.45	-10.06	-14.76
Centre	2013	3.72	-0.60	94.31	51.55	-0.69	-7.23	-0.96	-1.90	3.09	-2.97	2.53	-1.50	-7.05	-9.72
Centre	2014	2.20	1.85	17.57	13.71	-5.81	0.40	0.25	2.58	19.00	5.32	0.62	-3.83	-4.50	-5.39
Centre	2015	2.38	3.23	3.44	2.97	-2.72	-3.59	1.12	3.28	50.00	19.45	-6.44	2.96	-0.25	0.59
Centre	2016	1.80	2.93	-1.13	-0.17	-3.55	-4.40	0.16	2.65	332.21	156.67	-4.59	9.95	0.29	2.01
Centre	2017	2.76	4.14	0.34	2.93	3.16	0.08	0.42	3.78	2.07	2.25	-2.06	-6.28	1.97	3.74
Centre	2018	0.96	3.90	-3.45	-2.66	-5.87	1.75	-0.13	4.33	7.30	6.01	15.79	2.01	1.00	3.39
Lisbon Metropolitan Area	2012	-4.94	-6.57	-3.93	-5.15	-6.09	-15.05	-7.10	-6.24	5.04	-0.20	5.05	-2.35	-11.85	-14.92
Lisbon Metropolitan Area	2013	-1.64	-2.61	35.86	16.69	-12.04	-8.86	-4.30	-5.19	4.11	-7.43	0.69	-2.63	-8.11	-13.12
Lisbon Metropolitan Area	2014	2.25	1.66	11.69	11.91	-6.32	-15.17	-2.19	-0.43	2.63	-4.09	5.46	-0.45	-4.08	-5.61
Lisbon Metropolitan Area	2015	3.52	3.84	3.79	8.90	2.25	0.38	-0.74	1.89	12.82	13.35	12.94	0.29	0.15	1.39
Lisbon Metropolitan Area	2016	4.08	3.36	2.23	6.37	-3.30	-4.77	-0.09	0.93	110.80	5.82	-4.30	8.52	1.89	-1.33
Lisbon Metropolitan Area	2017	5.41	6.25	1.36	3.25	1.14	6.46	1.44	6.18	4.04	2.08	0.00	5.96	4.23	3.86
Lisbon Metropolitan Area	2018	3.45	4.21	2.69	1.94	-3.37	-1.49	0.78	1.60	5.31	5.85	-4.19	2.87	7.14	4.81
Alentejo	2012	-5.19	-6.33	-1.71	-2.60	-3.87	2.34	-5.15	-5.00	21.88	61.40	0.00	1.23	-12.50	-19.09
Alentejo	2013	1.21	-1.21	18.07	12.83	8.62	-2.25	-2.94	-4.59	2.56	39.13	2.08	-1.66	-5.79	-11.10
Alentejo	2014	2.06	1.89	10.53	8.37	5.29	4.28	0.08	0.24	-5.00	-10.16	7.14	11.20	-7.44	-4.83
Alentejo	2015	2.06	3.06	3.65	4.29	-5.53	0.27	-0.18	2.03	57.89	17.39	0.95	-2.08	-2.39	0.82
Alentejo	2016	2.69	3.18	3.90	3.31	1.06	1.74	0.05	1.74	328.33	146.67	1.89	3.15	0.19	0.65
Alentejo	2017	2.79	4.08	1.73	5.53	-1.58	3.87	1.91	0.74	2.33	1.50	-5.56	3.21	1.97	3.04
Alentejo	2018	2.33	3.95	1.97	3.54	1.60	1.46	2.52	4.38	4.18	-3.25	2.94	-1.41	4.22	5.71
Algarve	2012	-5.93	-9.16	-3.51	-4.91	8.89	-4.93	-5.44	-10.14	25.00	6.38	5.88	-1.38	-15.09	-23.93
Algarve	2013	-0.28	-2.31	20.50	16.94	-12.24	-17.45	-0.50	-4.43	5.00	-42.00	3.70	-0.88	-9.42	-15.28
Algarve	2014	5.80	5.55	32.94	23.81	-2.33	-4.57	-0.95	-1.60	0.00	3.45	3.57	-1.73	-3.23	-0.61
Algarve	2015	8.93	8.68	11.40	13.14	-14.29	1.20	0.85	2.87	100.00	80.00	-6.90	-2.19	2.76	6.98
Algarve	2016	4.96	7.56	-4.92	-1.03	2.78	-4.14	0.39	-0.56	323.81	253.70	-1.85	5.46	3.94	5.79
Algarve	2017	6.68	8.13	5.40	6.38	-2.70	15.43	3.25	6.14	-1.12	-0.52	7.55	1.97	9.70	10.94
Algarve	2018	4.42	6.08	-3.30	3.16	11.11	2.67	5.04	4.49	13.64	14.74	8.77	2.89	6.25	12.26

Table 1b. Number of companies and employees in growth rates (%), over the period 2011-2018 and across the Portuguese Mainland NUTS 2, for the several economic sectors (Continuation)

		Companies-Wholesale and retail trade; repair of motor vehicles and motorcycles	Employees-Wholesale and retail trade; repair of motor vehicles and motorcycles	Companies-Transport and storage	Employees-Transport and storage	Companies-Accommodation, catering and similar	Employees-Accommodation, catering and similar	Companies-Information and communication activities	Employees-Information and communication activities	Companies-Real estate activities	Employees-Real estate activities	Companies-Consulting, scientific, technical and similar activities	Employees-Consulting, scientific, technical and similar activities	Companies-Administrative and support service activities	Employees-Administrative and support service activities
North	2012	-3.64	-4.29	-3.15	-4.87	-1.80	-5.24	0.60	1.19	0.15	-7.43	-1.95	-3.41	-2.74	-3.70
North	2013	-1.57	-1.29	-1.92	-3.79	-1.68	-2.62	0.77	3.02	0.25	-6.27	-0.71	-0.86	1.86	0.40
North	2014	-2.21	0.00	-2.15	5.78	0.04	1.76	1.67	7.53	2.71	0.22	2.21	4.20	4.67	6.70
North	2015	0.53	2.70	-1.41	3.77	4.18	6.38	6.57	10.70	7.56	6.97	3.45	4.78	4.73	9.13
North	2016	-0.43	2.08	0.10	5.13	2.97	7.33	5.29	2.53	9.02	10.81	3.63	4.47	6.15	7.37
North	2017	-0.20	2.34	2.72	3.69	5.51	8.32	8.08	17.41	12.49	11.33	4.99	6.81	6.17	6.22
North	2018	0.38	3.69	10.85	5.18	7.42	9.20	8.12	13.20	10.20	10.18	2.57	4.54	3.11	4.42
Centre	2012	-4.48	-5.59	-4.87	-5.07	-2.76	-6.18	-0.62	-3.07	-1.91	-14.04	-3.60	-4.62	-4.15	-5.71
Centre	2013	-2.70	-3.14	-3.72	1.08	-2.43	-4.73	4.29	4.03	-2.05	-1.90	-1.52	-1.30	1.30	0.10
Centre	2014	-1.96	-0.57	-2.35	3.72	1.04	1.91	1.28	12.79	2.05	0.85	1.46	2.40	4.98	3.62
Centre	2015	-0.22	2.06	-1.49	2.73	3.57	5.42	7.40	5.86	6.72	6.56	3.20	4.17	7.22	7.55
Centre	2016	-1.15	1.31	-0.64	4.66	3.20	6.05	6.60	3.96	8.34	8.73	1.87	1.49	4.69	6.84
Centre	2017	-0.55	2.06	2.71	4.08	4.38	6.65	5.20	9.16	10.26	11.89	3.77	5.42	6.79	8.67
Centre	2018	-1.87	1.21	0.06	3.73	4.22	6.78	6.37	7.50	8.72	7.59	2.72	4.57	1.38	10.20
Lisbon Metropolitan Area	2012	-5.56	-6.56	-3.10	-4.37	-1.79	-6.16	-1.31	0.53	-2.43	-6.78	-4.44	-4.48	-3.93	-7.80
Lisbon Metropolitan Area	2013	-3.44	-4.30	-1.10	-1.93	-2.44	-2.34	0.71	1.27	0.54	-2.66	-1.81	1.80	-0.06	-0.30
Lisbon Metropolitan Area	2014	-2.37	-1.40	-1.98	-0.05	3.42	2.91	2.56	0.96	7.76	6.45	2.10	5.42	8.42	5.99
Lisbon Metropolitan Area	2015	-0.04	2.43	-0.60	1.85	11.91	6.84	4.25	5.25	10.99	12.17	2.25	2.10	6.45	5.62
Lisbon Metropolitan Area	2016	-0.84	1.88	2.39	1.86	10.10	9.08	4.71	3.32	14.65	13.15	2.99	3.49	6.98	3.48
Lisbon Metropolitan Area	2017	-0.96	3.17	9.58	4.27	10.68	10.34	8.95	5.65	17.23	14.92	4.27	4.36	8.44	10.18
Lisbon Metropolitan Area	2018	-1.49	3.53	24.33	6.18	10.22	8.06	7.14	7.66	13.86	14.60	1.36	5.99	2.34	1.33
Alentejo	2012	-5.60	-5.81	-4.44	-7.22	-4.43	-6.15	-4.29	-4.88	-4.90	-10.45	-4.79	-4.47	-5.62	-6.81
Alentejo	2013	-4.23	-4.32	-4.04	2.94	-3.58	-5.70	5.65	6.17	-2.62	-11.40	-1.52	-0.73	0.04	0.45
Alentejo	2014	-1.62	0.12	-3.86	1.90	-0.38	0.74	1.48	10.64	2.41	0.97	1.07	2.86	2.41	-1.91
Alentejo	2015	-0.08	0.33	-0.29	5.01	3.85	5.17	3.27	15.93	5.98	5.29	3.53	4.88	4.23	4.23
Alentejo	2016	-1.02	0.58	-0.66	5.65	2.26	5.15	8.10	9.76	10.43	6.51	1.43	2.65	5.79	7.80
Alentejo	2017	-1.21	1.22	2.43	7.13	3.49	5.25	12.54	10.42	10.53	14.63	4.26	6.52	8.35	11.97
Alentejo	2018	0.24	1.46	2.45	6.31	3.65	7.59	3.47	2.53	10.15	12.25	2.59	1.50	2.33	6.80
Algarve	2012	-6.07	-8.69	-2.57	-11.57	-2.18	-5.73	4.66	-3.38	-4.39	-8.28	-5.94	-7.69	-4.43	-4.81
Algarve	2013	-2.56	-4.96	-0.11	-3.69	-0.30	-0.54	-4.66	-2.65	-1.55	1.29	-1.41	-1.41	2.01	2.02
Algarve	2014	-1.06	0.87	-0.85	5.90	10.79	7.80	5.78	13.24	4.14	5.00	3.15	3.85	9.52	12.13
Algarve	2015	-0.53	2.65	2.03	4.89	32.52	14.52	5.04	5.36	8.75	10.13	4.06	6.41	9.53	14.54
Algarve	2016	-0.40	2.79	2.93	8.71	11.29	10.43	3.20	4.88	10.40	12.68	5.08	4.88	9.76	20.02
Algarve	2017	-0.20	3.85	6.10	5.43	8.98	9.27	6.20	13.16	11.82	8.86	5.67	8.70	11.40	14.07
Algarve	2018	-0.47	2.90	9.20	9.76	9.61	7.87	9.85	15.21	9.61	11.13	3.01	4.17	5.26	2.69

Table 1c. Number of companies and employees in growth rates (%), over the period 2011-2018 and across the Portuguese Mainland NUTS 2, for the several economic sectors (Continuation)

		Companies-Education	Employees-Education	Companies-Human health and social support activities	Employees-Human health and social support activities	Companies-Artistic, show, sports and recreational activities	Employees-Artistic, show, sports and recreational activities	Companies-Other service activities	Employees-Other service activities
North	2012	-8.57	-7.72	-1.77	-0.11	-3.74	-2.36	-2.04	-3.96
North	2013	-2.13	-4.58	-0.46	-0.13	-1.41	1.24	1.45	0.39
North	2014	-0.61	0.46	1.51	1.90	3.35	0.90	2.27	1.61
North	2015	-3.06	-1.64	4.77	5.62	8.05	7.42	3.85	2.27
North	2016	-0.77	-0.51	5.58	6.01	8.68	11.32	3.96	3.72
North	2017	4.12	2.56	5.66	6.58	9.82	11.84	5.14	3.93
North	2018	3.98	3.93	4.27	5.64	4.12	5.70	5.22	5.19
Centre	2012	-8.13	-7.85	-0.77	-2.49	-4.51	-5.99	-3.06	-4.58
Centre	2013	-3.09	-2.22	1.11	0.52	-0.25	-1.47	-0.54	-1.45
Centre	2014	-0.78	-0.13	3.83	3.87	4.36	4.44	1.98	2.29
Centre	2015	-1.99	0.40	4.37	5.90	4.32	6.26	3.63	2.34
Centre	2016	-0.30	-2.20	4.91	5.35	6.53	7.50	2.36	2.09
Centre	2017	4.27	3.22	4.89	5.73	8.79	8.46	3.14	3.28
Centre	2018	2.47	1.86	4.18	10.46	3.02	4.43	3.40	2.12
Lisbon Metropolitan Area	2012	-6.23	-5.12	-2.40	-0.94	-4.33	-4.26	-8.60	-12.00
Lisbon Metropolitan Area	2013	-2.68	-2.95	-1.20	1.09	-1.96	-0.19	-3.26	-3.80
Lisbon Metropolitan Area	2014	2.80	0.73	2.66	3.45	2.70	2.56	-0.57	0.75
Lisbon Metropolitan Area	2015	2.17	2.72	2.71	3.81	4.17	8.23	1.68	1.44
Lisbon Metropolitan Area	2016	1.86	1.89	2.38	4.23	7.98	9.00	2.00	2.07
Lisbon Metropolitan Area	2017	2.83	1.57	2.96	5.26	8.89	9.13	4.86	2.70
Lisbon Metropolitan Area	2018	0.02	2.82	2.13	4.06	1.39	6.11	1.92	1.80
Alentejo	2012	-10.25	-11.32	-2.10	-1.50	-6.31	-5.89	-5.36	-4.75
Alentejo	2013	-1.77	-2.04	-1.22	-1.14	-0.53	0.75	-1.84	-2.07
Alentejo	2014	-2.80	-0.11	5.25	5.12	1.54	2.87	2.22	2.46
Alentejo	2015	-3.53	-2.47	4.86	5.98	5.42	2.12	0.99	13.66
Alentejo	2016	-1.92	-1.95	7.54	6.13	6.20	6.87	3.63	10.03
Alentejo	2017	2.83	3.33	5.23	4.74	7.43	13.90	2.26	-2.62
Alentejo	2018	2.14	1.78	3.11	3.95	3.02	2.12	2.69	4.18
Algarve	2012	-9.41	-8.57	-1.64	0.62	-8.83	-8.26	-7.13	-9.04
Algarve	2013	-0.88	-1.85	-2.35	-0.41	0.20	4.77	0.71	-1.67
Algarve	2014	1.26	0.96	3.14	3.29	7.53	11.14	1.72	2.91
Algarve	2015	2.96	3.04	4.03	7.89	7.38	5.79	5.94	5.39
Algarve	2016	3.77	3.96	3.07	3.61	8.26	8.73	5.93	7.42
Algarve	2017	1.21	1.68	3.58	5.53	11.31	10.55	9.32	5.56
Algarve	2018	3.76	5.11	2.52	4.02	4.12	7.63	4.95	7.28

ing, forestry and fishing; extractive industries; and electricity, gas, steam, hot and cold water and cold air. In turn, in general, there are positive and statistically significant correlations between the number of

Table 2. Weight of each sector in the total economy (%), for each year in each region, relatively to the number of companies

Region	Year	Companies-Agriculture, animal production, hunting, forestry and fishing	Companies-Extractive industries	Companies-Manufacturing industries	Companies-Electricity, gas, steam, hot and cold water and cold air	Companies-Water collection, treatment and distribution; sanitation, waste management and depollution	Companies-Construction	Companies-Wholesale and retail trade; repair of motor vehicles and motorcycles	Companies-Transport and storage	Companies-Accommodation, catering and similar	Companies-Information and communication activities	Companies-Real estate activities	Companies-Consulting, scientific, technical and similar activities	Companies-Administrative and support service activities	Companies-Education	Companies-Human health and social support activities	Companies-Artistic, show, sports and recreational activities	Companies-Other service activities
North	2011	3.50	0.11	9.36	0.08	0.13	8.83	24.14	1.87	7.50	0.97	2.42	9.64	10.78	6.28	7.85	1.98	4.59
Centre	2011	5.71	0.19	7.15	0.07	0.13	11.68	23.84	2.27	7.58	0.87	1.91	9.15	10.44	5.79	6.52	2.06	4.64
Lisbon Metropolitan Area	2011	1.59	0.04	3.53	0.09	0.08	6.62	18.89	2.24	6.55	2.26	3.38	14.07	16.91	4.90	8.89	3.92	6.03
Alentejo	2011	18.23	0.23	5.36	0.04	0.12	7.15	21.82	1.95	9.33	0.67	1.46	7.13	9.55	5.14	5.14	2.01	4.68
Algarve	2011	6.45	0.08	3.25	0.03	0.09	11.11	20.81	1.67	13.44	0.77	4.18	8.04	12.32	4.09	5.64	2.82	5.23
North	2012	3.61	0.11	9.37	0.09	0.11	8.41	24.08	1.88	7.63	1.01	2.50	9.79	10.85	5.94	7.98	1.97	4.66
Centre	2012	5.94	0.19	7.15	0.08	0.14	11.00	23.84	2.26	7.72	0.91	1.96	9.24	10.48	5.57	6.77	2.05	4.71
Lisbon Metropolitan Area	2012	1.61	0.03	3.45	0.09	0.09	6.14	18.76	2.28	6.77	2.35	3.47	14.15	17.09	4.84	9.13	3.94	5.79
Alentejo	2012	18.90	0.23	5.36	0.05	0.13	6.60	21.72	1.96	9.41	0.68	1.46	7.16	9.50	4.86	5.31	1.98	4.67
Algarve	2012	6.61	0.09	3.27	0.04	0.10	10.03	20.78	1.73	13.97	0.86	4.25	8.04	12.51	3.93	5.89	2.73	5.16
North	2013	11.22	0.10	8.66	0.09	0.11	7.37	22.08	1.72	6.99	0.94	2.34	9.05	10.30	5.42	7.40	1.81	4.40
Centre	2013	11.13	0.18	6.83	0.08	0.14	9.85	22.36	2.10	7.26	0.91	1.85	8.77	10.23	5.20	6.60	1.98	4.52
Lisbon Metropolitan Area	2013	2.22	0.03	3.36	0.10	0.10	5.73	18.42	2.30	6.71	2.41	3.55	14.12	17.36	4.79	9.17	3.93	5.70
Alentejo	2013	22.05	0.25	5.14	0.05	0.13	6.15	20.55	1.86	8.96	0.71	1.41	6.97	9.39	4.72	5.18	1.95	4.53
Algarve	2013	7.99	0.08	3.26	0.04	0.10	9.11	20.31	1.73	13.97	0.82	4.20	7.95	12.80	3.91	5.77	2.74	5.21
North	2014	13.82	0.09	8.38	0.08	0.11	6.90	20.91	1.63	6.77	0.93	2.33	8.96	10.44	5.21	7.28	1.81	4.36
Centre	2014	12.80	0.17	6.70	0.10	0.13	9.21	21.45	2.00	7.18	0.91	1.85	8.71	10.51	5.05	6.71	2.02	4.51
Lisbon Metropolitan Area	2014	2.43	0.03	3.21	0.10	0.10	5.38	17.59	2.20	6.79	2.41	3.74	14.10	18.41	4.81	9.21	3.95	5.54
Alentejo	2014	23.88	0.25	5.04	0.05	0.13	5.57	19.81	1.75	8.75	0.70	1.41	6.90	9.42	4.50	5.34	1.94	4.54
Algarve	2014	10.04	0.07	3.05	0.04	0.09	8.33	18.99	1.62	14.63	0.82	4.13	7.75	13.25	3.74	5.62	2.79	5.01
North	2015	13.97	0.08	8.27	0.10	0.10	6.77	20.50	1.56	6.87	0.97	2.44	9.04	10.66	4.93	7.43	1.91	4.42
Centre	2015	12.94	0.15	6.62	0.14	0.12	8.97	20.91	1.93	7.26	0.95	1.93	8.78	11.01	4.83	6.84	2.06	4.57
Lisbon Metropolitan Area	2015	2.43	0.03	2.96	0.11	0.11	5.20	16.98	2.11	7.34	2.43	4.01	13.93	18.93	4.75	9.14	3.97	5.44
Alentejo	2015	24.25	0.24	4.93	0.08	0.13	5.33	19.40	1.71	8.90	0.71	1.47	7.00	9.62	4.25	5.49	2.00	4.49
Algarve	2015	10.27	0.06	2.83	0.07	0.09	7.86	17.34	1.52	17.80	0.79	4.12	7.40	13.32	3.54	5.37	2.75	4.87
North	2016	13.45	0.08	8.14	0.29	0.10	6.72	19.96	1.53	6.92	1.00	2.60	9.16	11.07	4.78	7.68	2.03	4.49
Centre	2016	12.56	0.08	6.51	0.61	0.11	8.84	20.30	1.88	7.36	1.00	2.05	8.78	11.32	4.73	7.04	2.15	4.59
Lisbon Metropolitan Area	2016	2.39	0.03	2.96	0.22	0.10	5.09	16.18	2.08	7.76	2.45	4.42	13.78	19.46	4.65	8.99	4.12	5.33
Alentejo	2016	24.53	0.23	4.80	0.31	0.13	5.20	18.70	1.66	8.86	0.75	1.58	6.91	9.91	4.06	5.75	2.07	4.53
Algarve	2016	9.30	0.06	2.70	0.27	0.08	7.78	16.45	1.49	18.87	0.78	4.34	7.41	13.93	3.50	5.27	2.84	4.92
North	2017	12.87	0.08	7.95	0.29	0.09	6.73	19.32	1.53	7.09	1.05	2.84	9.33	11.40	4.83	7.87	2.16	4.58
Centre	2017	12.27	0.15	6.36	0.60	0.11	8.77	19.65	1.88	7.48	1.02	2.20	8.87	11.77	4.80	7.19	2.28	4.61
Lisbon Metropolitan Area	2017	2.30	0.03	2.85	0.22	0.09	5.04	15.20	2.16	8.15	2.53	4.91	13.63	20.02	4.53	8.78	4.26	5.31
Alentejo	2017	24.28	0.22	4.76	0.31	0.12	5.16	17.97	1.65	8.92	0.82	1.70	7.01	10.45	4.06	5.89	2.16	4.51
Algarve	2017	9.19	0.05	2.62	0.25	0.08	8.00	15.39	1.48	19.28	0.78	4.55	7.34	14.55	3.32	5.12	2.96	5.04

continued on following page

Table 2. Continued

		Companies- Agriculture, animal production, hunting, forestry and fishing	Companies- Extractive industries	Companies- Manufacturing industries	Companies- Electricity, gas, steam, hot and cold water and cold air	Companies- Water collection, treatment and distribution; sanitation, waste management and depollution	Companies- Construction	Companies- Wholesale and retail trade; repair of motor vehicles and motorcycles	Companies- Transport and storage	Companies- Accommodation, catering and similar	Companies- Information and communication activities	Companies- Real estate activities	Companies- Consulting, scientific, technical and similar activities	Companies- Administrative and support service activities	Companies- Education	Companies- Human health and social support activities	Companies- Artistic, show, sports and recreational activities	Companies- Other service activities
North	2018	12.54	0.07	7.79	0.30	0.10	6.87	18.81	1.64	7.38	1.10	3.03	9.28	11.40	4.87	7.96	2.18	4.67
Centre	2018	11.73	0.14	6.29	0.64	0.12	8.77	19.10	1.86	7.72	1.07	2.37	9.02	11.81	4.87	7.42	2.32	4.72
Lisbon Metropolitan Area	2018	2.28	0.02	2.77	0.22	0.09	5.22	14.48	2.60	8.69	2.62	5.41	13.36	19.80	4.38	8.67	4.17	5.23
Alentejo	2018	24.19	0.22	4.77	0.32	0.12	5.25	17.60	1.65	9.04	0.83	1.83	7.03	10.45	4.05	5.93	2.18	4.53
Algarve	2018	8.51	0.05	2.63	0.27	0.08	8.15	14.67	1.55	20.24	0.82	4.77	7.24	14.67	3.30	5.03	2.95	5.06

Table 3. Weight of each sector in the total economy (%), for each year in each region, relatively to the number of employees

Region	Year	Employees-Agriculture, animal production, hunting, forestry and fishing	Employees-Extractive industries	Employees-Manufacturing industries	Employees-Electricity, gas, steam, hot and cold water and cold air	Employees-Water collection, treatment and distribution, sanitation, waste management and depollution	Employees-Construction	Employees-Wholesale and retail trade; repair of motor vehicles and motorcycles	Employees-Transport and storage	Employees-Accommodation, catering and similar	Employees-Information and communication activities	Employees-Real estate activities	Employees-Consulting, scientific, technical and similar activities	Employees-Administrative and support service activities	Employees-Education	Employees-Human health and social support activities	Employees-Artistic, show, sports and recreational activities	Employees-Other service activities
North	2011	1.94	0.32	29.46	0.09	0.70	12.53	21.76	2.94	6.03	1.16	1.29	5.24	6.49	2.84	4.04	0.97	2.20
Centre	2011	4.02	0.49	25.30	0.09	0.80	12.96	22.03	4.27	6.65	1.01	1.13	5.30	5.72	2.85	3.96	0.98	2.45
Lisbon Metropolitan Area	2011	0.93	0.09	8.05	0.46	0.95	8.44	21.83	5.91	8.44	4.43	1.50	8.03	19.42	2.83	4.58	1.50	2.61
Alentejo	2011	15.46	1.27	17.25	0.03	0.92	9.46	21.81	3.25	8.10	0.57	1.07	4.54	6.55	2.58	3.49	1.02	2.63
Algarve	2011	4.57	0.16	4.61	0.03	1.36	13.44	21.10	3.03	21.60	0.60	3.46	5.34	8.99	2.43	3.90	2.38	3.01
North	2012	2.00	0.29	29.84	0.08	0.73	11.39	21.98	2.95	6.03	1.24	1.26	5.34	6.60	2.77	4.26	1.00	2.23
Centre	2012	4.22	0.47	25.88	0.10	0.84	11.77	22.15	4.32	6.65	1.04	1.04	5.38	5.75	2.80	4.12	0.98	2.49
Lisbon Metropolitan Area	2012	0.94	0.09	8.08	0.50	0.99	7.69	21.84	6.05	8.47	4.76	1.50	8.21	19.16	2.88	4.85	1.53	2.46
Alentejo	2012	16.07	1.39	17.50	0.05	0.99	8.17	21.93	3.22	8.11	0.58	1.02	4.63	6.52	2.45	3.67	1.02	2.68
Algarve	2012	4.79	0.16	4.56	0.04	1.47	11.26	21.21	2.95	22.41	0.64	3.49	5.42	9.42	2.44	4.32	2.41	3.02
North	2013	4.62	0.27	29.47	0.09	0.71	10.61	21.42	2.80	5.80	1.27	1.17	5.23	6.54	2.61	4.20	1.00	2.21
Centre	2013	6.44	0.44	25.54	0.10	0.84	10.69	21.59	4.39	6.38	1.09	1.02	5.34	5.79	2.75	4.16	0.97	2.47
Lisbon Metropolitan Area	2013	1.13	0.08	7.87	0.47	0.99	6.86	21.46	6.09	8.50	4.95	1.50	8.58	19.62	2.87	5.04	1.57	2.43
Alentejo	2013	18.36	1.37	16.90	0.07	0.98	7.36	21.24	3.36	7.74	0.62	0.91	4.65	6.63	2.42	3.67	1.04	2.65
Algarve	2013	5.73	0.14	4.46	0.02	1.49	9.76	20.63	2.91	22.82	0.63	3.62	5.47	9.84	2.45	4.40	2.58	3.04
North	2014	5.50	0.24	29.52	0.09	0.67	10.03	20.86	2.89	5.75	1.32	1.14	5.31	6.79	2.55	4.16	0.99	2.19
Centre	2014	7.19	0.43	25.73	0.10	0.79	9.93	21.08	4.47	6.38	1.20	1.01	5.37	5.89	2.70	4.25	0.99	2.48
Lisbon Metropolitan Area	2014	1.24	0.07	7.70	0.44	0.97	6.37	20.81	5.99	8.60	4.92	1.57	8.90	20.45	2.84	5.13	1.59	2.41
Alentejo	2014	19.52	1.41	16.63	0.06	1.07	6.87	20.88	3.36	7.66	0.67	0.91	4.70	6.38	2.38	3.79	1.05	2.67
Algarve	2014	6.72	0.12	4.16	0.02	1.39	9.19	19.72	2.92	23.31	0.68	3.60	5.38	10.46	2.35	4.31	2.72	2.96
North	2015	5.48	0.23	29.41	0.09	0.64	9.78	20.66	2.89	5.90	1.41	1.18	5.36	7.15	2.42	4.24	1.02	2.16
Centre	2015	7.17	0.40	25.74	0.12	0.79	9.67	20.84	4.45	6.51	1.24	1.04	5.42	6.14	2.62	4.36	1.02	2.46
Lisbon Metropolitan Area	2015	1.30	0.06	7.56	0.48	0.93	6.22	20.53	5.88	8.85	4.99	1.69	8.75	20.80	2.81	5.13	1.65	2.35
Alentejo	2015	19.76	1.37	16.46	0.07	1.02	6.72	20.32	3.42	7.81	0.76	0.92	4.78	6.46	2.25	3.89	1.04	2.94
Algarve	2015	7.00	0.12	3.94	0.04	1.25	9.05	18.62	2.81	24.56	0.66	3.65	5.27	11.02	2.22	4.28	2.64	2.87
North	2016	5.26	0.23	29.23	0.15	0.63	9.69	20.37	2.93	6.11	1.40	1.26	5.41	7.41	2.33	4.34	1.10	2.16
Centre	2016	6.95	0.38	25.67	0.29	0.84	9.59	20.51	4.53	6.71	1.25	1.10	5.34	6.37	2.49	4.46	1.07	2.44
Lisbon Metropolitan Area	2016	1.34	0.06	7.38	0.50	0.98	5.94	20.24	5.79	9.34	4.98	1.85	8.76	20.83	2.77	5.17	1.74	2.32
Alentejo	2016	19.78	1.35	16.23	0.17	1.02	6.56	19.81	3.50	7.96	0.81	0.95	4.75	6.74	2.14	4.00	1.08	3.14
Algarve	2016	6.44	0.10	3.64	0.12	1.23	8.90	17.80	2.84	25.21	0.64	3.83	5.14	12.30	2.15	4.12	2.67	2.87
North	2017	5.05	0.23	28.99	0.16	0.61	9.49	20.04	2.92	6.37	1.58	1.35	5.56	7.57	2.29	4.45	1.18	2.16
Centre	2017	6.87	0.36	25.58	0.29	0.76	9.55	20.10	4.52	6.87	1.31	1.19	5.41	6.65	2.47	4.53	1.11	2.42
Lisbon Metropolitan Area	2017	1.30	0.06	7.38	0.48	0.98	5.80	19.65	5.68	9.70	4.96	2.00	8.61	21.60	2.65	5.12	1.79	2.24

continued on following page

Table 3. Continued

		Employees-Agriculture, animal production, hunting, forestry and fishing	Employees-Extractive industries	Employees-Manufacturing industries	Employees-Electricity, gas, steam, hot and cold water and cold air	Employees-Water collection, treatment and distribution; sanitation, waste management and depollution	Employees-Construction	Employees-Wholesale and retail trade; repair of motor vehicles and motorcycles	Employees-Transport and storage	Employees-Accommodation, catering and similar	Employees-Information and communication activities	Employees-Real estate activities	Employees-Consulting, Consulting, scientific, technical and similar activities	Employees-Administrative and support service activities	Employees-Education	Employees-Human health and social support activities	Employees-Artistic, show, sports and recreational activities	Employees-Other service activities
Alentejo	2017	20.06	1.35	15.71	0.17	1.01	6.49	19.26	3.60	8.05	0.85	1.05	4.87	7.26	2.12	4.03	1.18	2.94
Algarve	2017	6.34	0.11	3.57	0.11	1.16	9.13	17.09	2.77	25.48	0.67	3.85	5.17	12.97	2.02	4.02	2.73	2.80
North	2018	4.85	0.22	28.68	0.17	0.62	9.47	19.92	2.95	6.66	1.72	1.43	5.57	7.58	2.29	4.51	1.20	2.18
Centre	2018	6.44	0.35	25.69	0.29	0.74	9.51	19.58	4.52	7.07	1.35	1.23	5.45	7.05	2.42	4.81	1.12	2.38
Lisbon Metropolitan Area	2018	1.27	0.06	7.19	0.48	0.97	5.83	19.52	5.79	10.06	5.12	2.20	8.75	21.00	2.61	5.11	1.82	2.19
Alentejo	2018	19.98	1.31	15.77	0.15	0.96	6.60	18.80	3.69	8.33	0.84	1.14	4.75	7.46	2.08	4.03	1.16	2.94
Algarve	2018	6.16	0.11	3.52	0.12	1.12	9.66	16.58	2.87	25.91	0.73	4.03	5.07	12.56	2.00	3.94	2.77	2.83

Table 4. Pairwise correlation matrix between the number of companies for the several economic sectors

	CTO	CAG	CEX	CMA	CEL	CWA	CCO	CWH	CTR	CAC	CIN	CRE	CCN	CAD	CED	CHU	CAR	COT
CTO	1.000																	
CAG	0.5277*	1.000																
	(0.001)																	
CEX	0.4703*	0.6540*	1.000															
	(0.002)	(0.000)																
CMA	0.8428*	0.7547*	0.7240*	1.000														
	(0.000)	(0.000)	(0.000)															
CEL	0.5658*	0.5316*	0.3822*	0.4773*	1.000													
	(0.000)	(0.000)	(0.015)	(0.002)														
CWA	0.9693*	0.5670*	0.6397*	0.8730*	0.5428*	1.000												
	(0.000)	(0.000)	(0.000)	(0.000)	(0.000)													
CCO	0.9068*	0.5611*	0.7363*	0.9075*	0.5330*	0.9533*	1.000											
	(0.000)	(0.000)	(0.000)	(0.000)	(0.000)	(0.000)												
CWH	0.9675*	0.5748*	0.6221*	0.9282*	0.4909*	0.9767*	0.9636*	1.000										
	(0.000)	(0.000)	(0.000)	(0.000)	(0.001)	(0.000)	(0.000)											
CTR	0.9547*	0.301	0.3733*	0.6820*	0.4886*	0.9228*	0.8457*	0.8947*	1.000									
	(0.000)	(0.060)	(0.018)	(0.000)	(0.001)	(0.000)	(0.000)	(0.000)										
CAC	0.9626*	0.4433*	0.3619*	0.7901*	0.5801*	0.9084*	0.8607*	0.9077*	0.9247*	1.000								
	(0.000)	(0.004)	(0.022)	(0.000)	(0.000)	(0.000)	(0.000)	(0.000)	(0.000)									
CIN	0.7782*	-0.004	-0.065	0.3293*	0.3691*	0.6763*	0.5203*	0.6288*	0.8870*	0.7767*	1.000							
	(0.000)	(0.983)	(0.691)	(0.038)	(0.019)	(0.000)	(0.001)	(0.000)	(0.000)	(0.000)								
CRE	0.8561*	0.161	0.012	0.4927*	0.4742*	0.7445*	0.6179*	0.7162*	0.9054*	0.8995*	0.9501*	1.000						
	(0.000)	(0.322)	(0.942)	(0.001)	(0.002)	(0.000)	(0.000)	(0.000)	(0.000)	(0.000)	(0.000)							
CCN	0.9364*	0.244	0.204	0.6136*	0.4620*	0.8665*	0.7554*	0.8467*	0.9746*	0.9101*	0.9449*	0.9476*	1.000					
	(0.000)	(0.129)	(0.206)	(0.000)	(0.003)	(0.000)	(0.000)	(0.000)	(0.000)	(0.000)	(0.000)	(0.000)						
CAD	0.8893*	0.171	0.100	0.5121*	0.4754*	0.8040*	0.6715*	0.7654*	0.9492*	0.8894*	0.9761*	0.9774*	0.9862*	1.000				
	(0.000)	(0.291)	(0.541)	(0.000)	(0.002)	(0.000)	(0.000)	(0.000)	(0.000)	(0.000)	(0.000)	(0.000)	(0.000)					
CED	0.9852*	0.5141*	0.5515*	0.8891*	0.5017*	0.9782*	0.9426*	0.9918*	0.9344*	0.9383*	0.7104*	0.7903*	0.8983*	0.8324*	1.000			
	(0.000)	(0.001)	(0.000)	(0.000)	(0.001)	(0.000)	(0.000)	(0.000)	(0.000)	(0.000)	(0.000)	(0.000)	(0.000)	(0.000)				
CHU	0.9852*	0.4076*	0.3361*	0.7544*	0.5363*	0.9295*	0.8412*	0.9246*	0.9703*	0.9532*	0.8654*	0.9138*	0.9791*	0.9462*	0.9589*	1.000		
	(0.000)	(0.009)	(0.034)	(0.000)	(0.000)	(0.000)	(0.000)	(0.000)	(0.000)	(0.000)	(0.000)	(0.000)	(0.000)	(0.000)	(0.000)			
CAR	0.8289*	0.065	0.008	0.4052*	0.4282*	0.7327*	0.5932*	0.6898*	0.9184*	0.8281*	0.9946*	0.9637*	0.9680*	0.9908*	0.7648*	0.9039*	1.000	
	(0.000)	(0.689)	(0.962)	(0.010)	(0.006)	(0.000)	(0.000)	(0.000)	(0.000)	(0.000)	(0.000)	(0.000)	(0.000)	(0.000)	(0.000)	(0.000)		
COT	0.9813*	0.3852*	0.3417*	0.7355*	0.5270*	0.9281*	0.8472*	0.9207*	0.9792*	0.9459*	0.8743*	0.9094*	0.9837*	0.9496*	0.9544*	0.9968*	0.9129*	1.000
	(0.000)	(0.014)	(0.031)	(0.000)	(0.001)	(0.000)	(0.000)	(0.000)	(0.000)	(0.000)	(0.000)	(0.000)	(0.000)	(0.000)	(0.000)	(0.000)	(0.000)	

Note: CTO, Companies-Total; CAG, Companies-Agriculture, animal production, hunting, forestry and fishing; CEX, Companies-Extractive industries; CMA, Companies-Manufacturing industries; CEL, Companies-Electricity, gas, steam, hot and cold water and cold air; CWA, Companies-Water collection, treatment and distribution; sanitation, waste management and depollution; CCO, Companies-Construction; CWH, Companies-Wholesale and retail trade; repair of motor vehicles and motorcycles; CTR, Companies-Transport and storage; CAC, Companies-Accommodation, catering and similar; CIN, Companies-Information and communication activities; CRE, Companies-Real estate activities; CCN, Companies-Consulting, scientific, technical and similar activities; CAD, Companies-Administrative and support service activities; CED, Companies-Education; CHU, Companies-Human health and social support activities; CAR, Companies-Artistic, show, sports and recreational activities; COT, Companies-Other service activities. *, statistically significant at 5%.

companies for the several economic sectors, exception for the agriculture, animal production, hunting, forestry and fishing sector and extractive industries, where in some cases the coefficient of correlation with other sectors (for example those related with: information and communication activities; real estate; consulting and technical-scientific activities; and administrative services) has not statistical significance. The context for the correlations between the number of employees (table 5) follows a pattern similar to that described for the number of companies.

Tables 6a and 6b present the results for panel data regressions considering the logarithm of employees as function of the logarithm of companies and the logarithm of total passengers transported by land transport companies (as proxy for the transport costs). From the all variables related with the number of passengers and weight of goods transported analysed before, the logarithm of total passengers transported by land transport companies was that with more statistically satisfactory results. This model was

Table 5. Pairwise correlation matrix between the number of employees for the several economic sectors

	ETO	EAG	EEX	EMA	EEL	EWA	ECO	EWH	ETR	EAC	EIN	ERE	ECN	EAD	EED	EHU	EAR	EOT
ETO	1.000																	
EAG	0.289	1.000																
	(0.071)																	
EEX	0.211	0.7781*	1.000															
	(0.190)	(0.000)																
EMA	0.7161*	0.7120*	0.6500*	1.000														
	(0.000)	(0.000)	(0.000)															
EEL	0.7501*	-0.204	-0.282	0.089	1.000													
	(0.000)	(0.207)	(0.078)	(0.585)														
EWA	0.9471*	0.028	-0.012	0.4616*	0.9077*	1.000												
	(0.000)	(0.865)	(0.940)	(0.003)	(0.000)													
ECO	0.9139*	0.4318*	0.4476*	0.9022*	0.4470*	0.7632*	1.000											
	(0.000)	(0.005)	(0.004)	(0.000)	(0.004)	(0.000)												
EWH	0.9974*	0.275	0.230	0.7211*	0.7380*	0.9448*	0.9259*	1.000										
	(0.000)	(0.086)	(0.154)	(0.000)	(0.000)	(0.000)	(0.000)											
ETR	0.8877*	-0.039	-0.077	0.3307*	0.9558*	0.9818*	0.6619*	0.8842*	1.000									
	(0.000)	(0.812)	(0.639)	(0.037)	(0.000)	(0.000)	(0.000)	(0.000)										
EAC	0.8974*	-0.078	-0.205	0.3807*	0.9093*	0.9623*	0.6846*	0.8827*	0.9425*	1.000								
	(0.000)	(0.635)	(0.204)	(0.015)	(0.000)	(0.000)	(0.000)	(0.000)	(0.000)									
EIN	0.7768*	-0.216	-0.282	0.119	0.9854*	0.9279*	0.4782*	0.7669*	0.9592*	0.9306*	1.000							
	(0.000)	(0.182)	(0.078)	(0.464)	(0.000)	(0.000)	(0.002)	(0.000)	(0.000)	(0.000)								
ERE	0.9107*	-0.016	-0.144	0.4397*	0.8724*	0.9510*	0.7127*	0.8926*	0.9149*	0.9909*	0.9006*	1.000						
	(0.000)	(0.921)	(0.375)	(0.005)	(0.000)	(0.000)	(0.000)	(0.000)	(0.000)	(0.000)	(0.000)							
ECN	0.9391*	0.027	-0.047	0.4343*	0.9229*	0.9948*	0.7324*	0.9324*	0.9816*	0.9705*	0.9452*	0.9607*	1.000					
	(0.000)	(0.870)	(0.775)	(0.005)	(0.000)	(0.000)	(0.000)	(0.000)	(0.000)	(0.000)	(0.000)	(0.000)						
EAD	0.7939*	-0.206	-0.277	0.147	0.9819*	0.9368*	0.5036*	0.7836*	0.9611*	0.9441*	0.9981*	0.9165*	0.9532*	1.000				
	(0.000)	(0.202)	(0.084)	(0.367)	(0.000)	(0.000)	(0.001)	(0.000)	(0.000)	(0.000)	(0.000)	(0.000)	(0.000)					
EED	0.9910*	0.194	0.175	0.6561*	0.7858*	0.9690*	0.8949*	0.9945*	0.9194*	0.9074*	0.8147*	0.9105*	0.9560*	0.8294*	1.000			
	(0.000)	(0.232)	(0.280)	(0.000)	(0.000)	(0.000)	(0.000)	(0.000)	(0.000)	(0.000)	(0.000)	(0.000)	(0.000)	(0.000)				
EHU	0.9900*	0.207	0.111	0.6211*	0.8288*	0.9754*	0.8507*	0.9830*	0.9342*	0.9392*	0.8502*	0.9453*	0.9743*	0.8635*	0.9868*	1.000		
	(0.000)	(0.200)	(0.495)	(0.000)	(0.000)	(0.000)	(0.000)	(0.000)	(0.000)	(0.000)	(0.000)	(0.000)	(0.000)	(0.000)	(0.000)			
EAR	0.9170*	-0.019	-0.141	0.3992*	0.9250*	0.9777*	0.6948*	0.9028*	0.9610*	0.9931*	0.9459*	0.9873*	0.9885*	0.9566*	0.9256*	0.9591*	1.000	
	(0.000)	(0.909)	(0.385)	(0.011)	(0.000)	(0.000)	(0.000)	(0.000)	(0.000)	(0.000)	(0.000)	(0.000)	(0.000)	(0.000)	(0.000)	(0.000)		
EOT	0.9949*	0.243	0.185	0.6702*	0.7869*	0.9629*	0.8966*	0.9955*	0.9171*	0.9055*	0.8073*	0.9073*	0.9530*	0.8223*	0.9949*	0.9901*	0.9254*	1.000
	(0.000)	(0.130)	(0.254)	(0.000)	(0.000)	(0.000)	(0.000)	(0.000)	(0.000)	(0.000)	(0.000)	(0.000)	(0.000)	(0.000)	(0.000)	(0.000)	(0.000)	

Note: ETO, Employees-Total; EAG, Employees-Agriculture, animal production, hunting, forestry and fishing; EEX, Employees-Extractive industries; EMA, Employees-Manufacturing industries; EEL, Employees-Electricity, gas, steam, hot and cold water and cold air; EWA, Employees-Water collection, treatment and distribution; sanitation, waste management and depollution; ECO, Employees-Construction; EWH, Employees-Wholesale and retail trade; repair of motor vehicles and motorcycles; ETR, Employees-Transport and storage; EAC, Employees-Accommodation, catering and similar; EIN, Employees-Information and communication activities; ERE, Employees-Real estate activities; ECN, Employees-Consulting, scientific, technical and similar activities; EAD, Employees-Administrative and support service activities; EED, Employees-Education; EHU, Employees-Human health and social support activities; EAR, Employees-Artistic, show, sports and recreational activities; EOT, Employees-Other service activities. *, statistically significant at 5%.

obtained considering the New Economic Geography developments ((Krugman, 1996, 1998a, 1998b, 2007, 2011). The option for the more adjusted approach (cross-sectional time-series FGLS regression or RE GLS regression with AR (1) disturbances) taken into account the statistical tests results for cross sectional independence, heteroscedasticity and autocorrelation. The results for the coefficients of regression, related with the number of companies, show that they are positive and with statistical significant for the all economic sectors, exception for the administrative and support service activities where the coefficient has not statistical significance. This coefficient of regression associated with the number of companies is stronger for the manufacturing industries, as expected because this sector is usually one of those with higher increasing returns to scale.

The coefficient for the logarithm of total passengers transported by land transport companies has not statistical significance for the following sector: agriculture, animal production, hunting, forestry and

Table 6a. Results from panel data regressions, over the period 2011-2018 and across the Portuguese Mainland NUTS 2, with the logarithm of employees as dependent variable

Economic activities	Total	Agriculture, animal production, hunting, forestry and fishing	Extractive industries	Manufacturing industries	Electricity, gas, steam, hot and cold water and cold air	Water collection, treatment and distribution; sanitation, waste management and depollution	Construction	Wholesale and retail trade; repair of motor vehicles and motorcycles	Transport and storage
Model	Cross-sectional time-series FGLS regression	Cross-sectional time-series FGLS regression	RE GLS regression with AR(1) disturbances	Cross-sectional time-series FGLS regression	Cross-sectional time-series FGLS regression	Cross-sectional time-series FGLS regression	Cross-sectional time-series FGLS regression	Cross-sectional time-series FGLS regression	Cross-sectional time-series FGLS regression
Constant	-0.564* (-5.600) [0.000]	1.895* (5.460) [0.000]	-0.657 (-0.560) [0.575]	-1.266* (-3.120) [0.002]	-9.258* (-9.820) [0.000]	-0.254 (-1.590) [0.112]	-1.021* (-5.540)	-0.773* (-5.610) [0.000]	-1.610* (-4.590) [0.000]
Logarithm of companies	0.852* (39.880) [0.000]	0.847* (30.960) [0.000]	0.961* (9.150) [0.000]	1.397* (27.500) [0.000]	0.509* (6.870) [0.000]	0.140* (4.780) [0.000]	0.878* (24.560) [0.000]	0.687* (23.270) [0.000]	0.840* (8.730) [0.000]
Logarithm of total passengers transported by land transport companies	0.189* (17.220) [0.000]	0.006 (0.410) [0.685]	0.165* (2.550) [0.011]	-0.015 (-0.450) [0.655]	0.725* (11.010) [0.000]	0.445* (28.960) [0.000]	0.190* (10.210) [0.000]	0.287* (18.270) [0.000]	0.260* (4.790) [0.000]
Pesaran's test of cross sectional independence (absolute value)	6.574* [0.000]	3.104* [0.001]	1.476 [0.140]	3.160* [0.001]	0.755 [0.450]	2.756* [0.005]	0.974 [0.330]	5.450* [0.000]	4.808* [0.000]
Modified Wald test for groupwise heteroskedasticity	3218.320* [0.000]	131.270* [0.000]	7.650 [0.176]	1031.150* [0.000]	744.060* [0.000]	19.410* [0.001]	19.800* [0.001]	29.570* [0.000]	6.980 [0.222]
Wooldridge test for autocorrelation	510.781* [0.000]	30.945* [0.005]	43.370* [0.002]	38.903* [0.003]	62.503* [0.001]	3.793 [0.123]	71.458* [0.001]	83.712* [0.000]	142.677* [0.000]

Note: *, statistically significant at 5%.

fishing; manufacturing industries; and education. On the other hand, has statistical significance, but negative values for the next cases: real estate activities; and artistic, show, sports and recreational activities.

PERSPECTIVES FOR THE PORTUGUESE ECONOMY AFTER THE SHOCKS FROM THE COVID-19

Considering the average (over the period considered) weight of the number of employees for each one economic sector over the total municipality economy, the elasticities with the models estimated before and the weight of each municipal economy in the total of the respective region, it was possible to predict the logarithm of employees at municipal level (figure 3). Specifically, to obtain the logarithm of employees at municipal level, the following steps were followed:

1. Find the weight, by year, of the number of employees in each sector, over the total municipal economy;
2. Get the weight average (over the period considered) of the number of employees in each sector over the total municipal economy;

Table 6b. Results from panel data regressions, over the period 2011-2018 and across the Portuguese Mainland NUTS 2, with the logarithm of employees as dependent variable (Continuation)

Economic activities	Accommodation, catering and similar	Information and communication activities	Real estate activities	Consulting, scientific, technical and similar activities	Administrative and support service activities	Education	Human health and social support activities	Artistic, show, sports and recreational activities	Other service activities
Model	Cross-sectional time-series FGLS regression	RE GLS regression with AR(1) disturbances	Cross-sectional time-series FGLS regression	Cross-sectional time-series FGLS regression	Cross-sectional time-series FGLS regression	RE GLS regression with AR(1) disturbances	Cross-sectional time-series FGLS regression	RE GLS regression with AR(1) disturbances	Cross-sectional time-series FGLS regression
Constant	0.662 (0.850) [0.395]	-3.029* (-5.130) [0.000]	1.416* (6.480) [0.000]	-1.325* (-8.780) [0.000]	-2.417* (-5.220) [0.000]	-1.450* (-7.650) [0.000]	-0.468* (-4.640) [0.000]	0.316 (0.680) [0.499]	-0.193* (-2.220) [0.026]
Logarithm of companies	0.631* (3.740) [0.000]	1.289* (17.290) [0.000]	1.200* (20.700) [0.000]	0.702* (13.240) [0.000]	0.231 (0.920) [0.358]	0.779* (20.770) [0.000]	0.769* (26.670) [0.000]	1.170* (23.440) [0.000]	0.888* (24.480) [0.000]
Logarithm of total passengers transported by land transport companies	0.223* (3.640) [0.000]	0.117* (2.200) [0.028]	-0.146* (-4.220) [0.000]	0.267* (7.860) [0.000]	0.606* (4.180) [0.000]	0.216 (9.940) [0.000]	0.180* (9.820) [0.000]	-0.072* (-2.220) [0.027]	0.089* (4.760) [0.000]
Pesaran's test of cross sectional independence (absolute value)	3.281* [0.001]	1.041 [0.298]	3.904* [0.000]	2.494* [0.012]	1.212 [0.225]	0.461 [0.645]	1.299 [0.193]	0.860 [0.389]	0.726 [0.468]
Modified Wald test for groupwise heteroskedasticity	330.240* [0.000]	2.970 [0.704]	74.270* [0.000]	3806.530* [0.000]	311.620* [0.000]	0.890 [0.970]	165.920* [0.000]	9.650 [0.085]	2166.970* [0.000]
Wooldridge test for autocorrelation	9.892* [0.034]	10.049* [0.033]	24.893* [0.007]	23.505* [0.008]	222.269* [0.000]	7.912* [0.048]	45.029* [0.002]	11.235* [0.028]	7.999* [0.047]

Note: *, statistically significant at 5%.

3. Multiplication of these averages by the respective elasticities obtained in the previous section, to obtain a global elasticity by weighted average, at municipal level, for the logarithm of companies and for the logarithm of total passengers transported by land transport companies;
4. Multiplication of these global elasticities by the respective annual average logarithms, in each region (for companies and total passengers transported by land transport companies);
5. Sum of these values to obtain the logarithm of employees predicted at municipal level. These values were adjusted by the annual average weight of the total number of employees in each municipality over the total regional.

This information at municipal level allows to better discuss the Covid-19 impacts with a finer analysis.

Figure 4, obtained through the QGIS (2020) software and the shapefiles available in dados.gov (2020), shows the municipal distribution of the number of employees and number of employees predicted, respectively, across the Portuguese Mainland. The data show that, in fact, there are an agglomeration of employees in the littoral, namely around Oporto and Lisbon.

Analysing the figure 5, for increasing and decreasing in the number of passengers transported during the pandemic context, the results reveal that the more affected municipalities with changes in the flow of passengers are those close Lisbon. This is a conclusion for the passengers flow assessment, but, also, for the transport costs analysis. In other words, this means that potential reductions in the transport

Figure 3. Evolution of the logarithm of employees observed and logarithm of employees predicted, in average over the period 2011-2018, across the Portuguese municipalities (278 municipalities)

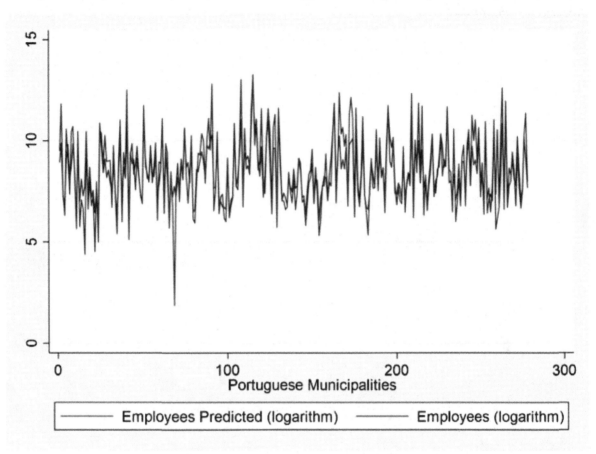

Figure 4. Distribution of the total employees and total predicted employees across the Portuguese municipalities, in average over the period 2011-2018

Figure 5. Distribution of the total predicted employees across the Portuguese municipalities, in average over the period 2011-2018, with an increase of 10% and 50% and a decrease of 50% and 85% in the passengers transported

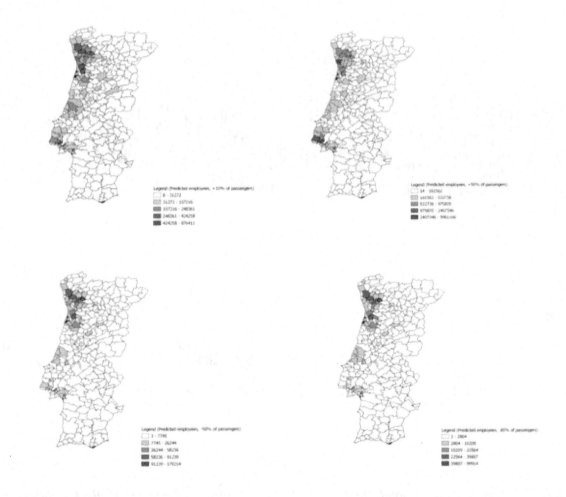

cost few impact the economic distribution across the Portuguese municipalities, with exception for the municipalities around Lisbon.

These findings are consistent with the information published by the Portuguese organism for the official statistics (INE, 2020b). In fact, the municipalities with higher density and greater human mobility in public transportation are, also, those with bigger pandemic incidence and where it is needed to implement more restrictions to the mobility. Furthermore, in the municipalities on the outskirts of Lisbon, this was where there were a significant percentage of employees engaged in telework (INE, 2021). In any case, the measures to reduce mobility to face the risks of contagion had an impact across the country (INE, 2020c), however with great heterogeneity (INE, 2020a).

CONCLUSION

Considering the actual framework around the world, the main objective of this work was to explore the regional Portuguese context before the Covid-19 scenario and with these outputs discuss the potential implications from this pandemic shocks. For that, it was considered data, disaggregated at regional and municipal level for the period 2011-2018, from the Statistics Portugal for the number of companies, employees and passengers transported, following the developments from the New Economic Geography. This statistical information was explored through panel data approaches and georeferenced files.

The data analysis highlighted the agglomeration of the companies and employees in the North and Lisbon Metropolitan Area regions, confirming the Oporto and Lisbon as two poles of economic growth. In fact, considering the NEG developments, companies and employees are two important variables for the spatial economic dynamics. This context claims for more adjusted public policies to reverse these tendencies that, as referred by the NEG theory, in general, are self-reinforced processes, involving increasing returns to scale, market size and transport costs. On the other hand, the number of passengers transported by road or land transports is higher around Lisbon, however, the passengers are transported more kilometres in the North. In turn, the service activities have higher relevance in the different Portuguese Mainland regions what may become the Portuguese economy more vulnerable to the Covid-19 context.

The results for the correlation matrix analysis between the several economic sectors present that, in general, the different economic activities are correlated for the number of companies and employees, exception for the agricultural and fishing sector and for the extractive industries that, because their specificities, have weaker correlations with other activities. In turn, the panel data regressions show that the number of companies explains significantly the number of employees. This level of explanation is greater for the manufacturing industries, as expected, considering that usually this a sector with great increasing returns to scale.

In terms of Covdi-19 impact in the Portuguese municipalities it is expected that the shock will higher in the municipalities around Lisbon, because is where the decreasing in the number of employees is greater considering the social confinement and the consequent reduction in the passengers flows. This analysis, also, shows that potential reductions in the transport costs (to increase the number of passengers) may have little impact in the remaining Portuguese municipalities.

In future researches could be interesting to compare these results with other approaches and other data. In fact, there are not many studies for the Portuguese context considering the New Economic Geography developments. However, researches in these fields could bring more insights to understand the real impact from the transport costs reduction in the regional asymmetries. This is important to support the design of adjusted transport public policies.

ACKNOWLEDGMENTS

This work is funded by National Funds through the FCT - Foundation for Science and Technology, I.P., within the scope of the project Refª UIDB/00681/2020. Furthermore we would like to thank the CERNAS Research Centre and the Polytechnic Institute of Viseu for their support.

REFERENCES

Branco, A., Parejo Moruno, F. M., Lopes, J. C., & Rangel Preciado, J. F. (2016). Changes in world cork industry location. An historical perspective. *Revista De Estudios Regionales*, *106*, 55–78.

Bui, M. T. T., & Preechametta, A. (2019). Will manufacturing investors go to border zones? The case of central Thailand. *International Journal of Emerging Markets*. doi:10.1108/IJOEM-10-2018-0567

Camoes, J., Lobato, C. T., Beires, F., & Gomes, E. (2021). Legionella and SARS-CoV-2 Coinfection in a Patient With Pneumonia—An Outbreak in Northern Portugal. *Cureus*, *13*(1), e12476. doi:10.7759/cureus.12476 PMID:33552790

Chatti, W., Ben Soltane, B., & Abalala, T. (2019). Impacts of Public Transport Policy on City Size and Welfare. *Networks and Spatial Economics*, *19*(4), 1097–1122. doi:10.100711067-019-09451-y

Commendatore, P., Kubin, I., & Sushko, I. (2020). A propos Brexit: On the breaking up of integration areas – an NEG analysis. *Spatial Economic Analysis*, *0*(0), 1–24. doi:10.1080/17421772.2019.1701702

Couto, G., Castanho, R. A., Pimentel, P., Carvalho, C., Sousa, A., & Santos, C. (2020). The Impacts of COVID-19 Crisis over the Tourism Expectations of the Azores Archipelago Residents. *Sustainability*, *12*(18), 7612. doi:10.3390u12187612

Csonka, A., & Fertő, I. (2019). Structural change and agglomeration in the Hungarian pork industry. *European Planning Studies*, *0*(0), 1–15. doi:10.1080/09654313.2019.1687652

da Costa, E. M., & da Costa, N. M. (2020). The Covid-19 Pandemic Process in Mainland Portugal. A Geographical Analysis of the First 100 Days. *Finisterra-Revista Portuguesa De Geografia*, *55*(115). Advance online publication. doi:10.18055/Finis20361

da Silva, S. M. (2021). Building trust, resilient regions, and educational narratives: Municipalities dealing with COVID-19 in border regions of Portugal. *European Educational Research Journal*, *14749041211029732*(5), 636–666. Advance online publication. doi:10.1177/14749041211029733

dados.gov. (2020). *Shapefile of Portuguese municipalities*. /pt/datasets/concelhos-de-portugal/

Fujita, M., & Krugman, P. (2004). The new economic geography: Past, present and the future. *Papers in Regional Science*, *83*(1), 139–164. https://doi.org/10.1007/s10110-003-0180-0

Gonzalez-Val, R., & Pueyo, F. (2019). Natural resources, economic growth and geography. *Economic Modelling*, *83*, 150–159. https://doi.org/10.1016/j.econmod.2019.02.007

Gopalan, S., Nguyen Trieu Duong, L., & Rajan, R. S. (2020). Trade configurations in Asia: Assessing de facto and de jure regionalism. *World Economy*, *43*(4), 1034–1058. https://doi.org/10.1111/twec.12907

Goto, H., & Minamimura, K. (2019). Geography and Demography: New Economic Geography With Endogenous Fertility. *The Japanese Economic Review*, *70*(4), 537–568. https://doi.org/10.1111/jere.12213

Hinzmann, S., Cantner, U., & Graf, H. (2019). The role of geographical proximity for project performance: Evidence from the German Leading-Edge Cluster Competition. *The Journal of Technology Transfer*, *44*(6), 1744–1783. https://doi.org/10.1007/s10961-017-9600-1

Illario, M., Zavagli, V., Ferreira, N. L., Sambati, M., Teixeira, A., Lanata, F., Pais, S., Farrell, J., & Tramontano, D. (2020). The Frailty of the Invincible. *Translational Medicine @ UniSa, 23*, 1–15.

Imran, M., HuSen, A., Kaleem, M., Bangash, A. K., Din, N. U., & Sobia. (2020). Effect of regional factor productivity on manufacturing sector: The case of Sino-Pak economic ties. *Financial Innovation, 6*(1), 5. doi:10.1186/s40854-019-0163-z

INE. (2020c). *Mobilidade da população ao nível regional no contexto da pandemia COVID-19.* https://www.ine.pt/xportal/xmain?xpid=INE&xpgid=ine_destaques&DESTAQUESdest_boui=465143606&DESTAQUESmodo=2

INE. (2020d). *Several Statistics.* https://www.ine.pt/xportal/xmain?xpgid=ine_main&xpid=INE

INE. (2020a). *Indicadores de contexto demográfico e da expressão territorial da pandemia CO-VID-19 em Portugal: COVID-19: Uma leitura do contexto demográfico e da expressão territorial da pandemia.* https://www.ine.pt/xportal/xmain?xpid=INE&xpgid=ine_destaques&DESTAQUESdest_boui=455108654&DESTAQUESmodo=2

INE. (2020b). *Indicadores de contexto e de impacto socioeconómico da pandemia COVID-19 em Portugal: COVID-19: O que distingue as 19 frequesias em estado de calamidade do resto da AML?* https://www.ine.pt/xportal/xmain?xpid=INE&xpgid=ine_destaques&DESTAQUESdest_boui=443697541&DESTAQUESmodo=2

INE. (2021). *Indicadores de contexto demográfico e da expressão territorial da pandemia COVID-19 em Portugal: No contexto da pandemia COVID-19 a Área Metropolitana de Lisboa concentrou quase metade do emprego em teletrabalho.* https://www.ine.pt/xportal/xmain?xpid=INE&xpgid=ine_destaques&DESTAQUESdest_boui=493705905&DESTAQUESmodo=2

Jin, L., Wang, C., Zhang, H., Ye, Y., Du, Z., & Zhang, Y. (2020). Evolution and Mechanism of the 'Core-Periphery' Relationship: Micro-Evidence from Cross-Regional Industrial Production Organization in a Fast-Developing Region in China. *Sustainability, 12*(1), 189. https://doi.org/10.3390/su12010189

Kim, H. Y., & McCann, P. (2020). Japanese contributions to regional science.-+. . *Papers in Regional Science, 99*(2), 389. doi:10.1111/pirs.12522

Krugman, P. (1996). 'Urban concentration: The role of increasing returns and transport costs. *International Regional Science Review, 19*(1–2), 5–30. https://doi.org/10.1177/016001769601900202

Krugman, P. (1998a). Space: The final frontier. *The Journal of Economic Perspectives, 12*(2), 161–174. https://doi.org/10.1257/jep.12.2.161

Krugman, P. (1998b). What's new about the new economic geography? *Oxford Review of Economic Policy, 14*(2), 7–17. https://doi.org/10.1093/oxrep/14.2.7

Krugman, P. (2007). The 'New' Economic Geography: Where Are We? In M. Fujita (Ed.), Regional Integration in East Asia: From the Viewpoint of Spatial Economics (pp. 23–34). https://doi.org/10.1057/9780230626607_2.

Krugman, P. (2011). The New Economic Geography, Now Middle-aged. *Regional Studies, 45*(1), 1–7. https://doi.org/10.1080/00343404.2011.537127

Li, H., Cai, H., & Chakraborty, S. (2019). Market Access, Labor Mobility, and the Wage Skill Premium: New Evidence from Chinese Cities. *Open Economies Review, 30*(5), 947–973. https://doi.org/10.1007/s11079-019-09546-6

Lopes, A. S., Sargento, A., & Carreira, P. (2021). Vulnerability to COVID-19 unemployment in the Portuguese tourism and hospitality industry. *International Journal of Contemporary Hospitality Management, 33*(5), 1850–1869. https://doi.org/10.1108/IJCHM-11-2020-1345

Martinho, V. (2021). *Economics of Tourism in Portugal: Impacts of the COVID-19 Pandemic.* Springer International Publishing. doi:10.1007/978-3-030-65200-5

Melenotte, C., Silvin, A., Goubet, A.-G., Lahmar, I., Dubuisson, A., Zumla, A., Raoult, D., Merad, M., Gachot, B., Henon, C., Solary, E., Fontenay, M., Andre, F., Maeurer, M., Ippolito, G., Piacentini, M., Wang, F.-S., Ginhoux, F., Marabelle, A., … Zitvogel, L. (2020). Immune responses during COVID-19 infection. *Oncoimmunology, 9*(1), 1807836. doi:10.1080/2162402X.2020.1807836

Morales, J. R. (2020). Perpetuating regional asymmetries through income transfers. *Spatial Economic Analysis, 0*(0), 1–24. https://doi.org/10.1080/17421772.2020.1714705

Pato, M. L. (2020). Short food supply chains—A growing movement. The case study of the Viseu Dao Lafoes Region. *Open Agriculture, 5*(1), 806–816. https://doi.org/10.1515/opag-2020-0077

Pengfei, N., Yangzi, Z., & Qingfeng, C. (2019). The Influence of Housing Prices on Urban Competitiveness: Review and Prospects. *Chinese Journal of Urban and Environmental Studies, 7*(3), 1950009. https://doi.org/10.1142/S234574811950009X

QGIS. (2020). *QGIS project.* https://www.qgis.org/en/site/

Quintino, D. D., & Ferreira, P. (2021). Diesel prices in Brazil: A dynamic fractional integration analysis. *Economics and Business Letters, 10*(2), 116–125. doi:10.17811/ebl.10.2.2021.116-125

Rocha, A., & Perobelli, F. (2020). Spatial distribution of logistics services in Brazil: A potential market analysis. *Regional Science Policy and Practice, 12*(1), 185–217. doi:10.1111/rsp3.12224

Rodrigues, M., Gelabert, P. J., Ameztegui, A., Coll, L., & Vega-Garcia, C. (2021). Has COVID-19 halted winter-spring wildfires in the Mediterranean? Insights for wildfire science under a pandemic context. *The Science of the Total Environment, 765*, 142793. https://doi.org/10.1016/j.scitotenv.2020.142793

Sabat, I., Neuman-Bohme, S., Varghese, N. E., Barros, P. P., Brouwer, W., van Exel, J., Schreyogg, J., & Stargardt, T. (2020). United but divided: Policy responses and people's perceptions in the EU during the COVID-19 outbreak. *Health Policy (Amsterdam), 124*(9), 909–918. https://doi.org/10.1016/j.healthpol.2020.06.009

Sannigrahi, S., Pilla, F., Basu, B., Basu, A. S., & Molter, A. (2020). Examining the association between socio-demographic composition and COVID-19 fatalities in the European region using spatial regression approach. *Sustainable Cities and Society, 62*, 102418. https://doi.org/10.1016/j.scs.2020.102418

Sara, G., Mangano, M. C., Berlino, M., Corbari, L., Lucchese, M., Milisenda, G., Terzo, S., Azaza, M. S., Babarro, J. M. F., Bakiu, R., Broitman, B. R., Buschmann, A. H., Christofoletti, R., Deidun, A., Dong, Y., Galdies, J., Glamuzina, B., Luthman, O., Makridis, P., … Helmuth, B. (2021). The Synergistic Impacts of Anthropogenic Stressors and COVID-19 on Aquaculture: A Current Global Perspective. *Reviews in Fisheries Science & Aquaculture*. doi:10.1080/23308249.2021.1876633

Skalkos, D., Kosma, I. S., Chasioti, E., Skendi, A., Papageorgiou, M., & Guine, R. P. F. (2021). Consumers' Attitude and Perception toward Traditional Foods of Northwest Greece during the COVID-19 Pandemic. *Applied Sciences-Basel, 11*(9), 4080. doi:10.3390/app11094080

Stata. (2020). *Stata: Software for Statistics and Data Science*. https://www.stata.com/

Teixeira, A. C. (2006). Transport policies in light of the new economic geography: The Portuguese experience. *Regional Science and Urban Economics, 36*(4), 450–466. https://doi.org/10.1016/j.regsci-urbeco.2006.01.002

Teresiene, D., Keliuotyte-Staniuleniene, G., Liao, Y., Kanapickiene, R., Pu, R., Hu, S., & Yue, X.-G. (2021). The Impact of the COVID-19 Pandemic on Consumer and Business Confidence Indicators. *Journal of Risk and Financial Management, 14*(4), 159. https://doi.org/10.3390/jrfm14040159

Wiberg, M. (2020). Capital controls and the location of industry. *World Economy, 43*(4), 871–891. https://doi.org/10.1111/twec.12908

Yi, L., & Yao, L. (2019). Comprehensive Assessment and Policy Suggestions on Building Multi-Level National Service Centers. *Chinese Journal of Urban and Environmental Studies, 7*(3), 1950010. https://doi.org/10.1142/S2345748119500106

Zuev, D., & Hannam, K. (2021). Anxious immobilities: An ethnography of coping with contagion (Covid-19) in Macau. *Mobilities, 16*(1), 35–50. https://doi.org/10.1080/17450101.2020.1827361

Conclusion

The authors have concluded that COVID-19 changed lives and economic structures. This means that the areas presented in the 28 chapters have changed because of a new reality. Society has shown new ways to do things but also to get things. The methodology used after and during the COVID-19 to improve new ways of production, education and personal income. In fact, according to the authors, COVID-19 has proven that society needs to move faster towards new economic and social values. However, the government and organizations must introduce new social and economic policies to compensate for the loss of business and the market's ability to improve goods and services. Indeed, COVID-19 has proven that organizations and citizens are grappling with new ways of being in society. The authors point out three main areas to improve the resilience of citizens and organizations: government factors, health system factors and cultural factors. The most important area is to improve and create new mechanisms to renew the social and economic background.

In conclusion, according to the authors, COVID-19 will open a new way to improve the well-being of citizens and the ability to change economic and social patterns towards sustainability in the future. Moreover, COVID -19 has influenced all economic sectors and changed social and economic policies towards competitiveness and cooperation in all sectors. The final question should be: are we better now?

Compilation of References

Aafjes-van Doorn, K., Zilcha-Mano, S., Graham, K., Caldari, A., Barber, J. P., Chambless, D. L., & Milrod, B. (2019). The Role of Safety Behaviors in Panic Disorder Treatment: Self-Regulation or Self-Defeat? *Journal of Contemporary Psychotherapy*, *49*(4), 203–212. doi:10.100710879-019-09432-9

Aarikka-Stenroos, L., & Sakari Makkonen, H. (2014). Industrial buyers' use of references, word-of-mouth and reputation in complex buying situation. *Journal of Business and Industrial Marketing*, *29*(4), 344–352. doi:10.1108/JBIM-08-2013-0164

Aarons, H. (2020). *A practical introduction to survey design: a beginner's guide*. SAGE Publications Ltd.

Abaci, S., Robertson, J., Linklater, H., & McNeill, F. (2021). Supporting school teachers' rapid engagement with on-line education. *Educational Technology Research and Development*, *69*(1), 29–34. doi:10.100711423-020-09839-5 PMID:33052183

Abdoli-Sejzi, A. (2015). Augmented Reality and Virtual Learning Environment. *Journal of Applied Sciences Research*, *11*(8), 1–5.

Aberbach, J. D., & Rockman, B. A. (2002). Conducting and Coding Elite Interviews. *PS, Political Science & Politics*, *35*(4), 673–676. doi:10.1017/S1049096502001142

Addis, M., & Holbrook, M. B. (2001). On the conceptual link between mass customisation and experiential consumption: An explosion of subjectivity. *Journal of Consumer Behaviour*, *1*(1), 50–66. doi:10.1002/cb.53

Adhikari, S.P., Meng, S., Wu, Y., Mao, Y., Ye, R., Wang, Q., Sun, C., Sylvia, S., Rozelle, S., Raat, H., & Zhou, H. (2020). *A literature review of 2019 Novel Coronavirus during the early outbreak period: Epidemiology, causes, clinical manifestation and diagnosis, prevention and control*. Academic Press.

Aghekyan-Simonian, M., Forsythe, S., Suk Kwon, W., & Chattaraman, V. (2012). The role of product brand image and online store image on perceived risks and online purchase intentions for apparel. *Journal of Retailing and Consumer Services*, *19*(3), 325–331. doi:10.1016/j.jretconser.2012.03.006

Agmeka, F., Wathoni, R. N., & Santoso, A. S. (2019). The Influence of Discount Framing towards Brand Reputation and Brand Image on Purchase Intention and Actual Behaviour in e-commerce. *Procedia Computer Science*, *161*, 851–858. doi:10.1016/j.procs.2019.11.192

Agrawal, S., De Smet, A., Poplawski, P., & Reich, A. (2020). *Beyond hiring: How companies are re-skilling to address talent gaps. In Organization Practice and McKinsey Accelerate*. McKinsey & Company.

Agrebi, S., & Jallais, J. (2015). Explain the intention to use smartphones for mobile shopping. *Journal of Retailing and Consumer Services*, *22*, 16–23. doi:10.1016/j.jretconser.2014.09.003

Aguinis, H., & Burgi-Tian, J. (2021). Talent management challenges during COVID-19 and beyond: Performance management to the rescue. *BRQ Business Research Quarterly*, *24*(3), 233–240. doi:10.1177/23409444211009528

Aithal, P., & Aithal, S. (2016). Impact of on-line education on higher education system. *International Journal of Engineering Research and Modern Education*, *1*(1), 225–235.

Al-Azawei, A., Parslow, P., & Lundqvist, K. (2016). Barriers and opportunities of e-learning implementation in Iraq: A case of public universities. *The International Review of Research in Open and Distributed Learning*, *17*(5), 126–146. doi:10.19173/irrodl.v17i5.2501

Aldrich, D. P., & Yoshida, T. (2020). How Japan stumbled into a pandemic miracle. *Current History (New York, N.Y.)*, *119*(818), 217–221. doi:10.1525/curh.2020.119.818.217

Aldrich, H. E. (1999). *Organizations Evolving* (Vol. L). Sage.

Alexandre, A. F. (2021). *Metodologia científica: princípios e fundamentos*. Blucher. doi:10.5151/9786555062229

Alkhamisi, A. O., & Muhammad, M. M. (2013). Rise of Augmented Reality: Current and Future Application Areas. *International Journal of Internet and Distributed Systems*, *1*(04), 25–34. doi:10.4236/ijids.2013.14005

Allee, V. (2009). Value-creating networks: Organizational issues and challenges. *The Learning Organization*, *16*(6), 427–442. doi:10.1108/09696470910993918

Almeida, A., & Azevedo, A. (2016). A multi-perspective performance approach for complex manufacturing environments. *Journal of Innovation Management*, *4*(2), 125–155. doi:10.24840/2183-0606_004.002_0007

Al-Qahtani, A., & Higgins, S. (2013). Effects of traditional, blended and e-learning on students' achievement in higher education. *Journal of Computer Assisted Learning*, *29*(3), 220–234. doi:10.1111/j.1365-2729.2012.00490.x

Altieri, M. A., & Nicholls, C. I. (2020). Agroecology and the reconstruction of a post-COVID-19 agriculture. *The Journal of Peasant Studies*, *47*(5), 881–898. doi:10.1080/03066150.2020.1782891

Altinay, L., & Paraskevas, A. A. (2008). *Planning Research in Hospitality and Tourism*. Elsevier Ltd.

Amblard, M. (2010). *La rationalité - mythes et réalité*. L'Harmattan.

Ameen, N., Hosany, S., & Tarhini, A. (2021). Consumer interaction with cutting-edge technologies: Implications for future research. *Computers in Human Behavior*, *120*, 106761. Advance online publication. doi:10.1016/j.chb.2021.106761

Américo, B. (2021). *Método De Pesquisa Qualitativa: Analisando fora da caixa a Prática de Pesquisar Organizações*. Alta Books.

Anadolu, A. J. A. N. S. (2020). *AA Yerli Solunum Cihazının Üretim Aşamalarını Görüntüledi*. 30 Nisan 2021 tarihinde https://www.aa.com.tr/tr/bilim-teknoloji/aa-yerli-solunum-cihazinin-uretim-asamalarini-goruntuledi/1821021

Anadolu, A. J. A. N. S. (2020). *ASELSAN İle USHAŞ Arasında Sözleşme İmzalandı*. https://www.aa.com.tr/tr/ekonomi/aselsan-ile-ushas-arasinda-sozlesme-imzalandi/1871703

Anderson, K., Arrow, J., & Pines, D. (Eds.). (1988). *The Economy as an Evolving Complex System*. Addison-Wesley.

Andrade Braga, A. (2009). Netnography: A naturalistic approach towards online interaction. In B. J. Jansen, A. Spink, & I. Taksa (Eds.), *Handbook of Research on Web Log Analysis* (pp. 488–505). IGI Global. doi:10.4018/978-1-59904-974-8.ch024

Andriopoulos, C., & Lewis, M. W. (2009). Exploitation-exploration tensions and organizational ambidexterity: Managing paradoxes of innovation. *Organization Science*, *20*(4), 696–717. doi:10.1287/orsc.1080.0406

Angel, P., Jenkins, A., & Stephens, A. (2018). Understanding entrepreneurial success: A phenomenographic approach. *International Small Business Journal*, *36*(6), 611–636. doi:10.1177/0266242618768662

Ansari, Z. N., & Kant, R. (2017). A state-of-art literature review reflecting 15 years of focus on sustainable supply chain management. *Journal of Cleaner Production*, *142*, 2524–2543. doi:10.1016/j.jclepro.2016.11.023

Anthony, B. Jnr, & Noel, S. (2021). Examining the adoption of emergency remote teaching and virtual learning during and after COVID-19 pandemic. *International Journal of Educational Management*, *35*(6), 1136–1150. doi:10.1108/IJEM-08-2020-0370

Antoine, M. (2018). *Unveiling the organisational identity: A spatial approach based on the office. The case of ORES Picardy Wallonia transition towards an activity-based workspace* (Doctoral dissertation). Université catholique de Louvain, Louvain-la-Neuve, Belgique.

Anvari, R. D., & Norouzi, D. (2016). The impact of e-commerce and R&D on economic development in some selected countries. *Procedia: Social and Behavioral Sciences*, *229*, 354–362. doi:10.1016/j.sbspro.2016.07.146

Anzai, A., & Nishiura, H. (2021). "Go To Travel" campaign and travel-associated coronavirus disease 2019 cases: A descriptive analysis, July–August 2020. *Journal of Clinical Medicine*, *10*(3), 398. doi:10.3390/jcm10030398 PMID:33494315

Appiah, M., & Van Tonder, F. (2018). E-Assessment in Higher Education: A Review. *International Journal of Business Management and Economic Research*, *9*(6), 1454–1460.

Appio, F., Frattini, F., Petruzzelli, A. & Neirotti, P. (2021). Digital Transformation and Innovation Management: A Synthesis of Existing Research and an Agenda for Future Studies. *Journal of Product Innovation Management*, *38*(1), 4-20.

Arends, R. (2008). Aprender a ensinar (7th ed.). McGraw Hill Edition.

Argyris, C., & Schön, D. A. (1996). *Organizational Learning II: Theory, Method, and Practice*. Addison-Wesley.

Arnold, V.I. (1979). Catastrophe theory. *Nature*, *10*, 54-63.

Arnold, V. I. (1975). Critical points of smooth functions, *Proc. of International Congress of Mathematicians*, 19-40.

Arnold, V. I. (1979). Catastrophe theory. *Nature*, (10), 54–63.

Arnould, E. J., & Price, L. L. (1993). River Magic: Extraordinary Experience and the Extended Service Encounter. *The Journal of Consumer Research*, *20*(1), 24–45. doi:10.1086/209331

Arthur, W. B. (1999). Complexity and the economy. *Science*, *284*, 107-109.

Arthur, W. B. (2013). *Complexity economics: A different framework for economic thought*. Santa Fe Institute Working Paper. 2013-04-012.

Arthur, W. B. (2009). *The Nature of Technology: What it Is and How it Evolves*. Free Press.

Arthur, W. B., Durlauf, S. N., & Lane, D. A. (Eds.). (1997). *The Economy as an Evolving Complex System II*. Addison-Wesley.

Arumugam, T. (2020). Caring for Your Mental Health during MCO. *News Straits Times*. https://www.nst.com.my/news/nation/2020/03/578414/caring-your-mental-health-during-mco

Aryal, R. (2018). Kinship as a social capital in rural development: An anthropological perspective. *Dhaulagiri*, *12*, 88–97. doi:10.3126/dsaj.v12i0.22184

Asian Development Bank. (2021). *In the Spotlight*. https://www.adb.org/countries /bangladesh/main

Assaf, A., & Scuderi, R. (2020). COVID-19 and the recovery of the tourism industry. *Tourism Economics*, *26*(5), 731–733. doi:10.1177/1354816620933712

Azevedo, J. (2000). *O ensino secundário na Europa*. Edições Asa.

Bailey, D. E., & Kurland, N. B. (2002). A review of telework research: Findings, new directions, and lessons for the study of modern work. *Journal of Organizational Behavior: The International Journal of Industrial, Occupational and Organizational Psychology and Behavior*, *23*(4), 383–400. doi:10.1002/job.144

Bai, Q., & Tian, S. (2020). Innovate or die: Corporate innovation and bankruptcy forecasts. *Journal of Empirical Finance*, *59*, 88–108. doi:10.1016/j.jempfin.2020.09.002

Baker, S., Farrokhnia, R.A., Meyer, S., Pagel, M., & Yannelis, C. (2020). *How Does Household Spending Respond to an Epidemic? Consumption During the 2020 COVID-19 Pandemic*. doi:10.3386/w26949

Baldry, C. J., & Barnes, A. (2012). The Open-plan Academy: Space, Control and the Undermining of Professional Identity. *Work, Employment and Society*, *26*(2), 228–245. doi:10.1177/0950017011432917

Baldwin, R., & di Mauro, W. (2020). *Economics in the Time of COVID-19*. CEPR Press.

Bamber, P., Fernandez-Stark, K., & Taglioni, D. (2020). *Why Global Value Chains Remain Essential For COVID-19 Supplies*. VOX CEPR Policy Portal. https://voxeu.org/content/why-global-value-chains-remain-essential-covid-19-supplies

Banco de México. (2021). *Información sobre CoDi® Cobro Digital*. https://www.banxico.org.mx/sistemas-de-pago/codi-cobro-digital-banco-me.html

Baratali, E. (2016). Effective of Augmented Reality (AR) in marketing communication; a case study on brand interactive advertising. *International Journal of Management and Applied Science*, *2*(4), 133–137.

Barbierato, E., Campanile, L., Gribaudo, M., Iacono, M., Mastroianni, M., & Nacchia, S. (2021). Performance evaluation for the design of a hybrid cloud-based distance synchronous and asynchronous learning architecture. *Simulation Modelling Practice and Theory*, *109*, 102303. doi:10.1016/j.simpat.2021.102303

Barbieri, J. C., & Álvares, A. (2009). *Gestão de ideias para inovação contínua*. Bookman.

Barros, M. V., Salvador, R., de Francisco, A. C., & Piekarski, C. M. (2020). Mapping of research lines on circular economy practices in agriculture: From waste to energy. *Renewable & Sustainable Energy Reviews*, *131*, 109958. doi:10.1016/j.rser.2020.109958

Barroso, J. (2003). Organização e regulação do ensino básico e secundário, em Portugal: Sentidos de uma evolução. *Educação & Sociedade*, *24*(82), 63–92. doi:10.1590/S0101-73302003000100004

Bartsch, S., Weber, E., Büttgen, M., & Huber, A. (2020). Leadership matters in crisis-induced digital transformation: How to lead service employees effectively during the COVID-19 pandemic. *Journal of Service Management*, *32*(1), 71–85. doi:10.1108/JOSM-05-2020-0160

Baruch, Y. (2001). The status of research on teleworking and an agenda for future research. *International Journal of Management Reviews*, *3*(2), 113–129. doi:10.1111/1468-2370.00058

Barykin, S. Y., Kapustina, I. V., Kalinina, O. V., Dubolazov, V. A., Esquivel, C. A. N., Alyarovna, N. E., & Sharapaev, P. (2021). The sharing economy and digital logistics in retail chains: Opportunities and threats. *Academy of Strategic Management Journal*, *20*(2), 1–14.

Basilaia, G., & Kvavadze, D. (2020). Transition to online education in schools during a SARS-CoV-2 coronavirus (COVID-19) pandemic in Georgia. *Pedagogical Research*, *5*(4), 1–9. doi:10.29333/pr/7937

Batat, W. (2019). *Experiential Marketing: Consumer Behavior, Customer Experience and The 7Es* (1st ed.). Routledge. doi:10.4324/9781315232201

Batra, M. (2017). Customer experience – an emerging frontier in customer service excellence. *Competition Forum, 15*(1), 198–207.

Baumeister, R. & Leary, M. (1995). The Need to Belong: desire for interpersonal attachments as a fundamental human motivation. *Psychological Bulletin, 3*(117), 497-529.

Baum, S., & McPherson, M. (2019). The human factor: The promise & limits of online education. *Daedalus, 148*(4), 235–254. doi:10.1162/daed_a_01769

Bayraktutan, Y., & Solmaz, A. R. (2021). Türkiye'de Kovid-19 Salgını: İktisadi Önlemler ve Kısa Dönem Sonuçları Üzerine Bir Değerlendirme. In A. Çelik (Ed.), *Kovid-19 Sürecinde Türkiye'de Sosyal Politika* (pp. 17–46). Orion.

Bazeley, P. (2014). *Qualitative data analysis with nvivo + the coding manual for qualitative researchers*. Sage Publications.

BCG Executive Perspectives. (2021). *Investing to Win Talent*. Boston Consulting Group.

Beaunoyer, E., Dupéré, S., & Guitton, M. J. (2020). COVID-19 and digital inequalities: Reciprocal impacts and mitigation strategies. *Computers in Human Behavior, 111*, 106424. doi:10.1016/j.chb.2020.106424 PMID:32398890

Beck, K. (2022). *Manifesto para Desenvolvimento Ágil de Software*. https://agilemanifesto.org/iso/ptbr/manifesto.html

Behera, S. (2013). E-and M-Learning: A comparative study. *International Journal on New Trends in Education and Their Implications, 4*(3), 65–78.

Behsudi, A. (2020). Wish you were here: Tourism-dependent economies are among those harmed the most by the pandemic. *Finance & Development*. Retrieved from: https://www.imf.org/external/pubs/ft/fandd/2020/12/pdf/impact-of-the-pandemic-on-tourism-behsudi.pdf

Béland, L.P., Brodeur, A., & Wright, T. (2020). *The short-term economic consequences of Covid-19: exposure to disease, remote work and government response*. Academic Press.

Bell, J. A., & Nuzzo, J. B. (2022). *Global Health Security Index: Advancing Collective Action and Accountability Amid Global Crisis*. Retrieved from: www.GHSIndex.org

Benassi, J. L., & Amaral, D. C. (2007). Gerenciamento ágil de projetos aplicados ao desenvolvimento de produto físico. *Anais Simpósio de Engenharia de Produção*. https://simpep.feb.unesp.br/anterior.php?evento=1

Béné, C., Waid, J., Jackson-deGraffenried, M., Begum, A., Chowdhury, M., Skarin, V., Rahman, A., Islam, N., Mamnun, N., Mainuddin, K., & Amin, S.M.A. (2015). Impact of climate-related shocks and stresses on nutrition and food security in selected areas of rural Bangladesh. *Dhaka World Food Programme, 3*.

Ben-Eli, M. U. (2018). Sustainability: Definition and five core principles, a systems prespective. *Sustainability Science, 13*(5), 1337–1343. doi:10.100711625-018-0564-3

Bérastégui, P. (2021). *Teleworking in the aftermath of the Covid-19 pandemic: enabling conditions for a successful transition*. ETUI Research Paper-Policy Brief.

Berg, G., & Simonson, M. (2016). *Distance learning*. Encyclopedia Britannica.

Berkes, F., Colding, J., & Folke, C. (Eds.). (2003). *Navigating Social–Ecological Systems: Building Resilience for Complexity and Change*. Cambridge University Press.

Berman, S. J. (2012). Digital transformation: Opportunities to create new business models. *Strategy and Leadership, 40*(2), 16–24. doi:10.1108/10878571211209314

Bhadri, G. N., & Patil, L. R. (2022). Blended Learning: An Effective Approach for Online Teaching and Learning. *Journal of Engineering Education Transformations, 35*, 53–60.

Biedenbach, G., & Marell, A. (2010). The impact of customer experience on brand equity in a business-to- business services setting. *Journal of Brand Management, 17*(6), 446–458. doi:10.1057/bm.2009.37

Biggs, J., & Tang, C. (2011). *Teaching for quality learning at university* (4th ed.). McGraw-Hill.

Bilgin, M. H., Demir, E., Doker, A. C., & Karabulut, G. (2020). *How pandamics affect tourism: International evidence.* PMC.

Blacksip. (2021). Recovered from https://blacksip.com

Blitz, D. (1992). *Emergent Evolution: Qualitative Novelty and the Level of Reality.* Kluwer. doi:10.1007/978-94-015-8042-7

Bloomberg. (2021). https://www.bloomberg.co.jp/news/articles/2021-12-08/R3RS5ST0AFB401

Boersma, K., Büscher, M., & Fonio, C. (2022). Crisis management, surveillance, and digital ethics in the COVID-19 era. *Journal of Contingencies and Crisis Management, 30*(1), 2–9. doi:10.1111/1468-5973.12398

Bofinger, P., Dullien, S., Felbermayr, G., Fuest, C., Hüther, M., Südekum, J., & di Mauro, B. W. (2020). Economic Implications of the COVID-10 Crisis for Germany and Economic Policy Measures. In *Mitigating the COVID Economic Crisis: Act Fast and Do Whatever It Takes* (pp. 167–177). Centre for Economic Policy Research.

Bogdanov, A. A. (1934). Tectology or General Organizational Science. Academic Press.

Bogdanov, A. A. (1934). *Tectology or General Organizational Science.* Conjuncture Institute publishing house.

Boin, A., Kuipers, S., & Overdijk, W. (2013). Leadership in times of crisis: A framework for assessment. *International Review of Public Administration, 18*(1), 79–91. doi:10.1080/12294659.2013.10805241

Boltanski, L., & Thévenot, L. (1991). *De la justification.* Gallimard.

Bolton, R. N., Gustafsson, A., McColl-Kennedy, J., Sirianni, N. J., & Tse, D. K. (2014). Small details that make big differences: A radical approach to consumption experience as a firm's differentiating strategy. *Journal of Service Management, 25*(2), 253–274. doi:10.1108/JOSM-01-2014-0034

Bootle, R. (2009). *The Trouble with Markets: Saving Capitalism from Itself.* Nicholas Brealey Publishing.

Boston Consulting Group. (2019). *Mission Talent: Mass Uniqueness. A global challenge for one billion workers.* BCG.

Boyer, R., & Orléan, A. (1989). Les transformations des conventions salariales entre théorie et histoire. *Revista Economica, 42*(2), 233–272.

Bozkurt, A., Jung, I., Xiao, J., Vladimirschi, V., Schuwer, R., Egorov, G., Lambert, S., Al-Freih, M., Pete, J., Olcott, D. Jr, & Rodes, V. (2020). A global outlook to the interruption of education due to COVID-19 pandemic: Navigating in a time of uncertainty and crisis. *Asian Journal of Distance Education, 15*(1), 1–126.

Bozkurt, A., & Sharma, R. (2020). Emergency remote teaching in a time of global crisis due to CoronaVirus pandemic. *Asian Journal of Distance Education, 15*(1), i–vi.

Branco, A., Parejo Moruno, F. M., Lopes, J. C., & Rangel Preciado, J. F. (2016). Changes in world cork industry location. An historical perspective. *Revista De Estudios Regionales, 106*, 55–78.

Branded Media, E. F. (2020). *Las tienditas mexicanas recurrieron a la innovación digital.* https://www.elfinanciero.com.mx/mundo-empresa/las-tienditas-mexicanas-recurrieron-a-la-innovacion-digital/

Brasil, Ministério da Saúde. (2020). *Brasil confirma primeiro caso da doença.* https://www.saude.gov.br/noticias/agencia-saude/46435-brasil-confirma-primeiro-caso-de-novo-coronavirus

Bravo, E. R., Santana, M., & Rodon, J. (2015). Information systems and performance: The role of technology, the task, and the individual. *Journal Behaviour & Information Technology, 1*(3), 247–260. doi:10.1080/0144929X.2014.934287

Breen, K. (2016). *Why does inclusive growth matter?* The World Economic Forum.

Brege, S., & Brandes, O. (1993). The successful double turnaround of ASEA and ABB—Twenty lessons. *Strategic Change, 2*(4), 185–205. doi:10.1002/jsc.4240020403

Brem, A., Viardot, E., & Nylund, P. A. (2021). Implications of the coronavirus (COVID-19) outbreak for innovation: Which technologies will improve our lives? *Technological Forecasting and Social Change, 163*, 120451. doi:10.1016/j.techfore.2020.120451 PMID:33191956

Brockner, J., & James, E. H. (2008). Toward an understanding of when executives see crisis as opportunity. *The Journal of Applied Behavioral Science, 44*(1), 94–115. doi:10.1177/0021886307313824

Brown, B., & O'Hara, K. (2003). Place as a practical concern of mobile workers. *Environment & Planning A, 35*(9), 1565–1587. doi:10.1068/a34231

Buchanan, S., & McMenemy, D. (2012). Digital service analysis and design: The role of process modeling. *International Journal of Information Management, 32*(3), 251–256. doi:10.1016/j.ijinfomgt.2011.11.008

Bui, M. T. T., & Preechametta, A. (2019). Will manufacturing investors go to border zones? The case of central Thailand. *International Journal of Emerging Markets.* doi:10.1108/IJOEM-10-2018-0567

Bulearca, M., & Tamarjan, D. (2010). Augmented Reality: A Sustainable Marketing Tool? *Global Business and Management Research, 2*(2-3), 237–252.

Bundy, J., Pfarrer, M. D., Short, C. E., & Timothy Coombs, W. (2016). Crises and crisis management: Integration, interpretation, and research development. *Journal of Management, 43*(6), 1661–1692. doi:10.1177/0149206316680030

Burgos, D., & Ivanov, D. (2021). Food retail supply chain resilience and the COVID-19 pandemic: A digital twin-based impact analysis and improvement directions. *Transportation Research Part E, Logistics and Transportation Review, 152*, 1–20. doi:10.1016/j.tre.2021.102412 PMID:34934397

Burns, M. (2011). *Distance education for teacher training: modes, models, and methods.* Education Development Center-EDC.

Business in the Era of Stakeholders. (2022). *Harvard Business Review Russia.* Retrieved from: https://hbr-russia.ru/management/strategiya/biznes-v-eru-steykkholderov/

Byron, K., & Laurence, G. A. (2015). Diplomas, photos, and tchotchkes as symbolic self-representations: Understanding employees' individual use of symbols. *Academy of Management Journal, 58*(1), 298–323. doi:10.5465/amj.2012.0932

Cabot, J. (2018). WordPress: A Content Management System to Democratize Publishing. *IEEE Software, 35*(3), 89–92. doi:10.1109/MS.2018.2141016

Cabugueira, A. C. C. M. (2001). A nova economia e a educação. *Gestao e Desenvolvimento,* (10), 305–318. doi:10.7559/gestaoedesenvolvimento.2001.76

Cachón-Rodríguez, G., Prado-Román, C., & Blanco-González, A. (2021). The relationship between corporate identity and university loyalty: The moderating effect of brand identification in managing an institutional crisis. *Journal of Contingencies and Crisis Management, 29*(3), 265–280. doi:10.1111/1468-5973.12342

Cachón-Rodríguez, G., Prado-Román, C., & Zúñiga-Vicente, J. Á. (2019). The relationship between identification and loyalty in a public university: Are there differences between (the perceptions) professors and graduates? *European Research on Management and Business Economics, 25*(3), 122–128. doi:10.1016/j.iedeen.2019.04.005

Calvo-Porral, C., & Lévy-Manginb, J. (2017). Store brands' purchase intention: Examining the role of perceived quality. *European Research on Management and Business Economics, 23*(2), 90–95. doi:10.1016/j.iedeen.2016.10.001

Camoes, J., Lobato, C. T., Beires, F., & Gomes, E. (2021). Legionella and SARS-CoV-2 Coinfection in a Patient With Pneumonia—An Outbreak in Northern Portugal. *Cureus, 13*(1), e12476. doi:10.7759/cureus.12476 PMID:33552790

Carey, K. (2016). *The end of college: Creating the future of learning and the university of everywhere.* Riverhead Books.

Carlsson-Szlezak, P., Reeves, M., & Swartz, P. (2020). *What Coronavirus Could Mean for the Global Economy.* https://hbr.org/2020/03/what-coronavirus-could-mean-for-the-global-economy/

Carnevale, J. B., & Hatak, I. (2020). Employee adjustment and well-being in the era of COVID-19: Implications for human resource management. *Journal of Business Research, 116*, 183–187. doi:10.1016/j.jbusres.2020.05.037 PMID:32501303

Carrasqueira, H. (2016). *Economia e educação.* Working paper, ESGHT-UAlg.

Carù, A., & Cova, B. (2003). Revisiting consumption experience: A more humble but complete view of the concept. *Marketing Theory, 3*(2), 259–278. doi:10.1177/14705931030032004

Cavazotte, F., Lemos, A. H., & Villadsen, K. (2014). Corporate smart phones: Professionals' conscious engagement in escalating work connectivity. *New Technology, Work and Employment, 29*(1), 72–87. doi:10.1111/ntwe.12022

Cefrio. (2001). *Le télétravail: articuler qualité de vie et performance.* Cefrio.

CentroGeo-GeoInt-DataLab. (2021). *Covid-19 México Actualizado 22-02-2022.* https://datos.covid-19.conacyt.mx/

Chahad, J. P. Z. (2002). As modalidades especiais de contratos de trabalho e o emprego flexível no Brasil. *RDT- Revista de Direito do Trabalho, 28*(106), 76-95.

Chambers, R., & Conway, G. (1992). *Sustainable rural livelihoods: practical concepts for the 21st century.* Institute of Development Studies.

Chan, A. P. C., & Chan, A. P. L. (2004). Key performance indicators for measuring construction success. *Benchmarking, 11*(2), 203–221. doi:10.1108/14635770410532624

Chang, H., & Windeatt, S. (2016). Developing collaborative learning practices in an online language course. *Computer Assisted Language Learning, 29*(8), 1271–1286. doi:10.1080/09588221.2016.1274331

Chan, Y., Krishnamurthy, R., & Desjardins, C. (2020). Technology-Driven Innovation in Small Firms. *MIS Quarterly Executive, 19*(1), 1. doi:10.17705/2msqe.00024

Chardin. (1959). *The Phenomenon of Human Being.* Harper & Brothers.

Chatel, E., & Rivaud-Danset, D. (2004). L'économie des conventions: une lecture critique à partir de la philosophie pragmatiste de John Dewey. *Revue de philosophie économique, 13*(1), 49-76.

Chatti, W., Ben Soltane, B., & Abalala, T. (2019). Impacts of Public Transport Policy on City Size and Welfare. *Networks and Spatial Economics, 19*(4), 1097–1122. doi:10.100711067-019-09451-y

Chen, C. (2006). CiteSpace II: Detecting and visualizing emerging trends and transient patterns in scientific literature. *Journal of the American Society for Information Science and Technology, 57*(3), 359–377. doi:10.1002/asi.20317

Chen, C., Ibekwe-SanJuan, F., & Hou, J. (2010). The structure and dynamics of co-citation clusters: A multiple-perspective co-citation analysis. *Journal of the American Society for Information Science and Technology, 61*(7), 1386–1409. doi:10.1002/asi.21309

Chiavenato, I. (2014). *Gestão de pessoas: o novo papel dos recursos humanos nas organizações.* Manole.

Chin, G. L. (2004). *Agile project management: how to succeed in the face of changing project requirements.* Amacon.

Chopra, S., & Peter, M. (2007). *Supply chain management, strategy planning & operation* (3rd ed.). Pearson Prentice Hall. doi:10.1007/978-3-8349-9320-5_22

Chowdhury, R., Luhar, S., Khan, N., Choudhury, S. R., Matin, I., & Franco, O. H. (2020). Long-term strategies to control COVID-19 in low and middle-income countries: An options overview of community-based, non-pharmacological interventions. *European Journal of Epidemiology, 35*(8), 743–748. doi:10.100710654-020-00660-1 PMID:32656618

Christensen, C. M., Raynor, M., & McDonald, R. (2015). What is Disruptive Innovation. *Harvard Business Review, 93*(12), 44–53. PMID:17183796

Christopher, M. (1998). *Logistics and Supply Chain Management – Strategies for Reducing Cost and Improving Service* (2nd ed.). Pitman Publishing.

Chung, Dietz, Rab, & Townsend. (2020). *Ecosystem 2.0: Climbing to the next level.* McKinsey & Co.

CISCO. (2021). *O que é o Wi-Fi 6? Wi-Fi da próxima geração?* https://www.cisco.com/c/pt_pt/products/wireless/what-is-wi-fi-6.html

Clark, A. M. (1988). The qualitative-quantitative debate: Moving from positivism and confrontation to post-positivism and reconciliation. *Journal of Advanced Nursing, 27*(6), 1242–1249. doi:10.1046/j.1365-2648.1998.00651.x PMID:9663876

Clark, J. B. (2007). *Essentials of Economic Theory: As Applied to Modern Problems of Industry and Public Policy.* Ludwig von Mises Institute.

Clemente, M., Durand, R., & Roulet, T. (2017). The recursive nature of institutional change: An Annales School perspective. *Journal of Management Inquiry, 26*(1), 17–31. doi:10.1177/1056492616656408

Coase, R.H. (1988). The nature of the firm: origin, meaning, influence. *Journal of Law, Economics and Organization, 4.*

Cobo Martín, J. M. (2012). *Scimat, herramienta software para el análisis de la evolución del conocimiento científico: Propuesta de una metodología de evaluación* (Tesis Doctoral). Universidad de Granada, Granada.

Cochran, W. G. (2017). *Sampling Techniques* (3rd ed.). John Wiley & Sons.

Collins, A. M., Hislop, D., & Cartwright, S. (2016). Social support in the workplace between teleworkers, office-based colleagues and supervisors. *New Technology, Work and Employment, 31*(2), 161–175. doi:10.1111/ntwe.12065

Colm, L., & Ordanini, A. (2021). Facing supply chain disruptions: Strategies to ensure relational continuity. In R. Wilding (Ed.), *The impact of Covid-19 on supply chain management* (pp. 55–72). Proud Pen. doi:10.51432/978-1-8381524-2-0-4

Colquitt, J. A., & George, G. (2011). 'Publishing in AMJ – part 1: Topic choice'. *Academy of Management Journal, 54*(3), 432–435. doi:10.5465/amj.2011.61965960

Commendatore, P., Kubin, I., & Sushko, I. (2020). A propos Brexit: On the breaking up of integration areas – an NEG analysis. *Spatial Economic Analysis, 0*(0), 1–24. doi:10.1080/17421772.2019.1701702

Concanaco Servytur. (2020). *¿Qué es Mándamelo?* https://www.concanaco.com.mx/que-es-mandamelo/

Cooke, H., Lane, A., & Taylor, P. (2018) Open by degrees: a case of flexibility or personalization? In Enhancing Education Through Open Degree Programs and Prior Learning Assessment. IGI Global. doi:10.4018/978-1-5225-5255-0.ch008

Cooper, R. G. (2021). Accelerating innovation: Some lessons from the pandemic. *Journal of Product Innovation Management, 38*(2), 221–232. doi:10.1111/jpim.12565 PMID:33821086

Coordinación de Estrategia Digital Nacional de la Oficina de la Presidencia de la República - Medidas. (2021). *COVID-19 Medidas Económicas.* https://www.gob.mx/covid19medidaseconomicas

Cornford, T., & Shaikh, M. (2013). Introduction to Information Systems. In *Undergraduate study in Economics, Management, Finance and the Social Sciences.* University of London.

Corrado, Haskel, Jona-Lasinio, & Iommi. (2018). Intangible investment in the EU and US before and since the Great Recession and its contribution to productivity growth. *Journal of Infrastructure, Policy and Development, 2*(1).

Correa-Martínez, L., Kampmeier, S., Kümpers, P., Schwierzeck, V., Hennies, M., Hafezi, W., & Mellmann, A. (2020). A pandemic in times of global tourism: Superspreading and exportation of COVID-19 cases from a ski area in Austria. *Journal of Clinical Microbiology, 58*(6), 1–3. doi:10.1128/JCM.00588-20 PMID:32245833

Costas, J. (2013). Problematizing mobility: A metaphor of stickiness, non-places and the kinetic elite. *Organization Studies, 34*(10), 1467–1485. doi:10.1177/0170840613495324

Cousins, P. D., & Menguc, B. (2006). The Implications of Socialization and Integration in Supply Chain Management. *Journal of Operations Management, 24*(5), 604–620. doi:10.1016/j.jom.2005.09.001

Couto, G., Castanho, R. A., Pimentel, P., Carvalho, C., Sousa, A., & Santos, C. (2020). The Impacts of COVID-19 Crisis over the Tourism Expectations of the Azores Archipelago Residents. *Sustainability, 12*(18), 7612. doi:10.3390u12187612

COVID-19. Briefing Materials. (2020). Global health and crisis response. McKinsey & Company.

Cowling, M., Brown, R., & Rocha, A. (2020). Did you save some cash for a rainy COVID-19 day? The crisis and SMEs. *International Small Business Journal: Researching Entrepreneurship, 38*(7), 593–604. doi:10.1177/0266242620945102 PMID:35125601

CPD. (2020). *Dealing with COVID-19.* https://cpd.org.bd/dealing-with-covid-19/

Creswell, J. W. (2007). Five Qualitative Approaches to Inquiry. In Qualitative Inquiry & Research Design. Choosing among five approaches (pp. 68-72). Sage Publications Inc.

Csonka, A., & Fertő, I. (2019). Structural change and agglomeration in the Hungarian pork industry. *European Planning Studies, 0*(0), 1–15. doi:10.1080/09654313.2019.1687652

Cuneo, A., Milberg, S. J., Benavente, J. M., & Palacios-Fenech, J. (2015). The growth of private label brands: A worldwide phenomenon? *Journal of International Marketing, 23*(1), 72–90. doi:10.1509/jim.14.0036

Cupman, J. (2016). The Six Pillars of B2B Customer Experience Excellence. *MarketingProfs.* Available at: https://www.marketingprofs.com/articles/2016/29806/the-six-pillars-of-b2b-customer-experience-excellence

Cyprus Ministry of Education, Culture, Sport and Youth. (2012). Higher Education in Cyprus. Department of Higher and Tertiary Education, MOEC: Nicosia: PIO da Costa, E. M., & da Costa, N. M. (2020). The Covid-19 Pandemic Process in Mainland Portugal. A Geographical Analysis of the First 100 Days. *Finisterra-Revista Portuguesa De Geografia, 55*(115). Advance online publication. doi:10.18055/Finis20361

da Silva, S. M. (2021). Building trust, resilient regions, and educational narratives: Municipalities dealing with COVID-19 in border regions of Portugal. *European Educational Research Journal, 14749041211029732*(5), 636–666. Advance online publication. doi:10.1177/14749041211029733

Dabholkar, P. A. (1996). Consumer evaluations of new technology-based self-service options: An investigation of alternative models of service quality. *International Journal of Research in Marketing, 13*(1), 29–51. doi:10.1016/0167-8116(95)00027-5

Dabholkar, P. A., & Bagozzi, R. P. (2002). An attitudinal model of technology-based self-service: Moderating effects of consumer traits and situational factors. *Journal of the Academy of Marketing Science, 30*(3), 184–201. doi:10.1177/0092070302303001

dados.gov. (2020). *Shapefile of Portuguese municipalities.* /pt/datasets/concelhos-de-portugal/

Dahlquist, S. H., & Griffith, D. A. (2014). Multidyadic industrial channels: Understanding component supplier profits and original equipment manufacturer behavior. *Journal of Marketing, 78*(4), 59–79. doi:10.1509/jm.13.0174

Dakowska, D. (2019). *Decentring European higher education governance: The construction of expertise in the Bologna Process.* Routledge. doi:10.4324/9781351209557-5

Danchikov, E. A., Prodanova, N. A., Kovalenko, Y. N., & Bondarenko, T. G. (2021). Using different approaches to organizing distance learning during the COVID-19 pandemic: Opportunities and disadvantages. *Linguistics and Culture Review, 5*(S1), 587–595. doi:10.21744/lingcure.v5nS1.1444

Das, S., Rasul, M. G., Hossain, M. S., Khan, A. R., Alam, M. A., Ahmed, T., & Clemens, J. D. (2020). Acute food insecurity and short-term coping strategies of urban and rural households of Bangladesh during the lockdown period of COVID-19 pandemic of 2020: Report of a cross-sectional survey. *BMJ Open, 10*(12), e043365. doi:10.1136/bmjopen-2020-043365 PMID:33310813

Dastgerdi, A. S., De Luca, G., & Francini, C. (2020). *Reforming Housing Policies for the Sustainability of Historic.* MDPI.

DataMéxico. (2020) *Unidades económicas según sector económico en 2019.* https://datamexico.org/es/profile/geo/atizapan-de-zaragoza

Davenport, T. H., & Pearlson, K. (1998). Two cheers for the virtual office. *MIT Sloan Management Review, 39*(4), 51–65.

Davies, Diemand-Yauman, & van Dam. (2019, Feb.). Competitive advantage with a human dimension: From lifelong learning to lifelong employability. *McKinsey Quarterly.*

Davies, B., Diemand-Yauman, C., & van Dam, N. (2019). *Competitive advantage with a human dimension: From lifelong learning to lifelong employability. McKinsey Quarterly.*

Davitt, D. (2020). *UN World Tourism Organisation says "five to seven years" of growth could be lost through COVID-19.* Retrieved from: https://www.moodiedavittreport.com/un-world-tourism-organisation-says-five-to-seven-years-of-growth-could-be-lost-through-covid-19/

De Keyser, A., Verleye, K., Lemon, K. N., Keiningham, T. L., & Klaus, P. (2020). Moving the customer experience field forward: Introducing the touchpoints, context, qualities (TCQ) nomenclature. *Journal of Service Research, 23*(4), 433–455. doi:10.1177/1094670520928390

De la Rosa, E., & Ochoa, C. (2020). *Antad y Concanaco lanzan "Mándamelo", plataforma digital para 'tienditas'.* https://www.milenio.com/negocios/mandamelo-plataforma-digital-antad-concanaco-tienditas

De Pablos Heredero, C. (2012). *Organización y transformación de los sistemas de información en la empresa.* ESIC Editorial.

De Vito, A., & Gómez, J.-P. (2020). Estimating the COVID-19 cash crunch: Global evidence and policy. *Journal of Accounting and Public Policy*, *39*(2), 1–14. doi:10.1016/j.jaccpubpol.2020.106741

Deffayet, S. (2002). Nouvelles Technologies de l'Information et de la Communication (NTIC) et contrôle dans la relation managériale. *Recherches Sociologiques*, *33*(1), 27–48.

Del Valle, A. S. (2020). *The tourism industry and the impact of Covid-19, scenarios and proposals.* Global Journey Consulting.

Demetriou, L., Keramioti, L., & Hadjicharalambous, D. (2021). Examining the Relationship between Distance Learning Processes and University Students' Anxiety in Times of COVID-19. *European Journal of Social Sciences Studies*, *6*(2), 123–141. doi:10.46827/ejsss.v6i2.1012

Dennis, A., Antino, K., Rahimi, M., & Ayabakan, S. (2020). User reactions to COVID-19 screening chatbots from reputable providers. *Journal of the American Medical Informatics Association: JAMIA*, *27*(11), 1727–1731. doi:10.1093/jamia/ocaa167 PMID:32984890

Denso Wave Incorporated. (2021). Retrieved from http://www.qrcode.com

Dentoni, D., Pinkse, J., & Lubberink, R. (2021). Linking sustainable business models to socio-ecological resilience through cross-sector partnerships: A complex adaptive systems view. *Business & Society*, *60*(5), 1216–1252. doi:10.1177/0007650320935015

Destící, A. (2020). Covid-19 Seferberliği Üretimde Dönüşümü Getirdi. *Koç Grubu Bizden Haberler Dergisi*, *482*, 11–13.

Dewar, C., Keller, S., & Milhotra, V. (2022). *CEO Excellence: The Six Mindsets That Distinguish the Best Leaders from the Rest.* Scribner.

Diamond. (2021). *Tokushimaru's Present and Future.* https://diamond-rm.net/management/74592/

Dibrova, A. (2016). Virtual currency: New step in monetary development. *Procedia: Social and Behavioral Sciences*, *229*, 42–49. doi:10.1016/j.sbspro.2016.07.112

Dietz, Khan, & Rab. (2020). *How do companies create value from digital ecosystems?* McKinsey & Co.

Dietz, Khan, & Rab. (2020). *How do companies create value from digital ecosystems?* McKinsey & Company.

Díez-Martín, F., Blanco-González, A., & Díez-de-Castro, E. (2021). Measuring a scientifically multifaceted concept. The jungle of organizational legitimacy. *European Research on Management and Business Economics*, *27*(1), 100131. doi:10.1016/j.iedeen.2020.10.001

Díez-Martín, F., Miotto, G., & Cachón-Rodríguez, G. (2022). Organizational legitimacy perception: Gender and uncertainty as bias for evaluation criteria. *Journal of Business Research*, *139*, 426–436. doi:10.1016/j.jbusres.2021.09.073

Dionisio, M., Pinho, J. C., & Macedo, I. M. (2020). Resourced-based View and Internationalization in Social Enterprises : An exploratory study from Ashoka's Globalizer in Brazil. In International Marketing Trends (pp. 1–11). IGI Global.

Dionisio, M. A. (2021). The Impact of COVID-19: A Major Crisis or Just Another One? In *Cases on Small Business Economics and Development During Economic Crises* (pp. 207–217). IGI Global. doi:10.4018/978-1-7998-7657-1.ch010

Distribution Economics Institute of Japan. (2021). *Internet supermarkets growing dramatically under Covid-19*. https://www.dei.or.jp/aboutdei/column/20210215

Dito. (2020). *Dampak pandemi Covid-19 terhadap perekonomian Indonesia*. Jurnal Benefita. Universitas Sumatera Utara.

Dixon-Fyle, Hunt, & Prince. (2020). *Diversity wins: How inclusion matters*. McKinsey & Company.

Dodangh, J., Majid, M., & Nasehifar, V. (2010). Ranking of strategic plans in balanced scorecard by using electric method. *International Journal of Innovation, Management and Technology*.

Doğru, Ç. (2021). The Effects of Electronic Surveillance on Job Tension, Task Performance and Organizational Trust. *Business Systems Research: International Journal of the Society for Advancing Innovation and Research in Economy*, *12*(2), 125–143. doi:10.2478/bsrj-2021-0023

DoHouse. (2020). *The thought behind Ouen purcharging, "What is Ouen purcharging for you?"* https://www.dohouse.co.jp/kikulab/?p=14285

Dolega, L., Rowe, F., & Branagan, E. (2020). Going digital? The impact of social media marketing on retail website traffic, orders, and sales. *Journal of Retailing and Consumer Services*, *60*, 102501. Advance online publication. doi:10.1016/j.jretconser.2021.102501

Dollman, J. (2018). Social and environmental influences on physical activity behaviours. *International Journal of Environmental Research and Public Health*, *15*(1), 169. doi:10.3390/ijerph15010169 PMID:29361761

Donis, C., Perret, V., & Taskin, L. (2017). *Space, Place, and Scale: Critical Reflections on the New Spatial Turn in Organization Studies*. Academic Press.

Donthu, N., & Gustafsson, A. (2020). Effects of COVID-19 on business and research. *Journal of Business Research*, *117*, 284–289. doi:10.1016/j.jbusres.2020.06.008 PMID:32536736

Dörr, J. O., Licht, G., & Murmann, S. (2022). Small firms and the COVID-19 insolvency gap. *Small Business Economics*, *58*(2), 887–917. doi:10.100711187-021-00514-4

Dosi, G., Freeman, C., Nelson, R., Silverberg, G., & Soete, L. (1988). *Technical change and economic theory*. Printer Publisher Limited.

Dressler, M., & Paunovic, I. (2021). Sensing Technologies, Roles and Technology Adoption Strategies for Digital Transformation of Grape Harvesting in SME Wineries. *Journal of Open Innovation*, *7*(2), 123. doi:10.3390/joitmc7020123

Drever, E. (2006). *Using semi-structured interviews in small-scale research: A teacher's guide*. The SCRE Centre.

Drucker, P. F. (1976). *Uma era de descontinuidade*. Zahar.

Duan, L., & Zhu, G. (2020). Psychological interventions for people affected by the COVID-19 epidemic. *The Lancet. Psychiatry*, *7*(4), 300–302. doi:10.1016/S2215-0366(20)30073-0 PMID:32085840

Duarte, J. B. (2005). *O trabalho no domicílio do empregado: controle da jornada e responsabilidade pelo custeio dos equipamentos envolvidos*. https://migalhas.uol.com.br/depeso/12333/o-trabalho-no-domicilio-do-empregado--controle-da-jornada-e-responsabilidade

Dumas, M., & Ruiller, C. (2014). Le télétravail: Les risques d'un outil de gestion des frontières entre vie personnelle et vie professionnelle? *Management Avenir*, (8), 71–95. doi:10.3917/mav.074.0071

Dündar, N. (2020). Küresel salgınların makroekonomik etkileri üzerine bir araştırma. *Journal of Social and Humanities Sciences Research*, *7*(52), 837–852.

Dupuy, J. P. (1992). *Libéralisme et justice sociale: le sacrifice et l'envie*. Hachette.

Dupuy, J. P., Eymard-Duvernay, F., Favereau, O., Salais, R., & Thévenot, L. (1989). Economie des conventions. *Revista Economica*, *40*(2), 329–359.

Dussauge, P., Hart, S., & Ramanantsoa, B. (1992). *Strategic Technology Management – Integrating Product Technology into Global Business Strategies for the 1990s*. Wiley.

Duxbury, L., & Halinski, M. (2014). When more is less: An examination of the relationship between hours in telework and role overload. *Work (Reading, Mass.)*, *48*(1), 91–103. doi:10.3233/WOR-141858 PMID:24763352

Düzarat Şenak, A. (2021). *Pandemi Sürecinde Yerli Solunum Cihazı Üretimi ve Ortaklaşa Değer Yaratımı*. Eskişehir Osmangazi Üniversitesi, Sosyal Bilimler Enstitüsü, İşletme ABD, Yayınlanmamış Doktora Tezi.

Düzarat Şenak, A., & Girginer, N. (2021). *Bir Hizmet Ekosistemi Örneği Olarak Yerli Solunum Cihazı Üretimi. İktisadi ve İdari Bilimlerde Araştırma ve Değerlendirmeler-1*. Gece Publishing.

E-Commerce Info Platform. (2022). *E-Commerce Statistics*. https://www.eticaret.gov.tr/istatistikler/

Economy: A 10-point Action Plan to create a circular bioeconomy devoted to sustainable wellbeing. (n.d.). *The Solutions Journal*, *11*(2).

EGADE Business School. (2021). *Adaptabilidad al cambio, clave para transformar los negocios frente a COVID-19*. https://egade.tec.mx/es/blog/adaptabilidad-al-cambio-clave-para-transformar-los-negocios-frente-covid-19

EGADE Business School. (2021). *EGADE Future Forum - Reinvención del negocio en un entorno desafiante* [Video]. Youtube. https://www.youtube.com/watch?v=JBFYGU9cWrk&t=3447s

EGADE Business School. (2021). *EGADE Future Forum: Tendencias en Operaciones, Logísitca y Cadena de Suministro* [Video]. Youtube. https://www.youtube.com/watch?v=zPUJ5wcPDMk&t=1111s

EGADE Business School. (2021). *Exponen tendencias en operaciones, logística y cadena de suministro*. https://egade.tec.mx/es/blog/exponen-tendencias-en-operaciones-logistica-y-cadena-de-suministro

Egger, D., Miguel, E., Warren, S. S., Shenoy, A., Collins, E., Karlan, D., Parkerson, D., Mobarak, A. M., Fink, G., Udry, C., Walker, M., Haushofer, J., Larreboure, M., Athey, S., Lopez-Pena, P., Benhachmi, S., Humphreys, M., Lowe, L., Meriggi, N. F., ... Vernot, C. (2021). Falling living standards during the COVID-19 crisis: Quantitative evidence from nine developing countries. *Science Advances*, *7*(6), eabe0997. doi:10.1126ciadv.abe0997 PMID:33547077

Eisenhardt, K. M., & Graebner, M. (2007). Theory Building From Cases: Opportunities and Challenges. *Academy of Management Journal*, *50*(1), 25–32. doi:10.5465/amj.2007.24160888

Eisenhardt, K. M., & Martin, J. A. (2000). Dynamic capabilities: What are they? *Strategic Management Journal*, *21*(10-11), 1105–1121. doi:10.1002/1097-0266(200010/11)21:10/11<1105::AID-SMJ133>3.0.CO;2-E

Elsbach, K. D. (2003). Relating physical environment to self-categorizations: Identity threat and affirmation in a non-territorial office space. *Administrative Science Quarterly*, *48*(4), 622–654. doi:10.2307/3556639

Elsobeihi, M. M., & Abu Naser, S. S. (2017). Effects of Mobile Technology on Human Relationships. *International Journal of Engineering and Information Systems*, *1*(5), 110–125.

Emmett, J., Schrah, G., Schrimper, M., & Wood, A. (2020). *COVID-19 and the employee experience: How leaders can seize the moment. Organization Practice*. McKinsey & Company.

Eneyew, A., & Bekele, W. (2012). Determinants of livelihood strategies in Wolaita, southern Ethiopia. *Agricultural Research and Reviews*, *1*(5), 153–161.

Estrada, M. M. (2010). Realidade do teletrabalho no Brasil e nos tribunais brasileiros. *Revista Direito e Liberdade*, 193-116.

European Commission (EC). (2019). *2nd survey of schools: ICT in Education. Objective 1: Benchmark progress in ICT in schools*. Final report. Luxemburg: Publication Office of the European Union.

Eurostat. (2020). *Agriculture, Forestry and Fisheries Statistical book*. https://www.gpp.pt/images/Estatisticas_e_analises/Estatisticas/AgricolasEstruturais_Producao/AgricultureForestryFisheryStatistics_2020_Edition2020.pdf

Everything you need to know about 5G (Qualcomm 2020). (n.d.). https://www.qualcomm.com/5g/what-is-5g

Fagbolu, A. O. (2021). The reasons for failure of tourism small and medium scale enterprises (TSMEs) and possible strategies for restraining the failure. *Global Scientific Journals*, *9*, 576–580.

Fahmi, I. (2016). *Teori dan paraktik pengambilan keputusan kualitatif dan kuantitatif*. Rajawali Pers.

Fallows, J. W., Iyer, P., Potts, R., Becker, E., Crabtree, J., & de Juniac, A. (2021). The Future of Travel After the Coronavirus Pandemic: Travel and tourism will be changed forever. We asked seven leading thinkers for their predictions. *FP Insider*. Retrieved from: https://foreignpolicy.com/2020/06/13/travel-tourism-coronavirus-pandemic-future/

Favereau, O. (2002). Conventions and regulation. In R. Boyer & Y. Saillard (Eds.), *Régulation theory: the state of the art* (pp. 312–319). Routlege.

Feber, D., Lingqvist, O., Nordigaarden, D., & Seidner, M. (2022). *2022 and beyond for the packaging industry's CEOs: The priorities for resilience*. McKinsey & Company.

FeiaF. (2022). https://frutafeia.pt/

Felstead, A., Jewson, N., & Walters, S. (2005). The shifting locations of work: New statistical evidence on the spaces and places of employment. *Work, Employment and Society*, *19*(2), 415–431. doi:10.1177/0950017005053186

Fenu, G., & Pau, P. L. (2015). An Analysis of Features and Tendencies in Mobile Banking Apps. *Procedia Computer Science*, *56*, 26–33. doi:10.1016/j.procs.2015.07.177

Fernández-Rovira, C., Álvarez, J., Molleví, G., & Nicolas-Sans, R. (2021). The digital transformation of business. Towards the datafication of the relationship with customers. *Technological Forecasting and Social Change*, *162*, 120339. doi:10.1016/j.techfore.2020.120339

Ferreira Júnior, J. C. (2000). Telecommuting: o paradigma de um novo estilo de trabalho. *Revista de Administração de Empresas*, 8-17.

Firmino, A. (1999). Agriculture and landscape in Portugal. *Landscape and Urban Planning*, *46*(1-3), 83–91. doi:10.1016/S0169-2046(99)00049-3

Folke, C. (2006). Resilience: The emergence of a perspective for social–ecological systems analyses. *Global Environmental Change*, *16*(3), 253–267. doi:10.1016/j.gloenvcha.2006.04.002

Fontoura, I. H. N. da, & Reis, S. d. S. (2022). As consequências da modalidade home office às mulheres vítimas de violência doméstica e familiar e o papel do empregador. In *Anais da III Jornada de Desenvolvimento e Políticas Públicas*. Criciúma: Universidade do Extremo Sul Catarinense.

Food and Agriculture Organization of the United Nations. (2020). *Preventing the next global pandemic: sustainability and the One Health approach*. Retrieved from https://www.fao.org/sustainability/success-stories/detail/en/c/1300674/

Food and Agriculture Organization of the United Nations. (n.d.). *Sustainable Food and Agriculture*. Retrieved from https://www.fao.org/sustainability/background/en

Foo, L. P., Chin, M. Y., Tan, K. L., & Phuah, K. T. (2021). The impact of COVID-19 on tourism industry in Malaysia. *Current Issues in Tourism, 24*(19), 2735–2739. doi:10.1080/13683500.2020.1777951

Forecast, G. M. D. T. (2019). *Cisco visual networking index: global mobile data traffic forecast update, 2017-2022*. Retrieved from https://www.cisco.com/c/en/us/solutions/service-provider/visualnetworking-index-vni/index.html

Freeman, A., Becker, S., & Cummins, M. (2017). *The NMC/CoSN Horizon Report*. The New Media Consortium and Consortium for School Networking.

Frisch, R. (1933). Propagation problems and impulse problems in dynamic economics. In *Economic Essays in Honour of Gustav Cassel*. Allen and Unwin.

Fujita, M., & Krugman, P. (2004). The new economic geography: Past, present and the future. *Papers in Regional Science, 83*(1), 139–164. https://doi.org/10.1007/s10110-003-0180-0

Fukunaga, H. (2020). Toilet paper rumors and hoarding induced by the spread of coronavirus infections. *The NHK Monthly Report on Broadcast Research, 70*(7), 2–24.

Futi & Bumba. (2021). *Metodologia de elaboração de trabalhos científicos: uma abordagem de acordo com as normas APA e ABNT*. Curitiba: CRV.

Gaceta, U. N. A. M. (2020). *Mexicanos usan hasta 4 horas su WhatsApp*. https://www.fundacionunam.org.mx/unam-al-dia/mexicanos-usan-hasta-4-horas-su-whatsapp/

Gadde, N., Jakkali, B., Siddamallaih, H., & Babu, R. (2022). Quality of experience aware network selection model for service provisioning in heterogeneous network. *International Journal of Electrical & Computer Engineering, 12*(2).

Gala, D., & Patil, R. D. (2013). Consumer Attitude towards Private Labels in Comparison To National Brands International. *Journal of Business and Management Invention, 2*(5), 12–18.

Galanakis, C. M., Rizou, M., Aldawoud, T. M., Ucak, I., & Rowan, N. J. (2021). Innovations and technology disruptions in the food sector within the COVID-19 pandemic and post-lockdown era. *Trends in Food Science & Technology, 110*, 193–200. doi:10.1016/j.tifs.2021.02.002

Gallup. (2021). *State of the Global Workplace: 2021 Report*. https://www.gallup.com/workplace/349484/state-of-the-global-workplace.aspx

Gamage, S. H., Ayres, J. R., & Behrend, M. B. (2022). A systematic review on trends in using Moodle for teaching and learning. *International Journal of STEM Education, 9*(1), 1–24. doi:10.118640594-021-00323-x PMID:35096513

Garcia-Alonso, J., Krentz, M., Lovich, D., & Mingardon, S. (2020). Diversity, equity, and inclusion still matter in a pandemic. Boston Consulting Group.

Gates, B. (2020). Responding to Covid-19 - A once-in-a-century pandemic? *The New England Journal of Medicine, 382*(18), 1677–1679. doi:10.1056/NEJMp2003762 PMID:32109012

Gensse, P. (2003). Introduction générale. In M. Amblard (Ed.), *Conventions & management*. De Boeck Supérieur.

George, G., Howard-Grenville, J., Joshi, A., & Tihanyi, L. (2016). Understanding and tackling societal grand challenges through management research. *Academy of Management Journal, 59*(6), 1880–1895. doi:10.5465/amj.2016.4007

George, G., Lakhani, K., & Puranam, P. (2020). What has changed? The impact of Covid pandemic on the technology and innovation management research agenda. *Journal of Management Studies*, *57*(8), 1754–1758. doi:10.1111/joms.12634

Ghaderi, Z., & Paraskevas, A. (2021). Approaching Organizational Learning through Crisis Management. In *Organizational Learning in Hospitality and Tourism Crisis Management*. De Gruyter Publishing.

Ghose, B. (2020). *Why 2020 will see the birth of the 'trust economy'*. World Economic Forum.

Gil, A. C. (2019). *Métodos e Técnicas de Pesquisa Social* (7th ed.). Atlas.

Giovanis, E. (2018). The relationship between teleworking, traffic and air pollution. *Atmospheric Pollution Research*, *9*(1), 1–14. doi:10.1016/j.apr.2017.06.004

Giudice, F., Caferra, R., & Morone, P. (2020). COVID-19, the Food System and the Circular Economy: Challenges and Opportunities. *Sustainability*, *12*(19), 7939. doi:10.3390u12197939

Gjaja, Hutchinson, Farber, Brimmer, & Kahn. (2020). *Three Paths to the Future*. Boston Consulting Group Analysis.

Glaser, B., & Strauss, A. (1999). *The Discovery off rounded theory: Strategies for qualitative research*. Aldine Publishing.

Glynn, S. M., & Denise Muth, K. (1994). Reading and writing to learn science: Achieving scientific literacy. *Journal of Research in Science Teaching*, *31*(9), 1057–1073. doi:10.1002/tea.3660310915

Gögce, H., & Özmen, M. (2020). Hizmet Baskın Mantık ve Ortaklaşa Değer Yaratımı: Pazarlama Disiplini İçin Bütüncül Bir Değer Yaklaşımı. *Pazarlama Teorisi ve Uygulamaları Dergisi*, *5*(1), 1–18.

Golden, T. (2007). Co-workers who telework and the impact on those in the office: Understanding the implications of virtual work for co-worker satisfaction and turnover intentions. *Human Relations*, *60*(11), 1641–1667. doi:10.1177/0018726707084303

Gomes, M. J., & Costa, F. A. (2010). A Escola e a agenda digital europeia. *Educação, Formação & Tecnologias*, *3*(1), 1-5.

Gonzalez-Val, R., & Pueyo, F. (2019). Natural resources, economic growth and geography. *Economic Modelling*, *83*, 150–159. https://doi.org/10.1016/j.econmod.2019.02.007

Google. (2021). *Informes de Movilidad Local sobre el COVID-19, 2021*. https://www.google.com/covid19/mobility/

Gopalan, S., Nguyen Trieu Duong, L., & Rajan, R. S. (2020). Trade configurations in Asia: Assessing de facto and de jure regionalism. *World Economy*, *43*(4), 1034–1058. https://doi.org/10.1111/twec.12907

Gössling, S., Scott, D., & Hall, C. M. (2020). Pandemics, tourism and global change: A rapid assessment of COVID-19. *Journal of Sustainable Tourism*, *29*(1), 1–20. doi:10.1080/09669582.2020.1758708

Goto, H., & Minamimura, K. (2019). Geography and Demography: New Economic Geography With Endogenous Fertility. *The Japanese Economic Review*, *70*(4), 537–568. https://doi.org/10.1111/jere.12213

Govindan, K., Jafarian, A., & Nourbakhsh, V. (2015). Bi-objective integrating sustainable order allocation and sustainable supply chain network strategic design with stochastic demand using a novel robust hybrid multi-objective metaheuristic. *Computers & Operations Research*, *62*, 112–130. doi:10.1016/j.cor.2014.12.014

Gözen, M. (2019). Değer ve Değerleme Hakkında Kavramsal Ve Kuramsal Bir Çalışma. *Selçuk Üniversitesi Sosyal Bilimler Meslek Yüksekokulu Dergisi*, *22*(2), 374–382. doi:10.29249elcuksbmyd.481913

Grönroos, C. (2004). The Relationship Marketing Process: Communication, Interaction, Dialogue, Value. *Journal of Business and Industrial Marketing*.

Grönroos, C. (2006). Adopting a service logic for marketing. *Marketing Theory, 6*(3), 317–333. doi:10.1177/1470593106066794

Grubb, V. M. (2018). *Conflito de gerações: desafios e estratégias para gerenciar quatro gerações no ambiente de trabalho*. Autêntica Business.

Grubor, A., & Milovanov, O. (2017). Brand strategies in the era of sustainability. *Interdisciplinary Description of Complex Systems, 15*(1), 78–88. doi:10.7906/indecs.15.1.6

Grupo Bimbo. (2020). *Bimbo Contingo*. https://bimbocontigo.com/

Grytsenko, I., Borysenko, N., Sydorenko, N., Vashchuk, V., & Valuieva, I. (2022). Higher education institution: Distance learning and modern communicative opportunities. *Review of Education, 10*(1), e3318. doi:10.1002/rev3.3318

Guan, H., Okely, A. D., Aguilar-Farias, N., del Pozo Cruz, B., Draper, C. E., El Hamdouchi, A., Florindo, A. A., Jáuregui, A., Katzmarzyk, P. T., Kontsevaya, A., Löf, M., Park, W., Reilly, J. J., Sharma, D., Tremblay, M. S., & Veldman, S. L. (2020). Promoting healthy movement behaviours among children during the COVID-19 pandemic. *The Lancet. Child & Adolescent Health, 4*(6), 416–418. doi:10.1016/S2352-4642(20)30131-0 PMID:32458805

Guckenheimer, J. (1973). Bifurcation and catastrophe. In M. Peixoto (Ed.), *Dynamical Systems*. Academic Press.

Guckenheimer, J. (1973). Bifurcation and catastrophe. Proc. International Sympos. In M. Peixoto (Ed.), *Dynamical Systems*. Academic Press.

Guerrieri, V., Lorenzoni, G., Straub, L., & Werning, I. (2020). *Macroeconomic Implications of Covid-19: Can Negative Supply Shocks Cause Demand Shortages?* NBER Working Paper No: 26918.

Guest, G., MacQueen, K. M., & Namey, E. E. (2012). *Applied Thematic Analysis*. Sage. doi:10.4135/9781483384436

Guha Roy, D., Mahato, B., De, D., & Srirama, S. N. (2022). Quality of experience aware recommendation system with IoT data filtration for handshaking among users using MQTT-SN protocol. *Journal of Ambient Intelligence and Humanized Computing*, 1–16.

Guimarães, T. d. C., & Santos, B. S. M. (2022). Metodologias ágeis na construção civil: estudo de caso da construção modular off site aplicada no hospital m'boi mirim em São Paulo / agile methodologies in civil construction: a case study of offsite modular construction applied at hospital M'boi Mirin in São Paulo:. *BJD - Brazilian Journal of Development, 8*(1). doi:10.34117/bjdv8n1-143

Gules, H. K., & Özilhan, D. (2010). Kaynak Temelli Teori Bağlamında Üretim Ve Pazarlama Stratejilerinin İşletme Performansı Üzerine Etkisinin İncelenmesi. *Sosyal ve Ekonomik Araştırmalar Dergisi, 13*(19), 477–490.

Gultom, D. R. (2009). *Pengukuran kinerja perusahaan dengan balanced scorecard: studi kasus pada perusahaan perkebunan negara III (Persero) Medan*. Universitas Sumatra Utara.

Gummesson, E. (2006). Many-to-Many Marketing as Grand Theory: A Nordic School Contribution. Routledge.

Gummesson, E., & Mele, C. (2010). Marketing as Value Co-Creation Through Network Interaction and Resource Integration. *Journal of Business Market Management, 4*(4), 181–198. doi:10.100712087-010-0044-2

Guo, B., Wang, J., & Wei, S. X. (2018). R&D spending, strategic position and firm performance. *Frontiers of Business Research in China, 12*(1), 1–19. doi:10.118611782-018-0037-7

Guo, J., Feng, X. L., Wang, X. H., & van IJzendoorn, M. H. (2020). Coping with COVID-19: Exposure to COVID-19 and negative impact on livelihood predict elevated mental health problems in Chinese adults. *International Journal of Environmental Research and Public Health, 17*(11), 3857. doi:10.3390/ijerph17113857 PMID:32485859

Guttman, N., & Lev, E. (2021). Ethical Issues in COVID-19 Communication to Mitigate the Pandemic: Dilemmas and Practical Implications. *Health Communication*, *36*(1), 116–123. doi:10.1080/10410236.2020.1847439 PMID:33191801

Haber, İ. T. O. (2020). *Yeni ekosistemin ilk bebeği doğdu*. https://www.itohaber.com/haber/sektorel/211582/yeni_ekosistemin_ilk_bebegi_dogdu.html

Hadiwardoyo, W. (2020). Kerugian ekonomi nasional akibat PSBB. *Jurnal of Business and Entrepreneurship, 2*.

Hadjicharalambous, D., Demetriou, L., & Erotocritou, K. (2021). Exploring the quality of life and psychological symptoms of university students in Cyprus during the Covid-19 pandemic. *Journal of Social Science Research*, *17*, 2321–1091.

Haizer, J., & Render, B. (2010). *Manajemen operasi*. Salemba Empat.

Haken, H. (1977). *Synergetics. An Introduction*. Springer-Verlag.

Hall, C. M., Gossling, S., & Scott, D. (2015). *The Routledge Handbook of Tourism and Sustainability*. Routledge. doi:10.4324/9780203072332

Hall, M. C., Prayag, G., Fieger, P., & Dyason, D. (2020). Beyond panic buying: Consumption displacement and COVID-19. *Journal of Service Management*, *32*(1), 113–128. doi:10.1108/JOSM-05-2020-0151

Hamadani, J. D., Hasan, M. I., Baldi, A. J., Hossain, S. J., Shiraji, S., Bhuiyan, M. S. A., Mehrin, S. F., Fisher, J., Tofail, F., Tipu, S. M. U., Grantham-McGregor, S., Biggs, B.-A., Braat, S., & Pasricha, S.-R. (2020). Immediate impact of stay-at-home orders to control COVID-19 transmission on socioeconomic conditions, food insecurity, mental health, and intimate partner violence in Bangladeshi women and their families: An interrupted time series. *The Lancet. Global Health*, *8*(11), e1380–e1389. doi:10.1016/S2214-109X(20)30366-1 PMID:32857955

Hannan, M. T., & Freeman, J. (1977). The population ecology of organizations. *American Journal of Sociology*, *82*(5), 929–964. doi:10.1086/226424

Hannan, M. T., & Freeman, J. (1984). Structural inertia and organizational change. *American Sociological Review*, *49*(2), 149–164. doi:10.2307/2095567

Harari, Y. N. (2020). *Notas sobre a pandemia: e breves lições para o mundo pós-coronavírus*. Companhia das Letras.

Hartmann, N. N., & Lussier, B. (2020). Managing the sales force through the unexpected exogenous COVID-19 crisis. *Industrial Marketing Management*, *88*, 101–111. doi:10.1016/j.indmarman.2020.05.005

Hassan, V., Bellos, G. S. G., & Fawaz, R. (2021). Transportation twowards tourism sustainility: Case study of Lebanon. *Athens Journal of Tourism*, *8*(1), 177–192. doi:10.30958/ajt.8-3-3

Hauge, N., & Hauge, P. (2018). *B2B Customer Experience: A Practical Guide to Delivering Exceptional CX*. KoganPage.

Hausmann, R., & Gavin, M. (1996). *Securing stability and growth in a shock prone region: the policy challenge for Latin America*. Inter-American Development Bank. Working Paper. No. 315. Office of the Chief Economist.

Hayakawa, K., & Mukunoki, H. (2021). The impact of COVID-19 on international trade: Evidence from the first shock. *Journal of the Japanese and International Economies*, *60*, 101135. doi:10.1016/j.jjie.2021.101135

Hegel, G. W. F. (1892). The science of logics. In The Logic of Hegel (2nd ed.). Oxford University Press.

Hegel, G. W. F. (1892). The science of logics. In:The Logic of Hegel (2nd ed.). Oxford University Press.

Hernández, V. (2021). *GS1 México y AMVO confirman el músculo digital de las pymes*. https://retailers.mx/gs1-mexico-y-amvo-confirman-el-musculo-digital-de-las-pymes/

He, W., Zhang, Z. J., & Li, W. (2021). Information technology solutions, challenges, and suggestions for tackling the COVID-19 pandemic. *International Journal of Information Management*, *57*, 102287. Advance online publication. doi:10.1016/j.ijinfomgt.2020.102287 PMID:33318721

Hiertz, G. R., Denteneer, D., Max, S., Taori, R., Cardona, J., Berlemann, L., & Walke, B. (2010). IEEE 802.11s: The WLAN Mesh Standard. *IEEE Wireless Communications*, *17*(1), 104–111. doi:10.1109/MWC.2010.5416357

Highsmith, J. (2004). *Agile project management: creating innovative products*. Addison-Wesley.

Hinzmann, S., Cantner, U., & Graf, H. (2019). The role of geographical proximity for project performance: Evidence from the German Leading-Edge Cluster Competition. *The Journal of Technology Transfer*, *44*(6), 1744–1783. https://doi.org/10.1007/s10961-017-9600-1

Hirogaki, M. (2021). Online Consumer Behaviors Trigger Drastic Distribution Changes: The Case of Japan. In Impact of Globalization and Advanced Technologies on Online Business Models (pp. 303-321). IGI Global.

Hirst, A. (2011). Settlers, vagrants and mutual indifference: Unintended consequences of hot-desking. *Journal of Organizational Change Management*, *24*(6), 767–788. doi:10.1108/09534811111175742

Hislop, D., & Axtell, C. (2011). Mobile phones during work and non-work time: A case study of mobile, non-managerial workers. *Information and Organization*, *21*(1), 41–56. doi:10.1016/j.infoandorg.2011.01.001

Hodges, C., Moore, S., Lockee, B., & Trust, T. B. A. (2020). The difference between emergency remote teaching and online learning. *EDUCAUSE Review*, *27*(1), 1–9.

Hodgson, G. M. (2002). Reconstitutive downward causation: social structure and the development of individual agency. In Intersubjectivity in Economics: Agents and Structures. Routledge.

Hodgson, G.M. (1988). Competence and control in the theory of the firm. *Journal of Economic Behavior and Organization*, *35*(2), 179-201.

Hodgson, G.M. (1998). The approach of institutional economics. *Journal of Economic Literature, 36*(1), 166-192.

Hodgson, G. M. (1988b). *Economics and Institutions. A Manifesto for a Modern Institutional Economics*. Polity Press. doi:10.9783/9781512816952

Hodgson, G. M. (2003). The hidden persuaders: Institutions and individuals in economic theory. *Cambridge Journal of Economics*, *27*(2), 159–175. doi:10.1093/cje/27.2.159

Hodgson, G. M., & Knudsen, T. (2004). The firm as an interactor: Firms as vehicles for habits and routines. *Journal of Evolutionary Economics*, *14*(3), 281–307. doi:10.100700191-004-0192-1

Hohenstein, N.-O. (2022). Supply chain risk management in the COVID-19 pandemic: strategies and empirical lessons for improving global logistics service providers' performance. *The International Journal of Logistics Management*.

Hohenstein, N. O. (2022). Supply chain risk management in the COVID-19 pandemic: Strategies and empirical lessons for improving global logistics service providers' performance. *International Journal of Logistics Management*. Advance online publication. doi:10.1108/IJLM-02-2021-0109

Holbrook, M. B., & Hirschmann, E. C. (1982). The experiential aspects of consumption: Consumer fantasies, feelings and fun. *The Journal of Consumer Research*, *9*(2), 132–140. https://www.jstor.org/stable/2489122. doi:10.1086/208906

Holcombe, R. G. (2009). Product differentiation and economic progress. *The Quarterly Journal of Austrian Economics*, *12*(1), 17–35.

Holland, C. P., & Naudé, P. (2004). The metamorphosis of marketing into an information-handling problem. *Journal of Business and Industrial Marketing*, *19*(3), 167–177. doi:10.1108/08858620410531306

Holling, C. S. (1973). Resilience and stability of ecological systems. *Annual Review of Ecology and Systematics*, *4*(1), 1–23. doi:10.1146/annurev.es.04.110173.000245

Honkamaa, P., Jäppinen, J., & Woodward, Ch. (2007). *A Lightweight Approach for Augmented Reality on Camera Phones using 2D Images to Simulate in 3D*. VTT Technical Research Centre of Finland. doi:10.1145/1329469.1329490

Hoornweg, N., Peters, P., & Van der Heijden, B. (2016). Finding the optimal mix between telework and office hours to enhance employee productivity: A study into the relationship between telework intensity and individual productivity, with mediation of intrinsic motivation and moderation of office hours. In New Ways of Working Practices. Emerald Group Publishing Limited. doi:10.1108/S1877-636120160000016002

Hootsuite. (2021). *Digital 2021: A global digital overview*. Retrieved from https://datareportal.com/reports/digital-2021-global-overview-report

Hoque, A., Shikha, F. A., Hasanat, M. W., Arif, I., & Hamid, P. D. (2020). The Effect of Coronavirus (COVID-19) in the Tourism Industry in China. *Asian Journal of Multidisciplinary Studies*, *3*(1).

Hossain, M. I. (2021). COVID-19 Impacts on Employment and Livelihood of Marginal People in Bangladesh: Lessons Learned and Way Forward. *South Asian Survey*, *28*(1), 57–71. doi:10.1177/0971523121995072

How adaptive WiFi can solve your WFH woes. (2020). https://www.plume.com/homepass/blog/how-adaptive-wifi-can-solve-your-wfh-woes/

Howells, K. (2018). *The future of education and skills: education 2030: the future we want, OECD*. DES.

Huang, C., Wang, Y., Li, X., Ren, L., Zhao, J., Hu, Y., Zhang, L., Fan, G., Xu, J., Gu, X., Cheng, Z., Yu, T., Xia, J., Wei, Y., Wu, W., Xie, X., Yin, W., Li, H., Liu, M., ... Cao, B. (2020). Clinical features of patients infected with 2019 novel coronavirus in Wuhan, China. *Lancet*, *395*(10223), 395. doi:10.1016/S0140-6736(20)30183-5 PMID:31986264

Huang, Y., Savelsbergh, M., & Zhao, L. (2018). Designing logistics systems for home delivery in densely populated urban area. *Transportation Research Part B: Methodological*, *115*, 95–125. doi:10.1016/j.trb.2018.07.006

Huber, S. G., & Helm, C. (2020). COVID-19 and schooling: Evaluation, assessment and accountability in times of crises-reacting quickly to explore key issues for policy, practice and research with the school barometer. *Educational Assessment, Evaluation and Accountability*, *32*(2), 237–270. doi:10.100711092-020-09322-y PMID:32837626

Hugill, P. J. (2016). The Power of Knowledge: How Information and Technology Made the Modern World. *Journal of Historical Geography*, *52*, 123–124. doi:10.1016/j.jhg.2015.06.007

Humphries, J. E., Neilson, C., & Ulyssea, G. (2020). *The evolving impacts of COVID-19 on small businesses since the CARES Act*. Cowles Foundation Discussion Papers, EliScholar, Yale University. Retrieved from https://elischolar.library.yale.edu/cgi/viewcontent.cgi?article=1016&context=cowles-discussion-paper-series

Hunt, Layton, & Prince. (2015). *Diversity matters*. McKinsey & Company.

Hunt, Prince, Dixon-Fyle, & Yee. (2018). *Delivering through Diversity*. McKinsey & Company.

Hunt, Prince, Dixon-Fyle, & Yee. (2018). *Delivering Through Diversity*. McKinsey & Company.

Hunt, J. G., Boal, K. B., & Dodge, G. E. (1999). The effects of visionary and crisis-responsive charisma on followers: An experimental examination of two kinds of charismatic leadership. *The Leadership Quarterly*, *10*(3), 423–448. doi:10.1016/S1048-9843(99)00027-2

Hürríyet, G. (2020). *Yerli solunum cihazinin uretim aşamalari göruntülendi.* https://www.hurriyet.com.tr/teknoloji/yerli-solunum-cihazinin-uretim-asamalari-goruntulendi-41505171

Hussain, M., Ahmed, N., Ahmed, M., Iqubal, Z., & Sarma, N. (2022). QoS Provisioning in Wireless Mesh Networks: A Survey. *Wireless Personal Communications, 122*(1), 157–195.

Iberahim, H. (2021). Designing online and distance learning: Aid pedagogical approach for creative and critical thinking course. *The Insight Journal.*

Ibn-Mohammed, T., Mustapha, K. B., Godsell, J. M., Adamu, Z., Babatunde, K. A., Akintade, D. D., ... Koh, S. C. L. (2020). A critical review of the impacts of COVID-19 on the global economy and ecosystems and opportunities for circular economy strategies. *Resources, Conservation and Recycling,* 105169.

Iivari, N., Sharma, S., & Ventä-Olkkonen, L. (2020). Digital transformation of everyday life–How COVID-19 pandemic transformed the basic education of the young generation and why information management research should care? *International Journal of Information Management, 55,* 102183.

Illario, M., Zavagli, V., Ferreira, N. L., Sambati, M., Teixeira, A., Lanata, F., Pais, S., Farrell, J., & Tramontano, D. (2020). The Frailty of the Invincible. *Translational Medicine @ UniSa, 23,* 1–15.

ILO. (2021). *Country policy responses.* https://www.ilo.org/global/topics/coronavirus/regional-country/country-responses/lang--en/index.htm#MX

IMF. (2020). *The Great Lockdown.* IMF.

IMF. (2021). *Fiscal Monitor: Government Support Is Vital as Countries Race to Vaccinate.* IMF.

Impact, E. (2022). *The ESG conundrum: How investors and companies can find common purpose in ESG.* The Economist Group.

Imran, M., HuSen, A., Kaleem, M., Bangash, A. K., Din, N. U., & Sobia. (2020). Effect of regional factor productivity on manufacturing sector: The case of Sino-Pak economic ties. *Financial Innovation, 6*(1), 5. doi:10.1186/s40854-019-0163-z

INE. (2020a). *Indicadores de contexto demográfico e da expressão territorial da pandemia COVID-19 em Portugal: COVID-19: Uma leitura do contexto demográfico e da expressão territorial da pandemia.* https://www.ine.pt/xportal/xmain?xpid=INE&xpgid=ine_destaques&DESTAQUESdest_boui=455108654&DESTAQUESmodo=2

INE. (2020b). *Indicadores de contexto e de impacto socioeconómico da pandemia COVID-19 em Portugal: COVID-19: O que distingue as 19 frequesias em estado de calamidade do resto da AML?* https://www.ine.pt/xportal/xmain?xpid=INE&xpgid=ine_destaques&DESTAQUESdest_boui=443697541&DESTAQUESmodo=2

INE. (2020c). *Mobilidade da população ao nível regional no contexto da pandemia COVID-19.* https://www.ine.pt/xportal/xmain?xpid=INE&xpgid=ine_destaques&DESTAQUESdest_boui=465143606&DESTAQUESmodo=2

INE. (2020d). *Several Statistics.* https://www.ine.pt/xportal/xmain?xpgid=ine_main&xpid=INE

INE. (2021). *Indicadores de contexto demográfico e da expressão territorial da pandemia COVID-19 em Portugal: No contexto da pandemia COVID-19 a Área Metropolitana de Lisboa concentrou quase metade do emprego em teletrabalho.* https://www.ine.pt/xportal/xmain?xpid=INE&xpgid=ine_destaques&DESTAQUESdest_boui=493705905&DESTAQUESmodo=2

Instituto Nacional de Estadística. Geografía e Informática. (2021). *Censos Económicos 2019.* https://www.inegi.org.mx/default.html

International Organization for Standardization. (2019). *Security and resilience – Business continuity management systems – Requirements* (ISO 22301:2019). https://www.iso.org/obp/ui#iso:std:iso:22301:ed-2:v1:en

Internet World Stats. (2021). Retrieved from https://www.internetworldstats.com/emarketing.htm

Ionescu-Somers, A., & Tarnawa, A. (2020). *Diagnosing COVID-19 Impacts on Entrepreneurship Exploring policy remedies for recovery. Global Monitor.* Retrieved from https://www.gemconsortium.org/reports/covid-impact-report

Ishibashi, M., & Sekiya, N. (2021). Exploratory Study on the Spread of Rumors and Psychological Factors Related to COVID-19. *Japanese Journal of Risk Analysis, 31*(2), 123–132.

Ishikawa, T.(2012). Emergency mobile supply of goods in the regional retail channel: case studies and challenges. *The Journal of Marketing and Distribution, 2012*(499), 22-29.

Ishizuka, Y. (2012). *Changes in consumption trends due to the Great East Japan Earthquake. Macroeconomic Analysis Project.* The Asia Pacific Research Institute.

Islam, M. S. (2021). COVID-19 and the construction industries in Dhaka, Bangladesh. *Academic Letters, 193*(6), 3971. Advance online publication. doi:10.20935/AL3971

Islam, S., Islam, R., Mannan, F., Rahman, S., & Islam, T. (2020). COVID-19 pandemic: An analysis of the healthcare, social and economic challenges in Bangladesh. *Progress in Disaster Science, 8,* 100135. doi:10.1016/j.pdisas.2020.100135 PMID:34173450

Islam, T., Pitafi, A. H., Arya, V., Wang, Y., Akhtar, N., Mubarik, S., & Xiaobei, L. (2021). Panic buying in the COVID-19 pandemic: A multi-country examination. *Journal of Retailing and Consumer Services, 59,* 102357. doi:10.1016/j.jretconser.2020.102357

İşsever, H., İşsever, T., & Öztan, G. (2020). COVID-19 Epidemiyolojisi. *Sağlık Bilimlerinde İleri Araştırmalar Dergisi, 3,* 1–13.

Ivanov, D. (2020). Predicting the impacts of epidemic outbreaks on global supply chains: A simulation-based analysis on the coronavirus outbreak (COVID-19/SARS-CoV-2) case. *Transportation Research Part E, Logistics and Transportation Review, 136,* 1–14. doi:10.1016/j.tre.2020.101922 PMID:32288597

Ivanov, D., & Das, A. (2020). Coronavirus (COVID-19/SARS-CoV-2) and supply chain resilience: A research note. *International Journal of Integrated Supply Management, 13*(1), 90–102. doi:10.1504/IJISM.2020.107780

Jagpal, S., & Spiegel, M. (2011). Free samples, profits, and welfare: The effect of market structures and behavioral modes. *Journal of Business Research, 64*(2), 213–219. doi:10.1016/j.jbusres.2010.02.001

Jain, R., Aagja, J., & Bagdare, S. (2017). Customer experience–a review and research agenda. *Journal of Service Theory and Practice, 27*(3), 642–662. doi:10.1108/JSTP-03-2015-0064

James, E. H., Wooten, L. P., & Dushek, K. (2011). Crisis management: Informing a new leadership research agenda. *The Academy of Management Annals, 5*(1), 455–493. doi:10.5465/19416520.2011.589594

James, P., Magee, L., Scerri, A., & Steger, M. B. (2015). *Urban Sustainability in Theory and Practice: Circles of Sustainability.* Routledge.

Janssens, W., Pradhan, M., de Groot, R., Sidze, E., Donfouet, H. P. P., & Abajobir, A. (2021). The short-term economic effects of COVID-19 on low-income households in rural Kenya: An analysis using weekly financial household data. *World Development, 138,* 105280. doi:10.1016/j.worlddev.2020.105280

Jauch, L. R., & Glueck, W. F. (2004). *Strategic management and business policy* (9th ed.). McGraw-Hill.

Jin, L., Wang, C., Zhang, H., Ye, Y., Du, Z., & Zhang, Y. (2020). Evolution and Mechanism of the 'Core-Periphery' Relationship: Micro-Evidence from Cross-Regional Industrial Production Organization in a Fast-Developing Region in China. *Sustainability*, *12*(1), 189. https://doi.org/10.3390/su12010189

Johns, T., & Gratton, L. (2013). The Third Wave of Virtual Work. *Harvard Business Review*. https://hbr.org/2013/01/the-third-wave-of-virtual-work

Johnson, A., Jacovina, M., Russell, D., & Soto, C. (2016). Challenges and solutions when using technologies in the classroom. In *Adaptive Educational Technologies for Literacy Instructions.l* (pp. 13–30). Routledge. doi:10.4324/9781315647500-2

Jonathan Davidson. (2020). *Global Traffic Spikes. No Panic at the Cisco!* https://blogs.cisco.com/news/global-traffic-spikes-no-panic-at-the-cisco

Jones, M. (1997). Out of the office, out of control. *Psychology Today*, *30*(2).

Jones, P., & Comfort, D. (2020). A commentary on the COVID-19 crisis, sustainability and the. service industries. *Journal of Public Affairs*, *40*(2), 1–5. doi:10.1002/pa.2164 PMID:32837318

Jurs, P., & Kulberga, I. (2021). Pedagogical challenges in Distance Learning during COVID-19 conditions–Experience of Latvia. *World Journal on Educational Technology: Current Issues*, *13*(4), 947–955. doi:10.18844/wjet.v13i4.6278

Kafa, A., & Pashiardis, P. (2020). *Coping with the Global Pandemic COVID-19 Through the Lenses of the Cyprus Education System.* CCEAM.

Kakkos, N., Trivellas, P., & Sdrolias, L. (2015). Identifying Drivers of Purchase Intention for Private Label Brands. Preliminary Evidence from Greek Consumers. *Procedia: Social and Behavioral Sciences*, *175*(12), 522–528. doi:10.1016/j.sbspro.2015.01.1232

Kalgotra, P., Gupta, A., & Sharda, R. (2021). Pandemic information support lifecycle: Evidence from the evolution of mobile apps during COVID-19. *Journal of Business Research*, *134*, 540–559. doi:10.1016/j.jbusres.2021.06.002 PMID:34565948

Kamran, M. (2020). *Global Sustainability Overview and Role of Policy Instruments for Sustainable Tourism Management in Pakistan* [PhD Thesis]. Faculty of Geography and Tourism, Rovira I Virgili University, Tarragona, Spain.

Kansiime, M. K., Tambo, J. A., Mugambi, I., Bundi, M., Kara, A., & Owuor, C. (2021). COVID-19 implications on household income and food security in Kenya and Uganda: Findings from a rapid assessment. *World Development*, *137*, 105199. doi:10.1016/j.worlddev.2020.105199 PMID:32982018

Kaplan, R. S., & dan Norton, D. P. (2000). Balance scorecard, menerapkan strategi menjadi aksi. Terjemahan. Penerbit Erlangga.

Kaplan, R. S., & Norton, D. P. (2004). *Strategy maps: convert intangible assets into tangible outcomes.* Harvard Business School Press.

Kapsargina, S., Shmeleva, Z., & Olentsova, J. (2019). *The use of LMS-MOODLE in the implementation of a point-rating system of evaluation in the discipline "Foreign language".* 19th International Multidisciplinary Scientific GeoConference SGEM.

Karageorgos, C., Kriemadis, A., Travlos, A., & Kokaridas, D. (2021). Planning and Implementing Total Quality Management In Education: The Case Of Cyprus. *International Journal of Educational Management and Innovation*, *2*(1), 1–12. doi:10.12928/ijemi.v2i1.2627

Karalee, A., Gourévitch, M. S., Sterman, M., Quarta, L., & Close, A. S. (2020). Digital acceleration is just a dream without a new approach to tech. Boston Consulting Group.

Katrijn, G. (2012). New Products: The Antidote to Private Label Growth? *JMR, Journal of Marketing Research, 49*(3), 408–423. doi:10.1509/jmr.10.0183

Kaufmann, H. (2002). Construct 3D: An augmented reality application for mathematics and geometry education. *Proc. 10th ACM International Conference on Multimedia*, 656-657.

Kaushal, V., & Srivastava, S. (2021). Hospitality and tourism industry amid COVID-19 pandemic: Perspectives on challenges and learnings from India. *International Journal of Hospitality Management, 92*, 102707. doi:10.1016/j.ijhm.2020.102707 PMID:33024348

Kazekami, S. (2020). Mechanisms to improve labor productivity by performing telework. *Telecommunications Policy, 44*(2), 101868. doi:10.1016/j.telpol.2019.101868

Kebede, A., & Bhattacharya, S. (2022) Student Engagement Awareness Dashboard for Asynchronous E-learning Environment. ICT Systems and Sustainability, 737-749. doi:10.1007/978-981-16-5987-4_74

Kelliher, C., & Anderson, D. (2010). Doing more with less? Flexible working practices and the intensification of work. *Human Relations, 63*(1), 83–106. doi:10.1177/0018726709349199

Kemenkes, R. I., McLeod, J. R., & Schell, G. P. (2011). *Sistem informasi manajemen.* Salemba Empat.

Kementrian Kesehatan Republik Indonesia. (2020). *Peraturan menteri kesehatan republik indonesia nomor 9 tahun 2020 tentang pedoman pembatasan sosial berskala besar dalam rangka percepatan penanganan corona virus disease 2019 (covid-19).* Author.

Kemp, E., Borders, A., Anaza, N., & Johnston, W. (2018). The heart in organizational buying: Marketers' understanding of emotions and decision-making of buyers. *Journal of Business and Industrial Marketing, 33*(1), 19–28. doi:10.1108/JBIM-06-2017-0129

Kendall, K. E., & Kendall, J. E. (2011). *Systems Analysis and Design* (8th ed.). Pearson Education, Inc.

Keneally, Brimmer, & Gjaja. (2020). *To Restart Economies, Governments Need a Social Interactions Budget.* BCG.

Kentnor, H. (2015). Distance education and the evolution of online learning in the United States. *Curriculum and Teaching Dialogue, 17*(1), 21-34.

Keynes, J. M. (1936). *The General Theory of Employment? Interest and Money. The Selected Works.* Harcourt, Brace and Company.

Khalid, U., Okafor, L. E., & Burzynska, K. (2021). Does the size of the tourism sector influence the economic policy response to the COVID-19 pandemic? *Current Issues in Tourism, 24*(19), 2801–2820. doi:10.1080/13683500.2021.1874311

Khan, K. S., Mamun, M. A., Griffiths, M. D., & Ullah, I. (2020). The mental health impact of the COVID-19 pandemic across different cohorts. *International Journal of Mental Health and Addiction*, 1–7. PMID:32837440

Khan, R. T. (2014). Synthesis of Constructs for Modeling Consumers' Understanding and Perception of Eco-Labels. *Sustainability, 6*(4), 2176–2200. doi:10.3390u6042176

Khosrow-Pour, M. (2022). *Research Anthology on Business Continuity and Navigating Times of Crisis* (Vols. 1–4). Information Resources Management Association.

Kim, H. Y., & McCann, P. (2020). Japanese contributions to regional science.-+. . *Papers in Regional Science*, *99*(2), 389. doi:10.1111/pirs.12522

Kim, J., Kim, J., & Wang, Y. (2021). Uncertainty risks and strategic reaction of restaurant firms amid COVID-19: Evidence from China. *International Journal of Hospitality Management*, *92*, 1–21. doi:10.1016/j.ijhm.2020.102752 PMID:33223596

Kim, R. Y. (2020). The Impact of COVID-19 on Consumers: Preparing for Digital Sales. *IEEE Engineering Management Review*, *48*(3), 212–218. doi:10.1109/EMR.2020.2990115

Kinzig, A. P., Ryan, P., Etienne, M., Elmqvist, T., Allison, H. E., & Walker, B. H. (2006). Resilience and regime shifts: Assessing cascading effects. *Ecology and Society*, *11*(1), 20. doi:10.5751/ES-01678-110120

Kíper, M. (2018). *Dünyada Ve Türkiye'de Tıbbi Cihaz Sektörü Ve Strateji Önerisi*. TTGV – T/2013/002.

Kissler, S. M., Tedijanto, C., Goldstein, E., Grad, Y. H., & Lipsitch, M. (2020). Projecting the transmission dynamics of SARS-CoV-2 through the post-pandemic period. *Science*, *368*(6493), 860–868. doi:10.1126cience.abb5793 PMID:32291278

Kiwi México. (2021). *Acepta pagos a distancia*. https://conkiwi.com/luchacovid/tienditacerca?utm_source=tiendita_cerca&utm_medium=organico&utm_=

Klein, T., & Ratier, D. (2012). L'impact des TIC sur les conditions de travail. Centred'Analyse Stratégique, La documentation française, Rapports et documents, n° 49, 328 p.

Klein, V. B., & Todesco, J. L. (2021). COVID-19 crisis and SMEs responses : The role of digital transformation. *Knowledge and Process Management*, *28*(2), 117–133. doi:10.1002/kpm.1660

Komori, M. (2020). The toilet paper fiasco triggered by social networking sites. *Kokumin Seikatsu*, *99*, 4-5.

Kondratiev, N. D. (1984). The Long Wave Cycle (G. Daniels, Trans.). Richardson and Snyder.

Konishi, Y., Saito, T., Ishikawa, T., Kanai, H., & Igei, N. (2021). How did Japan cope with COVID-19? Big data and purchasing behavior. *Asian Economic Papers*, *20*(1), 146–167.

Kontopoulos, K. M. (1993). *The Logic of Social Structure*. Cambridge University Press. doi:10.1017/CBO9780511570971

Korhonen, J., Nuur, C., Feldmann, A., & Birkie, S. E. (2018). Circular economy as an essentially contested concept. *Journal of Cleaner Production*, *175*, 544–552. doi:10.1016/j.jclepro.2017.12.111

Korneta, P., & Rostek, K. (2021). The Impact of the SARS-CoV-19 Pandemic on the Global Gross Domestic Product. *International Journal of Environmental Research and Public Health*, *18*(10), 5246. doi:10.3390/ijerph18105246 PMID:34069182

KOSANO. (2021). *Koronavirüs (Covid-19)'a Yönelik Alınan Tüm Tedbirler*. https://kosano.org.tr/koronavirus-covid-19a-yonelik-alinan-tedbirler/

Koutselini, M. (2019). *Strengthening Institutions for Quality Assurance - Seminar on Quality Assurance of Distance Learning (E-Learning) Programs of Study*. Cyprus Ministry of Education, Culture, Sport and Youth.

Kozlenkova, I. V., Samaha, S. A., & Palmatier, R. W. (2014). Resource-based theory in marketing. *Journal of the Academy of Marketing Science*, *42*(1), 1–21. doi:10.100711747-013-0336-7

KPMG. (2020). *Cyprus Education sector - Trends, challenges and opportunities*. KPMG Limited.

Kramer, A., & Kramer, K. Z. (2020). The potential impact of the Covid-19 pandemic on occupational status, work from home, and occupational mobility. *Journal of Vocational Behavior*, *119*, 103442. doi:10.1016/j.jvb.2020.103442 PMID:32390661

Kreiner, N. C., & Ram, Y. (2020). National tourism strategies during the Covid-19 pandemic. *Annals of Tourism Research*, *103076*. Advance online publication. doi:10.1016/j.annals.2020.103076 PMID:33100431

Krishnan, Mischke, & Remes. (2018). Is the Solow paradox back? *McKinsey Quarterly*.

Krugman, P. (2007). The 'New' Economic Geography: Where Are We? In M. Fujita (Ed.), Regional Integration in East Asia: From the Viewpoint of Spatial Economics (pp. 23–34). https://doi.org/10.1057/9780230626607_2.

Krugman, P. (1996). 'Urban concentration: The role of increasing returns and transport costs. *International Regional Science Review*, *19*(1–2), 5–30. https://doi.org/10.1177/016001769601900202

Krugman, P. (1998a). Space: The final frontier. *The Journal of Economic Perspectives*, *12*(2), 161–174. https://doi.org/10.1257/jep.12.2.161

Krugman, P. (1998b). What's new about the new economic geography? *Oxford Review of Economic Policy*, *14*(2), 7–17. https://doi.org/10.1093/oxrep/14.2.7

Krugman, P. (2011). The New Economic Geography, Now Middle-aged. *Regional Studies*, *45*(1), 1–7. https://doi.org/10.1080/00343404.2011.537127

Kuhlman, T., & Farrington, J. (2010). What is Sustainability? *Sustainability*, *2*(11), 3436–3448. doi:10.3390u2113436

Kumar, N., & Steenkamp, E. M. J. B. (2007). Private Label Strategy-How to Meet the Store Brand Challenge. Harvard Business School Press.

Kumudumali, S. H. (2020). *Impact of COVID-19 on Tourism Industry: A Review*. Munich Personal RePEc Archive (MPRA). MPRA Paper No. 102834. Retrieved from: https://mpra.ub.uni-muenchen.de/102834/

Kupelian, B., & Clarry, R. (2021). *Predictions for 2021: From the Great Lockdown to the Great Rebound*. Global Economy Watch. PwC.

Kuppelwieser, V. G., & Klaus, P. (2020). Measuring customer experience quality: The EXQ scale revisited. *Journal of Business Research*, *126*(C), 624–633. doi:10.1016/j.jbusres.2020.01.042

Kurland, N. B., & Egana, T. D. (1999). Telecommuting: justice and control in the virtual organization. *Organization Science*, 500-513. https://www.jstor.org/sTable/2640368

Kushwaha, A. K., Kar, A. K., & Dwivedi, Y. K. (2021). Applications of big data in emerging management disciplines: A literature review using text mining. *International Journal of Information Management Data Insights*, *1*(2), 100017. doi:10.1016/j.jjimei.2021.100017

Kutlu, R. (2020). Yeni Koronavirüs Pandemisi ile İlgili Öğrendiklerimiz, Tanı ve Tedavisindeki Güncel Yaklaşımlar ve Türkiye'deki Durum. *Turkish Journal of Family Medicine and Primary Care*, *14*(2), 329–344. doi:10.21763/tjfmpc.729917

Kutz, M. (2016). *Introduction to e-commerce: Combining business and information technology*. bookboon.com Ltd.

Kuwayama, M., Ariu, T., Kato, M., & Sugita, J. (2013). Analysis of Consumer Attitudes, Values, and Behavior after the Great East Japan Earthquake from a CSR Perspective. *Journal of Japan Society for Business Ethics Study*, *20*, 129–146.

Kvale, S. (2007) Doing Interviews. London: Sage.

Kyodo News. (2022). *Japan formally decides to end COVID-19 quasi-emergency next week*. https://english.kyodonews.net/news/2022/03/bc188041dee7-panel-oks-japan-ending-covid-19-quasi-emergency-next-week.html

L'Hoest, R. (2001). The European dimension of the digital economy. *Inter Economics*, *36*(1), 44–50. doi:10.1007/BF02927909

Lacanilao Arnould, P. (2018). *What is Sustainable Tourism & Why is it Important?* Retrieved from https://visit.org/blog/en/what-is-sustainable-tourism/#:~:text=Definition%20of%20Sustainable%20Tourism%20Sustainable%20tourism%20is%20a,Unfortunately,%20most%20people%20do%20not%20travel%20this%20way

Lai, I. K. W., & Wong, J. W. C. (2020). Comparing crisis management practices in the hotel industry between initial and pandemic stages of COVID-19. *International Journal of Contemporary Hospitality Management*, *32*(10), 3135–3156. doi:10.1108/IJCHM-04-2020-0325

Laloux, F. (2019). *Reinventing Organizations*. Diatenio.

Lal, R., Brevik, E. C., Dawson, L., Field, D., Glaser, B., Hartemink, A. E., Hatano, R., Lascelles, B., Monger, C., Scholten, T., Singh, B. R., Spiegel, H., Terribile, F., Basile, A., Zhang, Y., Horn, R., Kosaki, T., & Sánchez, L. B. R. (2020). Managing soils for recovering from the COVID-19 pandemic. *Soil Systems*, *4*(3), 46. doi:10.3390oilsystems4030046

Lampel, J., Shamsie, J., & Shapira, Z. (2009). Experiencing the improbable: Rare events and organizational learning. *Organization Science*, *20*(5), 835–845. doi:10.1287/orsc.1090.0479

Lampikoski, T., Westerlund, M., Rajala, R., & Möller, K. (2014). Green innovation games: Value-creation strategies for corporate sustainability. *California Management Review*, *57*(1), 88–116. doi:10.1525/cmr.2014.57.1.88

Lapointe, D. (2020). Reconnecting tourism after COVID-19: The paradox of alterity in tourism areas. *Tourism Geographies*, *22*(3), 633–638. doi:10.1080/14616688.2020.1762115

Larson, P., Carr, P., & Dhariwal, K. (2005). SCM Involving Small Versus Large Suppliers: Relational Exchange and Electronic Communication Media. *The Journal of Supply Chain Management*, *41*(1), 18–29. doi:10.1111/j.1745-493X.2005.tb00181.x

LaSalle, D., & Britton, T. A. (2003). *Priceless: Turning ordinary products into extraordinary experiences*. Harvard Business School Press.

Laudon, K. C., & Laudon, J. P. (2019). *Management Information Systems Managing the Digital Firm* (16th ed.). Pearson Education Limited.

Lay, C., Allman, B., Cutri, R., & Kimmons, R. (2020) Examining a Decade of Research in Online Teacher Professional Development. Frontiers in Education, 5, 167.

Lazaretti, B. (2020). *94% das firmas aprovam home office, mas 70% vão encerrar ou manter em parte*. https://economia.uol.com.br/noticias/redacao/2020/07/28/94-das-empresas-aprovam-home-office-mas-75-nao-o-manterao-apos-pandemia.htm

Lazarus, R. S., & Folkman, S. (1984). *Stress, appraisal, and coping*. Springer publishing company.

Leap by McKinsey. (2021). *2021 global report: The state of new-business building*. McKinsey & Co.

Leap by McKinsey. (2021). *Global Report: The state of new-business building*. McKinsey & Co.

Lee, C. D., & Daiute, C. (2019). Introduction to Developmental Digital Technologies in Human History, Culture, and Well-Being. *Human Development*, *62*(1-2), 5–13. doi:10.1159/000496072

Leeflang, P. S. H., Verhoef, P. C., Dahlström, P., & Freundt, T. (2014). Challenges and solutions for marketing in a digital era. *European Management Journal*, *32*(1), 1–12. doi:10.1016/j.emj.2013.12.001

Lee, S. M., & Trimi, S. (2021). Convergence Innovation in the Digital Age and in the COVID-19 Pandemic Crisis. *Journal of Business Research*, *123*, 14–22. doi:10.1016/j.jbusres.2020.09.041 PMID:33012897

Lee, W.-I., Cheng, S.-Y., & Shih, Y.-T. (2010). Effects among product attributes, involvement, word-of-mouth, and purchase intention in online shopping. *Asia Pacific Management Review*, *22*(4), 223–229. doi:10.1016/j.apmrv.2017.07.007

Lemon, K. N., & Verhoef, P. C. (2016). Understanding customer experience throughout the customer journey. *Journal of Marketing*, *80*(6), 69–96. doi:10.1509/jm.15.0420

Lerner, J., & Keltner, D. (2001). Fear, anger, and risk. *Journal of Personality and Social Psychology*, *81*(1), 146–159. doi:10.1037/0022-3514.81.1.146 PMID:11474720

Letaifa, S.B., Gratacap, A., & Isckía, T. (2013). Understanding Business Ecosystems: How Firms Succeed in the New World of Convergence. *De Boeck*, 22-29.

Levasseur, R. E. (2012, April). People skills: Leading virtual teams - a change management perspective. *Interfaces*, *42*(2), 213–216. doi:10.1287/inte.1120.0634

Levin, B. (2000). Putting students at the centre in education reform. *Journal of Educational Change*, *1*(2), 155–172. doi:10.1023/A:1010024225888

Levitt, B., & March, J. G. (1988). Organizational learning. *Annual Review of Sociology*, *14*(1), 319–340. doi:10.1146/annurev.so.14.080188.001535

Levy Yeyati, E., & Filippini, F. (2021). *Social and economic impact of COVID-19*. Brookings Global Working Paper #158 Global Economy and Development program at Brookings. Retrieved from https://www.brookings.edu/research/social-and-economic-impact-of-covid-19/

Lian, F., & … . (2015). Monetary and Image Influences on the Purchase Decision of Private Label Products in Malaysia. *Journal of Advanced Management Science*, *3*(4), 312–318.

Liguori, E., & Winkler, C. (2020). From offline to online: Challenges and opportunities for entrepreneurship education following the COVID-19 pandemic. *Sage (Atlanta, Ga.)*, *3*(4), 346–351. doi:10.1177/2515127420916738

Li, H., Cai, H., & Chakraborty, S. (2019). Market Access, Labor Mobility, and the Wage Skill Premium: New Evidence from Chinese Cities. *Open Economies Review*, *30*(5), 947–973. https://doi.org/10.1007/s11079-019-09546-6

Lima, M. A., & Soares, A. d. (May 2014). O secretário executivo e a tecnologia da informação: um estudo sobre a utilização de recursos tecnológicos pelos profissionais da cidade de Belém/PA. *Revista de Gestão e Secretariado*, *5*(2), 138-157. https://www.revistagesec.org.br/secretariado/article/view/254

Lindsey-Mullikin, J., & Borin, N. (2017). Why strategy is key for successful social media sales. *Business Horizons*, *60*(4), 473–482. doi:10.1016/j.bushor.2017.03.005

Lin, W., Shao, Y., Li, G., Guo, Y., & Zhan, X. (2021). The psychological implications of COVID-19 on employee job insecurity and its consequences: The mitigating role of organization adaptive practices. *The Journal of Applied Psychology*, *106*(3), 317–329. doi:10.1037/apl0000896 PMID:33871269

Lin, X., Featherman, M., Brooks, S. L., & Hajli, N. (2018). Exploring gender differences in online consumer purchase decision making: An online product presentation perspective. *Information Systems Frontiers*, *21*(5), 1187–1201. doi:10.100710796-018-9831-1

Lin, Y., & Wu, L. Y. (2014). Exploring the role of dynamic capabilities in firm performance under the resource-based view framework. *Journal of Business Research*, *67*(3), 407–413. doi:10.1016/j.jbusres.2012.12.019

Liu, J. J., Bao, Y., Huang, X., Shi, J., & Lu, L. (2020). Mental health considerations for children quarantined because of COVID-19. *The Lancet Child & Adolescent Health*, *4*, 347–349. doi:10.1016/S2352-4642(20)30096

Lonergan, E., & Blyth, M. (2020). *Angrynomics*. Columbia University Press. doi:10.2307/j.ctv13840ch

Lopes, A. S., Sargento, A., & Carreira, P. (2021). Vulnerability to COVID-19 unemployment in the Portuguese tourism and hospitality industry. *International Journal of Contemporary Hospitality Management*, *33*(5), 1850–1869. https://doi.org/10.1108/IJCHM-11-2020-1345

Lorencowicz, E., Baptista, F., Silva, L. L., & Marques da Silva, J. R. (2014). *Sustainable agriculture–Poland and Portugal*. Academic Press.

Lotka, A. J. (1920). Analytical note on certain rhythmic relations in organic systems. *Proceedings of the National Academy of Sciences of the United States of America*, *6*(7), 410–415. doi:10.1073/pnas.6.7.410 PMID:16576509

Lotka, A. J. (1925). *Elements of Physical Biology*. Williams & Wilkins.

Lunde, L. K., Fløvik, L., Christensen, J. O., Johannessen, H. A., Finne, L. B., Jørgensen, I. L., ... Vleeshouwers, J. (2022). The relationship between telework from home and employee health: A systematic review. *BMC Public Health*, *22*(1), 1–14. PMID:34983455

Madaleno, R., Wilson, H., & Palmer, R. (2007). Determinants of Customer Satisfaction in a Multi-Channel B2B Environment. *Total Quality Management & Business Excellence*, *18*(8), 915–925. doi:10.1080/14783360701350938

Maechler, N., Sahni, S., & van Ooostrun, M. (2016). *Improving the business-to-business customer experience.* https://www.mckinsey.com/business-functions/marketing-and-sales/our-insights/improving-the-business-to-business-customer-experience

Mahlangu, V. (2018). *The good, the bad, and the ugly of distance learning in higher education*. Trends in E-learning. doi:10.5772/intechopen.75702

Malík, A., Masood, T., & Kousar, R. (2020). Reconfiguring and ramping-up ventilator production in the face of COVID-19: Can robots help? *Journal of Manufacturing Systems*, *15*, 1–26. PMID:33082617

Malone, T. W. (2018). *Superminds. The Surprising Power of People and Computers Thinking Together*. Little, Brown Spark.

Malone, T. W. (2018). *Superminds. The Surprising Power of People and Computers Thinking Together*. Oneworld Publications.

Mandal, S. C., Boidya, P., Haque, M. I. M., Hossain, A., Shams, Z., & Mamun, A. A. (2021). The impact of the COVID-19 pandemic on fish consumption and household food security in Dhaka city, Bangladesh. *Global Food Security*, *29*, 100526. doi:10.1016/j.gfs.2021.100526 PMID:35155095

Mandviwalla, M., & Flanagan, R. (2021). Small business digital transformation in the context of the pandemic. *European Journal of Information Systems*, *30*(4), 359–375. doi:10.1080/0960085X.2021.1891004

Mann, S., & Holdsworth, L. (2003). The psychological impact of teleworking: Stress, emotions and health. *New Technology, Work and Employment*, *18*(3), 196–211. doi:10.1111/1468-005X.00121

Manyika, J., Birshan, M., Smit, S., Woetzel, J., Russell, K., Purcell, L., & Ramaswamy, S. (2021). *Companies in the 21st century. A new look at how corporations impact the economy and households*. Discussion paper. McKinsey Global Institute. Retrieved from: www.mckinsey.com/mgi

Manzur, E., Olavarrieta, S., Hidalgo, P., Farías, P., & Uribe, R. (2011). Store brand and national brand promotion attitudes antecedents. *Journal of Business Research, 64*(3), 286–291. doi:10.1016/j.jbusres.2009.11.014

Marinko, Š., Domingo, R. S., & Małgorzata, P. (2021). Impact of COVID-19 on the travel and tourism industry. *Technological Forecasting and Social Change, 163*, 1–14. doi:10.1016/j.techfore.2020.120469

Markezine. (2020). https://markezine.jp/article/detail/34347

Marshall, C., & Rossman, G. B. (2016). Designing Qualitative Research. *Sage (Atlanta, Ga.)*.

Martarello, R. de A., & Ferro, D. (2021). Entrepreneurship and innovation in informal productive enterprises: Development of process innovation in a floral arrangement company. *Iberoamerican Journal of Entrepreneurship and Small Business, 11*(1). doi:10.14211/ibjesb.e1985

Martin, S., & Trang, M. (2018). Creating Personalized Learning Using Aggregated Data from Students' Online Conversational Interactions in Customized Groups. Learning Engineering for Online Education, 144-165.

Martin, A., Markhvida, M., Hallegatte, S., & Walsh, B. (2020). Socio-economic impacts of COVID-19 on household consumption and poverty. *Economics of Disasters and Climate Change, 4*(3), 453–479. doi:10.100741885-020-00070-3 PMID:32838120

Martinho, V. (2021). *Economics of Tourism in Portugal: Impacts of the COVID-19 Pandemic*. Springer International Publishing. doi:10.1007/978-3-030-65200-5

Marx, K. (1995). *Capital: A New Abridgement*. Oxford University Press.

Matarazzo, M., Penco, L., Profumo, G., & Quaglia, R. (2021). Digital transformation and customer value creation in Made in Italy SMEs : A dynamic capabilities perspective. *Journal of Business Research, 123*(February), 642–656. doi:10.1016/j.jbusres.2020.10.033

Mattar, F. N. (2012). *Pesquisa de Marketing: edição compacta*. Atlas.

Mattila, M., Yrjölä, M., & Hautamäki, P. (2021). Digital transformation of business-to-business sales: What needs to be unlearned? *Journal of Personal Selling & Sales Management, 41*(2), 113–129. doi:10.1080/08853134.2021.1916396

Maymina, E., Puzynya, T., & Egozaryan, V. (2018). Digital economy in education: Perspectives and development perspectives. *Revista ESPACIOS, 39*(38), 30.

Mazzucato, M. (2013). *The Entrepreneurial State: Debunking Public vs. Private Sector Myths*. Anthem Press.

McChesney, I.-G. (1991). *The Brundtland Report and sustainable development in New Zealand. Information Paper, 25*. Centre for Resource Management Lincoln University and University of Canterbury.

McColl-Kennedy, J., Mohamed Zaki, M., Lemon, K. N., Urmetzer, F., & Neely, A. (2019). Gaining customer experience insights that matter. *Journal of Service Research, 22*(1), 8–26. doi:10.1177/1094670518812182

McConnell, M., & Schaninger, B. (2019, Jan.). *Are we long—or short—on talent? McKinsey Quarterly.*

McGann, M., Murphy, M. P., & Whelan, N. (2020). Workfare redux? Pandemic unemployment, labour activation and the lessons of post-crisis welfare reform in Ireland. *The International Journal of Sociology and Social Policy, 40*(9/10), 963–978. doi:10.1108/IJSSP-07-2020-0343

McIntyre, D. P., Srinivasan, A., & Chintakananda, A. (2021). The persistence of platforms: The role of network, platform, and complementor attributes. *Long Range Planning, 54*(5), 101987. doi:10.1016/j.lrp.2020.101987

McKee, M., & Stuckler, D. (2020). If the world fails to protect the economy, COVID-19 will damage health not just now but also in the future. *Nature Medicine, 26*(5), 640–642. doi:10.103841591-020-0863-y PMID:32273610

McKercher, B. (1993). The unrecognized threat to tourism: Can tourism survive 'sustainability'? *Tourism Management, 14*(2), 131–136. doi:10.1016/0261-5177(93)90046-N

McKinsey & Co. (2020). *The State of Fashion 2021 BOF McKinsey & Co.* https://www.mckinsey.com/industries/retail/our-insights/state-of-fashion

McKinsey & Company. (2020). *The path to the next normal.* https://www.mckinsey.com/~/media/McKinsey/Featured%20Insights/Navigating%20the%20coronavirus%20crisis%20collected%20works/Path-to-the-next-normal-collection.pdf

Means, B., Bakia, M., & Murphy, R. (2014). *What research tells us about where, when and how.* Routledge. doi:10.4324/9780203095959

Mei, M. Q. (2014). Learning to innovate: The role of ambidexterity, standard, and decision process. Frederiksberg: Copenhagen Business School (CBS).

Mekni, M., & Lemieux, A. (2014). Augmented reality: Applications, challenges, and future trends. *Applied Computational Science Proceedings of the 13th International Conference on Applied Computer and Applied Computational Science*, 23-25.

Melanthiou, Y., Thrassou, A., & Vrontis, D. (2017). A value-based transcription of student choices into higher education branding practices. *Global Business and Economics Review, 19*(2), 121–136. doi:10.1504/GBER.2017.082574

Melenotte, C., Silvin, A., Goubet, A.-G., Lahmar, I., Dubuisson, A., Zumla, A., Raoult, D., Merad, M., Gachot, B., Henon, C., Solary, E., Fontenay, M., Andre, F., Maeurer, M., Ippolito, G., Piacentini, M., Wang, F.-S., Ginhoux, F., Marabelle, A., … Zitvogel, L. (2020). Immune responses during COVID-19 infection. *Oncoimmunology, 9*(1), 1807836. doi:10.1080/2162402X.2020.1807836

Meletiou-Mavrotheris, M., Mavrou, K., & Rebelo, P. V. (2021). The Role of Learning and Communication Technologies in Online Courses' Design and Delivery: A Cross-National Study of Faculty Perceptions and Practices. *Frontiers in Education, 11*, 1–17. doi:10.3389/feduc.2021.558676

Mello, A. (1999). *Teletrabalho (telework): o trabalho em qualquer lugar e em qualquer hora.* Qualitymark.

Mendonça, M. (2010). *A inclusão dos home offices no setor residencial no município de São Paulo.* Tese de Doutorado: Curso de Tecnologia da Arquitetura, Faculdade de Arquitetura e Urbanismo, Universidade de São Paulo. São Paulo. Accessed Sep. 2021, available at https://www.teses.usp.br/teses/disponiveis/16/16132/tde-25112010-145910/pt-br.php

Mendy, Stewart, & VanAkin. (2020). *A leader's guide: Communicating with teams, stakeholders, and communities during COVID-19. Organization Practice.* McKinsey & Company.

Mendy, A., Stewart, M. L., & VanAkin, K. (2020). *A leader's guide: Communicating with teams, stakeholders, and communities during COVID-19. April. In Organization Practice.* McKinsey & Company.

Mercado Solidario. (2021). *Mercado Solidario.* https://mercadosolidario.gob.mx/

Merchant, K. A., & der Stede, W. A. (2017). *Management control systems performance measurement, evaluation, and incentives.* Pearson.

Meyer, S. (2020). *Understanding the Covid-19 effect on online shopping behaviour.* BigCommerce. https://www.bigcommerce.com/blog/covid-19 ecommerce/#conclusion

Meyer, A. D., Brooks, G. R., & Goes, J. B. (1990). Environmental jolts and industry revolutions: Organizational responses to discontinuous change. *Strategic Management Journal*, 93–110.

Mheidle, R. A. (2020). *The impact of hiking on sustainable development in Moukhtara*. A Graduation Project Submitted in partial fulfillment of the requirements for the License Degree in Tourism Management, presented at the Lebanese University, Beirut.

Michael, H. (2020). *Dampak coronavirus terhadap ekonomi global. Bank indonesia.* https://www.bi.go.id/id/publikasi/ekonomi-keuangan-kerjasama-

Milanovic, B. (2019). Capitalism, Alone: The Future of the System that Rules the World. Harvard University Press. doi:10.4159/9780674242852

Miles, M. B., Huberman, A. M., & Saldaña, J. (2014). *Qualitative Data Analysis: A Methods Sourcebook*. Sage.

Miller, D., & Chen, M.-J. (1994). Sources and consequences of competitive inertia: A study of the US airline industry. *Administrative Science Quarterly*, *39*(1), 1–23. doi:10.2307/2393492

Ministério da Educação (ME). (2020). *Orientações para a Recuperação e Consolidação das Aprendizagens ao Longo do Ano Letivo de 2020/2021*. Ministério da Educação.

Ministry of Commerce. (2021). *Covid-19 Trade Precautions*. https://covid19.ticaret.gov.tr/

Ministry of Economy, Trade and Industry. (2020). https://www.meti.go.jp/covid-19/mask.html

Ministry of Education, Culture, Sports and Youth. (2020). *Annual Report 2020*. Republic of Cyprus.

Ministry of Education, Culture, Sports, and Youth. (2022). *Higher Education Statistics*. Republic of Cyprus.

Ministry of Family and Social Services. (2021). https://www.ailevecalisma.gov.tr/tr-tr/haberler/bakan-selcuk-sosyal-koruma-kalkani-kapsaminda-yaptigimiz-yardimlarin-tutari-45-5-milyar-liraya-yaklasti/

Ministry of Health. (2021). *COVID-19 Bilgilendirme Platformu*. https://covid19.saglik.gov.tr/

Ministry of Internal Affairs and Communications. (2020). *Report on Information Distribution Survey on New Coronavirus Infections*. https://www.soumu.go.jp/menu_news/s-news/01kiban18_01000082.html

Minsky, H. P. (2008). *Stabilizing an Unstable Economy*. McGraw-Hill.

Mises. (1998). *Human Action: A Treatise on Economics*. Yale University Press.

Miyaki, Y. (2011). Growing awareness of "ethical consumption" in the wake of the earthquake. *Life Design Report*, (200), 38-40.

Miyaki, Y. (2020). The Corona Disaster and Attitudes toward Sustainable Consumption Behavior: From the New Coronavirus Awareness Survey and the Post-Earthquake Survey. *Life Design Report 2020*.

Miyazaki, A. D., Grewal, D., & Goodstein, R. C. (2005). The effect of multiple extrinsic cues on quality perceptions: A matter of consistency. *The Journal of Consumer Research*, *32*(1), 146–153. doi:10.1086/429606

Miyazu, K. (2022) Corporate Marketing IT Strategy with Consideration of Consumer Sentiment During COVID-19 Pandemic. *St. Andrew's University Economic and Business Review*, *63*(3).

Mofijur, M., Rizwanul Fattah, I. M., Asraful Alam, M., Saiful Islam, A. B. M., Chyuan Ong, H., Ashrafur Rahman, S. M., Najafi, G., Ahmed, S. F., Uddin Alhaz, M., & Mahliaa, T. M. I. (2020). Impact of COVID-19 on the social, economic, environmental and energy domains: Lessons learnt from a global pandemic. *Sustain Prod Consum.*, *26*, 343–359. doi:10.1016/j.spc.2020.10.016 PMID:33072833

Mohmmed, A. O., Khidhir, B. A., Nazeer, A., & Vijayan, V. J. (2020). Emergency remote teaching during Coronavirus pandemic: The current trend and future directive at Middle East College Oman. *Innovative Infrastructure Solutions*, *5*(3), 1–11. doi:10.100741062-020-00326-7

Mokyr, J. (2005). The intellectual origins of modern economic growth. *Journal of Economic History, 65*(2), 285 – 351.

Monitor, I.L.O. (2020). *COVID-19 and the world of work. Updated estimates and analysis.* ILO.

Moorthy, V., Restrepo, A. M. H., Preziosi, M. P., & Swaminathan, S. (2020). Data sharing for novel coronavirus (COVID-19). *Bulletin of the World Health Organization*, *98*(3), 150. doi:10.2471/BLT.20.251561 PMID:32132744

Morales, J. R. (2020). Perpetuating regional asymmetries through income transfers. *Spatial Economic Analysis*, *0*(0), 1–24. https://doi.org/10.1080/17421772.2020.1714705

Moral-Munoz, J. A., López-Herrera, A. G., Herrera-Viedma, E., & Cobo, M. J. (2019). Science mapping analysis software tools: A review. In Springer handbook of science and technology indicators. Springer. doi:10.1007/978-3-030-02511-3_7

Mulyadi, & Setyawan, J. (2000). *Sistem perencanaan dan pengenalian manajemen* (2nd ed.). Jakarta: Salemba Empat.

Mulyadi. (2001). *Balanced scorecard alat manajemen kontemporer untuk memperlipatgandakan kinerja keuangan perusahaan.* Jakarta: Salemba Empat.

Munyar, V. (2020a). Yerli Ventilatörün Kolektif Öyküsü. *Dünya Gazetesi.*

Munyar, V. (2020b). O Solunum Cihazının Seri Üretimi İçin Milli Seferberlik Ruhu Oluştu. *Dünya Gazetesi.*

Murray, A., Skene, K., & Haynes, K. (2017). The circular economy: An interdisciplinary exploration of the concept and application in a global context. *Journal of Business Ethics*, *140*(3), 369–380. doi:10.100710551-015-2693-2

Nadkarni, S., & Prügl, R. (2021). Digital transformation: A review, synthesis and opportunities for future research. *Management Review Quarterly*, *71*(2), 233–341. doi:10.100711301-020-00185-7

Nagel, L. (2020). The influence of the COVID-19 pandemic on the digital transformation of work. *The International Journal of Sociology and Social Policy*, *40*(9/10), 861–875. doi:10.1108/IJSSP-07-2020-0323

Nakajima,O. (2020). Masks depleted and skyrocketing due to spread of new corona infection. *The Journal of New Product Liability*, (5), 85-92.

National Institute of Infectious Diseases. (2020). *Field Briefing: Diamond Princess COVID-19 Cases.* https://www.niid.go.jp/niid/en/2019-ncov-e/9407-covid-dp-fe-01.html(accessed 21 March 2022,)

Nguyen, H., & Dar Santos, B. (2020). *Acute Impact of COVID-19 on the Global Ventilator Industry.* BlackOre Research Inc. http://www.blackore.com/sites/default/files/researchpdfs/blackore_hoovest_analytics__ventilator_industry_analysis_2020-11-22.pdf

Nguyen, V.-H., Sukunesan, S., & Huynh, M. (2021). Analyzing Australian SME Instagram Engagement via Web Scraping. *Pacific Asia Journal of the Association for Information Systems*, *13*(2), 11–43. doi:10.17705/1pais.13202

Nihon Housou Kyoukai. (2020, Jan. 16). *NHK News Web.* Author.

Nikkei, M. J. (2020b). Tokyu Store, DX, and Synops are collaborating to make the store a test site for ordering and and reduce the burden of back-office. Academic Press.

Nikkei, M.J. (2020a). *The goal is not to be unmanned, but to add value by saving supermarkets and people.* Academic Press.

Nikkei. (2020). https://www.nikkei.com/article/DGXMZO56173900Y0A220C2EA5000/

Niles, M. T., Bertmann, F., Belarmino, E. H., Wentworth, T., Biehl, E., & Neff, R. (2020). The early food insecurity impacts of COVID-19. *Nutrients*, *12*(7), 2096. doi:10.3390/nu12072096 PMID:32679788

Nishinippon. (2020). *APA Hotel to accept infected patients.* https://www.nishinippon.co.jp/item/o/597779/

Nisiforou, E. A., Kosmas, P., & Vrasidas, C. (2021). Emergency remote teaching during Covid-19 pandemic: Lessons learned from Cyprus. *Educational Media International*, *58*(2), 1–7. doi:10.1080/09523987.2021.1930484

Noguchi, H., Sano, S., Kitakaze, Y., & Aoki, Y. (2012). One Year After 3.11, Exploring Changes in Consumer Sentiment: From Survey Data. *Marketing Journal*, *31*(4), 4–21.

Nor Asshidin, N. H., Abidin, N., & Borhan, H. B. (2016). Consumer Attitude and Uniqueness towards International Products. *Procedia Economics and Finance*, *35*, 632–638. doi:10.1016/S2212-5671(16)00077-0

Norberg, J., & Cumming, G. S. (2006). *Complexity Theory for a Sustainable Future.* Columbia University Press.

North, D. (1997). *The process of economic change.* Research Paper. 128. World Institute for Development Economics Research.

North, D. (2005). *Understanding the Process of Economic Change.* Princeton University Press.

North, D. C. (1981). *Structure and Change in Economic History.* W. W. Norton & Co.

North, D. C. (1990). *Institutions, Institutional Change and Economic Performance.* Cambridge University Press. doi:10.1017/CBO9780511808678

Novacek, Lee, & Krentz. (2021). *It's time to reimagine diversity, equity, and inclusion.* Boston Consulting Group.

Noyes, J. A., Welch, P. M., Johnson, J. W., & Carbonneau, K. J. (2020). A systematic review of digital badges in health care education. *Medical Education*, *54*(7), 600–615.

Nurul, A. H. (2016). The Relationship of Attitude, Subjective Norm and Website Usability on Consumer Intention to Purchase Online: An Evidence of Malaysian Youth. *Procedia Economics and Finance*, *35*, 493–502. doi:10.1016/S2212-5671(16)00061-7

O'Dwyer, B. (2004). Qualitative data analysis: illuminating a process for transforming a 'messy' but 'attractive' 'nuisance. In *The real life guide to accounting research* (pp. 391–407). Elsevier. doi:10.1016/B978-008043972-3/50025-6

Obeng, K., & Ugboro, I. (2008). Effective strategic planning in public transit systems. *Transportation Research*, *44*(3), 420–439. doi:10.1016/j.tre.2006.10.008

Ochi, Y.(2021) Tourism and Economy Recovery Initiatives-Go To Travel Campaign Project in Japan. *Journal of Leisure and Tourism*, (8), 75-84.

Ochoa, C. (2021). *Más de 100 mil tienditas han logrado reabrir este año, pero con otros giros: Anpec.* https://www.milenio.com/negocios/tienditas-logran-reabrir-2021-giros-anpec

OECD iLibrary. (2021). *The Digital Transformation of SMEs.* https://www.oecd-ilibrary.org/sites/bdb9256a-en/index.html?itemId=/content/publication/bdb9256a-en

OECD. (2019). *Trends Shaping Education 2019*. OECD Publishing.

OECD. (2019). *Unpacking E-commerce: Business models, trends and policies*. OECD Publishing. Retrieved from https://www.oecd-ilibrary.org/science-and-technology/unpacking-e-commerce_23561431-en

OECD. (2020a). *Rebuilding tourism for the future: COVID-19 policy responses and recovery*. Retrieved from OECD: https://www.oecd.org/coronavirus/policy-responses/rebuilding-tourism-for-the-future-covid-19-policy-responses-and-recovery-bced9859/

OECD. (2020b). *OECD Policy Responses to Coronavirus (COVID-19): Tourism Policy Responses to the coronavirus (COVID-19)*. Retrieved from: https://www.oecd.org/coronavirus/policy-responses/tourism-policy-responses-to-the-coronavirus-covid-19-6466aa20/

Office of the Law Commissioner. (2014). *The Institutions of Tertiary Education Laws 1996 To 2013*. Printing Office of The Republic of Cyprus.

Okamoto, G. (2020). Knightmare uncertainty. *IMF Finance & Development, 57*(3).

Okamoto, G. (2020). Knightmare Uncertainty. *IMF Finance & Development, 57*(3).

Oliveira, F. R. D., Santos, R. F. D., França, S. L. B., & Rangel, L. A. D. (2020). Strategies and challenges for the circular economy: A case study in Portugal and a panorama for Brazil. *Brazilian Archives of Biology and Technology, 63*, 63. doi:10.1590/1678-4324-2020180646

Omar, N. A., Nazri, M. A., Ali, M. H., & Alam, S. S. (2021). The panic buying behavior of consumers during the COVID-19 pandemic: Examining the influences of uncertainty, perceptions of severity, perceptions of scarcity, and anxiety. *Journal of Retailing and Consumer Services, 62*, 102600. doi:10.1016/j.jretconser.2021.102600

OMS, Organização Mundial da Saúde. (2020). *OMS declara emergência de saúde pública de importância internacional por surto de novo coronavírus*. Fonte: OPAS Organização Pan-Americana de Saúde: https://www.paho.org/pt/news/30-1-2020-who-declares-public-health-emergency-novel-coronavirus

Ooi, J., & Yazdanifard, R. (2015). The Review of the Effectivity of the Augmented Reality Experiential Marketing Tool in Customer Engagement. *Global Journal of Management and Business Research: EMarketing, 15*(8), 12–17.

Orlosky, J., Kiyokawa, K., & Takemura, H. (2017). Virtual and Augmented Reality on the 5G highway. *Journal of Information Processing, 25*(0), 133–141. doi:10.2197/ipsjjip.25.133

Otache, I. (2020). The effects of the Covid-19 Pandemic on the Nigeria's economy and possible coping strategies. *Asian Journal of Social Sciences and Management Studies, 7*(3), 173–179. doi:10.20448/journal.500.2020.73.173.179

Otubanjo, O. (2013). A Discourse Approach to Brand Leadership Management. *International Journal of Marketing Studies, 5*(2), 131–137. doi:10.5539/ijms.v5n2p131

Ozcariz-Fermoselle, M. V., de Vega-Luttmann, G., de Jesús Lugo-Monter, F., Galhano, C., & Arce-Cervantes, O. (2019). Promoting Circular Economy Through Sustainable Agriculture in Hidalgo: Recycling of Agro-Industrial Waste in Production of High Nutritional Native Mushrooms. In *Climate Change-Resilient Agriculture and Agroforestry* (pp. 455–469). Springer. doi:10.1007/978-3-319-75004-0_26

Pakhomova, T. O., Komova, O. S., Belia, V. V., Yivzhenko, Y. V., & Demidko, E. V. (2021). Transformation of the pedagogical process in higher education during the quarantine. *Linguistics and Culture Review, 5*(S2), 215–230. doi:10.21744/lingcure.v5nS2.1341

Palahí, M., Pantsar, M., Costanza, R., Kubiszewski, I., Potočnik, J., Stuchtey, M., ... Dixson-Declève, S. (2020). *Investing in Nature to Transform the Post COVID-19*. Academic Press.

Pallares, M. A. (2013). *Tienditas, una mina para 8 empresas*. https://www.elfinanciero.com.mx/archivo/tienditas-una-mina-para-empresas-1/

Palvia, S., Aeron, P., Gupta, P., Mahapatra, D., Parida, R., Rosner, R., & Sindhi, S. (2018). Online education: Worldwide status, challenges, trends, and implications. *Journal of Global Information Technology Management, 21*(4), 233–241. doi:10.1080/1097198X.2018.1542262

Pamboukian, S., & Kanaane, R. (2020). Práticas docentes na educação superior tecnológica: A formação de competências demandadas dos profissionais na economia digital. *Revista Educação -. UNG-Ser, 15*(2), 32–47.

Pandey, S. K., & Mookerjee, A. (2018). Assessing the role of emotions in B2B decision making: An exploratory study. *Journal of Indian Business Research, 10*(2), 170–192. doi:10.1108/JIBR-10-2017-0171

Pang, J., Keh, H. T., & Peng, S. (2009). Effects of advertising strategy on consumer-brand relationships: A brand love perspective. *Frontiers of Business Research in China, 3*(4), 599–620. doi:10.100711782-009-0029-8

Pantano, E., & Rocco, S. (2012). Modeling innovative points of sales through virtual and immersive technologies. *Journal of Retailing and Consumer Services, 19*(3), 279–286. doi:10.1016/j.jretconser.2012.02.002

Parisi, C., & Bekier, J. (2022). Assessing and managing the impact of COVID-19: A study of six European cities participating in a circular economy project. *Accounting, Auditing & Accountability Journal, 35*(1), 97–107. doi:10.1108/AAAJ-08-2020-4837

Park, S., Choi, G. J., & Ko, H. (2020). Information technology-based tracing strategy in response to COVID-19 in South Korea-privacy controversies. *Journal of the American Medical Association, 323*(21), 2129–2130. doi:10.1001/jama.2020.6602 PMID:32324202

Parmenter, D. (2020). *Key performance indicators : developing, implementing, and using winning KPIs*. Wiley.

Parvatíyar, A., & Sheth, J. N. (1995). The Evolution of Relationship Marketing. *International Business Review, 4*(4), 397–418. doi:10.1016/0969-5931(95)00018-6

Pascariu, G. C. (2009). The Relationship Between Tourism And Sustainable Development In The European Context. *Annals of Faculty of Economics, University of Oradea, Faculty of Economics, 1*(1), 293–298.

Pato, M. L. (2020). Short food supply chains—A growing movement. The case study of the Viseu Dao Lafoes Region. *Open Agriculture, 5*(1), 806–816. https://doi.org/10.1515/opag-2020-0077

Patton, M. (2014). *Qualitative Research & Evaluation Methods*. Sage.

Paul, A., Nath, T. K., Mahanta, J., Sultana, N. N., Kayes, A. I., Noon, S. J., Jabed, M. A., Podder, S., & Paul, S. (2021). Psychological and livelihood impacts of COVID-19 on Bangladeshi lower income people. *Asia-Pacific Journal of Public Health, 33*(1), 100–108. doi:10.1177/1010539520977304 PMID:33289393

Paul, S. K., & Chowdhury, P. (2021). A production recovery plan in manufacturing supply chains for a high-demand item during COVID-19. *International Journal of Physical Distribution & Logistics Management, 51*(2), 104–125. doi:10.1108/IJPDLM-04-2020-0127

Pauwelyn, J. (2020). Export Restrictions in Times of Pandemic: Options and Limits Under International Trade Agreements. *Journal of World Trade, 5*(5), 727–747. doi:10.54648/TRAD2020031

Payne, G., Blanco-González, A., Miotto, G., & Del-Castillo, C. (2021). Consumer Ethicality Perception and Legitimacy: Competitive Advantages in COVID-19 Crisis. *The American Behavioral Scientist*. Advance online publication. doi:10.1177/00027642211016515

Pearson, C. M., & Clair, J. A. (1998). Reframing crisis management. *Academy of Management Review*, 23(1), 59–76. doi:10.2307/259099

Pego, A. (2014). *Sistemas e tecnologias de informação no turismo em espaço rural: estudo da região Algarve* [Dissertação de Mestrado]. Lisboa: Universidade Aberta.

Pego, A. (2020a). New Challenges for the Tourism Sector in the Algarve Region Based on Evaluation of the Circular Economy. In Strategic Business Models to Support Demand, Supply, and Destination Management in the Tourism and Hospitality Industry (pp. 185-199). IGI Global. doi:10.4018/978-1-5225-9936-4.ch010

Pego, A. C. (2020b). Circularity in Portugal: Features of New Business Challenges. In Networked Business Models in the Circular Economy (pp. 224-240). IGI Global.

Pego, A. C. H. C. D. (2019). Os sistemas colaborativos na Educação: Os valores pedagógicos e educacionais. *Desenvolvimento e Sociedade*, 4(7), 31-36. https://www.researchgate.net/profile/Ana-Pego/publication/338232231_Os_sistemas_colaborativos_na_Educacao_Os_valores_pedagogicos_e_educacionais/links/5e09efe44585159aa4a5d7dd/Os-sistemas-colaborativos-na-Educacao-Os-valores-pedagogicos-e-educacionais.pdf

Pego, A. C. H. C. D., & de Matos, M. D. R. A. (2017). O impacto dos sistemas e tecnologias de informação no turismo em espaço rural na região do Algarve. *Dos Algarves: A Multidisciplinary e-Journal*, (25), 39-59. http://dosalgarves.com/index.php/dosalgarves/article/view/5

Pelletier, C., & Cloutier, L. M. (2019). Conceptualising Digital Transformation in SMEs: An Ecosystemic perspective. *Journal of Small Business and Enterprise Development*, 26, 855–876.

Peltoniemí, M., & Vuorí, E.K. (2004). Business Ecosystem as the New Approach to Complex Adaptive Business Environments. *Frontier of e-Business Research*, 20-22.

Pengfei, N., Yangzi, Z., & Qingfeng, C. (2019). The Influence of Housing Prices on Urban Competitiveness: Review and Prospects. *Chinese Journal of Urban and Environmental Studies*, 7(3), 1950009. https://doi.org/10.1142/S234574811950009X

PepsiCo. (2021). *Seis maneras de apoyar a las tienditas con la digitalización*. https://www.pepsico.com.mx/noticias/historias/seis-beneficios-de-impulsar-la-inclusion-digital-de-las-tienditas

PepsiCo-CoDi. (2020). *Citibanamex, PepsiCo y Amigo PAQ impulsan la inclusión financiera digital de tienditas a través de CoDi®*. https://www.pepsico.com.mx/noticias/boletines-de-prensa/citibanamex-pepsico-y-amigo-paq-impulsan-inclusion-financiera-de-tienditas

Pereira, G., & Rodrigues, D. A. (2021). Transformação digital em pequenos negócios no contexto da pandemia da COVID-19: uma revisão da literatura. *Revista de Gestão Do Unilasalle*, 1–11.

Perveen, A. (2016). Synchronous and asynchronous e-language learning: A case study of virtual university of Pakistan. *Open Praxis*, 8(1), 21–39. doi:10.5944/openpraxis.8.1.212

Peteraf, M., Di Stefano, G., & Verona, G. (2013). The elephant in the room of dynamic capabilities: Bringing two diverging conversations together. *Strategic Management Journal*, 34(12), 1389–1410. doi:10.1002mj.2078

Pew Research Center. (2021). *Citizens in Advanced Economies Want Significant Changes to Their Political Systems*. Pew Research Center.

Phillips, J. (2016). *Ecommerce Analytics. Analyze and Improve the Impact of Your Digital Strategy*. Pearson Education, Inc.

Phillipson, J., Gorton, M., Turner, R., Shucksmith, M., Aitken-McDermott, K., Areal, F., Cowie, P., Hubbard, C., Maioli, S., McAreavey, R., Souza-Monteiro, D., Newbery, R., Panzone, L., Rowe, F., & Shortall, S. (2020). The COVID-19 pandemic and its implications for rural economies. *Sustainability*, *12*(10), 3973. doi:10.3390u12103973

Picchi, F. (2020). *Home office forçado vai mudar a forma como trabalhamos nas empresas*. Época Negócios Online. https://epocanegocios.globo.com/colunas/Enxuga-Ai/noticia/2020/04/home-office-forcado-vai-mudar-forma-como-trabalhamos-nas-empresas.html

Picciano, A. (2017). Theories and frameworks for online education: Seeking an integrated model. *Online Learning*, *21*(3), 166–190. doi:10.24059/olj.v21i3.1225

Pilipenko, A. I., Pilipenko, Z. A., & Pilipenko, O. I. (2021). Rebuilding a stronger business in the uncertain post-CO-VID-19 future: Factor of intellectually autonomous and adequately socialized employees. In Adapting and Mitigating Environmental, Social, and Governance Risk in Business. IGI Global.

Pilipenko, A. I., Pilipenko, Z. A., & Pilipenko, O. I. (2022). Dialectics of self-movement of resilient companies in the economy and society post COVID-19: patterns of organizational transformations of networking interactions. In Challenges and Emerging Strategies for Global Networking Post COVID-19. IGI Global.

Pilipenko, O. I., Pilipenko, Z. A., & Pilipenko, A. I. (2021). Theory of Shocks, COVID-19, and Normative Fundamentals for Policy Responses. IGI Global.

Pilipenko, A. I., Pilipenko, Z. A., & Pilipenko, O. I. (2021). Rebuilding a stronger business in the uncertain Post-COV-ID-19 future: Factor of intellectually autonomous and adequately socialized employees. In M. Ziolo (Ed.), *Adapting and Mitigating Environmental, Social, and Governance Risk in Business. (A volume in the Advances in Business Information Systems and Analytics (ABISA) Book Series)*. IGI Global. doi:10.4018/978-1-7998-6788-3.ch009

Pilipenko, O. I., Pilipenko, Z. A., & Pilipenko, A. I. (2022). COVID-19 shock and Schumpeterian "creative destruction": Self-enforcing companies and self-development of the future dynamic economy. In M. Khosrow-Pour (Ed.), *Research Anthology on Business Continuity and Navigating Times of Crisis* (Vols. 1–4). Information Resources Management Association. doi:10.4018/978-1-6684-4503-7.ch057

Pine, B. (2015). How B2B companies create economic value by designing experiences and transformations for their customers. *Strategy and Leadership*, *43*(3), 2–6. doi:10.1108/SL-03-2015-0018

Pine, B. J. II, & Gilmore, J. H. (1999). *The experience economy*. Harvard Business School Press.

Poeta, C., & Maragall, J. (2021). *Glossary Of Tourism Terms*. World Tourism Organization. Retrieved from: https://www.unwto.org/glossary-tourism-terms

Portway, K. (2021). Creating Medical Marvels: How Lasers Have Played Their Part in the pandemic, Including Making Medical Devices. Keely Portway Reports. *Europa ScienceLaser Systems Europe*, *50*, 12.

Pressman, R. S. (2014). *Software engineering. a practitioner's approach*. Edit. McGraw Hill.

Price, H. J., & Murnan, J. (2004). Research Limitations and the Necessity of Reporting Them. *American Journal of Health Education*, *35*(2), 66–67. doi:10.1080/19325037.2004.10603611

Prigogine, I., & Stengers, I. (1983). *Order Out of Chaos: Man's New Dialogue with Nature*. Bantam Books.

Prime, H., Wade, M., & Browne, D. T. (2020). Risk and resilience in family well-being during the COVID-19 pandemic. *The American Psychologist*, *75*(5), 631–643. doi:10.1037/amp0000660 PMID:32437181

Priyono, A., & Moin, A. (2020). *Identifying Digital Transformation Paths in the Business Model of SMEs during the COVID-19 Pandemic*. Academic Press.

Priyono, A., Moin, A., & Putri, V.N.A.O. (2020). Identifying Digital Transformation Paths in the Business Model of SMEs during the COVID-19 Pandemic. *Journal of Open Innovation, 6*, 104.

Prove. (n.d.). *PROVE-Promoting and Selling*. Retrieved from http://www.prove.com.pt/www/english.T9.php

Pujawan, I. N. (2005). *Supply chain management*. Surabaya: Gundawidya.

Pulido-Martos, M., Cortés-Denia, D., & Lopez-Zafra, E. (2021). Teleworking in Times of COVID-19: Effects on the Acquisition of Personal Resources. *Frontiers in Psychology, 12*, 2485. doi:10.3389/fpsyg.2021.685275 PMID:34248789

Pyöriä, P. (2011). Managing telework: Risks, fears and rules. *Management Research Review, 34*(4), 386–399. doi:10.1108/01409171111117843

QGIS. (2020). *QGIS project*. https://www.qgis.org/en/site/

Quinet, C. (1994). Herbert Simon et la rationalité. *Revue française d'économie, 9*(1), 133-181.

Quintino, D. D., & Ferreira, P. (2021). Diesel prices in Brazil: A dynamic fractional integration analysis. *Economics and Business Letters, 10*(2), 116–125. doi:10.17811/ebl.10.2.2021.116-125

Rabbi, I., & Ullah, S. (2013). A survey on augmented reality challenges and tracking. *Acta Graphica, 24*(1-2), 29–46. https://hrcak.srce.hr/102430

Radovilsky, Z. (2015). *Business Models for E-Commerce*. Cognella Academic Publishing.

Raghuram, S. (1998). Telework: managing distances in a connected world. *Strategy Business*. https://www.strategy-business.com/article/9530?gko=f82ad

Raghuram, S. (2001). Factors contributing to virtual work adjustment. *Journal of Management*, 383-405. https://www.researchgate.net/publication/228751940_Factors_contributing_to_virtual_work_adjustment

Rahman, T., Moktadir, M. A., & Paul, S. K. (2021). Key performance indicators for a sustainable recovery strategy in health-care supply chains: COVID-19 pandemic perspective. *Journal of Asia Business Studies*.

Rahman, H. Z., & Matin, I. (2020). *Livelihoods, coping, and support during COVID-19 crisis*. BRAC Institute of Governance and Development.

Rajan, R. G. (2010). *Fault Lines: How Hidden Fractures Still Threaten the World Economy*. Princeton University Press.

Ramli, N. S. (2017). A review of marketing strategies from the European chocolate industry. *Journal of Global Entrepreneurship Research, 7*(10), 1–17. doi:10.118640497-017-0068-0

Ramos-Rodríguez, A.-R., & Ruíz-Navarro, J. (2004). Changes in the intellectual structure of strategic management research: A bibliometric study of the Strategic management journal, 1980–2000. *Strategic Management Journal, 25*(10), 981–1004. doi:10.1002mj.397

Ranney, M. L., Gríffeth, V., & Jha, A. K. (2020). Critical Supply Shortages— The Need for Ventilators and Personal Protective Equipment during the Covid-19 Pandemic. *The New England Journal of Medicine, 382*(18), 41–54. doi:10.1056/NEJMp2006141 PMID:32212516

Rasmussen, E., & Corbett, G. (2008). Why Isn't Teleworking Working? *New Zealand Journal of Employment Relations*, 20-32. http://www.nzjournal.org/33(2)Rasmussen.pdf

Rassool, R., & Dissanayake, R. (2019). Digital Transformation for Small & Medium Enterprises: With Special focus on Sri Lankan Context as an Emerging Economy. *International Journal of Business and Management Review*, 7(4), 59–76.

Rawls, J. B. (1971). *A Theory of Justice*. Harvard University Press. doi:10.4159/9780674042605

Redacción Negocios. (2020). *Grupo Modelo lanza plataforma de tienditas con servicio a domicilio*. https://www.milenio.com/negocios/coronavirus-grupo-modelo-lanza-plataforma-abastecer-despensa

Reeves, T. C. (2003). Storms clouds on the digital education horizon. *Journal of Computing in Higher Education*, 15(1), 3.

Registre, J. F. R., Danthine, É., Ouellet, A. M., Cachat-Rosset, G., & Saba, T. (2022). Effet du télétravail sur la santé psychologique et la performance des travailleurs durant la pandémie de la COVID-19. *Psychologie du Travail et des Organisations*.

Reinhart, C. M., & Rogoff, K. S. (2009). *This Time Is Different. Eight Centuries of Financial Folly*. Princeton University Press.

Renda, A., Schwaag Serger, S., & Tataj, D. (2022). *Industry 5.0, a transformative vision for Europe: governing systemic transformations towards a sustainable industry*. https://data.europa.eu/doi/10.2777/17322

Reyes, G., Olmos, S., & Hernández, M. (2016). Private Label Sales through Catalogs with Augmented Reality. In Handbook of Research on Strategic Retailing of Private Label Products in a Recovering Economy. IGI Global.

Reynaud, J.-D. (1991). Pour une sociologie de la régulation sociale. *Sociologie et Sociétés*, 23(2), 13–26. doi:10.7202/001632ar

Rice, A. L. (2013). *The Enterprise and Its Environment: A System Theory of Management Organization*. Psychology Press. doi:10.4324/9781315013756

Richardson, J. (2010). Managing flexworkers: Holding on and letting go. *Journal of Management Development*, 29(2), 137–147. doi:10.1108/02621711011019279

Richardson, J., & McKenna, S. (2014). Reordering spatial and social relations: A case study of professional and managerial flexworkers. *British Journal of Management*, 25(4), 724–736. doi:10.1111/1467-8551.12017

Rietveld, J., & Schilling, M. A. (2021). Platform Competition: A Systematic and Interdisciplinary Review of the Literature. *Journal of Management*, 47(6), 1528–1563. doi:10.1177/0149206320969791

Rigby, D., Elk, S., & Berez, S. (2020). *Ágil do jeito certo: transformação sem caos*. Benvirá.

Rinekso, A. and Muslim, A. (2020) Synchronous online discussion: Teaching English in higher education amidst the covid-19 pandemic. *Journal of English Educators Society*, 5(2), 155-162.

Riobó, I. J. (2015). *TecsMedia: Análisis de tendencias: Realidad Aumentada y Realidad Virtual*. Instituto Tecnológico de Aragón. Retrieved from https://www.aragon.es/documents/20127/674325/Estudio%20Prospectiva%20Analisis%20de%20tendencias%20RA%20y%20RV%20con%20formato.pdf/45cb187d-55a4-9577-a0ce-476fa0ed1b06

Rizka, A., Hida, N., & Dewi, Y. R. (2021). Marketing Strategies Through Instagram to Increase Sales. In BISTIC (Vol. 193, pp. 273–277). Academic Press.

Robinson, J. (1980). Time in economic theory. Kyklos, 33(2), 219–29.

Robinson, K. (1992). Accounting Numbers As "Inscription": Action At a Distance and the Development of Accounting. *Accounting, Organizations and Society*, 17(7), 685–708. doi:10.1016/0361-3682(92)90019-O

Rocha, A., & Perobelli, F. (2020). Spatial distribution of logistics services in Brazil: A potential market analysis. *Regional Science Policy and Practice*, 12(1), 185–217. doi:10.1111/rsp3.12224

Rodrigues, A. R. P., & Costa, W. L. (2019, February). Percepções sobre os processos de ensino e aprendizagem do ensino superior. *Simpósio*, (7).

Rodrigues, M. D. L. (2012). Os desafios da política de educação no século XXI. *Sociologia, problemas e práticas*, (68), 171-176.

Rodrigues, M. D. L., & Silva, P. A. (2016). A constituição e as políticas públicas em Portugal. *Sociologia, Problemas e Práticas*, 13-22.

Rodrigues, M., Gelabert, P. J., Ameztegui, A., Coll, L., & Vega-Garcia, C. (2021). Has COVID-19 halted winter-spring wildfires in the Mediterranean? Insights for wildfire science under a pandemic context. *The Science of the Total Environment, 765*, 142793. https://doi.org/10.1016/j.scitotenv.2020.142793

Rodríguez-Nogueira, Ó., Leirós-Rodríguez, R., Benítez-Andrades, J. A., Álvarez-Álvarez, M. J., Marqués-Sánchez, P., & Pinto-Carral, A. (2021). Musculoskeletal pain and teleworking in times of the COVID-19: Analysis of the impact on the workers at two Spanish universities. *International Journal of Environmental Research and Public Health, 18*(1), 31. doi:10.3390/ijerph18010031 PMID:33374537

Rogerson, C. M., & Rogerson, J. M. (2020). COVID-19 tourism impacts in South Africa: Government and industry responses. *Geo Journal of Tourism and Geosites, 31*(3), 1083–1091. doi:10.30892/gtg.31321-544

Rogoff, K. (2020). *Mapping the COVID-19 Recession.* Retrieved from: https://www.project-syndicate.org/commentary/mapping-covid19-global-recession-worst-in-150-years-by-kenneth-rogoff-2020-04

Rong, C., Zhao, G., & Yan, L. (2014). *Erdal Cayirci, Hongbing Cheng.* Wireless Network Security. doi:10.1016/B978-0-12-416689-9.00010-1

Rosenfield, C. L., & Alves, D. A. (2011). Autonomia e trabalho informacional: o teletrabalho. *Dados, 54*(1), 207-233. https://www.scielo.br/scielo.php?script=sci_arttext&pid=S0011-52582011000100006&lng=en&nrm=iso

Roth Cardoso, H. H., Dantas Gonçalves, A., Dambiski Gomes de Carvalho, G., & Gomes de Carvalho, H. (2020). Evaluating innovation development among Brazilian micro and small businesses in view of management level: Insights from the local innovation agents program. *Evaluation and Program Planning, 80*(December), 101797. doi:10.1016/j.evalprogplan.2020.101797

Roth, F. (2019). Intangible capital and labor productivity growth: A review of the literature. *Hamburg Discussion Papers in International Economics*, 4.

Rubio, N., Villaseñor, N., & Oubiña, J. (2015). Consumer identification with store brands: Differences between consumers according to their brand loyalty. *Business Research Quarterly, 18*(2), 111–126. doi:10.1016/j.brq.2014.03.004

Russo, I., Confente, I., Gligor David, M., & Cobelli, N. (2017). The combined effect of product returns experience and switching costs on B2B customer re-purchase intent. *Journal of Business and Industrial Marketing, 32*(5), 664–676. doi:10.1108/JBIM-06-2016-0129

Rust, R. T. (2020). The future of marketing. *International Journal of Research in Marketing, 37*(1), 15–26. doi:10.1016/j.ijresmar.2019.08.002

Ruszczyk, H. A., Rahman, M. F., Bracken, L. J., & Sudha, S. (2021). Contextualizing the COVID-19 pandemic's impact on food security in two small cities in Bangladesh. *Environment and Urbanization, 33*(1), 239–254. doi:10.1177/0956247820965156 PMID:34253941

Ryutu Biz. (2021). https://www.ryutsuu.biz/strategy/n051843.html

Sabat, I., Neuman-Bohme, S., Varghese, N. E., Barros, P. P., Brouwer, W., van Exel, J., Schreyogg, J., & Stargardt, T. (2020). United but divided: Policy responses and people's perceptions in the EU during the COVID-19 outbreak. *Health Policy (Amsterdam)*, *124*(9), 909–918. https://doi.org/10.1016/j.healthpol.2020.06.009

Sağlik Bakanliği, T. C. (2020). *Covid-19 Bilgilendirme Sayfası*. https://covid19.saglik.gov.tr

Sakamoto, M., Matsuda, J., & Inakura, N. (2021) *Hoarding behavior during the COVID-19 pandemic and Consumer Trouble - Implications for Consumer Education*. Research Discussion Paper, International Consumer Policy Research Center (ICPRC).

Salais, R., Baverez, N., Reynaud, B. (1986). *L'invention du chômage*. Presses Universitaires de France Raveau.

Salais, R., Chatel, E., & Riveau-Danset, D. (1998). *Institutions et conventions, la réflexivité de l'action économique*. Raison Pratique, École des Hautes Études en Sciences Sociales. doi:10.4000/books.editionsehess.10492

Salehi, H., Shojaee, M., & Sattar, S. (2015). Using E-Learning and ICT courses in educational environment: A review. *English Language Teaching*, *8*(1), 63–70.

Samaniego-Erazo, G., Esteve-González, V., & Vaca, B. (2015). Teaching and Learning in digital worlds: strategies and issues in higher education. In M. B. Mercè Gisbert (Ed.), *Teaching and Learning in Digital World: Strategies and Issues in Higher Education* (pp. 129–136). Publicacions Universitat Rovira.

Samson, D. (2020). Operations/supply chain management in a new world context. *Operations Management Research*, *13*(1), 1–3. doi:10.100712063-020-00157-w

Sánchez, S. (2020*). Concanaco y Antad lanzan 'Mándamelo', una plataforma de venta en línea para las 'tienditas'*. https://www.forbes.com.mx/negocios-concanaco-y-antad-lanzan-mandamelo-una-plataforma-en-linea-para-las-tienditas/

Sánchez, A. M., Pérez, M. P., de Luis Carnicer, P., & Jiménez, M. J. V. (2007). Teleworking and workplace flexibility: A study of impact on firm performance. *Personnel Review*, *36*(1), 42–64. doi:10.1108/00483480710716713

Sandberg, J. (2005). How do we justify knowledge produced within interpretive approaches? *Organizational Research Methods*, *8*(1), 41–68.

Sandbu, M. (2020). The post-pandemic brave new world. *Finance & Development, 57*(4).

Sandbu, M. (2020). *The Economics of Belonging*. Princeton University Press.

Sannigrahi, S., Pilla, F., Basu, B., Basu, A. S., & Molter, A. (2020). Examining the association between socio-demographic composition and COVID-19 fatalities in the European region using spatial regression approach. *Sustainable Cities and Society*, *62*, 102418. https://doi.org/10.1016/j.scs.2020.102418

Santomauro, D. F., Mantilla Herrera, A. M., Shadid, J., Zheng, P., Ashbaugh, C., Pigott, D. M., Abbafati, C., Adolph, C., Amlag, J. O., Aravkin, A. Y., Bang-Jensen, B. L., Bertolacci, G. J., Bloom, S. S., Castellano, R., Castro, E., Chakrabarti, S., Chattopadhyay, J., Cogen, R. M., Collins, J. K., ... Ferrari, A. J. (2021). Articles Global prevalence and burden of depressive and anxiety disorders in 204 countries and territories in 2020 due to the COVID-19 pandemic. *Lancet*, *398*(10312), 1700–1712. doi:10.1016/S0140-6736(21)02143-7 PMID:34634250

SantomeroA. (1996). *The Regulatory and Public Policy Agenda for Effective Intermediation in Post Socialist Economies*. Available at SSRN: https://ssrn.com/abstract=7913

Sara, G., Mangano, M. C., Berlino, M., Corbari, L., Lucchese, M., Milisenda, G., Terzo, S., Azaza, M. S., Babarro, J. M. F., Bakiu, R., Broitman, B. R., Buschmann, A. H., Christofoletti, R., Deidun, A., Dong, Y., Galdies, J., Glamuzina, B., Luthman, O., Makridis, P., ... Helmuth, B. (2021). The Synergistic Impacts of Anthropogenic Stressors and COVID-19 on Aquaculture: A Current Global Perspective. *Reviews in Fisheries Science & Aquaculture*. doi:10.1080/23308249.2021.1876633

Saraiva, A., & Boas, B. V. (2020). Com quarentena e dólar, notebook tem maior alta de preço em 7 anos. *Valor Econômico Online*. https://valor.globo.com/empresas/noticia/2020/07/20/com-quarentena-e-dolar-notebook-tem-maior-alta-de-preco-em-7-anos.ghtml

Sarfraz, Z., Sarfraz, A., Iftikar, H. M., & Akhund, R. (2021). Is COVID-19 pushing us to the Fifth Industrial Revolution (Society 5.0)? *Pakistan Journal of Medical Sciences*, *37*(2), 591–594. https://doi.org/10.12669/pjms.37.2.3387

Sargeant, J. (2012). Qualitative Research Part II: Participants, Analysis, and Quality Assurance. *Journal of Graduate Medical Education*, *4*(1), 1–3. doi:10.4300/JGME-D-11-00307.1 PMID:23451297

Sariyalcinkaya, A. D., Altun, E., & Erümit, A. K. (2022). Managing Distance Learning Systematically: The Change of the LMS and Virtual Classroom Paradigm. In *Handbook of Research on Managing and Designing Online Courses in Synchronous and Asynchronous Environments* (pp. 352–379). IGI Global. doi:10.4018/978-1-7998-8701-0.ch018

Satterthwaite, D. (2004). *The under-estimation of urban poverty in low and middle-income nations* (Vol. 14). Iied.

Saunders, M. N. K., Lewis, P., & Thornhill, A. (2019). *Research Methods for Business Students* (8th ed.). Pearson.

Saykili, A. (2018). Distance education: Definitions, generations and key concepts and future directions. *International Journal of Contemporary Educational Research*, *5*(1), 2–17.

Schelling. (1993). *System of Transcendental Idealism*. University of Virginia Press.

Schmidt, C. (2004). The analysis of semi-structured interviews. A Companion to Qualitative Research (pp. 253–258). Sage.

Schmitt, B. (1999). Experiential marketing. *Journal of Marketing Management*, *15*(1-3), 53–67. doi:10.1362/026725799784870496

Schneider, S. L., & Council, M. L. (2021). Distance learning in the era of COVID-19. *Archives of Dermatological Research*, *313*(5), 389–390. doi:10.100700403-020-02088-9 PMID:32385691

Schumpeter, J. A. (1947). The creative response in economic history. *The Journal of Economic History*, *7*(2), 149–159. doi:10.1017/S0022050700054279

Schumpeter, J. A. (1949). *The Theory of Economic Development: An Inquiry into Profits, Capital, Credit, Interest, and the Business Cycle*. Harvard University Press.

Schumpeter, J. A. (1961). *The Theory of Economic Development*. Oxford Univ. Press.

Schwab, K. (2016). *The Fourth Industrial Revolution*. Geneva: World Economic Forum.

Schwab, K., & Malleret, T. (2020). *COVID-19: The Great Reset*. World Economic Forum.

Schwab, K., & Thierry, M. (2020). *COVID-19: The Great Reset*. World Economic Forum.

Schwarz, J. A., & Tan, B. (2021). Optimal sales and production rollover strategies under capacity constraints. *European Journal of Operational Research*, *294*(2), 507–524. doi:10.1016/j.ejor.2021.01.040

Scuotto, V., Nicotra, M., Del Giudice, M., Krueger, N., & Gregori, G. L. (2021). A microfoundational perspective on SMEs' growth in the digital transformation era. *Journal of Business Research*, *129*, 382–392.

Sebrae. (2020). *O impacto da pandemia de coronavírus nos pequenos negócios.* Author.

Sebrae. (2021). *O Impacto da pandemia de coronavírus nos Pequenos Negócios – 13ª edição.* Author.

Secretaria de Salud. (2020). *Jornada Nacional de Sana Distancia.* https://www.gob.mx/cms/uploads/attachment/file/541687/Jornada_Nacional_de_Sana_Distancia.pdf

Secretaría de Salud. (2021). *Quédate en casa.* https://coronavirus.gob.mx/quedate-en-casa/

Seitz, J., & Rigotti, T. (2018). How do differing degrees of working-time autonomy and overtime affect worker well-being? A multilevel approach using data from the German Socio-Economic Panel (SOEP). *German Journal of Human Resource Management, 32*(3-4), 177–194. doi:10.1177/2397002218780630

Shaikh, A. A., & Karjaluoto, H. (2015). Mobile banking adoption: A literature review. *Telematics and Informatics, 32*(1), 129–142. doi:10.1016/j.tele.2014.05.003

Shambhu, N. S., & Prasanna, S. (2021). Influence of conditional holoentropy-based feature selection on automatic recommendation system in the E-commerce sector. *Journal of King Saud University-Computer and Information Sciences.* Advance online publication. doi:10.1016/j.jksuci.2020.12.022

Shammi, M., Bodrud-Doza, M., Islam, A. R. M. T., & Rahman, M. M. (2021). Strategic assessment of COVID-19 pandemic in Bangladesh: Comparative lockdown scenario analysis, public perception, and management for sustainability. *Environment, Development and Sustainability, 23*(4), 6148–6191. doi:10.100710668-020-00867-y PMID:32837281

Shanka, M. S., & Menebo, M. M. (2022). When and How Trust in Government Leads to Compliance with COVID-19 Precautionary Measures. *Journal of Business Research, 139*, 1275–1283. doi:10.1016/j.jbusres.2021.10.036

Sharma, P., Leung, T. Y., Kingshott, R. P. J., Davcik, N. S., & Cardinali, S. (2020). Managing uncertainty during a global pandemic: An international business perspective. *Journal of Business Research, 116*, 188–192. doi:10.1016/j.jbusres.2020.05.026 PMID:32501304

Sharma, S., Mahajan, S., & Rana, V. (2019). A semantic framework for e-commerce search engine optimization. *International Journal of Information Technology, 11*(1), 31–36. doi:10.100741870-018-0232-y

Sharma, T., & Bashir, M. (2020). Use of apps in the COVID-19 response and the loss of privacy protection. *Nature Medicine, 26*(8), 1165–1175. doi:10.103841591-020-0928-y PMID:32457443

Sheppard, J. P., & Chowdhury, S. D. (2005). Riding the wrong wave: Organizational failure as a failed turnaround. *Long Range Planning, 38*(3), 239–260. doi:10.1016/j.lrp.2005.03.009

Sheth, J. (2020). Impact of Covid-19 on consumer behavior: Will the old habits return or die? *Journal of Business Research, 117*, 280–283. doi:10.1016/j.jbusres.2020.05.059 PMID:32536735

Shohel, M. M. C., Shams, S., Ashrafuzzaman, M., Alam, A. S., Al Mamun, M. A., & Kabir, M. M. (2022). Emergency remote teaching and learning: Digital competencies and pedagogical transformation in resource-constrained contexts. In *Handbook of Research on Asian Perspectives of the Educational Impact of COVID-19* (pp. 175–200). IGI Global. doi:10.4018/978-1-7998-8402-6.ch011

Shukla, M., Dos Santos, R., Fong, A., & Lu, C.-T. (2017). DERIV: Distributed brand perception tracking framework. *Journal of Big Data, 4*(17), 1–23. doi:10.1109/ICMLA.2016.0069

Siebel, T. M. (2019). *Digital Transformation: Survive and Thrive in an Era of Mass Extinction.* Rosetta Books.

Sigala, M. (2020). Tourism and COVID-19: Impacts and implications for advancing and resetting industry and research. *Journal of Business Research, 117*, 312–321. doi:10.1016/j.jbusres.2020.06.015 PMID:32546875

Simonson, M., Zvacek, S., & Smaldino, S. (2019). *Teaching and Learning at a Distance: Foundations of Distance Education* (7th ed.). IAP Information Age Publishing.

Singh, K., & Yip, G. S. (2000). Strategic lessons from the Asian crisis. *Long Range Planning, 33*(5), 706–729. doi:10.1016/S0024-6301(00)00078-9

Singh, S., Prakash, C., & Ramakríshna, S. (2020). Three-dimensional Printing in the Fight Against Novel Virus CO-VID-19: Technology Helping Society During an Infectious Disease Pandemic. *Technology in Society, 62*(06), 101–135. doi:10.1016/j.techsoc.2020.101305 PMID:32834232

Singh, U. S. (2021). A study on the revolution of consumer relationships as a combination of human interactions and digital transformations. *Materials Today: Proceedings*. Advance online publication. doi:10.1016/j.matpr.2021.05.578

Sipior, J. C. (2020). Considerations for development and use of AI in response to COVID- 19. *International Journal of Information Management, 55*, 102170. Advance online publication. doi:10.1016/j.ijinfomgt.2020.102170 PMID:32836632

Sirén, C., Hakala, H., Wincent, J., & Grichnik, D. (2016). Breaking the Routines: Entrepreneurial Orientation, Strategic Learning, Firm Size, and Age. *Long Range Planning*. Advance online publication. doi:10.1016/j.lrp.2016.09.005

Skalkos, D., Kosma, I. S., Chasioti, E., Skendi, A., Papageorgiou, M., & Guine, R. P. F. (2021). Consumers' Attitude and Perception toward Traditional Foods of Northwest Greece during the COVID-19 Pandemic. *Applied Sciences-Basel, 11*(9), 4080. doi:10.3390/app11094080

Slutsky, E. (1937). The summation of random causes as the source of cyclic processes. Econometrica, 5(2), 105–146. doi:10.2307/1907241

Small, H. (1973). Co-citation in the scientific literature: A new measure of the relationship between two documents. *Journal of the American Society for Information Science, 24*(4), 265–269. doi:10.1002/asi.4630240406

Smilanski, S. (2017). *Experiential Marketing* (2nd ed.). KoganPage.

Smith, J. (1972). *Interviewing in market and social research*. Routledge & Kegan Paul.

Smith, V., & Darvas, J. (2017). Encouraging Student Autonomy through Higher Order Thinking Skills. *Journal of Institutional Research, 6*(1), 29–34. doi:10.9743/JIR.2017.5

Smit, S., Hirt, M., Dash, P., Lucas, A., Latkovic, T., Wilson, M., Greenberg, E., Buehler, K., & Hjartar, K. (2020). *Crushing coronavirus uncertainty: The big 'unlock' for our economies. To safeguard lives and livelihoods, we must restore confidence. In Strategy & Corporate Finance Practice.* McKinsey & Company.

Snyder, C. R. (Ed.). (1999). *Coping: The psychology of what works.* Oxford University Press. doi:10.1093/med:psych/9780195119343.001.0001

Soares, F. (2020). Pandemia expõe as fragilidades do nosso sistema de avaliação. *Revista Educação Online.* RFM. Accessed 24 Jan. 2022, available at https://revistaeducacao.com.br/2020/11/03/avaliacao-chico-soares/

Sohel, M. S., Hossain, B., Alam, M. K., Shi, G., Shabbir, R., Sifullah, M. K., & Mamy, M. M. B. (2021). COVID-19 induced impact on informal migrants in Bangladesh: A qualitative study. *The International Journal of Sociology and Social Policy.*

Solihin, I. (2009). *Pengantar manajemen.* Erlangga.

Solihin, I. (2014). *Pengantar bisnis.* Erlangga.

Soylu, Ö. B. (2020). Türkiye Ekonomisinde Covid-19'un Sektörel Etkileri. *Avrasya Sosyal ve Ekonomi Araştırmaları Dergisi, 7*(5), 159–185.

Spante, M., Hashemi, S., Lundin, M., & Algers, A. (2018) Digital competence and digital literacy in higher education research: Systematic review of concept use. Cogent Education, 5(1).

Specialty Food. (2020). *Organic and sustainable foods receive "coronavirus boost".* Retrieved from https://www.specialityfoodmagazine.com/news/organic-and-sustainable-foods-receive-coronavirus-boost

Spena, T.R., Trequa, M., & Bifulco, F. (2016). Knowledge Practices For An Emerging Innovation Ecosystem. *International Journal of Innovation Technology Management, 13.*

Sperry, R. W. (1964). *Problems Outstanding in the Evolution of Brain Function.* American Museum of Natural History.

Sperry, R. W. (1969). A modified concept of consciousness. *Psychological Review, 76*(6), 532–536. doi:10.1037/h0028156 PMID:5366411

Spiggle, S. (1994). Analysis and interpretation of in qualitative data in consumer research. *The Journal of Consumer Research, 21*(3), 491–503. doi:10.1086/209413

Srivastava, P. (2019). Advantages & disadvantages of e-education & e-learning. *Journal of Retail Marketing & Distribution Management, 2*(3), 22–27.

Stanislawski, S., Ohira, S., & Sonobe, Y. (2015). Consuming to help—Post-disaster consumption in Japan. *Asia-Pacific Advances in Consumer Research, 11,* 76–79.

Stata. (2020). *Stata: Software for Statistics and Data Science.* https://www.stata.com/

Statista. (2021). Retrieved from https://www.statista.com

Statista. (2022). *Social Media Advertising.* Retrieved February 26, 2022, from https://www.statista.com/outlook/dmo/digital-advertising/social-media-advertising/worldwide

Stead, J. G., & Stead, W. E. (2013). The Coevolution of Sustainable Strategic Management in the Global Marketplace. *Organization & Environment, 26*(2), 162–183. doi:10.1177/1086026613489138

Stemn, E., Bofinger, C., Cliff, D., & Hassall, M. E. (2018). Failure to learn from safety incidents: Status, challenges and opportunities. *Safety Science, 101,* 313–325. doi:10.1016/j.ssci.2017.09.018

Stephan, W., & Stephan, C. W. (1985). Intergroup Anxiety. *The Journal of Social Issues, 41*(3), 157–175. doi:10.1111/j.1540-4560.1985.tb01134.x

Stephan, W., Stephan, C. W., & Gudykunst, W. B. (1999). Anxiety in intergroup relations: A comparison of anxiety/uncertainty management theory and integrated threat theory. *International Journal of Intercultural Relations, 23*(4), 613–628. doi:10.1016/S0147-1767(99)00012-7

Stich, V., Zeller, V., Hicking, J., & Kraut, A. (2020). Measures for a successful digital transformation of SMEs. *Procedia CIRP, 93,* 286–291.

Stinchcombe, A. L. (1965). Social structure and organizations. In Handbook of Organizations. Academic Press.

Stonehouse, G., & Snowdon, B. (2007). Competitive Advantage Revisited: Michael Porter on Strategy and Competitiveness. *Journal of Management Inquiry, 16*(3), 256–273. doi:10.1177/1056492607306333

Štreimikienė, D., Baležentis, T., Volkov, A., Ribašauskienė, E., Morkūnas, M., & Žičkienė, A. (2021). Negative effects of covid-19 pandemic on agriculture: Systematic literature review in the frameworks of vulnerability, resilience and risks involved. *Economic Research-Ekonomska Istraživanja*, 1-17.

Strielkowski, W. (2020). *International Tourism and COVID-19: Recovery Strategies.* doi:10.20944/preprints202003.0445.v1

Studies, C., Cv, O., & Abadi, K. (2018). Analisis saluran distribusi kayu (studi kasus di cv. Karya abadi, Manado). *Jurnal EMBA: Jurnal Riset Ekonomi, Manajemen. Bisnis Dan Akuntansi, 6*. Advance online publication. doi:10.35794/emba.v6i3.20444

Subekti, A. (2021). Covid-19-triggered online learning implementation: Pre-service English teachers' beliefs. *Metathesis: Journal of English Language, Literature, and Teaching, 4*(3), 232–248. doi:10.31002/metathesis.v4i3.2591

Sullivan, C. (2003). What's in a name? Definitions and conceptualisations of teleworking and homeworking. *New Technology, Work and Employment, 18*(3), 158–165. doi:10.1111/1468-005X.00118

Sundaram, R., Sharma, R. & Shakya, A. (2020). Digital Transformation of Business Models: A Systematic Review of Impact on Revenue and Supply Chain. *International Journal of Management, 11*(5), 9-21.

Sustainability. (2021). Retrieved from Academic Impact: https://academicimpact.un.org/content/sustainability.

Tackie, H. N. (2022). (Dis)Connected: Establishing Social Presence and Intimacy in Teacher-Student Relationships During Emergency Remote Learning. *AERA Open, 8*. Advance online publication. doi:10.1177/23328584211069525

Taladriz, C. C. (2019) Technology to empower relationships, interactions and emotions in the classroom. *2019 IEEE Global Engineering Education Conference*, 1493-1498. 10.1109/EDUCON.2019.8725076

Taleb, N. N. (2007). The Black Swan: The Impact of the Highly Improbable. The Random House Publishing Group.

Taleb, N. N. (2012). *Antifragile: Things That Gain from Disorder*. Random House Trade Paperbacks.

Tanzi, V. (2011). *Government versus Markets: The Changing Economic Role of the State*. Syndicate of the Press of the University of Cambridge.

Taplett, F. B., Krentz, M., Dean, J., & Novacek, G. (2019). Diversity is just the first step. Inclusion comes next. Boston Consulting Group.

Tashiro, T. (2020). We got 100 million yen! Hida beef at home project" with Corona's marketing of local products. *Economic Monthly Report, 87*, 2-8. https://www.think-t.gr.jp/pdf/award_01.pdf

Taskin, L. (2006). Télétravail: Les enjeux de la déspatialisation pour le Management Humain. *Revue Interventions économiques. Papers in Political Economy*, (34).

Taylor, J. (2020). How Dhaka's urban poor are dealing with Covid-19. *Urban Matters, 1*.

TCMB. (2021). *Koronavirüsün Ekonomik ve Finansal Etkilerine Karşı Alınan Tedbirler*. https://www.tcmb.gov.tr/wps/wcm/connect/TR/TCMB+TR/Main+Menu/ Duyurular/Koronavirus/

Teece, D. J. (2009). *Dynamic capabilities and strategic management*. Academic Press.

Teece, D. J. (2007). Explicating dynamic capabilities: The nature and microfoundations of (sustainable) enterprise performance. *Strategic Management Journal, 28*(13), 1319–1350. doi:10.1002mj.640

Teece, D. J. (2016). Dynamic capabilities and entrepreneurial management in large organizations: Toward a theory of the (entrepreneurial) firm. *European Economic Review, 86*, 202–216. doi:10.1016/j.euroecorev.2015.11.006

Teece, D. J., Pisano, G., & Shuen, A. (1997). Dynamic capabilities and strategic management. *Strategic Management Journal, 18*(7), 509–533. doi:10.1002/(SICI)1097-0266(199708)18:7<509::AID-SMJ882>3.0.CO;2-Z

Teixeira, A. C. (2006). Transport policies in light of the new economic geography: The Portuguese experience. *Regional Science and Urban Economics, 36*(4), 450–466. https://doi.org/10.1016/j.regsciurbeco.2006.01.002

Tellis, G. J. (2013). Unrelenting Innovation: How to Build a Culture for Market Dominance. John Wiley & Sons.

Teresiene, D., Keliuotyte-Staniuleniene, G., Liao, Y., Kanapickiene, R., Pu, R., Hu, S., & Yue, X.-G. (2021). The Impact of the COVID-19 Pandemic on Consumer and Business Confidence Indicators. *Journal of Risk and Financial Management, 14*(4), 159. https://doi.org/10.3390/jrfm14040159

Thatcher, S. M., & Zhu, X. (2006). Changing identities in a changing workplace: Identification, identity enactment, self-verification, and telecommuting. *Academy of Management Review, 31*(4), 1076–1088. doi:10.5465/amr.2006.22528174

The business case for inclusive growth. (2018). In *Deloitte Global Inclusive Growth Survey*. Deloitte Touche Tohmatsu Limited.

The Coca-Cola Company. (2020). *Hablemos de tienditas.* https://www.coca-colamexico.com.mx/noticias/comunidad/hablemos-de-tienditas

The Economist Intelligence Unit. (2020). *COVID-19 and the crisis for higher education.* Report. London: The Economist Intelligence Unit Limited.

Thom, R. (1969). Topological models in biology. *Topology, 8,* 313-36.

Thom, R. (1974). Catastrophe theory: its present state and future perspectives. Dynamical Systems-Warwick. Lecture Notes in Mathematics. Math., 468, 366–372.

Thomsen, T. U., Holmqvist, J., von Wallpach, S., Hemetsberger, A., & Belk, R. W. (2020). Conceptualizing unconventional luxury. *Journal of Business Research, 116,* 441–445. doi:10.1016/j.jbusres.2020.01.058

Thorik, S. H. (2020). Efektivitas pembatasan sosial berskala besar di indonesia dalam penanggulangan pandemi covid-19. *Jurnal: Hukum dan Keadilan, 4*(1).

Tiendita Cerca. (2021). *La tienda de la esquina en la puerta de tu casa.* https://www.tienditacerca.com/

Tietze, S., & Nadin, S. (2011). The psychological contract and the transition from office-based to home-based work'. *Human Resource Management Journal, 21*(3), 318–334. doi:10.1111/j.1748-8583.2010.00137.x

Tight, M. (2016). Phenomenography: The development and application of an innovative research design in higher education research. *International Journal of Social Research Methodology, 19*(3), 319–338.

Tigre, P. B. (2019). *Gestão da inovação: uma abordagem estratégica, organizacional e de gestão de conhecimento.* Atlas.

Tih, S., & Lee, K. H. (2013). Perceptions and Predictors of Consumers' Purchase Intentions for Store Brands: Evidence from Malaysia. *Asian Journal of Business and Accounting, 6*(2), 105–136.

Timuş, A. (2020). Circular agriculture development in the post-COVID-19 era. Competitiveness and sustainable development, 2, 14-14.

Tjiptono, F. (2014). *Pemasaran jasa – prinsip, penerapan, dan penelitian.* Andi Offset.

TOBB. (2021). *İş Dünyası Korona İçin Ekonomik Tedbirler.* https://tobb.org.tr/Sayfalar/20200323-covid-destegi.php/

Toriumi, F., & Lim, D. (2021). Information Sharing During the Pandemic. *Yokokan Rengo Conference.* https://www.jstage.jst.go.jp/article/oukan/2021/0/2021_A-4-4/_pdf/-char/ja

Toussaert, S. (2021). Upping uptake of COVID contact tracing apps. *Nature Human Behaviour, 5*(2), 183–184. doi:10.103841562-021-01048-1 PMID:33479504

Traxler, J. (2018). Distance learning-Predictions and possibilities. *Education Sciences, 8*(1), 35. doi:10.3390/educsci8010035

Tremblay, D. G. (2001). Le télétravail: Les avantages et inconvénients pour les individus et les défis de gestion des RH. La GRH dans la société de l'information.

Tremblay, D.-G., Chevrier, C., & Et Di Loreto, M. (2006). Le télétravail à domicile: Meilleure conciliation emploi-famille ou source d'envahissement de la vie privée? *Revue Interventions Economiques, 34*(34), 1–16. doi:10.4000/interventionseconomiques.689

Trouche, L., Rocha, K., Gueudet, G., & Pepin, B. (2020). Transition to digital resources as a critical process in teachers' trajectories: The case of Anna's documentation work. *ZDM*, 1-15.

Tsiakkiros, A., & Pashiardis, P. (2002). Strategic planning and education: The case of Cyprus. *International Journal of Educational Management, 16*(1), 6–17. doi:10.1108/09513540210415505

Tuncay, T., Musabak, I., Gok, D. E., & Kutlu, M. (2008). The relationship between anxiety, coping strategies and characteristics of patients with diabetes. *Health and Quality of Life Outcomes, 6*(1), 1–9. doi:10.1186/1477-7525-6-79 PMID:18851745

Tunggal, A. W. (2011). *Pokok-pokok performance measurement dan balanced scorecard.* Harvindo.

Turan, A., & Çelíkyay, H. H. (2020). Türkiye'de KOVİD-19 ile Mücadele: Politikalar ve Aktörler. *Uluslararası Yönetim Akademisi Dergisi, 3*, 1–25.

Turban, E. (2018). *Electronic Commerce 2018. A Managerial and Social Networks Perspective* (9th ed.). Springer Nature. doi:10.1007/978-3-319-58715-8

Türkíyeti Cumhuríyetí Cumhurbaşkanliği Strateji Ve Bütçe. (2020). *On Birinci Kalkınma Planı.* www.sbb.gov.tr

TURKSTAT. (2021). https://data.tuik.gov.tr/

Turnea, E. S., Neştian, Ş. A., Tiţă, S. M., Vodă, A. I., & Guţă, A. L. (2020). Dismissals and Temporary Leaves in Romanian Companies in the Context of Low Demand and Cash Flow Problems during the COVID-19 Economic Lockdown. *Sustainability, 12*(21), 8850. doi:10.3390u12218850

Turner, S. M., Beidel, D. C., Dancu, C. V., & Stanley, M. A. (1989). An empirically derived inventory to measure social fears and anxiety: The Social Phobia and Anxiety Inventory. *Psychological Assessment, 1*(1), 35–40. doi:10.1037/1040-3590.1.1.35

Tursunbayeva, A., Di Lauro, S., & Antonelli, G. (2022). Remote work at the time of COVID-19 pandemic and beyond: A scoping review. *HR Analytics and Digital HR Practices*, 127-169.

Uber. (2020a). *Supporting you during the Coronavirus.* https://www.uber.com/en-HK/blog/supporting-you-during-coronavirus-v1/

Uber. (2020b). *An update on COVID-19 financial assistance.* Retrieved from: https://www.uber.com/en-HK/blog/supporting-you-during-coronavirus/

Uchiyama, H., & Marchand, E. (2012). Object detection and pose tracking for augmented reality: recent approaches. *18th Korea-Japan Joint Workshop on Frontiers of Computer Vision (FCV)*.

Udny, Y. G. (1927). *On a method of investigating periodicity* (Vol. 226; D. Series, Trans.). Royal Society.

Ugur, N. G., & Akbıyık, A., (2020). Impacts of COVID-19 on global tourism industry: A cross-regional comparison. *Tourism Management Perspectives*, 36.

Uğur, N. G., & Akbıyık, A. (2020). Impacts of COVID-19 on global tourism industry: A cross- regional comparison. *Tourism Management Perspectives*, *36*, 100744. doi:10.1016/j.tmp.2020.100744 PMID:32923356

Ulaga, W. (2018). The journey towards customer centricity and service growth in B2B: A commentary and research directions. *AMS Review*, *8*(1/2), 80–83. doi:10.100713162-018-0119-x

Ulas, D. (2019). Digital Transformation Process and SMEs. *Procedia Computer Science*, *158*, 662–671.

UNCTAD. (2021). *Review of Maritime Transport 2021*. New York: United Nations Publications.

UNDP Istanbul International Center For Private Sector in Development. (2020). Lessons Learned and Strategies fro Local Manufacturing of PPE for Covid-19 Response Based on Literature Review. In *Experience and Case Study from Turkey*. USHAŞ.

United States Bureau of Labor Statistics. (2022). *Labor Force Statistics From the Current Population Survey*. Retrieved from https://www.bls.gov/cps/effects-of-the-coronavirus-covid-19-pandemic.htm# table1

UNWTO. (2020a). *International tourism growth continues to outpace the global economy*. Retrieved from: https://www.unwto.org/international-tourism-growth-continues-to-outpace-the-economy

UNWTO. (2020b). *COVID-19 Related Travel Restrictions: A Global Review for Tourism*. Retrieved from https://webunwto.s3.eu-west1.amazonaws.com/s3fspublic/2020-04/TravelRestrictions - 28 April.pdf

UNWTO. (2020c). *World Tourism Organization Underscores Tourism's Importance for COVID-19 Recovery in Audience with the King of Spain*. Retrieved from https://www.unwto.org/news/unwto-underscores-tourisms-importance-for-covid-19-recovery-in-meeting-with-the-king-of-spain

UNWTO. (2020d). *Impact assessment of the covid-19 outbreak on international tourism*. Retrieved from: https://www.unwto.org/impact-assessment-of-the-covid-19-outbreak-on-international-tourism

UNWTO. (2021). *Sustainable Development*. Retrieved from: https://www.unwto.org/sustainable-development

Våland, M. S., & Georg, S. (2018). Spacing identity: Unfolding social and spatial-material entanglements of identity performance. *Scandinavian Journal of Management*, *34*(2), 193–204. doi:10.1016/j.scaman.2018.04.002

Van de Vord, R., & Pogue, K. (2012). Teaching time investment: Does online really take more time than face-to-face? *International Review of Research in Open and Distributed Learning*, *13*(3), 132–146. doi:10.19173/irrodl.v13i3.1190

Van Eck, N. J., & Waltman, L. (2014). CitNetExplorer: A new software tool for analyzing and visualizing citation networks. *Journal of Informetrics*, *8*(4), 802–823. doi:10.1016/j.joi.2014.07.006

Van gorp, J. C. (2005). Using key performance indicators to manage energy costs. *Strategic Planning for Energy and the Environment*, *25*(2), 9–25.

Vargo, S. L., Akaka, M. A., & Vaughan, C. M. (2017). Conceptualizing value : A service-ecosystem view. *Journal of Creating Value*, *3*(2), 1–8. doi:10.1177/2394964317732861

Vargo, S. L., Koskela-Huotari, K., & Vink, J. (2020). Service-Dominant Logic: Foundations and Applications. In E. Bridges & K. Fowler (Eds.), *The Routledge Handbook of Service Research Insights and Ideas* (pp. 3–23). Routledge. doi:10.4324/9781351245234-1

Vargo, S. L., & Lusch, R. F. (2004). Evolving to a New Dominant Logic for Marketing. *Journal of Marketing, 68*(1), 1–17. doi:10.1509/jmkg.68.1.1.24036

Vargo, S. L., & Lusch, R. F. (2004). Evolving to a New Dominant Logic. *English, 68*(January), 1–17.

Vargo, S. L., & Lusch, R. F. (2008). Service-Dominant Logic: Continuing The Evolution. *Journal of the Academy of Marketing Science, 36*(1), 1–10. doi:10.100711747-007-0069-6

Vargo, S. L., & Lusch, R. F. (2016). Institutions and axioms: An extension and update of service-dominant logic. *Journal of the Academy of Marketing Science, 44*(1), 5–23. doi:10.100711747-015-0456-3

Vargo, S. L., Maglio, P. P., & Akaka, M. A. (2008). On value and value co-creation: A service systems and service logic perspective. *European Management Journal, 26*(3), 145–152. doi:10.1016/j.emj.2008.04.003

Veblen, T. B. (1899). *The Theory of the Leisure Class: An Economic Study in the Evolution of Institutions*. Macmillan.

Verheyen, G. (2019). Scrum: a pocket guide. Hertogenbosch: Van Haren Publishing.

Verhoef, P. C., Lemon, K. N., Parasuraman, A., Roggeveen, A., Tsiros, M., & Schlesinger, L. A. (2009). Customer experience creation: Determinants, dynamics and management strategies. *Journal of Retailing, 85*(1), 31–41. doi:10.1016/j.jretai.2008.11.001

Vernadsky, W. (1998). The Biosphere. Springer-Verlag Inc. doi:10.1007/978-1-4612-1750-3

Vinuto, J. (2014). A amostragem em bola de neve na pesquisa qualitativa: um debate em aberto. *Temáticas*, 203–220.

Volterra, V. (1926). Fluctuations in the abundance of a species considered mathematically. Nature, 118, 558–560.

Volterra, V. (1931). *Leçons sur la Théorie Mathématique de la Lutte pour la Vie*. Gauthier-Villars.

von Bertalanffy, L. (1968). General System Theory: Foundations, Development, Applications. University of Alberta.

Wabi2you. (2021). *WABI*. https://www.wabicasa.com/

Wakashima, K., Asai, K., Kobayashi, D., Koiwa, K., Kamoshida, S., & Sakuraba, M. (2020). The Japanese version of the Fear of COVID-19 scale: Reliability, validity, and relation to coping behavior. *PLoS One, 15*(11), e0241958.

Walker, J. (2014). *Internet Security*. doi:10.1016/B978-0-12-416689-9.00007-1

Walley, L. E. E., & Taylor, D. W. (2002). Opportunists, Champions, Mavericks? A Typology of Green Entrepreneurs. *Greener Management International*. doi:10.9774/GLEAF.3062.2002.su.00005

Wang, Y.-S., Yeh, C.-H., & Liao, Y.-W. (2013). What drives purchase intention in the context of online content services? The moderating role of ethical self-efficacy for online piracy. *International Journal of Information Management, 33*(1), 199–208. doi:10.1016/j.ijinfomgt.2012.09.004

Wapshott, R., & Mallett, O. (2012). The spatial implications of homeworking: A Lefebvrian approach to the rewards and challenges of home-based work. *Organization, 19*(1), 63–79. doi:10.1177/1350508411405376

Ward, N., & Shaba, G. (2001). Teleworking: an assessment of sociopsychological factors. *Facilities, 19*(1), 61-71. https://www.emerald.com/insight/content/doi/10.1108/02632770110362811/full/html

Watanabe, T. (2014). Chins Up! Discovery of Ethical Consumption after the Great Earthquake in Northeastern Japan. *Tokyo Keizai Law Review, 26*, 311–342.

Webber, S. S. (2011). Dual organizational identification impacting client satisfaction and word of mouth loyalty. *Journal of Business Research, 64*(2), 119–125. doi:10.1016/j.jbusres.2010.02.005

Webster, F. E. (2000). Understanding the relationships among brands, consumers, and resellers. *Journal of the Academy of Marketing Science, 28*(1), 17–23. doi:10.1177/0092070300281002

Wechsler, B. (1995). Coping and coping strategies: A behavioural view. *Applied Animal Behaviour Science, 43*(2), 123–134. doi:10.1016/0168-1591(95)00557-9

WEF. (2018). *The Inclusive Growth and Development Report*. World Economic Forum.

Weissman, D. (2000). *A Social Ontology*. Yale University Press.

Wengler, S., Hildmann, G., & Vossebein, U. (2021). Digital transformation in sales as an evolving process. *Journal of Business and Industrial Marketing, 36*(4), 599–614.

Wernerfelt, B. (1984). A resource-based view of the firm. *Strategic Management Journal, 5*(2), 171–180. doi:10.1002mj.4250050207

What is Ripe Atlas? (2022). https://atlas.ripe.net/about/

Wheelen, T. L., & Hunger, D. J. (2004). *Concepts in strategic management and business policy*. Prentice Hall.

White, W. (2009). Modern macroeconomics is on the wrong track. Finance & Development, 46(4), 15-18.

WHO. (2020). *Director-general's opening remarks at the media briefing on COVID-19*. https://www.who.int/dg/speeches/detail/who-director-general-s-opening-remarks-at-the-media-briefing-on-covid-19

WHO. (2020). *The COVID 19 global pandemic*. Parliamentary Budget Office.

WHO. (2021). *Coronavirus*. World Health Organization. Retrieved from: https://www.who.int/health-topics/coronavirus#tab=tab_1

Wiberg, M. (2020). Capital controls and the location of industry. *World Economy, 43*(4), 871–891. https://doi.org/10.1111/twec.12908

Wiener, N. (1930). *Generalized Harmonic Analysis* [Doctoral dissertation]. Acta Mathematica.

Wi-Fi Alliance. (2018). *Wi-Fi Alliance® introduces Wi-Fi 6*. https://www.wi-fi.org/news-events/newsroom/wi-fi-alliance-introduces-wi-fi-6

Wi-Fi EasyMesh (Wi-Fi Alliance). (n.d.). https://www.wi-fi.org/discover-wi-fi/wi-fi-easymesh

Wijayanto, I. H., Soeaidy, M. S., & Rochmah, S. (2014). Tourism Based on the Model of Strategic Place Triangle (A Case Study in Wisata Bahari Lamongan). *Journal of Indonesian Tourism and Development Studies, 2*(3), 114–119. doi:10.21776/ub.jitode.2014.002.03.04

Wikipedia/Sustainability. (2021). Retrieved from Sustainability: https://en.wikipedia.org/wiki/Sustainability

Wiklund, J., & Shepherd, D. (2003). Aspiring for, and achieving growth: The moderating role of resources and opportunities. *Journal of Management Studies, 40*(8), 1919–1941.

Williams, A., Whiteman, G., & Kennedy, S. (2021). Cross-scale systemic resilience: Implications for organization studies. *Business & Society*, *60*(1), 95–124. doi:10.1177/0007650319825870

Williamson, O. E. (1985). *The Economic Institutions of Capitalism: Firms, Markets, Relational Contracting*. Academic Press.

Willman-Iivarinen, H. (2017). The future of consumer decision making. *European Journal of Futures Research*, *5*(14), 1–12. doi:10.100740309-017-0125-5

Winchester, M., & Romaniuk, J. (2008). Negative brand beliefs and brand usage. *International Journal of Market Research*, *50*(3), 355–375. doi:10.1177/147078530805000306

Wolfe, P. (2019). Télétravail: 62% des employeurs canadiens permettent cette pratique. *Infopresse*, 18-19.

Woodward, C., & ... . (2007). Virtual and augmented reality in the Digital building project. *International Journal of Design Sciences and Technology*, *14*(1), 23–40.

Word Health Organization. (2021). www.who.int

World Bank. (2018). *World Development Report 2018: Learning to Realize Education's Promise*. World Bank.

World Bank. (2020). *The COVID-19 pandemic: shocks to education and policy responses*. World Bank Report.

World Bank. (2021). *The World Bank in Bangladesh*. https://www.worldbank.org/ en/ country/bangladesh/overview

World Economic Forum. (2020). *The Future of Nature and Business. New Nature Economy*. Report II. World Economic Forum.

World Economic Forum. (2020a). *Emerging Pathways towards a Post-COVID-19 Reset and Recovery*. Chief Economists Outlook. World Economic Forum.

World Economic Forum. (2020a). *Latin America and Caribbean Travel & Tourism Competitiveness Landscape Report: Assessing Regional Opportunities and Challenges in the Context of COVID-19*. Retrieved from: https://www.weforum.org/reports/latin-america-and-caribbean-travel-tourism-competitiveness-landscape-report-in-the-context-of-covid-19

World Economic Forum. (2020b). *Blogs and Opinions*. Retrieved from: https://reports.weforum.org/travel-and-tourism-competitiveness-report-2019/blogs-and-opinions/

World Health Organization. (2022). *Statement on Omicron sublineage BA.2*. Retrieved from https://www.who.int/news/item/22-02-2022-statement-on-omicron-sublineage-ba.2

Worldometers. (2021). *COVID-19 coronavirus pandemic*. https://www.worldometers.info/coronavirus/

Woyo, E. (2021). The Sustainability of Using Domestic Tourism as a Post-COVID-19 Recovery Strategy in Distressed Destination. In *Information and Communication Technologies in Tourism 2021* (p. 489). Naminia: Conference Paper. 10.1007/978-3-030-65785-7_46

Wren-Lewis, S. (2020). The Economic Effects of a Pandemic. In *Mitigating the COVID Economic Crisis: Act Fast and Do Whatever It Takes* (pp. 109–112). Centre for Economic Policy Research.

Wright, A., Murray, J. P., & Geale, P. (2007). A phenomenographic study of what it means to supervise doctoral students. *Academy of Management Learning & Education*, *6*(4), 458–474.

WTTC. (2020a). *The World Travel & Tourism Council (WTTC) represents the Travel & Tourism sector globally*. Retrieved from https://wttc.org/en-gb/COVID-19/Global-Protocols-for-the-New-Normal

WTTC. (2020b). *WTTC unveils "Safe Travels" – new global protocols to restart the Travel & Tourism sector.* Retrieved from https://wttc.org/News-Article/WTTC-unveils-Safe-Travels-new-global-protocols-to-restart-the-Travel-Tourism-sector

Wysokińska, Z. (2021). A review of the impact of the digital transformation on the global and European economy. *Comparative Economic Research, 24*(3), 75–92. doi:10.18778/1508-2008.24.22

Xie, J., Luo, S., Furuya, K., & Sun, D. (2020). Urban parks as green buffers during the COVID-19 pandemic. *Sustainability, 12*(17), 6751. doi:10.3390u12176751

Xu, D., & Jaggars, S. (2011). The effectiveness of distance education across Virginia's community colleges: Evidence from introductory college-level math and English courses. *Educational Evaluation and Policy Analysis, 33*(3), 360–377. doi:10.3102/0162373711413814

Yamagata-Lynch, L. C. (2014). Blending Online Asynchronous and Synchronous Learning. *International Review of Research in Open and Distributed Learning, 15*(2), 189–212. doi:10.19173/irrodl.v15i2.1778

Yang, K., Kim, J., Min, J., & Hernandez-Calderon, A. (2020). Effects of retailers' service quality and legitimacy on behavioral intention: The role of emotions during COVID-19. *Service Industries Journal, 41*(1-2), 84–106. doi:10.1080/02642069.2020.1863373

Yang, S., Ning, L., Jiang, T., & He, Y. (2021). Dynamic impacts of COVID-19 pandemic on the regional express logistics: Evidence from China. *Transport Policy, 111*, 111–124. doi:10.1016/j.tranpol.2021.07.012

Yanik & Ajans. (2020). *Yerli solunum cihazı 30'dan fazla ülkede insanlara nefes oluyor.* https://www.aa.com.tr/tr/saglik/yerli-solunum-cihazi-30dan-fazla-ulkede-insanlara-nefes-oluyor/2214339

Yeh, S. S. (2021). Tourism recovery strategy against COVID-19 pandemic. *Tourism Recreation Research, 46*(2), 188–194. doi:10.1080/02508281.2020.1805933

Yesilyurt, M., & Yalman, Y. (2016). Security threats on mobile devices and their effects: Estimations for the future. *International Journal of Security and Its Applications, 10*(2), 13–26. doi:10.14257/ijsia.2016.10.2.02

Yi, L., & Yao, L. (2019). Comprehensive Assessment and Policy Suggestions on Building Multi-Level National Service Centers. *Chinese Journal of Urban and Environmental Studies, 7*(3), 1950010. https://doi.org/10.1142/S2345748119500106

Yin, R. K. (1983). *The Case Study Method: An Annotated Bibliography.* Sage.

Yin, R. K. (2014). Applied social research methods series: Vol. 5. *Case study research : design and methods.* doi:10.1097/FCH.0b013e31822dda9e

Yin, R. K. (2017). *Case Study Research and Applications: Design and Methods.* Sage.

Yuan, J., Zeng, A. Y., Skibniewski, M. J., & Li, Q. (2009). Selection of performance objectives and key performance indicators in public-private partnership projects to achieve value for money. *Construction Management and Economics, 27*(3), 253–270. doi:10.1080/01446190902748705

Yulianti, A. (2020). *Knowledge management: learning organization di rs seri VIII.* http://mutupelayanankesehatan.net/sample-levels/19-headline/3437-keberlangsungan-usaha-rs-di-masa-covid-19-apakah-akan-menuju-new-normal-perspektif-learning-organization

Yu, S. J. (2012). The dynamic competitive recommendation algorithm in social network services. *Information Sciences, 187*, 1–14. doi:10.1016/j.ins.2011.10.020

Zeeman, E. C. (1977). *Catastrophe Theory: Selected Papers.* Addison-Wesley.

Zendjebil, I. M. (2008). Outdoor Augmented Reality: State of the Art and Issues. *10th ACM/IEEE Virtual Reality International Conference (VRIC 2008)*, 177-187.

Zenker, S., & Kock, F. (2020). The coronavirus pandemic–A critical discussion of a tourism research agenda. *Tourism Management*, *81*, 104164. doi:10.1016/j.tourman.2020.104164 PMID:32518437

Zhou, S., Battaglia, M., & Frey, M. (2018). Organizational learning through disasters: A multi-utility company's experience. *Disaster Prevention and Management*, *27*(2), 243–254. doi:10.1108/DPM-11-2017-0290

Ziolo, M. (Ed.). (2021). Adapting and Mitigating Environmental, Social, and Governance Risk in Business. IGI Global. doi:10.4018/978-1-7998-6788-3

Zolkiewski, J., Story, V., Burton, J., Chan, P., Gomes, A., Hunter-Jones, P., O'Malley, L., Peters, L. D., Raddats, C., & Robinson, W. (2017). Strategic B2B customer experience management: The importance of outcome-based measures. *Journal of Services Marketing*, *31*(2), 172–184. doi:10.1108/JSM-10-2016-0350

Zuev, D., & Hannam, K. (2021). Anxious immobilities: An ethnography of coping with contagion (Covid-19) in Macau. *Mobilities*, *16*(1), 35–50. https://doi.org/10.1080/17450101.2020.1827361

Zupic, I., & Cater, T. (2015). Bibliometric methods in management and organization. *Organizational Research Methods*, *18*(3), 429–472. doi:10.1177/1094428114562629

About the Contributors

Ana Pego holds a Ph.D. in Geography and Territorial Planning (Universidade Nova de Lisboa, Portugal), an MBA (Open University, Portugal) and a BSC in Economics (Universidade de Évora, Portugal). She is an integrated researcher at CICS Nova- Research Center in Social Sciences; in her research, she focuses on the circular economy, offshore energy, smart cities and tourism. She is a coordinator of five European projects as Erasmus and Horizon Europe. She is an author of several articles about offshore energy clusters, tourism, and the circular economy. She also collaborates with Open University in Macroeconomics and Business Management classes.

* * *

Aminat Kikelomo Abdul Kadir is a student of the Department of Creative and Tourism, Faculty of Humanities, Management and Social Sciences, Kwara State University, Malete, Nigeria.

Rita Ambarwati is a permanent lecturer in the Faculty of Business Law and Social Sciencees, Muhammadiyah University of Sidoarjo, who teaches several subjects including: industrial management, human resource management, marketing management, and marketing strategies. The fourth daughter of the couple Mr. H.Sudarso and Mrs. Hj. Sri Asmaningwati was born in Surabaya, April 7, 1980, who began her career as a banking practitioner in 2000 2012 and has been a trainer and operational management lecturer since 2017. The educational background of researchers include: Bachelor of Management, Wijaya Putra University in Surabaya (graduated in 2003). S-2 Master of Technology Management, ITS 10 November Surabaya (graduated in 20I1), and S-3 Doctoral Program in Management, Brawijaya University in Malang (graduated in 2014). The author is involved in research and Community service both funded by Ristekdikti and an independent fund on the implementation of good governance in public government services.

Bruno Bandeira is Bachelor of Business Administration from the Pontifical Catholic University of São Paulo PUC SP, Brazil.

João Barros Neto is Coordinator of the Extension Course in Applied Leadership at the Pontifical Catholic University of São Paulo - PUC (COGEAE). Graduated in Administration with Major in Foreign Trade from Faculdade Associada de São Paulo (1991), specialization in Production Administration and Industrial Operations from Fundação Getúlio Vargas - FGV SP (1993), Master in Administration from Pontifical Catholic University of São Paulo (1998) and Doctorate in Social Sciences and Post-Doctorate from the Pontifical Catholic University of São Paulo (2002). He is currently a member of the Group of Excellence in Higher Education Institutions - GIES of the Regional Administration Council of São Paulo - CRA SP and Assistant Professor at the Pontifical Catholic University of São Paulo - PUC SP at the Faculty of Economics, Administration, Accounting and Actuarial - Department of Administration, Epistemological Area of Personnel Management. Has experience in Administration, with an emphasis on Organizational Behavior, acting on the following topics: leadership, social responsibility, people management, skills. He has 36 books published as author, co-author and organizer, in addition to several articles.

Yusuf Bayraktutan was born in Erzurum. He completed his undergraduate and postgraduate education at Ankara University Faculty of Political Sciences, Gazi University and Atatürk University, Wichita State University and Oklahoma State University, USA. He worked as a research assistant in Atatürk University, Faculty of Economics and Administrative Sciences, and as an assistant professor in the Economics Department of Cumhuriyet University. He became an associate professor in 2005 and professor in 2010 at Kocaeli University, Faculty of Economics and Administrative Sciences, Department of Economics. In the same department, he teaches Economic Development and International Economics; He has served as the chairman of his department, Dean of the Graduate College, and Kandıra Vocational High School. He is Advisor to the Chamber of Commerce of Kocaeli and member of the publication / advisory / referee board of many national and international journals. He is the author of almost two hundred national and international publications in the form of books, book chapters, articles, papers, etc.

Georges Bellos is a Lebanese-Greek and Dutch author. Born in Beirut, he has continued most of his education in Lebanon, except for the college years between France and the USA. Geologist by training, and holder of a master's degree in geology, and a license in archeology, and a master's degree in archeology, he is oriented towards management and management, then asserts itself in education sciences. He is currently invested in several research projects in Management and management, geology, archeology and tourism, for his PhD given that he is applying for a PhD for the year 2021-2022. In order to see his research, please consult his profile on ResearchGate (https://www.researchgate.net/profile/Georges-Bellos/), its official page on Academia.edu (https://liu-lb.academia.edu/GeorgesBellos) and its page secondary at Academia.edu (https://independent.academia.edu/GBel).

Alicia Blanco-González is a Professor of Marketing in Business Economics Department at Rey Juan Carlos University (Madrid). Alicia is Vice-President of European Academy of Management and Business Economics Her research interests include organizational legitimacy, SCR and consumer behavior. ORCID: 0000-0002-8509-7993.

Francesca Bonetti is a Senior Lecturer (Associate Professor) in Marketing at the London College of Fashion, University of the Arts London, London, UK, and a Visiting Lecturer at universities across Europe, the USA and Asia. She is currently a Visiting Scholar at USC Marshall School of Business, conducting a research project on technological innovation in the fashion and creative industries across the USA West Coasts (Los Angeles area), UK (London area) and Europe. Her research interests focus on business technological innovation across cultures in the fashion and creative industries, and the digital transformation of retailing. Her PhD (University of Manchester, UK, 2020) explored the adoption of consumer-facing technologies in fashion retail settings from a managerial perspective. Her interests also include luxury fashion retailing in China and the consumption of fashion goods by Asian consumers.

Her work is published in academic journals such as the Journal of the Academy of Marketing Science, Journal of Retailing and Consumer Services, and the International Journal of Technology Marketing, among others, and in a number of books. She has international industry experience in marketing communications and retail and business development in the fashion and apparel sector. She currently consult for fashion brands, retailers and startup companies on distribution strategies, communications strategies and the use of consumer-facing technology.

Gabriel Cachón-Rodríguez is a Lecturer at the University Rey Juan Carlos of the Department of Business Economics in the Marketing and Market Research area. Doctorate from the University Rey Juan Carlos. MBA from EUDE-Business School. Master's Degree in Senior Management from the University Rey Juan Carlos. Member of the European Academy of Management and Business Economics (AEDEM). His lines of research focus on intangible assets of marketing and education in the university sector. His papers have been published as book chapters in editorials of recognized international prestige (ESIC), as well as in journals that occupy top positions or prominent positions in various categories of the JCR Social Science Edition or SJR of Scopus (European Research on Management and Business Economics, Corporate Social Responsibility and Environmental Management, Cuadernos de Gestión). ORCID: 0000-0002-4228-2881.

Laura Colm is Researcher in Marketing and Sales and at SDA Bocconi. Her research activities focus on B2B and industrial marketing, services marketing, as well as the interface of marketing and sales. She is Head of Core Team of SDA Bocconi's Mobius Lab on user-centric, smart, and sustainable mobility, as well as member of the Commercial Excellence Lab (CEL). She authored articles, books, and chapters on these subjects. Her work as been published among others in the Journal of Marketing, Journal of Service Research, and Italian Journal of Marketing (former Mercati e Competitivitaì). Her most recent book is "Forgiare il futuro – L'effectuation theory e il percorso imprenditoriale di Loccioni" (Egea, 2021). Laura won a teaching award at Bocconi University in 2021, the ASFOR GSE Research/Greenleaf Publishing annual best case study award in 2016, and the Lyam Glynn research scholarship by AMA-SERVSIG and Arizona State University in 2014. She also teaches courses with a main focus on e-commerce, services marketing, and qualitative research methods. She is ad hoc reviewer for the Journal of Service Research, Journal of Service Management, and Asia Pacific Journal of Tourism Research. Laura earned a PhD in Marketing Management from the University of Stuttgart, and a MSc in Marketing Management, as well as a BSc in Business Administration and Management from Bocconi University.

Maria Constantinou holds an MBA (with distinction) from the University of Roehampton (UK), a degree in Home Economics and Ecology from the Harokopion University of Athens (GR), and a Certificate in Accounting. She works at the Cyprus Ministry of Education, Culture, Sport and Youth as a teacher of House Economics and Ecology in secondary education. She is also teaching Nutrition and Dietetics, Hygiene, and other related courses at a higher education institution in Cyprus.

Ana Cruz-Suárez is an Assistant Professor of Management in Rey Juan Carlos University. Her research lines are: Organizational legitimacy and sustainability. ORCID: 0000-0001-5525-3695.

Cristina Del-Castillo-Feito has a degree in of Management and Business Economics (Carlos III Universty). Master in Master in Advanced Management (Rey Juan Carlos University). Assistant Professor in Rey Juan Carlos University. Professional experience in marketing and business development in the Renewable Energy sector. Her research lines are: Legitimacy, Corporate Social Responsibility, Sustainability, Intangible assets management ORCID: 0000-0002-7903-1365

Regina Diaz is a PhD student in Administrative Sciences. She studied Accounting and has a Master's Degree in Finance. Her research revolves around Digital Transformation and the opportunities that Mexico has in this field. Regina has been working for companies such as KPMG, Coca Cola Femsa, Hewlett Packard and PepsiCo for 20 years, therefor she has extensive experience working with large suppliers. Regina works as a Teaching Assistant for the Tecnológico de Monterrey collaborating with the creation of material for classes and grading assignments.

Marcelo Dionisio is a post-doctoral student at Pontifical Catholic University in Rio, PHD from Coppead/UFRJ (Rio de Janeiro, Brasil) and MBA from Institut Superieur de Gestion (Paris, France) with specializations at Pace University (New York, USA) and International Management University of Asian (Tokyo, Japan). 25 years of experience within multinational companies such as P&G and Japan Tobacco and for the last 10 years as entrepreneur in import & retail and as business consultant to foreign companies seeking oportunities in the Brazilian market.

Çağlar Doğru (Ph.D.) is an associate professor at the department of management and organization and he serves as the advisor to the Rector at Ufuk University. He was graduated from Business Administration at Hacettepe University and received his master's and a doctoral degree in management from Gazi University in Turkey. Before academic studies, he was employed as the human resource manager and the assistant general manager for nearly ten years in prestigious international companies in Turkey. He completed various national and international projects professionally. He has published numerous articles, books, and chapters on organizational behavior, leadership, management, and human resource management. His researches focus on leadership styles, innovation, creativity, employee behaviors, and sustainability. He also serves as the editor in various international journals and books. Furthermore, he advises to international large-scale companies.

Olukemi Adedokun Fagbolu holds a PhD in Hospitality and Tourism Management from the Assumption University, Thailand. Currently, she is working as a Lecturer I in the department of Tourism Studies, National Open University of Nigeria. Her research interests cover hospitality and tourism management education, tourism destination development, marketing and management, and hospitality and tourism entrepreneurship and business management.

Nuno Felizardo holds a MSc in Maritime Electronic Systems Engineering and a postgraduate in Project Management. The main expertise areas are: Data Network, Software Feature Specification and Systems Engineering. In the past, he assumed several roles since field engineer, technical support engineer, QA engineer until systems engineer. Currently, he is Broadband Product Manager at NOS Innovation, a Portuguese telecommunications company, where he is the leader of the Technical Product team.

Andrea Girardi is a PhD Student at University of Modena and Reggio Emilia (Italy) and University of Trento (Italy).

Nuray Girginer was born in Eskişehir in 1967. She graduated from Department of Statistics, Faculty of Science at Anadolu University in 1992. She received her master's degree in 1994 and Ph.D. degree in 2001 from Department of Quantitative Methods, Institute of Social Science, Anadolu University. Since 1994, she has been working as a faculty member at Eskişehir Osmangazi University, Faculty of Economics and Administrative Sciences, Department of Business. She continued her academic career as an associated professor during 2009-2014, and she has been working as a professor since 2014 at the same university. She is head of Department of Business and vice-dean of Faculty of Economics and Administrative Sciences,Eskişehir Osmangazi University. Hermajorfields are operationsresearch,mathematical modeling, quantitative methods, multivariate statistical analysis, data analysis, and econometric analysis.

Viana Hassan is actively involved in academic and research work in Tourism & Cultural Management in Lebanon and Malta. She got her Ph.D. in Tourism Management and Cultural from Saint Joseph University, Beirut. Her Thesis was entitled "Medical Tourism in Lebanon". She has more than 15 years of tourism experience in many related Travel and Tourism Fields, varying from airline sales experience (MEA), to Co-management several Lebanese Travel agencies. She is an Experienced Lecturer with more than 15 years' experience at several universities in Lebanon (Lebanese University, A.U. L, Lebanese International University, Islamic University) and the Institute of Tourism Studies, Malta, Scholars School Business UK and Rushford Business School -Geneva with a demonstrated history of working in the Higher education industry, Skilled in Tourism Management, Customer service, Branding, Event Management, and Medical Tourism. Dr. Viana has participated in international conferences in multiple countries, including Athens, Paris, Vienna, Dubai, Beirut, Valencia, and has published papers in peer review

Mitsunori Hirogaki is currently an Associate Professor of Marketing Strategy at Kyushu University, Graduate School of Economics, Department of Business and Technology Management (QBS Business School), where he teaches Marketing Strategy and International Marketing. He also teaches Marketing Research and Consumer Behaviour at Ehime University and teaches Marketing at Nikkei Business School. His current research focuses on cross-cultural consumer behaviour in international marketing and marketing strategies in mature, developed societies. He has published numerous papers in international journals such as International Review of Retail, Distribution and Consumer Research; International Journal of Entrepreneurship and Small Business; Micro and Macro Marketing; International Journal of Technology Transfer and Commercialisation; and International Journal of Business and Globalisation. He is a member of the Japanese Economic Association, Japan Society of Marketing and Distribution, Kyushu Association of Economic Science and Japan Association for Consumer Studies.

Elena Marcoulli holds an MA degree in International Relations and European Studies from the University of Kent (UK), a BSc degree in Psychology from the Open University UK, a degree in Spanish Language and Civilisation from the Hellenic Open University (GR), and a degree in Translation from the Ionian University (GR). She works at the Cyprus Ministry of Education, Culture, Sport and Youth as a Spanish teacher in secondary education. She is a member of the Association of Professors of Spanish Language (APECHI) and a member of the Pancyprian Union of Graduate Translators and Interpreters.

Vítor João Pereira Domingues Martinho is Coordinator Professor with Habilitation at the Polytechnic Institute of Viseu, Portugal, and holds a Ph.D. in Economics from the University of Coimbra,

Portugal. He was President of the Scientific Council, President of the Directive Council and President of the Agricultural Polytechnic School of Viseu, Portugal, from 2006 to 2012. He participated in various technical and scientific events nationally and internationally, has published several technical and scientific papers, is referee of some scientific and technical journals and participates in the evaluation of national and international projects.

Nuno Martins is a principal engineer on the Home Gateways development team for the RDK-b projects. He participated in European Research projects (ULOOP, TIMBUS) and is currently on MIRAI and turntable. Martins received his Msc Software Engineering degree, focused on network and distributed computing, from Nova University of Lisbon, Portugal. Aside from his work at NOS on the Home Gateways, other areas of interest are cybersecurity, IoT solutions, and piloting small drones.

Doni Maryono, SM. born in Blitar, March 03, 1981. Primary education was achieved at SDN Sumberasri IV. Education is achieved at SMPN 2 Nglegok and SMAN I Blitar. S1 education in Business Management Study Program was completed at Muhammadiyah University of Sidoarjo completed in 2020. Now the author is completing his master's study in management at Muhammadiyah University of Sidoarjo. The author has worked since 2009 at the Sidoarjo Hospital until now, and in several hospitals in the Sidoarjo area.

Raul Montalvo Corzo has dedicated his research and teaching work to microeconomic theory and applied it to the economy of a business, industrial organization, econometrics, game theory and global business, areas on which he has extensively written. Amongst his publications and intellectual contributions the following stand out: the co-authorship of 6 books, 10 book chapters, 15 scientific articles, diverse publications and participation in numerous newspapers, specialized journals and radio and tv programs. Dr. Corzo has been an associate researcher in applied macroeconomics and optimum stochastic control in the Centro de Investigación y Docencia Económicas and has worked in the private sector in the field of insurance. He has also acted as a consultant in projects for a range of businesses. He has been active as a member in various professional organizations such as Coparmex Jalisco's Economic Analysis Committee, the Committee for Economic Development and the Board of the US Chamber of Commerce, the Consultative Board of Advisors of the Secretariat of Economic Promotion of the State of Jalisco, the Jalisco Academy of Sciences and the Institute of Statistics and Geography. He is also a member of the SNI (Sistema Nacional de Investigadores), Level 1, Conacyt. In addition to his role as Director of EGADE Business School Guadalajara, Dr. Montalvo has served as the Director of the Graduate School of Administration on the Guadalajara campus and of the Graduate School of Administration and Business Administration. He has been a visiting professor in countries such as as the UK, Peru, Equador, Colombia, Panama, France and the US and has delivered a SNOC (Small Network Online Course) for the GNAM (Global Network for Advanced Management) consortium. He has completed short term programs in economic geography and overlapping generations in the Technical University of Lisbon; business and the Chinese market in Fundan University and Peking university; data visualization at the Stevens Institute of Technology and Entrepreneurship at Babson College.

Andrey I. Pilipenko graduated from Leningrad State University (Faculty of Mathematics and Mechanics) in 1972. In 1984 he received his degree of Candidate of Physics and Mathematics Sciences at the Institute of Physical Chemistry of the USSR Academy of Sciences. In 1998 he received his degree of Doctor of Pedagogical Sciences at the Russian Academy of Education. For more than 40 years he worked as full Professor at many Russian Universities: All-Russian Correspondence Financial and Economic Institute (VSFEI), People's Friendship University of Russia (RUDN), Lomonosov Moscow State University, Russian Presidential Academy of National Economy and Public Administration (RANERA) (last work), etc. He was invited as Professor by Gumilyov Eurasian National University (Kazakhstan). He has more than 130 publications (in Russian and in English), including ones indexed by RISC (RF), Scopus, Web of Science. His scientific interests lie in the field of mathematical modeling of processes of cyclical changes in economics and finance in terms of a synergistic approach to nonlinear fluctuations and waves; adaptation of the Heisenberg uncertainty principle in the choice of management decisions in public finance; stochastic processes in the context of shocks theory; the theory of psychological and cognitive barriers in education and the mechanisms of self-organization (education and socialization) and self-development of a human embedded into the human-created systems' self-movement.

Olga I. Pilipenko graduated from Moscow State Institute for Foreign Relations (MGIMO University) in 1975. In 1981 she got her degree of Candidate of Economic Sciences at the Institute of Latin America of the USSR Academy of Sciences. In 1994 she got a degree of Doctor of Economic Sciences at Lomonosov Moscow State University. She worked as full Professor for many Russian Universities: All-Russian Correspondence Financial and Economic Institute (VSFEI), People's Friendship University of Russia (RUDN), Lomonosov Moscow State University, Russian Presidential Academy of National Economy and Public Administration (RANERA) (last work). In the late 1990s, she was invited as a researcher to the Institute of Technology of Hearning and to Aarhus University (Denmark) under the interstate exchange program. She has more than 130 publications (in Russian and in English), including ones indexed by RISC (RF), Scopus, Web of Science. Her scientific interests lie in the field of bifurcation effects' modeling in global financial markets in connection with shocks; interaction of factors of global financial stability, monetary circulation, and public finance; of dialectic lows of self-movement of human-created systems in economy, society, technological structures; of economic and social policies interaction for the coronavirus pandemic; of self-organization of economic and financial systems in the context of the theory of shocks.

Zoya A. Pilipenko received the following degrees at Lomonosov Moscow State University: Doctor of Economic Sciences (Finance and World Economy) (2013), Candidate of Economic Sciences (Finance and World Economy) (2004), Master in Economics (2003) and Bachelor in Economics (2001). She started her professional career in Finance at Insurance Company "Gefest" (Russia, Moscow, in 2003) and at the Joint Stock Company "Sberbank" (Russia, Moscow, in 2004), where she estimated the required rate of return on offered banking services and actual profitability of credit services in particular. For the last 15 years she has been working for the Central Bank of Russia. In her current role as Advisor to the Head of Platforms Operators and Information Services Supervision Division at the Financial Market Infrastructure Department she is deeply involved in the process of CRA's supervision enhancement and standardization, methodologies validation requirements' formation, as well as mapping framework development and market structure analysis. She has teaching and research experience: more than 60 publications in Russian and in English (indexed by RISC (RF), Scopus, etc.). She has got certificates in Banking and Finance from practical seminars in Great Britain, Luxembourg, Austria, Italy, and France. She has got certificates in Banking and Finance from practical seminars in Great Britain, Luxembourg, Austria, Italy and France. Her research interests lie in the field of shocks theory and self-organization laws of systemic integrity in economy and finance, as well as monetary and fiscal policies' formation on financial markets at national and global levels due to the coronavirus pandemic.

Gerardo Reyes Ruiz is an Actuary by training from the Faculty of Sciences-UNAM; he studied a Specialty in Econometrics in the Postgraduate Studies Division of the Faculty of Economics-UNAM; He obtained a Master's and Doctorate (with a scholarship from CONACYT and the Carolina Foundation) in Business Studies (actuarial profile) from the Faculty of Economics and Business of the University of Barcelona, Spain. In the Doctorate he graduated with the highest honors awarded to a thesis of this nature, that is, he obtained the qualification of Excellent Cum Laude. Later he did a postdoctoral stay at the Center for Economic, Administrative, and Social Studies (CIECAS) of the National Polytechnic Institute (IPN). His work experience has been in public education institutions (UNAM, UAEM, IPN, Centro de Estudios Superiores Navales-CESNAV) where he has taught classes in Bachelor's, Specialty, Masters and Doctorate degrees. In some of these institutions, he developed several research projects, including Basic Science, forming and creating Research Networks (both nationally and internationally). All this accumulated experience allowed him to enter the National System of Researchers (SNI), Social Area, of Mexico (he has the appointment of Level I National Researcher). He is currently attached to the Center for Superior Naval Studies (CESNAV), Mexico.

Aslisah Senak holds a Bachelor degree in Business Administration from Anadolu University and a Master's degree in International Relations from Galatasaray University. She started her career in marketing for a multinational company and has been involved in sales and business development activities respectively. She has been living and working in Frankfurt, Milano and Paris before she started working as a business development consultant back in Turkey. She speaks English, French and Italian. She has a PhD degree in Business Administration at Osmangazi University in Eskisehir and other than her PhD dissertation titled 'Local Production of Ventilators Amid Pandemic and Value Co-creation', she has studies on effects of globalization on small and medium sized enterprises, R&D efficiency and innovation efficiency.

Carlos Silva has more than 10 years experience in telco operator. Currently, he is the head of Internet Services at NOS Innovation, a Portuguese telco operator. He' responsible for the broadband product development, including not only the CPEs but the hole home network. Carlos holds a master's degree in Electrotechnical Engineering in Instituto Superior Técnico.

Joana Sousa holds an MSc in Biomedical Engineering with expertise in the areas of biosignal processing, innovation management and marketing strategy. She was partner in Unlimited-Hashtag.com, a start-up combining technological skills and business expertise to provide support for the innovation process from conception to market. In Unlimited-Hashtag.com, she was responsible for conducting research in biomedical signal processing, features extraction, pattern recognition, continuous patient monitoring and development of new biosignal techniques for research, health and sports. She is an independent expert in the European Community's H2020 framework, which provides funding for research and innovation. She is also Innovation Consultant at NOS Innovation, a Portuguese telecommunications company. She was R&D project coordinator at PLUX–Wireless Biosignals, SA, and Innovation sub-director at Edge Innovation, leading innovative projects and managing innovation in the Health, IT, communications areas.

Alessandra Vecchi is a Reader in International Fashion Management at London College of Fashion where she is a Co-Investigator of the "Business of Fashion, Textiles and Technology" research project (https://bftt.org.uk/). She is an Associate Professor in the Department of Environmental and Prevention Sciences (DEPS) at the University of Ferrara in Italy. Prior to that, she was an Assistant Professor in the Department of Management at the University of Bologna in Italy where from 2012 to 2018 she had a Marie Curie Fellowship.

George Yiapanas is the Finance Manager of GSP Stadium in Nicosia, CY, with more than twenty [20] years of experience in the sports industry. He is also a lecturer in the field of sustainable strategic management at the University of Roehampton (UK), and a special scientist in sports management at the University of Nicosia (CY). He is the founder and owner of GKY Sports Management, a sports consultancy. He holds a PhD in Sports Management from the University of Nicosia (CY), an MA degree (with distinction) in Management from the University of Wolverhampton (UK), a degree in Accounting from the BPP University (UK), a Certificate in Football Management and in Security Management. He is a board member of the Cyprus Association for Sports Management (CyASM), and a member of the EuroMed Research Business Institute (SMEMAB/EMRBI). His primary research interests lie in the areas of strategic management, sustainability, sports governance, and sports safety management.

Index

A

Academic staff readiness 301
accommodation 101, 218, 232, 234-235, 237, 387-388, 447, 451
agglomeration processes 444-445
agile management 324, 327-330, 333-334, 340
Agriculture Sector 417, 428
AI 38, 48-49, 252, 258, 270, 299
and inclusion principles 36, 38, 40
anxiety 193, 239-247, 249-250, 319, 330, 336, 339-340, 371-372, 376, 385
Augmented Reality 24, 26, 271, 276, 293-300

B

B2B Marketing 18
B2B Relationship 35
Balanced Scorecard 429-431, 434-435, 439-443
bibliometric methodology 239-240
Bibliometric methods 240-241, 250
bio-economy 417
blurring 193-194, 204
business model 48, 153-154, 158-159, 162, 208, 210, 212, 218, 228, 361-362, 364, 417-418, 425-426

C

case vignette 19, 23, 35
catering 232, 234, 237, 387, 447, 451, 459-460
Ceremonial expenses 370
circular economy 57, 150, 253, 415, 417-419, 421-423, 425-428
co-citation analysis 239, 241, 246, 248, 250
collaboration 1-16, 26, 119, 214, 253, 255, 267, 307, 312, 335, 361, 371, 409-410, 422
consumer behavior 19, 32, 117, 239, 245, 247, 249, 344, 425
Consumer Survey 344

consumers 19, 23, 35, 40, 57, 97, 109, 124-125, 128, 150, 159, 208, 212-213, 216-217, 219, 225, 239-240, 244, 246-247, 249-250, 253, 273-277, 279, 291-293, 296, 298-299, 325, 344-346, 348-350, 362, 417-418, 421-426, 428, 431, 436-439, 441, 469
corporate ecosystems 36, 38-39, 47-49
COVID-19 1-3, 5-14, 16, 18-25, 27-28, 30, 33, 35-38, 43, 45, 50, 52-53, 55, 61-62, 64, 66-98, 102, 106, 109, 113, 115-119, 123, 129, 131-135, 137-141, 146-147, 149-155, 158-162, 164-168, 172, 177, 179, 187-194, 197, 201, 206, 209-211, 213-216, 222, 224, 226-230, 232-240, 246-252, 258, 266-271, 295-298, 301-302, 306, 309-310, 315-322, 324-325, 328-330, 333, 338, 340, 344-346, 348-356, 358-361, 363-364, 366-368, 370-378, 381-389, 391-394, 397-406, 415, 417, 424-425, 427, 429, 432-433, 440-446, 461-462, 465-469
COVID-19 pandemic 1, 3, 5-9, 11-12, 35, 37, 43, 45, 50, 52, 55, 61-62, 68-70, 74-77, 81-83, 85, 91-94, 109, 116-119, 123, 129, 131-132, 135, 137-141, 146-147, 149-153, 158-160, 162, 165, 167, 177, 179, 187, 192-194, 209, 213, 215, 222, 228, 230, 232, 234-238, 247-249, 252, 258, 266-267, 269, 271, 295-296, 301-302, 306, 309-310, 315-316, 318-322, 324-325, 328-330, 333, 338, 340, 344-345, 348-350, 352, 354, 356, 364, 366, 368, 370-372, 374, 376, 378, 381-384, 386-387, 398, 401, 415, 425, 427, 429, 440-442, 445, 466, 468-469
crisis 9-10, 13-14, 30, 34, 44, 50, 63-64, 67, 94, 112-114, 117, 120, 142, 147-151, 154, 159, 161-162, 167, 186, 188, 190-191, 193-194, 197-198, 201, 210-211, 215, 224, 227, 229, 248-249, 252-253, 257-258, 265, 268-269, 273, 296, 301-302, 306-307, 309, 311, 314-315, 317, 319, 327, 330, 337, 346, 350, 354-355, 357-373, 376-377, 380-382, 384, 387, 391-392, 394, 400, 403, 424, 444, 466
crisis management 14, 248, 354-355, 357-358, 364-368
customer experience 18-19, 21-22, 32-35, 262

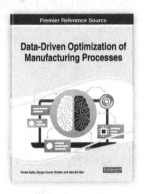
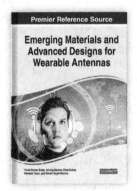

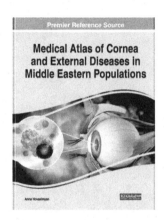
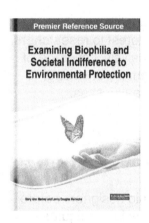
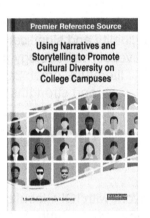

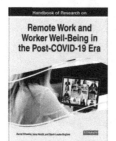

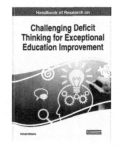

Printed in the United States
by Baker & Taylor Publisher Services